THE MILITARY ORDERS

Volume 2

Welfare and Warfare

edited by

Helen Nicholson

editorial committee
Malcolm Barber, Peter Edbury, Anthony Luttrell,
Jonathan Phillips, Jonathan Riley-Smith

Ashgate

Aldershot • Brookfield USA • Singapore • Sydney

This edition copyright © 1998 by Helen Nicholson

Published by   Ashgate Publishing Limited
                    Gower House, Croft Road,
                    Aldershot, Hampshire GU11 3HR
                    Great Britain

                    Ashgate Publishing Limited
                    Old Post Road,
                    Brookfield, Vermont 05036–9704
                    USA

ISBN 0–86078–679–X

British Library Cataloguing-in-Publication Data
The military orders
    Volume 2: Welfare and warfare
    1. Military religious orders—Europe—History—Congresses
    2. Hospitalers—History—Congresses
    I. Nicholson, Helen
    271.7'91

U.S. Library of Congress Cataloging-in-Publication Data
The Military Orders Volume 2. Welfare and Warfare/
edited by Helen Nicholson
    Includes bibliographical references and index.
    1. Military religious orders—History—Congresses.
    2. Hospitalers—History—Congresses. 3. Templars—
    History—Congresses. 4. Teutonic Knights—History—
    Congresses. I. Nicholson, Helen
    CR4701.M55 1994
    271'.05—dc20

Typeset by Stanford Desktop Publishing Services, Northampton
Printed in Great Britain on acid-free paper at MPG Books Ltd, Bodmin, Cornwall.

Contents

Part II   Warfare

Part III   Life Within the Military Orders

Part IV   Relations with the Outside World

List of Illustrations

List of Tables

Abbreviations

AHN OO.MM	Archivo Histórico Nacional, Madrid, Ordenes Militares
AOL	*Archives de l'Orient Latin*
APV	Archives of the Grand Priory, Venice
ASVen	Archivio di Stato, Venice
BN	Bibliothèque Nationale de France
CH	*Cartulaire général de l'Ordre des Hospitaliers de Saint-Jean de Jérusalem, 1100–1310*, ed. J. Delaville le Roulx, 4 vols (Paris, 1894–1906)
CSM	Archives of the *Cinque Savii alla Mercanzia*
CT	*Cartulaire général de l'Ordre du Temple 1119?–1150. Recueil des chartes et des bulles relatives à l'ordre du Temple*, ed. Marquis d'Albon (Paris, 1913)
Cont WT	*La Continuation de Guillaume de Tyr (1184–1197)*, ed. M.R. Morgan, Documents relatifs à l'histoire des croisades, 14 (Paris, 1982)
Crusades	*A History of the Crusades*, gen. ed. K.M. Setton, 2nd edn, 6 vols (Madison, 1969–89)
Eracles	*L'Estoire de Eracles Empereur et la Conqueste de la Terre d'Outremer*, in *RHC Occid*, 1.2 (Paris, 1859)
Malta, Cod.	Archives of the Order of St John, National Library of Malta, Valletta
MGH SS	*Monumenta Germaniae Historica. Scriptores*
MO, 1	*The Military Orders: Fighting for the Faith and Caring for the Sick*, ed. M. Barber (Aldershot, 1994)
NLM	National Library of Malta, Valletta
PL	*Patrologia Latina*
PPTS	Palestine Pilgrims' Text Society
PUTJ	*Papsturkunden für Templer und Johanniter*, ed. R. Hiestand, 2 vols (Göttingen, 1972–84)
QuStDO	Quellen und Studien zur Geschichte des Deutschen Ordens

RHC   *Recueil des Historiens des Croisades*
  Occid   *Historiens occidentaux*
  Or   *Historiens orientaux*
  DArm   *Documents arméniens*
RHGF   *Recueil des Historiens des Gaules et de la France*
ROL   *Revue de l'Orient Latin*
RRH   Regesta Regni Hierosolymitani and Additamentum, ed. R. Röhricht
              (Innsbruck, 1893–1904)
RS   Rolls Series
RSJ   *The Rule of the Spanish Military Order of St James, 1170–1493,*
              ed. E. Gallego Blanco (Leiden, 1971)
RT   *La Règle du Temple*, ed. H. de Curzon (Paris, 1886)
SDO   *Die Statuten des Deutschen Ordens nach den ältesten Handschriften,*
              ed. M. Perlbach (Halle, 1890)
SRP   *Scriptores Rerum Prussicarum*, ed. T. Hirsch *et al.* (Leipzig,
              1861)
WT   Guillaume de Tyr, *Chronique*, ed. R.B.C. Huygens, Corpus
              Christianorum, Continuatio Medievalis, 63, 63A (Turnholt,
              1986)

List of Contributors

David F. Allen is Lecturer in Modern History at the University of Birmingham. He has published several articles about the Order of St John's history in early modern Europe and the New World, in which he has tried to integrate the Order's history with the better known mainstream of European and colonial history.

Carlos de Ayala is *profesor titular* of the Universidad Autónoma of Madrid. He holds a doctorate in Medieval History (1985) and has led two research projects into the military orders in Castile and León in the Middle Ages.

Malcolm Barber is Professor of History at the University of Reading. His publications include *The Trial of the Templars* (1978), *The New Knighthood: A History of the Order of the Temple* (1994) and *The Two Cities: Medieval Europe from 1050 to 1320* (1992).

Carlos Barquero Goñi is a Research Assistant at the Universidad Autónoma of Madrid. He has published a number of articles on the Hospitallers in Spain. His most recent work is a study of the Hospitaller commandery of Mallen in the Middle Ages (1996).

Karl Borchardt works in the Department of History at the University of Würzburg. His most recent book, *Die Cölestiner: Eine Mönchsgemeinschaft des späteren Mittelalters*, has just been published. He has been a collaborator of the *Monumenta Germaniae Historica*, Munich, and of the Deutsches Historisches Institut, Rome. He is currently preparing a study on the Hospitallers in central Europe in collaboration with Dr Anthony Luttrell.

Jochen Burgtorf is Instructor in Medieval History at the Heinrich-Heine-University, Düsseldorf. He is currently working on a doctoral thesis on the high dignitaries in the headquarters of the Hospitallers and the Templars from the twelfth to the early fourteenth centuries.

Simonetta Cerrini is working on the history of the Templars and a new edition of their Rule, and has recently completed her doctoral thesis at the University of Paris IV-Sorbonne: 'Une expérience neuve au sein de la spiritualité médiévale: l'ordre du Temple (1120–1314). Etude et édition des règles latine et française' which will be published by Brepols in the *Corpus Christianorum Cont. Med.* She has participated in numerous conferences on the military orders, and has organized two conferences on the Templars.

Bernhard Demel, OT is Director of the Zentralarchiv des Deutschen Ordens and Rector of the Teutonic Order's church of St Elizabeth in Vienna. Since 1985 he has been Secretary to the Internationalen Historischen Komission zur Erforschung des Deutschen Ordens. He has researched extensively into the Teutonic Order and into the ecclesiastical and cultural history of Moravia and Silesia.

Mark Dupuy is a Graduate Assistant at Louisiana State University, where he is currently pursuing a doctoral degree.

Susan Edgington is Senior Lecturer at Huntingdonshire Regional College. Besides her continuing work on the edition and English translation of Albert of Aachen's *Historia*, she researches various aspects of the early crusading period. A translation with commentary of Walter the Chancellor's *Bella Antiochena*, produced jointly with Thomas Asbridge, will appear shortly.

Klaus van Eickels has studied History and Latin at Düsseldorf, Munich and Aix-en-Provence. His doctoral thesis (1993) examined the Rhenish bailiwick of the Teutonic knights. Since 1994 he has been Wissenschaftlicher Assistent at the University of Bamberg, where he is preparing a *habilitation*-thesis on the Anglo-French treaty negotiations of the twelfth and thirteenth centuries.

Sven Ekdahl is Lecturer in History at the University of Göteborg, Wissenschaftlicher Angestellter at the Geheimes Staatsarchiv Preussischer Kulturbesitz, Berlin, and also President of the North-East German Cultural Institute, Lüneburg. His publications include *Die Schlacht bei Tannenberg 1410. Quellenkritische Untersuchungen*, vol. 1: *Einführung und Quellenlage* (1982) (vol. 2 is in progress). He is at present working on the second volume of an edition of *Das Soldbuch des Deutschen Ordens 1410–1411*.

Alan Forey has taught in the universities of Oxford, St Andrews and Durham. He has published extensively on the military orders. His publications include *The Military Orders from the Twelfth to the Early Fourteenth Centuries* (1992).

Luis García-Guijarro Ramos is Lecturer in Medieval History at the University of Zaragoza, Huesca. He has researched into various aspects of military and monastic orders in medieval Spain. His publications include *Papado, Cruzadas y Ordenes Militares, siglos XI–XIII* (1995), a comparative analysis of the structure of the international military orders and of the role they played in the Latin Church.

Libor Jan works on Medieval History at the Department of History in the Faculty of Philosophy, University of Masaryk, Brno, Czech Republic. He researches into the military orders and the history of Moravia in the thirteenth and fourteenth centuries, and in particular has been collaborating with Vít Jesenský in research into the building activity of the medieval military orders.

Vít Jesenský works for the Regional Office for Conservation in Central Bohemia, Czech Republic, as a field recorder of historic buildings. He also researches into the history of architecture. He publishes regularly. His main area of research is the building activity of the medieval military orders, and he and Libor Jan have been collaborating in this field since their student days.

Fotini Karassava-Tsilingiri was born in Athens, Greece. She is an architect and art historian working for the Greek Archaeological Service in the Section for the Ancient Monuments of Attica. Her main research interest is the architecture of the Hospitallers in Rhodes in the fifteenth century.

Benjamin Z. Kedar is Professor of History at the Hebrew University of Jerusalem. He has been president of the Society for the Study of the Crusades and the Latin East since 1995. His main publications are *Merchants in Crisis* (1976), *Crusade and Mission* (1984) and *The Franks in the Levant, the 11th to the 14th Centuries* (1993).

Anthony Luttrell studied at Oxford, Madrid, Rome and Pisa, taught at Swarthmore College in Pennsylvania, Edinburgh, Malta and Padua, and was Assistant Director and Librarian of the British School at Rome. He works and publishes extensively on the Hospitallers of Rhodes, on medieval Malta, on the English in the Levant and on various archaeological projects.

Christoph T. Maier is Wissenschaftlicher Assistent und Lehrbeauftragter in Medieval History at the University of Zürich. He has published several articles on the military orders and crusade propaganda in the Middle Ages and is the author of *Preaching the Crusades: Mendicant Friars and the Cross in the Thirteenth Century* (1994).

Victor Mallia-Milanes is Dean of the Faculty of Arts and Head of the Department of History at the University of Malta. His special research interest is Venice, the Order of St John, and Malta in the early modern period, on which he has published extensively. His publications include *Venice and Hospitaller Malta 1530–1798: Aspects of a Relationship* (1992) and *Hospitaller Malta 1530–1798: Studies on Malta and the Order of St John of Jerusalem* (1993).

Sophia Menache is an Associate Professor of Medieval History at the University of Haifa, Israel. She has published numerous articles on western society during the thirteenth and fourteenth centuries. Her books include *The Vox Dei: Communication in the Middle Ages* (1990), *L'Humor en chaire: Le rire dans l'Eglise médiévale* (1994), and a monograph *Pope Clement V* (1998).

Klaus Militzer is Professor of Medieval History at the University of Bochum. His publications on the military orders centre particularly upon the history of the Teutonic Order in Germany, Prussia and Livonia, and include *Die Entstehung der Deutschordensballien im Deutschen Reich* (1981) and *Ritterbrüder im livländischen Zweig des Deutschen Ordens* (1993) (with Lutz Fenske).

Piers Mitchell's research interests lie in the archaeology of disease and the history of medicine of the crusades. Pursuit of these two fields concurrently enables the construction of his hypotheses based on textual evidence to be tested using archaeological methods. The rest of the time he works as a surgeon in a London teaching hospital.

Johannes Adriaan Mol is Research Fellow at the Fryske Akademy in Leeuwarden. He has published several books and articles on Frisian medieval history and on the history of the military orders in the Netherlands.

Helen Nicholson is Lecturer in Medieval History at the University of Wales, Cardiff, and works on the military orders and various related subjects. Her most recent book is *Chronicle of the Third Crusade: a Translation of the Itinerarium Peregrinorum et Gesta Regis Ricardi* (1997).

António Pestana de Vasconcelos holds an MA in Medieval History from the University of Oporto, Portugal and researches into the Portuguese military orders, especially the Order of Christ. He has published 'Os Santos das Ordens Militares no Agiologio Lusitano de Jorge Cardoso', in *Via Spiritus – Revista de História da Espiritualidade e do Sentimento Religioso* (1996).

Jonathan Phillips is Lecturer in Medieval History at Royal Holloway College, University of London. He is the author of *Defenders of the Holy Land. Relations* *between the Latin East and the West 1119–87* (Oxford, 1996) and is now working on a major study of the Second Crusade.

Paula Pinto Costa holds an MA in Medieval History from the University of Oporto, Portugal, and researches into the military orders in Portugal. Her publications include a number of articles on the military orders, most recently: 'A Ordem do Hospital no Primeiro Século da Nacionalidade', in *Actas do II Congresso Histórico de Guimarães. Sociedade, administração, cultura e igreja em Portugal no século XII*, 5 (1997).

Denys Pringle is a Principal Inspector of Ancient Monuments, Scotland, and formerly Assistant Director of the British School of Archaeology, Jerusalem. He has published many reports, monographs and books on the medieval archaeology of Italy, North Africa, the Middle East and Scotland. Among his books are *The Red Tower (al-Burj al-Ahmar)* (1986) and vols 1 and 2 of a projected three-volume work, *The Churches of the Crusader Kingdom of Jerusalem: A Corpus* (1993–).

Jonathan Riley-Smith is Dixie Professor of Ecclesiastical History at the University of Cambridge, and Honorary Vice-President of the Society for the Study of the Crusades and the Latin East. He is the author of many books and articles on the military orders, the Western settlements in Palestine and the crusades, including *The Knights of St John in Jerusalem and Cyprus, c. 1050–1310* (1967) and most recently *The First Crusaders, 1095–1131* (1997).

José Manuel Rodríguez García holds an MA in Medieval History from the University of Salamanca. He is currently working on a PhD thesis on 'The Crusade in the Kingdoms of León and Castile, 1000–1350', under the supervision of Professor C. de Ayala, at the Universidad Autónoma of Madrid.

Jürgen Sarnowsky is Professor of Medieval History at the University of Hamburg. He is a specialist in scholastic thought in the later Middle Ages, as well as the history of the Teutonic Order and the Order of St John. His books and articles include *Die Wirtschaftsführung des Deutschen Ordens in Preussen, 1382–1454* (1993).

Johannes Schellakowsky holds an MA from the University of Würzburg. He is currently working on a doctoral thesis on the relationship between King Frederick William I of Prussia and his aristocracy.

Christopher Toll is Professor of Semitic Philology at the University of Copenhagen, Denmark. He has published books and articles on Arabic literature, dialects, science and numismatics, and on Hebrew and Aramaic subjects. He is a member of the Royal Danish Academy of Sciences and Letters and of the Royal Swedish Society of Letters in Uppsala, a Knight of Justice of the Order of St John in Sweden and Librarian of the Order.

Theresa M. Vann is the Malta Curator at the Hill Monastic Manuscript Library, St John's University, Collegeville, Minnesota. She has worked extensively on the Spanish military orders and is preparing an on-line catalogue of the archives of the Order of St John.

Editor's Preface

This volume contains papers from the second conference on the military orders, which was held on 5–8 September 1996 at the Museum of St John, St John's Gate, Clerkenwell, London, under the auspices of the London Centre for the Study of the Crusades. The conference was planned as a sequel to the very successful conference on the military orders held in September 1992; it is intended that a third conference will be held in 2000. The second conference included scholars from nineteen countries who presented between them a total of fifty-three papers on subjects covering a chronological period from the eleventh century to the present day and a geographical spread from Portugal to the Middle East, and Malta to the Baltic States. A large proportion of these papers has been published here.

Unlike the first conference, the papers given at the second did not divide easily into sections dealing with distinct military orders. For the purposes of publication, it was thought best to divide them according to broad subject categories: medical work, military activity, internal organization and life, and relations with rulers and donors; with the papers in each section arranged in general chronological order.

The success of this conference was due to lengthy and meticulous planning by the organizing committee, chaired by Jonathan Riley-Smith and administered by Rosemary Bailey and Helen Gribble, together with Peter Edbury, Malcolm Barber, Carolyn Brownhill, Anthony Luttrell, Jonathan Phillips and Pamela Willis. The St John Historical Society and the St John Ambulance Association also gave most welcome assistance. In the production of the book, the advice and expertise of the editorial committee has been invaluable. I am also indebted to Judi Upton-Ward for her professional care and patience as secretary and copy-editor, and her many valuable suggestions. Thanks are also due to John Smedley, Ruth Peters and Ellen Keeling of Ashgate Publishing for their advice and support.

Address by Father Bernhard Demel, OT

Allocutio in missa die dominica (8 September 1996) in ecclesia s. Joannis Baptistae in civitate Londoniensi

Fratres et Sorores in Domino nostro Jesu Christo! Saluto vos omnes in initio novae hebdomadae. Vos estis parati non solum ad audiendum novissimarum cognitionum de 'ordinibus sic – dictis militaribus', de eorum rebus et factis pro hospitalitate et de re militari eorum, sed etiam interne ordinati ad celebrandum diem solis, nempe diem, qui est consecratus per resurrectionem Domini nostri Jesu Christi, redemptoris omnium hominum. Quis autem dicit, vel tantum dicere audeat, hae in civitate Londoniensi auditae praelectiones sunt inutiles pro multis hodiernis hominibus et propterea inserviunt tantum pro aliquibus specialistis – sicut vos estis – mihi videtur errare. Rationes meae ad istam quaestionem utilitatis nostrarum enuntiationum sunt hae tres, quae post collapsum doctrinae communisticae ortae sunt vel de novo inveniuntur:

1. Primo loco nomino revitalisticum et fundamentaliticum doctrinam de 'Islam'; quia – praeter alia – ante paucas hebdomadas factus est incitator pro morte episcopi Romano-catholici in Oran/Algeria, pro interfectione monachorum ibidem ex Ordine Cisterciensium reformato – sic dictis Trappistico – et causa intolerantiae contra christianos in parte meridonale rei publicae Sudanae. Videmus in multis territoriis Europae et aliis territoriis mundi, quod doctrina Mohammed prophetae, praesertim ea de Schiitis, non facit aliquam coniunctionen vel signat tolerantiam veram cum elementis doctrinae humanisticae, quae ex fundamento judaico-christiano per tempora illuminationis ante fere ducentos annos nobis communia et pro evolutione et libertate omnium hominum – fidelium et infidelium – necessaria sunt. Ubi Islam adhuc est in minoritate, ibi requirit et accipit ex aliorum tolerantia oratoria et aedificia ad exercendam istam fidem. Sed e contra: conceditne Islam etiam omnia privilegia suis minoritatibus, ubi est in maioritate? Hic existunt defectus, exempla multa intolerantiae crassae et etiam persecutiones usque ad mortem eorum, qui non adhaerent doctrinis Prophetae Mohammed, inveniuntur. Ex tempore medii aevi et postea scimus, quod nos debemus invigilare pro istis principibus religioso-humanisticis, quae inserviunt omnibus hominibus. Intolerantia nulla est utilis pro habitationibus terrae! Nostra scientifica investigatio de ordinibus militaribus potest multa elementa praebere,

quomodo hoc sine laesione conscientiae omnium hominum fieri potest. Initiis malae viae obstate carissimi auditores, ergo dico!

2. Secundo commemoro 'Nationalismum'. Dominus noster Jesus Christus proclamat diversis verbis et actionibus (confer *Concilium 31 December 1995*, pp. 487–492) universalem salvificam voluntatem Dei ergo omnes homines, non tantum erga credentes. Pax Romana, relativa stabilitas pacis in tempore Caesaris Augusti, et una usque ad syncretismum fere omnium formarum religionum parata tolerantia Romanorum praebebat religioni christianae bonas possibilitates. Pro propaganda doctrina christiana et eius universalismi forma usque ad persecutiones Imperii Romani ista pax erat valde utilis, si excipiuntur persecutiones usque ad tempora Constantini. Post tempora istius imperatoris videmus duas vias evolutionis: via religionis in regno byzantinistico cum maxima coniunctione inter rem publicam et religionem, quae praeparabat – sic dictum – Caesaropapismum et ecclesias dictas autocephales in Bulgaria, Serbia, Romania et Russia quae usque hodie non se seperant ab immissione rei publicae in res internas ecclesiarum. Alteram viam veniebat ecclesia occidentalis papalis, quae evolvebat doctrinam de duobis regnis, de regno spirituale et mundano. Papa Gregorius VII aggressivo modo pugnavit pro libertate Ecclesiae de immissione imperatorum et aliorum virium temporalium. Secundam meam privatam opinionem ecclesia catholica ab hinc usque ad tempora illuminationis et speciatim revolutionis in Francia et postea saeculo peracto non feliciter defendebat principia humanistica memorata. Propterea accipiebat multa incommoda et ergo etiam revolutio sovietica saeculo nostro oriri potuit. Nationalismus sensu stricto orta est saeculo duodevigesimo, (*Concilium* pp. 490 ff., 495 ff.) et habet influxum maximum usque hodie, sicut exempla balcanica demonstrant. Hodie et adhuc in Graecia perseverat coincidentia religionis et nationis – ne dicam nationalismi – quae facit nova problemata, exempli gratia in insula Cypro cum Turcis intolerantibus: nationalismus quocumque modo pugnat in se cum universalismo christiano – ergo est magna periclitatio pro vita et evolutione hominis secundum principia religioso – humanistica.

3. Tertio nomino Saecularismum in omni forma – ergo interpretationem evolutionam omnium hominum sine aliqua verae fidei forma et historica cognitione de bonis fructibus religionis verae. Etsi saecularismus characterisatus progredi videatur, non habet sufficientem statum et fundamentum pro tolerantia vera, sine qua vita moderna hodie et in futuro vere existere non potest. Non habet apodicticum, ab omnibus acceptatum et realizatum fundamentum religiosum in doctrina Dei, omnibus ad salutem promulgatum. Potest tantum omnia facere, ne partes in societate pugnant inter se et contra alienos et extraneos.

Nos investigatores temporum cruciferorum in Palaestina, Rhodos, Malta, Russia, in regionibus balticis et aliis partibus terrae nostrae et postea contra Turcos usque ad finem saeculi duodevigesimi nominati in fontibus ut 'inimicos christianae nominis' debemus attenti esse et exempla ex historia praebere ne tota familia hominum per ista tria falsa et ideologica movimenta detrimentum capiat et corrumpatur. Videant omnes vere instructi, ut praebent bonam medicinam suis auditoribus, praeparatam ex propria et aliorum hominum instructorum bona conscientia, ex illuminatione antiqui et novi testamenti Dei ergo nos homines querentes! Jesus Christus, cuius memoriam passionis et resurrectionis nunc celebrare incipimus, pro nobis et omnibus ei adhaerentibus est vera lux, bona via, veritas illuminans omnia et vita in praesenti et futuro. Ipse neminem fallit; econtra omnes edocet ad veram et felicem formam suae vitae. Propterea volumus nunc audire suum verbum, quod manet in aeternum, et iam eorum, qui eius nomine qua propheta vel aliter missi fuerunt. Eius memoria sacramentalis crucis at resurrectionis evocat nos ex falsis fundamentis in praeterito et praesenti et praeparat ad coenam aeternam in suo regno, ubi omnia aenigmata – adhuc existentia – suas solutiones invenient.

Confiteor . . .

Introduction

Jonathan Riley-Smith

Academic interest in the military orders has been growing for the last decade or so. Perhaps one should be surprised that there had been comparatively little before. The military orders have always been intrinsically important, as great orders of the Church (two of which have survived into modern times), as economic and political forces in many western European countries and as the creators of unusual polities – the order-states in Prussia and on Rhodes and Malta. Each of these was a theocracy governed by an elite class of brother-knights originating from outside the state's boundaries, who had taken full religious vows, isolated themselves from the population and conducted aggressive warfare: the raids of the Teutonic Knights into Lithuania; the caravans, or naval cruises, of the Knights Hospitallers in the Mediterranean, east of Greece before 1522, west of it from 1530 to 1798; and the Hospitallers' use of the *corso*, which in some ways resembled licensed piracy with the element of holy war added to it. But it sometimes takes a catalyst for the significance of a subject to European history to be generally recognized and in this case the catalyst has been radical developments in crusade studies, within which the orders are usually contextualized. Crusade historians have begun to turn from their conventional field of endeavour in Palestine and Syria to the West, where the roots of crusading lay, and in doing so they have become more conscious of the wealth of documents in European archives, many of which relate to the orders. Theatres of war like Spain and Prussia, in which they played prominent roles, are now being treated as true expressions of the crusading movement and therefore of significance to everyone, and the early modern period, in which the Hospitallers of St John were a leading force, is attracting much more attention.

It was in response to growing interest that in 1992 the London Centre for the Study of the Crusades (comprising the Library and Museum of The Most

Venerable Order of St John and the Department of History of Royal Holloway University of London) staged its first conference, the proceedings of which were published two years later.[1] A second conference, the proceedings of which make up this volume, was held in 1996, and a third is planned for the year 2000. The editors of the two volumes of proceedings, Malcolm Barber and Helen Nicholson, have not had an easy task, but the range of topics covered in them by scholars from all over the world demonstrates the scale of the international effort now being devoted to the subject and justifies the decision to hold regular meetings at which ideas could be exchanged and progress assessed.

Publications reveal shifts in intellectual emphasis and the appearance of the two volumes within four years enables one to conduct a brief analysis of the titles of the seventy-four papers listed in their contents. Many have general themes, covering all or several of the orders, but of those which are specific, twenty-eight concentrate on the Hospitallers, thirteen on the Teutonic Knights and only eleven on the Templars. The weight of research on the Hospital of St John and the Teutonic Order is not surprising. Both are in being today, the latter as an order of priests, the former almost unchanged; and as a national institution, the Teutonic Order naturally attracts German scholars. In spite of unfortunate *lacunae* – most of the fourteenth-century documents from Rhodes are missing, for example – the Hospital must be one of the best served of the orders of the Church in terms of its surviving archival material, and new sources are still being discovered, even for the twelfth-century hospital in Jerusalem, as one paper in this volume demonstrates. At first sight it is surprising that the history of the Temple, the most famous – indeed notorious – of the military orders appears to be relatively unappealing. One explanation is that historians' interests tend to follow the availability of sources – without evidence, past events are non-events – and the bulk of the Templars' central archives have long been lost, although the paper on the Rule in this volume shows what can still be done with a well-known document. It is, nevertheless, odd that there is so little new research on the Templars' provincial masterships and commanderies, because there is plenty of material on these scattered about in western archives, some of it transcribed for the Marquis d'Albon and conveniently brought together in a collection in the *Bibliothèque Nationale*. Perhaps the *Institut de Recherche et d'Histoire des Textes* at Orléans, where important work on the orders in France is proceeding, will give us a lead in this respect.

The Iberian military orders are considered in six papers, although this gives a misleading impression of the extent of the contribution to both conferences made by Spanish and Portuguese historians, who are responsible for ten papers in all; others by them deal with the military orders in general or with the commanderies of the international orders in Spain. The conference of 1992 was the one at which the large Iberian contingent of historians burst upon the

---

[1] M. Barber (ed.), *The Military Orders. Fighting for the Faith and Caring for the Sick* (Aldershot, 1994).

international scene and it has become clear that they are now a major force in research; it looks as though there are more scholars working on the crusades in the Iberian peninsula than in France and Italy.

Twenty-four papers deal with the east Mediterranean theatre of war, but nearly as many, twenty-one, are concerned with the supporting roles of the commanderies in western Europe, or with European perceptions of the orders' performance. This is an expression of the growing interest in the European convents, where most of the brothers resided and on which the headquarters relied for recruits, cash and *matériel*. The pioneering work of Michael Gervers and Anne-Marie Legras, who view the subject not as local or regional historians but as historians of the military orders concerned with regional issues, is beginning to bear fruit. And while sixteen papers report research on aspects of warfare, no less than eleven are concerned with the care of the sick and fifteen with internal religious life, a sign that the orders are increasingly being recognized as religious institutes as much as fighting machines. Out of such an approach, spearheaded over the years by Alan Forey and Anthony Luttrell, a more rounded picture is being drawn, in which the brothers are seen to have been concerned with more than warfare. Administration, in which they had great expertise, medicine (in the cases of St John, St Lazarus and the Teutonic Order) and the maintenance of their spiritual life were just as important to them.

Only four papers in the two volumes deal with architecture and five with archaeology, although these are topics which are among the most exciting in military order studies, given the quality of the surviving buildings and the wide public support generated by the interest in commandery buildings shown by national governments all over Europe, by the excavation of Belvoir in the 1960s and the discovery that it was the first datable concentric castle, by the emerging importance of Acre, and particularly of the Hospitaller compound in it, as an archaeological treasure trove, and by the detailed work undertaken by Denys Pringle and others on minor sites in Palestine. Recognizing that the conferences have been more attractive to historians than to archaeologists and architectural experts, we plan to involve representatives from the many military order museums throughout Europe in 2000.

Seven papers are concerned with the orders in the early modern period and three relate to the years after 1800. Early modern Malta is becoming a major field of research and more and more scholars are likely to be working on it, making use of the large quantities of source material there and throughout the rest of Europe. It will be interesting to see how nineteenth-century studies develop. The government of the Hospital (now more commonly called the Order of Malta) in Rome in the middle of the century was one of the most remarkable the order ever had. Inheriting a chaotic situation, the product of demoralization, fragmentation and near bankruptcy in the wake of the French Revolution and the seizure of Malta by Napoleon, it restored unity, preserved the notion of sovereignty established by Grand Master Pinto a century before in the face of attempts by national governments to convert the priories in their territories into state orders, abolished the *langues* and replaced them with national associations, and, most radical of all, persuaded the order to abandon its military functions, which were now out of date, and to concentrate on the nursing of the sick. Three papers consider aspects of interesting mutations of the Hospital and the Teutonic Order, the Protestant branches, two of which, in Germany and Holland, have had almost continuous history since the Reformation. No one, however, has yet offered a paper on the twentieth century, when the Teutonic Order became one of priests and when there emerged a plethora of orders of St John: Catholic, Protestant, Orthodox, some recognized (by outside bodies and each other), some not, some romantic, some masonic, and a few reputedly engaged in activities almost as colourful as those of which the Templars were accused seven centuries ago. The history of the military orders has something in it for everyone.

1

A Twelfth-Century Description of the Jerusalem Hospital

Benjamin Z. Kedar

In his *Die Vassallen Christi*, published in 1988, Berthold Waldstein-Wartenberg drew attention to an unknown description, extant in a single Munich manuscript, of charitable activities performed in the Jerusalem hospital. Without specifying his reasons, Waldstein-Wartenberg presented this description as the work of an anonymous German monk who visited Jerusalem before 1187. He went on to utilize it in his discussion of the Hospitallers' care of the sick and provision for foundlings, but unfortunately chose to dispense with references to specific passages of the quite long text.[1] Moreover, a comparison of his presentation with the manuscript suggests that his readings must have been in some crucial cases faulty. Yet such flaws do not detract from the importance of Waldstein-Wartenberg's discovery, one of the most exciting that have been made in crusade studies in recent years.

It is symptomatic of the communications barriers in our profession that so significant a discovery – made by a scholar who did not publish in mainstream journals – has been virtually overlooked: suffice it to mention that Waldstein-Wartenberg's book has not been listed in the *Bulletin* of the Society for the Study of the Crusades and the Latin East.[2] To the best of my knowledge, the Munich text (though not Waldstein-Wartenberg's utilization of it) has been alluded to in current research only once, and then only briefly. In his paper on

---

[1] B. Waldstein-Wartenberg, *Die Vassallen Christi: Kulturgeschichte des Johanniterordens im Mittelalter* (Vienna, 1988), pp. 110–18, 134–5, 357–60, 422.

[2] In her quite negative review of the book, M.-L. Favreau-Lilie mentioned as one of its redeeming features the use of an unknown report on the care of the sick in the Jerusalem hospital in the second half of the twelfth century, but she did not point out the singularity of the discovery: *Deutsches Archiv für Erforschung des Mittelalters*, 46 (1990), 256. Waldstein-Wartenberg's presentation has been recently utilized by Marie-Luise Windemuth, *Das Hospital als Träger der Armenfürsorge im Mittelalter*, Sudhoffs Archiv. Beihefte 36 (Stuttgart, 1995), pp. 69–70.

From *The Military Orders. Volume 2. Welfare and Warfare*. ed. Helen Nicholson. Copyright © 1998 by Helen Nicholson. Published by Ashgate Publishing Ltd, Gower House, Croft Road, Aldershot, Hampshire, GU11 3HR, Great Britain.

the Hospitallers' medical tradition, Anthony Luttrell mentioned a Latin treatise dealing with hospitals, doctors and patients that is extant in a Munich manuscript, observing that 'nothing in it indicated that it was describing the Hospitallers' hospital.'[3]

An examination of the Munich text leaves no doubt that it was indeed the Hospitallers' hospital in Jerusalem that was being dealt with. Early in his treatise the anonymous author reveals that it is the '*hospitale beati Iohannis*' he is about to extol;[4] later he states that he has been describing the care conferred on sick pilgrims '*in hospitali sancti Iohannis apud Ierosolimam*'.[5] Elsewhere he observes that the brothers of the hospital are active '*non solum in Ierosolima*', and immediately afterwards he alludes to the '*hospitale in Ierusalem*' as their main establishment.[6] Waldstein-Wartenberg was therefore right to date the text before the fall of Jerusalem in 1187.[7] On account of similarities between the text and the Hospitaller statutes of 1182 one is tempted to date the text between 1182 and 1187; but of course it is possible that the statutes merely codified prevailing practices. In any case, the Munich text presents a description of the Jerusalem hospital, possibly in the 1180s, by an eyewitness who tells us that he stayed in it for some time.[8]

Who was this eyewitness? Waldstein-Wartenberg consistently referred to him as a German monk, but did not give his reasons for doing so. Possibly it was the anonymous writer's mention of *talenta* and *solidi* that led Waldstein-Wartenberg to consider him a German, as the talent was a unit of account then current in Germany.[9] Yet this is not conclusive, since it is possible that our author, who affects a linguistic purity, chose to speak of *talenta*, which are attested in classical literature, rather than of bezants, which he may have considered a neologism. His frequent biblical citations, as well as his quotations from Ovid and Horace,[10] suggest that he was a cleric. And a cleric of considerable learning, for his vocabulary is remarkably rich: he writes, for instance, that the brother who supervises the care of the sick is called '*quasi anthonomasice hospitalarius*'; the sick women have been assigned a palace which, like that of the sick men, is '*amfractuose per vicos distinctum*'.[11]

Unfortunately, the anonymous author did not find his match in the scribe whose copy of the treatise has come down to us. Carelessly duplicating words

---

[3] A. Luttrell, 'The Hospitallers' Medical Tradition: 1291–1530', in *MO*, 1, p. 68.

[4] Clm. 4620, fols 134r, 135r; the text is tentatively edited in the appendix to the present article.

[5] Fol. 138v.

[6] Fol. 137r; also, fol. 139v.

[7] Waldstein-Wartenberg, p. 112.

[8] Clm. 4620, fol. 135r.

[9] P. Spufford believes that the talent was current in Bavaria: *Handbook of Medieval Exchange* (London, 1986), p. xxi. But see a Frisian use of talents and solidi in the years 1085–1106: W. Jesse, *Quellenbuch zur Münz- und Geldgeschichte des Mittelalters* (Halle, 1924), no. 103 (p. 38).

[10] Clm. 4620, fol. 134v.

[11] Fols 138r, 138v.

or syllables, the scribe apparently misconstrued some of the less common expressions, probably skipping words or even passages. His carelessness and limitations can be gauged by comparing other texts he copied with their critically edited counterparts: for example, where the *Josephi historiographi tractatus de exordio sacrae domus Hospitalis jerosolimitani* has '*Bohamunt*', our scribe writes '*Scamunt*';[12] when one pope states: '*Sed quod dolentes referimus*', our scribe garbles the statement by writing '*volentes referimus*';[13] where another pope grants the hospital the right that excommunicated persons '*a divino officio non coartentur*', our scribe skips the crucial '*non*';[14] and where still another pope writes '*tam exemptis quam non exemptis*', our scribe gives only the first two words, and changes, a few lines below, '*hujusmodi*' into '*hujusmode*', and '*eidem indulto*' into '*eadem indulto*',[15] and so forth. Such carelessness explains why the extant text of the treatise is very corrupt, with several sentences incomprehensible. Moreover, the text breaks off in mid-sentence, with the scribe having left blank the remaining five lines of his last page.

The codex, now in the Bavarian State Library, Munich, was formerly the property of the monastery of Benediktbeuern. It is rather astonishing to note that no less a student of Hospitaller history than Jean Delaville Le Roulx had dealt with this codex and came tantalizingly close to dealing with the treatise of our concern. In the introduction to his *Cartulaire*, published in 1894, Delaville Le Roulx stated that the codex is interesting for Hospitaller history, as beyond various fragments from the Patristic literature it contains several pieces referring to the Order of the Hospital, the last of them being a '*traité inconnu sur l'Hôpital*'.[16] Yet Delaville Le Roulx wasted no further words on this unknown work which is, of course, the anonymous treatise we are concerned with. Similarly, in the Munich Library's catalogue that appeared in the same year, 1894, the work is rather inexhaustively described as '*tractatus alius*'.[17] Only Günter Glauche's recent catalogue, published in 1994, accurately presents the text as a fragment '*über Krankenpflege bei den Johannitern*', refers to Waldstein-Wartenberg's book and dates the manuscript to the mid-fourteenth century.[18]

The treatise, as preserved in the Munich manuscript, consists of three parts, or *distinctiones*. The first amounts to a laudation of Christian charity, which culminates in the statement that it is most fitting for the House of Charity, the forerunner of all virtues, to take the Lord's precursor for its patron.[19] The

---

[12] *RHC Occid*, 5.2, p. 409; Clm. 4620, fol. 118r.

[13] *CH*, no. 1908 (2, p. 381); Clm. 4620, fol. 128v.

[14] *CH*, no. 911 (1, p. 578); Clm. 4620, fol. 131v.

[15] *CH*, no. 2981 (3, p. 5); Clm. 4620, fol. 132r.

[16] *CH*, 1, p. clxxv.

[17] *Catalogus codicum latinorum Bibliotecae regiae Monacensis*, 1.2: *Clm 2501–5250* (Munich, 1894), p. 218.

[18] G. Glauche, *Katalog der lateinischen Handschriften der Bayerischen Staatsbibliothek München, Clm 4501–4663* (Wiesbaden, 1994), pp. 210–14.

[19] Clm. 4620, fol. 134v.

second *distinctio*, which takes up more than one half of the treatise as it has come
down to us, describes the works of charity bestowed on the sick in the
Jerusalem hospital. It is in this part that the admission of the sick, the beds,
clothing, food and medical care with which they were provided, and the tasks
of the staff that attended to their needs are dealt with in detail; it concludes
with a short section on the treatment of sick and pregnant women. The rubric
of the third *distinctio* promises to deal with the attention given to orphans and
adults; but shortly after the care of orphans (or rather foundlings) has been dealt
with, and as our author turns his attention to noble pilgrims who, unwilling to
spend their own money, accept the Order's hospitality, the text breaks off. At
present there is no way to know whether the original treatise contained further
distinctiones and whether these described the military activities of the
Hospitallers; the possibility cannot be ruled out.

The abundant information contained in the treatise includes details that
specify or extend existing knowledge as well as totally new facts. Let me give
just one example of the first kind before going on to the second.

The statutes of 1182 mention that the hospital used to receive and nourish
all infants cast away by their parents.[20] Our author speaks more specifically –
and probably more realistically – of little children cast away by their *mothers*,
who were brought to the hospital by the first who found them; of mothers who
secretly, with forehead covered, deposited their infants at the hospital; and of
mothers who, having given birth to twins, retained one of the children and
delivered the other to St John. The foundlings were entrusted to nurses, each
of whom – be their number one thousand – received twelve talents a year and,
on each major holiday, a meal equal to that of the brothers in quantity and
variety. Moreover, the nurses were under constant supervision. Often they had
to bring the children to the hospital, where each was inspected by the sisters
of the house; and if these found that a child had been badly attended, it was
committed to the custody of another nurse. We are told that these children were
known, especially in the Latin East, as *filii beati Iohannis*. On reaching adulthood
they were given the choice to serve the one who had raised them – St John –
or 'to embrace the seductive allurements of the frivolous world.'[21] The passage
implies that in Frankish Jerusalem the abandonment of infants by poor
mothers was quite common. If so, Jerusalem may have been conspicuous in
this respect, for John Boswell has claimed that, except for Scandinavia, there
is little evidence for the abandonment of children in twelfth-century Europe.[22]

The first of the new pieces of information concerns admission. Our author
relates that, with the sole exception of lepers, the hospital admits all sick, of
whichever origin and status and of both sexes, and 'as this holy house rightly

---

[20] *CH*, no. 627 (1, p. 428).

[21] Clm. 4620, fol. 139r–v.

[22] J. Boswell, *The Kindness of Strangers: The Abandonment of Children in Western Europe from Late
Antiquity to the Renaissance* (London, 1988), pp. 275–95.

understands that the Lord invites all to salvation, wishing no one to perish, also men of pagan creed find in it mercy, and also Jews, if they flock to it.'[23] Thus, according to our eyewitness, pagans – that is, Muslims – and Jews were admitted to the hospital.[24] This is an extraordinary statement that may entail a modification of the accepted view about the exclusively Christian character of twelfth-century Frankish Jerusalem. (Indeed, the presence of non-Christians in the hospital may be also hinted at in the stipulation of the statutes of 1182 that those who cannot eat pork or mutton should be given chicken).[25]

The second new piece of information concerns what in modern parlance might be called the Hospitallers' field medical service. Our author relates that whenever the Christians move out on an expedition against the pagans, those who are wounded in battle seek help in tent hospitals, where they are attended to. Those who need further care are transported – on camels, horses, mules and donkeys – to the hospital in Jerusalem, or to closer retreats. And if the beasts of burden belonging to the hospital do not suffice for the transportation, the Hospitallers hire beasts belonging to others; and if these, too, do not suffice, the wounded get on the mounts of the brothers, with the brothers themselves – even the noble ones – returning on foot.[26] This description makes for a better understanding of the report that after the battle of Montgisard in 1177, in which 1,100 Franks met their death, 750 seriously wounded men were taken in by the Hospital.[27]

In the twelfth century, field hospitals seem to have been a rarity. In the Muslim realm, one of the earliest was equipped in about 1120, in Iraq, by the *mustawfī* 'Azīz al-Dīn: 200 Bactrian camels transported the hospital, which consisted of tents and was staffed by physicians and attendants who had instruments and medications at their disposal.[28] Thus, at the time our author wrote his treatise, the Hospitallers appear to have been in the forefront in this regard, whether influenced by Oriental practices or not.

---

[23] Clm. 4620, fol. 135r.

[24] It may be noted that in Visigothic Spain in about 600, the *xenodochium* of Merida provided medical care to slaves and free men, Christians and Jews: Paulus Emeritanus Diaconus, *De vita patrum Emeritensium*, in PL, 80, col. 139; C.F. Heusinger, 'Ein Beitrag zur ältesten Geschichte der Krankenhäuser im Occidente', *Janus. Zeitschrift für Geschichte und Literatur der Medizin*, 1 (1846), 772–3; K. Sudhoff, 'Aus der Geschichte des Krankenhauswesens im früheren Mittelalter in Morgenland und Abendland', *Sudhoffs Archiv für Geschichte der Medizin*, 21 (1929), 182.

[25] *CH*, no. 627 (1, p. 428); Jonathan Riley-Smith's suggestion.

[26] Clm. 4620, fol. 137r.

[27] The report, first edited by J. Ficker in 1852, was republished by R. Röhricht, *Beiträge zur Geschichte der Kreuzzüge*, 2 (Berlin, 1878), note 45 on pp. 127–8; for a translation and discussion see [K.] Herquet, 'Die Doppelschlacht von Ramle-Montgisard (1177) nach einer urkundlichen Darstellung des Großmeisters Roger de Molins', *Wochenblatt der Johanniter-Ordens-Balley Brandenburg*, 23 (1882), 254–8.

[28] R. Levy, *A Baghdad Chronicle* (Cambridge, 1929), p. 212, after *Histoire des Seldjoucides de l'Iraq, par al-Bondari, d'après Imād ad-Dīn al-Kātib al-Isfahānī*, ed. Th. Houtsma (Leiden, 1889), p. 137.

Another new piece of information allows us to make some guesses about the hospital's size and location. Our author reports that the *palacium infirmorum* was divided into eleven *vici*, or wards. This number could be doubled whenever the number of sick exceeded the palace's capacity: in that case, the brothers would give up their dormitory to the sick and lie on the ground wherever they found a place. The sick women had a *palacium* of their own, divided into an unspecified number of *vici*.[29]

Unfortunately, our author does not specify how many male sick could be accommodated in the eleven *vici*. John of Würzburg, whose pilgrimage has been recently redated by Robert Huygens to the early 1160s, reports that at the time of his visit there were up to 2000 sick in the various *mansiones* of the hospital. Theoderich – who according to Huygens's redating probably visited Jerusalem in 1169 – writes that he saw in the *palatium* more than 1000 beds.[30] It is now possible to explain this discrepancy by assuming that John saw the hospital during an emergency, with both the *palacium* and the dormitory occupied by the sick, whereas Theoderich's visit took place at a more normal juncture. Such reasoning ties in with the report about the battle of Montgisard, according to which the 900 sick who had been in the Jerusalem hospital before the battle were joined by 750 men who were seriously injured in it.[31] In other words, in normal times the hospital could probably accommodate some 900 or 1000 sick.[32] As in each of the eleven *vici* there were one *magister* and twelve *clientes*,[33] the total number of attendants was 143. If we assume that on a given day there were 1000 sick in the *palacium*, we arrive at seven sick per attendant; and if we assume that the number of sick was only 900, the respective figure is 6.3. A ratio of 6.3 to seven patients per attendant is not markedly different from present-day ratios: for example, at the Hadassah Hospital, Jerusalem, the ratio is five to six patients per nurse. Yet the twelfth century also knew much lower ratios: at the hospital of the Pantocrator monastery in Constantinople, which John Comnenus founded in 1136, thirty-six attendants served fifty sick, a ratio of 1.4 patients per attendant![34]

---

[29] Clm. 4620, fols 135v, 138v.

[30] *Peregrinationes tres. Saewulf, John of Würzburg, Theodericus*, ed. R.B.C. Huygens, Corpus Christianorum, Continuatio Mediaevalis, 139 (Turnhout, 1994), pp. 131, 157–8. Similarly, Ludolph of Suchem relates in the early fourteenth century that in the erstwhile Hospitaller *palatium* there is a pilgrims' hospice that can easily accommodate 1,000 men: Ludolph of Suchem, *De itinere Terrae Sanctae liber*, ed. F. Deycks, Bibliothek des Litterarischen Vereins in Stuttgart, 25 (Stuttgart, 1851), p. 81. The above texts are assembled in E.E. Hume, *Medical Work of the Knights Hospitallers of Saint John in Jerusalem* (Baltimore, 1940), pp. 14–18.

[31] See note 27 above.

[32] Cf. Waldstein-Wartenberg, p. 110.

[33] Clm. 4620, fol. 135v.

[34] P. Gautier, 'Le Typikon du Christ Sauveur Pantocrator', *Revue des études byzantines*, 32 (1974), 9–10. In addition to the thirty-six assistants and servants, there were eleven physicians.

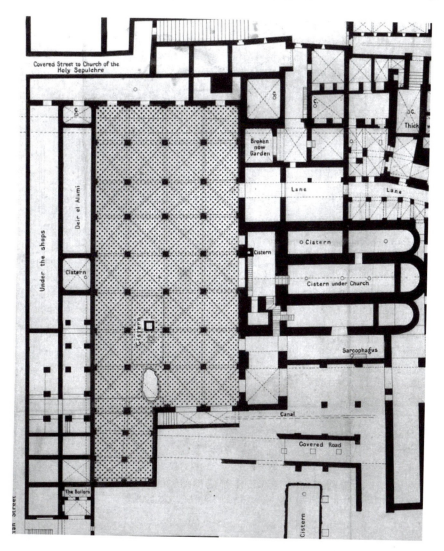

Figure 1.1   Plan of the north-western part of the Muristan, or Hospital of the Knights of St John at Jerusalem, by C. Schick. The shaded area represents the probable location of the hospital's eleven wards.

Where was the *palacium infirmorum* located? Conrad Schick, in an article published posthumously in 1902, convincingly argued that it was situated in a large building the remains of which were discovered in the north-western part of the Muristan, just to the west of Sancta Maria Maior.[35] Waldstein-Wartenberg, on the other hand, sought the *palacium* in a still larger complex in the south-eastern part of the Muristan.[36] However, according to my count the number of aisles in the said complex is thirteen, whereas in the large building in the north-west, where Schick located the *palacium*, I count eleven sections (eight large and three small), running from west to east, which may well be identified with the eleven *vici* of our treatise (Figure 1.1).

The eight large sections cover an area of 230 by 120 feet, the three small ones an area of 52 by 48 feet. Could 900 to 1000 beds have stood there? Neither the statutes of 1182 nor the treatise give the beds' measurements. However, the municipal statutes of Marseilles of 1253 state that the minimum space allotted to a pilgrim on a ship sailing to the Holy Land should be 6½ *palmae* long and 2½ *palmae* wide,[37] with a *palma* amounting to about 10 inches.[38] To reconstruct a twelfth-century Jerusalem hospital bed on the basis of a thirteenth-century Marseillais ship space allotment is not the best procedure conceivable, yet in the absence of better data let us experiment with what we have. Remembering the stipulation of the statutes of 1182 that *les liz des malades fucent fait en longeur et en larjour au plus covenable que estre poyssent à reposer*, and the statement of our author that the beds were 'beautifully wrought',[39] let us add 12 per cent to the Marseillais minima, and arrive at a bed that measures 73 by 28 inches. Positing a space of 18 inches between the beds within a row, and a space of 30 inches between the rows, we arrive at 837 beds in the eight large sections and 72 beds in the three small ones, or 909 beds in all.

Finally, what can we learn from the treatise about the relative position of the Frankish hospital in Jerusalem among contemporaneous Oriental counterparts?

---

[35] C. Schick, 'The Muristan, or the Site of the Hospital of St John in Jerusalem', *Palestine Exploration Fund. Quarterly Statement* (1902), 49–50 and plan. Schick died on 23 December 1901: see A. Carmel, *Christen als Pioniere im Heiligen Land. Ein Beitrag zur Geschichte der Pilgermission und des Wiederaufbaus Palästinas im 19. Jahrhundert* (Basel 1980), opposite p. 178. Schick's hypothesis was accepted by E.J. King, *The Knights Hospitallers in the Holy Land* (London, 1931), pp. 65–6; J. Riley-Smith, *The Knights of St John in Jerusalem and Cyprus, c. 1050–1310* (London, 1967), p. 247; M. Benvenisti, *The Crusaders in the Holy Land* (Jerusalem, 1970), pp. 59, 62; see also D.S. Richards, 'Saladin's Hospital in Jerusalem: Its Foundation and Some Later Archival Material', in *The Frankish Wars and their Influence on Palestine*, ed. K. Athamina and R. Heacock (Birzeit, 1994), p. 72.

[36] Waldstein-Wartenberg, pp. 108–10.

[37] *Les Statuts municipaux de Marseille*, 4.25, ed. R. Pernoud (Monaco and Paris, 1949), p. 158; also p. xlviii. The passage was utilized by J. Prawer, *The Latin Kingdom of Jerusalem: European Colonialism in the Middle Ages* (London, 1972), p. 201.

[38] See M. Mendelssohn, *Handbuch der Münz-, Maaß- und Gewichtskunde* (Potsdam, 1855; repr. Neustrelitz, 1994), pp. 18 (Genoa), 35 (Naples), 37 (Nizza), 38 (Palermo); L.C. Bleibtreu, *Handbuch der Münz-, Maaß- und Gewichtskunde* (Stuttgart, 1863), pp. 306 (Naples), 326 (Nizza), 332 (Palermo).

[39] *CH*, no. 627 (1, p. 426); Clm. 4620, fol. 135v.

Several details mentioned by our author recall Byzantine *typika* and descriptions of medical practice in the Muslim realm,[40] but they do not throw new light on the question – repeatedly if inconclusively discussed in the literature[41] – as to whether the model for the Jerusalem hospital should be sought in Byzantium or in the world of Islam. Evidence bearing on this issue appears, however, in a virtually overlooked passage by Ibn Jubayr, the Muslim pilgrim from Granada who passed through Frankish Galilee in 1184. Ibn Jubayr writes that he saw near Palermo churches set apart for the Christian sick: 'in their cities,' he reports, 'they have some such, along the lines of the Muslim hospitals, and we have seen some such [belonging] to them in Acre and Tyre. We marvelled at such solicitude.'[42] Evidently, the Frankish and Sicilian hospitals were sufficiently similar to Muslim ones to elicit so unequivocal an observation. On the other hand, Ibn Jubayr's designation of the Christian establishments as churches betrays an awareness of the ecclesiastical character that distinguished them from the Islamic hospitals, which were founded by rulers and administered by government officials.

Our treatise, however, leaves little doubt as to the relative backwardness of the Jerusalem hospital. Comparable institutions in the Muslim and Byzantine spheres were divided into specialized wards. Thus in Aḥmad ibn Ṭūlūn's hospital in al-Fusṭāṭ, founded in 872, each ward was earmarked for a different disease or for surgical operations.[43] The Hospital of the Pantocrator in Constantinople, founded in 1136, was divided into five wards: one for patients who sustained wounds or fractures, another for patients with ophthalmological or stomach problems, a third for sick women, and the remaining two for other patients.[44] Our author, on the other hand, while repeatedly referring to the *vici*

---

[40] I intend to discuss these parallels in a future publication.

[41] E. Wickersheimer, 'Organisation et législation sanitaires au Royaume franc de Jérusalem', *Archives internationales d'histoire des sciences*, 4 (1951), 699; A. Philipsborn, 'Les Premiers hôpitaux au Moyen Age (Orient et Occident)', *La nouvelle Clio*, 6 (1954), 161; Riley-Smith, p. 335; T.S. Miller, 'The Knights of St John and the Hospitals of the Latin West', *Speculum*, 53 (1978), 723–33.

[42] Ibn Jubayr, *The Travels*, ed. W. Wright and M.J. de Goeje (Leiden, 1907), p. 330; my thanks to Prof. Etan Kohlberg for his translation. The passage, appearing in a chapter dealing with Sicily, has not been noted by historians of the crusades; it was partially utilized by R.F. Bridgman, 'Evolution comparée de l'organisation hospitalière en Europe et en pays d'Islam. Influences mutuelles au Moyen Age et à la Renaissance', in *Atti del primo congresso europeo di storia ospitaliera, 6–12 giugno 1960* (Reggio Emilia, 1962), p. 234.

[43] S. Hamarneh, 'Development of Hospitals in Islam', *Journal of the History of Medicine*, 17 (1962), 373. On wards in other Islamic hospitals see A. Issa Bey, *Histoire des Bimaristans (Hôpitaux) à l'époque islamique* (Cairo, 1928), p. 4; C. Elgood, *A Medical History of Persia and the Eastern Caliphate from the Earliest Times until the Year 1932* (Cambridge, 1951), pp. 177–8. Islamic hospitals stood out for their wards for the mentally ill: M. Dols, 'Insanity in Byzantine and Islamic Medicine', *Dumbarton Oaks Papers*, 38 (1984), 142.

[44] Gautier, p. 82; see also P.S. Codellas, 'The Pantocrator, the Imperial Byzantine Medical Center of XIIth Century AD in Constantinople', *Bulletin of the History of Medicine*, 12 (1942), 392–410. For a general survey see T.S. Miller, 'Byzantine Hospitals', *Dumbarton Oaks Papers*, 38 (1984), 53–63.

of the Jerusalem hospital, does not even hint that these wards might have specialized in different diseases.

Again, the number of physicians in the Jerusalem hospital was strikingly low: four resident physicians[45] for 900 to 1000 sick! On the other hand, the tenth-century 'Aḍudī Hospital in Baghdad had twenty-four physicians – in 1068 their number was raised to twenty-eight – and the Pantocrator Hospital had eleven physicians attending just fifty sick.[46] Probably some of the 900 to 1000 Jerusalem inmates were feeble rather than ill, and did not require much medical care. Also, the scarcity of doctors in the Jerusalem hospital may have been partially offset by more intensive work: whereas Ibn Jubayr reports that in the 'Aḍudī Hospital doctors visited the sick every Monday and Thursday, and that the doctors of the hospital Nūr al-Dīn established in Damascus visited the sick early each morning,[47] our author reports that in the Jerusalem hospital doctors made their rounds twice a day.[48] The Jerusalem hospital must have been conspicuous for its sheer size: the 3,344 square yards of its eleven wards dwarf the 165 square yards of the purported wardrooms of Nūr al-Dīn's hospital.[49] Still, from a professional viewpoint, the Jerusalem hospital lagged significantly behind its counterparts – and probable models – in the Muslim and Byzantine spheres. In this respect, as in several others, twelfth-century Latins still played Third World *vis-à-vis* the First and Second Worlds of the realms of Islam and Byzantium.

And yet, while from the standpoint of Oriental medicine the hospital must have appeared quite backward, it amounted to an entirely new departure when considered in a Western context. It has been pointed out recently that when, in late eleventh-century southern Italy, Constantine the African translated from the Arabic *The Complete Book of the Medical Art* by 'Alī ibn al-'Abbās al-Majūsī, he suppressed the advice to visit hospitals in order to gain medical knowledge there; evidently hospitals in which such knowledge could have been acquired did not exist in the West at the time.[50] Indeed, physicians attached to Western hospitals appear in the documentation only from the

---

[45] Clm. 4620, fol. 136v; *CH*, nos 627, 690 (1, pp. 426, 458).

[46] On the 'Aḍudi Hospital see Elgood, pp. 160–71; Hamarneh, 369–70. For the Pantocrator Hospital see note 34 above.

[47] *The Travels of Ibn Jubayr*, tr. R.J.C. Broadhurst (London, 1952), pp. 234–5, 286. For Damascus, see also D. Jetter, 'Zur Architektur islamischer Krankenhäuser', *Sudhoffs Archiv für Geschichte der Medizin und der Naturwissenschaften*, 45 (1961), 266–7.

[48] Clm. 4620, fol. 136v.

[49] Calculations based on Schick, pp. 49–50 and plan; E. Herzfeld, 'Damascus: Studies in Architecture – I', *Ars Islamica*, 9 (1942), 5–6 (text and plan); Y. Tabbaa, 'Geometry and Memory in the Design of the Madrasat al-Firdows in Aleppo', in *Theories and Principles of Design in the Architecture of Islamic Societies* (Cambridge, Mass., 1988), p. 28 (plan).

[50] D. Jacquart, 'Le Sens donné par Constantin l'Africain à son oeuvre: les chapitres introductifs en arabe et en latin', in *Constantine the African and 'Alī ibn al-'Abbās al-Maǧūsī. The* Pantegni *and Related Texts*, ed. C. Burnett and D. Jacquart (Leiden, 1994), p. 79.

thirteenth century onwards, and even then no hospital seems to have had more than a single physician.[51] Thus the four doctors of the Jerusalem hospital, so pathetically few when regarded from Baghdad or Constantinople, amount to a dramatic innovation when viewed from Rome, Paris or London.

APPENDIX

A provisional edition of Clm. 4620, fol. 132v–139v[*]

Sicut absurdum nimis est, ymo prophanam abhominationis sapit insaniam, in Dei mirabilibus oblocucione malignari erronei, ita et valde perniciosum esse arbitramur, cognita immensitatis nostri Salvatoris tacere magnalia, quia tanto periculosius eius laudes formidolosa taciturnitate reticentur, quanto gloriosius pia vocis exultacione promulgantur. Cum igitur per universa mundi climata animator omnium Deus infinita misericordie opera cum servis suis exercuerit, nusquam tamen excellentius, nusquam manifestius quam in partibus Syrie, in quibus, sola caritate incitante, toti<us>[a] humani generis salutem misericorditer operatus est. Nam cum hominem inobediencie tabe fraudulenta, suggestione dyabolica, persuasione femina contaminatum, paradysi voluptatum immunem, condoleret, caritas Deum traxit ad terras, ne is, que<m>, alto divine bonitatis consilio sibi conformem, omni carens invidia Deus beatitudinis sue participem disposuerat, in eternum exularet. Triplici ergo Dominus caritatis vinculo innodatus, cuius iocundo admonicionis fomitem crebro sentiens implicitum, pius ad humane imbecillitatis decliv<i>a descendit. In Nazareth civitate Galilee, celesti paranympho Gabriele previo, caritate trahente in utero virginis intemerate spiritu sancto voluit concipi. Secreto, quod ipse novit, incarnatus cum nostre carnis substantia, in Bethlehem pro nobis dignatus est nasci, cuius tamen principium nequit comprehendi. Post multa tandem mirificanda et manifesta opera, quibus indubitanter verus Deus et verus homo cognosci poterat, dure cervicis populus, generacio prava, genus perversum, gens iudaica

---

[51] For example, E. Wickersheimer, 'Médecins et chirurgiens dans les hôpitaux du moyen âge', *Janus. Archives internationales pour l'histoire de la médecine et la géographie médicale*, 32 (1928), 1–11.

[*] I should like to thank Dr Susan Edgington and Dr Günter Glauche for their help with the transcription of this text, and especially Professor Robert B.C. Huygens, who checked the transcription against photostats of the manuscript, corrected a large number of mistakes, offered various conjectures, identified several quotations, and saved me from sundry pitfalls. Nevertheless, Professor Huygens believes that the text is unpublishable, since even he could not decipher or understand much more than he has already corrected. Yet as most of the text is now comprehensible and as it contains significant information, I decided to present this tentative edition, the remaining deficiencies of which are, of course, my own responsibility. I must reiterate that I do not understand several sentences; their number exceeds that of the bracketed question marks, which merely denote words about whose reading I am not certain. Hopefully this provisional text will allow readers to offer further, or better, conjectures.

[a] < > denotes text added by the editor.

in Ierusalem eum colaphis cesit, sibi odi<bi>lia[?] irrogavit, sputo conspuit, spinis coronavit, in derisu adoravit, cruci affixit, manus et pedes illius clavis perforavit, aceto fellito potavit, postea lancea latus suum perforavit; ad hec omnia pro nobis sed et pro irrogantibus ipsis pie perpaciendi illum transduxit caritas, pro quo angelice multitudinis, si vellet, utique decertasset potestas, sicut ipse ad beatum Petrum, servi auriculam amputantem, dixit: *An putas* quod *non possum rogare Patrem meum et exhibebit mihi modo plus quam .xii.* /fol. 133r/ *legiones angelorum.*[1] Nam que[a] humani vigoris violentia illum poterat molestare, cuius pedibus se mare calcabile prebuit, pro cuius angustia terra tremuit, duriciam suam petra[b] dirupit, templum vela decidit,[2] sol splendoris sui radios ascendit? Que cum vidissent et invidi, testimonium perhibebant veritati, dicentes: *Vere Filius Dei erat iste.*[3] Sola igitur ad tantas pressuras pro homine sustinendas Deum incitavit caritas, ad quas creatori suo ingerendas dyabolica hominem animavit iniquitas. Ex tanti siquidem immanitate sceleris dominica caro consternata patri nescia, iniquorum manibus pro alieno delicto subdenda, et cum no<n>dum tunc teneretur a perfidis, sudorem effudit saguineum tamquam future passionis presagium. Hinc et ait: *Tristis est anima mea usque ad mortem.*[4] Que tristicia satis innotuit cum ipse ter prostratus terre oraret, dicens: *Pater, si* fieri potest, *transeat a me calix iste.*[5] Nullius revera terrene potestatis impulsu coarctatus dixit: 'si fieri potest,' sed tantum desuper date, secundum quod dixit ad Pylatum: *Non haberes potestatem adversum me ullam nisi tibi datum esset desuper.*[6] Quo namque humani furoris consternaretur strepitu, quo plecti posset nutu, eius dominationi omnia subduntur et termino, qui solo verbo cuncta creavit ex nichilo, sicut per psalmistam dictum est: *Dixit et facta sunt* omnia, *mandavit et creata sunt* universa.[7] Sed nec etiam aliqua necessitate sua cogente pro nobis passus est Dominus, cuius regnum inestimabiliter gloriosum nullius indiget apposicione ut melioraretur, nullius auxilio ut roboraretur, iuxta illud: Nec *oculus vidit*[c] nec *auris audivit nec in cor hominis ascendit* quanta *preparavit Deus* diligentibus se.[8] Deus enim, ut dicit apostolus, prius dilexit nos, quare et pro nobis venit,[9] nec tamen eo quod nostrum sibi consorcium in aliquo esset necessarium, sed ineffabili bonitate sua tantum congratulativum, quod Iudea, tamquam bestiali sensualitate vegetata consilio superbie, super se ipsam, quanta[?] incredula celestium beneficiorum ingrata Deum ad se venientem

---

[a] MS: qui.   [b] MS: petram.   [c] audivit *struck out before* vidit.

---

[1] Mt 26, 53.
[2] cf. Mt 27, 51.
[3] Mt 27, 54.
[4] Mt 26, 38; Mk. 14, 34.
[5] Mt 26, 39.
[6] Jn 19, 11.
[7] Ps 32, 9.
[8] 1 Cor 2, 9.
[9] cf. 1 Jn 4, 19.

respuit, miracula facientem non credidit, in homine latentem non agnovit, unde et ipse Dominus: *Filios enutrivi et exaltavi, ipsi autem* graviter *spreverunt me.*[10] Et per prophetam quasi voce querula dixit: *O vos omnes qui transitis per viam*[11] etc. Nam que tristitia gravior, quis magis coangustans dolor, quam ut creatura creatorem, opus opificem, filius patrem, pecus pastorem, /fol. 133v/ sceleratus innocentem, servus dominum turpi morti condempnet? Hoc tamen persuadente caritate celestis sustinuit misericordia, que ut expedit nimis prestabilis est malitia. Manifestum est ergo quod sola caritas, ut audacter loquar, Deum coegit a celi descendere solio ut homo angelorum frueretur contubernio,[a] supremum mirabiliter protraxit ad yma ut[b] miserabiliter elapsum hominem erigeret ad suprema, Deum atrahens nodolo illa que avit amplexu ut incarceratum hominem a tartareo expediret occasu. Celestis per caritatem sic ad terras inclinata est potestas, ut ad celos humana extolleretur infirmitas. Deus humanatus per hanc humiliter tulit conversacionem hominum, ut homines magnifice concives efficeret angelorum, per istam excelsi regis gloria[c] manifesta est in terris et pax data hominibus bone voluntatis,[12] Deum adducendo lucem in tenebras perfudit et servilem humane depressionis condicionem in veram libertatem redegit. Quis enim sufficeret caritatis magnificentiam exprimere, que regem glorie in femineo ventre servi formam fecit induere, non deflorata tamen virginalis uteri castitate? Cui celorum non poterat sufficere amplitudo, illum caritas puellari reclusit in gremio. Per hanc casta ubera regem lactaverunt angelorum, qui omni carni nutis prestat edulium. Cui celestium subditur celsitudo,[d] per caritatem visum[?] deportatur virgineo. Instigante caritate, puellaria illum brachia meruerunt baiulare, in cuius digito tota dependet moles terre.[13] Qui iugi laude celestibus modulis angelicus opes decantat et ordo, infinita[e] caritate humili pro nobis reclinata est in presepio. Sic caritas Deum pro homine humiliavit in terris, ut eo sublimius hominem exaltaret in celis. O ineffabilis virtus caritatis, que sola magistravit omnipotentem, traxit incommutabilem, ligavit insuperabilem, vulneravit impassibilem, eternum fecit mortalem. Licet enim Deus omnipotens sit, se tamen a vinculis caritatis expedire non potuit, nam et cum quadrifido etiam nexu sibi alligavit. Quia illum misericordie brachiis amplexata complosis manibus pietatis tenuit, circa tameratis[?] digitis benignitatis ipsum invectendo humilitatis pectori visu efficacissimo astrinxit. Istas namque irremissiva frequentia sibi collaterales habet avertas[?] et tamquam earum asistrix humanorum continuo famulatu suffraganeos. Quare et omnium caritatis

---

[a] contur *deleted before* contubernio.   [b] MS: ut *bis.*   [c] MS: gloriam.   [d] amplitudo *deleted before* celsitudo.   [e] MS: infinitia.

[10] Is 1, 2.
[11] Lam 1, 12.
[12] cf. Lk 2, 14.
[13] cf. Is 40, 12.

deliciarum /fol. 134r/ conscie in cellulam amenitatis hostio producunt aperto
secretarios ipse preambule. Iste merces pias dulcore caritatis imbuunt, cuius
et presentiam limpido illis in nutu ostendunt. Hec proculdubio semita iusticie,
methodus direccionis, via rectitudinis, per quam ad Deum curritur, per quam
ad Deum venitur, via Dei est ad homines et via hominis ad Deum. Via est
Domini ad hominem[a] deducens et hominem ad Deum dirigens, via est per
quam Deus venit ad terras, per quas humanas degustavit molestias, per quam
ad celos retrogradi nostras adportavit iniurias. Via est per quam corda humilium
ad Deum eriguntur et per quam vota precum ante conspectum divine maiestatis
protenduntur. Via est vias distortas[b] extendens[c] et vias rectas producens, via
que directo tramite secreta celestia penetrat et oberrantes a tortuoso amfractu
iniquitatis exorbitat. De hac enim via dicit apostolus: *Adhuc excellentiorem viam
vobis demonstr*abo.[14] Revera de caritate dixit, cuius excellentiam, cuius vim
retenturam, cuius redivivum dulcedinis saporem presenserat cum diceret:
*Quis non separabit a caritate Christi, tribulacio an angustia an persecucio an fames
an nudita<s> an gladius.*[15] *Certus sum quia neque mors neque vita neque angeli
neque principatus* neque potestates *neque instantia neque futura neque fortitud*o *neque
profundum neque altitudo neque creatura aliqua poterit nos separare a caritate Dei.*[16]
Et vera via est caritas, quia via superexcellens et supereminens est. Superexcellens namque omnis viduatur virtus que caritatis anulo non subarratur, que
vinculo illius non constringatur. Unde apostolus: *Si li<n>guis hominum loquar
et angelorum, caritatem non hab*uero, *factus sum velud es sonans aut cymbalum
tinniens. Et si habuero prophetiam et omnem scientiam et noverim* in scientia *omnia
et* si *habuero omnem fidem, ita ut montes transferam, caritatem autem non habuero,
nichil sum. Et si distribuero in cibos pauperum omnes facultates meas et tradidero corpus
meum* ita *ut ardeam, caritatem autem non habuero, nichil mihi prodest,*[17] et ideo
superexcellens. Supereminens est quoniam ab illa omnes alie virtutes sumunt
exordium et primeve originis sue contrahunt eminentiam. Quare in sacro
eloquio bene per oleum intelligitur, quia sicut cuilibet alii liquori appositum
supereminet oleum, sic et caritas aliarum omnium superexcellitur celsitudini
virtutum. Unde ipsa sola et Deus meruit dici et est hinc <quod> beatus
Johannes, qui super pectus dominicum in cena recubuit utpote hauriens
secretum, de quo bibit divinitatis sacramentum, cui etiam postmodum in
extasi rapto[d] secreta revelata sunt celestia, dixit:[e] /fol. 134v/ *Deus caritas est.*[18]
Et ut expressam ydemptitatem caritatis cum Deo nobis insinuaret, adiecit: *Et*

---

[a] deum *deleted before* hominem.   [b] in *deleted before* distortas.   [c] ostendens *struck out before*
extendens.   [d] MS: raptum.   [e] celestia dixit *bis.*

[14] 1 Cor 12, 31.
[15] Rom 8, 35.
[16] Rom 8, 38–39.
[17] 1 Cor 13, 1–3.
[18] 1 Jn 4, 16.

qui manet in caritate, in Deo manet, et Deus in eo.[19] Sed quia hec tanta domina eodem Deo nostra tempora prescivit futura plurima periculosa, ut in quibus iuxta propheticum ewangeliste sermonem: Super*habundat iniquitas*, querende multitudinis *refrigescit caritas*,[20] prope Domini nostri sepulcro ac Calvarie loco quedam voluptatis sue thalamum quasi amoris posuit privilegio, unde in Ierosolima, velud ad quam omnium nationum populi peregre confluunt, voluntatem suam homines instruant et opera sibi accepta *occul<a>ta fide*[21] dilectoribus suis manifestaret. Et ideo ne redemptos suos et inprobos[?] ti[?] lutee obscenitatis volutabro defedatos amitteret, vel in tenebroso ignorancie devio aberrare permitteret, hunc enim thalamum suum frequens usus hominum 'hospitale beati Iohannis' app<e>llat, quod racione non vacat.[a] Nam cum karitas maxima sit virtutum, bene domus sue illum construit sponsum quo, atestante Christo, *non surrexit maior inter natos mulierum*,[22] ut sic maioritate maioritati consueta felix fieret matrimonium iuxta illud poete gentilis: *Si qua volens apte nube<re>, nube pari.*[23] Dignum et fuit ut domus omnibus contanda[?] illo gauderet marito, qui utriusque veneratur apostolo. Intus veneracione Iacob et Esau reperiuntur concordes, illi domui pater familias competenter preficitur, in qua fere omnium li<n>guarum[b] conveniunt varietates. Item pauperum tam generale habitaculum illi congrue maritavit caritas, quem in celis cum excellentia spirituali ditavit paupertas. Congruum itaque fuit et valde consentaneum ut caritas, omnium preambula virtutum, precursorem Domini domus sue recolligeret patronum. Hec enim domus erogative caritatis gemina proroganter doceatur, hec eius patronus prerogante gratia[c] Christi testimonio sublimatur. Sed licet huius reverende excellencia laude, ymo magis laude digna per orbem terrarum longe lateque famosa promulgacione[d] sit diffusa, tamen dignum duxi pro mee modulo parvitatis absque ornatu rethorico sive leporis elegantia in medium proferre, quanta in ea sanctitas exhibicionesque misericordie opera usque peregre divina prestante gratia prefectus *oculis subiecta fidelibus*[24] adnotatarum[e][?]. Et quoniam antiquata veterum inolevit consuetudo, quod non solum mundi sectatores, sed et religiosi proch dolor viri, homines pompose preciosarum vestium fastu[f] splendidos corvi[?] vultu, sermone blando, /fol. 135r/ adulatoriis gule irritamentis preveniunt, pauperes econtrario fronte lurida, li<n>gue asperitate, federe[g] obliquo exasperant, ideo

---

[a] MS: vocat.   [b] MS *adds*: fere liguarum.   [c] MS: gratie.   [d] MS: permulgacione.   [e] MS: adnotararum [?].   [f] MS: faustu.   [g] MS: sedere.

---

[19] 1 Jn 4, 16.

[20] Mt 24, 12.

[21] On the expression *fidem ... oculatam* see *Lettres de Jacques de Vitry*, ed. R.B.C. Huygens (Leiden, 1960), p. 73, note to Letter 1, line 66.

[22] Mt 11, 11.

[23] Ovid, *Epistulae Heroidum*, 9, 32.

[24] Horace, *Ars poetica*, 181.

paupertate, vere religionis vere exploratrice, mihi conscia cunctis ignotus plebeo amictu velatus clientem componens, predictam domum aliquamdiu cohabitavi, ut sic sublimium oculorum me non laterent offendicula et modicos secretos[a] facilius penetrarem recessus et ita vigilanti cura quanto diligentius potui latitante cum cautela fraternitatis domus illius unanimitatem indigui. Ne veridice narracionis[b] explanacionem falsitatis deturparet admixtio et ne probosi mendacii tremebundi me dampnaret auditorum castigatio, ab illis ergo huiusmodi propositi nostri summamus inicium, quos in ea domo caritate suadente, beato Iohanne volente, primiciavit[?] fidelium.

Secunda inchoat distinccio demonstrans que et quanta et qualiter exhibentur infirmis in hospitali.

In primis igitur et primi dominacionis primatum in hospitali predicto optinent pauperes infirmi quacumque infirmitate detenti; sola excipitur lepra, que nescio qua communi omnium hominum exasperacione odibilis evitatur et, aliorum communione sibi denegata, tamquam solitudinis in devio seponitur. Sed omnes alii, cuiuscumque infirmitatis labore cruciati aliena indigentes cura ut convalescant, famulatu alieno ut comedant, alieni ducatus sustentacione ut ambulent, immo et quibuscumque sive in toto corpore sive in qualibet parte naturalis potentie denegatur officium, illis pie sibi prerogatur divinum. Et sicut *non est personarum acceptor Deus*,[25] cuiuscumque nacionis cuiuscumque condicionisque et utriusque sexus infirmi recolliguntur in ista domo ut, Domini misericordia, quanto accumulatur multitudo languencium, tanto ibi augmentatur numerositas dominorum. Quin ymo, sane intelligens domus hec sancta quod omnes Dominus ad salutem invitans neminem vult perire,[26] pagane professionis homines in ea etiam misericordiam inveniunt, sed et Iudei, si affluunt, ut pro quibus seipsum affligentibus oravit Dominus, dicens: *Pater* ignosce *illis* quia ne*sciunt quid faciunt*.[27] In quo etiam beata domus celestem viriliter amplectitur doctrinam, quia dicitur: *Diligite inimicos vestros* et *benefacite hiis qui oderunt vos*;[28] et alibi: 'Diligendi sunt amici in Deo et inimici propter Deum.' Item si pauperum egrotantium natura vicium fuerit defecta,[c] ut proprii vigoris beneficio beati Iohannis hospitale non possint adire, misericorditer /fol. 135v/ per villam queruntur et a famulis hospitalarii<s> humiliter advehuntur. Infirmis igitur ad sanctum hospitale confluentibus primo divinum representatur remedium: nam sacerdotibus ibidem commorantibus, peccatorum suorum rubigine propalata et salutifera penitencie suscepta medicina celesti reficiuntur alimonia, deinde ab uno fratrum hospitalis in suum producuntur

---

[a] MS: modicus secretus.   [b] ratio *deleted before* narracionis.   [c] MS: defectam.

---

[25] Acts 10, 34.
[26] cf. Ez 18, 32.
[27] Lk 23, 34.
[28] Mt 5, 44; Lk. 6, 27.

palacium. Est enim ad hoc unus frater constitutus ut infirmos patienter et benigne suscipiat, secundum quod dicit apostolus: *Suscipite infirmos, patientes estote ad omnes.*[29] In palacium vero producti super culci<t>ras plumarias in lectis tornatilibus[a] cubantur, ne vel algore pavimenti vel ex duricia contristentur albis interponuntur linteaminibus, culcitris consutilibus et aliis villosis coopertoriis superpositis; ne vel aliorum pannorum ledantur asperitate, constringantur vel frigore, pallia eis traduntur de domo, et sine pellibus et pellicii vel pelles, quibus induantur cum ad deserviendum nature surrexerint, sed et setulares ne vel immundicia pedibus surgentium adhereat vel ne vel marmoreum frigus nocivum[b] plantis subsistat.

De magistris vicorum et clientibus.

Est enim palacium infirmorum per undecim vicos distinctum, in aliis vero super duplum hic numerus augmentatur. Multotiens tamen contingit quod, amplitudine palacii non sufficiente languencium multitudini, dormitorium fratrum cum lectis suis est ab infirmis preoccupatum, ipsis fratribus hac illac prout potuerunt terre accubantibus. Unusquisque vicus diligenti unius fratrum custodie committitur, qui adductos humiliter egrotos suscipiat, preassignato modo cubet, singulorum exuvias singulatim[c] in unum colligatas fideliter custodiat, quas infirmis convalescentibus reddat. Sed quia quasi humane imbecillitati est innatum unum solum hominem tot diversis tante multitudinis administracionibus non posse sufficere, singulis fratribus, qui singulis presunt vicis, duodecim clientes admittuntur suffraganei: quot sunt vici, tot sunt fratres super eos magistri et tot clientu<m>. Duodeni clientes isti vivunt de bonis domus quamdiu in eo ministraverint et in recessu suo donis aureis consolantur. Istorum officium est sedula cura suis invigilare infirmis, sic, quod nec etiam unus illorum tantum in os palacii absque magistri sui licencia excedat. Lectos infirmorum habent parare, scilicet culcitra<s> divertendo emollire, quia pluma indurescit conglomerata /fol. 136r/ que mollior sit dispersa, linteamina oportet extendere, infirmos cubare, cooperire, erigere, ad successivos thalamos magis debiles adducere, inter brachia ut quantotiens opus est portare ac reportare, aquam cum manutergio honorifice infirmorum manibus ministrare, gausape comesturis aponere, panem in cophinis afferre, qui a fratribus domus apponitur egris equa porcione, videlicet duos panes inter duos: unus omnibus in domo illa commorantibus in discreta communione generalis, alius similaceus privatus ad opus infirmancium factus. Quo nonnisi soli cottidie vescuntur egroti, quod intuitu misericordie nemo ambigat fieri, scilicet ne huiusmodi panis assiduitate fastidita bene conditum eger nauseet tamquam insipidum, sed grata varietate gustu leviter[d] decepto, alterius blandicias avidi gula saporet. Vinum eis etiam[e] a fratribus apponitur, famulis vasa quibus infundatur

---

[a] MS: tornatililibus. [b] MS: nociva. [c] MS: singularum. [d] MS: leniter. [e] etiam *added in margin*, que *struck out before* a fratribus.

---

[29] 1 Th 5, 14.

adaptantibus, tenentur[a] et famuli delicata cibaria in privata coquina parare. Habent enim infirmi duas coquinas, unam tam maribus quam feminis egrotantibus communem, aliam privatam. In communi eis grossiora parantur cibaria, ut carnes porcine, arietine et huiusmodi, prima videlicet, tercia et quinta feria omni temporali, quo legis nostre indulgentia carnibus vescuntur. Aliis vero diebus plus[?] pulmento ex farris simila[b] facto[c] et ciceres, que a fratribus et sororibus domus ac peregrinis nobilibus de hac coquina ministrantur infirmis, predictis fratribus vicorum cum suis ministris per vicos suos inter prandendum deambulantibus ac diligenter adnotantibus qui famelico appetitu, qui parum, qui non prenominata degustant cibaria, ut aut parum aut non cogustantibus confestim a privata coquina subpleant carnes gallinarum vel pullorum sive columbarum aut perdicum aut agnorum vel edorum vel alia huiusmodi, aut pro tempore ova vel pisces. Ista enim pretaxati fratres vicis prestituti tenentur emere. Nam singulis ebdomadis unusquisque illorum suscipit de thesauro domus .xxx. solidos vel .xxv. vel .xx. secundum augmentum et diminucionem numerositatis egrotancium, quibus talia delicata que extra domum sunt querenda[d] infirmis suis emat cibaria.[e] Supplent etiam preter numerata, sicut poma granata, pira, prunia,[f] castaneas, amigdalas, uvas et pro tempore eisdem passas ficus et eas /fol. 136v/ similiter passas lactucas, cicoreas, radices, portulacas, petrosilinum, apium, cucumeres, cytroles, cucurbitas, melones palestinos et alia multa, de quibus longum esset enarrare per singula, ut sic strophi[g] fastidientis ingluviem saltem pro tempore multa extingant quam reverberare singula non sufficiunt, vel quia diversi diversis laborant egritudinibus, quibus predictorum aliqua sunt prestantia. Eorundem aliis alia sunt nociva, ideo illis plura offeruntur, ut unius pregustati nocumentum alterius subinducti vel adnichilare satagat vel temperare remedium.

De theoricis quatuor preoccupantibus.

Sed quoniam inferioris phisice prorsus ignari nonnisi ceco casu plura degustantibus huiusmodi possunt exhibere temperamentum, sanctus hospitalis conventus theoricorum peritie fideli practicorum cure infirmos suos sancte commisit ac provide. Sancte, ne in illa domo Dei aliquid deesset infirmis in quo humana facultas eis posset esse prestabilis; provide, ne curabiles egritudines per continuata similia vel nociva contraria fientur incurabiles, et sic fomenta languoris aut causas mortis eger reperiret in illis, que sue speraret effectiva salutis. Propter ergo cum infame periculum evitandum, sunt enim in hospitali quatuor medici phisicam docti, ita domus stipendiarii, ut aliquam curam infirmis hospitalis alienam non presumant, qui et iuramento constringuntur quod nullius admonicione,[h] plura nullius dissuasione, pauci hora exspectent ab hospitali queque ad salutem infirmorum suorum noverint necessaria, hinc

---

[a] MS: teneretur.   [b] MS: similia.   [c] MS: facta.   [d] MS: querendi.   [e] Supplicat etiam preter numerata *struck out after* cibaria.   [f] MS: prinia.   [g] MS: strothi.   [h] MS: admonicioni; ergo *deleted after* admonicioni.

in electuariis, inde in aliis medicinis, quia de suo nulla egris medici subpeditant medicamenta, sed de domo illis ministrantur omnia. Distribuuntur medici per vicos ut quisque discreta sciat cognicione quos habeat infirmos curare, ne unius vici respectu alterius tediosam multitudinem alter eorum propter alterum aspernaretur, vel ne confusa commixtione in vicum eundem assidue concurrerent, et aliqua alterna fiducia die aliquo sine cura preterirent. Omni autem die in mane et vespere suos tenentur infirmos visitare, urinas, pulsus qualitates iuxta tenorem artis sue attendere. Cum autem ad visitandos infirmos accedunt, secum quisque illorum duos assumit[a] clientes de vico quem est per-ambulaturus[b] et primo perambulato alios duos resumit de alio et sic deinceps, ut unus syropum, oximel, electuaria et alias medicinas egris conferentes portet, alter urinas ostendat, iudicatas abiciat, urinalia emundet,[c] quam cui dietam medicus iniungat similiter cum servo suo diligenter in-/fol. 137r/-telligat, minutorem ad infirmos suos vel etiam infirmos ad minutorem adducat.

De minutoribus infirmorum.

Habent enim suos minutores infirmi, qui tenentur eos omni die, quecumque hora fuerit, minuere. Qui et beate domus sunt stipendiarii sicut et medici. Sic igitur circa consultam phisicorum suorum discrecionem preassignatis, sed et multo pluribus, egri utuntur cibariis. Quare secundum generalem medicorum prohibicionem quedam cibaria nunquam illis in hospitali proponuntur, ut faba, lens, squille, murene, nec etiam scrofe. Nam ut generalis phisicorum teneat assercio, feminine humidorum animalium carnes, ad masculin<or>um animalium generis comparate,[d] duriores, grossiores, viscosiores, indigestibil-iores in suo genere reperiuntur. Inde fit quod si quando huiusmodi carnes apponantur sanis, nunquam autem ibi dantur egrotis, quod divinam utique redolet misericordiam.

De cyrugicis hospitalis.

Et ut omnimodam pietatis gratiam infirmis suis gloriosum hospitale non desistat exhibere, preter prefatos theoricos cyrugicos tenet stipendiarios, ut de sauciis curam habeant quotquot ad ipsum confugiunt. Qui et vere confugiunt, quia non solum in Ierosolima, immo et quocienscumque ierosolimitana Chris-tianitas contra paganos in expedicione exierit, in ea vulnerati quocumque voluerint ad hospitalia profugiunt tentoria tamquam asilum[?][e] iure hereditario[f] sibi deputatum. Illic eis, qualiscumque ibi potest, adhibetur plena[g] cura. Et non[h] curatos illinc super camelos, equos, mulos, asinos ad hospitale in Ierusalem sive ad propinquiora hospitalis receptacula provehuntur[?],[i] ubi sicut et in hospitali custodiuntur. Et si in provehendis sauciis propria hospitalis non habundaverint iumenta, ipsi revera hospitalarii aliena conducunt; que si adhuc non sufficiunt, ipsorum fratrum equitaturas saucii ascendunt, ipsis fratribus, etiam nobilibus, hac ingruente necessitate pedes redeuntibus, ut sic aperte

---

[a] MS: assumunt.   [b] MS: preambulaturus.   [c] MS: emundent.   [d] MS: comparare.   [e] MS: an͡lium.   [f] iū *deleted before* sibi.   [g] MS: pena.   [h] MS: nunc[?].   [i] MS: propheūtur.

demonstrent se non sibi quod habent apropriare, sed et se et si qua sunt sua infirmorum esse. Hoc tenore, hac pietate, hoc caritatis intuitu, beatum hospitale hinc practicantes theoricos, inde cyrugicos et minutores tenet stipendiarios. O quam beata domus, quod beate considerans lapidibus virtutes, herbis vires a creatore misericorditer insitas, ut scilicet homo per eas a primo primi parentis excessu corruptibilis nature incommodis in hoc suo possit mederi exilio, <...>, o quam felix in hac sua institutione /fol. 137v/ conventus, qua[a] felicis Samaritani factus est imitator, qui de curandis proximis etiam in agone contendit. Nam ut singula singulis atribuamus, huius conventus[b] proximi viri sunt katholici omnium nacionum peregrini, qui cottidie in partibus illis incidunt in latrones, quia et in diversarum egritudinum grav<e>dines et occursu assiduo in paganorum insultationes, quos bene conventus quasi stabulario committit curandos, cum eis adhibet medicos, cum quibus tamquam cum stabulario de duobus denariis[30] satis congrue convenit, ex quo eis pro adhibita cura stipendia et procuraciones impendit; medicis tamen nichil super egrotantibus, nam ut predictum est, de thesauro domus omnia emuntur medicamenta, que pro egris curandis ipsi medici adiudicant utilia. Ecce qualiter felix congregatio sanctorum hospitalis fratrum obstrusum iacens aurum in stercore pia exponit opum exhibicione et spiritualis intelligentie granum recolligit, quod arescentis ystorie mollior palea delirescit.

Item de clientibus vicorum et etiam de fratribus.

Sed quasi adiuncticulo ad sepedictos infirmorum clientes redeamus. Quibus propter egros suos sedulo custodiendos nocturna deputatur vigilia, in omni vico contubernali[c] vicissitudine per binarium alternata. Ipsis etiam incumbit lampades accendere, que more solito ante infirmos consueverunt ardere a crepusculo donec rucilante aurora nostri superficiem emisperii sol ortus sui splendore irradiaverit. Sunt enim in omni vico tres vel quatuor lampades preter crucibulos, lumen non languidum per omnes vicos diffundentes, ne ad secessum deambulantes infirmi tenebrosum evagacionis subeant errorem, aut offendicula incurrant aliquam superflue prestitura lesionem. Ministri siquidem ad vigilandum per singulos vicos contub<er>niati tenentur infirmos suos deambulacione assidua visitare, ut in sompnis denudatos cooperiant, male iacentes componant, sacerdotes distric<t>os adducant, mortuos in monasterium deferant, debilibus in quibuscumque molestiis subveniant, sicientes[d] potent. Nam duorum vigilancium in vico unus vicum suum primo pedetentim perambulat, candelam ceream et crossam a sinistris et vinum in ciato deferendo a dextris, continua vociferatione ac pia proclamat, dicens: 'Domini, vinum ex parte Dei,' quod et *omni petenti*[31] humili porrectione propinat. Perambulato sic utroque vico convigilator suus assumpta candela vitreolo ereo aquam frigidam

---

[a] MS: quam.   [b] MS: consuetus.   [c] MS: contubermali.   [d] sacien *deleted before* sicientes.

---

[30] cf. Lk 10, 35.
[31] Lk 6, 30.

defert per vicum, similiter acclamando: Aquam ex parte Dei. In reditu suo ipsemet vel socius eius nichil refert utrum[a] /fol. 138r/ illorum, sed iuxta opcionis sue affectum in lebete parvulo, in fluctuante siphilo[b] iterato regressu aquam calidam deportat, sua etiam propalante acclamacione contrarii violentia clementi accidens illatum dicit: 'Aquam calidam in nomine Dei.' Sicque verso inde parvis mediantibus in tristiciis orarii per totum noctis curriculum. Eodem modo se habent et alii per alios vicos binarii. Sed ne duos servos humilis conventus solis relinquat mercenariis per nocturni tranquillitatem[c] silencii custodiendos, mox finito completorio piam per omnes vicos tocius palacii egrorum acomodabilem facit processionem, quo fratrum previo cum lucerna, reliquo cum candela, ut convenienter videant fratres si aliquid incompositum, aliquid indecens, si aliquid illic pietati apparuerit inimicum. Et si contumelia, que semper angarioso tumultu misericordie ac pacis unioni novercatur, partes suas inibi ausu temerario intercalaverit,[d] illorum assensu fit emendatum. Hac vero finita processione omni nocte modo hiis duobus, modo illis duobus fratribus, nunc huius noctis, nunc illius instituitur vigilia, ut unus eorum usque ad matutinas pervigilet, alius deinceps. Qui vice sua candelam deportantes in manibus modesto incessu vicos circumeunt, diligenter inspiciunt si vel adhibiti vigiles dormierint, vel si ex desidiosa illorum incuria infirmis aliquo indiguerint. Et quemcumque vigilium in aliquo excedentem repererunt, dabit penas in crastinum, nudus[e] per totum vapulans palacium. Si etiam econtra[f] egro illorum quispiam contumeliosus fuerit in verbis aut insolens in officiis, similiter castigacionis scutica[g] corrip<i>tur. Sed assiduus[h] in excessibus a tali privatur obsequio, alio statim loco illius subinducto. Frater humilitatis transgressu[i] adversus egros contumax, per .xl. dies vel amplius eo terre assidens sine omni honore mense, in pane et aqua penitebit, nisi et hic iusticie rigor alicuius interventu nobilis temperetur. Omnibus enim tam magistris vicorum quam clientibus suis ac medicis unus fratrum subponitur, qui quasi anthonomasice 'hospitalarius' in domo sua illa nuncupatur. Nam velud singularem ac precipuam de omnibus ad infirmos pertinentibus curam habet, unde et ministris eorum iuxta beate domus institucionem tenetur disponere, transgressus emendare, delinquentibus pro qualitate commissorum statutas penas irrogare. Est et quidam alius frater, habens super se ministros quibus incumbit omnium fratrum capita lavare, barbas aptare, capillorum luxus tondere. Isti omni ebdomada, scilicet secunda ac quinta feria, in calida aqua omnium egrorum pedes abluere <tenentur>. Cum pumi-/fol. 138v/-ceo lapide plantarum sordes abscalpunt, delicato postmodum manutergio extergunt. Insuper et omni die infirmis epulantibus predictus frater iste cum uno subditorum sibi singulos vicos unus hinc alius inde perambulat, a[j] dextris turibula, sportulas incensu

---

[a] MS: utrum *bis.*   [b] MS: sisphilo.   [c] in *deleted before* tranquillitatem.   [d] MS: interculaverit.
[e] MS: nudum.   [f] MS: contra.   [g] MS: scutico.   [h] MS: assidius.   [i] MS: transgresso.
[j] MS: ad.

semiplenas, a sinistris deportat odoriferi thuris flagrancia, unicuique officiose oblata. Quos cum aqua benedicit, subsequens aspersione salutifera omnes satagit irrorare.

De portantibus feminis et de earum ministris.

Hec eadem in omnibus[a] revera et per omnia egrotantibus feminis inibi adhibetur. Et cum que suum pro se habe<a>nt palacium, ad conformitatem predicti amfractuose per vicos distinctum, suam etiam habent coquinam privatam, habent etiam ministras privato famulatu suo ascriptas, sicut mares prenotavimus habere ministros. Pregnantes prout et alie quotquot volunt ad hospitale confugiunt ut illic parturiant. Nam illic cum parvulis suis pia vigilantia custodiuntur, balneis confoventur, quo ad pristine sanitatis convale<sce>ntia<m> respiraverint. In purificacione sua que habent necessaria sibi de beata domo subpeditantur, ut candele et similia. Infantulum suum si vel paupertate aut egritudine incumbente non valens vel novercali austeritate non curans enutrire, sed illo[b] a visceribus maternis secluso abierit,[c] a pio certe conventuali[d] confestim nutrici alendus committitur. Omni enim quindena[e] dierum completa, tam masculinorum egrotantium lectis quam feminarum linteamina imponuntur dealbata, immo et quotiens hic vel alia, non incommoda sustinens, ea commaculaverint, totiens recenter suscipiet lota, etiam si vigesies in die illa humane infirmitatis pudibundi necessitas ingruisset. Hec est cure misericordia quam egris in hospitali sancti Iohannis apud Ierosolimam peregrinis ego teste Deo vidi exhibitam, cui et totis viribus meis gratias refero, tam gloriosa me in domo sua vidisse. Sed et que alia ibidem viderim sanis erogata cum pupillis tum adultis, hinc maribus, inde feminis nostre civitati fratres, non sit honerosum ascultare: auris namque divinis acommoda operibus tanto salubri<us> pio imprimit animo veritatem, quanto periculosius vage menti frivolose narracionis admictio vanitatem. Et sicut non in dictis, ita nec itaque in dicendis aut decolorans venenum adulacionis aut se immiscebit deturpans scrupulus falsitatis, nisi forte mea in aliquo decepta, puritate tamen mentis illesa, /fol. 139r/ aberraverit consciencia. *Explicit de infirmis.*

Incipit tercia distinctio de sanis pupillis adultis maribus et feminis.

Quecumque igitur puerpera alias quam in hospitali quacumque de causa parturierit, non habens quo vagientis nuditatem parvuli obvolvat, hospitale commiserans cum omni festinatione transmissam sibi pannorum administrat opulentiam, quasi ad piam revocans memoriam quod cum animalia universa contra inclementiam aeream nascantur premunita, ut iumenta cum pilis, aves cum plumis, pisces cum squamis, testudines cum conchis, solus homo nudus et inhermis nascitur. Quare beata domus tenere non obaudiens vagitus infancie, primeve calamitatis rigorem celeri procursu festinat emollire, ne vel dona

---

[a] revera *deleted after* omnibus.   [b] MS: illa.   [c] habuerit *deleted before* abierit.   [d] MS: conventualii.   [e] dierum *deleted before* quindena.

Deo tam accepta morosa manus denigret, vel intensa nuditatis austeritate subumbrat parvulus tamquam verecundus effugiat. Sic patrocinante clementia similes similibus[a] compati, sic non devio prestigio proprie carnis nos edocet misereri. Si vero puerpere, aut inedia desolate aut insolito nature cursu materne pietatis oblite, parvulos suos abiecerint, a primis inventoribus ad hospitale deportati humillime suscipiuntur, nutricibus illico quesitis lactis alimonia educandi committuntur, sed robustiori cibo confortandi in ipsa domo enutriuntur. Sed vero matres clanculo fronte obducta infantes illic abiciunt, immo a multis, iam cognita domus[b] illius misericordia, si qua gemellos fuerit enixa, uno retento reliquum beato Iohanni nutriendum nullo rebellante palam relinquo. Attamen si tantum et unius mater illum quocumque circumstante incomodo non sufficiat enutriente, summo magistro domus suum propalat decidium. Si ergo egritudo fuerit in causa, continuo pius vir ille puerum fideli alterius nutricis custodie deputat. Si vero paupertas nutriendo[c] infantulo, convenit magister cum illa tamquam de alio cum aliena, confestim insuper sibi aliquo collato consolatorii emolumenti beneficio. Nutrices itaque talium abiectorum scilicet filiorum beati Iohannis adoptorum singule, licet essent mille, .xii. habent talenta per annum et in omni sollempnitate .ix. lectionum de cibariis domus procurantur, sicut[d] et ipsi fratres tam in porcionum quantitatibus quam in ferculorum varietatibus. Sed ne in custodiendis parvulis, ut mos[e] est in alienis, torpeant, /fol. 139v/ nutrices frequenter illos ad hospitale secum tenentur deferre, ut sorores domus quasi materna circumspectione singulos visitent et male servatos aliarum nutricum custodie committant. Sunt namque in hospitali sorores matrone in diebus processive, viduali continentia, honestate mulieres religiose. Que quia curam infantulis[f] debitam melius[g] noverunt quam mares, ideo earum[h] sanctitati addicitur parvulos visitare, humilem super illos vigilanciam gerere. Nec inmerito, cum isti tales pupilli, et quamvis parentibus, quos sibi dedit natura, superstitibus orphani, sola misericordissime pietatis adopcione, communi vocabulo in illis partibus 'filii beati Iohannis' nuncupantur. Et filie, etate tamen sufficiente, aliquibus adaptantur officiis, quibus iuxta Tullianum dogma inopem provecti in erumpna possint rarum defendere.[32] Adultorum vero subditur obcioni utrum nutritori suo beato maluerint servire Iohanni an cavillantis mundi seductorias illecebras amplecti.

Nobiles peregrini, propriis parcentes sumptibus vel non valentes fodere aut erubescentes mendicare,[33] hospitalis petito subsidio illic honorifice recolliguntur, eodem alimento illis ac fratribus per omnia communicato, nullius tamen ab eis subieccione famulatus exhibita quamdiu inibi[i] perendinaverint,[j]

---

[a] MS: sileribus.   [b] MS: domo.   [c] MS: te[?] *before* nutriendo.   [d] MS: quod *before* sicut. [e] MS: mox.   [f] MS: in famulis.   [g] MS: initius[?].   [h] MS: eorum.   [i] MS: inhibi.   [j] MS: peremdinaverit.

[32] Possibly alluding to Cicero, *De officiis* 2, 70.
[33] cf. Lk 16, 3.

nisi quis divino admonitu spontanee voluntatis pro ductu se Christi velit
pauperibus inclinare in cibi eorum ac potus administracione. Sed hac <admin-
istracione> quamplures illorum, mundum consulentes, proprie iactantia mentis
seipsos exuentes tamquam bruta stabilitate, irretiti nausatico contemptu
fastidiunt, male intelligentes quam periculosum sit panem ociosum ea in
domo comedere. Proculdubio nimis est gloriosum servire[a] domos et quas
habet beatus Iohannes hac illac per Ierosolimam diffusas, istis talibus peregrinis
sola hospitalitatis misericordia satagunt hospitalarii gratis accomodare. Et si eas
negociatoribus pro gratuito possint precio conducere [*here the text breaks off*].

---

[a] est *deleted before* servire.

2

Medical Care in the Hospital of
St John in Jerusalem

Susan Edgington

Two manuscripts have recently come to light which relate to the hospital of St John in Jerusalem in the 1180s, one a version in Old French of the statutes of Roger des Moulins, the other a description by a pilgrim who was treated in the hospital.[1] Each provides important new information about the hospital's organization and procedures; together they enable a radical review of the hospital's development and function in the twelfth century, and the practice of medicine there. The two texts are independent and they vary in detail, as one would expect from two documents which were framed for quite different purposes. The extent of their essential agreement is more significant: both emphasize the importance of prayer, of comfort, of diet, and appear to place physic only in fourth place.

Nevertheless, an understanding of the doctors' role is crucial to defining the nature and function of the hospital in the later twelfth century. The statutes contain two references: the first is general, that the doctors 'should earnestly study the qualities of the sick and of their illnesses, inspect their urine and give syrups, electuaries and other things necessary to the sick, forbidding contrary things and giving profitable ones';[2] the second is more specific: the weakest patients were to have their own physician, who would swear by the saints or

---

[1] I am grateful to Dr A. Luttrell who drew both of these manuscripts to my attention: (1) Vatican Lat. 4852, fols 89r–105r. I also thank Ms Katja Klement, who sent me a copy of her unpublished doctoral thesis, '"Von Krankenspeisen und Ärzten ..." Eine unbekannte Verfügung des Johannitermeisters Roger des Moulins (1177–1187) im Codex Vaticanus Latinus 4852' (Salzburg, June 1996); (2) Munich Clm. 4620, fols 132v–139v. The Bayerische Staatbibliothek kindly provided a printout, and I had the opportunity of comparing transcriptions with Professor Benjamin Kedar at the Military Orders Conference, 1996. A provisional edition of this manuscript is printed above, pp. 13–26.

[2] Vatican, fol. 89r.

would vow to do all in his power to look after the sick without asking anything of them.[3] This matches Pope Lucius III's decree of 1184/5: 'that in the house of the hospital there should always be five doctors and three surgeons, at whose disposition should be administered those things which are necessary for the infirm, both foodstuffs and other things ...'; other versions specify four doctors and four surgeons.[4]

The pilgrim-author agrees that there were four doctors, who were learned in physic. They were salaried, employed exclusively in the hospital, and bound by oath. They were to know the nature of the sick and to use electuaries and other medicines. Twice a day they visited the sick and checked urine and pulse, accompanied by two serjeants, one of whom carried syrups, oxymel, electuaries and other medicines; the other held up urine samples, discarded them when seen and cleaned the urine flasks, and recorded the doctor's dietary instructions or arranged for the bloodletter to attend.[5]

The reference in the statutes to the alternative oath is significant, as it is presumably a provision for non-Christians. This is a reminder of the high status enjoyed by Jewish and other Oriental doctors in the Holy Land, as reported by William of Tyre and other observers.[6] The employment of such doctors was both sanctioned and regulated. A procedure for licensing doctors is recorded in the *Assises des Bourgeois de Jerusalem*.[7] This collection dates from the 1240s, the chapters which deal with medical subjects being from the thirteenth century,[8] at which date they show there was a system of examination and licensing which established a professional body of physicians who treated the households of urban Franks. It is from this body that doctors would be recruited for stipendiary posts in the hospital of St John, and the areas of knowledge which were examined were probably those identified in the printed statutes of the Hospitallers, 1181: 'for the sick in the hospital of Jerusalem there should be engaged four wise doctors, who are qualified to examine urine, and to diagnose different diseases, and are able to administer appropriate medicines.'[9]

In view of their expertise, the doctor:patient ratio which can be deduced from the anonymous description is a striking 4:1,000. There was evidently a practised routine for ward-rounds, as described by the pilgrim-author; nevertheless there is a strong indication in the ratio – which no contemporary appears to have

---

[3] Ibid., fol. 99v.

[4] *Acta Pontificum Romanorum Inedita*, 2, ed. J. v. Pflugk-Harttung (Stuttgart, 1884), no. 441 (p. 389); cf. *PUTJ*, no. 172 (p. 361).

[5] Munich, fols 136v–137r.

[6] WT, XVIII.34 (pp. 859–60); XX.31 (pp. 956–7); cf. C. Cahen, *Orient et Occident au temps des Croisades* (Paris, 1983), doc. 13 (pp. 235–6) and WT, XXI.1 (p. 961).

[7] 'Livre des Assises de la Cour des Bourgeois', *RHC Lois*, 2, p. 169.

[8] J. Prawer, *Crusader Institutions* (Oxford, 1980), pp. 358–90.

[9] *CH*, 1, no. 627 (p. 426).

considered inadequate – that few patients were in need of extensive medical attention. This may be confirmed by the language of the statutes: the four general doctors are *mièges*, while for the very weakest patients a *fisicien* is employed.

The statutes make no reference to the surgeons, who are described by the anonymous pilgrim specifically in relation to the treatment of the wounded. The pilgrim-author describes the surgeons as 'hands-on' doctors, or *practici*, in contrast to the general doctors who are described as *theorici*. He is here making a distinction which was first made by Aristotle.[10] The surgeons seem to have been underemployed compared with the doctors, except in time of emergency; for example, after the battle of Montgisard, in 1177, 750 seriously wounded men were treated in the hospital, which already held 900 patients.[11]

The only specific reference to medical treatment is found in the case of the battle casualties: '*O quam beata domus, quod beate considerans lapidibus virtutes, herbis vires ...*'('O what a fortunate house, blessedly contemplating the strength in stones, the power in plants ...'). The reference could be rhetorical, but since the author explains a few lines later '*de thesauro domus omnia emuntur medicamenta que pro egris curandis ipsi medici adiudicant utilia*' ('from the treasury of the house all medicaments are bought which the doctors themselves judge useful for curing the ill'), it may be assumed that stones and plants were used therapeutically. The use of herbs is widely attested in the period by well-worn copies of Dioscorides and pseudo-Apuleius in medieval collections. One of these, the Latin Alphabetical Dioscorides, was produced at Salerno, and probably authored by Constantine the African.[12] Non-Salernitan works on herbs included the late-eleventh-century Macer Floridus's *De viribus herbarum*, whose title may have been in the mind of the pilgrim-author.[13]

The use of stones, or lithotherapy, does not have such a well-known history, yet there are many lapidaries extant in European collections.[14] For example, the fourth section of Hildegard of Bingen's *Physica* (*c.* 1151–8) is a lapidary.[15] The principle behind the use of stones is that each has a humoral property (hot, cold, moist or dry), and so can be used to counter an excess of the opposite humour in the patient. They were used in three ways: worn as amulets, applied topically, or taken internally. Although lithotherapy is little used today, it was a dynamic form of therapy in the twelfth century, as much-glossed manuscripts demonstrate.

---

[10] J.M. Riddle, 'Theory and practice in medieval medicine', *Viator*, 5 (1974), 158–84 (at 161).

[11] R. Röhricht, *Beiträge zur Geschichte der Kreuzzüge*, 2 (Berlin, 1878), no. 45, pp. 127–8.

[12] J.M. Riddle, 'The Latin Alphabetical Dioscorides', *Proceedings of the XIIIth International Congress for the History of Science, Acts Section IV* (Moscow, 1971), 204–9.

[13] Riddle, 'Theory and Practice', p. 171.

[14] J.M. Riddle, 'Lithotherapy in the Middle Ages: Lapidaries Considered as Medical Texts', *Pharmacy in History*, 12 (1970), 39–50.

[15] *PL*, 197, cols 1247–66.

The plants used in medicaments in the hospital are not named, although we know that electuaries consisted largely of sugar: in the printed statutes of Roger des Moulins the prior of Mont Pèlerin was to send to Jerusalem annually two quintals of sugar (a hundredweight) for making electuaries, syrups and other medicines, and the bailiff of Tiberias was to send the same amount.[16] The oxymel mentioned by the pilgrim-author was a vinegar and honey mixture.

In contrast to the lack of information about medical treatments, the lists of foodstuffs in both texts are almost obsessively detailed. This is the key to understanding the function of the hospital in the later twelfth century. The medieval doctor, working in the tradition of Hippocrates and Galen, believed that the science of medicine consisted of three parts: the study of 'natural' things; of 'non-natural' things, and of 'extra-natural' things. Natural things were the elements, the temperaments, the humours, the faculties – the physiology of the human body as then understood. Illnesses, their causes and symptoms were extra-natural. There were also six non-natural things essential to preserve human life: (1) air; (2) movement and rest; (3) eating and drinking; (4) sleeping and waking; (5) repletion and excretion; (6) the soul's moods.[17] To maintain good health, moderation and balance were important, and if a body deviated from a state of well-being, then it could be restored to health by a change of lifestyle. Doctors often preferred to prescribe an adjustment in food and drink, for example, because it was gentler than pharmaceutics.

Thus, alongside the herbals and lapidaries already mentioned, there was an important genre of medical writing called the dietary, or in Latin *Regimen sanitatis*. Dietaries covered all the six categories of non-naturals, but the dominant section in every one dealt with food and drink. An example of the dietary is the *Kitāb Kāmil aṣ-ṣinā'a aṭ-ṭibbiya* (The Complete Book of the Medical Art) by the Persian al-Majūsī (d. 994). After sections discussing air and physical activity, the third section begins with a definition of what are considered drugs, poisons, remedial foods and pure foods, and explains their classification according to qualities: hot, cold, dry, moist or balanced. Then their action, from strong to weak, is explained, and their substance: 'subtle', 'gross' or 'middling'. There follows a taxonomy of foodstuffs, plant and then animal, and a full listing, each foodstuff with its quality, action and substance. At the end of the list are a chapter on honey and sugar, one on wine, and a final one on medicinal drinks such as oxymel. Three sections on the other 'non-naturals', dealing with the importance of sleep, of elimination and of controlling one's moods, complete the book.[18]

A comparison of the contents of al-Majūsī's foodstuff list with those in the two texts leaves little doubt that dietary regulation was the predominant form

---

[16] *CH*, 1, no. 627 (p. 427).

[17] M. Ullmann, *Islamic Medicine* (Edinburgh, 1978), p. 97; M.W. Adamson, *Medieval Dietetics: Food and Drink in Regimen Sanitatis Literature from 800 to 1400* (Frankfurt am Main, 1995), p. 20.

[18] Ullmann, pp. 99–102; Adamson, pp. 43–7.

of therapy in the hospital. This raises the question of whether it was imposed by doctors who had been trained in the Islamic tradition and had read dietaries in Arabic, or if there was another explanation for its acceptance.

'Alī ibn al-'Abbās al-Majūsī is better known in western Europe as Haly Abbas, and his *Kitāb Kāmil aṣ-ṣina'a aṭ-ṭibbiya* was twice translated into Latin: by Constantine the African between 1070 and 1080 as *Liber pantegni*, and again in 1127 by Stephen of Pisa. Stephen studied at Salerno before going to Antioch where he made the new translation, which is usually known as the *Liber regius*, 'The Royal Book', a translation of the book's alternative title *Kitāb al-Malakī*.[19] Stephen's translation is known to have been in use in western Europe in 1140.[20] Just as the *Kitāb al-Malakī* dominated Arabic medicine until Avicenna's *Canon* displaced it, so the translations dominated Western medicine until overtaken by the same work.

Although it is possible that the Order of St John adopted Galen's ideas on dietary regulation, as mediated by Haly Abbas and other Arabic writers, in the East, the Salernitan connection merits further examination. Amalfitan merchants founded (or refounded) the hospital in the eleventh century and there were continued links with southern Italy.[21] Bohemond of Antioch had been treated at Salerno and his father, Robert Guiscard, knew and respected Constantine the African.[22] Soon after the Christians captured Jerusalem, in 1101, Roger I of Sicily sent 1,000 bezants to be shared equally between the Holy Sepulchre, the king's army and the hospital.[23] His son granted privileges to the Order in the late 1130s, in consideration of their charitable work.[24]

In view of these indications, the alternative case for Byzantine influence, argued by T.S. Miller, must be reconsidered.[25] Miller's argument rests heavily on the *typikon* of the Pantokrator Hospital in Constantinople, dated 1138. The *typikon* is unique in the detailed information it gives about the organization of the great hospital founded by Emperor John Comnenus and his empress

---

[19] Ullmann, pp. 53–4; Adamson, p. 42.

[20] *Constantine the African and 'Ali ibn al-'Abbas al-Maǧusi*, ed. C. Burnett and D. Jacquart, Studies in Ancient Medicine, 10 (Leiden, 1994), pp. vii–viii.

[21] J. Riley-Smith, *The Knights of St John in Jerusalem and Cyprus 1050–1310* (London, 1967), p. 36.

[22] Orderic Vitalis, *Historia Ecclesiastica*, ed. and tr. M. Chibnall (Oxford, 1969–1980), 4, VII.7 (pp. 28/29). Bohemond's stepmother Sichelgaita acquired her skill in poisons there too (pp. 30/31); cf. William of Apulia, *Gesta Roberti Wiscardi*, ed. M. Mathieu (Palermo, 1961), pp. 248–9. See also F. Newton, 'Constantine the African and Monte Cassino: New Elements and the Text of the *Isagoge*', in *Constantine the African*.

[23] Albert of Aachen, *Historia*, ed. S.B. Edgington, Oxford Medieval Texts (forthcoming), VII.62.

[24] *CH*, 1, no. 119 (p. 99).

[25] T.S. Miller, 'The Knights of Saint John and the Hospitals of the Latin West', *Speculum*, 53 (1978), 709–33. See also M.W. Dols, 'The Origins of the Islamic Hospital: Myth and Reality', *Bulletin of the History of Medicine*, 6 (1987), 367–90 (at 370–1).

Irene of Hungary.[26] A comparison with the two texts referring to the Jerusalem hospital is instructive. There are at least four key differences: firstly, the Pantokrator Hospital was devised to accommodate a maximum of sixty-one patients, more normally fifty; secondly, it was divided into specialized wards – one for wounds, one for patients with complaints of the eyes or stomach, plus a ward for women – and two general wards; thirdly, the ratio of doctors to patients was 1:4 (not counting two general practitioners and two surgeons who staffed the dispensary); fourthly, the prescribed diet was completely vegetarian. Such discrepancies are sufficient to demonstrate that the Hospitallers in Jerusalem were either ignorant of the details of Byzantine *xenodochia*, or they viewed them as irrelevant because they considered the function of the hospital was different. The same would be true of Islamic hospitals, which were also organized along highly specialized lines and in addition were secular in nature. An essential difference between the Jerusalem hospital and possible Eastern models is that they were conceived and established according to a plan, while it evolved in response to a unique set of circumstances.

As is well known, at the beginning of the twelfth century the hospital took care of paupers and pilgrims, functioning as a hostel or hospice. Its distinctive role as a 'place of public charity for the care of the sick' – a hospital – had emerged by the period of our two documents. It appears from charter evidence that Roger II of Sicily was first to recognize a changing role in the late 1130s when he described the hospital as 'a house providing continuous lodging and comfort for the poor and infirm' (*domus ... pauperibus et infirmis continuum prestat hospitium et levamen*). Soon afterwards Pope Innocent II praised the hospital: 'For the poor and indigent are refreshed there, and many-faceted services of humanity are shown towards the infirm, and those tired by different labours and dangers get back their strength and are restored ... so that they are able to go forth more safely ...'[27] Since the vocabulary of charters is conservative, by 1140 the hospital was certainly catering for people described as *infirmi*. This is usually translated as 'sick', but it should be noted that the patients were not described as *aegri*, that is to say ill or diseased. Observers still classed all inmates as paupers: for example Frederick I Barbarossa who made a grant in 1156 to 'the holy hospital which is in Jerusalem, where indeed we saw with our own eyes the merciful works rendered to Christ's poor,' though two years later he added *advenas et peregrinos* – strangers and pilgrims.[28] Of all the charters dated before 1187, only one describes the beneficiaries of the Order's activities as ill (*egroti*) and that is dated 1175 and refers to the hospital at Acre.[29]

---

[26] P. Gautier, 'Le Typikon du Christ Sauveur Pantocrator', *Revue des études byzantines*, 32 (1974), 1–145.

[27] *CH*, 1, nos 119, 124, 130 (pp. 99, 103, 107). Previous popes had referred only to pilgrims and poor, e.g. Paschal II, 1113 (*CH*, 1, no. 30, pp. 29–30); Calixtus II, 1119–24 (no. 47, pp. 39–40).

[28] *CH*, 1, nos 246, 270 (pp. 185–6, 203–4).

[29] *CH*, 1, no. 471 (pp. 323–4).

All the extant textual evidence corroborates the strong impression conveyed by the 'new' texts that the primary purpose of the hospital in Jerusalem, even in the 1180s, was to restore to health pilgrims and poor people who were suffering from exhaustion and malnutrition, and perhaps old age or chronic ailments: Riley-Smith has pointed out that Jerusalem was not a pilgrimage goal for those looking to be healed, but rather a place where people went to die.[30] In short, in normal times the overwhelming concern of the hospital was not *curing* but *caring*, which within the frame of contemporary scientific knowledge meant an emphasis on spiritual and physical comfort, and on dietary regulation in accordance with humoral theory. The modern analogy is not the hospital, but the convalescent home.

The organizational structure within which this purpose was accomplished was described in Raymond du Puy's *Rule*, which dates from the middle of the twelfth century (before 1153), and which has been shown to draw on the Augustinian *Praeceptum*, a document with much emphasis on good food and comfortable conditions for the infirm, and reliance on the advice of doctors in these matters.[31] Lucius III, confirming the *Rule* in 1184/5, certainly believed that the Order followed St Augustine: *canonicis regularibus beati Augustini regula concessa est*.[32] This means that, while the hospital probably based its medical practice on Salernitan ideas, it looked for its organization and ethos to a model popular in more northerly parts of Europe. Dickinson has shown that in the eleventh and twelfth centuries houses of regular canons spread slowly in Italy, but flourished in France, Flanders and lower Lorraine.[33]

A different hypothesis may thus be proposed. A hostel, or hospice, for pilgrims existed in 1099. After the capture of Jerusalem its growth was exponential, in direct proportion to the influx of pilgrims.[34] Many of these were infirm, and hence a specialized role evolved over a period of about thirty years, which was recognized by Raymond's *Rule* and by the massive rebuilding programme in the mid-century. The arrangements for the care of the infirm represent a fusion of two contemporary western European movements: the expansion of the Augustinian canons, and the influence of Salernitan medicine. The size and efficiency of the resulting institution excited the admiration of eyewitnesses, including the unknown writer of the Munich text.[35]

---

[30] J. Riley-Smith, *The First Crusade and the Idea of Crusading* (London, 1986), p. 24.

[31] Riley-Smith, *Knights of St John*, pp. 46–52. For the rule of St Augustine see: L. Verheijen, *Nouvelle approche de la Règle de Saint Augustin*, Vie Monastique, 8 (Maine et Loire, 1980).

[32] *Acta Pontificum*, no. 441 (p. 389).

[33] J.C. Dickinson, *The Origins of the Austin Canons, and their Introduction into England* (London, 1950), pp. 40–8.

[34] Cf. K. Park, 'Medicine and society in medieval Europe, 500–1500' in *Medicine and Society*, ed. A. Wear (Cambridge, 1992), pp. 59–90.

[35] Cf. the well-known descriptions by John of Würzburg and Theoderich, tr. A. Stewart, PPTS, 5 (London, 1896), texts B and D, and the reference by Benjamin of Tudela, *The Itinerary of Benjamin of Tudela*, ed. M.N. Adler (London, 1907), p. 22. All saw the hospital *c.* 1160–70.

3

Arabic Medicine and Hospitals in the Middle Ages: a Probable Model for the Military Orders' Care of the Sick

Christopher Toll

Medicine and magic are concepts which have characterized humanity's view of sickness: on the one hand something which has its cause in the body and can be an object of medical treatment, on the other something with an external origin, provoked by the evil eye or caused by the Devil or by an evil spirit. This latter concept is still alive, as when someone who has fallen severely ill exclaims: 'What have I done to have to suffer this?' Thus, leprosy was considered as a curse by Europeans but recognized as an infectious disease by the Arabs.

I should like to begin this presentation of medieval Arabic medical care, which probably influenced the medical care of the crusaders, by describing how these two concepts confronted each other 800 years ago. The Arab Knight Usāmah ibn Munqidh, in the middle of the twelfth century, relates what his uncle had told him:

> A Frankish ruler wrote to my uncle asking him to send a doctor to treat some of his followers who were ill. My uncle sent a Christian called Thabit. After only ten days he returned and we said: 'You cured them quickly!' This was his story: They took me to see a knight who had an abscess on his leg, and a woman with consumption. I applied a poultice to the leg, and the abscess opened and began to heal. I prescribed a cleansing and refreshing diet for the woman.
>
> Then there appeared a Frankish doctor, who said: 'This man has no idea how to cure these people!' He turned to the knight and said: 'Which would you prefer, to live with one leg or to die with two?' When the knight replied that he would prefer to live with one leg, he sent for a strong man and a sharp axe. They arrived, and I stood by to watch. The doctor supported the leg on a block of wood and said to the man: 'Strike a mighty blow and cut cleanly!' And there, before my eyes, the fellow struck the knight one blow, and then another, for the first had not finished the job. The marrow spurted out of the leg, and the patient died instantaneously.

From *The Military Orders. Volume 2. Welfare and Warfare.* ed. Helen Nicholson. Copyright © 1998 by Helen Nicholson. Published by Ashgate Publishing Ltd, Gower House, Croft Road, Aldershot, Hampshire, GU11 3HR, Great Britain.

Then the doctor examined the woman and said: 'She has a devil in her head
who is in love with her. Cut her hair off!' This was done, and she went back to
eating her usual Frankish food, garlic and mustard, which made her illness worse.
'The devil has got into her brain', pronounced the doctor. He took a razor and cut
a cross on her head and removed the bone so that the inside of the skull was laid
bare. This he rubbed with salt; the woman died instantly. At this juncture I
asked whether they had any further need of me, and as they had none I came away,
having learnt things about medical methods that I never knew before.[1]

One of the benefits of the crusades was that the Franks in Syria and in Egypt
met with modern medical care and well-equipped hospitals, which could
serve as models for their own hospitals and those of Europe in the thirteenth
century.

We speak of 'Arabic' medicine because the medical literature was in Arabic,
but we have to bear in mind that many doctors in medieval Near Eastern international society were Syrians, Greek, Persians or Turks, though writing in
Arabic, the learned language of that time. And although many doctors were
Christians, Jews or Samaritans, we also speak of 'Islamic' medicine, because
it was part of the Islamic culture.

The Muslim caliphate was founded in the Hellenistic world, which extended
from Rome to India and had been dominated politically by two great powers,
Byzantium and Persia, and culturally by the Greek heritage, cultivated at
universities in Alexandria in Egypt, Nisibis in Mesopotamia, and Gondēshāpūr
in Persia[2] where Indian medicine was also known.

Arabs in leading positions would, of course, have consulted Christian, Jewish
and Persian doctors with a Greek medical education, and we know that these
doctors also had Arab students. But ordinary people knew only the magic cures:
you could, for instance, tie a thread around the arm of a fever patient; if
someone untied it, the fever went over to that person. Another popular remedy
was that of the magical squares. Do you want to have a remedy against fever?
Then write these squares on an egg, put the egg in a piece of blue cloth, roast
it on a fire without the piece of cloth being consumed, eat the egg and put the
shell in a piece of cloth to hang around the neck:

4	9	4
8	5	4
8	1	6[3]

[1] Translation by F. Gabrieli, *Arab Historians of the Crusades* (London, 1969), pp. 76–7. See also
Usāmah Ibn Munqidh, *An Arab-Syrian Gentleman and Warrior in the Period of the Crusades*, tr. P.K.
Hitti (New York, 1929), pp. 162–3, where this anecdote is followed by two others, showing more
successful results of Frankish medical treatment.

[2] A Nestorian centre of learning, with a medical school and a hospital, founded in the middle
of the sixth century.

[3] From M. Ullmann, *Die Medizin im Islam* (Leiden and Cologne, 1970), p. 254.

Often these magical prescriptions, which are not the result of experiment, end with the notice 'Tried'. The following is a tried method against baldness: 'If one burns the bones of the sand grouse and boils up the ashes from these with the oil made from unripe olives and with this rubs the head of a bald person, the hair will grow again'.[4] This popular medicine was later on ascribed to the Prophet Muḥammad, and the so-called prophetical medicine has survived until now – in the bazaars of the Near East you can still buy amulets and magical substances against inexplicable illnesses.

The Arab-Muslim conquests in around 640 incorporated the Hellenistic centres of learning into the caliphate. In the eighth century the Arabs began systematically to assimilate Greek medical science. The incentive came from the caliph al-Manṣūr (754–75, grandfather of the famous caliph of the *Arabian Nights*, Hārūn al-Rashīd). Suffering from an illness of the stomach, which nobody in Baghdad could cure, he summoned the director of the hospital in Gondēshāpūr, a Syrian Christian, whose family for eight generations was to serve as doctors in Iraq, often as court physicians.[5]

Hārūn al-Rashīd's son, the caliph al-Ma'mūn (813–33), founded an academy in Baghdad and collected for its library Greek manuscripts which were translated into Arabic.[6] Thus hundreds of medical works became available, such as the works of Hippocrates and Galen, and the pharmacological *Materia medica* of Dioscorides.

From Galen the Arabs inherited humoral pathology. This theory is based on the idea that illnesses are caused by a disproportion of the corporal fluids and their qualities. Thus blood is warm and humid, phlegm is cold and humid, yellow bile is warm and dry, and black bile is cold and dry.[7] If these fluids and their qualities are not balanced, an illness arises, and the task of the physician is to restore the balance. Cold and humid illnesses, such as migraine and diarrhoea, could be cured by cauterization. This concept is still alive among people who believe that a cold with its surplus of cold and humid phlegm is caused by having been exposed to coldness and wetness and is cured by staying warm and dry. Although medical science today knows this concept to be wrong, it was a scholarly theory which sought the source of an illness in the body itself and not in external influences like evil spirits.

The success of Muslim medicine can be attributed not only to the theories inherited from Greek medicine but also to the common sense of the physicians. A Jewish physician Isḥāq al-Isrā'īlī, in Europe called Isaac Israeli or Isaac Judaeus, said in the tenth century: 'The doctor does not bring about recovery, he prepares the way so that Nature, which does the real work, can bring about

---

[4] Ibid., p. 110.

[5] Ibid., p. 108.

[6] The famous *Bayt al-Ḥikma*, 'House of Wisdom', inspired by the centre of learning in Gondēshāpūr (for both, see *Encyclopaedia of Islam*, new edn (Leiden and Paris, 1960).

[7] See Ullmann, *Islamic Medicine* (Edinburgh, 1978) pp. 57–60.

recovery'.[8] Isaac Israeli, by the way, has left a very accurate description of tuberculosis.[9]

His contemporary, the Persian physician al-Majūsī, wrote a comprehensive medical work, *Al-Kitāb al-Malakī* (The Royal Book), to supplant Hippocrates, whom he found too short, Galen, whom he found too verbose, and other authors, whose works he found badly translated, incomplete or too bulky and thus too expensive. This work was translated into Latin several times in Europe, the last time as late as 1539.[10]

Al-Majūsī was of the opinion that human beings choose their own manner of living, so that good or bad health depends on their own behaviour, as distinguished from the animals, who act instinctively.[11] A patient could thus often be cured by a changed way of life, and diet was often to be preferred to medicine, the effect of which could be too strong. Pure air, exercise, baths, warm clothes, good sleeping habits – too much sleep increases the phlegm, too little makes the body dry – and controlling one's temper lead to good health. These rules of life were explained on the basis of humoral pathology, but being sensible they were successful.

Medical treatment was often offered in the patient's home. From the tenth century doctors made daily visits to the prisons. Villages in the country were also regularly visited by doctors. What interests us in this context is, however, the medical care offered in hospitals.

The difference between European and Arab hospitals at this time was a result of the different view of the causes of illness which I have mentioned. The European hospitals in the Middle Ages aimed at caring for patients rather than healing them, or at isolating them, for instance in *leprosoria*. In the Arab hospitals the patients were treated by use of the scholarly medical methods of the time: medicinal, surgical or psychiatrical, as the case might be, and students

---

[8] For the quotation, see A. Bar-Sela and H.E. Hoff, 'Isaac Israeli's Fifty Admonitions to the Physicians', *Journal of the History of Medicine*, 17 (1962), no. 11 (252); H.D. Isaacs, 'Some Clinical Methods Used by the Arabs in the Middle Ages', *Proceedings of the XXIII International Congress of the History of Medicine*, 1 (London, 1974), 83; S. Jarcho, 'Guide for Physicians (Musar harofim) by Isaac Judaeus (880?–932?), Translated from the Hebrew', *Bulletin of the History of Medicine*, 15 (1944), no. 11 (184); M. Levey, *Medical Ethics of Medieval Islam with Special Reference to al-Ruhāwī's 'Practical Ethics of the Physician'*, Transactions of the American Philosophical Society, new ser. 57.3 (Philadelphia, 1967), p. 95.

[9] Isaac Israeli, 'On Fevers', an abridged Latin translation by Constantine the African in the eleventh century and printed in Lyon in 1515; parts of the section on tuberculosis are translated into English in J.D. Latham, 'Isaac Israeli's "Kitāb al-Hummayat" and the Latin and Castilian texts', *Journal of Semitic Studies*, 14 (1969), 84 ff.

[10] Also known as the *Kitāb Kāmil aṣ-ṣinā'a aṭ-ṭibbiya* (*The Complete Book of the Medical Art*). The title 'The Royal Book' refers to the author's patron, Sultan 'Aḍud al-Dawla, who founded the famous 'Aḍudi hospital in Baghdad *c.* 980 (see text below). Parts of the Arabic text have been translated, see Ullmann, *Medizin*, p. 141 ff.

[11] Ullmann, *Medicine*, p. 97 ff.

were trained to be physicians. Another difference was that while European hospitals were managed by the Church and the monastic orders, all people employed in the Muslim hospitals were laity, many of them not even Muslims but Christians or Jews.

The first known hospital in the Muslim world was established in Baghdad under the caliph al-Manṣūr in 766, after the model of that in Gondēshāpūr in Persia. It was followed by other hospitals endowed by the famous Barmaki wazir family, by the caliph Hārūn al-Rashīd and his successors and by the rulers of the new dynasties emerging from the tenth century onwards.[12]

When Christian merchants in 1036 founded a lodging house and a hospital for pilgrims in Jerusalem, the hospital was probably of the more primitive European kind with the aim of caring for sick and tired pilgrims but without much contact with Muslim medical science and treatment. But after the crusaders had established themselves in the Near East in the twelfth century, in time they became acquainted with Muslim culture, they learnt to build Arab houses, they dressed as Muslims, ate Muslim food and no doubt they consulted Muslim doctors when they fell ill. So when the crusaders took over the Christian lodging house in Jerusalem, they could hardly remain ignorant of the Muslim hospitals which had by then a tradition several centuries old. Thus, by the end of the twelfth century, the Knights of St John, or Hospitallers, as the Arabs also called them, ought to have been able to transform the lodging house into a modern hospital after the Muslim pattern.[13] When Sultan Saladin conquered Jerusalem in 1187, he took over the hospital, enlarged it and named it after himself. Later it fell into decay and in 1458 it was destroyed by earthquake.

In 1156 Saladin's predecessor, Sultan Nūr al-Dīn, completed the greatest hospital in Damascus, al-Nūri, which he equipped with a library where medicine was taught and discussed. After their rounds, the doctors wrote down in the hospital's register the diet and medication for each patient. In charge of the hospital was the sultan's court physician.[14]

---

[12] D.M. Dunlop and G.S. Colin, 'Bîmâristân', *Encyclopaedia of Islam*.

[13] See E.E. Hume, 'Medical Work of the Knights Hospitallers of St John of Jerusalem', *Bulletin of the History of Medicine* (1938), 399–405. However, as B.Z. Kedar makes clear in 'A Twelfth-Century Description of the Jerusalem Hospital' in this volume, the Jerusalem hospital was backward in its treatment of the sick in comparison to Muslim hospitals. For the theory that Byzantium and not Islamic society provided the Knights with the inspiration for their hospital in Jerusalem, see T.S. Miller, 'The Knights of St John and the Hospitals of the Latin West', *Speculum*, 53 (1978), 709–33. Although in other spheres of daily life, such as clothing, food and so on, Arab influence seems to have been much stronger than Byzantine influence, this paper does not aim at excluding the possibility of a certain influence from Byzantium.

[14] S. Hamarneh, 'Development of Hospitals in Islam', *Journal of the History of Medicine*, 17 (1962), 371 ff.; A. Terzioglu, 'Das Nureddin-Krankenhaus in Damaskus', *Historia hospitalium*, 11 (1976), 59–75.

The famous 'Aḍudi hospital in Baghdad had twenty-four doctors, distributed amongst the different wards.[15] Both this hospital and al-Nūri have been described by the traveller Ibn Jubayr, who visited them in the 1180s.[16]

Hospitals usually had wards for male and female medicinal, surgical, ophthalmological, psychiatric, orthopaedic, dysentery and fever cases and a ward for convalescents; they contained an outpatient clinic, a pharmacy, a library, a lecture hall and a public bath. Hospital administration was led by a director with the same standing as a minister. As hospitals were pious foundations, all treatment, in hospital or at home, was free, as also were burial costs when patients died. Socio-economic rehabilitation of patients leaving hospitals was also taken care of. No difference was made between men and women, free men and slaves.[17]

Drugs were listed in pharmacological works, which in Latin translation were to be used in Europe until the seventeenth century. The physician's prescription was given to an apothecary who prepared the medicine but, as already mentioned, dietary control was preferred.

In surgery, tumours were removed and amputations performed, children were delivered by means of forceps, and catgut was used for ligatures of intestinal wounds. Dental surgery extracted roots and made use of bridgework of gold and silver thread. Plastic surgery was used to remove warts on the nose, to repair a broken nose bone, to correct uneven teeth, to amputate supernumerary fingers or to separate adherent fingers, to sew up damaged noses, lips and ears and to remove abnormal accumulation of fat in the pectoral tissue of men. The most original results were attained in eye surgery, for example cataract operations. Arab surgical operations and instruments were not surpassed in Europe until the eighteenth century.[18]

Mental diseases were also treated, not brutally as often happened in Europe, but on an equal footing with physical illnesses. To this treatment belonged a change of climate, beautiful surroundings such as gardens with running water, stimulating medicine and musical and occupational therapy: reading, fishing, hunting, playing chess. Choirs, music bands, storytellers, dancers and comic performers entertained the sick. Mental obsessions could be treated by suggestion.[19]

---

[15] Hamarneh, 369 ff.

[16] Ibn Jubayr, *The Travels of Ibn Jubayr*, tr. R.J.C. Broadhurst (London, 1952), pp. 234 ff., 296.

[17] A. Terzioglu, *Mittelalterliche islamische Krankenhäuser*, Diss. (Berlin, 1968).

[18] See *Albucasis on Surgery and Instruments*, ed. and tr. M.S. Spink and G.L. Lewis (Berkeley and Los Angeles, 1973) which deals with the chapter on surgery in a textbook on medicine written by the physician Abū'l-Qāsim al-Zahrāwi in Cordoba (d. after 1009). This influenced European surgery into the eighteenth century: Ullmann, *Medizin*, p. 149 ff.

[19] E. Bay, 'Islamische Krankenhäuser im Mittelalter unter besonderer Berücksichtigung der Psychiatrie', Diss. (Düsseldorf, 1967); see also J.O. Leibowitz, 'A Mental Hospital in Bagdad as Described by Benjamin of Tudela (12th cent.)', *Proceedings of the XXIII International Congress of the History of Medicine* 1972, 1 (London 1974), p. 412.

A doctor could be on duty at the hospital two days and two nights a week. His activities started with the round when he, followed by his students, listened to the complaints of the patients and gave his prescriptions to the personnel. After the round the doctor studied medical works in the hospital library and discussed problems with colleagues and students.

After an accident with a fatal outcome caused by bad medical treatment in 931, the caliph ordered all Baghdad physicians to be examined by his court physician, and those who did not qualify for a licence were to be barred from practice.[20] Handbooks for this examination are preserved and show us what was expected from an authorized physician. Such examinations may have been introduced among the Franks in the Kingdom of Jerusalem before the same steps were taken in 1140 by King Roger II of Sicily, a country which was also subject to Muslim influence.

But whatever the result of this control, God would judge on the Last Day, when the patients held their doctors responsible for their mistakes and when, as one Arab physician says, the speaking tongues will become silent, but the silent urinals will speak.

To conclude: we know that the medical knowledge of the Arabs was introduced into Europe via Sicily and Italy, particularly Salerno (through Constantine the African, d. 1087), and via Spain. We do not know, or at least I do not know, how much of this knowledge was assimilated by the crusaders. Given the interest of the military orders in medical care, however, it would seem strange if they did not take over, along with certain heraldic devices,[21] Damascus steel, textiles, food, and so on, the medical knowledge of the Arabs with whom they lived in intimate contact and whose customs they to a great extent imitated.

---

[20] Ullmann, *Medizin*, p. 226. On the examination of physicians, see A.Z. Iskander, 'Galen and Rhazes on Examining Physicians', *Bulletin of the History of Medicine*, 36 (1962), 362–5.

[21] A.H. Christie, 'Islamic Minor Arts and their Influence upon European Work', in *The Legacy of Islam*, ed. T. Arnold and A. Guillaume (Oxford, 1931, repr. 1968), pp. 108–51; L.A. Mayer, *Saracenic Heraldry* (Oxford, 1933).

4

The Archaeological Approach to the Study of Disease in the Crusader States, as Employed at Le Petit Gerin

Piers Mitchell

INTRODUCTION

The crusades were responsible for great changes in the lives of those who left Europe for the eastern Mediterranean, and many of these changes had a direct impact on the health of crusaders. Quite apart from the obvious widespread trauma expected in an invading army, they had to travel through inhospitable terrain varying from snow-clad mountains to arid deserts.[1] The lack of sanitation predisposed them to gastrointestinal diseases such as dysentery,[2] while the frequent sieges and scarcity of food have left many records of malnutrition.[3]

Even after the various crusader states had been established, the European inhabitants continued to suffer. The cultures they brought with them were often inappropriate for the Middle East. Food stored at room temperature would have decomposed faster in the hot weather in the county of Tripoli than it did in the West, and so needed to be handled and stored differently. Farming techniques successful in northern France would not have worked so well in arid parts of the kingdom of Jerusalem, and Latin farmers may have experienced dietary deficiencies in consequence. The states of the Middle East also grew crops such as sugar cane, dates and figs[4] which would have been new

---

[1] Odo of Deuil, *De Profectione Ludovici VII in Orientem*, ed. and tr. V.G. Berry (New York, 1948), p. 117; Ambroise, 'The History of the Holy War' in *Three Old French Chronicles of the Crusades*, tr. E.N. Stone (Washington, 1939), p. 85.

[2] John of Joinville, *The Life of St Louis*, ed. N. de Wailly, tr. R. Hague (London, 1955), p. 24.

[3] Raymond d'Aguilers, *Historia Francorum Qui Ceperunt Iherusalem*, tr. J.H. Hill and L.L. Hill (Philadelphia, 1968), p. 59.

[4] Burchard of Mount Zion, *A Description of the Holy Land AD 1280*, tr. A. Stewart, PPTS, 12 (London, 1896), pp. 99–102; Nāsir-i-Khusrau, *Diary of a Journey Through Syria and Palestine in 1047 AD*, tr. G. Le Strange, PPTS, 4 (London, 1888), pp. 6–7.

From *The Military Orders. Volume 2. Welfare and Warfare*. ed. Helen Nicholson. Copyright © 1998 by Helen Nicholson. Published by Ashgate Publishing Ltd, Gower House, Croft Road, Aldershot, Hampshire, GU11 3HR, Great Britain.

to many crusaders. These sugary products might be expected to accelerate the development of tooth decay if eaten regularly. There were also new diseases endemic in this area such as schistosomiasis and dracunculiasis.[5] Factors such as these make the study of disease during the crusades more complex and interesting than perhaps anywhere else in Europe or the Middle East in the medieval period.

METHODS USED TO STUDY DISEASE IN PAST POPULATIONS

Until recently most research into disease during the crusades was based on textual evidence.[6] Fortunately there are many useful contemporary records available such as legal documents, historical accounts of military campaigns and pilgrim records of journeys to the Holy Places. These have enabled great advances to be made in understanding medical practice at the time. The first studies of two valuable manuscripts form the basis of other articles of this conference compilation.[7] Texts also have the potential to give valuable descriptions of disease. However, any such descriptions must be viewed with caution as they were written from a medieval perspective of disease and we are reading them from a modern one. Furthermore, the records we have were not even written by physicians of the time but by clerics and scholars, which creates further potential for ambiguous information.

Archaeology is an approach which is not hampered by many of these problems and the specialty involved with analysis of human skeletal remains for evidence of disease is termed palaeopathology. This has the great advantage that it is relatively objective and not reliant on a contemporary description. Remains can be studied for the wide range of diseases we now know exist and we are not limited to those diseases which had been identified by the medieval period. Visual inspection of bones may be supplemented with X-ray imaging of suspect areas, detailed examination of bone structure using microscopy, trace element analysis and also DNA analysis of that genetic material still present. Together with lesions of bone, evidence of disease which may be found include kidney and gall stones, calcified parasites, and eggs of parasitic worms from the gut preserved in latrine pits. While diagnosing individual cases of various diseases is obviously important, study of human skeletal remains allows research at the level of a population rather than just an individual. The prevalence of particular conditions can be calculated and compared with other

---

[5] P.B. Adamson, 'Schistosomiasis in Antiquity', *Medical History*, 20 (1976), 176–88; P.B. Adamson, 'Dracontiasis in Antiquity', *Medical History*, 32 (1988), 204–9.

[6] P.D. Mitchell, 'Leprosy and the Case of King Baldwin IV of Jerusalem: Mycobacterial Disease in the Crusader States of the 12th and 13th Centuries', *International Journal of Leprosy and Other Mycobacterial Diseases*, 61 (1993), 283–91; S. Edgington, 'Medical Knowledge in the Crusading Armies: the Evidence of Albert of Aachen and Others' in *MO*, 1, pp. 320–6.

[7] *Idem*, 'Medical Care in the Hospital of St John in Jerusalem', Chapter 2 of this collection; B. Kedar, 'A Twelfth-Century Description of the Jerusalem Hospital', Chapter 1 of this collection.

relevant groups. Life expectancy and population structure can be assessed by knowing the age at death of each member of a community.[8]

As with any method of research there are limitations to palaeopathology. Unless remains are exceptionally well preserved, as with dessicated Egyptian mummies or the bog bodies of northern Europe,[9] usually only bones are left. This is obviously a problem when trying to study diseases which affect only soft tissues and leave no obvious evidence in skeletal material. If in a cemetery, the remains may become mixed with others by the digging of later graves and it can be difficult to distinguish the bones of one individual from those nearby. After hundreds of years in the ground the bones are often fragmentary and this usually reduces the amount of information which can be deduced from the remains. Moreover, in contrast to research based on manuscripts, archaeology is expensive. It takes a large team several years to excavate a site using a wide range of equipment, unlike the study of a text by one scholar.

PALAEOPATHOLOGY OF LE PETIT GERIN (PARVUM GERINUM)

There has been little work on human skeletal remains from the twelfth and thirteenth centuries in the eastern Mediterranean. This is partly explained by the fact that countries understandably show more interest in excavating their own heritage than the remains left by invaders from Europe. Furthermore, bones do not make tourist attractions in the way that an excavated castle might, and are harder for a non-specialist to appreciate in a museum compared with a pot or weapon. In consequence these excavations are often seen as a financial drain.

One site which has been excavated[10] is that of Le Petit Gerin (Tel Jezreel, Israel) which overlooked the Jezreel Valley, 17 km south of Nazareth. This was a village of local Syrian Christians owned by the Knights Templar, who manned a fortified tower in the twelfth century. The human skeletal remains were recovered from the cemetery of the village church.[11] The fact that these individuals lived all their lives in the Levant means that any evidence of disease found on those buried during the crusader period must be related to life in the crusader states. This is in contrast to Frankish cemeteries, where those who died may have developed diseases either in the Levant or in

---

[8] D. Ortner and W.G.J. Putschar, *Identification of Pathological Conditions in Human Skeletal Remains* (Washington, 1985); D.R. Brothwell, *Digging Up Bones*, 3rd edn (London, 1981).

[9] *Mummies, Disease and Ancient Cultures*, ed. A. Cockburn and E. Cockburn (Cambridge, 1983); P.V. Glob, *The Bog People*, tr. R. Bruce-Mitford (London, 1977).

[10] D. Ussishkin and J. Woodhead, 'Excavations at Tel Jezreel 1990–1991', *Tel Aviv*, 19 (1992), 3–56; *idem*, 'Excavations at Tel Jezreel 1992–1993. Second Preliminary Report', *Levant*, 26 (1994), 1–48.

[11] M. Bradley, 'Preliminary Assessment of the Mediaeval Christian Burials from Tel Jezreel', *Levant*, 26 (1994), 63–5.

Europe before they travelled East. In this way, study of local inhabitants allows a more representative assessment of disease in the crusader period.

The remains of thirty-four immature individuals were recovered from the site before the close of excavation.[12] In contrast to adults, infants and children in the medieval period typically experienced acute infections, malnutrition and parasitic infestation as occurs in the Third World today. One notable example was that of an infant with meningitis (Figure 4.1). The internal aspect of the occipital bone at the back of the skull demonstrated a thin layer of periosteal new bone deposition. Meningitis is the term used to describe an infection which causes inflammation of the layers of tissue between the skull and the brain and would have triggered the new bone production. As it takes approximately one week for new bone to be produced in response to a stimulus,[13] this meningitis must have been present for at least that long. It is possible that tuberculosis, typically slow to develop, was the cause of death.

Adults from the medieval period are more likely to show evidence of chronic conditions on their bones. They were still susceptible to epidemics as contemporary records show,[14] but most diseases which left signs on their skeletons were not instrumental in their deaths. By the close of the excavation only six adults had been recovered and it is likely that most of the adults from the site were buried elsewhere. One area of particular relevance to a population in the crusader period is that of trauma resulting from the use of weapons. A good example from Le Petit Gerin is that of a male twenty to thirty years old who suffered a blow which cut clean through the acromion of his left scapula (shoulder blade). The edge is straight with no evidence of splintering (Figure 4.2), which suggests that a thin blade such as a sword was responsible. A number of styles including the curved sabre were known to have been used in the Levant at that time from their representation in artwork and the margins of manuscripts.[15] The early evidence of healing visible at the cut edge suggests the man survived the attack for at least a week. As a result we cannot know if the attack took place at Le Petit Gerin itself, or if he was elsewhere in the kingdom and lived long enough to return home. Chronicles record that the settlement was attacked a number of times in the twelfth century: the forces of Saladin destroyed the village on the night of 9–10 September 1184[16] and it

---

[12] P.D. Mitchell, 'Pathology in the Crusader Period: Human Skeletal Remains from Tel Jezreel', *Levant*, 26 (1994), 67–71; *idem*, 'Further Evidence of Disease in the Crusader Period Population of Le Petit Gerin (Tel Jezreel, Israel)', *Tel Aviv*, 24(1) (1997), 169–79.

[13] C.G. Barber, 'The Detailed Changes Characteristic of Healing Bone in Amputated Stumps', *Journal of Bone and Joint Surgery*, 12 (1930), 353–9.

[14] William of Tyre, *A History of Deeds Done Beyond the Seas*, ed. and tr. E.A. Babcock and A.C. Krey (New York, 1943), 1, p. 309; John of Joinville, pp. 128–9.

[15] D.C. Nicolle, *Arms and Armour in the Crusading Era 1050–1350* (New York, 1988), 1, pp. 156–83, 198–221 (text); 2, pp. 715–32, 736–50 (illustrations).

[16] Ralph of Diss, *Opera Historica*, 2 vols, ed. W. Stubbs, RS, 68 (London, 1876), 2, p. 28.

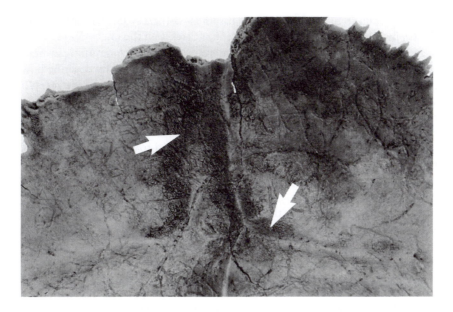

Figure 4.1   Meningitis in an infant. Periostosis in the occipital bone

Figure 4.2   Sword wound to the left scapular bone

fell once again to Saladin's nephew Husam al-Muhammad after the battle of Hattin in July 1187.[17]

Dental caries are well known to be more prevalent in communities where sugar cane is consumed regularly.[18] Contemporary texts vividly describe how people both enjoyed eating the cane itself and also made use of the refined sugar as a syrup and in the crystallized form.[19] A number of sugar cane refineries from the crusader states are known, such as that at Jericho.[20] It was a major crop and industry of the states with both local consumption and export to Europe and other parts of the eastern Mediterranean. A number of sugar pots have been recovered from Le Petit Gerin,[21] confirming its consumption at the site. The presence of the marshy Jezreel Valley below would have allowed local cultivation of the canes, but it is not known for sure if this was farmed and possibly processed locally, as the twelfth-century village remains unexcavated. The hypothesis that dental caries would have been more severe in crusader-period populations where sugar cane was grown and processed compared with other farming areas or cities is a highly plausible one. However, although cases of dental caries, periodontitis and dental abscess have been found at this site, the small adult sample cannot be sufficiently representative to allow a reasonable assessment of the dental health of the whole community.

While caries can lead to dental abscess formation around the roots of an infected tooth, the pain and difficulty in eating is not the only unpleasant consequence. Bacteria from the abscess can spread via the blood to other organs including bone, a condition termed osteomyelitis.[22] Two cases from Le Petit Gerin suffered with osteomyelitis, one in the sacrum at the base of the spine and the other in the ulna at the right elbow. The former did have a dental abscess but unfortunately no fragments of jaw have survived from the latter. As neither showed signs of local trauma or infection in overlying tissues, a haematogenous source of the bacteria is most likely and an origin such as a dental abscess is very plausible.

FURTHER RESEARCH NECESSARY AT OTHER CRUSADER SITES

The hypothesis regarding a possible geographical relationship between dental caries and sugar cane consumption is only one of a number of questions where

---

[17] Abū Shāma, 'Le Livre des Deux Jardins', *RHC Or*, 4, p. 301.

[18] J.E. Frenken, P. Rugarambu and J. Mulder, 'The Effect of Sugar Cane Chewing on the Development of Dental Caries', *Journal of Dental Research*, 68 (1989), 1102–4.

[19] Burchard of Mount Zion, pp. 99–100.

[20] B. Pörée and A. Padgett, 'The crusader and Medieval Sugar-Mill of Jericho (Tawahin as-Sukkar site): Elements of Conservation and Restoration Studies', *Bulletin of the Society for the Study of the Crusades and the Latin East*, 16 (1996), 38–9.

[21] A. Grey, 'The Pottery of the Later Periods from Tel Jezreel – an Interim Report', *Levant*, 26 (1994), 51–62.

[22] N.M. Rubin, R.J. Sanfillipo and R.S. Sadoff, 'Vertebral Osteomyelitis Secondary to Oral Infection', *Journal of Oral Maxillofacial Surgery*, 49 (1991), 897–900.

archaeology may provide valuable information. Study of battlefield cemeteries should be able to demonstrate the types of wounds which resulted from warfare in this period and highlight the contrasting styles of combat and weapons employed by each side. It would be interesting to know if those living in rural areas would have experienced more trauma than those in cities, as defences against attack from raiding parties, bandits or armies would have been less effective. The effect on other areas of health from living in towns rather than in the countryside is another necessary line of research. Many cities had filthy streets, experienced periodic sieges with associated malnutrition and some, such as Acre, were infamous for the violent and immoral activities of many inhabitants.[23]

Another area awaiting clarification is whether Frankish farmers in crusader settlements,[24] with their European culture and farming techniques, would have been less productive than the local farmers whose ancestors would have passed down methods appropriate for the hot and sometimes arid Middle East. Comparing signs of malnutrition and calculating life expectancy in Latin and local farming communities may help towards a conclusion.

A further hypothesis concerns the diagnosis of 'leprosy' as perceived by medieval physicians. While it is known that true leprosy definitely did exist in the crusader states,[25] it is unclear exactly which diseases were labelled by contemporary physicians under the umbrella term of 'leprosy'; there is some evidence that syphilis may have been confused with true leprosy in the medieval Middle East. Cases of treponemal disease have been excavated from Europe[26] dating well before Columbus and 1492, confirming that the group of diseases was present hundreds of years before his voyage to the New World. The Order of St Lazarus was established to accommodate those with a medieval diagnosis of 'leprosy' in the crusader states, and excavation of their cemeteries should provide definitive information on the diseases of those admitted to the Order. Observations from archaeological approaches to each of these hypotheses can then be compared with the studies of disease based on textual evidence, further enriching our understanding of disease patterns.

---

[23] Ibn Jubayr, *The Travels of Ibn Jubayr*, tr. R.J.C. Broadhurst (London, 1952), p. 318; John of Joinville, p. 181.

[24] D. Pringle, 'Magna Mahumeria (al-Bira): the Archaeology of a Frankish New Town in Palestine', in *Crusade and Settlement*, ed. P.W. Edbury (Cardiff, 1985), pp. 147–68; R. Ellenblum, 'Colonization Activities in the Frankish East: The Example of Castellum Regis (Mi'ilya)', *English Historical Review*, 111 (1996), 104–23.

[25] Mitchell, 'Leprosy'.

[26] A. Stirland, 'Pre-Columbian Treponematosis in Medieval Britain', *International Journal of Osteoarchaeology*, 1 (1991), 39–47; C. Roberts, 'Treponematosis in Gloucester, England: a Theoretical and Practical Approach to the Pre-Columbian Theory', in *L'Origine de la Syphilis en Europe: Avant ou Après 1493?* ed. O. Dutour, G. Palfi, J. Berato, J.-P. Brun (Paris, 1994), pp. 101–8.

CONCLUSION

Palaeopathology is a research tool which is sadly under-utilized in the study of health and disease in the crusader states. While it is more expensive and time-consuming than literary research, it can provide relatively objective information about a population which is unavailable from other sources. It also avoids the problems associated with studying disease from a medieval viewpoint and allows an assessment of ill health in a community from a modern perspective.

5

The Role of Hospitals in the Teutonic Order

Klaus Militzer

The Teutonic Order arose from small beginnings in the twelfth century. Its foundation passed without ceremony; there was nothing to indicate that it would expand so rapidly in the first half of the thirteenth century. In 1190, during the siege of Acre, a hospital was founded by citizens of Bremen and Lübeck who were taking part in the Third Crusade. This hospital was dedicated to sick and wounded German crusaders, and according to the Order's own tradition the citizens stretched out a ship's sail in order to give shade to the care of sick and wounded.[1] We do not know exactly how the care of the sick was organized, but it seems certain that the newly founded hospital was managed by a lay fraternity with a master. A similar arrangement had been introduced into hospitals in German cities and was the most modern form of organization at that time.[2] Therefore it is possible that the citizens of Bremen and Lübeck committed the new foundation to the care of such a fraternity.

The form of organization adopted by the citizens did not remain in place for long. When Duke Frederick of Swabia arrived at Acre in October 1190 he took the hospital under his protection, and from that time on it played a role in Staufen politics. Perhaps the lay fraternity was transformed into an order, but we do not know the precise circumstances, nor when this happened; no rule of this order has come down to us. Then, in 1198, the hospital was transformed

---

[1] M.-L. Favreau, *Studien zur Frühgeschichte des Deutschen Ordens*, Kieler Historische Studien, 21 (Stuttgart, 1974), pp. 35–63; U. Arnold, 'Entstehung und Frühzeit des Deutschen Ordens. Zu Gründung und innerer Struktur des Deutschen Hospitals von Akkon und des Ritterordens in der ersten Hälfte des 13. Jahrhunderts', in *Die geistlichen Ritterorden Europas*, ed. J. Fleckenstein and M. Hellmann, Vorträge und Forschungen, 26 (Sigmaringen, 1980), pp. 81–107.

[2] S. Reicke, *Das deutsche Spital und sein Recht im Mittelalter*, Kirchenrechtliche Abhandlungen, 111–114 (Stuttgart, 1932), 1, pp. 53–71.

into a military order. The brethren were to observe the rule of the Templars in military affairs and the rule of the Hospitallers in matters of hospitality.[3]

Some historians maintain that military functions were assigned to the hospital before this transformation, referring to the fact that in 1193 Henry of Champagne had given the hospital a section of the defences of Acre next to the gate of St Nicholas. But as the hospital was obliged only to repair this part of the fortifications this obligation was more financial than military, and so we would suggest that there was no military involvement before 1198. After the transformation the military function became more dominant.[4] Nevertheless, the Order continued to support hospitals even after 1198; it had and retained an official for caring for the sick. He was the *Spittler*, or hospitaller, who ranked among the *Großgebietiger*, the leading officials in the Order's headquarters under the Grand Master (*Hochmeister*).[5] The first *Spittler* that we know of was a knight brother, Henry, in 1208.[6] The main hospital of the Order remained in Acre until 1291, and was not moved when the Order's headquarters were transferred to the castle of Montfort.[7]

After the loss of Acre in 1291 the Grand Master transferred his headquarters to Venice; the *Großgebietiger* were also usually based there.[8] According to the statutes promulgated by Siegfried of Feuchtwangen (1303–9) or Gottfried of Hohenlohe (1297–1303), a *Spittler* lived in the headquarters in Venice, and he was ordered not to cross the Alps without permission.[9] But it is not clear from the statutes whether the Order supported a hospital in Venice or even whether it had a hospital there at all.[10] The absence of any evidence for a Venice hospital suggests that its existence is improbable.[11]

---

[3] Favreau, pp. 64–73.

[4] U. Arnold, 'Vom Feldspital zum Ritterorden. Militarisierung und Territorialisierung des Deutschen Ordens (1190–ca.1240)', in *Balticum. Studia z dziejów polityki gospodarki i kultury XII–XVII wieku, ofiarowane Marianowi Biskupowi w siedemdziesiątą rocznicę urodzin*, ed. Z.H. Nowak (Torun, 1992), pp. 27–8; A. Forey, *The Military Orders. From the Twelfth to the Early Fourteenth Centuries* (London, 1992), pp. 19–20.

[5] F. Milthaler, *Die Großgebietiger des Deutschen Ritterordens bis 1440*, Schriften der Albertus-Universität. Geisteswissenschaftliche Reihe, 26 (Königsberg and Berlin, 1940), pp. 23–5, 39–40, 85–91.

[6] *Tabulae Ordinis Theutonici ex regii tabularii Berolinensis codici potissimum*, ed. E. Strehlke (Berlin, 1869, repr. Toronto and Jerusalem, 1975), p. 35.

[7] C. Probst, *Der Deutsche Orden und sein Medizinalwesen in Preußen: Hospital, Firmarie und Artz bis 1525*, QuStDo, 29 (Bad Godesberg, 1969), p. 37.

[8] Milthaler, pp. 43–4.

[9] *SDO*, p. 145.

[10] Thus Probst, p. 38 and Milthaler, p. 44.

[11] K. Forstreuter, *Der Deutsche Orden am Mittelmeer*, QuStDO, 2 (Bonn, 1967), p. 56, and U. Arnold, 'Der Deutsche Orden und Venedig', in *Militia Sacra*, ed. E. Coli, M. de Marco and F. Tommasi (Perugia, 1994), p. 149, state that in 1300 a *Spittler* named Conrad of Babenberg is mentioned in Famagusta. In fact, a careful reading of the relevant document reveals that he was probably in Venice: see the document printed in *Notai Genovesi in Oltremare: Atti rogati a Cipro di Lamberto di*

In 1309 the Grand Master transferred his headquarters to Marienburg in Prussia. The *Spittler* accompanied him but set up his residence in Elbing, where the Hospital of the Holy Ghost, which was already in existence by the middle of the thirteenth century, became the Order's main hospital.[12] The supreme hospitaller (*Oberster Spittler*), as he was called, did not manage the hospital by himself; that was the task of the under-hospitaller (*Unterspittler*).[13] The supreme hospitaller had to govern the old commandery or preceptory of Elbing, which was also already in existence before his arrival. As a member of the *Großgebietiger* he belonged to the council of the Grand Master. So he was not a minister of public health nor an inspector general of all hospitals in Prussia;[14] as the under-hospitaller's superior he was responsible for the main hospital of the Order in Elbing, but only with general oversight, not directly.

According to the rule of the Teutonic Order the *Spittler* could claim an exceptional position. Unlike other officials who had to render accounts for their office, he was not expected to render an account of the hospital's expenses. His hospital was financially independent with its own income and he could demand contributions without any interference from other officials of the Order, only being obliged to inform the Grand Master of the hospital's economic position now and then; this enabled the *Spittler* to give the best care to the sick and poor.[15] These regulations, which were laid down for the headquarters and its hospital in the Latin East and were already valid about 1200, were written into the rule about 1250, and became standard for the Order's other hospitals. Many hospitals in other regions were financially independent with their own incomes, with no external control over their expenses. The possessions of these hospitals could be allocated specifically to them, for their use alone. These hospitals were able to develop into separate economic units, independent of the economies of the preceptories to which they belonged. An example of this development is the hospital in Nuremberg, the most important hospital in the bailiwicks under the *Deutschmeister*, the master of the Order's possessions in Germany.[16] However, the Order did not usually distribute properties specifically to individual hospitals. For most of the hospitals in the bailiwicks such a development cannot be proven and probably did not occur. This may have been the result of a decision reached by the

---

Sambuceto (3 Iuglio–3 Agosto 1301), ed. V. Polonio, Collana Storica di fonti e studi, 31 (Genoa, 1982), no. 140 (pp. 156–7).

[12] Probst, pp. 44–5, 64–7; B. Jähnig, 'Das Entstehen der mittelalterlichen Sakraltopographie von Elbing', *Beiträge zur Geschichte Westpreußens*, 10 (1987), 40–1.

[13] Probst, p. 67.

[14] Milthaler, pp. 87–91.

[15] *SDO*, p. 107.

[16] K. Militzer, 'Wirtschaftstätigkeit ländlicher und städtischer Deutschordenshäuser', in *Zur Wirtschaftsentwicklung des Deutschen Ordens im Mittelalter*, ed. U. Arnold, QuStDO, 38 (Marburg, 1989), p. 6; *Die ältesten Urbare der Deutschordenskommende Nürnberg*, ed. G. Pfeiffer. Veröffentlichung der Gesellschaft für fränkische Geschichte, 10.10 (Neustadt an der Aisch, 1981), pp. 81–153.

chapter general before 1289, by which smaller hospitals with only a few properties were managed by cellarers (*Kellnern*), who were obliged to render accounts.[17] The properties of these hospitals were not separate from the goods of the preceptories to which they were attached.

Because of its emergence from a hospital fraternity the Teutonic Order was regarded as a competent manager of hospitals even after its transformation into a military order. Emperors, kings, lords, noblemen and citizens donated hospitals in Italy, southern France and in the German Empire. In 1200 the archbishop of Magdeburg and the burgrave of Magdeburg transferred a place near Halle on the River Saale to the Order for the building of a hospital.[18] Two years later the citizens of Bozen (Bolzano) granted the Order their hospital[19] and the following year the archbishop of Salzburg donated his hospital in Friesach.[20] In fact, by 1230 the Order had received at least twenty-six hospitals.[21] In the years that followed the middle of the century the Order received another four hospitals, among them the hospital of St Elizabeth in Marburg[22] and the hospitals in Lengmoos and Sterzing on the route to the Brenner Pass.[23] In the fourteenth century some small hospitals were added, such as those in Bilin (Bilina) in Bohemia in 1302,[24] in Neubrunn in Franconia in 1311,[25] and in Aken on the River Elbe in 1355.[26] The last three hospitals hardly expanded at all because the Order did not support them; we have only a small amount of evidence about other hospitals in Italy.[27] After the middle of the thirteenth century contemporaries no longer had any confidence in the

---

[17] *SDO*, p. 137.

[18] R. Wolf, *Das Deutsch-Ordenshaus St Kunigunde bei Halle an der Saale*, Forschungen zur thüringisch-sächsischen Geschichte, 7 (Halle an der Saale, 1915), pp. 6–10; *Urkundenbuch der Deutschordensballei Thüringen*, ed. K.H. Lampe, Thüringische Geschichtsquellen, new ser. 7 (Jena, 1936), pp. 1–2.

[19] *Tiroler Urkundenbuch*, 2, ed. F. Huter (Innsbruck, 1949), no. 543; U. Arnold, 'Die Ballei und das Land. Mittelalter, in *Der Deutsche Orden in Tirol. Die Ballei an der Etsch und im Gebirge*, ed. H. Noflatscher, QuStDO, 43 (Marburg, 1991), p. 130.

[20] U. Arnold, 'Die Gründung der Deutschordensniederlassung Friesach in Kärnten 1203', in *Festschrift für Hans Thieme*, ed. K. Kroeschell (Sigmaringen, 1986), pp. 37–41.

[21] Other figures: Probst, p. 39; Reicke, 1, pp. 112–32.

[22] U. Braasch-Schwersmann, *Das Deutschordenshaus Marburg. Wirtschaft und Verwaltung einer spätmittelalterlichen Grundherrschaf*, Untersuchungen und Materialien zur Verfassungs- und Landesgeschichte, 11 (Marburg, 1989), pp. 6–15.

[23] F.-H. Hye, 'Die Ballei an der Etsch und die Landkommende Bozen', in *Der Deutsche Orden in Tirol. Die Ballei an der Etsch und im Gebirge*, QuStDO, 43, pp. 330–1.

[24] *Preußisches Urkundenbuch* (hereafter *Preuß. UB*), 1.2, ed. A. Seraphim (Königsberg, 1909), no. 776; *Regesta diplomatica nec non epistolaris Bohemiae et Moraviae*, 2.6, ed. J. Emler (Prague, 1874), no. 1927.

[25] K.H. Lampe, 'Die Entstehung der Deutschordenskommende Prozelten', *Wertheimer Jahrbuch für Geschichte, Volks- und Heimatkunde des Main-Tauberlandes, 1955* (1956), 41–2.

[26] E. Behr, 'Zur Geschichte der Deutschordenskommende Aken', *Geschichtsblätter für Stadt und Land Magdeburg*, 31.2 (1896), 222–6.

[27] Probst, pp. 37–9; M. Tumler, *Der Deutsche Orden im Werden, Wachsen und Wirken bis 1400* (Vienna, 1955), pp. 75–7.

Order's management of hospitals; it had lost its credibility as a hospital order and its competence in that field.

In 1289, two years before the fall of Acre, the chapter general had to impress upon the brethren that the sick and poor were their masters, whom they had to serve.[28] Burchard of Schwanden, the last Grand Master to have resided at least for part of his magistracy in Acre had to admonish the commanders of bailiwicks (*provinciales*, or *Landkomture*), that the hospitals were reserved for the poor and the sick and not for the brethren. If a house was burdened with too many brothers, they should be sent to other houses. On no account were the incomes of hospitals to be used for the upkeep of the brethren.[29] This instruction was repeated by Burchard's successor, Conrad of Feuchtwangen, in 1292, but he restricted its application to those houses with ancient hospitals.[30]

Some historians link these instructions to the reduction of hospitality in the Teutonic Order after the end of the thirteenth century, others to the loss of the Latin East by the Christians, because, they say, many brethren fled from the Latin East to the bailiwicks, occupied the hospitals and consumed their incomes.[31] Such a view can hardly be supported, as most of the brethren in the Latin East lost their lives fighting against the Muslims; in fact, it is probable that no brothers of the Teutonic Order escaped from the besieged and conquered city of Acre in 1291.[32] Therefore refugee brethren from the Latin East cannot be the reason for the decline of hospitality in the bailiwicks. Symptomatic of the decline may be the fact that the Teutonic Order did not care for the refugees of Acre in Cyprus as did the Hospitallers and even the Templars.[33] So we must ask whether the Teutonic Order reduced its involvement as a result of the loss of its headquarters and main hospital in Acre, or whether it began to reduce it before the fall of Acre, this event merely accelerating an already existing development.

In recent years Klaus van Eickels, who has published a book about the bailiwick of Koblenz, has argued that the Teutonic Order had used the income of the hospitals for its military engagements and not for the sick and poor alone. As he has dealt with this subject, I refer the reader to his work.[34]

---

[28] *SDO*, p. 137.

[29] Ibid., p. 140.

[30] Ibid., p. 141.

[31] See, for instance, Probst, p. 39.

[32] U. Arnold, 'Deutschmeister Konrad von Feuchtwangen und die "preußische Partei" im Deutschen Orden am Ende des 13. und zu Beginn des 14. Jahrhunderts', in *Aspekte der Geschichte. Festschrift für Peter Gerrit Thielen zu seinem 65. Geburtstag*, ed. U. Arnold, S. Schröder and G. Walzik (Göttingen, 1990), pp. 22–42.

[33] M.-L. Favreau-Lilie, 'The Military Orders and the Escape of the Christian Population from the Holy Land in 1291', *Journal of Medieval History*, 19 (1993), 223.

[34] See his article in this volume, 'Knightly Hospitallers or Crusading Knights? Decisive Factors for the Spread of the Teutonic Knights in the Rhineland and the Low Countries, 1216–1300'. See also his *Die Deutschordensballei Koblenz und ihre wirtschaftliche Entwicklung in Spätmittelalter* (Marburg, 1995).

The Order used its hospitals in this way not only in the bailiwick of Koblenz but in other bailiwicks too, although it is necessary to qualify this statement. In Nuremberg in Franconia, for instance, it appears that the Order had established its own hospital rather than acquiring it from the citizens.[35] But even if the Order did obtain the hospital in this way, it extended and developed it at its own cost. This became the Teutonic Order's most important hospital in the German Empire, the main hospital in the region of the *Deutschmeister* and of the branch of the Order in the bailiwicks.[36] The hospital in Marburg was also extended by the Order: about the middle of the thirteenth century a new hospital building was erected. However, the Order then lost interest in the foundation.[37] Both hospitals, in Marburg and in Nuremberg, had already needed the attention of Grand Master Burchard of Schwanden. In 1284 or 1285 he transferred the Order's preceptory in Griefstedt near Erfurt to support the hospital in Marburg and in 1287 the preceptory in Hüttenheim to support the hospital in Nuremberg.[38] Yet Burchard of Schwanden was an exception in the sequence of masters, and his successors did not follow his example. In the fourteenth century the citizens of both towns, Marburg and Nuremberg, complained that the Order was not doing its duty and was receiving rich beneficiaries in the hospitals rather than caring for the sick and poor.[39] In Nuremberg, Conrad Groß deemed it necessary to found the Hospital of the Holy Ghost in 1331 because the Order's existing hospital had failed to provide adequate welfare in a large medieval town.[40] The new hospital soon became more important than the old one.

As in Nuremberg and Marburg, all the hospitals which the Order maintained became institutions for providing for the wealthy. This became a continuous trend but there were notable exceptions. In the main hospital in Nuremberg, for instance, care for the sick and poor continued, although, as we have seen, the new Hospital of the Holy Ghost superseded the Order's older Hospital of St Elizabeth. In 1340 Henry of Zipplingen, commmander of the preceptory in Donauwörth, established ten new prebends and – more important for our subject – five beds for sick people in the Order's hospital at Donauwörth. The five beds were reserved for those ill with fever, raving madness or dysentery. These beds still existed in the sixteenth century, when the city's council

[35] Thus D.J. Weiß, *Die Geschichte der Deutschordens-Ballei Franken im Mittelalter*, Veröffentlichungen der Gesellschaft für fränkische Geschichte, 9.39 (Neustadt an der Aisch, 1991), p. 34.

[36] K. Militzer, 'Der Deutsche Orden in den großen Städten des Deutschen Reichs', in *Das Verhältnis des Deutschen Ordens zu den Städten in Livland, Preussen und im Deutschen Reich*, ed. U. Arnold, QuStDO, 44 (Marburg, 1993), pp. 196–7.

[37] Braasch-Schwersmann, p. 233–4.

[38] K. Militzer, *Die Entstehung der Deutschordensballeien im Deutschen Reich*, QuStDO, 16 (Marburg, 1981), pp. 97, 116.

[39] Braasch-Schwersmann, pp. 235–6; see also Weiß, pp. 363–4.

[40] U. Knefelkamp, *Das Heilig-Geist-Spital in Nürnberg vom 14.–17. Jahrhundert*, Nürnberger Forschungen, 26 (Nuremberg, 1989).

obtained a right to reserve them.[41] In 1340 the *Deutschmeister*, Wolfram of Nellenburg, probably one of the few reformers to hold this office, founded a new hospital in Mergentheim in Franconia. This hospital was not managed by the Order's brethren, however; it was only under the superintendence of an official of the Order.[42] Wolfram's foundation was more typical of its age than that of Henry of Zipplingen. With only a few exceptions, new foundations were no longer managed by the Order's brethren.

In 1242 the cardinal legate William of Modena decided that all hospitals in Prussia should be under the direction of the Teutonic Order.[43] The hospital in Thorn was under the Order's control from 1257, but the hospital in Elbing was managed by *provisores*, perhaps a lay confraternity.[44] When the Grand Master transferred his headquarters from Venice to Marienburg in 1309, the supreme hospitaller took up residence in Elbing and the hospital there accordingly became the Order's principal hospital. Another hospital, in Preußisch-Holland ('Prussian Holland'), in the territory of the commandery of Elbing, was managed by a lay *provisor* under the supreme hospitaller's superintendence. Other hospitals in Prussia were associated with houses of the Order and included in the administration of the preceptories. In other cases, such as Danzig and Königsberg, the Grand Master held the superintendence.[45] Besides the Order, bishops and cities supported and managed hospitals.[46] In the fourteenth and fifteenth centuries new hospitals were erected under the superintendence of the Order. During this time the Order's hospitals in Prussia continued to develop along the same lines they had followed earlier in the West. In the fifteenth century the people of Prussian cities were complaining about the Order's hospitals just as people living in the German Empire had done, and were making the same criticism that only the rich were admitted as beneficiaries.[47]

The achievements of Byzantine and Arab medicine were not introduced into Germany and Prussia. For instance, physicians did not serve in the hospitals, either in the bailiwicks or in Prussia, not even in the main hospitals. However, physicians would examine the Grand Masters and important officials, and from the mid-fourteenth century there were physicians attached to the Master's court.[48] Sometimes they were sent by the Masters to the preceptories to examine sick brethren, but they were not sent into the ordinary hospitals, which

---

[41] Weiß, pp. 249, 364.

[42] Ibid., pp. 223, 331; K. Heck and A. Herrmann, *Der Deutsche Orden und Mergentheim* (Mergentheim, 1986), p. 35.

[43] *Preuß. UB*, 1.1, ed. R. Philippi (Königsberg, 1882), no. 138 (pp. 102–3).

[44] Probst, pp. 43–5.

[45] Ibid., pp. 48–50.

[46] Ibid., pp. 86, 89.

[47] Ibid., pp. 90–2.

[48] Ibid., pp. 160–75.

generally continued to be the homes of wealthy beneficiaries as in the bailiwicks and did not develop into hospitals in a modern sense. The Hospitallers in Rhodes were more progressive than the Teutonic Order in the bailiwicks or in Prussia.

In Livonia the Order of the Swordbrothers was founded as a military order; it did not found or support hospitals. After losing the battle at the Saule in 1236, it was incorporated into the Teutonic Order in 1237. The Teutonic Order followed in the Swordbrothers' footsteps and did not found or support hospitals in Livonia. In contrast to the Prussian branch under the *Landmeister*, and after 1309 under the Grand Master, the Livonian branch had no hospitals throughout its history until its end in 1562.[49]

All preceptories had their own infirmaries for their brothers, which were separated from the hospitals. According to the statutes, brethren who suffered from particular illnesses such as fever, dysentry, diarrhoea or festering wounds had to enter the infirmary.[50] The ruins at the base of the castle of Montfort were formerly believed to be the infirmary of this convent; but in fact the building seems to have been a mill and later on a guest house for important visitors,[51] although this is not quite certain. In Montfort and Acre the grand commander (*Großkomtur*), not the supreme hospitaller, governed the infirmary. We do not know much about separate buildings for sick brethren in the preceptories of the German bailiwicks. It seems that the infirmaries were integrated into the preceptory building complex. For most of the thirteenth century there were no infirmaries in the combat area of the Baltic region, although surely the Order cared for its wounded and sick brethren. Those who were no longer capable of bearing arms were sent back to the bailiwicks to end their lives in a preceptory.[52] It was probably after the last rebellion of the Prussians at the end of the thirteenth century that the Order started to build infirmaries in Prussia. In the fourteenth century there was no preceptory without an infirmary, which was usually situated in the castle's inner courtyard and reserved for knight, sergeant and priest brothers.[53] Sometimes there were infirmaries for lay servants in the outer courtyards of the castles.[54]

---

[49] M. Hellmann, 'Der Deutsche Orden und die Stadt Riga', in *Das Verhältnis des Deutschen Ordens zu den Städten in Livland, Preussen und in Deutschen Reich*, QuStDO, 44, p. 10; see also F. Benninghoven, *Der Orden der Schwertbrüder. Fratres Milicie Christi de Livonia*, Ostmitteleuropa in Vergangenheit und Gegenwart, 9 (Cologne and Graz, 1965), pp. 54–62.

[50] *SDO*, p. 70; Probst, p. 105.

[51] W. Hubatsch, 'Montfort und die Bildung des Deutschordensstaates im Heiligen Lande', *Nachrichten der Akademie der Wissenschaften in Göttingen*, Phil.-hist. Klasse 1966, 5 (1966), 186–99 and Probst, p. 109 speak of an infirmary; for a different opinion see R.D. Pringle, 'A Thirteenth-Century Hall at Montfort Castle in Western Galilee', *The Antiquaries Journal*, 66 (1986), 68–75.

[52] Probst, p. 111.

[53] Ibid.

[54] Ibid., pp. 118–30.

Infirmaries were built in Livonian preceptories too, but we know little about them. For instance, a *Spittler* was caring for the sick and old brethren in Fellin during the fifteenth century.[55] There must have been such infirmaries in other castles of the Livonian branch of the Order.

To sum up, from the thirteenth century onwards the Order took over hospitals for their goods and income, which it wanted to use to support its wars in the Latin East, Prussia and Livonia. Some hospitals remained, as in Marburg or Nuremberg, but they changed their character and became homes for rich beneficiaries, who could buy a bed or room with food and clothing included. These hospitals were no longer houses for the sick and poor. Exceptions such as the foundation in Donauwörth were rare. From the fourteenth century the city councils tried to obtain influence over these hospitals – with success. They supported their own hospitals, which replaced those of the Order; caring for the sick and poor had become a municipal task in the cities.

We can observe the same trend in Prussia with a certain time lag. The supreme hospitaller was not a minister of public health. He only had to manage the main hospital in Elbing, assisted by an under-hospitaller. In Livonia the Order supported no hospitals. In both countries, from the end of the thirteenth century the Order was developing infirmaries for sick and old brethren. In the subsequent period nearly every preceptory had its own infirmary situated in the inner courtyard of the castle; but only the Grand Master had paid physicians living in the Order's headquarters. These physicians could be sent to officials or brethren in Prussia, but they did not practise in public hospitals. The Teutonic Order never reached the standards of medical care the Hospitallers employed in Jerusalem or in Rhodes.[56]

---

[55] L. Fenske and K. Militzer, *Ritterbrüder im livländischen Zweig des Deutschen Ordens*, Quellen und Studien zur baltischen Geschichte, 12 (Cologne, Weimar and Vienna, 1993), p. 757.

[56] See B.Z. Kedar's article in this volume, 'A Twelfth-Century Description of the Jerusalem Hospital' (Chapter 1).

6

Welfare and Warfare in the
Teutonic Order: a Survey

Bernhard Demel, OT

In the earliest statutes of the Teutonic Order, which date to about 1244, we read the following:

> *Quia vero ordo iste prius hospitalia quam miliciam habuit, sicut ex nomine eius liquidius edocetur, statuimus, quod in principali domo, vel ubi magister decreverit cum consilio capituli, semper hospitale teneatur. In aliis vero locis, si hospitale iam ante factum cum loco et redditibus fuerit oblatum, poterit provincialis terre de prudenciorum fratrum consilio illud recipere, si voluerit. In domibus autem aliis ordinis, que sine hospitali sunt, non fiat hospitale absque magistri ordinis ordinacione speciali cum consilio fratrum prudenciorum.*[1]

(But, because this order was a hospital before it became a military order, so that it may better live up to its name we resolve that there should always be a hospital in the principal house or wherever the master decrees with the advice of the chapter. In other places, if a hospital has already been built and is offered with the place and its revenues, the provincial commander may receive it if he wishes, after taking advice from the more prudent brothers. In other houses of the Order, however, where there is no hospital, no hospital should be established without the special ordinance of the Master, with the advice of the more prudent brothers.)

These regulations summarize the obligations of the Teutonic Order, and allude to its origins during the Third Crusade when the first members – priests and laymen vowed to poverty, chastity and obedience – had to help the

---

[1] *SDO* (repr. Hildesheim and New York, 1975), p. 31. For the date, see U. Arnold, 'Die Statuten des Deutschen Ordens. Neue amerikanische Forschungsergebnisse', *Mitteilungen des Instituts für Österreichische Geschichtsforschung*, 83 (1975), 145. For the history of the Order's rules and statutes, I. Sterns, 'The Statutes of the Teutonic Knights. A Study of the Religious Chivalry', PhD thesis (University of Pennsylvania, 1969); E. Volgger, *Die Regeln des Deutschen Ordens in Geschichte und Gegenwart* (Lana, 1985). For the current rules and statutes see *Das Ordensbuch. Die Regeln und Statuten des Deutschen Ordens* (Vienna, 1996).

From *The Military Orders. Volume 2. Welfare and Warfare*. ed. Helen Nicholson. Copyright © 1998 by Helen Nicholson. Published by Ashgate Publishing Ltd, Gower House, Croft Road, Aldershot, Hampshire, GU11 3HR, Great Britain.

sick and wounded during the siege of Acre (1189–91).[2] Throughout the Order's
history – as the so-called *Deutsche Hospitalbruderschaft*, the fraternity of the
Hospital of the Germans (1190–98/9),[3] as a military order (1199–1929), and as
a religious order of the Roman Catholic Church (1929 to the present)[4] – the
Teutonic Order has observed its obligation to care for the sick and the dying.[5]
It soon received houses with hospitals in the Holy Land and the adjoining
territories, and also in the towns of the Empire and along the routes through
the Alps.[6] As examples I would mention the principal house at Acre held from
1190 or 1191;[7] the oldest house in the Empire with a hospital for the poor at
Halle in 1200;[8] the hospital with a church at Bozen, South Tyrol, granted in

---

[2] *SDO*, pp. 159–60; H.E. Mayer, *Geschichte der Kreuzzüge*, 8th edn (Stuttgart, Berlin and Cologne,
1995), pp. 125–38; E. Eickhoff, *Friedrich Barbarossa im Orient. Kreuzzug und Tod Friedrich I.*
(Tübingen, 1977), pp. 1–179, esp. pp. 167–9; R. Hiestand, '*Precipua tocius christianismi columpna.*
Barbarossa und der Kreuzzug', in *Friedrich Barbarossa. Handlungsspielräume und Wirkungsweisen des
staufischen Kaisers*, ed. A. Haverkamp (Sigmaringen, 1992), pp. 51–108.

[3] U. Arnold, 'Entstehung und Frühzeit des Deutschen Ordens. Zu Gründung und innerer
Struktur des Deutschen Hospitals von Akkon und des Ritterordens in der ersten Hälfte des 13.
Jahrhunderts', in *Die geistlichen Ritterorden Europas*, ed. J. Fleckenstein and M. Hellmann, Vorträge
und Forschungen, 26 (Sigmaringen, 1980), pp. 81–107.

[4] For the history of the Teutonic Order, *Tabulae Ordinis Theutonici ex regii tabularii Berolinensis
codici potissimum*, ed. E. Strehlke (Berlin, 1869, repr. Toronto and Jerusalem, 1975); M. Tumler
and U. Arnold, *Der Deutsche Orden. Von seinem Ursprung bis zur Gegenwart*, 5th edn (Bad Münstereifel,
1992); I. Sterns, 'The Teutonic Knights in the Crusader States', in *Crusades*, 5, pp. 315–78; H.
Nicholson, *Templars, Hospitallers and Teutonic Knights. Images of the Military Orders, 1128–1291*
(London and New York, 1993); U. Arnold, '800 Jahre Deutscher Orden', *Westpreussen Jahrbuch*, 40
(1990), 5–20; *idem*, 'Eight Hundred Years of the Teutonic Order', in *MO*, 1, pp. 223–35; also the
studies by J.M. Powell (pp. 236–44), K. Guth (pp. 245–52), J. Sarnowsky (pp. 253–62), S. Ekdahl
(pp. 263–9), K. Militzer (pp. 270–7), and B. Demel (pp. 278–9) in the same volume; B. Demel,
'Hospitalität und Rittertum im Deutschen Orden', in *Der Deutsche Orden und die Ballei Elsaß-
Burgund. Die Freiburger Vorträge zur 800-Jahr-Feier des Deutschen Ordens*, ed. H. Brommer
(Bühl/Baden, 1996), pp. 33–56; *idem*, 'Der Deutsche Orden und die Krone Frankreichs in den
Jahren 1648–1789', ibid., pp. 97–188 (and the other studies in this volume); J. Sarnowsky, *Die
Wirtschaftsführung des Deutschen Ordens in Preußen (1382–1454)* (Cologne, Weimar and Vienna,
1993). For the Order's history from the beginning to the present, see the catalogues: *800 Jahre
Deutscher Orden*, ed. G. Bott and U. Arnold (Gütersloh and Munich, 1990); *Kreuz und Schwert. Der
Deutsche Orden in Südwestdeutschland, in der Schweiz und im Elsaß*, ed. U. Arnold, B. Leipold and A.
Soffner (Mainau, 1991); *Ritter und Priester. Acht Jahrhunderte Deutscher Orden in Nordwesteuropa*, ed.
U. Arnold, *et al.* (Alden-Biesen, 1992); *Die Leechkirche. Hügelgrab-Rundbau-Ordenshaus*, ed. G.M.
Dienes, F. Leitgeb and H. Leitgeb (Graz, 1993). For recent research in this connection see the
published volumes of the QuStDO (Bonn, [Bad] Godesberg, Marburg, Bozen and Lana, 1966–).

[5] Demel, 'Hospitalität'.

[6] S. Reicke, *Das deutsche Spital und sein Recht im Mittelalter*, Kirchenrechtliche Abhandlungen,
111–114 (Stuttgart, 1932, repr. Amsterdam, 1970), 1, pp. 112–49.

[7] *SDO*, pp. 159–60.

[8] R. Wolf, *Das Deutsch-Ordenshaus St Kunigunde bei Halle an der Saale*, Forschungen zur thüringisch-
sächsischen Geschichte, 7 (Halle an der Saale, 1915), pp. 6–10; B. Sommerlad, *Der Deutsche Orden
in Thüringen* (Halle an der Saale, 1931), p. 5; K. Militzer, *Die Entstehung der Deutschordensballeien im
Deutschen Reich*, QuStDO, 16, 2nd edn (Marburg, 1981), p. 34.

1202;[9] and, on the route from Venice to Vienna, the house with the Hospital of St Mary Magdalen at Friesach in Carinthia which dates from 1203 and was the oldest established house in the province or *Ballei* (bailiwick) of Austria.[10] The hospital at Nuremberg began its existence in 1209 and lasted throughout the Middle Ages and then from the time of the Reformation to the Treaty of Pressburg (1805), which saw the end of the Order as a member of the Empire and the expulsion of the Order from Germany by Napoleon (1809).[11] For around two centuries in the Middle Ages the hospital at Nuremberg was the greatest hospital anywhere in the Empire. Dieter Weiss supposes that it owed its origins to the initiative of the Order itself and not to other institutions or the inhabitants of Nuremberg. Alongside the *Komtur* or commander, the principal ecclesiastical official in the house at Nuremberg, we also hear of an administrator of the hospital, which received many donations in the city of Nuremberg and the surrounding district.[12] The hospital was dedicated to St Elizabeth of Marburg, the second patron saint of the Order after the Virgin Mary. From 1234 the Order also held the hospital at Marburg which St Elizabeth had founded and where she had lived until her death in 1231. At Marburg the Order built one of the most famous gothic churches of the Middle Ages, which became a centre of pilgrimage, especially in the fourteenth century.[13]

In his thesis Christian Tenner has made a special study of the history of the hospitals in the *Ballei Franken*, the bailiwick of Franconia, and has discussed

---

[9] U. Arnold, 'Die Ballei und das Land. Mittelalter', in *Der Deutsche Orden in Tirol. Die Ballei an der Etsch und im Gebirge*, ed. H. Noflatscher, QuStDO, 43 (Bozen and Marburg, 1991), pp. 125–70 (at p. 130).

[10] W. Wadl, 'Friesachs historische Entwicklung. Ein Überblick', in *Die profanen Bau- und Kunstdenkmäler der Stadt Friesach*, ed. B. Kienzl, *et al.* (Vienna, 1991), pp. 1–71, esp. pp. 29–30; B. Demel, 'Zur Geschichte der Johanniter und des Deutschen Ordens in Kärnten', in *Symposium zur Geschichte von Millstadt und Kärnten*, ed. F. Nikolasch, (1992), pp. 76–99, esp. pp. 82–4.

[11] C. Tenner, 'Die Ritterordensspitäler im süddeutschen Raum (Ballei Franken). Ein Beitrag zum frühesten Gesundheitswesen', Diss. (Munich, 1969), pp. 52–8, 105–26, 130–8 and *passim*; D.J. Weiss, *Die Geschichte der Deutschordens-Ballei Franken im Mittelalter* (Neustadt an der Aisch, 1991), pp. 31, 232–7. For Napoleon, see F. Täubl, *Der Deutsche Orden im Zeitalter Napoleons*, QuStDO, 4 (Bonn, 1966), pp. 101–76.

[12] Weiss, pp. 34–6.

[13] *Elisabeth, der Deutsche Orden und ihre Kirche. Festschrift zur 700jährigen Wiederkehr der Weihe der Elisabethkirche Marburg 1983*, ed. U. Arnold and H. Liebing, QuStDO, 18 (Marburg, 1983); B. Demel, 'Die Heilige Elisabeth von Thüringen – Patronin des Deutschen Ordens', *Archiv für Kirchengeschichte von Böhmen-Mähren-Schlesien*, 12 (1993), 74–96; M. Werner, '*Mater Hassiae – Flos Ungariae – Gloria Teutoniae*. Politik und Heiligenverehrung im Nachleben der hl. Elisabeth von Thüringen', in *Politik und Heiligenverehrung im Hochmittelalter*, ed. J. Petersohn (Sigmaringen, 1994), pp. 449–540. For the church and pilgrimage, see J. Michler, *Die Elisabethkirche zu Marburg in ihrer ursprünglichen Farbigkeit*, QuStDO, 19 (Marburg, 1984); K.E. Demandt, 'Verfremdung und Wiederkehr der Heiligen Elisabeth', *Hessisches Jahrbuch für Landesgeschichte*, 22 (1972), 112–61, esp. 134–9.

the hospitals at Speyer, Ellingen, Öttingen, Neubrunn-Prozelten, Donauwörth, Mergentheim and Frankfurt-Sachsenhausen.[14] In addition to the bailiwick of Franconia, which was under the rule of the *Deutschmeister* or German Master, answerable only to the Grand Master as the head of the whole Order,[15] the province of Bohemia also possessed hospitals.[16] To mention just one example, the hospital at Neuhaus, in the southern part of the kingdom of Bohemia, had twelve residents and was possibly founded in 1255.[17]

After the transfer of the Grand Master's residence from Venice to the castle of Marienburg in September 1309, the house of Elbing with its commander (one of the grand commanders and known as the *Oberster Spittler*, supreme hospitaller) became the principal hospital in Prussia. Later on there was a *Spittler* (hospitaller) at the commandery of Christburg, another settlement in the Order's Prussian territories. After the end of the Thirteen Years' War (1454–66), the *Oberster Spittler* became the commander in the newly built house of 'Prussian Holland' and from 1467 in the chief commandery of Brandenburg. Subsequently he had the house in Osterode to support him in his duties, although this arrangement ended in 1511. Hospitals existed in 'Prussian Holland' and Osterode until the demise of the Order in eastern Prussia in 1525.[18] As we know from Klaus Neitmann's recent investigations, the Grand Master visited the hospitals in all the provinces.[19] There is hardly any information about the hospitals in the Livonian sector of the Order's lands. We know only of hospitals at Riga and Reval; whether any existed in the other Livonian houses remains a matter for future research.[20]

---

[14] Tenner, pp. 45–52, 58–60. For Frankfurt-Sachsenhausen, see B. Demel, 'Die Sachsenhäuser Deutschordens-Kommende von den Anfängen bis zum Verkauf an die Katholische Gemeinde Frankfurt am Main im Jahre 1881 – Versuch einer Gesamtübersicht', *Archiv für mittelrheinische Kirchengeschichte*, 23 (1971), 37–72; H. Mann, 'Die Reichsstadt Frankfurt und die Deutschordenskommende Sachsenhausen', ibid., 47 (1995), 11–43.

[15] Deutschordens-Zentralarchiv (hereafter DOZA), Vienna, MS 411, pp. 90–101; B. Demel, 'Der Deutsche Orden und seine Besitzungen im südwestdeutschen Raum vom 13. bis 19. Jahrhundert', *Zeitschrift für Württembergische Landesgeschichte*, 31 (1972), 16–73.

[16] J. Hemmerle, *Die Deutschordens-Ballei Böhmen in ihren Rechnungsbüchern 1382–1411*, QuStDO, 22 (Bad Godesberg, 1967), pp. 11–22; B. Demel, 'Der Deutsche Orden in Mähren und Schlesien', *Jahrbuch der Schlesischen Friedrich-Wilhelms-Universität zu Breslau*, 32 (1991), 29–68. There were hospitals in the Order's Silesian territory at Freudenthal and Braunseifen: DOZA Mei[stertum] 139/1–10, 140/1–14, 141/1–5.

[17] Hemmerle, p. 17; F. Kavka, *Jindrichuv Hradec 1293/1993* (Budejovice, 1992), p. 25.

[18] C. Probst, *Der Deutsche Orden und sein Medizinalwesen in Preußen: Hospital, Firmarie und Arzt bis 1525*, QuStDo, 29 (Bad Godesberg, 1969), pp. 63–92. For the background for this period, M. Burleigh, *Prussian Society and the German Order. An Aristocratic Corporation in Crisis c. 1401–1466* (Cambridge, 1984). For hospitals in Prussia, J. Rink, *Die christliche Liebestätigkeit im Ordensland Preussen bis 1525* (Freiburg i. B., 1911).

[19] K. Neitmann, *Der Hochmeister des Deutschen Ordens in Preußen – ein Residenzherrscher unterwegs. Untersuchungen zu den Hochmeisteritineraren im 14. und 15. Jahrhundert* (Cologne and Vienna, 1990), pp. 41–54.

[20] D. Jetter, *Das europäische Hospital. Von der Spätantike bis 1800* (Cologne, 1986), p. 46.

The sixteenth century saw the loss of the rest of Prussia (1525) and then of the Livonian territories (1561/2).[21] As a consequence of the Reformation in the Empire, knights and priests left the Order. They served the Protestant princes or civic leaders in Hesse, Thuringia, Westphalia and Saxony as Lutherans, and then in the third quarter of the seventeenth century as Calvinist members of the Teutonic Order.[22] What remained of the Order in the Holy Roman Empire became '*des adels getreuer Aufenthalt*', a residence for the aristocracy, or, more exactly, '*ain Spital undd sonnderlich Zuflucht unnd uffenthalt des Adels teutscher nacion*', a hospice and special refuge and residence of the German nobility, where the knights serving in the Order were maintained in an aristocratic lifestyle.[23] During the wars of the sixteenth[24] and seventeenth centuries,[25] the Order suffered major financial problems and loss of its properties, although its continued existence within the Empire after the Peasants' War was assured in 1527–30, when the holder of the amalgamated posts of Grand Master and German Master was incorporated into the imperial power structure, where he ranked after the archbishops but ahead of the bishops and abbots.[26]

In readiness for new problems the Order reformed its statutes in 1606.[27] Between the time of the Reformation and the Treaty of Utrecht-Baden of 1714 there were wars against the Turks to the east and south of the Empire,[28] and

---

[21] *Ritterbrüder im livländischen Zweig des Deutschen Ordens*, ed. L. Fenske and K. Militzer (Cologne, Weimar and Vienna, 1993), pp. 11–70, esp. pp. 11, 16, 46.

[22] See the so-called Ri[tterakten] in DOZA. For Hesse, see B. Demel, 'Von der katholischen zur trikonfessionellen Ordensprovinz. Entwicklungslinien in der Personalstruktur der hessischen Deutschordensballei in den Jahren 1526–1680/81', in *Elisabeth, der Deutsche Orden*, ed. Arnold and Liebing, pp. 186–281. For Westphalia, see ibid., p. 191. My study on Saxony and Thuringia is forthcoming.

[23] See, for example, the imperial diploma of 17 July 1530 in DOZA; H. Boockmann, *Der Deutsche Orden. Zwölf Kapitel aus seiner Geschichte*, 4th edn (Munich, 1994), pp. 194–6; A. Herrmann, *Der Deutsche Orden unter Walther von Cronberg (1525–1543). Zur Politik und Struktur des 'Teutschen Adels Spitale' im Reformationszeitalter*, QuStDO, 35 (Bonn and Godesberg, 1974), pp. 220–43; K. Oldenhage, *Kurfürst Erzherzog Maximilian Franz als Hoch- und Deutschmeister (1780–1801)*, QuStDO, 34 (Bad Godesberg, 1969), pp. 45–93; V. Press, '"Des deutschen Adels Spital". Der Deutsche Orden zwischen Kaiser und Reich', in *Der Deutsche Orden in Tirol*, ed. Noflatscher, pp. 1–42.

[24] For detailed figures, see the Haus-, Hof- und Staatsarchiv, Vienna, Mainzer Erzkanzler Archiv, Reichstags Akten, Faszikel (hereafter HHStA, MEA, RTA, Fasz.) 77, A, fols 194r–197r. See also DOZA, Merg[entheim], 284/1, fols 140r–150v.

[25] For the losses before 1634, Staatsarchiv Ludwigsburg, Germany, Bestand 298, Büschel 198 (hereafter StAL, Bs, Bü).

[26] Demel, 'Die Deutsche Orden und die Krone Frankreichs', pp. 103–13.

[27] See DOZA, MS 790. Also *Sammlung der neuesten Regeln, Statuten und Verwaltungsvorschriften des deutschen Ritterordens 1606–1839* (Vienna, 1840), pp. 70–155.

[28] W. Schulze, *Reich und Türkengefahr im späten 16. Jahrhundert. Studien zu den politischen und gesellschaftlichen Auswirkungen einer äußeren Bedrohung* (Munich, 1978); H. Noflatscher, *Glaube, Reich und Dynastie. Maximilian der Deutschmeister (1558–1618)*, QuStDO, 11 (Marburg, 1987), pp. 173–91; J.P. Niederkorn, *Die europäischen Mächte und der 'Lange Türkenkrieg' Kaiser Rudolfs II. (1593–1606)* (Vienna, 1993); M. Braubach, *Prinz Eugen von Savoyen*, 5 vols (Vienna, 1963–5); E. Zöllner, *Geschichte Österreichs*, 8th edn (Vienna and Munich, 1990), pp. 187–327.

– particularly during the reign of Louis XIV – against the kingdom of France to the west.[29] During these troubled centuries we cannot detect any significant hospital activity in the remaining commanderies. Large and small hospitals existed in the new residence of the Grand Master at Mergentheim (1525–1809), notably the *Carolinum* for sick and wounded soldiers;[30] and there was a hospital in the territory of the commandery at Frankfurt-Sachsenhausen.[31] Grand Master Franz-Ludwig of Pfalz-Neuburg (1694–1732) made provision for hospital care after the long wars in the Empire, building a new hospital at Mergentheim on the River Tauber, which he mentioned in a letter dated 1724 to the president of the Order's central court at Mergentheim.[32] After 1705 the old hospital was reconstructed in the residence of the important Franconian commander (the *Landkomtur*) at Ellingen, and it received new statutes approved by the Grand Master in 1736.[33]

In 1809 Napoleon dissolved the Teutonic Order in the German territories; but it survived in the Austrian Empire where it was reorganized between 1834 and 1840.[34] It then had just two provinces: 'Austria' and 'Etsch' (abolished in 1810 but revived at the beginning of 1836) and the so-called 'Masterdom' in Silesia and Moravia.[35]

The institution of the nuns of the Teutonic Order was re-established in Tyrol with a mother house at Lanegg, and in Silesia with the houses in Freudenthal and Troppau founded between 1837 and 1841. Their vocation was the education of girls and the care of patients in the municipal hospitals and their own infirmaries.[36]

As for the remaining knights, Archduke and Grand Master Wilhelm (1863–94) re-established new offices in the imperial army. The money came from the knights themselves and from the members of the newly founded orga-

---

[29] Demel, 'Der Deutsche Orden und die Krone Frankreichs', pp. 97–188.

[30] DOZA, MS 436, fols Anhang 65r–71r. See also fols Anhang 72r–77r for the so-called 'Große und kleine Armenhaus' (also in StAL, Bs 236, Bü 215). For the other hospitals at Mergentheim see fols Anhang 10r–64r.

[31] H. Wolter, 'Die Bedeutung der geistlichen Orden für die Entwicklung der Stadt Frankfurt am Main', *Archiv für mittelrheinische Kirchengeschichte*, 26 (1974), 25–43 (at 37).

[32] DOZA, G[eneral] K[apitel] 730/7, Punkt 3 (general chapter of 1700); DOZA, H[och]m[eister] 500 (letter of 15 August 1724 from Grand Master Franz Ludwig to the governor at Mergentheim). Also DOZA, GK 737/7, Punkt 2 and 3 (grand chapter of 1736); Demel, 'Hospitalität', pp. 40–1.

[33] R. Grill, 'Die Deutschordens-Landkommende Ellingen', Diss. (Erlangen, 1957), p. 79. For the organization of this hospital in the early eighteenth century, see Tenner, pp. 176–84; also H.H. Hofmann, *Der Staat des Deutschmeisters* (Munich, 1964), pp. 288, 474. In the Ellingen hospital the old women had their own rooms, but at Nuremberg the women lived together in one room. See the letter dated 9 April 1716 to the grand commander at Ellingen: DOZA, V[aria], no. 3681.

[34] U. Gasser, *Die Priesterkonvente des Deutschen Ordens*, QuStDO, 28 (Bonn and Bad Godesberg, 1973), pp. 10–19.

[35] There are many as yet unexamined documents and papers in DOZA. See Täubl, p. 174; B. Demel, 'Der Deutsche Orden in Schlesien und Mähren in den Jahren 1742–1918' *Archiv für Kirchengeschichte von Böhmen-Mähren-Schlesien*, 14 (1997), 7–62.

[36] E. Gruber, *Deutschordensschwestern im 19. und 20. Jahrhundert. Wiederbelebung, Ausbreitung, und Tätigkeit 1837–1971*, QuStDO, 14 (Bonn and Bad Godesberg, 1971), pp. 6–167.

nizations, the *Ehrenritter* (1866) and the *Marianer* (1871), made up of nobles from the Austro-Hungarian Empire and other European states. Their donations were used for the construction of the Order's first modern hospital, used for example during the Serbo-Bulgarian War in 1885 in cooperation with the Order of Malta. We currently have some knowledge of the cooperation between the two Orders in the Austro-Hungarian Empire during service in both peace and war, but a thorough study of the development of their medical services in the nineteenth and early twentieth centuries is needed.[37]

The nuns of the Teutonic Order first served in the military hospital at their mother house at Lanegg in 1859. In 1864 a military hospital was organized by nuns in Schleswig in northern Germany during the war against Denmark. A new hospital was built at Friesach in Carinthia in 1880; this still exists and has been enlarged as the only hospital now owned by the Order. In the First World War nuns of the Order were employed as nurses helping to move the sick and wounded from high up in the Alps to the hospitals in the villages.[38]

The reorganization of the Order after the First World War with the demise of the Habsburgs was difficult, but the care by the nuns and priests for the sick, the wounded and the dying continued. All these activities were destroyed by the Nazis in Austria after September 1938 and in the Sudetenland after February 1939 when the Order was dissolved. Following the Second World War, the new government of Czechoslovakia expelled the German priests and nuns from their offices, hospitals and parishes, and they moved to Germany and Austria. In Germany a new province for the sisters and priests was developed with the traditional obligations of pastoral care and welfare for the sick.[39]

This survey cannot discuss every aspect of the subject. It must be pointed out, however, that from medieval times to the late twentieth century the Order has maintained its obligations to help the sick and the dying, to educate the young and to bring help where needed in accordance with its means and in obedience to its statutes.

During the Third Crusade the brotherhood of the Teutonic Order was founded to take care of the sick and pilgrims. Eight years later, on 19 February 1199, Pope Innocent III approved the transformation of this religious corporation into a military order of the Roman Catholic Church.[40] It continued

---

[37] G. Müller, *Die Familiaren des Deutschen Ordens*, QuStDO, 13 (Marburg, 1980), pp. 77–102; Gruber, pp. 118–20; Demel, 'Hospitalität', pp. 52–4; M. Deeleman, *Der Deutsche Ritterorden, einst und jetzt* (Vienna, 1903), pp. 84–102; D. Wehner, 'Das Feldsanitätswesen des Deutschen Ritterordens von 1871 bis zum Vorabend des Ersten Weltkrieges', thesis (Constance, 1995).

[38] Gruber, pp. 99–105, 108–18, 137–40; Wadl, pp. 29–30.

[39] A. Wieland, 'Vom Ritterorden zu den Regeln von 1929', in *Die Regeln*, ed. Volgger, pp. 231–74; B. Demel, 'Der Deutsche Orden in den Jahren 1918 bis 1989', in *Il tessuto cristiano della Mitteleuropa (1919–1989)*, ed. F. Tassin (Goricia, 1994), pp. 201–15, esp pp. 202–11.

[40] *Tabulae*, no. 297; U. Arnold, 'Vom Feldspital zum Ritterorden. Militarisierung und Territorialisierung des Deutschen Ordens (1190–*c*. 1240)', in *Balticum. Studia z dziejów polityki gospodarki i kultury XII–XVII wieku, ofiarowane Marianowi Biskupowi w siedemdziesiątą rocznicę urodzin*, ed. Z.H. Nowak (Toruń, 1992), pp. 25–36.

as a military order until 1929.[41] Insofar as its means allowed and in association
with the Templars and the Knights of St John, it was involved in the conquest
and defence of the Christians' possessions in the Holy Land until the final loss
of Acre in 1291.[42] In the meantime it also became involved in the affairs of the
Empire and the Baltic region.[43] In all its houses the Order served pilgrims
bound for Jerusalem, Rome and the shrine of St James in Spain. After the
Order's unfortunate experiences in trying to establish a new state in
Siebenbürgen, Grand Master Hermann of Salza (1209–39) made sure of the
assistance of Emperor Frederick II. This was granted in the Golden Bull of
Rimini of March 1226 with the result that it was possible for the Order to help
Piast Duke Conrad of Masovia against the pagan Prussians.[44]

In 1230–31 the Order began the conquest of Prussia. The wars, backed by
newly built castles, ended in 1283 following the second Prussian rebellion
(1260).[45] In 1236-37 the pope had agreed to the union of the Teutonic Order
with the so-called Swordbrothers (*Fratres Milicie Christi de Livonia*), and the
Order thereby gained influence in Livonia.[46] However, it did not have the
complete authority there that it had in Prussia owing to the opposition of towns
such as Riga and its archbishop, and Reval following the Order's purchase of
Estonia with the territories of Harrien and Wierland in 1346.[47]

---

[41] Tumler and Arnold, pp. 8–87; Wieland, 'Vom Ritterorden'.

[42] E. Stickel, *Der Fall von Akkon. Untersuchungen zum Abklingen des Kreuzzugsgedankens am Ende des 13. Jahrhunderts* (Bern and Frankfurt, 1975). See the studies in *Acri 1291. La fine della presenza degli ordini militari in Terra Santa e i nuovi orientamenti nel XIV secolo*, ed. F. Tommasi (Perugia, 1996).

[43] B. Schumacher, *Geschichte Ost- und West Preußens*, 7th edn (Würzburg, 1987), pp. 24–142, and notes on pp. 334–58; Boockmann, pp. 10–291.

[44] I. Matison, 'Zum politischen Aspekt der Goldenen Bulle von Rimini', in *Acht Jahrhunderte Deutscher Orden in Einzeldarstellungen*, ed. K. Wieser, QuStDO, 1 (Bad Godesberg, 1967), pp. 49–55. For the text of the bull and the diplomatic problems it presents, see E. Weise, 'Interpretation der Goldenen Bulle von Rimini (März 1226) nach dem kanonischen Recht', ibid., pp. 15–47.

[45] Schumacher, pp. 34–43; Boockmann, pp. 93–114. See also the studies in *Der Deutschordensstaat Preussen in der polnischen Geschichtsschreibung der Gegenwart*, ed. U. Arnold and M. Biskup, QuStDO, 30 (Marburg, 1982); A. Nowakowski, *Arms and Armour in the medieval Teutonic Order's State in Prussia*, Studies on the history of ancient and medieval art of warfare, 2 (Lódź, 1994). For the fortresses, U. Arnold, 'Zur Entwicklung der Deutschordensburg in Preussen', in *Die Ausgrabungsergebnisse der Deutschordensburgen Graudenz und Roggenhausen*, ed. H. Jacobi (Braubach, 1996), pp. 84–103.

[46] F. Benninghoven, *Der Orden der Schwertbrüder. Fratres Milicie Christi de Livonia*, Ostmitteleuropa in Vergangenheit und Gegenwart, 9 (Cologne and Graz, 1965), pp. 321–87.

[47] M. Hellmann, 'Die Stellung des livländischen Ordenszweiges zur Gesamtpolitik des Deutschen Ordens vom 13. bis zum 16. Jahrhundert', in *Von Akkon bis Wien. Studien zur Deutschordensgeschiche vom 13. bis zum 20. Jahrhundert*, ed. U. Arnold, QuStDO, 20 (Marburg, 1978), pp. 6–13 (at p. 12); also R. Wittram, *Baltische Geschichte. Die Ostseelande Livland, Estland, Kurland 1180–1918. Grundzüge und Durchblicke* (Munich, 1954, repr. Darmstadt, 1973), pp. 36–41.

Until the loss of Livonia in 1561/2, the Order was the greatest military power in the Baltic area.[48] After the transfer of the Grand Master's residence from Venice to the castle of Marienburg in September 1309, relations with Lithuania and other territories bordering Prussia became important. In 1398 Grand Master Conrad of Jungingen (1393–1407) regained the island of Gotland from the pirates, the so-called 'Vitalian Brothers', using a fleet owned by the Order and so secured control of trade in the Baltic for the members of the Hanse.[49] However, with the defeat at the battle of Tannenberg/Grunwald (15 July 1410),[50] the first Treaty of Thorn (1411)[51] and the founding of the Prussian Union (1440),[52] the situation began to deteriorate seriously. In the second Treaty of Thorn (October 1466) at the end of the Thirteen Years' War (1454–66), the Order lost the western part of Prussia, including the important Hanseatic cities of Elbing, Danzig and Thorn. From 1457 the Grand Master had to fix his new residence at Königsberg, where hitherto the *Ordensmarschall*, one of the grand commanders, had coordinated the *Litauenreisen* (military expeditions into Lithuania) and other military activities.[53]

---

[48] Wittram, *Baltische Geschichte*, pp. 64–73; U. Arnold, 'Livland als Glied des Deutschen Ordens in der Epoche Wolters von Plettenberg', in *Wolter von Plettenberg. Der größte Ordensmeister Livlands*, ed. N. Angermann (Lüneburg, 1985), pp. 23–45; M. Hellmann, 'Wolter von Plettenberg. Bedingungen und Beweggründe seines Handelns', ibid., pp. 47–69, esp. pp. 65–6.

[49] B. Eimer, *Gotland unter dem Deutschen Orden und die Komturei Schweden zu Arsta* (Innsbruck, 1966), pp. 119–72. For the Teutonic Order as a member of the Hanse, K. von Schlözer, *Die Hansa und der Deutsche Ritter-Orden in den Ostseeländern* (Stuttgart, 1851–3, repr. Wiesbaden, 1966); T.H. Lloyd, *England and the German Hanse, 1157–1611: A study of their trade and commercial diplomacy* (Cambridge, 1991), pp. 51–72, 112–44, 174–93, 287, 371; S. Jenks, *England. Die Hanse und Preußen Handel und Diplomatie 1377–1474* (Cologne and Vienna, 1992); F. Benninghoven, 'Die Gotland-feldzüge des Deutschen Ordens 1398–1408', *Zeitschrift für Ostforschung*, 13 (1964), 421–77; *idem*, 'Die Vitalienbrüder als Forschungsproblem' in *Kultur und Politik im Ostseeraum und im Norden, 1350–1450*, ed. S Ekdahl, Acta Visbyensia, 4 (Visby, 1973), pp. 41–52.

[50] H. Baranowski and I. Czarcinski (with additions by M. Biskup), *Bibliografia bitwy pod Grunwaldem i jej Tradycji* (Toruń, 1990); S. Ekdahl, *Die Schlacht bei Tannenberg 1410. Quellenkritis-che Untersuchungen*, 1 (Berlin, 1982); *idem*, *Das Soldbuch des Deutschen Ordens 1410/11*, 1 (Cologne and Vienna, 1988).

[51] Schumacher, p. 127; Z.H. Nowak, 'Waffenstillstände und Friedensverträge zwischen Polen und dem Deutschen Orden', in *Träger und Instrumentarien des Friedens im hohen und späten Mittelalter*, ed. J. Fried, Vorträge und Forschungen, 43 (Sigmaringen, 1996), pp. 391–403, esp. p. 395.

[52] E. Weise, *Das Widerstandsrecht im Ordensland Preußen und das mittelalterliche Europa* (Göttingen, 1955); K.E. Murawski, *Zwischen Tannenberg und Thorn. Die Geschichte des Deutschen Ordens unter dem Hochmeister Konrad von Erlichshausen 1441–1449* (Göttingen, 1953), pp. 95–104; Boockmann, pp. 205–12; K. Neitmann, 'Die Außenpolitik des Deutschen Ordens zwischen preußischen Ständen und Polen-Litauen (1411–1454)', in H-J. Schuch, *Westpreußen Jahrbuch*, 42 (Münster, 1991), pp. 49–64.

[53] Schumacher, p. 137; Boockmann, pp. 151–69, 207–10; L. Dralle, *Der Staat des Deutschen Ordens in Preussen nach dem II. Thorner Frieden. Untersuchungen zur ökonomischen und ständepolitis-chen Geschichte Altpreußens zwischen 1466 und 1497* (Wiesbaden, 1975), pp. 9–13; Nowak, pp. 397, 402–3. For this period of the Order's history, see also Burleigh, *Prussian Society*.

When the last Prussian Grand Master, Albert of Brandenburg-Ansbach, adopted the Lutheran faith in 1525, Lutheranism was introduced into Prussia and the Order, which was at the time involved in wars against the Poles, lost control there.[54] Only in the Holy Roman Empire and in Italy did the Order continue. The *Deutschmeister* Walther of Cronberg (1526/27–43) was appointed administrator of the vacant Grand Master's office by the Emperor Charles V, and at the Imperial Diet of Augsburg in 1530 Walther was installed as the new head of the Order. From this time the offices of Grand and German Master (*Hoch- und Deutschmeister*) were combined. The Order suffered grievously during the widespread warfare of this period (the war against the Poles, the Peasants' War and the Schmalkaldian War of 1546–7), especially at its remaining houses at the centre of the Empire on the Rivers Tauber and Neckar.[55] The Order lost its houses in Bohemia, Moravia, Silesia,[56] Spain and elsewhere.[57] It was therefore necessary to consolidate and reform its medieval structure, and this was done in the general chapter of 1606 at the new residence at Mergentheim.[58] The Order then had to suffer the depredations of the Thirty Years' War (1618–48)[59] and could only raise the money to pay the *Schwedische Satisfaktionsgelder*, which supported the foreign troops in the Empire, by resorting to credit.[60]

The Order continued to play some role in the military affairs of the Empire. From 1593 the archduke and Grand Master, the Habsburg Maximilian I (1585/90–1618), directed the emperor's troops as chief commander in Hungary; in the two years following, the grand chapter of the Order approved 150 horse and 100 foot for these campaigns.[61] Later the Teutonic knight Johann Caspar

---

[54] W. Hubatsch, *Albrecht von Brandenburg-Ansbach. Deutschordens-Hochmeister und Herzog in Preußen 1490–1568*, 2nd edn (Cologne, 1965), pp. 139–83; U. Arnold, 'Luther und die Reformation im Preußenland', in *Martin Luther und die Reformation in Ostdeutschland und Südosteuropa*, ed. U. Huter and H-G. Parplies (Sigmaringen, 1991), pp. 27–44.

[55] Hubatsch, pp. 74–137; Herrmann, pp. 23–97; B. Demel, 'Mergentheim-Residenz des Deutschen Ordens (1525–1809)', *Zeitschrift für Württembergische Landesgeschichte*, 34/5 (1975/6), 185–8. For the position of the *Hoch-* und *Deutschmeister*, Demel, 'Der Deutsche Orden und die Krone Frankreichs', pp. 97–109.

[56] Demel, 'Mähren und Schlesien', pp. 42–4.

[57] DOZA, Wel[schland], boxes 124/1–154 (containing many hitherto-unknown documents and papers). For these sources, see my forthcoming study.

[58] Noflatscher, *Glaube, Reich und Dynastie*, pp. 245–87.

[59] DOZA, Liga-Akten 62/3 (1646–49), 62/1 (1649–50).

[60] For the decision of Grand Master Leopold Wilhelm of Austria (1641–62) regarding the payment of this money on 30 November 1648, see StAL, Bs 298, Bü 199. For the background, A. Oschmann, *Der Nürnberger Exekutionstag 1649–1650. Das Ende des Dreißigjährigen Krieges in Deutschland* (Münster/Westphalia, 1991), pp. 41–6, 354–61.

[61] For the achievements of Grand Master Maximilian and his successors from 1593 to 1725 and the Teutonic knights, DOZA, Wel 153/1, no. 82/n9; Noflatscher, *Glaube, Reich und Dynastie*, pp. 175–91; Niederkorn, pp. 11, 13 f., 76, 345, 401, 421, 453 f., 459 f., 462, 470, 471–5, 479 f., 485–91, 493 f.

of Stadion, from the province of Alsace-Burgundy, joined the troops around Vienna at the beginning of the Thirty Years' War, and then served Emperor Ferdinand II as *Hofkriegsratspräsident* (minister of war) from 1619 until 1624.[62] The commander of Austria, (*Landkomtur*) Guidobald of Starhemberg (1657–1737), joined in the battle against the Turks at Zenta (11 September 1697)[63] and his successor, Johann Joseph Philipp *Reichsgraf* of Harrach zu Rohrau, played a major part in the battle of Belgrade (16 August 1717) under Prince Eugene of Savoy.[64] For many years the wars against the Turks, which threatened the Order's possessions in Austria and Styria, provided the opportunity for Teutonic knights of other provinces of the Order to serve in the imperial army and, after 1695/96, in the famous regiment of the *Hoch- und Deutschmeister*.[65] Teutonic knights also fought against the Turks in Crete in 1668,[66] and they served and fought with the imperial forces to defend the Empire on various fronts.[67] The Order's statutes and the subsequent grand chapters laid down that in times of peace the novice knights could serve their three probationary periods on Malta on the so-called 'Caravans'.[68] At the siege of Vienna in 1683 Coadjutor Ludwig Anton of Pfalz-Neuburg (1679–84) was appointed *Obrist Veldt Wachtmeister* (major general) by his brother-in-law, Emperor Leopold I. Before his early death this Grand Master fought against the Turks and, from 1689, in the Rhineland against the troops of Louis XIV. As the elected coadjutor of Mainz (after 1691), he was the commander of the town's own troops, and from 1692/3 he assumed military direction of the whole electorate of Mainz.[69] During the Wars of Spanish and Polish Succession

---

[62] O. Regele, *Der österreichische Hofkriegsrat 1556–1848* (Vienna, 1949), p. 74.

[63] B. Demel, 'Die Beziehungen der Starhemberger zum Deutschen Orden', in *1933–1993. Festschrift 60 Jahre Katholische Österreichische Landsmannschaft Starhemberg* (Vienna, 1993), pp. 33–56, esp. pp. 37, 52–3.

[64] Braubach, 3, pp. 354–7. Harrach was the leading general on the left wing at the battle of Belgrade. See P. Stenitzer, 'Die Deutschordensprovinz Österreich unter der Führung des Komturs und Balleioberen Johann Joseph Philipp Graf Hararch (1678–1764)', Diss. (Vienna, 1992); Regele, p. 76 (for Harrach as *Hofkriegsratspräsident*).

[65] B. Demel, 'Der Deutsche Orden und das Regiment Hoch- und Deutschmeister von 1695–1918 – Überblick und neue Erkenntnisse', in *300 Jahre Regiment Hoch- und Deutschmeister 1696–1996* (Vienna, 1996), pp. 2–28. After 23 February 1595 (DOZA, V 1062) all knights killed by the Turks were considered to be *in nomine Jesu entschlaffen*.

[66] DOZA, Exercitium Militare, 116/1. These documents were not used by W. Kohlhaas, *Candia 1645–1669. Die Tragödie einer abendländischen Verteidigung mit dem Nachspiel Athen 1687* (Osnabrück, 1978), pp. 125–46.

[67] Important papers in DOZA, Ritter-Akten. H. Hartmann, 'Deutschordensritter in den Kriegen des 17. und 18. Jahrhunderts', in Arnold, *Von Akkon bis Wien*, pp. 228–49. For example, a knight of the Teutonic Order, Franz Josef Baron of Reinach, died on 28 January 1795 as captain in the *Fränkischen Kreiskompanie*, which the Order, as a member of the Franconian *Kreis*, had to support: DOZA, V 1378, 1815, 3071.

[68] *Sammlung der neuesten Regeln*, p. 116.

[69] M. Lehner, *Ludwig Anton von Pfalz-Neuburg (1660–1694). Ordensoberhaupt – General – Bischof*, QuStDO, 48 (Marburg, 1994), pp. 83–6, 135–175.

(1701–14; 1733–5) troops of the Order fought under Prince Eugene.[70] The Austrian knight and coadjutor of the Austrian *Ballei*, Field Marshal Harrach, was Prince Eugene's right-hand man in the Polish War of Succession near Heidelberg and Heilbronn in the Swabian *Reichskreis*.[71] Teutonic knights also served in the imperial army in the wars against King Frederick II of Prussia and revolutionary France, in the armies of the various *Reichskreise* and as officers in the *Hoch- und Deutschmeister* regiment. The famous Archduke Charles of Austria, who was Grand Master (without having taken religious vows) for three years from 1801 until 1804, resigned as the head of the Order in favour of his younger brother, Anton Victor. Charles then served as chief commander in the new Austrian Empire until 1809.[72]

After the loss of all their possessions in the former Holy Roman Empire and their restriction to the territory of the Austrian Empire, the Teutonic knights had to prove their military skills in the army and the general staff, as did the last knight of the Order, Frederick of Belrupt-Tissac.[73] Grand Master Archduke Wilhelm (1863–94) was the only chief commander of the regiment of the *Hoch- und Deutschmeister* to fight with his troops at the battle of Königgrätz (3 July 1866). He was wounded in this battle but subsequently went on to become an artillery expert.[74] The last knightly Grand Master, Archduke Eugen (1894–1923), held a leading position in the Austro-Hungarian army, rising to the rank of field marshal in 1916.[75]

After the end of the First World War and following negotiations with the successor states to the Austro-Hungarian Empire, Pope Pius XI reformed the Order so that it became a purely religious order with no knightly brethren.[76] The priests, coming from the convents at Lana in South Tyrol (founded in 1855), Troppau in Silesia (1866), Laibach in Slovenia (1917) and Gumpold-skirchen in Austria (1924), engaged in pastoral care, charitable work and

---

[70] Demel, 'Hoch- und Deutschmeister', pp. 6–7; Braubach, 3, pp. 15–234; 5, pp. 199–362.

[71] DOZA, G[eheime] K[onferenz]-P[rotokolle], 1733–35.

[72] Täubl, pp. 83–6; H. Hertenberger and F. Wiltschek, *Erzherzog Karl. Der Sieger von Aspern* (Graz, Vienna and Cologne, 1983), pp. 134–293.

[73] 'Offiziersbelohnungantrag für Friedrich Graf Belrupt-Tissac im Ersten Weltkrieg', in *A[ustellungs] – K[atalog] 800 Jahre Deutscher Orden*, p. 296.

[74] Demel, 'Hoch- und Deutschmeister', p. 10; G. Müller, pp. 77–98. For Archduke Wilhelm's decoration after the battle of Königgrätz, *AK 996–1995. Ostarrichi Österreich. Menschen Mythen Meilensteine*, ed. E. Bruckmüller and P. Urbanitsch (= Katalog des Niederösterreichischen Landesmuseums new ser., 388) (Horn, 1996), pp. 114–15.

[75] E.F. Hoffmann, 'Feldmarschall Svetozar Boroevic von Bojna. Österreich-Ungarns Kriegsfront an den Flüssen Isonzo und Piave', Diss. (Vienna, 1985), pp. 27–9, 33, 44, 47, 53–5, 60–86, 112, 131, 159, 171–5, 237–8, 246; M. Rauchensteiner, *Der Tod des Doppeladlers. Österreich-Ungarn und der Erste Weltkrieg* (Graz, Vienna and Cologne, 1993), pp. 544, 545, 555 and *passim*.

[76] Wieland, pp. 249–74. For the negotiations, DOZA, Ballei Österreich Korrespondenz, Box 25/1; Demel, 'Der Deutsche Orden in den Jahren 1918', pp. 201–2.

various educational activities.[77] They were forced to confront fresh problems in Fascist Italy and Czechoslovakia and had to develop new forms of religious involvement in the new youth movement.[78] After the Order's abolition in Austria by the Nazi government at the beginning of September 1938[79] and soon afterwards, in February 1939, in the Sudetenland, and then later by the governments in Yugoslavia and Czechoslovakia whence the Order's priests and sisters were expelled to Germany and Austria, new problems were created that could not easily be solved.[80] Since the Second Vatican Council and the collapse of the Soviet bloc, the Order has had to face new political situations in its charitable and educational work.[81] The Order is preparing new initiatives in pastoral care for the next century, such as the foundation of a new province in Slovakia for priests and sisters, and in medical care in its German province. Regular information about these activities will appear in its quarterly journal, *Deutscher Orden*.

---

[77] Gasser, pp. 83–281. For Gumpoldskirchen, *Mitteilungen des Deutschordens* no. 9/10 (September–October 1924), p. 28; D. Heyderer, *Die Geschichte der Österreichischen Brüderprovinz des Deutschen Ordens. Vom Untergang der Monarchie bis zur Gegenwart*, Master's thesis (Vienna, 1994), pp. 18–19.

[78] D. Langhans, *Der Reichsbund der deutschen katholischen Jugend in der Tschechoslowakei 1918–1938* (Bonn, 1990), pp. 27, 40, 43, 106–8, 135, 141, 191, 221, 230, 231, 244, 255–8.

[79] M. Liebmann, *Theodor Innnitzer und der Anschluß. Österreichs Kirche 1938* (Graz, Vienna and Cologne, 1988), pp. 177, 186 f.; E. Weinzierl, *Prüfstand. Österreichs Katholiken und der National-sozialismus* (St Gabriel/Mödling, 1988), p. 132.

[80] Demel, 'Deutsche Orden in den Jahren 1918', pp. 204–9.

[81] B. Demel, 'Die Pfarrei Schottenfeld in Wien und der Deutsche Orden', in *Pfarre St Laurenz am Schottenfeld 1786–1986*, ed. J. Kellner (St Pölten and Vienna, 1986), pp. 189–211, esp. pp. 196–9.

7

Knightly Hospitallers or Crusading Knights? Decisive Factors for the Spread of the Teutonic Knights in the Rhineland and the Low Countries, 1216–1300

Klaus van Eickels

In the Rhineland, as in other parts of the Empire, the Teutonic Knights did not begin their expansion until about a generation after their Order was first founded as a field hospital during the siege of Acre in 1190. In 1216 they received their first donations at Koblenz and Cologne and by the end of the 1220s they had acquired most of the nuclei from which the bailiwick of Koblenz and its main houses were to emerge later in the century.[1]

It is obvious that the years after 1216 were crucial in the rise of the Teutonic Knights to their later position as one of the three great military orders. Although they had already been established as a knightly order in 1198, it was only during this period that they received the decisive papal privileges that granted them equality with the Templars and the Hospitallers of St John.[2] Within a few years, a wave of donations transformed the hitherto relatively insignificant community into the leading military order in the Empire.

It is therefore by no means unimportant to ask how the Teutonic Knights conceived of themselves during these years and how they were perceived by

---

[1] This paper is based on my PhD thesis, published as: K. van Eickels, *Die Deutschordensballei Koblenz und ihre wirtschaftliche Entwicklung im Spätmittelalter* QuStDo 52 (Marburg, 1995), pp. 17–35. It therefore focuses mainly on the Rhineland and the southern Low Countries, that is, the bailiwick of Koblenz. The corresponding development in the northern Low Countries has been studied recently by J.A. Mol, 'Vechten of verplegen. Ontstaan en begintijd van het huis en de balije van Utrecht van de Duitse Orde', *Jaarboek Oud Utrecht* (1993), 45–66.

[2] The papal privileges for the Teutonic Order are most conveniently accessible in *Tabulae ordinis Theutonici ex tabularii regii Berolinensis codici potissimum*, ed. E. Strehlke (Berlin, 1869, repr. Toronto and Jerusalem, 1975), nos 296 ff.; cf. J. Voigt, *Geschichte des Deutschen Ordens in seinen zwölf Balleien in Deutschland* (Berlin, 1857), 1, pp. 352–449; H. Kluger, *Hochmeister Hermann von Salza und Kaiser Friedrich II* (Marburg, 1987), pp. 20–30; van Eickels, pp. 36–40.

their contemporaries and especially by their benefactors. Were they seen as hospitallers of knightly origin or as knights of Christ who, like the Hospitallers of St John, administered hospitals alongside their main task of defending the Holy Land?

In a series of articles published between 1962 and 1969, one of the then leading Rhenish regional historians, Herbert Neu, argued that the early spread of the Teutonic Knights in the Rhineland was primarily fostered by their ability to manage hospitals. This ability was rooted, according to Neu, in their original vocation to serve the sick and especially in their acquaintance with the highly developed culture of Eastern hospitals.[3]

At first glance this explanation is far from implausible, since most of the early donations the Order received in the Rhineland and in Flanders consisted of hospitals. The main house of the emerging Rhenish bailiwick at Koblenz was probably created in 1216, when the archbishop of Trier conveyed to the Order the dilapidated possessions of a local hospital founded by one of his predecessors.[4] In the same year, a second commandery was founded at Cologne, where a wealthy citizen, Henry Halverogge, endowed the Order with a hospital he had recently founded.[5] In 1219 the Order received a hospital at Oudenburg in Flanders[6] and at least two, probably three, further donations of Flemish hospitals were to follow before 1225.[7]

The number of hospitals transferred to the Order is indeed impressive, all the more so as the other bailiwicks in the Empire also received similar donations in their early years. Yet it would be short-sighted to infer from this observation that the Order owed its early expansion to its reputation as a good administrator of hospitals.

---

[3] H. Neu, *Die Entwicklung des Deutschen Ritterordens im Rheinland. Akademische Festrede aus Anlaß der Rektoratsübergabe in der Pädagogischen Hochschule Köln* (Bonn, 1962); *idem*, 'Die Aufnahme des Deutschen Ordens im Rheinland (mit besonderer Berücksichtigung der ursprünglichen Zielsetzung des Ordens)', in *Acht Jahrhunderte Deutscher Orden (Festschrift M. Tumler)*, ed. K. Wieser, QuStDO, 1 (Bonn, 1967), pp. 165–74; *idem*, 'Das Rheinland und der Deutsche Orden'; *idem, Zur Geschichte des Deutschen Ordens* (Cologne, 1969), pp. 1–26, esp. p. 4.

[4] *Urkundenbuch der jetzt die preußischen Regierungsbezirke Koblenz und Trier bildenden Territorien*, 1, ed. H. Beyer (Koblenz, 1860), no. 419; 3, ed. L. Eltester and A. Goerz (Koblenz, 1874), no. 53; cf. A. Diederich, *Das Stift St Florin zu Koblenz* (Göttingen, 1967), pp. 204–7; *Regesta Pontificum Romanorum: Germania Pontificia X (Erzbistum Trier)*, ed. E. Boshof (Göttingen, 1992), pp. 350–2; van Eickels, pp. 19–21.

[5] *Urkundenbuch des Deutschen Ordens*, 2, ed. J.H. Hennes (Mainz, 1861), nos 9–11; cf. W. Peters, 'Zur Gründung des St Katharinen-Hospitals in Köln Anfang des 13. Jahrhunderts', *Jahrbuch des Kölnischen Geschichtsvereins*, 61 (1990), 59–70; van Eickels, pp. 21–4.

[6] cf. note 12 below.

[7] In 1221 Beatrix of Massemen endowed the Order with a hospital she had founded herself (*De oorkonden van Pitsenburg*, 1, ed. A. Jamees (Antwerpen, 1991), nos 17 ff.) and in 1225 Arnold of Oudenaarde did the same with a hospital at Velzeke (ibid., no. 54). It was probably during these years that the Order received the hospital at Vilvoorde which it resigned in 1238 (ibid., appendix IV).

In fact, there are several reasons for calling this assumption into question. First of all, the rule of the Order does not give any priority to hospital service. Although the circumstances in which the Order had first emerged did not fall into oblivion, the new knightly Order established in 1198 was given the rule of the Templars, and it was only a supplementary stipulation that, as to the hospitals of the Order, the respective clauses of the rule of the Hospitallers were to be followed. Moreover, these clauses did not undergo any specific modifications. They were taken over unchanged when the Teutonic Knights finally put their statutes into writing in the mid-thirteenth century.[8] Obviously these clauses did not play a central part in the everyday life of the Order, and thus they escaped the process of gradual adaptation.

Secondly, a medieval hospital must not be mistaken for an institution of efficient social welfare. The founders of hospitals were interested in the efficient administration of their hospital only insofar as it was necessary for the salvation of their own souls. In committing their foundation to the Teutonic Knights they made clear that in their eyes this step promoted their own blessedness. This does not necessarily mean, however, that they thereby wanted to further the functioning of their foundation as a charitable institution for the sick, the poor and wandering pilgrims.

Thirdly, all the donations of hospitals mentioned above coincide with the intense propaganda that accompanied the Fifth Crusade.[9] The Fourth Lateran Council had promulgated indulgences for those who supported crusaders; these indulgences far exceeded the spiritual benefits a founder of a hospital could hope to gain from the prayers of the poor who were supported by his foundation. It was therefore in the interest of the founder or his successors to convert the hospital into a donation to a military order. The protection which canon law provided for charitable foundations should have made such a procedure impossible. Yet the Teutonic Knights, like the Hospitallers of St John, could argue that their Order as a whole was at least nominally a hospital. They thus escaped the reproach that they were alienating the donated goods of an incorporated hospital if they used them for their activities in the East.

When Archbishop Theoderic of Trier transferred the hospital of St Nicholas at Koblenz to the Teutonic Order in 1216, he did so to the glory of the Virgin Mary, to the support of the Holy Land and to the relief of the poor ('*ad honorem beate virginis et succursum terre sancte et pauperum alimoniam*').[10] The Teutonic Knights thus received the hospital as a donation designed to further

---

[8] *SDO*, pp. 31 ff.; cf. I. Sterns, 'The Statutes of the Teutonic Knights. A Study in Religious Chivalry', PhD thesis (Pennsylvania, 1969), p. 87.

[9] P. Pixton, 'Die Anwerbung des Heeres Christi. Prediger des Fünften Kreuzzuges in Deutschland', *Deutsches Archiv*, 34 (1978), 166–91; J. Powell, *Anatomy of a Crusade 1213–1221* (Philadelphia, 1986); C. Neuhausen, 'Köln und die Kreuzzüge', *Geschichte in Köln*, 31 (1992), 23–50.

[10] Cf. note 4 above.

their general purposes, which in fact consisted of these three activities. The secular canons of St Florin, who had hitherto administered the hospital, agreed to the transfer, since they retained the main building of the hospital which they needed as a refectory. By giving the goods to the Teutonic Knights, they avoided the obligation to erect a new hospital. The Teutonic Order, meanwhile, by virtue of its status as a hospital, could reorganize these possessions as the basis for a new commandery.

In the same period the preaching of the crusade reached a peak in the Rhineland as in the rest of western Europe. As a result of this intense propaganda Henry Halverogge handed over to the Teutonic Knights the hospital of St Catherine, which he had founded at Cologne.[11] He did so not because he was looking for a capable administrator of his foundation, but 'in order to glorify the Virgin Mary and the Holy Cross', as the town council put it in a letter to the papal judges delegate concerned with the matter a few years later. Henry Halverrogge thus converted his foundation into a donation to a crusading order, which entitled him to the spiritual benefits such a donation implied. His change of mind must have come about quite suddenly: the town council had just reached a compromise with the canons of St Severin which compensated them for the loss of income from funerals held in the hospital's cemetery.

In a similar way, the gifts of Flemish hospitals can be traced back to crusading propaganda and experience. During the siege of Damietta, Gilles Berthout and his wife made over to the Teutonic Order a chapel and a hospital in their dominion of Oudenburg.[12] In their charter they praise the great expenses the Teutonic Knights incurred in the Holy Land fighting the infidels and supporting the poor; obviously, their donation was aimed at these tasks in the East. Another Flemish noble, Gilbert of Zottegem, who had witnessed the charter of Gilles Berthout, followed his example immediately after his return from the crusade. Moreover, he induced his mother and his feudal overlord to endow the Teutonic Order with hospitals they had founded in the villages of Massemen and Velzeke.[13]

Apparently the legal position of the Teutonic Order as a hospital sufficed to legitimize the conversion of a local hospital into a donation which supported the Order's activities in the Holy Land. Whether such a conversion was considered meritorious, however, was a different question, the answer to which depended largely on the general level of enthusiasm evinced for the idea of crusading. Having reached its peak during the Fifth Crusade, this enthusiasm cooled considerably in the 1230s. As far as the Empire was

---

[11] Cf. note 5 above.

[12] *De oorkonden van Pitsenburg*, 1, nos 9–11; cf. van Eickels, pp. 26, 28 (note 50 ff.) and 229 ff.

[13] Cf. note 7 above.

concerned, it could not be revived even when the news spread in 1244 that Jerusalem had been lost.

In 1245 Sibert of Dülken and his wife handed over to the Order a hospital they had founded at Neuss three years before.[14] The charter of transfer contains an explicit clause stipulating that none of the hospital's receipts should be passed on to the Order's brethren beyond the sea.[15] Sibert of Dülken and his wife had given their hospital to the Teutonic Knights because they wanted the Order to defend their foundation against the rival claims of their relatives, but they wanted it to function as a local charitable institution. Their expectations were the exact opposite of those of Duke Walram of Limburg in 1221 when he endowed the Order with a hospital at Luxembourg, expressing the hope that the brethren would be able to send a part of its income to the Holy Land.[16]

The changed attitude of the general public towards crusading forced the Teutonic Knights to reconsider the importance of hospital service. Clearly they were not considered first-rate hospital administrators; at least they did not receive any further donations of hospitals. Running a charitable institution was a locally visible activity, however, likely to attract the attention of benefactors who might otherwise not find the Order appealing. Even in this instance, however, other motives for endowing the Teutonic Order with donations remained more important or became so (for example parental bonds and, above all, the wish to participate in the spiritual merits that the Order enjoyed thanks to its papal privileges of indulgence). It is therefore not astonishing that the affiliation of lay men and women to the Order became the primary means by which the Teutonic Knights expanded, whereas the hospitals of the Order were maintained on a rather reduced level only.

The Order gave up or closed down its Flemish hospitals after a short time, but it maintained its hospitals at Cologne and Koblenz until the mid-fourteenth century, and even received a few donations for them.[17] At Koblenz the

---

[14] *Urkundenbuch des Deutschen Ordens*, 2, nos 64, 65, 67; cf. van Eickels, pp. 33–5.

[15] *Urkundenbuch des Deutschen Ordens*, 2, no. 64: '*[fratres domus Theutonice] de dicte domus proventibus [...] nichil diminuant nec ad usus fratrum transmarinorum convertant*'. For a similar example from Bremen cf. *Bremisches Urkundenbuch*, 1, ed. D.R. Ehmck and W. v. Bippen (Bremen, 1873), no. 225.

[16] Staatsarchiv Ludwigsburg, Germany, Bestand 352, Büschel 117, no. 2: '*[...] attendentes sollercius et considerantes devocius, quod, cum predicta domus minus sufficiens esset pauperibus et fere nichil caritatis inpenderet peregrinis et transeuntibus, quod per fratres Theutonice domus egenis et languentibus ad ipsam domum concurrentibus maiora de cetero sint habenda beneficia et caritatis amplioris gratia conferenda et terre sancte de fructibus eiusdem domus ab ipsis fratribus aliquid sit mittendum*'; photograph in: *Ritter und Priester. Acht Jahrhunderte Deutscher Orden in Nordwesteuropa*, ed. U. Arnold *et al.* (Alden-Biesen, 1992), pp. 62 ff.

[17] van Eickels, pp. 195 ff. (with references): around 1280 the commandery was granted the right to close a path passing in front of the hospital, because the noise disturbed the holy service in the chapel as well as the poor and the sick in the hospital. The following year the commander and the brethren of the house of the Teutonic Order at Koblenz bought a piece of land adjacent to

commandery finally abolished its hospital when it needed space to extend its own buildings in the second half of the fourteenth century. The hospital of St Catherine at Cologne came under the jurisdiction of the town council at about the same time.[18] Again, the altered rank of hospital service seems to be indicative of a more far-reaching change in the Order and its image: in the same period – more precisely after 1371 – donations to the Order ceased abruptly;[19] obviously, the Teutonic Knights were no longer able and willing to compete for alms with other religious houses.

In conclusion, the Teutonic Knights received their early donations as an order of crusaders. They only attached a certain degree of importance to the administration of their hospitals once the general enthusiasm for crusading had cooled down, since local charity only became a factor of some consequence in the stiffening competition between old and new privileged orders at this point. They therefore maintained some of the hospitals received early in the thirteenth century, especially urban ones, until the bailiwicks and commanderies in the Empire finally became institutions which confined themselves to providing a living for their own members.

---

the hospital and received a donation '*nomine domus sue predicte et infirmorum inibi decumbencium ac nomine subsidii terre sancte*'. Another donation was given to them in 1297 '*in promotionem infirmorum hospitalis domus eiusdem*'. In 1299 the hospital received a rent of 2 marks, a quarter of which was to be used to board the sick in the hospital one day a year. In 1318 the city of Koblenz and the archbishop of Trier endowed the commandery with land needed to enlarge the hospital building. The hospital is last mentioned in 1344 in a letter of indulgence which contains a clause prohibiting that it be advertised outside the chapel and the hospital of the commandery. By the end of the fourteenth century, the Order had built a new wing of the commandery in place of the former hospital.

[18] van Eickels, pp. 196 ff.: the hospital is referred to in donations of 1250 and 1297; it is last mentioned in 1349, when the commandery granted a room in the hospital to a layman affiliated to the Order: Historisches Archiv der Stadt Köln, Katharinen D.O., Urk. 1/335. A list of hospitals compiled for the town council of Cologne in 1470 mentions three communal *provisores* for a hospital '*apud sanctam Katharinam*': *Akten zur Geschichte der Verwaltung und Verfassung der Stadt Köln im 14. und 15. Jahrhundert*, ed. W. Stein (Bonn, 1895), 2, p. 476.

[19] van Eickels, pp. 81 ff.

8

Archbishop Henry of Reims and the Militarization of the Hospitallers

Jonathan Phillips

In 1173–4 Jobert, the Master of the Hospitallers, sent a letter to Archbishop Henry of Reims in which he asked for a property in his diocese.[1] Such requests do not appear to have been commonplace. An examination of the timing, tone and content of this letter may reveal why Jobert made such an approach. This investigation may help to shed more light on the turbulent period in the Hospitallers' history when their level of involvement in military affairs provoked serious concern within the Order itself and in the wider Church. This paper will also consider the reasons why Jobert chose to approach Archbishop Henry in particular. In the course of this discussion it will be possible to see the existence of a network of ties between the Hospitallers and a group of leading figures in western Europe who were interested in the defence of the Holy Land.

The most remarkable aspect of Jobert's letter is its emphasis on the Hospitallers' spiritual and pastoral activities. The Master mentioned their continual prayers for Archbishop Henry and all Christians and he made a separate reference to the intercessory prayers offered by the brothers. He also expressed the hope that by serving the poor of Christ the Order would be rewarded by God.[2] In highlighting the Hospitallers' religious work Jobert chose to omit any explicit information about their military role, although he did note that the 'limbs of Christ are weary from diverse occupations', which may be an oblique reference to the fact that the Order engaged in warfare.[3] The explanation for the tone of this letter probably lies in the contemporary debate concerning the militarization of the Hospitallers, an issue that had

---

[1] *CH*, no. 438. See also Henry of Reims, 'Epistolae', *RHGF*, 16, pp. 199–200.

[2] *CH*, no. 438.

[3] Ibid.

emerged most noticeably during the controversial mastership of Gilbert of Assailly (1163–69/70).[4] Gilbert did much to encourage the Order's participation in military affairs and soon after he took office a number of Hospitallers were killed in the battle of Artah (1164).[5] Gilbert's mastership also saw an expansion of the Order's landholdings in sensitive border areas. In 1170 the Hospitallers assumed control of 'Arqa and 'Akka, two castles that commanded the routes from Homs to the coast and to Baalbek.[6] In the same year Prince Bohemond III of Antioch gave the Order territory to the east of the River Orontes centred on the Muslim-held settlement of Afāmīya.[7] Gilbert also oversaw the acquisition of a series of castles. Prior to his mastership the Hospitallers had owned seven castles, but he secured rights over a further eleven, agreed to help defend the walls of Sidon and negotiated theoretical claims to six other fortresses.[8]

The most high-profile military action of the time concerned King Amalric of Jerusalem's ongoing efforts to capture Egypt. Towards the end of his mastership Gilbert brought the Hospitallers into some disrepute by promoting their involvement in one of these campaigns. In 1168 he promised to support Amalric's planned invasion with 500 knights and 500 turcopoles. In return for this the Order would receive the town of Bilbais and generous rents throughout the land.[9] Such rewards would never be forthcoming because in late 1168 Amalric launched an ill-judged attack which led to Nūr al-Dīn taking power in Egypt. The failure of this expedition provoked a serious crisis in the Latin East because it meant that the settlers had to face the combined strength of Muslim Syria and Egypt for the first time. More importantly for the Hospitallers, William of Tyre reports rumours that Gilbert had been personally responsible for persuading Amalric to initiate the invasion – a folly compounded by the fact that the attack broke existing treaties with the Muslims. The Master was said to have been motivated solely by greed and his reputation suffered badly as a result.[10]

The financial repercussions of Gilbert's tenure as master might help to explain why the Hospitallers needed to ask Archbishop Henry for a gift of property. William of Tyre wrote that Gilbert had exhausted all the treasures of the Hospital, borrowed more money and spent that as well.[11] A letter from Pope Alexander III to the preceptor dated 20 June 1172 mentioned that the

---

[4] J.S.C. Riley-Smith, *The Knights of St John in Jerusalem and Cyprus 1050–1310* (London, 1967), pp. 60–3. On the Order's dual role see also H. Nicholson, *Templars, Hospitallers and Teutonic Knights: Images of the Military Orders 1128–1291* (Leicester, 1993), pp. 120–2.

[5] *CH*, no. 404.

[6] Ibid., no. 411.

[7] Ibid., no. 391.

[8] For a full list see Riley-Smith, p. 69.

[9] Ibid., p. 72.

[10] WT, pp. 917–18.

[11] Ibid.

Order was impoverished at this time.[12] Donations to properties in western Europe may also have been dropping in this period. Gervers has demonstrated that support for Hospitaller foundations in Essex declined during the 1160s and 1170s, and this could reflect a more general trend affecting the Order's holdings in France too.[13] In sum, therefore, the Hospitallers' financial and military standing had suffered much in the late 1160s and early 1170s.

Little is known about Jobert's period as master (1172–7), but it is believed that Gilbert's emphasis on warfare had faced some opposition from within the Order. Riley-Smith has argued that Jobert's issue of statutes concerned with the care of pilgrims and the service of the Church did not mean that his election was a reaction to the aggressive policies of Gilbert. Riley-Smith reasons that Jobert's successor, the warlike Roger des Moulins, was also known to have issued statutes concerned with pastoral responsibilities, and that Jobert himself continued with military affairs.[14] It is apparent that evidence on this topic is limited, but Jobert's letter to Henry of Reims – which Riley-Smith does not cite – does plainly emphasize the spiritual function of the Order. Even if Jobert was less enthusiastic about the Hospitallers engaging in warfare, he could not simply halt such involvement because to do so would have exposed the Holy Land to great danger. It might be suggested that Jobert had decided to play down further expansion of the Order's military function, rather than actually cutting back on these activities. It should also be noted that disquiet about the Hospitallers' military role extended further afield and a series of letters written by Pope Alexander III between 1168 and 1180 reminded the Hospitallers that their first duty was to care for the poor and that arms-bearing should take place only in certain prescribed situations, usually in times of crisis.[15]

It remains to consider why Master Jobert chose to turn to Henry of Reims for support. It is possible that similar appeals were directed to other important figures in the West, but they do not appear to have survived. The fact that Henry's career is particularly well documented may reinforce this point. A manuscript from the abbey of St Vaast at Arras contains over 500 letters, mostly sent to Henry by the papacy, but also including the work of other correspondents and some of the archbishop's own letters.[16] If Jobert had sent similar appeals elsewhere such action would emphasize the Order's need for assistance even further. It is essential, however, to indicate that the approach to Henry of Reims did not represent a shot in the dark and there existed

---

[12] *CH*, no. 434.

[13] M. Gervers, 'Donations to the Hospitallers in England in the Wake of the Second Crusade', *The Second Crusade and the Cistercians*, ed. M. Gervers (New York, 1992), pp. 155–62. *CH*, nos 439 and 440 show that some donations were still being made to the Order at this time.

[14] Riley-Smith, pp. 63–4.

[15] *CH*, nos 391, 434, 527.

[16] Henry of Reims, 'Epistolae', pp. 171–200.

compelling reasons to contact him. There is little doubt that he was seen as a great source of support by the Order. The Master described the Hospital as an institution that Henry valued, helped, protected and advised. Jobert claimed that 'as long as the house of the Hospital has your patronage and assistance it will always prosper ...'.[17] By what means had Henry come to be held in such esteem? The explanation for this appears to lie in his connections with the crusading movement and his part in a network of prominent individuals in the West associated with the defence of the Holy Land.

The seat of Henry's archbishopric – Reims – was located in the county of Champagne, a region closely linked with the crusading movement. Count Henry participated in the Second Crusade and in 1169 – after the fall of Egypt – the house of Champagne was specifically identified in a request for military help sent from the Holy Land. The embassy carrying this message was led by Archbishop Frederick of Tyre and he approached a member of the house of Champagne, Count Stephen of Sancerre, to be the husband of Sibylla of Jerusalem, daughter of King Amalric, although in the end no such marriage took place.[18]

In addition to his position as one of the leading churchmen in France, Archbishop Henry was a close confidant of his brother King Louis VII (1137–80). Louis had led the French contingent on the Second Crusade and in the course of the 1160s had been the target of a series of appeals from the Latin settlers in the Levant.[19] Through a study of this diplomatic process we can see the emergence of links between Henry and the Hospitallers. In 1166 Gilbert of Assailly had headed an embassy to the West sent by the kingdom of Jerusalem. In response to this, Pope Alexander III issued a crusading bull and Gilbert travelled into France where he probably met senior figures in the political and ecclesiastical hierarchy. As we have seen, in 1169 the settlers made another appeal for help. One aspect of this was a letter King Amalric sent to Henry outlining the desperate situation in the East and the need for assistance. It is also worth noting that the envoys who accompanied Frederick of Tyre included a group of Hospitallers. Pope Alexander reacted to this mission by issuing another crusading bull in support of the settlers. He then wrote to Henry of Reims and instructed him to summon the people of his province, to broadcast the crusade appeal and to issue indulgences. Henry was also directed to organize a council of all lay and ecclesiastical magnates to consider the defence of the Frankish East. A meeting in Paris in September 1169 did just this and gave the envoys from the Levant an opportunity to present their case to the leading men of France, although again they received little response.[20]

---

[17] *CH*, no. 438.

[18] J.P. Phillips, *Defenders of the Holy Land. Relations between the Latin East and the West, 1119–87* (Oxford, 1996), pp. 168–70, 176–9.

[19] Ibid., pp. 140–208.

[20] Ibid., pp. 151–4, 168–208.

It is possible to reconstruct further elements in the network of prominent individuals in western Europe who were connected with the Hospitallers. We can note, for example, that Henry of Reims was closely linked with Pope Alexander III. They had known each other since their youth and when a papal schism broke, in 1159, out Henry became one of Alexander's key representatives in his struggle against Frederick Barbarossa and the antipope Victor IV. In the course of the 1160s the archbishop undertook a series of negotiations with the imperial court and he provided Alexander with money. It is also of note that when Alexander was forced to flee from Rome in 1162 he chose to seek refuge in France.[21] This network can be highlighted further by indicating the close affinity between the Hospitallers and Pope Alexander, which was underpinned by the basic point that the Hospitallers were under papal protection and exempt from local episcopal jurisdiction.[22] In a situation where there were two popes this relationship could have become difficult, but it seems that the Hospitallers chose to support Alexander rather than Victor in the schism.[23]

This series of associations can be rounded out by noting two further episodes, incidents which also indicate that the Hospital was experiencing money problems around this period. First, in January 1166 Alexander wrote to Henry instructing him to organize financial help for the Order.[24] Secondly, in 1168/9 Alexander again contacted Henry directing him to act on behalf of the brothers. The pope had heard that the duke of Louvain had been withholding alms due to the Hospitallers from property in his lands. Alexander stressed how important the Hospitallers were and how much they deserved to be supported. Henry was directed to send messengers and letters to the duke ordering him to rectify the situation. If this did not happen the duke's lands were to be placed under interdict and he would be excommunicated.[25] The scale of ecclesiastical penalties being threatened demonstrated that Alexander viewed this matter with great seriousness.

In addition to this diplomatic and spiritual network, one final piece of evidence may reveal why the Hospitallers singled out Henry in particular for help, and why they believed that he would agree to their request for a property. In 1170 Henry gave the Templars a house in the city of Reims.[26] This indicated a willingness to provide backing for the military orders from his own lands. Jobert may have learned of this gift and might have hoped that Henry's

---

[21] M.W. Baldwin, *Alexander III and the Twelfth Century* (New York, 1968), pp. 52, 61, 77, 156.

[22] Riley-Smith, pp. 375–89.

[23] P.W. Edbury and J.G.Rowe, *William of Tyre: Historian of the Latin East* (Cambridge, 1988), pp. 127–8; I.S. Robinson, *The Papacy, 1073–1198* (Cambridge, 1990), pp. 241, 243.

[24] Alexander III, 'Epistolae', *PL*, 200, col. 328.

[25] Ibid., cols 524–5.

[26] P. Demouy, 'L'église de Reims et la croisade aux xi–xii siècles', *Les Champenois et la croisade. Actes des IVe journées rémoises du CRLMR* (Paris, 1989), p. 31.

generosity to the Templars might be replicated for the Hospitallers, especially in light of his earlier assistance for the brothers. The provision of a house would also help to give them a visible presence in an area where interest in the defence of the Latin East was already strong. Unfortunately there is no evidence that allows us to ascertain whether Henry agreed to Jobert's request and this intriguing episode ends in obscurity. In early 1173 Alexander wrote to Henry concerning another dispute over the Order's property and Henry died in 1175, thus ending the relevant correspondence.[27]

In conclusion, in the person of Henry of Reims the Hospitallers saw a man at the heart of a network of supporters of the Holy Land that also included the counts of Champagne, Louis VII and Pope Alexander III. Henry himself was viewed by the brothers as a protector and patron of the Order. The emphasis in Jobert's letter on the spiritual aspect of the Hospitallers' work may reflect contemporary concerns over the recent militarization of the Order. It is interesting that the tone of Jobert's appeal coincided closely with the views expressed in 1168–70 by Alexander III, Archbishop Henry's great friend and the Order's ecclesiastical protector. The pope wrote that the Hospitallers' prime duty was towards the poor and that the carrying of arms was not in the spirit of the original foundation.[28] The similarity of tone between Jobert's approach to Henry and Pope Alexander's views outlined above may well indicate that contemporary concerns over the Order's involvement in warfare were having some impact on the Hospitaller leadership and in consequence it was felt appropriate to draw the attention of one of their key supporters to the brothers' spiritual work, rather than their fighting capacities.

---

[27] Alexander III, 'Epistolae', col. 950.
[28] *CH*, no. 391 *ter*.

9

Templar Castles between Jaffa and Jerusalem

Denys Pringle

THE ROAD FROM JAFFA TO JERUSALEM

The main duty of the Templars that was enjoined upon them by Patriarch Warmund and others at the time of their formation around 1119–20 was 'that, as far as their strength permitted, they should keep the roads and highways safe from the menace of robbers and highwaymen, with especial regard for the protection of pilgrims'.[1] The Templars' activity in protecting pilgrims on the road between Jerusalem and the River Jordan in the twelfth century is attested by both documentary and archaeological evidence.[2] Here, however, I propose to focus on the road by which travellers reached Jerusalem from Jaffa and the coastal plain. In so doing my task is simplified considerably by the recent appearance of the second volume in the series, *Roman Roads in Judaea*, which, although primarily concerned with the Roman and Byzantine periods, also analyses the changing pattern of the road network between Jaffa and Jerusalem from the third millennium BC to the Ottoman period.[3]

In the Roman period, as in earlier centuries, the western part of the route between Jaffa and Lydda followed a well-trodden path through the coastal plain, avoiding any major river crossing. To the east of Lydda, however, where the ground begins to rise into the foothills (or Shephela), and then into the hills

The survey work in 1989 at Laṭrūn and Yālu was carried out under the auspices of the British School of Archaeology in Jerusalem and with the support of the Royal Archaeological Institute.

[1] WT, p. 554; tr. E.A. Babcock and A.C. Krey, *A History of Deeds Done beyond the Sea*, 2 vols, Columbia University Records of Civilization, Sources and Studies, 35 (New York, 1943), 1, p. 525; cf. M. Barber, *The New Knighthood: A History of the Order of the Temple* (Cambridge, 1994), pp. 6–9.

[2] D. Pringle, 'Templar Castles on the Road to the Jordan', in *MO*, 1, pp. 148–66.

[3] M. Fischer, B. Isaac and I. Roll, *Roman Roads in Judaea*, 2, *The Jaffa–Jerusalem Roads*, BAR International Series, 628 (Oxford, 1996).

of Judaea, a number of alternative routes were possible. In Roman times there were two principal ones: a northern route passing through Mod'in (Midiya) and the Beth Horon pass to connect with the Nāblus (Neapolis) road at Ḥawānīt, north of Jerusalem; and a southerly one through 'Amwās (Nicopolis, Emmaus), Bāb al-Wād and Abū Ghawsh. From 'Amwās another road ran north-east through the Shephela, skirting the edge of the hills; this connected the two principal roads and also gave access to other secondary routes, which penetrated the hills up the stream valleys or more often along the crests of the ridges separating them.[4]

In the late Roman and Byzantine periods the picture remained largely unchanged, though the number of settlements and of secondary routes connecting them increased substantially. The only major change was that between 'Amwās and Abū Ghawsh the southerly route shifted slightly to the north to pass through Yālu (Ailon).[5] In the Umayyad period, repairs to the road between 'Amwās and Jerusalem are attested by two milestones from the reign of 'Abd al-Malik (AD 685–705). With the foundation of Ramla as the administrative capital of *Filasṭīn* around 714/5 and the eclipse of Christian Lydda, the importance of the southerly route over the others was reinforced and the favoured route between 'Amwās and Jaffa also shifted south to pass through it. Secondary routes in the Shephela and hill country continued to be used, but by this time the Beth Horon route was of only secondary importance.[6]

The routes followed in the twelfth century were essentially those used in earlier times (see Figure 9.1); but it is clear from analysis of archaeological and documentary evidence that some were favoured over others. The main route through the coastal plain and Shephela followed that of the early Islamic period, passing from Jaffa to Yāzūr, Ramla, Gezer (Montgisart) and Laṭrūn. From there it continued through 'Amwās, Yālu, Bayt Nūbā, Khirbat Judayra, Bayt 'Inān, al-Qubayba (Parva Mahomeria), Biddū, Nabī Samwīl (Montjoie), Khirbat Farrāj and Bayt Ḥanīna, to meet the main Nāblus road at Ḥawānīt. As this route neared Jerusalem other more direct, though less easily passable, routes diverged from it: one at Biddū to pass through Bayt Sūrīq, Khirbat al-Lawza, Bayt Ṭulmā and Burj al-Tūt; and another from Nabī Samwīl (Montjoie), passing through Khirbat al-Burj (al-Kurūm) and Lifta. The southerly Roman road from Laṭrūn through Bāb al-Wād and Abū Ghawsh also remained in secondary use, as apparently did others from Lydda eastwards through the Shephela. But significantly, the northern Beth Horon road appears to have fallen out of use as a main thoroughfare in this period.[7]

During the twelfth century, the Templars possessed some houses in the northern *faubourg* of Jaffa, associated with a postern gate through which King

---

[4] Ibid., pp. 329–31, fig. 39.

[5] Ibid., pp. 331–4, fig. 40.

[6] Ibid., pp. 334–5, fig. 41.

[7] Ibid., pp. 335–6, fig. 42.

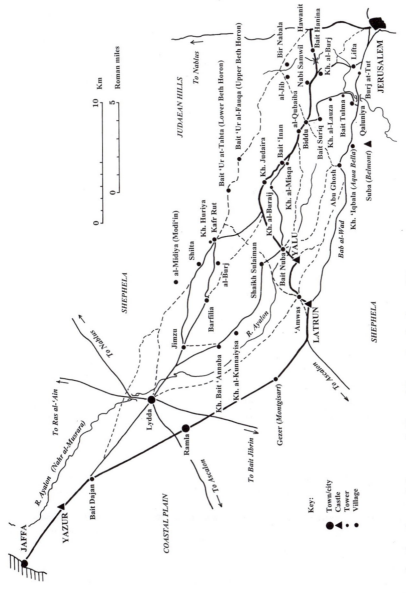

Figure 9.1 Map showing the roads between Jaffa and Jerusalem in the twelfth century

91

Richard I entered the town in August 1192.[8] They are also known to have possessed three castles between Jaffa and Jerusalem, each of which lay on the main road just described.

YĀZŪR

The first Templar castle that late twelfth-century travellers from Jaffa to Jerusalem would have reached before they came to Lydda was Yāzūr. This is referred to by different names in Frankish sources. An anonymous pilgrim text of *c.* 1131–43, for instance, calls it *Casale Balneorum* (Village of the Baths) and identifies it as the place 'where Nicodemus carved the wooden face in the likeness of the Saviour, which is now venerated at Lucca in Italy'.[9] In his French verse account of Richard I's campaign against Saladin between September 1191 and August 1192, Ambroise refers to Yāzūr as *Casel des Plains* (Village of the Plains); but while the Latin *Itinerarium Regis Ricardi* also calls it *Casellum/Casella de Planis* in the passages which correspond with Ambroise, in others it refers to the same place as *Casellum Balneorum* or *Casellum de Templo*.[10]

The date at which the Templars became associated with the village is uncertain. In 1158 and 1160, a chaplain of Yāzūr (*capellanus casalis Balneorum*), named Azo, appears together with the chaplain of Ramla as witness to two charters of Hugh of Ibelin, lord of Ramla.[11] This suggests that at that time the village was still in lay hands. The Templars' first recorded involvement with *casella de Planis* was in October 1191, when they rebuilt it following its destruction by Saladin a month earlier.[12] Subsequently, in November 1191, Richard based himself at Yāzūr (*casellum de Templo*), while negotiating with al-'Ādil in the plain between it and al-Sāfiriya (*casellum de Josaphat*).[13] In August 1192, having failed to take Jaffa, Saladin once more ordered his miners to destroy Yāzūr before withdrawing to Ramla.[14] It does not appear to have been

---

[8] *Itinerarium Regis Ricardi*, ed. W. Stubbs, RS, 38.1 (London, 1864), VI.15 (p. 409); D. Pringle, *The Churches of the Crusader Kingdom of Jerusalem: A Corpus*, 3 vols (in progress) (Cambridge, 1993–), 1, p. 266, fig. 79.

[9] *Descriptio locorum circa Hierusalem adiacentium*, ed. S. de Sandoli, *Itinera Hiersolymitana Cruce-signatorum (saec. XII–XIII)*, Studium Biblicum Franciscanum, Collectio Maior, 24 (Jerusalem, 1980), 2, p. 109.

[10] See references below.

[11] *Le Cartulaire du chapitre du Saint-Sépulcre de Jérusalem*, ed. G. Bresc-Bautier, Documents relatifs à l'histoire des croisades, 15 (Paris, 1984), no. 51 (pp. 136–8); no. 53 (pp. 140–2); *RRH*, no. 333 (p. 87); no. 360 (p. 94).

[12] Ambroise, *L'Estoire de la Guerre Sainte (1190–1192)*, ed. and tr. G. Paris (Paris, 1897), lines 7177–213; *Itinerarium Regis Ricardi*, IV.29 (pp. 289–90).

[13] *Itinerarium Regis Ricardi*, IV.31 (p. 296).

[14] Bahā' al-Dīn ibn Shaddād, *The Life of Saladin*, tr. C.W. Wilson, PPTS, 13 (London, 1897), CLXV–CLXVI (pp. 371, 373) (cf. CLXII [p. 361]); *Eracles*, 2, p. 196.

Figure 9.2   Yāzūr: tower from north

Figure 9.3   Yāzūr: tower, east wall showing round-headed splayed window

reoccupied by the Franks, and is described around 1239 as a former castle of the Templars, then in the hands of the sultan.[15] In the early fourteenth century, James of Verona describes *Jessur* as *castrum ... dirutum*.[16]

Yāzūr occupies a small hillock next to the main Jaffa to Jerusalem road. Since the abandonment of the Arab village in 1948, the central part of the site has been cleared and laid out as a park. The visible remains include the lower storey of a tower and a stretch of enclosure wall running north-west from it (Figure 9.2). The tower measures 12.8 by 12.6 m, with walls 2.8 to 2.9 m thick. The basement is enclosed by a barrel vault, with the opening for a timber stair in one corner. The east wall is pierced by a narrow embrasure with a rounded head (Figure 9.3), the splayed opening behind it being covered by a series of antique column drums forming lintels.[17] The tower's small internal size, some 50 m², suggests that it may have been a refuge or solar tower, rather than one containing a hall and intended for permanent residence.[18] It is therefore uncertain whether it may have been built by a secular owner earlier in the twelfth century, or should be associated with the Templars' reconstruction of 1191–2. Indeed, until the site is more closely investigated, it will be hard to tell what precisely the Templars contributed to it.

LAṬRŪN

After leaving Lydda and Ramla, the next Templar castle to be reached was Laṭrūn. Built on a low hill in the Shephela just south of 'Amwās, this castle commanded the point at which the southerly Roman road through Bāb al-Wād diverged from the main Ramla to Jerusalem road, and where both were met by the road from Ascalon. The strategic importance of such a position, surveying the principal routes into the hill country around Jerusalem from Ascalon, which until 1153 remained a Muslim city, appears to have been a principal reason for the castle's construction.

Laṭrūn's foundation is attributed by the *Chronica Aldefonsi imperatoris* to Count Rodrigo Gonzalez of Toledo, at a date which may be set between 1137 and 1141. Following a dispute with King Alfonso VII of Castile, the count

---

[15] P. Deschamps, 'Étude sur un texte latin énumérant les possessions musulmanes dans le royaume de Jérusalem vers l'année 1239', *Syria*, 23 (1942–3), 86–104, pls VII–VIII (at 94).

[16] R. Röhricht, 'Le pèlerinage du moine augustin Jacques de Vérone (1335)', *ROL*, 3, 155–302 (at 181).

[17] D. Pringle, *Secular Buildings in the Crusader Kingdom of Jerusalem: An Archaeological Gazetteer* (Cambridge, 1997), no. 233 (pp. 109–10), fig. 62, pls CX–CXIII; cf. V. Guérin, *Description géographique, historique et archéologique de la Palestine*, 1, *Judée*, 3 vols (Paris, 1868), 2, pp. 26–9; F.-M. Abel, 'Yazour et Beit Dedjan ou le Chastel des Plains et le Chastel de Maen', *Revue biblique*, 36 (1927), 83–9; *All that Remains: The Palestinian Villages Occupied and Depopulated by Israel in 1948*, ed. W. Khalidi (Washington, DC, 1992), pp. 261–2; Pringle, *Churches*, 2, no. 279 (pp. 377–8).

[18] Cf. D. Pringle, 'Towers in Crusader Palestine', *Château-Gaillard: Etudes de castellologie médiévale*, 16 (Caen, 1994), 335–50 (at 341–2).

set out abroad to Jerusalem, where he engaged in many battles with the Saracens and built a certain extremely strong castle facing Ascalon, called *Toron*; he also defended it strongly with knights, foot-soldiers and victuals, and gave it to the knights of the Temple.[19]

It appears that Count Rodrigo was himself serving with the Templars at this time, for Rorgo Fretellus, in dedicating a version of his *Description of the Holy Places* to him, addresses him as *impiger Machabeorum commilito, hospitatus ante Bethel, regis Salomonis in atrio* ('diligent fellow soldier of the Maccabees, lodged before Bethel in the court of King Solomon').[20]

Between 1169 and 1171 the Jewish traveller, Benjamin of Tudela, though writing in Hebrew, also refers to Laṭrūn, by a Spanish name, *Toron de los Caballeros*.[21] Unlike most other Frankish *toron* names, which usually represent the equivalent of the Arabic *tall* (or *tell*), meaning a small hill,[22] this name, which also appears later as *Toronum Militum* or *Toron des Chevaliers*, is therefore probably to be associated with the Spanish word for a tower (*torre, torreón*).

In September 1187, the Templars surrendered the castle to al-'Ādil, along with Gaza, in return for the release of their Grand Master, Gerard of Ridefort.[23] On 17 November 1191, Saladin established his camp on a hill beside Laṭrūn, but on 2 December he gave orders for the castle to be demolished.[24] First Richard I and then Saladin camped at Laṭrūn before the Treaty of Jaffa

---

[19] 'Chronica Aldefonsi imperatoris', ed. A. Maya Sanchez, in *Chronica Hispana saec. XII*, Corpus Christianorum, Continuatio Mediaevalis, 71 (Turnhout, 1990), I.48 (p. 172); cf. R. Hiestand, 'Un centre intellectuel en Syrie du Nord? Notes sur la personnalité d'Aimery d'Antioche, Albert de Tarse et Rorgo Fretellus', *Le Moyen-Age*, 100 (1994), 7–36 (at 29–32). I am grateful to Professor B.Z. Kedar for drawing my attention to this source.

[20] P.C. Boeren, *Rorgo Fretellus de Nazareth et sa description de la Terre Sainte: Histoire et Edition du Texte*, Koninklijke Nederlandse Akademie van Wetenschapen, Afdeling Letterkunde, Verhandelingen Nieuwe Reeks, 105 (Amsterdam, Oxford and New York, 1980), p. 54; cf. Hiestand, 'Un centre intellectuel', 30–1.

[21] *The Itinerary of Benjamin of Tudela*, ed. and tr. M.N. Adler (London, 1907), p. 26 note; *idem*, tr. A. Asher, in *Early Travels in Palestine*, ed. T. Wright, (London, 1848), p. 87; cf. J. Prawer, *The History of the Jews in the Latin Kingdom of Jerusalem* (Oxford, 1988), pp. 62–3.

[22] D. Pringle, 'A Castle in the Sand: Mottes in the Crusader East', *Château-Gaillard: Études de castellologie médiévale*, 17 (Caen, 1998), pp. 187–91.

[23] *Gesta Regis Henrici II*, ed. W. Stubbs, RS, 49, 2 vols (London, 1867), 2, p. 23; Ralph of Diss, *Opera Historica*, 2 vols, ed. W. Stubbs, RS, 68 (London, 1876), 2, p. 56; 'Imād al-Dīn al-Iṣfahānī, *Conquête de la Syrie et de la Palestine par Saladin*, tr. H. Massé, Documents relatifs à l'histoire des croisades, 10 (Paris, 1972), p. 100; Bahā' al-Dīn, p. 117; Abū Shāma, *Le livre des deux jardins* in *RHC Or*, 4, pp. 312–13; Ibn al-Athīr, *al-Kāmil fi'l-tarīkh*, in *RHC Or*, 1, p. 697; Abu'l-Fidā', in *RHC Or*, 1, p. 57; B.Z. Kedar, 'Ein Hilferuf aus Jerusalem vom September 1187', *Deutsches Archiv für Erforschung des Mittelalters*, 38 (1982), 112–22 (at 121); M.C. Lyons and D.E.P. Jackson, *Saladin: The Politics of the Holy War*, University of Cambridge Oriental Publications, 30 (Cambridge, 1982), p. 272.

[24] 'Imād al-Dīn, p. 348; Bahā' al-Dīn, pp. 303–4; Ambroise, *L'Estoire*, line 6858; *Itinerarium Regis Ricardi*, IV.23 (p. 280); J. Prawer, *Histoire du royaume latin de Jérusalem*, 2 vols, 2nd edn (Paris, 1975), 2, p. 83.

assigned it, in October 1192, to the territory controlled by the Muslims; but there is no suggestion in any of the sources describing these events that the castle was still serviceable.[25]

In March 1229, by the terms of Frederick II's treaty with the Ayyūbids, the Templars regained Laṭrūn and its appurtenances on condition that they did not fortify it.[26] In late 1243, however, a letter from the Grand Master, Armand of Périgord, to the Order's preceptor in England made it known that by then the Templars were planning to built a strong castle 'near Jerusalem above Toron' (*prope Jerusalem supra Toronum*) if sufficient help could be obtained from the barons of the kingdom.[27] Laṭrūn was evidently the intended location. In August 1244, however, the Khwarizmian Turks sacked Jerusalem, swept through Palestine from Laṭrūn (*a Nirone militum*) as far as Ascalon and Gaza and, combining with the Egyptians, imposed so crushing a defeat on the Franks at *la Forbie* on 17 October that the plan had no chance of ever being put into effect.[28]

None the less, Joinville tells us that in 1253 King Louis IX considered fortifying a hill between Jaffa and Jerusalem on which there had formerly been a castle at the time of the Maccabees; but he was dissuaded by the barons of the kingdom, who pointed out the difficulty of holding a place five leagues from the sea. This site also seems likely to have been Laṭrūn.[29] It appears, however, that the castle was never rebuilt after 1191; and in 1283, 'the province of al-Aṭrūn and its districts' were formally included in the sultan's possessions in the treaty made between Qalāwūn and the Franks of Acre.[30]

The castle now barely survives above basement level, and much of it is covered by rubble from the collapsed upper storeys. However, surveys undertaken by D. Bellamy for the Survey of Palestine in 1938 and by Matthew Pease and myself for the British School of Archaeology in Jerusalem in 1989 show that Laṭrūn began as a keep-and-bailey castle, with a central tower (some 14 m square, with walls 3–4 m thick) enclosed by a quadrangular enclosure with an external *talus* (see Figures 9.4–9.6). The outer wall measured

---

[25] *Itinerarium Regis Ricardi*, V.49 (p. 368); Roger of Howden, *Chronica*, ed. W. Stubbs, RS, 51, 4 vols (London, 1868–71), 3, pp. 174–5, 179; 'Imād al-Dīn, pp. 354, 379, 386; Bahā' al-Dīn, pp. 340–41, 376, 377, 390; *Cont WT*, p. 149.

[26] *Monumenta Germaniae Historica, Epistolae saeculi XIII. e Regestis Pontificium Romanorum Selectae per G.H. Pertz*, ed. C. Rodenberg, 2 vols (Berlin, 1883–7), 1, no. 384 (pp. 292–303); Prawer, *Histoire*, 2, p. 200 note 40.

[27] Matthew Paris, *Chronica majora*, ed. H.R. Luard, RS, 57, 7 vols (London, 1872–83), 4, p. 290.

[28] *Chronica de Mailros*, ed. J. Stevenson, Bannatyne Club, 49 (Edinburgh, 1835), p. 157; cf. Barber, pp. 143–7.

[29] On the supposed identification of Laṭrūn with Modi'in in this period, see Pringle, *Churches*, 2, p. 6.

[30] P.M. Holt, *Early Mamluk Diplomacy (1260–1290): Treaties of Baybars and Qalāwūn with Christian Rulers*, Islamic History and Civilization, Studies and texts, ed. U. Haarmann, 12 (Leiden, New York and Cologne, 1995), p. 75.

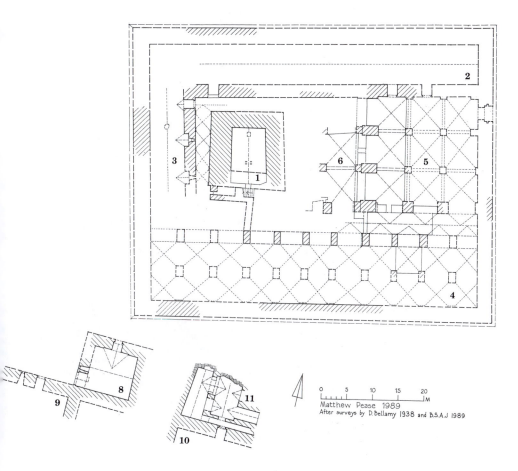

Matthew Pease 1989
After surveys by D. Bellamy 1938 and B.S.A.J 1989

Figure 9.4   Laṭrūn: plan of the castle at ground-floor level

Figure 9.5   Laṭrūn: south range (4), looking south-east from the main tower (1)

Figure 9.6   Latrūn: the main tower (1), west side

Figure 9.7   Laṭrūn: vaulted range (6) to east of main tower

Figure 9.8   Laṭrūn: south-west tower (8), inside of west wall, showing gateway defended by a machicolation in the vault above

some 72 m east-west by 55 m north-south, and was about 3 m thick, with a gate defended by a portcullis on the east. Against the inside face of the north wall was a continuous barrel vault (2), some 8 m wide, with at least two doors opening from the courtyard surrounding the tower. This courtyard was later infilled with other vaults: a barrel vault on the west (3), with the space between it and the tower also being covered over by a series of groin vaults; a block of groin vaults on the east (5–6), built in at least two stages (Figure 9.7); and another block on the south (4).

The rectangular nucleus of the castle was later enclosed by a polygonal outer *enceinte*, also with a *talus*, following roughly the shape of the hill and with two large towers and a gate tower (8) (Figure 9.8) on the south and another smaller one on the north-west. Another outer range of vaulted buildings, including stables, lies 100 m or so to the north.

It may be assumed that the knights' residence and chapel would have been located within the inner ward, probably on the first floor. Indeed, the chapel may possibly be identified with an area known as *al-kanīsa*, lying in the eastern part of the upper floor (above 5). If so, it would seem that as at Hospitaller Belvoir and Templar Sidon, the chapel was placed to command the inner gate, whose portcullis was in all probability operated from inside it (as in Edward I's castle at Harlech in north Wales).[31] This may also have been the original location of two triple capitals, delicately carved in the so-called 'Temple workshop' style, that were found in a village house in Laṭrūn in 1910 and taken to Istanbul in 1917.[32] These cannot be used, however, to support the claim by Helmuth Buschhausen that the castle was rebuilt between 1229 and 1245,[33] for the consensus of opinion among other art historians is that the products of the so-called 'Temple workshop' belong to the period before 1187;[34] and, as we have seen, the documentary and archaeological evidence suggests that the castle was not rebuilt after its destruction in 1191.

---

[31] D. Pringle, *Churches*, 1, no. 57 (pp. 120–2); 2, no. 242 (pp. 321–4); A.J. Taylor, *Harlech Castle* (Cardiff, 1980, repr. 1988), p. 24.

[32] H. Buschhausen, *Die süditalienische Bauplastik im Königreich Jerusalem von König Wilhelm II. bis Kaiser Friedrich II.*, Österreiche Akademie der Wissenschaften, Phil.-hist. Klasse, Dankschriften, 108 (Vienna, 1978), pp. 62–5, pls 1–21; J. Folda, *The Art of the Crusaders in the Holy Land, 1098–1187* (Cambridge, New York and Melbourne, 1995), pp. 452, 596 note 186, 597 note 213, 600 note 275, pls 10.16a–g; Z. Jacoby, 'The workshop of the Temple area in Jerusalem in the twelfth century: its origin, evolution and impact', *Zeitschrift für Kunstgeschichte*, 45 (1982), 325–94 (at 334–5, 337, 344, figs 25–6, 39). For further references and discussion, see Pringle, *Churches*, 2, pp. 7–9, pl. I.

[33] Buschhausen, pp. 61–2.

[34] Jacoby, 'The workshop of the Temple area', 376–85; *idem* 'The tomb of Baldwin V, king of Jerusalem (1185–1186), and the workshop of the Temple area', *Gesta*, 18.2 (1979), 3–14; V. Pace, 'Sculpture italienne en Terre Sainte ou sculpture des croisés en Italie? A propos d'un livre récent', *Cahiers de Civilisation médiévale*, 27 (1984), 251–7; M. Burgoyne and J. Folda, review of Buschhausen, *Die süditalienische Bauplastik*, in *The Art Bulletin*, 63.2 (1981), 321–4; Folda, *Art of the Crusaders*, pp. 441–56.

YĀLU (CHASTEL ARNOUL/ARNOLD)

The third Templar castle known to have existed on the Jerusalem to Jaffa road, and the next to be reached after Laṭrūn, was *Chastel Arnoul*, or *Arnold*. Although identified at various times with Khirbat al-Burayj (Palestine grid ref. 1584.1409)[35] and al-Burj (Qal'at Ṭanṭūra, grid ref. 1520.1455),[36] this castle is now more certainly associated with the remains of a substantial structure underlying the ruins of the Arab village of Yālu, which cover a low spur overlooking to the north the valley of the Ayalon (Wādi Muṣrāra).[37] Indeed, the name *Arnoul* may possibly be derived from the late Roman *Ailon* (or Arabic *Yālu*), rather than from a Frankish personal name, as the Latin form, *Arnaldi* (or *Arnulfi*), seems to imply. Be that as it may, the castle is first mentioned, though not of course in Templar hands, in October 1106, when the Egyptians from Ascalon raided Ramla and, having failed to take that city, turned their attention to a castle which Albert of Aachen calls *castellum Arnulfi*.[38] This, according to Albert, was a royal castle, built by Baldwin I in the mountains on the Jerusalem road as a point of defence for the surrounding area. After a siege of two days its commander, Geoffrey, castellan of the Tower of David, made a deal with the Muslims who, while sparing his life, proceeded to slaughter the other inhabitants and to throw down the newly constructed defences.[39]

The castle was rebuilt in 1132–3 by Patriarch Warmund and the people of Jerusalem, during the absence of King Fulk in Antioch. William of Tyre tells us that they

> assembled in full strength at a place near the ancient *Nobe* [Nob], which today is generally called *Beitenuble* [Bayt Nūbā]. There, on the slope of the hill at the

---

[35] F. de Saulcy, *Voyage en Terre Sainte*, 2 vols (Paris, 1865), 1, p. 87; and E. Rey, *Les Colonies franques de Syrie aux XIIe et XIIIe siècles* (Paris, 1883), p. 381.

[36] L.H. Vincent and F.M. Abel, *Emmaüs, sa basilique et son histoire* (Paris, 1932), pp. 367–9; G. Beyer, 'Das Gebiet der Kreuzfahrerherrschaft Caesarea in Palästina', *Zeitschrift des Deutschen Palästina-Vereins* (hereafter *ZDPV*), 59 (1936), 1–91 (at 47); *idem*, 'Die Kreuzfahrergebiete von Jerusalem und St Abraham', *ZDPV*, 65 (1942), 165–211 (at 178); *idem*, 'Die Kreuzfahrergebiete Süd-westpalästinas', *ZDPV*, 68 (1951), 148–281 (at 252); C.N. Johns, *Palestine of the Crusaders: A Map of the Country on Scale 1:350,000 with Historical Introduction & Gazetteer*, Survey of Palestine (Jaffa, 1937), p. 26; E. Hoade, *Guide to the Holy Land*, 9th edn (Jerusalem, 1978), p. 538.

[37] This identification was suggested by E. Robinson, *Biblical Researches in Palestine, Mount Sinai and Arabia Petraea*, 3 vols (London, 1841), 3, p. 63; cf. P. Deschamps, *Les châteaux des croisés en Terre-Sainte*, 2, *La défense du royaume de Jérusalem*, text + album, Bibliothèque archéologique et historique, 34 (Paris, 1939), pp. 9–10, 20; F.M. Abel, *Géographie de la Palestine*, 2 vols, 3rd edn (Paris, 1967), 2, pp. 240–1; M. Benvenisti, *The Crusaders in the Holy Land* (Jerusalem, 1970), pp. 281–2, 314–16; Fischer, Isaac and Roll, pp. 251–3.

[38] Prawer, *Histoire*, 1, pp. 277 note 36, 328 note 20, distinguishes between *castellum Arnoldi* (*Château Arnold*), which he identifies as Yālu, and *castellum Arnulfi* (*Château Arnoul*), which he equates with Qastal (grid ref. 1637.1336). Fischer, Isaac and Roll, p. 196, on the other hand, equate *castellum Arnulfi* with Laṭrūn. It seems more logical to assume that both names applied to Yālu.

[39] Albert of Aachen [Albertus Aquensis], *Liber Christianae Expeditionis* in *RHC Occid*, 4, X.10–14 (pp. 637–8); Deschamps, *Châteaux*, 2, p. 9 note 1; S. Runciman, *A History of the Crusades*, 3 vols (Cambridge, 1951–4), 2, pp. 90–1.

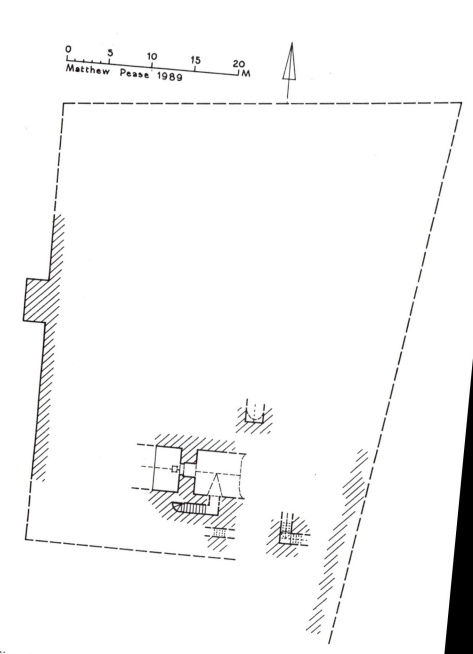

Figure 9.9 *Yālu: plan of the visible remains of the castle*

Figure 9.10   Yālu: internal doorway in the now-buried southern part of the castle

Figure 9.11   Yālu: west wall and projecting tower

entrance to the plain, on the road leading to Lydda and from there to the sea, they built a fortress of solid masonry to ensure the safety of the pilgrims passing along that route. In the narrow mountain pass, among defiles impossible to avoid, pilgrims were exposed to great danger. Here the people of Ascalon were accustomed to fall upon them suddenly. The work, when successfully accomplished, was called *Castellum Arnaldi*. Thus, by the grace of God and also because of this fortress, the road became much safer and the journey of pilgrims to and from Jerusalem was rendered less perilous.[40]

William of Tyre does not say to whom the castle-guard was entrusted when the fortress was completed. It seems, however, that the place lay in the diocese of Jerusalem, and therefore presumably in the royal domain, for in November 1136 the canons of the Holy Sepulchre granted the tithes of *castellum Arnaldi* to the bishop of Lydda along with those of the neighbouring Hospitaller village of *Bulbul*, in return for the bishop's confirmation of their possession of four villages in his diocese.[41]

Despite claims that *Castellum Arnaldi* was in Templar hands by the 1150s,[42] there is no definite evidence of such until February 1179, when the Hospitallers renounced some unspecified claims that they had made on certain Templar properties, including *Castellum Arnaldi*, Gaza and 'Ammān.[43]

The castle surrendered to Saladin soon after the battle of Ḥaṭṭīn in July 1187,[44] and was among those that al-'Ādil is supposed to have ordered to be destroyed in September 1191.[45] Richard I camped next to *castellum Arnaldi* on 10 June 1192, while *en route* between Laṭrūn and Bayt Nūbā;[46] and it is mentioned again when the Jerusalem pilgrims passed through it in September 1192.[47]

Little of this castle now survives above ground, though it is clear that much remains to be revealed by excavation (Figure 9.9). It appears to have had a roughly quadrangular plan (some 50 m east–west by 40 m north–south), and to have sat astride the neck of a spur. The main concentration of surviving structures is on the uphill side, to the south (Figure 9.10). This was also probably where the main gate lay, though its precise location is uncertain. On

---

[40] WT, XIV.8 (p. 640); Babcock and Krey, 2, p. 58.

[41] *Cartulaire du Saint-Sépulcre*, no. 61 (pp. 153–5); *RRH*, no. 165 (p. 41). The grant was confirmed in 1155, 1160 and 1164: *Cartulaire du Saint-Sépulcre*, no. 42 (1155) (pp. 115–19); no. 45 (1160) (pp. 123–7); no. 135 (1164) (pp. 261–6); *RRH*, no. 309 (1155) (p. 79); no. 352 (1160) (p. 91); no. 400 (1164) (p. 105).

[42] Benvenisti, p. 316; Barber, p. 88.

[43] *CH*, 1, no. 558 (pp. 378–9); J. Delaville le Roulx, *Documents concernant les Templiers* (Paris, 1882), no. 7 (p. 19); *RRH*, no. 572 (p. 152).

[44] Ralph of Diss, 2, p. 56; *Gesta Regis Henrici II*, 2, p. 23; cf. *de Expugnatione Terrae Sanctae Libellus*, ed. J. Stevenson, RS, 66 (London, 1875), pp. 209–62 (at pp. 229–30).

[45] *Itinerarium Regis Ricardi*, IV.23 (p. 280) (*Castrum Ernaldi*); Ambroise, *L'Estoire*, line 9810 (*Chastel Ernald*); Prawer, *Histoire*, 2, p. 83.

[46] *Itinerarium Regis Ricardi*, V.49 (pp. 368–9); Prawer, *Histoire*, 2, p. 94 note 32.

[47] *Itinerarium Regis Ricardi*, VI.33 (p. 435).

the west side there is a rectangular tower, 5 m wide, which projects 2.5 m (Figure 9.11).[48]

CONCLUSION

The fact that all three known Templar castles between Jaffa and Jerusalem were sited directly on the main road linking the two places would seem to suggest that protection of the road and those travelling on it was one of the principal concerns of their builders. Indeed, this purpose is specifically mentioned by William of Tyre in his description of the building of Yālu in 1132–3. In two and possibly all three cases, of course, the original builders had not been the Templars; and the chronology of their construction also casts doubt on the idea that they were planned as a system from the start. None the less, it seems reasonable to assume that the Order's acquisition of these three strong points was influenced by the consideration that protection of travellers was regarded as one of its primary duties.

Before the building of the railway in the late nineteenth century, it was barely possible to reach Jerusalem from Jaffa in a day. It is not impossible, therefore, that Laṭrūn, which lay roughly midway and was the largest of the three castles, would also have been associated with a road station, much as *le Destroit* south of Haifa and *Maldoim* on the Jericho road appear to have been.[49] As such it would also have been well placed to serve pilgrims travelling from or to Acre, which replaced Jaffa as the main point of disembarkation for Jerusalem in the early decades of the twelfth century.

Accounts of these castles' construction, however, indicate that their siting was also conditioned by broader strategic considerations, in particular the protection of central Palestine and Jerusalem itself against Egyptian raiding from Ascalon. Although Yālu is not recorded as a Templar possession until 1179, we first hear of its castle when it was raided by the Ascalonites in 1106; and it was specifically to protect travellers against raids from Ascalon that the castle was rebuilt in 1132–3. Laṭrūn was also built, between 1137 and 1141, to confront Ascalon. Indeed, it should be added to that group of castles, including Bayt Jibrīn (Beth Gibelin, 1136), Yibnā (Ibelin, 1141), Blanchegarde (Tall al-Ṣāfī, 1142) and Gaza (1150), that were constructed during the reign of King Fulk to contain Ascalonite raiding and serve as bases for colonization and for offensive action against the Muslim city.[50] The part played by the military

---

[48] Benvenisti, pp. 281–2, 314–16, photograph; D. Pringle, 'Survey of castles in the Crusader Kingdom of Jerusalem: preliminary report', *Levant*, 23 (1991), 87–91 (at 90–91); *idem*, *Secular Buildings*, no. 231 (pp. 108–9), fig. 61, pl. CVIII.

[49] Pringle, 'Templar Castles', p. 166.

[50] See M. Hoch, 'The Crusaders' Strategy against Fatimid Ascalon and the "Ascalon Project" of the Second Crusade', in *The Second Crusade and the Cistercians* ed. M. Gervers (New York, 1992), pp. 119–28; R.C. Smail, *Crusading Warfare (1097–1193)*, Cambridge Studies in Medieval Life and Thought, new ser., 3 (Cambridge, 1956), pp. 209–13; Hiestand, 'Un centre intellectuel', 31–2.

orders in this enterprise is illustrated by the granting of Bayt Jibrīn to the Hospitallers and of Gaza to the Templars.[51]

Unfortunately, we know too little of the Templars' other possessions between Jaffa and Jerusalem to assess what local administrative functions their castles in the area may also have served. The Hospitallers, for example, are known to have used Bayt Jibrīn as a centre for colonization; and a civilian settlement was already established outside the castle before the fall of Ascalon.[52] The same Order also had estate centres between Laṭrūn and Jerusalem at Belmont Castle (Ṣūba)[53] and at *Emmaus* (probably 'Amwās near Laṭrūn, though some prefer to identify it as Abū Ghawsh, which was also theirs).[54] One may suspect that the maintenance of a castle such as Laṭrūn would have required control of more than just the domain lands immediately surrounding it, but lack of documentation makes it impossible to tell what estates may have depended on it, and excavations have yet to shed light on the economic activities that may have been carried on within the castle's precincts.

---

[51] WT, XIV.22 (pp. 659–61) (Bayt Jibrīn); XVII.12 (pp. 775–7); XX.20 (pp. 937–9) (Gaza); Usāmah Ibn Munqidh, *An Arab-Syrian Gentleman and Warrior in the Period of the Crusades*, tr. P.K. Hitti, Columbia University Records of Civilization, Sources and Studies (New York, 1929), pp. 34–5.

[52] J. Prawer, *Crusader Institutions* (Oxford, 1980), pp. 119–26; cf. Pringle, *Churches*, 1, pp. 95–101.

[53] R.P. Harper and D. Pringle, 'Belmont Castle: a Historical Notice and Preliminary Report of Excavations in 1986', *Levant*, 20 (1988), 101–18.

[54] Pringle, *Churches*, 1, pp. 7–17, 52–9.

10

Before William of Tyre: European Reports on the Military Orders' Deeds in the East, 1150–1185

Helen Nicholson

William of Tyre's history of the kingdom of Jerusalem[1] has dominated our research into the military orders in the Holy Land for the period between the end of the Second Crusade and William's own death (1150–1185), and in general historians have been inclined to accept what William says about the Templars' and Hospitallers' deeds as being essentially the truth. Although it is recognized that he was prejudiced against these Orders for various reasons, it is assumed that if we subtract the exaggeration we arrive at a reasonable picture. There have been a number of studies of William's work in recent years which should have made us more cautious.[2] Yet William continues to dominate research because of his quality as an historian and the perceived lack of other narrative sources to compare to his version of events.

This tendency has been reinforced by medieval practice. After William of Tyre's history became well known in Europe, from 1190 onwards, Europeans writing about the Holy Land in the twelfth century usually relied on William or one of the French adaptations of his work for their information. So the fact that there were other points of view has been overlooked.

The other points of view are represented by some Muslim sources and a few twelfth-century European sources which were written before William's work was known in the West and so were not influenced by him. It is these European sources which are independent of William of Tyre that I want to consider. Comparing William of Tyre's account of the military orders to these sources

---

[1] The most recent edition is *Willelmi Tyrensis Archepiscopi Chronicon*, ed. R.B.C. Huygens, 2 vols, Corpus Christianorum, Continuatio Mediaevalis 63, 63A (Turnhout, 1986) (hereafter WT).

[2] For instance, P.W. Edbury and J.G. Rowe, *William of Tyre: Historian of the Latin East* (Cambridge, 1988); D. Vessey, 'William of Tyre and the Art of Historiography', *Medieval studies*, 35 (1973), 433–55.

not only clarifies the Orders' activities in the East but may also give us a clearer picture of how William worked and of his sources. I have referred in passing to these independent European sources in my book on images of the military orders,[3] but because they remain underused by historians of the military orders I think it is worthwhile setting them out in more detail.

I shall not include Walter Map among my independent European sources because, although he wrote before William of Tyre's work became well known in the West, I am not convinced that he was uninfluenced by William. His derogatory stories about the Templars and Nāṣir al-Dīn, and the Templars and the Assassins,[4] are very similar to William's stories and he is the only writer of the period apart from William who includes them in his work. He and William of Tyre were at the Third Lateran Council of 1179, where they both opposed the privileges of the regular clergy. I think it very likely that Walter Map acquired his stories about the Templars from William of Tyre or his fellow delegates at the Council.

I shall examine four incidents recounted by William of Tyre and consider what his contemporaries in Europe had to say about these incidents. The first of these incidents is the Templars' attempt to capture Ascalon in 1153.

William of Tyre's account of the 1153 siege of Ascalon is very well known.[5] In brief, when the wall of the city was breached, the Master of the Temple and forty of his brothers went forward and stood in the breach. They would not allow anyone else to enter, so that the Templars could claim all the booty from the city. The Muslims killed all the Templars, and hung their headless bodies from the walls; so the city was not taken, because of the Templars' greed. However, the Christians recovered, launched another attack and took the city.

Most contemporary European writers who mentioned the capture of Ascalon referred only briefly to the siege.[6] However, a handful of writers had more information. In the monastery of Anchin, near Douai, a chronicler wrote a continuation of Sigebert of Gembloux's chronicle, taking it to 1155, which included a detailed account of the capture of Ascalon. After describing how the wall was breached, it went on to say that the leader of the Templars broke into the city with his force and reached the city square, where they made a stand. However, the streets were narrow, the walls high, and they were

---

[3] H. Nicholson, *Templars, Hospitallers and Teutonic Knights: Images of the Military Orders, 1128–1291* (Leicester, 1993), pp. 43–4, 82–3, 160 notes 10, 16–22.

[4] Walter Map, *De Nugis Curialium*, ed. M.R. James, C.N.L. Brooke and R.A.B. Mynors (Oxford, 1983), pp. 62–6.

[5] WT, XVII.27 (2, pp. 798–9).

[6] 'Annales Ottenburani Isingrine maiores', ed. G.H. Pertz, *MGH SS*, 17, p. 313; 'Annales S. Jacobi Leodienses', ed. G.H. Pertz, *MGH SS*, 16, p. 641; Lambert Wattrelos, 'Annales Cameracenses', ed. G.H. Pertz, *MGH SS*, 16, p. 529; 'Annales Colonienses Maximi', ed. K. Pertz, *MGH SS*, 17, p. 765; 'Ex Libris de vita et miraculis Sancti Bernardi Clarevallensis abbas', ed. G. Waitz, *MGH SS*, 26, p. 112.

surrounded and crushed by the enemy. Their beheaded bodies were hung from the city walls. Three days later the Christians made another attack and captured the city.[7]

This account was copied by a chronicler at Affligem, in the duchy of Brabant,[8] who adds: 'A man who was present, and remained in the army throughout the siege, narrated all he knew to us.' So this is presented as a first-hand account, probably from a pilgrim from the West who joined the siege.

In short, we have an account which is overall very similar to William's, but with the added detail that the Templars reached the middle of the city before being surrounded and cut to pieces. It appears that as on other occasions (such as during the siege of Acre in the Third Crusade, on 4 October 1189)[9] the Templars proceeded too far ahead of the main body of the army and were cut off by the enemy.

We are left to ask why the rest of the Christian army did not follow them. It is possible that in the turmoil of battle the other leaders did not realize that the Templars had broken into the city until it was too late to go to their assistance. Was William's version of events based on accounts by Palestinian nobles who were present at the siege and wished to exonerate themselves from blame for not following the Templars into the city? William was not an eyewitness to the siege of Ascalon; he was reliant on other people's memories.

There is another account of the siege of Ascalon which was noted by Paul Riant and by F. Lundgreen:[10] the annals of Egmont, in Frisia.[11] This is so detailed that Riant suggested it was based on an eyewitness account given to the annalist by Scandinavian pilgrims who had been brought by King Baldwin III from Acre to assist in the siege. The Egmont annalist agrees with William in portraying the Templars as greedy, but blames the length of the siege on treachery by the Palestinian nobles. The Templars' greed is demonstrated here by their being unwilling to attack Ascalon because they used to make a large profit from raiding the caravans which came from Egypt every six weeks to relieve the garrison. However, when the breach was made in the wall many young men (not Templars) went in to attack the city, but were ambushed and killed. The Templars blazed with anger and launched a dawn attack on the city through the breach and, after killing many of the enemy, apparently withdrew. The capture of the city came a considerable time later, after the

---

[7] 'Sigebert Auctarium Aquicinense', ed. D.L.C. Bethmann, *MGH SS*, 6, p. 396.

[8] Ibid., p. 401.

[9] *Das Itinerarium Peregrinorum: eine zeitgenössische englishe Chronik zum dritten Kreuzzug in ursprunglicher Gestalt*, ed. H.E. Mayer, *Monumenta Germaniae Historica Schriften*, 18 (Stuttgart, 1962), p. 313.

[10] P. Riant, *Expéditions et Pèlerinages des Scandinaves en Terre Sainte au Temps des croisades* (Paris, 1865), p. 258; F. Lundgreen, *Wilhelm von Tyrus und der Templerorden*, Historische Studien Veröffentlicht von E. Ebering, Heft 97 (Berlin, 1911), pp. 89–93.

[11] 'Annales Egmundani', ed. G. Pertz, *MGH SS*, 16, pp. 458–9; *Fontes Egmundenses*, ed. O. Oppermann (Utrecht 1933), p. 161.

unmasking of the treachery of some of the Palestinian nobles, and was unrelated to the breach in the wall.

This is a difficult account, quite different from the rest, although it contains echoes of the events described by the Anchin and Affligem annals. It is not entirely pro-Templar, but is also hostile to the Palestinian Frankish nobility. The Egmont annalist seems to have been writing quite some time after the event, as the siege is dated to 1159. This may in fact be a romanticized, later version of events, reflecting more the western European distrust of the Palestinian Franks than what actually happened.

Nevertheless, even discounting the Egmont annals, the western European accounts of the Templars' attack on the breach in the wall at the siege of Ascalon in 1153 give us a more rounded and, I would suggest, a more probable picture of what occurred. The Anchin and Affligem chronicles appear to be based directly on recent eyewitness accounts, whereas William of Tyre was relying on more distant memories of events. The probable course of events was that the Templars were the first into the breach and stormed into the city with characteristic courage and enthusiasm but became separated from the main body of the Christian army, who perhaps did not immediately realize that they had broken into the city, or who were rather slow in following them. The Templars were massacred and the Muslims hung their headless bodies from the walls. Certain Palestinian commanders came under criticism for failing to follow the Templars into the breach, and when William of Tyre came to write his history they or their descendants were anxious to defend their reputation by insisting that the Templars had prevented them from following them in.

My second example is the Hospitallers' dispute with the patriarch of Jerusalem.[12] William of Tyre describes how the Hospitallers and Patriarch Fulcher of Jerusalem came into conflict over the Hospitallers' exemptions from the patriarch's authority, granted to them by the pope. The patriarch travelled to the West in the hope of having the exemptions revoked, but the Hospitallers bribed the pope to refuse the patriarch's request.

These events went more or less without comment from Western chroniclers. However, the dispute was reported by Gerhoh, provost of Reichersberg, writing in 1160–2 in his *De investigatione Antichristi* and *De quarta vigilia noctis*.[13] His account of the case is quite similar to William's, agreeing that the Hospitallers bribed Pope Hadrian; but he does point out that the patriarch was also to blame in exacerbating the dispute because he was 'too zealous in pressing his own case' ('*nimius causa propria exactor exstitit*').

The third incident to consider is William's story of the Templars and Nāṣir al-Dīn.[14] William places this immediately after his chapters dealing with the

[12] WT, XVIII.3, XVIII.6–8 (2, pp. 812–4, 817–21).

[13] Ed. E. Sackur, *MGH Libelli de Lite Imperatorum et Pontificum*, 3 (Hanover, 1897), pp. 378–9, 391; p. 510.

[14] WT, XVIII.9 (2, pp. 822–3).

Hospitallers' dispute with the patriarch of Jerusalem; it is told more in sorrow than in anger. The Templars killed 'Habeis' ('Abbās) and captured his son, 'Noseradin', a very bold man, the most outstanding warrior in Egypt, and held him prisoner for many days. He was eager to become a Christian and had begun to learn the rudiments of the Christian faith, but the Templars then sold him back to the Egyptians, who were demanding his death, for 60,000 gold coins. He returned shamefully to Egypt where he was torn to pieces.

A different version of this story was known in Europe. Another continuation of Sigebert of Gembloux's chronicle, written by a Premonstratensian monk from the diocese of Reims or Laon, states that in 1154: 'The king of Babylonia [Egypt] was killed by a certain man from his own provinces. While this man was fleeing with an endless load of treasure, he was killed by the Knights of the Temple. His son was captured and all that opulence and unequalled excess fell to them'.[15] The editor suggested that this was written in around 1155, soon after the event.

No other account of the Order's good fortune in capturing Nāṣir appears to have survived from this period. However, it seems likely that someone else did record it, because Guy of Bazoches included another account in his chronicle, written in the 1190s. Guy's chronicle drew extensively on William of Tyre's work, but surprisingly he did not follow William's account of this incident. He recorded that just before the death of Baldwin III of Jerusalem (1163) the caliph of Egypt was killed by his procurator, who fled and was killed when the Christians came on him. His son 'Nosseradin' and many men and treasures were captured. He fell by lot to the brothers of the Knights Templar, who then handed him over to his enemies to be punished.[16] Although the date is wrong, this is clearly the same incident.

Did this version of events come from a Templar newsletter to the West, announcing their success against the Muslims? It is certainly tempting to see this as the Templars' side of the story. There is no mention here of Nāṣir considering conversion to Christianity. Interestingly enough, the Muslim sources do not mention Nāṣir's conversion either, although they regard him as a murderer and traitor;[17] so it remains uncertain whether Nāṣir did convert. Perhaps the story that he had converted arose from the fact that the Egyptians hung his dead body on a cross at the city gate, a standard punishment for traitors.

---

[15] 'Continuatio Praemonstratensis', ed. D.L. Bethmann, *MGH SS*, 6, pp. 455–6.

[16] Guy of Bazoches, 'Cronosgraphia,' BN, lat. 4998, fol. 63r. I am indebted to Professor B. Kedar for supplying me with a copy of Guy's manuscript. Guy's account is also quoted by Aubrey des Trois Fontaines, ed. P. Scheffer-Boichorst, *MGH SS*, 23, p. 846.

[17] Isma'īl Abu'l-Fidā, *al-Mukhtaṣar fī akhbār al-bashar*, in 'Resumé de l'histoire des Croisades tiré des annales d'Abu'l-Feda', *RHC Or*, 1, pp. 30–1; Ibn al-Athīr, *al-Kāmil Fī'l-tarīkh*, in 'Extrait du Kamel-Altevarykh,' *RHC Or*, 1, p. 495.

So William's version of this incident seems to be distorted. I do not believe he distorted it himself; I think his sources were distorted and perhaps little better than hearsay. He included it as an illustration of how little the Templars cared for winning souls for Christ, and how much for money. However, he certainly did not invent it; it is based on a true incident.

My fourth example is William's account of King Amalric's attack on Egypt in 1168.[18] According to William of Tyre, the Master of the Hospital advised King Amalric to break his truce with Egypt and launch an invasion. The Master of the Temple disagreed. William approved of the Templars' stand, although he was inclined to think that the Order opposed the invasion only because the Hospitallers supported it.

There is one Western account of this campaign, in Lambert of Wattrelos's *Annals of Cambrai*,[19] which Jonathan Riley-Smith has noted in his book *The Knights of St John*.[20] Lambert states that he had heard about the events in the East from 'true-speaking men'. He describes the Master of the Hospital, Gilbert of Assailly, leading his own troops and capturing the castle of Barbastra, or Bilbais. The king of Jerusalem and the Master of the Temple also each led separate contingents.

This is an invaluable account as it is the earliest direct description we have of a Master of the Hospital as a military commander, and it reinforces William of Tyre's evidence of the Hospital's military commitments under Master Gilbert of Assailly. However, it also suggests that William has been slightly misleading; William implies that the Templars did not accompany the king to Egypt, illustrating their independence of royal authority. Yet Lambert informs us that they led their own contingent on the campaign. Whom are we to believe? As Lambert agrees with William on the Hospital as a military organization, it is possible that he is right about the Templars too. He has no axe to grind, whereas William has. Perhaps the Templars protested about the breaking of the truce, yet had no choice but to accompany the king.

In these instances I have described, we have independent European corroboration that the events happened much as William of Tyre states, although for the first three instances William was recording events at a greater distance, perhaps at third- or fourth-hand, and much later than the European source. So although William of Tyre is in fact not the best source as far as our view of the Templars is concerned for events at Ascalon and the capture of Nāṣir al-Dīn, there is no doubt that each event occurred in some form. I suggest that the differences between the European sources and William's account are due partly to the different sources used by each, but also to their different purposes

---

[18] WT, XX.5 (2, pp. 917–8).

[19] Lambert of Wattrelos, 'Annales Cameracenses', pp. 547–8.

[20] J. Riley-Smith, *The Knights of St John in Jerusalem and Cyprus, c. 1050–1310* (London, 1967), p. 72 note 2; p. 61 note 3.

in writing. William had a 'message' to convey to his readers in the East and later in the West, which led him to select some versions of events and reject others; part of this 'message' was that the Templars and Hospitallers were damaging the kingdom of Jerusalem, not helping it, so those who wanted to help the kingdom should not give money to these Orders.[21] The European sources, on the other hand, had no such agenda.

For the Hospitallers' dispute with the patriarch of Jerusalem and the invasion of Egypt, William of Tyre is the best source but in each case the European source provides a welcome second opinion and allows us to amend his picture slightly.

This leaves the question of why no independent European source mentioned other events of King Amalric's reign involving the Templars, such as the case of the Templars' murder of the Assassins' envoy, or King Amalric's hanging of twelve Templars who surrendered a fortress without waiting for relief.[22] Perhaps to those outside the Holy Land these incidents seemed insignificant. Or perhaps no one informed them, for if their main sources for events in the East were newsletters and appeals for aid from the Templars, then the Templars would hardly report these incidents.

These differences in agenda and sources are highlighted by a few Templar achievements which were recorded by European writers but not mentioned by William of Tyre. A letter of 13 November 1157 from Pope Hadrian IV to Archbishop Samson of Reims and his suffragans described a recent defeat near Banyas but concluded by describing two victories, including a successful Templar attack on a Muslim wedding party.[23] Presumably this letter was based on a newsletter from the East which had detailed the defeat but added news of victories to show that God was still helping the Christians. Neither William nor any other chronicler mentioned the Templars' victory, however, probably considering that it was too mundane to prove anything. William of Tyre's version of the battle of Montgisard in 1177 leaves the reader with the clear impression that the king was in charge, while no other single leader played an outstanding role. On the other hand, the account of the battle given by Ralph of Diss, dean of London, in his *Ymagines Historiarum*, concentrates on a charge by the Templars under their Master Odo of St Amand, which smashed the Muslim lines and won a victory for the Christians. William's version of events seems to be designed to show that despite his illness Baldwin IV was a vigorous and capable leader, and that God still supported the Christian forces of the kingdom of Jerusalem in battle.[24] Ralph of Diss had no such

---

[21] On Williams's 'message' see Edbury and Rowe, pp. 170–3; and also R.H.C. Davis, 'William of Tyre', in *Relations between East and West in the Middle Ages*, ed. D. Baker (Edinburgh, 1987), pp. 64–76.

[22] WT, XX.30 (2, pp. 954–5); XIX.11 (2, p. 879).

[23] Pope Hadrian IV, 'Lettres', in *RHGF*, 15, p. 682.

[24] WT, XXI.21 (22)–23 (24) (pp. 990–4); Ralph of Diss, *Opera Historica*, ed. W. Stubbs, 2 vols, RS, 68 (London, 1876), 1, p. 423; Edbury and Rowe, p. 77 and note 74.

agenda. His description of the Templars' charge may have been drawn from a pilgrim's account of the battle, or a Templar newsletter to the West.

None of the individual European sources I have described tells us much about the military orders in the Holy Land between 1150 and 1185. They give only brief glimpses of material which was passing from the East to the West, either carried by pilgrims to the Holy Land or by newsletters and appeals for aid. Most of this material is completely lost, because no one in the West considered it worth recording. What survives enables us to gain a somewhat broader picture of the Templars and Hospitallers in the Holy Land than William's history allows. And because it does not share William's disillusionment with these Orders, it gives us a better picture not only of the military orders but also of William's history itself.

11

Horses and Crossbows: Two Important Warfare Advantages of the Teutonic Order in Prussia

Sven Ekdahl

The thirteenth-century conquest of Livonia and Prussia by the Order of the Swordbrothers and its successor, the Teutonic Knights, would not have been possible if the numerically weaker knights and crusaders had not enjoyed certain advantages over the heathen peoples.[1] These included several innovations in military techniques as well as experience gained by Christians in the Holy Land and other theatres of war. One such innovation was the erection of permanent fortresses in stone or brick: the manufacture of bricks and mortar was unknown in the eastern Baltic until then.[2] Another innovation was the introduction of the crossbow, which, as a long-range weapon, proved to be superior to the spears and bows of the heathens.[3] The combination of these two developments made it possible for the Order's garrisons to withstand long sieges, provided they had sufficient supplies of food, weapons and crossbow bolts. Conquered territories were secured systematically with fortresses which were sited strategically in places suited to commerce and communications, most often along major river routes. These, together with the fortified larger towns, composed the backbone of the new military states in east-central Europe.[4]

---

[1] For literature about the conquest of Livonia and Prussia, see the references in the contributions concerning the Teutonic Order in *MO*, 1, pp. 223–79.

[2] S. Ekdahl, 'Die Rolle der Ritterorden bei der Christianisierung der Liven und Letten', in *Gli inizi del cristianesimo in Livonia-Lettonia. Atti del colloquio internazionale di storia ecclesiastica in occasione dell'VIII centenario della chiesa in Livonia (1186–1986)*, ed. M. Maccarrone, Pontificio comitato di scienze storiche, Atti e documenti, 1 (Vatican City, 1989), pp. 203–43 (at pp. 224–8).

[3] Ibid., pp. 225–6.

[4] F. Benninghoven, 'Die Burgen als Grundpfeiler des spätmittelalterlichen Wehrwesens im preussisch-livländischen Deutschordensstaat', in *Die Burgen im deutschen Sprachraum. Ihre rechts- und verfassungsgeschichtliche Bedeutung*, ed. H. Patze, 1, Vorträge und Forschungen, 19 (Sigmaringen, 1976), pp. 565–601. See also F. Borchert, *Burgenland Preussen. Die Wehrbauten des Deutschen Ordens und ihre Geschichte* (Munich and Vienna, 1987).

From *The Military Orders. Volume 2. Welfare and Warfare*. ed. Helen Nicholson. Copyright © 1998 by Helen Nicholson. Published by Ashgate Publishing Ltd, Gower House, Croft Road, Aldershot, Hampshire, GU11 3HR, Great Britain.

During the fourteenth century, particularly in Prussia, there were also fortifications of the traditional style which, like the heathen garrisons, were built
of timber and earth, in addition to the new stone and/or brick fortresses.[5] The
former were often constructed within a few weeks in the summer during
expeditions into enemy territory.[6]

The fortresses served to secure those territories which were already under
the control of the Order. However, it was also important that new military
operations could be carried out from them. With this, the third great innovation
in the Order's military technique came into its own: the heavy cavalry, against
which the heathen forces were in most cases inferior. Only when these
armoured cavalrymen could not use their strength to full advantage, as when
they were fighting in boggy terrain or with poor visibility, was it possible for
the light cavalry and infantry of the local population to defend themselves
successfully and win victories. An example of this was the important victory
of the Lithuanians and Semigallians over the Swordbrothers at Saule in 1236.[7]
Christian losses on the moor at Saule were so high that the Order of the
Swordbrothers was unable to recover and a year later it was amalgamated
with the Teutonic Order by a papal bull. Under normal conditions the armoured
cavalry, equipped with lances, spears and swords, was able to crush everything
in its path in one powerful attack. Their armour alone generally protected them
from the impact of spears and arrows; however, if his horse fell, the heavily
armed rider was very vulnerable because of his immobility. His life depended
on the quality and battle worthiness of his war-horse, his *destrier* (*dextrarius*).

These are not the only examples of military innovation. We should also
mention the heavy siege weapons, such as ballistas, catapults and trebuchets
(*Bliden*), battering rams (*Tümmlern*) and siege towers (*Ebenhöhen*), which were
also introduced by the Knights.[8] In the second half of the fourteenth century,
when the Teutonic Order was at war with the pagan Lithuanians, firearms were
added to the Christian arsenal. At first they were used mainly as siege guns,
firing large arrows, spears or stone shot.[9] However, in all these cases the

---

[5] M. Arszyński, 'Die Deutschordensburg als Wehrbau und ihre Rolle im Wehrsystem des
Ordensstaates Preussen', in *Ordines Militares. Colloquia Torunensia Historica*, ed. Z.H. Nowak
(Toruń, 1983–present), 6: *Das Kriegswesen der Ritterorden im Mittelalter* (1991), pp. 89–123. Cf. G.
Zabiela, *Lietuvos medinės pilys* (Vilnius, 1995); English summary 'Wooden Castles in Lithuania',
ibid., pp. 290–8.

[6] W. Paravicini, *Die Preussenreisen des europäischen Adels*, 1–2. Beihefte der Francia, 17.1–2
(Sigmaringen, 1989–95) (at 2, pp. 59–64).

[7] F. Benninghoven, *Der Orden der Schwertbrüder, Fratres Milicie Christi de Livonia*, Ostmit-
teleuropa in Vergangenheit und Gegenwart, 9 (Cologne and Graz, 1965), pp. 327–47; E. Gudavičius,
Kryžiaus karai Pabaltijyje ir Lietuva XIII amžiuje (Vilnius, 1989), pp. 45–6, 66; W.L. Urban, *The Baltic
Crusade*, 2nd edn (Chicago, 1994), pp. 184–7.

[8] Ekdahl, 'Die Rolle der Ritterorden', p. 227. For the use of such weapons see, for instance,
Wigand of Marburg's description of the siege of Kaunas in Lithuania in 1362: *SRP*, 2, p. 532.

[9] An analysis of the earliest mentions of firearms in the eastern Baltic is given by A. Mäesalu,
'Otepää püss ongi maailma vanimaid käsitulirelvi', *Kleio. Ajaloo ajakiri*, 4 (1996), 3–11 (at pp. 9–10).

element of surprise was short-lived. Innovations are notorious for the speed with which they spread and it was always only a question of time before the opponent became familiar with them and thus was able to develop and use them. In the first half of the fourteenth century stone or brick fortresses were increasingly replacing wood and earth constructions in Lithuania.[10] Moreover, Prussian or Lithuanian building techniques even began to be adopted partially within the territories of the Order.[11] Heavy siege weapons were known to the Lithuanians by this time. The first reliable mention of the use of firearms (*Lotbüchsen*) by the Teutonic Order occurs in a chronicle describing a siege in 1362.[12] Two decades later bombards were used by the Lithuanians against the fortresses of the Order.[13] In addition, the possession of large war-horses did not remain a long-term privilege of the Christians, since capture or purchase made it possible for the heathens to overcome this disadvantage to some extent.[14]

For the Teutonic Order it was always a battle against time to maintain its advantage by continual improvements in technique, hardware and horsepower. Comparisons with development in our age of modern technology and communication come to mind. In any case the better position in this medieval competition was held by the Teutonic Knights who, one may say, because of their money and excellent organization in the areas mentioned above, made a first-rate showing. That the Order proved in the end unable to survive in eastern Europe depended on quite different factors.

Here we need to take a closer look at two of the above-mentioned military advantages: the horse and the crossbow. A good illustration of these developments comes from the Prussian section of the Order, for which particularly detailed sources survive.[15] In addition to charters and chronicles there are also, from the last third of the fourteenth century, increasing amounts

---

[10] J. Jurginis, 'Entwicklung der Steinbauten in Litauen im 14.–15. Jahrhundert', in *Kultur und Politik im Ostseeraum und im Norden 1350–1450*, ed. S. Ekdahl, Acta Visbyensia, 4 (Visby, 1973), pp. 223–37. The last wooden castles vanished in the fourth decade of the fourteenth century, when they could no longer maintain a more significant defensive role. See Zabiela, p. 297.

[11] The Polish architectural historian Professor T. Poklewski (Łódź) works on this subject.

[12] John of Posilge, 'Prussian Chronicle', in *SRP*, 3, pp. 81–2. Cf. note 8. See also Paravicini, 2, p. 49, and the papers of an international conference on firearms used in the battlefield in the fourteenth to fifteenth centuries, held in Poland in 1994 and published in *Fasciculi Archaeologiae Historicae* (hereafter *FAH*), ed. A. Nadolski (from vol. 6, 1993, ed. T. Poklewski) (Łódź, 1986–present), 9 (1997).

[13] Wigand of Marburg, p. 613. See Paravicini, 2, p. 49.

[14] S. Ekdahl, 'Das Pferd und seine Rolle im Kriegswesen des Deutschen Ordens', in *Ordines Militares*, 6, pp. 29–47 (at p. 36).

[15] B. Jähnig, 'Die Quellen des historischen Staatsarchivs Königsberg zur Geschichte der deutsch-litauischen Beziehungen in der Zeit der Ordensherrschaft und des Herzogtums Preußen', in *Deutschland und Litauen, Bestandsaufnahmen und Aufgaben der historischen Forschung*, ed. N. Angermann and J. Tauber (Lüneburg, 1995), pp. 9–19. See also S. Ekdahl, 'Die preußisch-litauischen Beziehungen des Mittelalters. Stand und Aufgaben der Forschung in Deutschland', ibid., pp. 31–44.

of correspondence and various accounting books of the Order.[16] Furthermore there are several surviving travel accounts from crusaders, for the fourteenth century was the classical period of European noble pilgrimage to Prussia, which was the starting point for the military campaigns into Lithuania (*reysa* or *Litauenreisen*).[17] The best known are the two Prussian journeys of Henry Bolingbroke, earl of Derby, later King Henry IV of England, in the years 1390–1 and 1392.[18]

*   *   *

During the conquest of Prussia, the Knights became familiar with a small horse indigenous to that region, the so-called *Sweik* (*Schweike*).[19] This designation probably derives from a Baltic word meaning 'healthy' or 'strong'.[20] These animals had a stocky, muscular build and generally measured at the withers not much more than ten hands.[21] In a letter of 1427 the grand marshal called them 'little shaggy horses' ('*cleyne gerugete pherde*').[22] Although there is no reliable information concerning their colour, presumably they were light brown, fawn or grey and had a black dorsal stripe. Interestingly, this old breed of horse is still reared on stud farms in Lithuania where they are known as *Žemaitukai*.[23] The *Sweiks* were swift, tenacious and hardy. They served the

---

[16] S. Ekdahl, *Die Schlacht bei Tannenberg 1410. Quellenkritische Untersuchungen*, 1: *Einführung und Quellenlage*, Berliner Historische Studien, 8 (Berlin, 1982), pp. 77–106; J. Sarnowsky, *Die Wirtschaftsführung des Deutschen Ordens in Preussen (1382–1454)*, Veröffentlichungen aus den Archiven Preussischer Kulturbesitz, 34 (Cologne, Weimer and Vienna, 1993), pp. 14–23.

[17] See Paravicini, 1–2.

[18] Ibid., 1, p. 134; cf. note 95.

[19] F. Rünger, 'Herkunft, Rassezugehörigkeit, Züchtung und Haltung der Ritterpferde des Deutschen Ordens. Ein Beitrag zur Geschichte der ostpreussischen Pferdezucht und der deutschen Pferdezucht im Mittelalter', *Zeitschrift für Tierzüchtung und Züchtungsbiologie einschliesslich Tierernährung*, 2 (1925), 211–308 (at pp. 219–34). See also M. Töppen, 'Über die Pferdezucht in Preussen zur Zeit des Deutschen Ordens, nebst einigen Bermerkungen über die Sweiken', *Altpreussische Monatschrift*, 4 (1867), 681–702, and Ekdahl, 'Das Pferd', pp. 31–2.

[20] Cf. the Lithuanian adjective *sveikas*, 'healthy'.

[21] Cf. Rünger, 226–7.

[22] Ordensbriefarchiv (hereafter OBA), no. 4861. The documents on paper in the OBA are listed in *Regesta Historico-Diplomatica Ordinis S. Mariae Theutonicorum 1198–1525*, ed. E. Joachim and W. Hubatsch, Pars I, 1–3 (Göttingen, 1948, 1950, 1973). The parchments are listed in Pars II (Göttingen, 1948). There is an index of Pars I, 1–2, and Pars II (Göttingen, 1965). Pars I,3 also contains an index.

[23] Especially in Baisogala, about 100 km to the north of Kaunas. The total number of breeding females and males of the old small breed (not interbred) is only twenty-six and six respectively (information by Prof. J. Kulpys from the Lithuanian Veterinary Academy in Kaunas in September 1996). According to a description by R. Žebenka the *Žemaitukai* are small, of strong constitution, and have very powerful legs. They have a well developed chest. The head is small, the forehead wide. They have small, very lively ears and big, expressive eyes, which makes them look intelligent. The neck, especially of the stallions, is comparatively short, nicely bent and strong.

Figure 11.1   The Lithuanian Žemaitukai stem from the 'little shaggy horses' (Sveiks) of Prussia and the eastern Baltic

native Prussians and other peoples of the Baltic as saddle- and workhorses as well as war-horses. In the last case, however, it was only possible for the rider to be lightly armed with 'the native Prussian weapons' of spear, shield (*scutum Prutenicum*), plate armour (*Brünne*) and the Prussian helmet (a specific variety of the conical helmet).[24]

Although the *Sweiks*, because of their limited size, were not used by the Christian conquerors as cavalry horses, they were bred systematically by the Order.[25] They had a variety of uses, from which stemmed their designation as castle, yard, fish, beach, mill, hunting, forest, plough, field or draught *Sweiks*. For the Knights' courier service the so-called post *Sweiks* (*Briefsweiken*) were indispensable. However, these were not bred by the Order itself, but purchased from native Prussians. On campaign the *Sweiks* served the Knights as pack-horses to transport provisions, fodder and war materials. In Prussia they had the same function as the mules prescribed for the Order's use in the Holy Land.[26] Their pack-saddles were kept in the saddle-house or in the so-called *Karvan* (an Arabic word) where carts and equipment were also stored. The pack-horses had to be provided by Prussian peasants.[27] According to one chronicler, Wigand of Marburg, the Order first transported provisions to Lithuania on carts during a campaign in 1390, which seems to have been regarded at that time as remarkable.[28] Valuable insights into the composition of a baggage train are provided in an instruction concerning equipment for the journey to negotiations in Kaunas, Lithuania, at Christmas 1407. In addition to the delegation's 200 war-horses and saddle-horses there were between 450 and 500 draught horses to transport provisions and fodder in carts drawn by two animals. These were certainly *Sweiks*.[29]

When, after a hard struggle, the Prussians had been defeated by the Teutonic Order in the thirteenth century, the native nobles had to perform military service for the Knights against the Lithuanians and later also against the Poles, as light auxiliary troops (*equites Pruteni*).[30] Like the turcopoles in the Holy Land, they fought with their native weapons, with which they were familiar, 'according to the custom of the country', and thus we can assume that the *Sweiks* were employed as war-horses. The criterion for such service by Prussians was the possession of a small farm, often no more than one or two hides of land, as the expense of horse and equipment was not very great. A hide

---

[24] S. Ekdahl, 'Über die Kriegsdienste der Freien im Kulmerland zu Anfang des 15 Jahrhunderts', *Preussenland*, 2 (1964), 1–14 (at pp. 3–4).

[25] Rünger, 230–4; Töppen, 'Über die Pferdezucht', 686–8, 697–9.

[26] Cf. *SDO*, p. 103.

[27] Rünger, 231.

[28] '*In xlma fit reysa et ducunt secum victualia in plaustrum, quod ante ea non fuit visum.*' *SRP*, 2, p. 641. Usually carts could not be used during the campaigns because of the wild terrain.

[29] OBA, no. 957. See Ekdahl, 'Das Pferd', pp. 31, 42–3 note 31.

[30] Ekdahl, 'Über die Kriegsdienste', 3–4.

Figure 11.2   War-horse of the Teutonic Order of partly Arab blood. Municipal seal of Kulm, thirteenth century–first half of fourteenth century

Figure 11.3   Heavy war-horse of the Teutonic Order, without Arab blood. Municipal seal of Kulm, about 1400

(Hufe) corresponds to 16.8 hectares or about 42 acres. It is to be assumed that these light troops used the horse primarily as a means of transport, while they themselves fought on foot.

It was a different matter in the case of the heavy, non-indigenous war-horses, without which the Order would not have been able to achieve its successes against the heathens, and which were also a sign of their knightly pride – *omnis nobilitas ab equo*! During battle these horses had to be able to carry an armoured rider as well as (sometimes) their own protective attire in the form of covers or metal plates.[31] At first they were brought by the knights of the Order from their respective home countries, mainly from Thuringia, Saxony and Meissen, but later in the fourteenth century chargers were brought increasingly from Franconia, Swabia, Bavaria, the Rhineland and other parts of the Empire.[32] These horses, as well as those brought to the Order's lands by many crusaders, were probably mixed with Oriental, that is, Arab, blood. There can be no question of uniformity of the breeding stock used by the Order (from the thirteenth century onwards) because of the different places of origin of the horses used. Apart from thirteenth-century information that returning crusaders left their horses in Prussia,[33] evidence is available from 1322 which indicates that the Teutonic Order was breeding horses at that time. This evidence mentions a *pastura equorum* in Heiligenfeld in north-western Sambia (*Samland*) on which the horses of the brethren grazed.[34] In subsequent years period there were often reports in the chronicles about horses being seized in Prussia by the heathens during their battles and plundering expeditions.[35] However, it is Hermann of Wartberge who gives the first detailed description of a stud farm, near Insterburg, which fell into the hands of the Lithuanians in 1376. It had fifty mares, two stud-horses and sixty war-horses and foals.[36] At this time the records of transfer of the offices began, and these contain a great deal of information about horse breeding in the Order's lands.[37] According to Fritz Rünger, in around 1400 there were over thirty stud farms in Prussia

---

[31] Horse armour was introduced in the second half of the fourteenth century, yet very few knights owned it. A. Nowakowski, *Arms and Armour in the Medieval Teutonic Order's State in Prussia*, Studies on the History of Ancient and Medieval Art of Warfare, 2 (Łódź, 1994), pp. 105–9 (at p. 105).

[32] For the following, see Rünger.

[33] See, for instance, *SRP*, 1, p. 365.

[34] *Codex diplomaticus Prussicus. Urkunden-Sammlung zur ältern Geschichte Preussens aus dem königl. Geheimen Archiv zu Königsberg, nebst Regesten*, ed. J. Voigt (Königsberg, 1857), 2, no. 101.

[35] See *SRP*, 1–3.

[36] 'Item abstulerunt a castro Insterborg equirream vulgo "die stut" de 50 equabus et duos emissarios cum 60 dextrariis ac polledris.' *SRP*, 2, p. 110. See also Wigand of Marburg, p. 583.

[37] *Das grosse Ämterbuch des Deutschen Ordens*, ed. W. Ziesemer (Danzig, 1921, repr. Wiesbaden, 1968). Also see *Das Marienbucher Ämterbuch*, ed. W. Ziesemer (Danzig, 1916). Cf. M. Burleigh, *Prussian Society and the German Order. An aristocratic corporation in crisis, c. 1410–1466* (Cambridge, 1984), pp. 59–60.

on which the Order bred heavy warhorses. These were the so-called 'large (horse) stud farms' as opposed to the 'small (horse) stud farms' for the *Sweiks*.[38]

When fortresses were to be built there were always the questions of whether the site had sufficient grazing and meadowland for horse-breeding and whether it was possible to cultivate the necessary oats.[39] In addition, the soil needed to be as heavy and firm as possible for the breeding of horses for knights. If these conditions were not available, it was necessary to deliver horses and, if need be, fodder to the fortress. This was, for example, the case with the castle of Ragnit (north-east of Königsberg).[40] Castle environs had to be laid out to accommodate stables for the number of war- and saddle-horses required by the brethren (*Konventspferde*).[41] They also had to contain stores of fodder and the required number of saddles, pack-saddles, bridles, horseshoes, carts and sledges as well as the various devices, weapons and equipment necessary for mounted warfare.[42] In order to maintain these facilities and to protect and care for the horses, many stable hands and workers were required and their needs also had to be met. The surroundings had to be such that, where possible, hay could be harvested and delivery of taxes and dues made in the form of oats. Of all the dues paid to the Order, that paid in oats was the greatest.[43]

The breeding of horses was generally not carried out in the castles themselves but on the Order's estates (*Vorwerke*) and on the stud farms which were primarily located in lowlands, deltas and river valleys.[44] The most important of these were in the area of the Vistula, on the banks of the lagoon called *Frisches Haff*, and in Sambia, whereas the thin soil of East Pomerania was unsuitable for breeding heavy horses. There could not have been a uniform type of knight's steed because the breeding material was so very different and, anyway, the most important thing was the horses' suitability for warfare. However, certain qualities were essential in the breeding of such horses.[45] Size and weight were often decisive in cavalry battle. The neck of a knight's steed

---

[38] Rünger, 266–80, 295, 303 (map). See also Töppen, 'Über die Pferdezucht'.

[39] Rünger, 239, 255, 280.

[40] See, for instance, Ordensfoliant (hereafter OF) 8, p. 430; 10, no. 379; 11, pp. 249–50, 269, 559.

[41] For details concerning stables, etc., see Rünger, 281 and Ekdahl, 'Das Pferd', p. 41.

[42] See *Das grosse Ämterbuch* and *Das Marienburger Ämterbuch*. Cf. Z. Nowak, 'Die Vorburg als Wirtschaftszentrum des Deutschen Ordens im Preussen. Eine Fragestellung,' in *Zur Wirtschaftsentwicklung des Deutschen Ordens im Mittelalter*, ed. U. Arnold, QuStDO, 38 (Marburg, 1989), pp. 148–62.

[43] Rünger, 238–9; cf. Sarnowsky, table 3–4, pp. 193–4.

[44] Rünger, 253–5, 266–80, 303. See also H. Boockmann, 'Die Vorwerke des Deutschen Ordens in Preussen', in *Die Grundherrschaft im späten Mittelalter*, ed. H. Patze, 1, Vorträge und Forschungen, 27 (Sigmaringen, 1983), pp. 555–76.

[45] Rünger, 250–3. See also, for instance, A. Hyland, *The Medieval Warhorse from Byzantium to the Crusades* (Stroud, 1994).

[46] Archaeological and iconographic material prove that the war-horses of the thirteenth and fourteenth centuries were not as large as generally supposed. The heaviest horses were bred in

was often strongly arched and this increased the certainty of its stride. The breast was broad and muscular, the back had to be short, that is, strong enough to carry an armed rider. The strong and arched croup was split and bound with a deep-lying tail. For such a heavy body, powerful extremities and joints were necessary which, however, were not to appear awkward and crude. They had to be strong and sinewy, with firm knees and short fetlocks. These war-horses were different from modern heavy workhorses in that they had to possess a special temperament as well as ability and ease of movement, notwithstanding their heavy build.[46] Although black and white horses were favoured, colour was, for the practically minded Knights, only of secondary importance; therefore the horses mentioned in the inventories and lists have many different colours and markings.[47]

Here we shall deal only briefly with the breeding itself.[48] While the mares were primarily kept on the Order's estates and breeding farms, the stud-horses were mostly stabled in the castles, mainly for reasons of better supervision and care as well as the increased safety this location offered. For every stud-horse there were ten to seventeen mares. Stud-horses were used for breeding from the age of five years, and the mares one year earlier. Normally the mares were not used for ordinary work or military service, as they were kept exclusively for the purposes of breeding;[49] however, there were exceptions to this. As far as colts were concerned, most were gelded when they were three years old in order to perform military service as so-called 'monk horses' (*Mönchpferde, Mönchhengste*). This designation was used in order to make it clear that these were horses not capable of breeding. There were, of course, ungelded war-horses in the army of the Teutonic Order but it would be a mistake to believe that they were in the majority. As far as can be determined from the account books relating to horse breeding, the 'monk horses' predominated.[50]

Because colts were almost always rendered infertile by 'strangulation' of the spermatic cords (*Auswürgen*),[51] they were not castrated in the present sense of the word – as asserted in the older literature on the subject – but sterilized. As a result of this, an animal's male characteristics remained largely intact. The systematic sterilization also avoided the danger that, in the case of a defeat, the enemy could use captured horses to develop the breeding of their own large horses. In his notes on the regulation of the Order, Grand Master Paul of Rusdorf (1422–41), declared in 1427: 'Furthermore, nobody, except those

---

the provinces of the Lower Rhine, whereas, for instance, those from Spain and central Europe were smaller. See the interesting article by K. Militzer, 'Turniere in Köln,' in *FAH*, 8 (1995), pp. 55–66, esp. pp. 60–1.

[47] Rünger, 249–50.
[48] See ibid., 253–66.
[49] Ibid., 262, 287–8.
[50] Ibid., 287–8.
[51] Ibid., 265.

who own mares, should possess stallions [horses capable of reproduction], only monk horses. Also the lords shall not give stallions [ungelded steeds] to the brethren'.[52] When the same Grand Master two years later gave the Lithuanian Grand Duke Vytautas (Witold) a valuable horse as a gift, it was a temperamental, yet infertile warhorse (*ein fröhlicher Mönchhengst*).[53]

A further method of sterilization was performed by crushing the spermatic cords with two sharp-edged pieces of wood (*Kluppen*),[54] but this seems to have been applied less often. Occasionally genuine castration took place by the removal of the testicles. It can be assumed that these geldings were primarily used as draught or saddle-horses. Incidentally, it appears that, in Prussia there were people skilled in applying this technique to human beings; in 1437 Paul of Rusdorf issued a testimony for the 'testicle-doctor' (*Hodenarzt*) Master Nicholas, who was well practised in 'the cutting of children and other people'.[55]

Fritz Rünger calculates that around the year 1400 there were 13,887 horses in the castles, on the breeding farms and on the estates of the Teutonic Order in Prussia, of which 7,200 belonged to the breed of large military horse.[56] In addition there were the war- and saddle-horses of the brethren of the Order, which Max Töppen estimated at 2,250.[57] Thus one can assume that the Order was in possession of around 16,000 horses at this time.

The large horses were bred not only by the Teutonic Order, but also in the four bishoprics and on the estates of the German nobles who were under an obligation to perform military service.[58] Those who possessed more than 40 hides of land (672 hectares or about 1,680 acres) served with heavy armour on a covered horse (*dextrarius opertus* or *textus*), which had to be a stallion, and with at least two further horsemen as escorts (*Rossdienst*).

Those with 10 to 40 hides had to perform one or more services with 'plate' or other light weapons (*Platendienst*). Plates were made in the form of a 'poncho' consisting of rows of vertically or horizontally arranged iron plates riveted to leather or thick cloth. The horse was sterilized or castrated (a *spado*). With the increasing importance of the crossbow as a long-range weapon, armour became heavier and the plate service developed into service on a war-horse which was three to four times as expensive as a *Sweik*. Around 1400, a good warhorse cost 12 to 15 marks and a very good one 15 to 18 marks, whereas a *Sweik* could be had for 3 to 6 marks. Much greater sums were paid for excellent chargers – even sums as high as 70 marks.[59]

---

[52] '*Item sal nimant rossichen halden, sunder monchpferde, ussgenommen die da stutte halden. Ouch sullen die gebietiger den brudern nicht rossichen geben.*' OBA, no. 4849.

[53] OBA, no. 5135.

[54] Rünger, 265.

[55] OF, 13, p. 422.

[56] Rünger, 237.

[57] Töppen, 'Über die Pferdezucht', 693.

[58] For the following see Ekdahl, 'Über die Kriegsdienste'.

[59] *Das grosse Ämterbuch*, p. 4.

Important work has been published in recent years, mainly by the Polish researchers A. Nadolski and A. Nowakowski, concerning the arms and armour of the Teutonic Order.[60] This is based primarily on investigations of the inventories of the Order's stores which contain a wealth of information, sometimes including details of equestrian equipment. This rather late evidence can be complemented by reference to the laws of Grand Master Luther of Brunswick (1331–5), according to which the brethren of the Order were to do military service with weapons 'according to the customs of the country, that is plate or mail armour [*panzir*]'.[61] The laws of his successor, Dietrich of Altenburg (1335–41), prescribe the condition in which, among other things, saddles, harnesses and spurs were to be kept.[62]

*　　*　　*

The war between the Teutonic Order and Lithuania, which lasted about 140 years (1283–1411/1422), was characterized mostly by mutual devastation and pillage.[63] Full-scale battles were the exception rather than the rule. In addition there were sieges, expeditions to erect fortresses (*Baureisen*) and defensive measures in the event of an attack on their own territory (*Landwehr* and *Geschrei*). Particularly characteristic of the Order's war strategy was the winter expedition, the 'Lithuanian journey' (*reysa*) *par excellence*. Werner Paravicini has ascertained that between the years 1305 and 1409 there were over 300 campaigns from Prussia or Livonia into Lithuania and he has arranged them into a 22-page table.[64]

The Order's razzias were generally brief attacks (*Stossreisen*, *Ruckreisen*), but there were also longer campaigns which could last several weeks.[65] In all cases, good planning was a precondition for the success of the undertaking. The provision of sufficient fodder for the large number of horses was part of this. In winter, hay and oats had to be transported on pack-horses or sledges; in

---

[60] A. Nadolski, 'Die Forschungen über die Bewaffnung des Deutschen Ordens und seiner Gegner in Ostmitteleuropa,' in *Werkstatt des Historikers der mittelalterlichen Ritterorden. Quellenkundliche Probleme und Forschungsmethoden*, ed. Z. H. Nowak, *Ordines Militares*, 4 (1987), pp. 49–63; A. Nowakowski, 'New studies on the Arms and Armour in the Teutonic Order's State in Prussia. The Status Quo and Perspectives', in *FAH*, 5 (1992), pp. 83–9; *idem*, 'Some Remarks about Weapons Stored in the Arsenals of the Teutonic Order's Castles in Prussia by the End of the 14th and Early 15th Centuries', in *Ordines Militares*, 6, pp. 75–88; *idem*, Arms and Armour.

[61] *SDO*, p. 148.

[62] Ibid., p. 151.

[63] For literature, see S. Ekdahl, 'The Treatment of Prisoners of War during the Fighting between the Teutonic Order and Lithuania', in *MO*, 1, pp. 263–9. See also Paravicini, 2, esp. pp. 95–110. An important contribution was made by F. Benninghoven, 'Zur Technik spätmittelalterlicher Feldzüge im Ostbaltikum', *Zeitschrift für Ostforschung*, 19 (1970), 631–51.

[64] Paravicini, 2, pp. 20–41. The different types of campaigns are dealt with on pp. 52–66.

[65] Ibid., pp. 59–64; Ekdahl, 'Das Pferd', pp. 34–5.

[66] *Die litauischen Wegeberichte*, ed. T. Hirsch, *SRP*, 2 (1863), pp. 662–708.

summer the stages had to be planned so as to give the horses the opportunity
to graze. If necessary, fodder was also transported on pack-horses or carts
drawn by a team of two *Sweiks*. In favourable circumstances, stores or fields of
grain would be encountered in Lithuania. As is recounted in the Order's route
descriptions (*Wegeberichte*), depots for provisions and fodder were placed along
the line of march.[66] If these provisions had already been captured or destroyed
by the enemy when the army arrived, the situation became so acute that it was
often a matter of life or death. These raids were very dependent on the
weather: a winter that was too mild, too hard or very snowy made the wild
countryside (*Wildnis*) just as difficult to travel through as when there was too
much rain; a cold but not too snowy winter provided the most preferable
conditions. This would cause the waters and bogs to freeze over, thereby
helping rather than hindering the progress of the horses. In winter, the
excellent organization of the Teutonic Order came into its own. The heavy war-
horses were not ridden during the march because they had to be saved for their
military service. Other animals, palfreys, were available as saddle-horses. In
Latin these were designated usually as *palafredus*. In contrast to the war-
horses (*hengste*; mostly infertile, as already described), they were often referred
to in the sources of the Order only as 'horses' or sometimes also termed
'trotters'. Because of their soft stride the 'amblers' (nags) were particularly
prized. *Sweiks* almost certainly also served as saddle-horses.

The care of the horses' hooves was of great importance during the march.
In summer unhardened horseshoes were used, whereas in winter hardened
shoes were the rule. In the fortresses there had to be sufficient supplies of these;
thus in the forge of the Order's castle at Balga there were once over 13,000
horseshoes.[67]

When possible, the Order tried to transport part of its army and supplies along
the waterways, whereas the mounted army had to force its way through the wild
countryside in order to reach the Lithuanian settlements that were to be
ravaged. The tremendous performance of the horses during these forays is
difficult for us to imagine today, although authors such as the Austrian herald-
poet Peter Suchenwirt, as well as many other source documents, report on their
feats of endurance and prowess and the hardships they endured. Corre-
spondingly the losses of horses were very high, as a result not only of their direct
participation in warfare, but also of the harshness and privations of the journey
itself. Particularly dreaded was the wild terrain of *Grauden* which was east of
Sambia.

A good and reliable example of the losses of horses is provided by the
Order's own *Tresslerbuch* (treasurer's book), which records how twenty-four
German nobles from Kulmerland, who were obliged to perform military
service, lost no fewer than fifty chargers, trotting and other horses during a

---

[67] *Das grosse Ämterbuch*, p. 153.

campaign in Žemaitija (that is, western Lithuania) in the summer of 1402.[68] This entry was made only because the Order, according to the *Kulmer Handfeste* – a privilege from the year 1233 – was under an obligation to replace losses to the vassals of Kulmerland, if these losses occurred beyond the bounds of their normal military service.[69] But we may wonder whether the loss of horses was not, in reality, much higher, because it is possible that the losses of pack-horses (*Sweiks*) belonging to Prussian peasants were not replaced and for this reason were not mentioned in the records.

There was a section of the Order in Livonia which we have not dealt with here, despite the fact that it was often coordinated with the operations of the army of Prussia. Presumably, heavy war-horses were bred quite early in Livonia too, as the routes for military provisions across the sea were long and dependent on weather conditions.[70] In his description of the battles of the Königsberg-based Knights against the Prussians in Sambia in the years of 1262 and 1263, Peter of Dusburg writes in his chronicle that the brethren of the Livonian section of the Order came to their aid 'with many large warhorses' (*'cum multis et magnis dextrariis'*).[71] The Livonian visitation records of 1334 declare that commanders (*Komture*) and bailiffs (*Vögte*) were not allowed to give as presents or sell horses from the stud farms without the permission of the Livonian Master.[72] In a letter to the Grand Master in 1420 the Master in Livonia made it clear that it was impossible to penetrate Lithuania by water or with carts. Only with the help of pack-horses would a campaign be possible in this region.[73] In this respect the small indigenous *Sweiks* were irreplaceable also in Livonia.

In the thirteenth century the *Sweiks* were used by the Lithuanians too, particularly as a means of transport for their warriors, who fought on foot.[74] As a result of the confrontation with the technically superior methods of warfare of the Teutonic Order, a reorganization of their own military tactics became necessary. This development should be dated to the end of the thirteenth and beginning of the fourteenth centuries.[75] It included, among other things, the development of a cavalry with large horses and thus, necessarily, the establishment of stud farms. Scattered reports of these are found in the chronicles of the Order. We know that around 1367 the Lithuanian prince Kęstutis had

---

[68] *Das Marienburger Tresslerbuch der Jahre 1399–1409*, ed. E. Joachim (Königsberg, 1896; repr. Bremerhaven, 1973), pp. 217–19. See Ekdahl, 'Über die Kriegsdienste', 8.

[69] Ekdahl, ibid., 7–10.

[70] Cf. Ekdahl, 'Die Rolle der Ritterorden', pp. 220–1, 224.

[71] *SRP*, 1, p. 108.

[72] *SDO*, p. 163.

[73] *Liv-, Est- und Kurländisches Urkundenbuch nebst Regesten*, ed. F.G. v. Bunge, 5 (Riga, 1867), no. 2510. Cf. Ekdahl, 'Das Pferd', pp. 35–6.

[74] A. Nikžentaitis, 'Changes in the Organisation and Tactics of the Lithuanian Army in the 13th, 14th and the first half of the 15th century', in *FAH*, 7 (1994), pp. 45–53, esp. pp. 46–7.

[75] Ibid., pp. 48–9.

a stud farm with fifty mares in Kaunas[76] and there are also reports of a stud farm at another location.[77] As many as 400 horses were kept in one stud farm in Žemaitija around 1379.[78] It is to be assumed that the Lithuanians obtained breeding material for their large horses primarily during war and plundering campaigns into Prussia, as they did in 1376 at Insterburg when they attacked one of the Order's stud farms and seized its fifty mares, two stallions and sixty warhorses and foals.

In the course of the fourteenth century the 'non-Christians' increasingly became opponents which the Teutonic Order had to take seriously, as the knightly culture of western and central Europe was no longer unknown to them. It is not without reason that in an anonymous address composed in 1415 for the Council of Constance (presumably, however, not delivered) the Order complained that 'the non-believers of whom one is at present speaking now appear powerful everywhere, with shining armour, with warhorses [*geroesse*] and other military equipment'.[79] The author of this document knew what he was talking about, as five years previously the Order had suffered a devastating defeat at Tannenberg (in Polish known as Grunwald and in Lithuanian as Žalgiris) on 15 July 1410, by a joint Polish and Lithuanian army.[80] The turning point in the battle was achieved by the Lithuanians, admittedly not through the use of heavy cavalry, but by the old tactic of simulated retreat. This was not known to the mercenaries and crusaders of the Teutonic Order, who left their battle formations in an undisciplined manner to take up the pursuit, thereby exposing their flank so that strong Polish fighting units could penetrate the Order's army from the side.[81]

* * *

The defeat of 1410 marked the end of the Order's forays into Lithuania; now the question was one of survival.[82] Instead of the razzias which had involved a limited number of knights, the Order, like the Poles, was now engaged in campaigns involving large armies that advanced into enemy territory. War in the region was taking on the form which we know from the rest of Europe:

---

[76] *SRP*, 2, p. 88.

[77] Ibid., p. 559.

[78] Ibid., p. 592.

[79] S. Ekdahl, *Die 'Banderia Prutenorum' des Jan Długosz – eine Quelle zur Schlacht bei Tannenberg 1410*, Abhandlungen der Akademie der Wissenschaften in Göttingen, Philologisch-Historische Klasse, Dritte Folge, 104 (Göttingen, 1976), p. 11; Lithuanian edn S. Ekdahl, *Jono Dlugošo 'Prūsų vėliavos' Žalgirio mūšio šaltinis* (Vilnius, 1992), p. 19.

[80] Ekdahl, *Die Schlacht bei Tannenberg 1410*.

[81] *Idem*, 'Die Flucht der Litauer in der Schlacht bei Tannenberg', *Zeitschrift für Ostforschung*, 12 (1963), 11–19.

[82] For the following see Ekdahl, 'Das Pferd', pp. 36–7.

mercenaries replaced the crusaders, firearms increased in importance, castle sieges became a matter of routine. However, the conduct of warfare depended as much as before on the horse and its needs. Campaigns had to be planned so that as far as possible the army was self-supporting in enemy territory. It is not surprising, therefore, that they were carried out only in summer when fodder was available in the meadows and there was grain in the fields, or in autumn, when enemy stores could be plundered. This was the case in 1409, 1410, 1414, 1422 and 1431 as well as during the Thirteen Years' War of 1454–66. That the infantrymen still did not play an important role in the conduct of the war (except in the case of sieges) was not only a consequence of the superiority of the cavalry, but also because, unlike the horsemen, they could carry only limited provisions with them. Mounted troops were quicker, more mobile and could stand their ground longer in the field. The introduction of military techniques developed by the Hussites gave the infantry considerably increased importance, as stores of every kind were now transported on heavy wagons which could also be used for parts of the *Wagenburg*, the wagon laager.[83] The powerful draught horses needed to pull these wagons could also serve as saddle-horses, but did not need to be of the same quality as the knights' war-horses.

The Order's loss of horses at Tannenberg must have been enormous and the effect of that loss on the Knights' horse-breeding activities and their capacity to defend their lands, devastating.[84] The stud farms were also affected by the destruction that followed, and the horses were driven away. Only gradually was it possible to build up new breeding stock. Grand Master Henry of Plauen (1410–14) bought, among others, 140 mares of the heavy breed from the peasants in the Vistula delta for this purpose.[85] As the lack of stud-horses was particularly great, he had a number of such horses purchased abroad and brought to Prussia.[86] Considering the background situation, it is not surprising that the Order was no longer able to do without the help of mercenary troops, although as a result it experienced a severe financial crisis.[87] To these adversities must be added poor harvests and an increase in horse diseases, the effects of which are abundantly testified to in the correspondence of the Order. In such times of crisis it is understandable that large-breed horses, oats, yew wood for bows and other important materials were not exported. The ban on the export of horses and weapons following the Polish-Lithuanian Union in 1386 is well known.[88] Similar prohibitions and regulations followed in 1394, 1400, 1418, 1432

---

[83] Z. Żygulski, Jr., 'The Wagon Laager', in *FAH*, 7, (1994) pp. 15–20.

[84] Rünger, 266–80; Ekdahl, 'Das Pferd', pp. 36–7.

[85] *Das Marienburger Konventsbuch der Jahre 1399–1412*, ed. W. Ziesemer (Danzig, 1913), pp. 260–95. The Grand Master also bought mares from the Order's mercenaries: see OBA, no. 1373.

[86] Ekdahl, 'Das Pferd', p. 37.

[87] Sarnowsky, pp. 392–413.

[88] *Acten des Ständetage Preussens unter der Herrschaft des Deutschen Ordens*, ed. M. Töppen, 1 (Leipzig, 1878), p. 50. Cf. Ekdahl, 'Über die Kriegsdienste', 10–11.

and 1437. Horses were branded in order to prevent smuggling and illicit selling. Only the less militarily important *Sweiks* could be exported freely.

In order to maintain the military fitness of conscripts and mercenary troops, inspections and military reviews were held in the Order's lands. Attention was also paid to the quality of the horses. Some of the inspection lists have survived and provide valuable insights into the art of war as practised at the time.[89] The regulations concerning the hiring of mercenaries (*Söldnerbriefe*), are also rich sources of information.[90]

Occasionally horses were individually recorded according to their size, colour and other characteristics together with their value.[91] Good war-horses, like falcons, were regarded as valuable diplomatic gifts, for the Knights' horse breeding was highly prized in Europe. Letters from foreign princes requesting horses can be found in the Order's archives in Berlin. These requests were often met, but sometimes they were refused by the Grand Master in times of war or emergency.[92]

Most of the wounds suffered by the horses during the time of the crusades of the thirteenth and fourteenth centuries were caused by spears, arrows and swords, later mainly by the bolts of crossbows (Figure 11.4). The better protected the rider, the more often weapons were directed against his vulnerable horse. In a draft contract from 1433, there was an order that a wounded horse should be put out to grass if it was still not fit for service after six weeks of care.[93] The sources often speak of horse doctors and horse medicines. The Order's text *Liber de cura equorum* (now in the Austrian National Library) bears witness to the great importance of the medical treatment of horses in Prussia. This work, written in 1408 and dedicated to Grand Master Ulrich of Jungingen (1407–10), who fell at Tannenberg, may be regarded as the oldest German equine veterinary encyclopedia.[94]

* * *

---

[89] S. Ekdahl, 'Zwei Musterungslisten von Deutschordens-Söldnern aus den Jahren 1413 und 1431', in *Arma et ollae. Studia dedykowane Profesorowi Andrzejowi Nadolskiemu w 70 rocznicę urodzin i 45 rocznicę pracy naukowej. Sesja naukowa, Łódź, 7–8 maja 1992 r.*, ed. M. Głosek *et al.* (Łódź, 1992), pp. 49–61.

[90] On them see W. Rautenberg, 'Böhmische Söldner im Ordensland Preussen. Ein Beitrag zur Söldnergeschichte des 15. Jahrhunderts, vornehmlich des 13jährigen Städtekriegs, 1454–1466', 1–2, unpublished doctoral thesis (Hamburg, 1953. Very few copies, one of them in Geheimes Staatsarchiv, Berlin).

[91] Ekdahl, 'Zwei Musterungslisten', p. 59. Cf. H. Boockmann, 'Pferde auf der Marienburg', in *Vera Lex Historiae. Studien zu mittelalterlichen Quellen. Festschrift für Dieter Kurze*, ed. St. Jenks *et al.* (Cologne, Weimer and Vienna, 1993), pp. 117–26.

[92] Ekdahl, 'Das Pferd', p. 39.

[93] OF, 13, pp. 191–2.

[94] Österreichische Nationalbibliothek, Cod. 2977, fols 53v–115v. Ed. by O. Bederke, 'Liber de cura equorum. Bearbeitungen von Albertus und Jordanus Ruffus aus dem Deutschen Ritterorden', doctoral thesis (Hanover, 1962).

Figure 11.4   Swedish peasants fighting horsemen, sixteenth century

When, in the summer of 1390, Bolingbroke was preparing for his journey to Prussia he had, among other things, eighty longbows costing one shilling each and six broadbows, each at double the price, purchased for him.[95] They were packed in hemp, tied up with straps made from Hungarian leather and provided with a lock. In addition, there were four bundles of broad arrows. Perhaps the wood for these bows came from Prussia, as the tough and elastic yew wood was an important article of export of the *Ordensstaat*. Thus, in the year 1396 the commander of Ragnit deposited no less than 7,600 unworked wooden pieces for bows (*ywenbogenholcz*) and 1,150 of the same for crossbows (*knottelholcz*) with a Danzig citizen on the Grand Master's behalf.[96] We also know that Bolingbroke's bows were used in action because in a description of the siege of Vilnius (Lithuania) in autumn 1390 the Knights' chronicler, Posilge, writes: 'Also the Lord of Lancaster from England was there; he had many fine archers, who did much good'.[97] The impression is that Posilge was very impressed by the effectiveness of the English longbows.

The Teutonic Order had, from the very beginning, preferred the crossbow to the ordinary bow. The oldest recorded use of the European crossbow dates from the fourth century AD, and one comes across them again in the tenth.[98]

---

[95] *Rechungen über Heinrich von Derby's Preussenfahrten 1390–91 und 1392*, ed. H. Prutz (Leipzig, 1893), p. 33.

[96] S. Ekdahl, 'Die Armbrust im Deutschordensland Preussen zu Beginn des 15. Jahrhunderts', in *FAH*, 5 (1992), pp. 17–48 (at p. 21).

[97] *SRP*, 3, p. 164.

[98] For the history of the crossbow see R. Payne-Gallwey, *The Crossbow, Medieval and Modern, Military and Sporting. Its Construction, History and Management. With a treatise on the Balista and Catapult of the Ancients and an Appendix on the Catapult, Balista and the Turkish Bow* (first published 1903, 7th impression London, 1981). Also see J. Alm, *Europeiska armbost. En översikt*, Vaabenhistoriske aarbøger, V b (Copenhagen, 1947), and E. Harmuth, *Die Armbrust. Ein Handbuch* (Graz, 1986).

During the First Crusade the crossbow was in general use. In the eleventh and twelfth centuries important improvements were made which led to the further spread of this weapon. The trigger, the notch for the bolt, the nut and its socket, and the stirrup were introduced, and these were only some of the changes made. The stirrup was fixed to the stock and served for spanning the bow. Already in the statutes of the Teutonic Order there was mention of the workshop in which the crossbows with stirrups (as well as bows) were produced: *'Marschalus potest accipere de domo balistarum minores balistas aptas pedibus ad trahendum et arcus pro fratribus, quibus sive balistas sive arcus viderit expedire'.*[99]

Both long-range weapons – bows and crossbows – were forbidden at the Second Lateran Council in 1139 as 'deadly and hated by God'.[100] However, this prohibition, which was later repeated by the Church, was directed only against the use of bows and crossbows among Christians. Behind this, surely, lay the fear that the social order might break down if these simple but effective weapons became widespread among the lower classes and thus might threaten the superiority of the nobility and the Church. However, the Church permitted the use of these weapons against non-Christians. Thus, the crossbow was brought into Livonia and Prussia by the military orders in the thirteenth century and played an extremely important role there in the war against the heathens, a fact which has, as yet, been greatly underestimated.[101] It was an 'everyday' weapon, not only of the brethren of the Order, but also of its servants, local burghers and simple men-at-arms. However, in a later period that romanticized this era, it was given less attention than the arms and armour of the Knights.

In the thirteenth century important improvements were made to the crossbow. The wooden bow, up to that time the usual form of propulsion, was being replaced by the much more effective composite 'horn bow' – actually a 'horn-layer bow' made of horn, sinew and possibly fish-bone plates and strips of wood. Instead of pulling the bowstring with the hands, one now used a belt with a metal claw. In the fourteenth century further devices to aid drawing the bow, such as the cord and pulley (*Seilrolle*), goat's foot lever (*Geissfuss*), wooden lever (*Wippe*) and windlass (*Winde*) were introduced. However, the simple bows and wooden crossbows (*Knottelarmbrüste*) were retained for ordinary use. The Order's inventories mention these only occasionally, but sometimes Russian and Hungarian bows are itemized.[102]

---

[99] 'The marshal may receive from the crossbow workshop for the brothers smaller crossbows for drawing with the feet or bows, according as he sees crossbows or bows to be necessary for them.' *SDO*, p. 106.

[100] In the literature generally only crossbows are mentioned; see, for instance, Payne-Gallwey, p. 3. Cf. Ekdahl, 'Die Rolle der Ritterorden', p. 226 note 113.

[101] Ibid., pp. 225–6.

[102] Ekdahl, 'Die Armbrust', p. 21. Cf. Nowakowski, *Arms and Armour*, pp. 96–102. According to Nowakowski, it is not possible to guess the meaning of the term *knottelarmbrost* (p. 99). However, there is no doubt that it means a crossbow with a wooden bow.

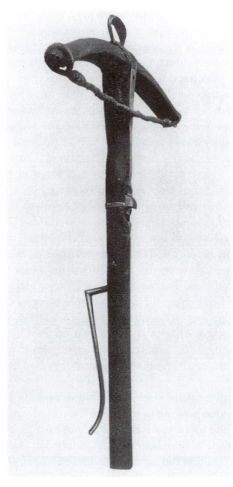

Figure 11.5   Crossbow with composite 'horn-layer' bow and revolving horn nut, fourteenth–fifteenth centuries

Figure 11.6   Composite 'horn-layer' bow of a crossbow in reflex position, fourteenth–fifteenth centuries

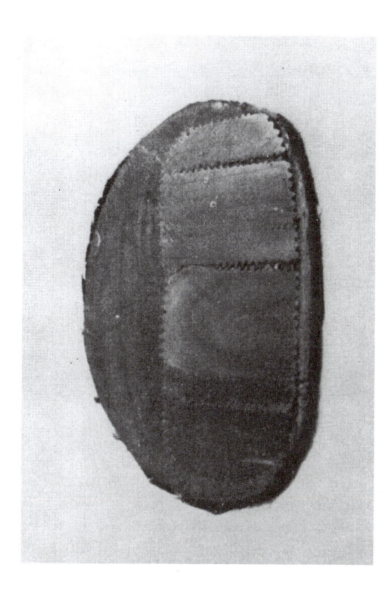

Figure 11.7   Cross-section of a 'horn-layer' bow, fourteenth–fifteenth centuries

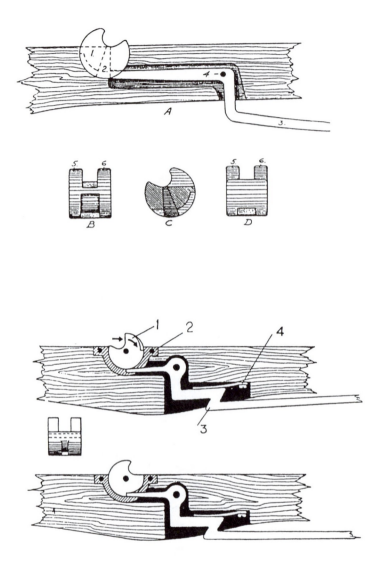

Figure 11.8   Crossbow lock and trigger without and with spring

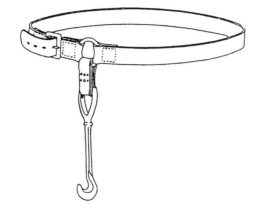

Figure 11.9   Belt and claw

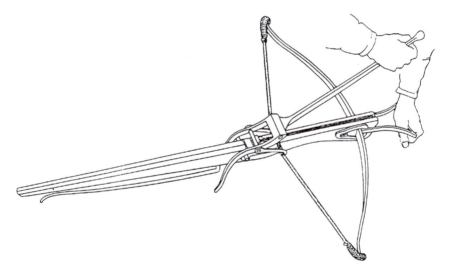

Figure 11.10   A crossbow being bent by a goat's foot lever

The new composite horn crossbow quickly demonstrated its superiority over the short bow and thus caused the introduction of the famous English longbow, which had functioned magnificently in important battles such as Crécy (1346), Poitiers (1356) and Agincourt (1415).[103] The secret of the effectiveness of these

---

[103] R. Hardy, *Longbow. A Social and Military History* (3rd edn repr. Frome and London, 1995). See also G. Rausing, *The Bow. Some Notes on its Origin and Development*, Acta archaeologica Lundensia, Papers of the Lunds Universitets Historiska Museum, 6 (Lund, 1967). For a general survey, see F. Lot, *L'art militaire et les armées au Moyen Age, en Europe et dans le Proche-Orient*, 1–2 (Paris, 1946).

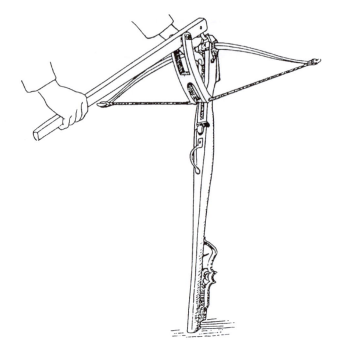

Figure 11.11   A crossbow being bent by a wooden lever

Figure 11.12   A crossbow being bent by cord and pulley

longbows was revealed only a few years ago, when in 1982 over 100 bows and 3,000 arrows were salvaged from Henry VIII's flagship, the *Mary Rose*, which sank in 1545.[104] Physicists established that these bows would have had draw-weights ranging from 45 kg to a truly astonishing 80 kg.[105] The long bodkin-headed arrows had a steel tip which was 10 cm long and could piece armour of 1.5 mm at a distance of 150 to 200 m. They hit their target at an angle of 50° and at a speed of around 35 m per second.[106] Despite these and other advantages, such as, for example, the fact that it could be shot up to six or seven times faster than the crossbow, the longbow did not replace the crossbow on the Continent. One reason is that the longbow was a weapon of the specialist, who needed to have practised its use from youth, whereas the drawing of the crossbow, made possible with the aid of a mechanical device, required no special training.

In the fifteenth century, to compete with the longbow and the emerging use of firearms, the crossbow was equipped with a powerful steel bow, with the help of which the draw-weight increased to up to 500 kg. In the case of the stirrup crossbow with a horn bow, the draw-weight was up to 150 kg.[107] The strong steel bows could be drawn only with the special help of mechanical devices such as a windlass (the so-called 'English winder') or the ratchet winder (the so-called 'German winder' or *cranequin*). Even after 1450, the crossbow was in no way inferior to hand-held firearms, and it was also used as a weapon of war in the sixteenth century. Then, however, the centuries-old superiority of this long-range weapon was over; but it did not completely disappear, as it is still used as a weapon of modern warfare by commando troops. One good reason for this is that an arrow or bolt makes no noise when shot and this still gives it an advantage over firearms under certain circumstances.

The crossbow played an essential role in the continuous competition between weapons of attack and weapons of defence in the Middle Ages and, because of continuous improvements in its construction, it contributed to the development of shields, helmets, armour and horse armour. One only needs to think of the pavises or the kettle-hats with their long protruding brims which were intended to protect the wearer from arrows and bolts, or of the ever-improving bodily protection in the form of *bascinets*, mail hauberks and different forms of plates in their various stages of development. In answer to this, the wooden shafts of the crossbow bolts were fitted with slanting rather than straight fletching and, as a result, when in flight the bolt rotated around its longitudinal axis. This spinning action was not so much intended to improve

---

[104] Hardy, pp. 194–236. See also G. Rees, 'The longbow's deadly secrets', *New Scientist*, 138, no. 1876 (5 June 1993), 24–5.

[105] Rees, p. 25. See also the table in Hardy, p. 213, as well as the analysis and technical considerations by P.L. Pratt, P.H. Blyth, P. Jones and other scientists in ibid., pp. 209–36.

[106] Rees, p. 25. See also Hardy.

[107] Harmuth, pp. 34, 38.

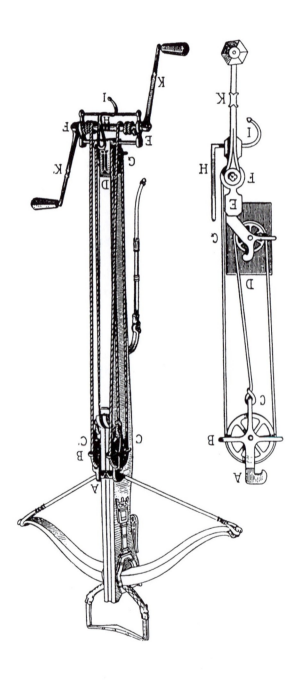

Figure 11.13   Strong western European crossbow with steel bow (Spanish origin) and windlass, about 1500

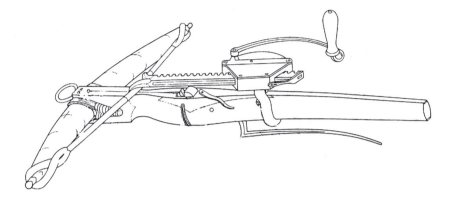

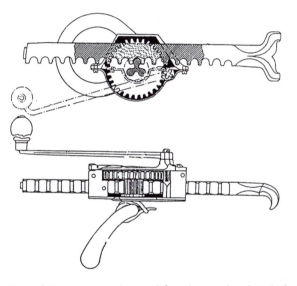

Figure 11.14   Central European crossbow with horn bow and racket winder (cranequin, 'German winder'), end of fifteenth century

the properties of flight as to enable the bolt, in a manner of speaking, to 'screw' into the armour rather than glancing off it. According to one chronicle the Swedish king Gustav Vasa taught the peasant soldiers in the province of Dalarna in Sweden in 1521 to produce bolts which were provided with slanting fletching 'so that they could hook themselves on to the armour and screw themselves through this'.[108] It is not surprising that, with this hectic pace of

---

[108] P. Svart, *Konung Gustaf I's Kronika*, ed. N. Edén (Stockholm, 1912), p. 21. The chronicle was written in the middle of the sixteenth century. Cf. Ekdahl, 'Die Armbrust', p. 20.

Figure 11.15   Bolt heads of different types from a common grave on the battlefield of Tannenberg/Grunwald, 1410

development, the non-Christian peoples of north-eastern Europe had great difficulty in keeping up with innovations. It was not only a question of quantity, but also of quality, and the Teutonic Order had the better capacity for both. Its need for crossbows, bolts and other equipment was met by its own comprehensive production which took place in its own workshops (*Schnitzhäuser*), located in the great castles. Also the larger towns in the Order's lands had their own crossbow makers and craftsmen who mounted the bolt heads on the shafts and made the fletching, and so on.[109]

It has been shown that during the first half of the fifteenth century the Order had eighteen *Schnitzhäuser* in which composite crossbows with bows made from billy-goat horn (*Bockhörner*), sinews and possibly fish-bone plates and wooden lasts were manufactured.[110] Throughout the whole of the Middle Ages simple and cheap crossbows made from yew wood were used in the country districts. In the Order's inventories they were, however, mentioned only occasionally, as *Knüttelarmbrüste* or *Knottelarmbrüste*.[111] Steel crossbows gained ground only very slowly in east-central Europe because in their case there was always the danger that the bow would break in cold weather. Horn crossbows, on the other hand, became about a third stronger in cold weather. In addition, the steel crossbow was slower. That it eventually replaced the horn crossbow was due not least to the fact that it could be produced more simply and therefore more cheaply.[112]

The Order's workshops produced horn crossbows on a scale that was probably unparalelled elsewhere in Europe.[113] An impression of this can be gained from inventories compiled each time new officers took charge, when the existing store of raw material for crossbow manufacture had to be listed.[114] To give only a few examples, in the *Schnitzhaus* of Marienburg in the year 1409 there were no fewer than 1,200 billy-goat horns and 36,000 sinews; also birch bark for 1,200 crossbows.[115] This bark was used to cover the bows to prevent them from drying out and to protect them from damp. In addition there was fish glue and glue obtained from the cooking of the neck hides of cattle. The 800 *Sternhorn* or *Storhorn*, used in the manufacture of the bows and mentioned in the inventories, have nothing to do with bulls' horns (*Stierhörner*), as was hitherto assumed to be the case. Instead they were horns from the great sturgeon (*Stör, Acipenser sturio*), that is, either the big ganoid scales or part of the head.[116] Plates made from these horns were fitted into the bow together

---

[109] Ibid., pp. 20–1.
[110] Ibid.
[111] See note 102 above.
[112] Ekdahl, 'Die Armbrust', p. 26.
[113] Harmuth, p. 78.
[114] For the following see Ekdahl, 'Die Armbrust', pp. 22–4.
[115] Ibid. and p. 45 with an edition of the inventory in question. Also see *Das Marienburger Ämterbuch*, pp. 144–6.
[116] Ekdahl, 'Die Armbrust', p. 22.

with sheets of billy-goat horn and with sinews in order to furnish it with greater strength and elasticity. The inventories also list 240 prepared nuts for the trigger mechanism, twenty-seven stags' antlers from which such nuts were turned, and twenty elk bones from which the material for the sockets was prepared. There was also wood for 340 stocks in various stages of preparation and 50 lb of flax thread from Flanders for the production of bowstrings. The quantity of equipment and special tools required needs no more than a mention here.[117] Crossbows were of different sizes and construction according to their purpose and manner of drawing. In addition to the simple forms by which the bowstring was drawn by a metal claw attached to the crossbowman's belt, there were many other mechanisms.

At the beginning of the fifteenth century, when the Teutonic Order was still at the height of its power, there were probably about 4,500 reserve crossbows and over one million crossbow bolts in Prussia.[118] After the defeat at Tannenberg (1410) the number was greatly reduced, as was the stock of horses.[119] Furthermore, the size of the field army, excluding the crusaders and mercenaries and those remaining to garrison the fortresses, can be estimated at something over ten thousand men, not including servants and camp followers.[120]

*   *   *

A simple crossbow such as the stirrup crossbow (*Steigbügelarmbrust*) weighed up to 4 kg, of which 2 kg were accounted for by the bow. This, like the stock, was about 90 cm in length and the sectional dimensions at the middle were about 23 by 54 mm. In the case of a long-range shot of something over 300 m the bolt, after about nine seconds, struck the ground steeply at an angle of 70°. Although the energy on impact fell to about half the initial energy, the shot was still effective up to 200 m.[121]

At the beginning of a battle the crossbow bolts were shot diagonally upwards for a distance of about 200 m towards the enemy lines (Figure 11.4). Among the hail of normal bolts it was also the practice to include *Heulbolzen* (whistling bolts) which produced a sharp whistling sound; in the Order's records they are referred to as *Bremsen* (gadflies).[122] Their purpose was to weaken the enemy and their horses psychologically, and to cause confusion. This effect was not produced by the sound as such, but by the fact that experience had shown that

---

[117] Ibid., pp. 23–6, 45.

[118] Benninghoven, 'Die Burgen', pp. 595–6.

[119] See the tables in Ekdahl, 'Die Armbrust', pp. 38–43.

[120] F. Benninghoven, 'Die Gotlandfeldzüge des Deutschen Ordens 1398–1408', *Zeitschrift für Ostforschung*, 13 (1964), 421–77, at p. 443.

[121] Harmuth, pp. 199–200.

[122] Ekdahl, 'Die Armbrust', p. 18. See also Harmuth, pp. 50, 175.

there was a relationship between the sound and pain; there was something like a 'Pavlovian Reflex' in both man and beast. An interesting parallel could be made with the German use of the Stuka dive-bomber in the Second World War, which, of course, used the same device of the association of a particular sound with danger, in order to cause the same effect – namely fear and confusion on the part of the enemy.

After such a punishing hail of bolts at the beginning of a battle, the crossbowmen moved forward in order to take aimed shots at a distance of up to 80 m, and thus to contribute to the further course of the battle. The great difference from the English longbowman lay in the often decisive fact that the longbowmen could shoot six or seven arrows before the crossbowmen could get off one shot (if they had mechanical winders).[123] The particular advantage of the crossbow as a weapon was that in the case of the siege or defence of fortresses and towns, it was often necessary to shoot from an angle or from small openings and to be able to keep the weapon drawn for a longer time.

As shown by the weapons and skeletons found in the mass graves of *Korsbetningen* near Visby on the Swedish island of Gotland, where, in the year 1361, a battle took place between a Danish army and local peasants, enormous numbers of crossbow bolts were shot.[124] The same was true in the case of sieges. Thus, in 1431 the commander of the Teutonic Order's castle at Rehden in Prussia complained that he had only 1,800 bolts and that these would not be enough for defence against an attack.[125] If one takes into consideration the fact that during a siege the attackers also shot thousands of bolts, it is easy to see why large supplies were needed on both sides.

Because the Knights in Livonia and Prussia did not have to fear a superior opponent equipped with English longbows, their composite horn crossbows remained the dominant, long-range weapon during the whole period of wars against the non-Christians and the Poles. This was so not only in the case of sieges but also in the many campaigns of war and devastation. Several surviving documents concerning the levy of troops and lists of equipment show that every second or third man in the Order's army was equipped with a crossbow. The overwhelming importance of this weapon is also shown in the chronicles, the Order's correspondence and the municipal *Kriegsbücher* (war books), of which one has survived, from the town of Elbing for the years 1384–1409.[126] In addition, there are several extant contracts with mounted mercenaries who came to Prussia from various parts of the Empire and were either armed with

---

[123] Payne-Gallwey, p. 37.

[124] B. Thordeman, P. Nörlund and B. E. Ingelmark, *Armour from the Battle of Wisby 1361*, 1 (Stockholm, 1939), p. 187.

[125] OBA, no. 5837.

[126] *Das Elbinger Kriegsbuch* (partly) ed. M. Töppen, Altpreussische Monatsschrift, 36 (1899), pp. 123–73.

spears (*Spiessen*) or crossbows.[127] After the conversion of Lithuania (1387) the flow of crusaders was reduced and for this reason the Teutonic Order had to make an effort to recruit the services of mercenaries.[128] This was particularly the case from 1409 onwards. A valuable remaining source for this fact is the *Soldbuch* (pay book) of the Teutonic Order for the years 1410–11 in which the payments to mercenaries are listed.[129]

The Genoese crossbowmen were counted among the most famous mercenaries of Europe in the later Middle Ages.[130] They were organized in companies and their powerful horn crossbows were drawn with windlasses. Their reputation, despite their defeat at the hands of the English longbowmen at Crécy in 1346 and at Poitiers in 1356, also reached Prussia. In 1394 Grand Master Conrad of Jungingen (1393–1407) employed 150 of them to take part in a planned siege campaign in Lithuania.[131] The negotiations were concluded with the help of Philip the Bold, duke of Burgundy. The Genoese were to demonstrate their prowess at the renewed siege of Vilnius (as in the year 1390 when Bolingbroke's longbowmen were present). They did this throughout the whole campaign, as the chronicler of the Order, Posilge, emphasizes with praise, although Vilnius castle could not be taken and the siege had to be abandoned after three weeks.[132] A letter from the Grand Master to Philip the Bold has survived, in which he offers thanks for wine received as well as the crossbowmen sent to him and confirms their good conduct.[133] In the year 1409 Genoese crossbowmen were again being recruited by Conrad's brother, Grand Master Ulrich of Jungingen, for the impending great war of the Teutonic Order against Poland-Lithuania. Details of this are, however, not known; the only remaining document is a letter to the Grand Master dated 11 July 1409 in which it is stated that 'Vytautas [the Lithuanian grand duke] knows very well

---

[127] E. Kutowski, 'Zur Geschichte der Söldner in den Heeren des Deutschordensstaates in Preussen bis zum ersten Thorner Frieden (1 February 1411)', *Oberländische Geschichtsblätter*, 14 (1912), 407–522.

[128] S. Ekdahl, 'Der Krieg zwischen dem Deutschen Orden und Polen-Litauen 1422', *Zeitschrift für Ostforschung*, 13 (1964), 614–51; M. Biskup, 'Das Problem der Söldner in den Streitkräften des Deutschordensstaates Preussen vom Ende des 14. Jahrhunderts bis 1525', in *Ordines Militares*, 6, pp. 49–74. See also Sarnowsky, pp. 402–13.

[129] *Das Soldbuch des Deutschen Ordens 1410/1411. Die Abrechnungen für die Soldtruppen*, 1, ed. S. Ekdahl, Veröffentlichungen aus den Archiven Preussischer Kulturbesitz, 23/1 (Cologne and Vienna, 1988).

[130] Harmuth, pp. 41–2. See also Lot.

[131] Posilge, p. 194. The chronicler Wigand of Marburg writes: '*Vocaverat eciam magister sagittarios de Genewel 150, cum quibus dominus Theodericus de Logendorff susceptis ibidem insigniis militaribus navigio venit in Prusziam, aliqui eorum nati erant de Francia, maior pars de Genewel, et veniunt in justa hora ad impugnandum infideles*': pp. 655–6. Nowakowski regards these mercenaries '*de Genewel*' as Swiss crossbowmen (*Arms and Armour*, p. 101). Cf. Paravicini, 2, pp. 154–5.

[132] *SRP*, 3, p. 196. Cf. ibid., 2, pp. 656, 660.

[133] *Codex diplomaticus Prussicus*, 5, no. 57 (p. 70).

that we have sent for the guests [that is, crusaders and mercenaries] and for Genoese crossbowmen [*genueren scucczen*]'.[134]

After the battle of Agincourt, members of the Teutonic Order became increasingly aware of the advantages of the English longbow, as can be established from a letter from Grand Master Paul of Rusdorf to Cardinal Henry Beaufort in about 1429. In this letter, which survives as a draft in the Order's archives, the Grand Master speaks of acquiring English longbowmen (*sagittarii*) for combat against the heretic Hussites in Bohemia.[135] In Prussia, however, the crossbow remained the most important long-distance weapon until the end of the fifteenth century; only then was it replaced by hand-held firearms. A document from the year 1433, concerning the equipment of wagons for the *Wagenburg* according to the Hussite pattern, states that at this time crossbows and hand firearms, called *Lotbüchsen*, should be regarded as of equal worth.[136]

In short, the crusades waged in north-eastern Europe by the knights of the Teutonic Order cannot be understood outside general European contexts. Developments in military architecture, weaponry, horse breeding and logistics influenced and promoted the Baltic crusades. It can be argued that the Order's success, however limited it turned out to be after the defeat of 1410, the Thirteen Years' War in the middle of the century and the Reformation in 1525, was based largely on the implementation of modern Western techniques, which it developed further. However, the knights of the Order also adopted and adapted local Prussian and Lithuanian material: fortifications of timber and earth, Lithuanian building techniques, local weapons like the Prussian helmet and shield, the Lithuanian spear and – last but not least – the 'little shaggy horses', the *Sweiks*. As is so often the case, the cross-fertilization of ideas and techniques rather than the crude domination of one culture over another was a key to success.

---

[134] OBA, no. 1093.

[135] Ibid., no. 5248.

[136] Ekdahl, 'Die Armbrust', p. 32; printed at ibid., p. 47.

12

The Hospitallers During Clement V's Pontificate: the Spoiled Sons of the Papacy?

Sophia Menache

From the perspective of the military orders, the pontificate of Clement V (1305–14) suggests a turning point in their traditional alliance with the papacy. During the long trial of the Templars, the pope can scarcely be said to have done his best to protect the brothers. Although the initiative of the arrest remains the rather dubious distinction of Philip the Fair, it was the pope who ordered the confinement of the Templars throughout Christendom (*Pastoralis praeeminentiae*, 22 November 1307).[1] Moreover, it was the pope who opposed the prelates' proposal at the Council of Vienne to give the Templars the right to defend their Order; and it was he who brought about the dissolution of the Temple 'by apostolic provision'.[2] One may argue that the case of the Templars was *sui generis*, and that Clement was left with no alternative *vis-à-vis* the 'Most Christian King'.

On the other hand, Philip the Fair had no interests in the faraway north-eastern borders of Christendom. Still, in 1305, Clement started an inquiry into the activities of the Teutonic Knights, who had been accused of causing serious harm to the Church in Livonia. The charges included the imprisonment of the archbishop of Riga, the continuous infringement of Church jurisdiction, the sale of castles and weapons to the Lithuanians, the impeding of the Christian mission, and a long list of acts of corruption and misbehaviour in the

---

[1] *Acta Imperii Angliae et Franciae ab anno 1267 ad annum 1313*, ed. F. Kern (Tübingen, 1911), no. 181 (pp. 120–2); *Acta Henrici VII Romanorum Imperatoris*, ed. F. Bonaini (Florence, 1877), no. 3 (pp. 6–8); *Constitutiones et acta publica imperatorum et regum, MGH, Legum IV*, 4.1, no. 300 (pp. 265–7); *Foedera, conventiones, literae ... inter reges Angliae ... ab ineunte saeculo duodecimo ... ad nostra usque tempora*, ed. T. Rymer, 10 vols (The Hague, 1739–45), 1.4, pp. 99–100.

[2] *Conciliorum Oecumenicorum Decreta*, ed. J. Alberigo *et al.* (Basel, 1962), p. 342. H. Finke, *Papsttum und Untergang des Templerordens*, 2 vols (Münster, 1907), 2, no. 146 (p. 299).

ranks of the Order.[3] Papal letters indicate the seriousness of the accusations against the Knights, who had abandoned warfare on Christ's behalf to wage war on the faithful: '*quod dimissa Christi militia, nunc contra Christi fideles armis nequitie bellum miserabile conferentes*' ('having set aside their service for Christ, they are now wickedly waging war with weapons against Christ's faithful').[4] The inquiry was still being carried out in 1310 when Clement nominated the archbishop of Bremen and Albert of Milan, a papal chaplain, to investigate the case.[5] During the Council of Vienne, there were well-founded expectations that the Livonian branch of the Teutonic Order would follow the fate of the Temple. Yet the proceedings were stopped in May 1313, and no noticeable results were forthcoming.[6]

Given these precedents, the title of this paper may appear contradictory, as it refers to the third great military order, the Hospital, as the 'spoiled sons of the papacy'. It is the thesis of this paper that Clement V's attitude to the Hospitallers was dictated by the dearest goal of his pontificate: the crusade. From the beginning of the pontificate up to the end of 1312, when papal crusading projects were closely connected with the Order of St John, the Hospitallers became the pope's close partners and, as such, achieved a vantage point in the *Curia*.

Clement V had ascended to the papacy fourteen years after the fall of crusader Acre, a most traumatic event in the annals of medieval Christendom.[7] Sylvia Schein argues that the pontificate of Clement V 'marked the beginning of serious and intensive efforts to launch a Crusade.'[8] Papal documentation, indeed, offers ample evidence of the pope's devotion to *Outremer*. In the encyclical that announced his coronation, Clement heralded his intention to concentrate efforts on the recovery of the Holy Land.[9] This was not just a rhetorical proclamation. Throughout his whole pontificate, the pope dedicated himself and curial resources entirely to the implementation of the crusade.[10] Political circumstances in the West seemed to be very propitious for the

---

[3] *Das Zeugenverhör des Franciscus de Moliano (1312)*, ed. A. Seraphin (Königsberg, 1912), pp. 1–145.

[4] *Regestum Clementis Papae V*, ed. O. St. Benedict, 8 vols, Bibliothèque des écoles françaises d'Athènes et de Rome (Rome, 1885–92), nos 5544, 6447, 7508.

[5] *Vetera Monumenta Poloniae et Lithuaniae gentiumque finitimarum historiam illustrantia, (1217–1409)*, ed. A. Theiner (Rome, 1860), nos 204, 206 (pp. 119–23). Albert was replaced in 1311 by Francis of Moliano, who went to Livonia with Archbishop Frederick of Riga and supported the excommunication of the knights.

[6] N. Housley, *The Avignon Papacy and the Crusade, 1305–1378* (Oxford, 1986), pp. 269–71.

[7] A. Luttrell, 'The Crusade in the Fourteenth Century', in *Europe in the Late Middle Ages*, ed. J.R. Hale, J.R.L. Highfield and B. Smalley (London, 1965), p. 124.

[8] S. Schein, *Fidelis Crucis: The Papacy, the West, and the Recovery of the Holy Land (1274–1314)* (Oxford, 1991), pp. 181–2.

[9] *Registrum Simonis de Gandavo diocesis Saresbiriensis, 1297–1315*, ed. C.T. Flower and M.C.B. Davies, 2 vols, Canterbury and York Society (Oxford, 1934), 1, pp. 220–3.

[10] *Regestum Clementis Papae V*, nos 750–3, 1247–8, 1250, 2148, 2987, 2988, 2992, 3010.

success of papal plans. The close alliance between Clement V and the kings of England and France and the peace process between them, which had been strengthened in 1308 by the marriage of Edward II and Isabelle of France, created the illusion of a united Christendom, one that was ready to renew the Just War against the infidel.[11]

The crusade, therefore, provided the main meeting point between Clement V and the Order of St John. On 6 June 1306, Clement summoned the Masters of the Temple and the Hospital 'to a consultation and deliberation about the recovery of the Holy Land.'[12] The meeting – during which the Master of the Temple submitted a full report – dealt with the unification of the military orders, a goal supported in many contemporary treatises.[13] The deliberations with the pope, however, did not bring about any substantial results. Soon after Fulk of Villaret arrived at the *Curia*, the trial of the Templars was in full swing, and Clement was obviously forced to rely only on the Hospital. On 11 August 1308, the pope proclaimed a Hospitaller *passagium particulare*, the main aims of which he defined in terms of the defence of Cyprus and Cilician Armenia and the obstruction of the Christians' illegal trade with the Muslims in the Mediterranean.[14] The pope also urged the Teutonic Knights – themselves still under papal investigation – to assist the Hospitallers (20 September 1308).[15]

A comparison, however, of the pope's declarations and those of Fr. Fulk of Villaret shows no little discrepancy. Fulk primarily viewed the expedition overseas as a means of concluding the conquest of Rhodes, where the Hospital had already won papal confirmation for the territories it had recovered from the Greeks and the Genoese.[16] From the Master's perspective, the consolidation of the Hospital's bastion in Rhodes would create a propitious basis from

---

[11] On the critical situation in Cilician Armenia and Cyprus and the close alliance between Clement and the Hospital, see my *Clement V* (Cambridge, 1998), pp. 101–12.

[12] *Regestum Clementis Papae V*, nos 1033, 10368–9; *Acta Clementis PP V 1303–14 e Regestis Vaticanis aliisque fontibus*, ed. F.M. Delorme and A.L. Tautu (Vatican, 1955), no. 8; Finke, 2, no. 23 (pp. 33–6).

[13] Finke, 2, nos 126, 128, 130 (pp. 240–1, 249, 253–4). On the reservations of James of Molay, *Le Dossier de l'affaire des Templiers*, ed. G. Lizerand (Paris, 1923), no. 1 (pp. 2–14); *Collectio actorum veterum*, ed. E. Baluze in *Vitae Paparum Avenionensium*, ed. G. Mollat, 4 vols (Paris, 1916–28), 3, pp. 145–54.

[14] *Regestum Clementis Papae V*, nos 2988–90; *The Register of John de Halton Bishop of Carlisle 1292–1324*, ed. W.N. Thompson, 2 vols, Canterbury and York Society, 12–13 (London, 1913), 2, pp. 41–50. L. Thier, *Kreuzzugsbemühungen unter Papst Clemens V. (1305–1314)* (Werl, Westphalia, 1973), pp. 79–82.

[15] *Regestum Clementis Papae V*, no. 3219; Thier, pp. 63–74; N. Housley, 'Pope Clement V and the Crusades of 1309–10', *Journal of Medieval History*, 8 (1982), 30–1.

[16] In his confirmation of the territories conquered by the Hospitallers, whom he called 'knights of Christ', Clement emphasized the importance of the conquest of Rhodes from the perspective of the total war that Christendom was fighting against the Infidel. '*Vos milites Christi ... per quos Deus omnipotens orientalem ecclesiam a paganorum spurcitia liberat christianique nominis inimicos expugnat ...*', *Regestum Clementis Papae V*, no. 2148; *Acta Clementis PP V*, no. 19.

which to launch an attack on Byzantium – then under the rule of Andronicus II, who had been excommunicated in 1307 – and even to recapture Antioch or Jerusalem within five years.[17] Eventually, the Hospitaller crusade did lead to the conquest of Rhodes and some neighbouring islands, but it hardly achieved the ambitious aims suggested by either the pope or the Master of the Hospital.

The commercial blockade of the Mediterranean also presented not a few challenges. The Venetians, for example, actively traded with Egypt and the ports along the Syrian coast.[18] Clement tried to stop this lucrative trade and threatened with excommunication all merchants implicated in contraband dealings. Those found guilty could be absolved, but only by apostolic mandate and provided that they handed over to the crusade a sum equal to the value of their illegal trade with Islam.[19] The pope also requested Philip IV to enforce the blockade on the southern ports of his kingdom and to punish all violators.[20] He wrote similar letters to the bishops of Pisa, Genoa, Ancona, Naples, Venice and Brindisi, whom he urged to enlist their flock in maintaining the Mediterranean blockade.[21]

Alongside these measures of a general nature, Clement made maximal effort to secure the free passage of the Hospitallers eastwards, a rather difficult objective, given the fractured nature of Christendom. The pope wrote to Charles II of Naples, the nominal king of Sicily, to assist the brothers when transferring horses and supplies to Cyprus (29 July 1306).[22] Further intensifying his efforts towards the passage, Clement urged the bishops of Viviers and Valence, the count of Savoy and the dauphin of Vienne (that is, prelates and princes who held fortresses along the Rhône) to allow the Hospitallers free movement through their territories and not to charge them any tolls (20 March 1309).[23] The pope repeated his order two weeks later, adding a threat of excommunication against all culprits who did not cooperate.[24] In parallel, Clement stimulated the always-reluctant Italian communes to relinquish their income from wages and taxes on the brothers moving eastwards.[25]

---

[17] B.Z. Kedar and S. Schein, 'Un projet de passage particulier proposé par l'Ordre de l'Hôpital 1306–1307', *Bibliothèque de l'Ecole des Chartes*, 137 (1979), 220–6.

[18] M.L. de Mas-Latrie, 'Traité des Vénetiens avec l'émir d'Acre en 1304', *AOL*, 1, 406–8; F.C. Hodgson, *Venice in the Thirteenth and Fourteenth Century. A Sketch of Venetian History from the Conquest of Constantinople to the Accession of Michele Steno, AD 1204–1400* (London, 1910), p. 323.

[19] *Regestum Clementis Papae V*, nos 2994–5, 5090. In Aragon, the money collected in this way was used to ransom Christian prisoners and to subsidize the *Reconquista* of Granada. J. Trenchs Odena, '*De Alexandrinis*: El comercio prohibido con los musulmanes y el papado de Aviñón durante la primera mitad del siglo XIV', *Anuario de estudios medievales*, 10 (1980), 276–9.

[20] *Regestum Clementis Papae V*, nos 2986, 2994–5.

[21] Ibid., nos 3088, 7118–19.

[22] Ibid., no. 1250.

[23] Ibid., no. 3825.

[24] Ibid., no. 3857.

[25] Ibid., no. 3218.

Clement's plan for the Hospitaller passage envisaged a force of 1,000 knights and 4,000 foot warriors, who would remain in the East for five years. To implement this plan, the pope committed the papal camera to contributing the considerable sum of 300,000 florins.[26] Another 100,000 florins were expected from Philip the Fair, which was rather wishful thinking, given the critical situation of the royal treasury.[27] The remainder of the expenses depended on the laity through their purchases of indulgences. Those who contributed the total amount of one passage to the Holy Land or even half this amount were granted plenary indulgence, while those who contributed twenty-four *livres tournois* received an indulgence for twenty-four years.[28] Clement refrained, however, from encouraging massive participation in the expedition, which remained the sole enterprise of the Hospital.[29]

Early in 1310, for the first time since the fall of Acre, a crusade headed to the East; the Hospitallers departed with a squadron of twenty-six or twenty-seven galleys under the leadership of Fr. Fulk of Villaret.[30] The pope's support of and leading role in the enterprise were indicated by the presence of his legate, Peter of Pleine Chassagne, bishop of Rodez.[31]

Once in the East, the army consolidated the rule of the Hospital in Rhodes, thereby facilitating the transfer of the Order's headquarters to the island, and conquered Kos and adjacent islands.[32] Although the expedition was diverted

[26] Ibid., no. 3753. *Registrum Simonis de Gandavo diocesis Saresbiriensis*, 3 vols, Canterbury and York Society (London, 1914–17), 1, pp. 305–6.

[27] *Regestum Clementis Papae V*, nos 2986, 3218, 5384; Finke, 2, no. 92 (pp. 154–8). See also the pope's letters to Philip IV requesting his financial help (6 June and 27 October 1309), *Collectio actorum veterum*, pp. 120–1, 105–8. The crystallization of the Hospitaller crusade was regarded by Philip as an insult against him and his kingdom. Indeed, the Hospitaller crusade undermined the king's rights to the tenth, a matter of crucial importance in Philip's reign. See the pope's apologetic response (27 October 1309), ibid., pp. 105–8.

[28] *Regestum Clementis Papae V*, nos 2987–90, 2996–7. *Continuationis chronici Guillelmi de Nangiaco, pars prima*, ed. H. Géraud, *Chronique latine de Guillaume de Nangis de 1113 à 1300 avec les continuations de cette chronique*, 2 vols (Paris, 1843), 1, p. 371.

[29] *Les Grandes chroniques de France*, ed. J. Viard, Société de l'histoire de France, 10 vols (Paris, 1920–53), 8, pp. 265–6; Jean de St Victor, *Prima Vita*, in *Vitae*, 1, p. 15; *Annales Paulini*, in *Chronicles of the Reigns of Edward I and II*, ed. W. Stubbs, 2 vols, RS, 76 (London, 1882), p. 266.

[30] *Continuationis chronici Guillelmi de Nangiaco*, 1, p. 376; Amalric Auger, *Sexta Vita*, in *Vitae*, 1, p. 98; Bernard Gui, *Quarta Vita*, in *Vitae*, 1, p. 67.

[31] The large list of papal privileges accorded the legate testify to Clement's concern about the crusade. *Regestum Clementis Papae V*, nos 3753, 3822, 3852–3, 4384, 4392, 4459, 4496–4516. See also the pope's letters to the kings of Cyprus (no. 4494), and Armenia (no. 4495); *Acta Clementis PP V*, nos 36a–c. F. Heidelberg, *Kreuzzugsversuche um die Wende des 13. Jahrhunderts* (Berlin, 1911), pp. 24–62.

[32] Bernard Gui, *Quarta Vita*, 1, pp. 62, 68; Amalric Auger, *Sexta Vita*, p. 93; *Les Grandes chroniques de France*, 8, p. 271. A. Luttrell, 'Feudal Tenure and Latin Colonization at Rhodes: 1306–1415', *English Historical Review*, 85 (1970), 755–75; *idem*, 'The Hospitallers of Rhodes: Prospectives, Problems, Possibilities', in *Die geistlichen Ritterorden Europas*, ed. J. Fleckenstein and M. Hellmann (Sigmaringen, 1980), pp. 243–66.

to the goals defined by Fulk of Villaret, the disregard of Clement's original plans did not cause any resentment between the Order and its sponsor. On the contrary, in 1314 Clement recompensed Peter of Pleine Chassagne with his nomination to patriarch of Jerusalem, a clear testimony of the pope's high appraisal of the Hospitaller crusade.

Still, the blockade of the Mediterranean presented many obstacles. In November 1311, the Hospitallers seized a Genoese ship coming out of Alexandria with a cargo of spices and refused to release it without papal authorization. The enraged Genoese ambassador endeavoured to persuade a Muslim prince – whose name is not mentioned in the sources – to imprison Rhodian merchants and other subjects of the Order in his territory. The Genoese further offered his Muslim accomplice a large subsidy of 50,000 golden florins to launch an expedition to drive the Hospitallers out of Rhodes. In the meantime, Genoese ships proceeded to take prisoner any knights they met and keep them in custody. The news of this disgraceful behaviour brought an immediate response from Clement, who sent a special nuncio, Bosolus of Parma, a canon of Tournai, to Genoa (26 November 1311). The pope also used the services of Henry of Luxembourg, the emperor-elect, to persuade the Genoese to offer some cooperation.[33]

The concurrence of interests between Clement V and the Hospital was not limited to the Mediterranean and Rhodes, but included Cyprus and Cilician Armenia as well.[34] This was a rather exceptional situation because of the fragile, ever-changing situation in the eastern Mediterranean. No wonder, then, that the essential agreement between the pope and the Order was translated into actual practice through a long series of papal privileges. In Cyprus, Clement tried to protect Hospitaller interests against the hostile policy of the regent, Amaury of Tyre, and his Templar allies. The pope gave the Hospitallers special permission to supply their ships with weapons and manpower from the island, in opposition to Amaury's specific prohibition (29 July 1306).[35] Clement also freed the Hospitallers in Majorca, Sicily and Achaia from the tenth while absolving them from any penalty they might incur for this reason.[36]

On 21 December 1307 – one year before the papal announcement of a new crusade but two months after the arrest of the Templars – Clement confirmed all Hospital privileges.[37] The request for such a confirmation was a rather common practice in the history of the military orders. Less common, however, was the large number of papal letters urging the prelates of Christendom to defend the Hospitallers and their property against attempts to harm the brothers and their Order by any person: '*quicunque vel cuiuscunque religionis,*

---

[33] *Regestum Clementis Papae V*, nos 7631–2.

[34] Ibid., nos 748, 750–1; *CH*, 3, no. 4515, 4, no. 4549; T.S.R. Boase, 'The History of the Kingdom', in *The Cilician Kingdom of Armenia*, ed. T.S.R. Boase (Edinburgh, 1978), pp. 29–30.

[35] *Regestum Clementis Papae V*, nos 1247–8.

[36] Ibid., nos 1250, 2693, 5284.

[37] Ibid., no. 2352.

conditionis aut status existant' ('anyone of no matter what religion, condition or estate').[38] A survey of papal documentation provides illuminating data with regard to the spread of the Hospital and the different attitudes the Order aroused (see Figure 12.1).[39] In the kingdom of France, the pope addressed numerous letters to the clergy.[40] This rather large quantity of correspondence may be explained by the threat posed by the arrest of the Templars to other military orders. The Hospitallers could easily have incurred the 'religious' devotion of the populace, who found the royal policy propitious ground for taking revenge on the privileged status of all military orders.[41] Clement, though, tried to give his request maximum scope. Still, the spread of papal letters was not uniform (that is, if all the letters were indeed registered). In England, Ireland, the Iberian peninsula and Hungary, only a few prelates were addressed. In contrast, papal letters were sent to a long list of prelates in Italy and Germany. One may wonder if this was a general letter of protection embracing the Hospital as a whole; if such was the case, its geographical scope lacks importance. On the other hand, the pope's emphasis on France, Germany and Italy and, conversely, the very few letters addressed to other areas suggest the diverging political status of the Hospitallers in Christendom. These differences may indicate varying degrees of antagonism not only to the Hospital but also to the Temple, the wealth of which was transferred to the Hospitallers by the Council of Vienne.

The most distinctive feature of the close alliance between Clement V and the Hospital was manifested at the Council of Vienne. Against the wishes of most prelates,[42] the constitution *Ad providam* transferred 'all that was in the possession of the Templars in the month of October 1307, when they were arrested in France ... to those who are ever placing their lives in jeopardy for the defense of the faith beyond the seas' (2 May 1312).[43] *Ad providam*, however,

---

[38] Ibid., nos 2371, 2387, 3381, 4986, 7427.

[39] The Hospitaller tongues were delimited according to the data provided by H.J.A. Sire, *The Knights of Malta* (New Haven and London, 1994), pp. 114, 159, 175, 190.

[40] *Regestum Clementis Papae V*, nos 2351, 2371, 2387, 3381, 4774.

[41] In some places, indeed, both Orders were confused, '*Fratres Hospitales in illis commorantes adhuc apud vulgus Templarii nominantur*'. *Chronica monasterii Sancti Bertini auctore Johanne Longo*, ed. O. Holder-Egger, *MGH SS*, 25, p. 796.

[42] According to the Aragonese representative to the council, 'Finally the pope told the prelates that he would like best to have their consent to the transfer of the property to the Order of St John, but that he was determined to do this with or without their agreement', Finke, 2, no. 146 (p. 299). The considerable interval between the council's two meetings, instead of the four days anticipated by Clement, may well point to the prelates' opposition to conveying additional property to the already wealthy Hospital.

[43] *Conciliorum Oecumenicorum Decreta*, p. 345; *Regestum Clementis Papae V*, nos 7885–6; *Calendar of Entries in the Papal Registers Relating to Great Britain and Ireland: Papal Letters*, 2, (1305–42), ed. W.H. Bliss (London, 1895), p. 95. Although the continuator of Guillaume de Nangis recognized that the transfer of Templar wealth to the Hospital was meant '*ad ejusdem terrae recuperationem sive subsidium possent effici fortiores ex ipsis*', he concluded, rather pessimistically, that '*ut apparuit processu temporis, facti sunt deteriores*'. See *Continuationis chronici Guiillelmi de Nangiaco*, 1, p. 392.

Figure 12.1   Destinations of papal letters concerning the Hospital

did not include Templar property in Castile, Aragon, Portugal and Majorca, the fate of which was left to the pope's later judgment.[44] The gift of the wealth of the Templars opened a new chapter in the history of the Hospital, which during the years to follow was engaged in endless conflict with prelates and princes who claimed their rights of advowson.

Philip the Fair took the initiative. In a letter of 24 August 1312 to the pope, Philip agreed to transfer the Templar wealth to the Hospital, on the condition of an overall reform of the Order *'tam in capite quam in membris'* ('root and branch').[45] The king specified that the goods of the Templars would be transferred to the Order of St John only 'after the deduction of necessary

[44] *Conciliorum Oecumenicorum Decreta*, p. 345; *Regestum Clementis Papae V*, no. 7886; Finke, 2, no. 146 (pp. 298–302).

[45] *Le Dossier*, nos 11–12 (p. 200).

expenses for the custody and administration of these goods' and provided that
this transfer caused no harm to the rights of the king, nobles and prelates of
France.[46] The stipulation of necessary reforms in the Hospital and the claim
of legitimate rights to Templar property appear as a serious warning in regard
to Philip's designs. Eventually, the king of France retained 260,000 *livres
tournois* from Templar resources: 200,000 *livres tournois* as compensation for his
and his ancestors' contributions to the Order and 60,000 *livres tournois* for the
expenses generated during the trial.[47] The king of France was soon followed
by other princes who were reluctant to relinquish such convenient income.[48]
To oppose their designs, Clement forbade the Hospitallers to sell their
property, old or new, to clergymen or the laity, a restriction probably meant to
protect the Order – and especially the former wealth of the Templars – from
external pressure.[49]

In the aftermath of the Council of Vienne, however, papal correspondence
shows a clear decline in support for the Hospital.[50] Anthony Luttrell has
convincingly demonstrated Clement's intentions for a complete reform of
the Order with close papal supervision over the distribution of its resources and
members, most of whom were expected to remain in the East. Whether this
plan was a result of the general hostility towards all exempt orders, a trend characteristic of the Council of Vienne, or an independent papal initiative,
Clement's death obviated the projected reform.[51] Only one letter in defence
of the Hospital appears in the papal registers after 1312; it concerns the
Comtat-Venaissin, and probably refers to an old feud over the property of the
Order.[52] In most cases, the pope called his old allies to order, in favour of either
the prince of Tarenteise or Amanieu, the archbishop of Auch.[53] Clement,
furthermore, instructed the Hospitallers to provide the duke of Athens with
four ships in order to protect this Catholic stronghold against the attacks of both
the Catalan Company and the schismatic Byzantines (14 January 1314).[54] In

---

[46] Ibid., p. 202. See the decision carried by the parliament of 1312, *Les Olim ou Registres des Arrêts
rendus par la cour du roi (1254–1318)*, ed. Comte Beugnot, 4 vols (Paris, 1839–48), 2, pp. 580–2.

[47] B. Causse, *Eglise, finance et royauté: La floraison des décimes dans la France du moyen âge*, 2 vols
(Lille, 1988), 1, p. 249.

[48] *Regestum Clementis Papae V*, nos 7952, 8862, 8961, 8973–4, 9383–6, 9496, 9618, 9984, 10166.
A full discussion of Edward II's attitude may be found in my *Clement V*, pp. 241–2.

[49] *Regestum Clementis Papae V*, nos 9398, 9835.

[50] Ibid., nos 8961–2, 8973–5.

[51] A. Luttrell, 'Gli Ospitalieri e l'eredità dei Templari, 1305–1378', in *I Templari: Mito e Storia*,
ed. G. Minnucci and F. Sardi (Siena, 1989), pp. 76–8.

[52] *Regestum Clementis Papae V*, no. 7671.

[53] Ibid., nos 7891, 8573.

[54] Ibid., no. 10168. In 1311 the duchy of Athens was conquered by the Catalan Company, which
had been called on to help against the Byzantines by the late duke. Clement outlawed the
Company and supported the lawful duke, Walter II of Brienne, grandchild of Walter of Châtillon,
constable of France. See *Chronique de Ramon Muntaner*, ed. J.A. Buchon, in *Collection des chroniques
nationales françaises écrites en langue vulgaire du XIIIe au XVe siècle*, 47 vols (Paris, 1827), 17, p. 250.

two curious letters of 29 May 1313, probably written at the request of Fulk of Villaret, Clement urged the prelates of Italy to help the Master in maintaining discipline within the ranks of the Order. This was a rather peculiar requirement in regard to an order that had so proudly defended its autonomy. On the other hand, these were the first symptoms of the crisis that in 1317 brought an end to the corrupt rule of Fulk of Villaret.[55] In 1314, the pope dismissed the prior of Aragon, Fr Ramon de Ampurias, who was charged with having a rich sexual life.[56]

One may conclude that the former close relationship between Clement V and the Hospitallers underwent a crucial alteration at the end of 1312. This change was not fortuitous. It corroborates the crucial importance that the pope attributed to the crusade, his former defence of the Hospital being just a means to advance the recovery of the Holy Land. According to Bertrand of Got, the pope's nephew, Clement became thoroughly disillusioned with minor crusading expeditions in the aftermath of the Council of Vienne and placed his hopes on a *passagium generale*, which the *Curia* might more easily control.[57] Philip the Fair was designated captain of the forthcoming enterprise and, as such, a six-year tenth was bestowed upon him. Clearly, therefore, the 'Most Christian King' inherited the privileged status of the Hospital in the papal camera and, perhaps more important still, on Clement's scale of priorities. Both Clement V and Philip the Fair, however, died in 1314, before a new crusade materialized.

---

[55] Fulk was eventually persuaded to resign, and in June 1319 Hélion of Villeneuve was elected to the mastership. A. Luttrell, 'Notes on Foulques de Villaret, Master of the Hospital, 1305–1319', in *Guillaume de Villaret Ier Recteur du Comtat Venaissin 1274, Grand Maître de l'Ordre des Hospitaliers de Saint Jean de Jérusalem, Chypre 1296* (Paris, 1985), pp. 76–90.

[56] *Regestum Clementis Papae V*, no. 9398.

[57] Norman Housley correctly claims that the pope's conclusion was not supported by past events. See his 'Pope Clement V and the Crusades of 1309–10', 41. *Lettres secrètes et curiales du pape Jean XXII relatives à la France*, ed. A. Coulon and S. Clemencet, 4 vols (Paris, 1900–1960), p. 614; Thier, p. 104.

13

English Contributions to the Hospitaller Castle at Bodrum in Turkey: 1407–1437

Anthony Luttrell

The English brethren of the Hospital only occasionally played a prominent role in its affairs and their presence in the East was never numerous.[1] Several early Masters were possibly English or Anglo-French[2] and a man such as Fr. Joseph de Chauncy, who served for many years as the Hospital's treasurer in Syria and also as Edward I's treasurer in England, was of considerable importance.[3] After 1312 the bulk of the Templars' English lands were absorbed by the Hospital and in 1338 there were approximately 116 Hospitaller brethren in England, that is 34 *milites*, 34 priests and 48 sergeants, together with some 50 fully professed Hospitaller sisters.[4] There were also a few English brethren at

---

[1] Standard outlines in E. King, *The Knights of St John in the British Realm*, rev. ed. (London, 1967), and H. Sire, *The Knights of Malta* (New Haven, 1994). Employing materials now in Valletta, National Library of Malta, Archives of the Order of St John, are L. Larking, *The Knights Hospitallers in England* (London, 1857); J. Delaville le Roulx, *Les Hospitaliers à Rhodes jusqu'à la mort de Philibert de Naillac: 1310–1421* (Paris, 1913); A. Mifsud, *The Knights Hospitallers of the Venerable Tongue of England in Malta* (Malta, 1916); H. Scicluna, *The Book of Deliberations of the Venerable Tongue of England: 1523–1567* (Malta, 1949); C. Tipton, 'The English Hospitallers during the Great Schism', *Studies in Medieval and Renaissance History*, 4 (1967); I. Cowan, P. Mackay and A. Macquarrie, *The Knights of St John of Jerusalem in Scotland* (Edinburgh, 1983). Not all these works are entirely reliable. Parts of the Hospital's English archive are reconstructed in the exemplary works of M. Gervers, most recently his *The Cartulary of the Knights of St John of Jerusalem in England*, part 2: *Prima Camera: Essex* (London, 1996). Much disparate material is available in the Venerable Order's library at Clerkenwell in London.

[2] For example, C. Humphery-Smith, *Hugh Revel: Master of the Hospital of St John of Jerusalem 1258–1277* (Chichester, 1994).

[3] J. Riley-Smith, *The Knights of St John in Jerusalem and Cyprus: c. 1050–1310* (London, 1967), p. 312.

[4] Larking, pp. lxi–iii *et passim*. Other lists of English commanderies and commanders, with financial data, in J. Miret y Sans, *Les Cases de Templers y Hospitallers en Catalunya* (Barcelona, 1910), pp. 400–2 (*c.* 1320); Madrid, Archivo Histórico Nacional, Ordenes Militares, Sección de Códices 602B, fols 10v–12 (1357); BN, MS Latin 13,824, fols 94v–95 (*c.* 1478).

From *The Military Orders. Volume 2. Welfare and Warfare.* ed. Helen Nicholson. Copyright © 1998 by Helen Nicholson. Published by Ashgate Publishing Ltd, Gower House, Croft Road, Aldershot, Hampshire, GU11 3HR, Great Britain.

Rhodes, probably fewer than ten,[5] but later, in 1445, a meeting of the English *langue* or tongue on Rhodes was attended by eleven brethren, while five were absent, another was ill and one more was serving on the island of Kos.[6] In the 1380s between 7,000 and 9,000 florins a year, and from 1400 to 1415 about 8,500 florins a year, were sent by the English to Rhodes as their *responsiones* and other dues;[7] that was over a sixth of the apparent total annual average of about 46,750 florins sent from the West between 1378 and 1399.[8]

The English Hospitaller *milites* or knight-brethren, many from the Midlands or the north of England, seldom belonged to the higher nobility. The Fr. Robert Luttrell of 1338 was the fourth son of Sir Geoffrey Luttrell,[9] while Fr. John l'Archer senior and Fr. John l'Archer junior, both Hospitaller *milites*, were presumably kinsmen of Fr. Thomas l'Archer, prior of England from 1321 *c.* to 1328; Fr. John l'Archer junior was prior of Ireland at the latest from 1345 until 1348.[10] Prior Thomas l'Archer was probably typical in coming from a non-knightly or sub-knightly provincial family of esquires who were at that time acquiring social status and heraldic seals.[11] Despite the formal regulations, many of the other *milites* listed in 1338 were relatively obscure in origin.[12]

More important was Fr. Robert Hales, who took part in the crusade which sacked Alexandria in 1365[13] and who became prior of England and was beheaded in 1381 after introducing a poll tax as royal treasurer.[14] The next prior, Fr. John Raddington, faced difficulties caused by the papal schism during which the English government, which supported the Roman popes, explicitly placed the defence of Christendom above local divisions and permitted English Hospitallers and their monies to go to Rhodes, even though the Master and convent there supported the Avignon papacy; these funds were to pass by way

---

[5] Researches in Malta and elsewhere would produce minimum but probably not total figures.

[6] Malta, Cod. 356, fol. 142.

[7] Incomplete figures in Tipton, 'The English Hospitallers', 99, 107–13, 118; add 15,190 ducats for 1378/80 (Malta, Cod. 322, fols 333–334); 5,000 ducats, 1409 (Cod. 339, fols 201, 206–207); 5,876 ducats, 1411 (fols 226–226v); 5,517 ducats, 1413/4 (fols 162v–163); 5,910 ducats, 1414/5 (fol. 169).

[8] Crude figures in A. Luttrell, *The Later History of the Maussolleion and its Utilization in the Hospitaller Castle at Bodrum = The Maussolleion at Halikarnassos: Reports of the Danish Archaeological Expedition to Bodrum*, 2.2 (Aarhus, 1986), pp. 144, 158 note 12, giving the average of 38,500 florins received at Avignon, to which an average of 8,250 florins from England is here added; these figures were atypical since many priories were paying no dues during the papal schism.

[9] J. Backhouse, *The Luttrell Psalter* (London, 1989), p. 28.

[10] Cf. Larking, pp. 11, 65, 208; Mifsud, pp. 78–80 *et passim*; Tipton, 'The English Hospitallers', *passim*; and *Registrum de Kilmainham: Register of Chapter Acts of the Hospital of Saint John in Ireland, 1326–1339*, ed. C. McNeill (Dublin, 1932), pp. 122–9. Detailed prosopographical research is required.

[11] The l'Archers are discussed in P. Coss, 'Knights, Esquires and the Origins of Social Gradation in England', *Transactions of the Royal Historical Society*, 6, ser. 5 (1995), 174–7.

[12] List in Larking, pp. lxi–ii.

[13] Malta, Cod. 319, fols 171–2.

[14] Tipton, 'The English Hospitallers', 95–100.

of Venice and not to go to Avignon. Raddington himself went repeatedly to Rhodes and accompanied Henry of Derby on his Jerusalem pilgrimage of 1392 and 1393 during which the future king twice stopped on Rhodes;[15] Raddington was probably killed in the disastrous crusade against the Turks at Nikopolis on the Danube in 1396.[16] Fr. Peter Holt, Prior of Ireland, was employed on diplomatic missions from Rhodes to the Byzantine imperial family, and in 1400 he arranged for the visit of Manuel II Palaeologus to London, accompanying him there;[17] the emperor stayed for a while in the Hospital's house at Clerkenwell.[18] Various English knights and nobles were at Rhodes between 1365 and 1367 during campaigns in Egypt and Cilician Armenia, after which others continued to reach the island *en route* for Jerusalem.[19]

The visits of the large contingent led by the Earl of Derby, later King Henry IV, helped to arouse English interest during several decades of difficulties at Rhodes caused by the non-payment of *responsiones* by many priories loyal to the Roman popes. In 1402 the Hospitallers lost their mainland castle at Smyrna to the Mongol ruler Timur, and a suitable replacement was judged essential. In 1407 or 1408 a new castle was constructed at Bodrum on the Anatolian mainland just across the sea from the Hospital's island of Kos. The fortification of this isolated peninsula constituted little strategic threat to the Turks, but it provided an escape route for Christians fleeing from Turkish captivity and it allowed the Hospital to present itself to Western public opinion as being in direct contact and confrontation with the infidel. By 1409 the Hospitallers were already claiming to have spent 70,000 florins on Bodrum and to be expending 7,000 ducats annually on their brethren and mercenaries there. In that year an indulgence for the castle was granted by the Pisan pope Alexander V, and it was confirmed in 1412 by his successor John XXIII. The Hospitallers' claims of losses and expenditures at Bodrum helped to raise funds and secure privileges and exemptions, so that the new castle was

---

[15] Ibid., 100–24; *idem*, 'The Irish Hospitallers during the Great Schism', *Proceedings of the Royal Irish Academy*, 69, C/3 (1970).

[16] A. Luttrell, 'Chaucer's Knight and the Mediterranean', *Library of Mediterranean History*, 1 (1994), 143–4. Raddington dined with the duke of Orleans, presumably in Paris, on 11 January 1394: London, British Library, Add. Charter 2909 (reference kindly supplied by Michael Bennett).

[17] D. Nicol, 'A Byzantine Emperor in England: Manuel II's Visit to London in 1400–1401', *University of Birmingham Historical Journal*, 12 (1969–70), 211–12. Cf. C. Tipton, 'Peter Holt Turcopolier of Rhodes and Prior of Ireland', *Annales de l'Ordre Souverain Militaire de Malte*, 12 (1964); J. Chrysostomides, *Monumenta Peloponnesiaca: Documents for the History of the Peloponnese in the 14th and 15th Centuries* (Camberley, 1995), nos 274–5, 277–9, 283, 289.

[18] '... and he was lodged atte the hous of Saynt John in Smythfeld': *Chronicles of London*, ed. C. Kingsford (Oxford, 1905), p. 267.

[19] C. Tyerman, *England and the Crusades: 1095–1588* (Chicago, 1988), pp. 280–8; A. Luttrell, 'English Levantine Crusaders: 1363–1367', *Renaissance Studies*, 2 (1988).

arguably a profit-making operation.[20] Even so, the expenses were considerable; a later, and certainly incomplete, estimate of 1467 calculated annual expenditures in the East at 54,000 florins, of which 7,200, or over an eighth, were allotted to Bodrum.[21]

Late in 1409, a dramatic financial crisis at Rhodes was alleviated by the arrival from England of 5,000 ducats, worth 8,000 florins, of *responsiones* sent by the Alberti of Florence on Venetian galleys; of this sum, 1,900 ducats were spent on Bodrum, 1,000 ducats for the mercenaries, 300 for the brethren's *stipendia* or pay and 600 for their *mensa* or table.[22] The English had long been reluctant to send money to France, to the Avignon popes or even perhaps to foreign Hospitallers living in comparative safety on Rhodes, but the transfer of funds specifically earmarked for Bodrum was more acceptable; there at least there was an element of direct confrontation with the infidel, though in reality this was described merely as *scaramuce* or skirmishes in 1409 when the captain was ordered to stop them lest they provoke serious Turkish retaliation.[23] In November 1411, after the Alberti had sent 5,876 ducats from London, the lieutenant master and convent at Rhodes reported that the English king and the English Hospitallers had insisted that this money go to Rhodes and nowhere else.[24] When in June 1413 Fr. Peter Holt the turcopolier, a senior officer at Rhodes, and the English brethren there, called upon the Hospitallers in England urgently to send those monies which had been raised for repairing and completing the towers and walls at Bodrum, all the *baliui* or officers and *proceres* or senior brethren of the convent explicitly promised that the money sent would be expended entirely on Bodrum.[25]

In 1409 both the English Crown and the Hospitaller Convent accepted the same pope, Alexander V, elected at the Council of Pisa.[26] A group of English Hospitallers, including Fr. Peter Holt, attended that council, and from March to June 1410 the Master of Rhodes, Fr. Philibert de Naillac, was in London as Alexander's envoy.[27] The English invested in Bodrum castle, of which Fr. Peter Holt was captain in 1412,[28] from the very beginning. In 1409 Henry Lord Fitzhugh secured customs exemptions for a *steynedcloth*, that is a tapestry or painted cloth, and for 38 sheaves of arrows, 13 bows and 72 bow strings to be

---

[20] Luttrell, *The Later History of the Maussolleion*, pp. 143–7 (misprinted in Tyerman, p. 314, as 700,000 florins).

[21] Malta, Cod. 283, fols 33–36.

[22] Malta, Cod. 339, fols 206v–207; (fols 143v–145 show one ducat worth 1.6 florins).

[23] Cod. 339, fol. 211v.

[24] 'Rex Anglie et Prior ac ceteri responsionum collectores ordinauerunt quod prefate responsiones debeant omnimodo ad conuentus portarj et non ad aliquem alium locum': Malta, Cod. 339, fols 226–226v.

[25] Cod. 339, fol. 251v.

[26] J. Wylie, *History of England under Henry the Fourth* (London, 1896), pp. 384–6.

[27] Delaville, pp. 309–11; M. Harvey, *Solutions to the Schism: A Study of Some English Attitudes 1378 to 1409* (St Ottilien, 1983), pp. 150 note 18, 157 note 54, 185–6.

[28] Malta, Cod. 339, fols 234, 235v.

sent to Rhodes for use at Bodrum.[29] In 1414 Sir William Fitzhugh, probably Henry's son, and William's wife Margary purchased Alexander V's Bodrum indulgence, receiving an illuminated parchment with a special seal issued at Clerkenwell by Fr. John Seyvill and Fr. William Hulles, 'procurators of this indulgence'.[30] A similar indulgence was sold at Temple Bruer in 1413 to John and Agnes Goby and their three children,[31] and another, which was issued for two persons by Fr. John Seyvill, also at Temple Bruer in 1414, survived in the papers of the Neville family of Holt.[32] In 1415 the lieutenant master and convent at Rhodes borrowed from Fr. Thomas Skipwith, turcopolier, and Fr. Richard Paule 2,000 ducats which had been raised through the Bodrum indulgence from the king, barons, knights, merchants and other faithful in England.[33] On 24 September 1418 Henry IV's half-brother, Cardinal Henry Beaufort, who was passing through Venice on his return from Jerusalem, secured a licence to export from Crete to Rhodes 200 wooden beams, 300 smaller beams and 500 cypress planks specifically for use at Bodrum.[34] At a more humble level, in 1429 John Pigot Esquire of York bequeathed 40 shillings for the castle's fabric and defence.[35]

In probably about 1430 the English *langue* constructed a tower at Bodrum. The French and Italian towers, the latter completed in 1436, were at the centre of the fortified peninsula, while other towers defended the outer landward approach to the castle. The English tower stood on the seaward side and was built into the walls above the water at the south-east corner of the peninsula.[36] It was a tall, oblong building measuring 10 by 15 m on the exterior with walls 2 m thick, which projected from the southern and eastern lines of

---

[29] *Calendar of the Close Rolls: Henry IV*, 2: *AD 1409–1413* (London, 1932), pp. 2–3; T. Rymer, *Foedera, Conventiones, Literes, ...*, 8 (London, 1709), p. 605, without stating that Fitzhugh was travelling to the East. A. Reeves, *Lancastrian Englishmen* (Washington, 1981), p. 81, assumes, merely on the basis of the arms at Bodrum, that Fitzhugh actually went to Rhodes. E. Jacob, *The Fifteenth Century: 1399–1485*, rev. edn (Oxford, 1976), p. 326, incorrectly states that Fitzhugh 'built a castle in Rhodes'.

[30] London, British Library, Cotton Charter IV, 31, printed in A. Oliver, 'Notes on the Heraldry at the Castle of Bodrum', *Ars Quatuor Coronatorum: Transactions of the Quatuor Coronati Lodge no. 2706, London*, 21 (1908), 86–7. The wax seal shows a castle with paschal lamb, banner and cross, inscribed '*sigillu[m].indulgencie.hospitalis. castri. sancti. petri*': E. King, *The Seals of the Order of St John of Jerusalem* (London, 1932), pp. 114–15; pl. XX (7–8).

[31] W. Lunt, *Financial Relations of the Papacy with England: 1327–1534*, 2 (Cambridge, Mass., 1962), p. 559.

[32] *Second Report of the Royal Commission on Historical Manuscripts* (London, 1874), p. 98: seal lost.

[33] Malta, Cod. 339, fol. 266v.

[34] G. Fedalto, *La Chiesa Latina in Oriente*, 3 (Verona, 1978), pp. 186–7. Beaufort returned to Venice on 10 September: G. Harriss, *Cardinal Beaufort: a Study of Lancastrian Ascendancy and Decline* (Oxford, 1988), p. 96; he had probably visited Rhodes.

[35] J. Hughes, *Pastors and Visionaries: Religion and Secular Life in Late Medieval Yorkshire* (Woodbridge, 1988), p. 22.

[36] Luttrell, *The Later History of the Maussolleion*, pp. 147–56; end-map.

the main sea walls. It was built of stones unequal in height and length laid in uneven courses, some being circular sections of classical columns. A west doorway led from the enclosed space outside and below the main south wall into a lower room; this connected upwards through a trapdoor into a fine chamber with three large rounded windows which were not gunports but had marble seats at each side; above it was another, barrel-vaulted, floor, and the roof was reached by stairs built within the walls. The room at ground level could more conveniently be entered directly from the main compound through a north door, which had a drawbridge. Below the lowest room were two separate cellars reached only through apertures in its floor.[37]

The building of towers became a national task. There were French and Italian towers both at Rhodes and at Bodrum. In 1445 the Italian *langue* at Rhodes encharged procurators to find and contract with masons to construct the tower of Italy there.[38] During the first part of the fifteenth century the Hospitallers built various towers in and around the island of Rhodes as well as on the surrounding islands, but the oblong tower above the sea at Bodrum with its grandiose residential upper chamber had no real parallel.[39] The English, who had no tower at Rhodes, built their Bodrum tower apparently in about 1430. In 1433 the Master at Rhodes issued a procuration to Fr. William Langstrother to receive monies in England which were still being collected from the Church and the laity for the building and *augmentacio* of Bodrum castle.[40] The English tower, which was dedicated to St Katharine, must have been completed some years before 1437 when an English Hospitaller serving at Bodrum protested that his servant was not being allowed to reside in or to be provided with his food in the tower, although this had previously been the custom because the English had built the tower. After hearing from Fr. Angelino Muscetula, who had been captain of Bodrum from about 1433 to 1436, that this had indeed been the practice when he was captain, the Master

---

[37] Brief description and drawings in R. Pullan, 'Description of the Castle of St Peter at Bodrum', in C. Newton, *A History of Discoveries at Halicarnassus, Cnidus, and Branchidae*, 2.2 (London, 1863), p. 661 and pls XXXVa–VIb; A Mauri, 'I Castelli dei Cavalieri di Rodi a Cos e a Budrúm (Alicarnasso)', *Annuario della R. Scuola di Atene*, 4–5 (1921–22), 309 (figs 23–4); old photograph in King, p. 66, and new ones in W. Müller-Wiener, *Castles of the Crusaders* (London, 1966), pls 148–51; photographs, plans and sections in S. Spiteri, *Fortresses of the Cross: Hospitaller Military Architecture (1136–1798)* (Malta, 1994), pp. 238–53. Restoration plans are held by the Museum Service in Ankara; early photographs survive in various collections. Evidently altered before 1522, the tower was shelled in 1917 and has been repeatedly and heavily restored. Corbels on the walls of the upper chamber may indicate an additional floor there.

[38] S. Fiorini and A. Luttrell, 'The Italian Hospitallers at Rhodes: 1437–1462', *Revue Mabillon*, 68 (1996), 229–30.

[39] Spiteri, pp. 63–258; see also A. Gabriel, *La Cité de Rhodes: MCCCX–MDXXII*, 2 vols (Paris, 1921–1923), 1, pp. 48–53, 63, 66–70; P. Pentz, 'The Medieval Period', in L. Sorensen and P. Pentz, *Excavations and Surveys in Southern Rhodes: the Post-Mycenaean Periods until Roman Times and the Medieval Period = Lindos*, 4.2 (Copenhagen, 1992).

[40] Malta, Cod. 350, fol. 224.

instructed that this custom should be maintained.[41] Subsequently, however, the English brethren, who were few in number, largely lost control of the tower which came to be occupied mainly by Spanish brethren.[42]

Placing numerous English arms on the tower evidently served to emphasize the claims of the English Hospitallers whose prestige at Rhodes was under threat. In January 1435 the prior, Fr. Robert Mallory, took a contingent of English Hospitallers and considerable quantities of plate to Rhodes in response to an appeal for its defence against Mamluk attacks. With him went John Lord Scrope, recently lord treasurer, who was licensed to leave England with twenty persons on a royal embassy to Rhodes and on pilgrimage to Jerusalem, while permits for Jerusalem were issued to his son-in-law Henry Lord Scrope of Bolton, to John de Vere, Earl of Oxford, and to others; John Lord Scrope had returned from Syria by October 1436.[43] This may have been the occasion when the English arms were placed on the newly built tower at Bodrum. At Rhodes John Scrope persuaded the Master, Fr. Antoni Fluviá, to restore to the turcopolier, always an Englishman, the rights and privileges which his office had formerly enjoyed, but that Master died and the king renewed the request in 1440 when he wrote eight letters to the new Master, Fr. Jean de Lastic, requesting appointments for various English brethren and demanding the confirmation of the new prior, Fr. Robert Botyll, whom he permitted to serve at Rhodes during the Mamluk siege of that year.[44] The English eventually secured the turcopolier's rights, but the bitterness of their resentment against the corrupt French monopoly at Rhodes was eloquently expressed in an outburst by Prior Botyll while he was presiding over the chapter general at Rome in 1446.[45]

The long frieze of escutcheons covered by a moulded lintel on the north face of the English tower was entirely atypical of normal Hospitaller practice. The

---

[41] Text in Appendix II.

[42] Further disputes in Malta, Cod. 76, fols 29v–30 (1480); Cod. 80, fol. 130v (1505); Cod. 81, fols 58–58v (1507), 83–83v (1508); Spanish graffiti in the tower, copied in 1856, are reproduced and discussed in Mauri, p. 336 and figs 39–45. P. Pedersen, *The Maussolleion Terrace and Accessory Structures = The Maussolleion at Halikarnassos: Reports ...*, 3.1 (Aarhus, 1991), pp. 33–4, 71, 194 notes 33–4 (fig. 46), demonstrates that materials from the terrace walls surrounding the Maussolleion were re-used in the English tower and elsewhere in the castle; the Hospitallers may by about 1430 have had access to the terrace walls or they may have used stones that had already been re-used in antiquity.

[43] Rymer, 10 (1710) pp. 600–1; *The Complete Peerage*, 13 vols, rev. edn (London, 1910–41), 11, p. 568 note (b). P. Field, 'Sir Robert Mallory, Prior of the Hospital of St John of Jerusalem in England: 1432–1439/40', *Journal of Ecclesiastical History*, 28 (1977), adds interesting detail.

[44] *Official Correspondence, Thomas Bekynton*, ed. G. Williams, 1 (London, 1872), pp. 78–89, 210–12; details concerning the turcopolier's rights in N. Iorga, *Notes et Extraits pour servir à l'Histoire des Croisades au XVe siècle*, 2 (Paris, 1899), p. 429.

[45] R. Valentini, 'Un Capitolo Generale degli Ospitalieri di S. Giovanni tenuto in Vaticano nel 1446', *Archivio Storico di Malta*, 7 (1936), 138, 155–6.

English had a fondness for displaying their arms. In 1393 Henry of Derby and his heralds had his arms and those of his many followers painted on wooden shields to be hung somewhere in the *castello* at Rhodes, while his contemporary Sir Hugh Hastings of Elsing left his arms in an unidentified *maison d'honneur* there.[46] They were presumably copying arrangements in Prussia where the Teutonic Order encouraged noble warriors, including various Englishmen who also visited Rhodes, such as Henry of Derby, Henry Lord Fitzhugh and Richard Beauchamp, Earl of Warwick, to display their arms in public as evidence of their service.[47] Many Rhodian buildings bore the Hospital's cross and the arms of the Master who was ruling at the time of their construction or repair;[48] at Bodrum the captain's arms were frequently shown as well.[49] The arms of the papacy, of France and of England were occasionally used at Rhodes. A small chapel in the main street bore a line of five escutcheons in which the Hospital's cross was flanked by the arms of the two Masters ruling from 1319 to 1353 and at each end by the arms of England, that to the right being quartered with those of France, which was not done before 1340; on another slab on this chapel the papal arms were placed between those of England and those of France.[50] However, the extensive display of the arms of individuals who were not Hospitallers was rare.

At Bodrum the French tower showed a line of five arms, with those of the papacy being flanked on each side by the lilies of France and then by those of the Hospital and the Master, Fr. Philibert de Naillac; below these were the arms of the rich Rhodian financier Dragonetto Clavelli, who died in 1414/5.[51] The English tower had the arms of England eight times, the Hospital's cross twice and fourteen escutcheons belonging to distinguished, and predominantly noble, English families which had presumably made financial contributions, probably for the castle in general, since at least some of the

---

[46] S. Düll, A. Luttrell and M. Keen, 'Faithful unto Death: the Tomb Slab of Sir William Neville and Sir John Clanvowe, Constantinople, 1391', *Antiquaries Journal*, 71 (1991), 182–3.

[47] W. Paravicini, *Die Preussenreisen des europäischen Adels*, 1 (Sigmaringen, 1989), pp. 115–35, 335–44; it seems unlikely that Richard Earl of Warwick and Henry Lord Fitzhugh actually visited Bodrum. Warwick did visit Jerusalem in 1408: Wylie, 3, pp. 178–9.

[48] Gabriel, 1, pp. 91–104; G. Gerola, 'Gli Stemmi superstiti nei Monumenti delle Sporadi appartenute ai Cavalieri di Rodi', *Rivista del Collegio Araldico*, 11–12 (1913–14); A. Kasdagli, 'Eisagogi stin Eraldiki tis Rodou', *Deltion Eraldikis kai Genealogikis Etairias Ellados*, 7 (1987–8). From 1355/65 onwards the Master's arms were shown on their *gigliati* coins.

[49] G. Gerola, 'Il Castello di S. Pietro in Anatolia ed i suoi Stemmi dei Cavalieri di Rodi', *Rivista del Collegio Araldico*, 13 (1915).

[50] F. de Belabre, *Rhodes of the Knights* (Oxford, 1908), figs 94–5, 97–8; Gabriel, 2, pp. 174–6; Gerola 'Gli Stemmi superstiti nei Monumenti', 81–5 (figs 7–8); Kasdagli, 36 (fig. 12). The predominance of the arms of England on this chapel remains unexplained. There is no convincing evidence that the chapel on the sea wall of the *castello* at Rhodes (datable 1382–96) belonged to the English, but it did show the arms of England and many other unidentified arms: Belabre, pp. 90–2, frontispiece, figs 73–6.

[51] Mauri, fig. 13; cf. Luttrell, *The Later History of the Maussolleion*, p. 198.

families had been involved with Bodrum well before the tower was built; there were no shields of individual Hospitallers, English or otherwise.[52] The families represented were of higher rank than the English brethren of the Hospital, many having members who were Knights of the Garter. The maintenance of Rhodes against the Turks did not require the presence of numerous expensive brethren but money for fortifications, mercenaries and supplies was essential. Allotting the English their own tower at Bodrum and allowing them to place upon it the arms of those who donated funds for the castle was one way of financing the Hospital, a multinational corporation which was active in the East but needed to raise money in the West.

APPENDIX I

The shields on the English tower[53]

Above the tower's west doorway are the arms of England surmounted by a lion; below them is a fairly large antique lion.[54] Across the north face are twenty-two escutcheons, mostly carved on individual slabs varying in size but arranged more or less symmetrically. In the centre are the arms of England surmounted by a lion [3]; on either side at an upper level is a plain Hospitaller cross [1–2], and on either side at a lower level is the long line of shields. Below that, in the centre, are three other shields on a single slab, possibly later additions [10–12]. Immediately on either side of the main central escutcheon [3] and at the lower level are six shields, three on each side, showing the arms of England and presumably representing members of the royal family [4–9]; those to the west [7–9] are also carved on a single slab.[55] Beyond these are eight shields to the east [left to right 13–20] and eight to the west [21–28], three of them [24–26] on a single slab. The arms, some not clearly identified, are or may be:

10 ?; 11 Woolf?; 12 Ingloss of Suffolk? or Sheffield?; 13 Harcourt or Grey; 14 Zouche; 15 De la Pole?; 16 Neville; 17 Percy; 18 Holland; 19 Beauchamp?; 20

---

[52] Details in Appendix I; it is not known who selected the arms and organized their display, or who supervised and carved the escutcheons.

[53] Drawings of 1853 by R. Pullan in London, British Library, Add. MSS 30,998, fols 50v–51, with identifications by R. Holmes in Pullan, p. 666; alternative identifications in C. Markham, 'The Display of English Heraldry at the Castle of Budrum (or Halicarnassus) in Asia Minor', *Proceedings of the Society of Antiquaries of London*, 2, ser. 14 (1891–3), 283–7; Gerola 'Il Castello di S. Pietro', 76; Mauri, 334 (fig. 38); E. Lyle Kalças, *Bodrum Castle and its Knights* (Smyrna, 1976), pp. 13–16 and fold-out. Mauri's numerations are those here given in square brackets; unfortunately it has not been possible to include a picture of these shields in the present volume.

[54] Müller-Wiener, pl. 150.

[55] Markham, pp. 283–4, identifies Henry IV, Humphrey Duke of Gloucester and John Beaufort Earl of Somerset, though he died in March 1410. Tom Blagg kindly reports that the shield blocks vary considerably in colour, size and type of stone, and that they appear not to have been made for their present position but seem likely to have come from other monuments.

Burleigh?; 21 Strange of Knokyn; 22 Talbot or Fitzalan; 23 Montagu; 24 Stafford; 25 Vere; 26 Courtenay; 27 Fitzhugh; 28 Halston or Cresson.[56]

APPENDIX II

Annotation dated 15 April 1437 in the Master's register[57]

Quia pro parte venerabilium fratrum lingue Anglie coram Reuerendissimo domino magistro querelanter expositum fuit, qualiter non permictebatur a nonnullis fratribus guaravane,[58] castri sancti Petri, quod frater dicte lingue, cum eius famulo ressideret apud turrim sancte Katerine dicti castri, Et dictus famulus suam pitanciam haberet in eandem, iuxta consuetudinem hactenus obseruatam, cum dictis fratribus propter constructionem dicte turris ab Anglicis factam. Qui Reuerendissimus dominus magister vocato domino admirato, olim dicti castri per quadrenium capitaneo,[59] eum interrogauit super consuetudine antedicta, et dixit se tempore sui capitaneatus, dictam consuetudinem seruasse. Et ideo idem Reuerendissimus dominus magister litteris suis mandauit presenti capitaneo vz. domino fratri Roberto de Diana quatenus ipse quoque dictam consuetudinem seruaret, et famulum in dicta turrj permicteret, ac pitanciam pro eodem dare mandaret. Postmodum uero idem venerabiles fratres a dicto Reuerendissimo domino magistro postularunt quatenus in registris cancellarie faceret continuarj consuetudinem antedictam ne deinceps nouiter ipsi fratres et eorum successores pro dicta causa perturbentur, qui dominus magister scribi mandauit predicta ad litteram per me fratrem Melchiorem secretarium[60] etc.

---

[56] Holmes in Pullan, p. 666; Markham, 284–5, and King, 67 note 1, ascribing various arms to particular individuals; the arms require further study.

[57] Malta, Cod. 352, fol. 132v.

[58] The caravan was the conventual brethren's obligation to a fixed period of service at Kos, Bodrum or elsewhere.

[59] Fr. Angelino Muscetula, Admiral on 30 April 1437 (Malta, Cod. 352, fols 190–190v), was captain of Bodrum by 11 May (Cod. 350, fol. 241v) and still in 1436 (Mauri, 299).

[60] Fr. Melchiore Bandini, the Master's secretary.

14

The Price of Hospitaller Crusading Warfare in the Eighteenth Century: the Maltese Consulate on Zante

Victor Mallia-Milanes

The late 1740s and 1750s were years of structural change in the relations between the republic of Venice and the Hospitaller Order of St John. Ever since Rhodian days these had been generally characterized by a tenacious element of mutual suspicion and aversion, intermittently marked by such inimical measures that ranged from the confiscation of Hospitaller estates on Venetian territory to the blocking of Venetian patricians aspiring to entry into the Order; from the dismissal and expulsion from Venice of all Hospitallers on the payroll of the republic to trade embargoes and the restriction of all forms of correspondence between the two; from orders to sink indiscriminately all ships flying the Hospitaller cross to instructions to seek, capture and conduct Venetian vessels to the port of Malta.

Behind this pervasive sense of mutual antagonism lay two major forces of friction. First, Venice's special relationship with the Ottoman Empire and its characteristic tolerance of non-Christians contrasted sharply with the Hospital's warlike function and activities towards Islam. The Order's relevance to Christian Europe depended on how successful its endeavour was to keep alive the idea of a crusade in its various manifest forms. This inherently defied by implication Venice's overriding political and economic interests. Secondly, the republic believed she could not comfortably trust the Hospitallers on yet another level. Venice's traditional distrust of the papacy, in both the latter's temporal and spiritual dimensions, had necessarily extended to the Hospital, an exempt Order of the Church which owed allegiance to no other secular sovereignty or diocesan authority than that exercised by the pope.[1]

---

[1] On this point, V. Mallia-Milanes, 'Corsairs Parading Crosses: the Hospitallers and Venice, 1530–1798', in *MO*, 1, pp. 103–12; for a wider treatment of the subject, *idem, Venice and Hospitaller Malta 1530–1798: Aspects of a Relationship* (Malta, 1992).

In the vain hope of containing Hospitaller and Maltese privateering in the Levant, Venice had opted rather clumsily to resort to the *sequestro* as the sole deterrent in her defence policy *vis-à-vis* the Hospital. It was a clumsy choice because it invariably proved ineffective in the short or long term, when other options had been open to the republic. Experienced Venetian patricians directly involved in the *Stato da Mar* had on several occasions seriously considered the problem and made some much more practical recommendations.[2] The painful truth about the *sequestro* and all the other related measures which the Venetian senate chose to decree against the Hospital was that they had failed to produce the desired effect. It was only the six-year-long *sequestro* of 1741–7 which appears to have ultimately convinced the republic of the hollowness of the whole approach.[3]

In April 1751 there could well have been no corsairs in the Levant under cover of either the Hospitaller cross or the magistral flag, as Grand Master Emmanuel Pinto, without straining credulity, reverently assured his consul at Corfu.[4] But there was a strikingly obvious incongruity between what Pinto notoriously claimed and what was actually happening. He had deliberately resolved to make no passing mention of the resurgence, one or two decades earlier, of Maltese privateering in the Levant, disguised under different shapes and forms. It was by then becoming common practice for resident representatives of foreign states on Malta to issue licences to corsairs on behalf of their respective sovereigns. Spain and Tuscany, Sardinia and Monaco were four classic examples, soon to be emulated later in the century by Corsica and Russia.[5]

This could not have been allowed to develop without the consent and connivance of an authoritarian magistracy such as Pinto's. The Venetian ambassador to the Roman *Curia* was well informed about this novel practice. This is attested by his knowledgeable observations to his Hospitaller counterpart on the disturbing activities of the Maltese corsair captain, Angelo Luri. Raimondo Mareghes, piloting a Maltese *filuca* towards the sheltering shores of Santa Maura as part of Luri's privateering team, declared on his arrest by the Venetian authorities that the entire eastern Mediterranean was currently infested with similar pirates.[6] Confronted, therefore, as Venice now was, by a new list of grievances against Maltese privateers, she chose this time to adopt such alternative measures as the suppression of Maltese consulates on Venetian islands, where Maltese corsairs had repeatedly sought shelter during their

---

[2] For the views of Niccolò Suriano, Filippo Pasqualigo, Nicolò Donato, Giovan Battista Michiel, see *idem*, 'Corsairs Parading Crosses', pp. 108–10.

[3] See *idem*, *Venice and Hospitaller Malta*, ch. 7.

[4] APV, *Sezione* III, *busta* 42, 17 May 1751.

[5] On the subject, V. Mallia-Milanes, 'Poised between Hope and Infinite Despair: Venetians in the Port of Eighteenth-Century Malta', *Library of Mediterranean History*, 3 (1996).

[6] *Idem*, *Venice and Hospitaller Malta*, pp. 207–8.

privateering operations.[7] The Maltese consulate on Corfu was the first to meet this fate, presumably on the grounds that Angelo Luri and most of his strong privateering team were subjects of the Hospitaller principality of Malta.[8] The second was that on Zante (Zàkinthos), and this is the subject of this paper.

* * *

Malta's consulate on Zante, along with those on Corfu and Napoli di Romania (Nauplia), owed their importance to the three islands' geographical position *vis-à-vis* the Hospital's permanent state of war with the Ottoman Porte.[9] Each constituted an intelligence-gathering centre of strategic interest to the Order, a ready source of first-hand information about the movements and whereabouts of the Turkish armada. It was this very sensitive nerve which the republic was endeavouring to impair or paralyse by denying the Hospital and its thriving corsairing industry access to a vital line of communication which had rendered both, through the ages, all the more capable of regulating their vigorous seasonal raiding operations in the Levant. Zuanne (or Giovanni) Ferrendino, a native of Zante, had been consul for Malta on Zante since 9 September 1746.[10] On 31 August 1754, the *Nobil Huomo* Berluzzi Valier, Venetian governor or *Provveditor* of Zante, suspended Ferrendino from his office and forced the consulate to close down, on orders from his superior Agostin Sagredo, *Provveditor Generale da Mar*. In accordance with the Senate decrees of 2 May 1739 and 2 April 1746, Ferrendino had been allegedly found wanting in what Sagredo called 'the integrity and legal requisites' of his consular office as defined by Venice's *Pien* (Full) *Collegio* on first endorsing Ferrendino's *commission consulaire*. Indeed, explained Sagredo, the republic had never formally recognized Ferrendino as 'consul for Malta'.[11]

Though correct at law, Venice's pretext for the dismissal of Ferrendino and for ordering the Grand Master's coat of arms to be taken down from above the consul's residence, 'where they had been for long displayed',[12] was too

---

[7] Ibid., pp. 207–10.

[8] Ibid., p. 209.

[9] See, for example, the Grand Master's letter to his consuls at Zante and Corfu, dated 3 April 1708, in V. Mallia-Milanes, 'Malta and Venice in the Eighteenth Century: A Study in Consular Relations', *Studi Veneziani*, 17–18 (1975–76), 273 note 26.

[10] Malta, Cod. 6429, fol. 56. Other Maltese consuls on Zante include: Magnifico Giovanni Faulignan ('Gallo in insula Zacinthi commoranti'), nominated on 5 February 1658 (Malta, Cod. 476, fol. 212v); Vittorio Faulignan, 23 December 1693 (Malta, Cod. 497, fol. 83r); Theodoro Andrizzi, 13 October 1704 (Malta, Cod. 6429, fol. 56); Canonico Francesco Mercati, 30 August 1782 (ibid.); and Canonico Demetrio Mercati, 23 November 1787 (ibid.).

[11] For the senate's decree of 2 May 1739, ASVen, CSM, 1st ser., *busta* 601, 8 August 1765; and *filza* 83, *carta* 113; for the decree of 2 April 1746, ibid., *filza* 99, *carta* 107; and *busta* 601, 8 August 1765.

[12] APV, *Sezione* III, *Affari marittimi, busta* 42, *Zante, deposizione del Ferrendino e altro*, fol. 17r.

lame by traditional practice. In the early 1740s,[13] Ferrendino's letters patent had passed through all the necessary formalities but, Pinto wrote to his ambassador in Rome,[14] 'they had been lost on their way from Venice to Zante'. The Venetian authorities on the island at the time appear to have accepted the explanation, as no further enquiries were made into the matter until August 1754:

> presumably (we believed) [wrote Pinto in 1754[15]] that all arguments [against our claim] could be easily demolished, either on the basis of the [Venetian] State's tolerance (Ferrendino having been notwithstandingly allowed to perform his consular duties for such a long time), or on the strength of the certainty of the existing records of our Letters Patent in Venice from where the necessary proofs could be ultimately obtained.

Venice's motives and real sentiments towards the Hospitaller government were too thinly veiled to have appeared at any time convincing. For, barely two days after his dismissal, the ill-fated Ferrendino found himself the target of a more searing accusation, which the republic's unconventional approach to the pernicious problem of Maltese privateering found so particularly expedient to exploit. This time the pretext concerned his alleged involvement in Paolo Marassi's pillaging operations years earlier on the southern Ionian island and its surrounding Venetian waters. The allegation was made by Giuseppe Luigi Reynaud, the French consul on Zante, in the form of a *querela* or legal complaint submitted to Agostino Sagredo in July 1754, the very time when Ferrendino was conveniently away from the island[16] on a private visit to Malta.[17] Marassi was a notorious Maltese corsair sailing under the protection of the prince of Monaco.[18] In January 1754 he was sailing on board his *sciambecchino* between Arcadia and Prodano in the Levant, where he seized a *cembero* (or smaller xebec) flying the Turkish flag and belonging to the Greek Marco di Gligori. Its cargo consisted of 1,500 barrels of wheat, a number of empty jars (*giarre vuote*), and 56 *oche* of silk, equivalent to about 70 kg.[19] To shelter from rough seas, Marassi conducted his prize safely to the port of Chieri on Zante.[20]

---

[13] Certainly before 1744, 'since the days of Receiver [Flaminio] Rovero': ibid.

[14] Ibid. His full name was Frà Maurizio Solaro di Breglio, bailiff of Armenia. He was Piedmontese.

[15] Ibid.

[16] See ibid., fol. 6: 'Copia tratta dalla scrittura di querela presentata in mano di S.E. Provveditor Generale da Mar Agostino Sagredo, dal signor Giuseppe Luigi Raynaud, Console di sua Maestà Cristianissima nel Zante'.

[17] '[A] causa de suoi interessi': ibid., fol. 19r.

[18] On Marassi and his privateering activity, Mallia-Milanes, 'Poised between Hope and Infinite Despair', *passim*.

[19] An *ocha* or *occa* was a unit of weight roughly equivalent to 1.25 kg. It is still in use in some Middle Eastern countries.

[20] See testimony of Francesco Zerafa, 23 March 1754: APV, *Sezione* III, *Affari marittimi, busta* 42, fol. 9v.

Reynaud's claim rested on two serious accusations: first, that Giovanni Ferrendino illegitimately secured the purchase of the stolen silk from the Maltese corsair for the 'ridiculous' price (*a vil prezzo*) of 112 *zecchini* (the silk, he claimed, had been originally chartered at Coron by the French dragoman Sarando Papadopolo, to be consigned to Costantin Balsamo at either Zante or Corfu); and secondly, that Ferrendino had been dealing regularly with the corsair and repeatedly providing him with all his needs and necessary supplies. The Maltese consul, conscious of his guilt, alleged Reynaud, sought to escape punishment by secretly fleeing the island of Zante.[21]

Reynaud's subterfuge worked. On 2 September 1754 Sagredo issued another set of instructions, exhorting the governor of Zante to see immediately to the execution of what he cautiously termed 'the provisional confiscation of Ferrendino's property to the tune of 500 Zecchini, which you should then forward to me in Cephalonia'.[22]

* * *

Grand Master Pinto, with his hypersensitive power-consciousness, reacted vehemently both to Venice's rough enactment of justice and to Reynaud's malicious slander.[23] The controversial dismissal of Ferrendino and the closure of the Maltese consulate betrayed an arrogant and unfriendly behaviour, which, he deplored, proved greatly prejudicial to his magistracy's representation. Without just grounds or sufficient knowledge of the facts, the excessive use of armed force in the confiscation of the consul's private property (including the most essential household furniture and goods), reminiscent of the Serenissima's old methods, was as damaging to his honour as to his material well-being. Spoiled overnight of all his belongings, Ferrendino, along with his numerous family,[24] faced acute financial difficulties,[25] living shabbily like a poor wretch (*da meschino*) and feeling compelled to seek both shelter and sustenance from his friends, without ever having been given the opportunity to prove his innocence.[26]

In his petition to the Grand Master, drawn up by Fra Carolus Farrugia *Auditor* and dated 13 March 1754, Ferrendino defined the *querela* simply as 'alien to the truth', maliciously coloured with the sole intent of rendering him odious to the Venetian government. The petition, supported by documentary evidence, consisted of a detailed *memoriale* of all that had happened. That same day, Grand Master Pinto ordered his *Curia* in Valletta to conduct what he called

---

[21] Ibid., fol. 6, *passim*.

[22] Ibid., fol. 7v.

[23] See, for example, ibid., fol. 17, Pinto's letter to the bailiff of Armenia, 30 May 1754.

[24] See ibid., fols 4r–5r, Ferrendino's petition to Pinto, 13 March 1754, *passim*.

[25] Ibid., fol. 17, Pinto to the bailiff of Armenia, 30 May 1754.

[26] Ibid., fols 4r–5r, *passim*.

a *processo informativo*. All those who were involved in Marassi's privateering venture and happened to be in Malta at the time were to be cross-examined. These included Giuseppe Elia Luri, the Greek consul on Malta; Captain Paolo Marassi and his brother Michele, another corsair; Francesco Zerafa, for the previous three years employed on Paolo Marassi's privateer, first as *scalco* (steward) and then as *cammerotto* (cabin boy); and Michele Treti, captain of a *filuca*, and Theodoro Galluzzi, *secondo tenente*, both of whom, like Zerafa, had worked with the corsair for the last three years. From the evidence produced under oath between 18 March and 1 April 1754,[27] corroborated by other independent documentation, it resulted that Reynaud's allegations were invariably false in substance and detail.

There was no evidence that Giovanni Ferrendino had ever furnished corsair Marassi or his privateering team with either help or provisions. Every time the consul had sought to get in touch with the corsair at the port of Chieri, he was simply obeying instructions from the Venetian governor of Zante. This is supported by two letters written by Francesco Maria Grimani, Valier's predecessor, to Ferrendino. In the one dated 23 January 1754,[28] he refers to

> the firm stand you have taken in conformity with the instructions I had given you by word of mouth these last few days, regarding the captain of the corsair ship which anchored at the port of Chieri. This [reads the letter] should have persuaded him to leave harbour ... I must point out, however, that he has still remained where he was, without paying the slightest thought to the trouble which his presence there could possibly create. I therefore urge you once more to strongly order him to leave without further delay, to keep away from these waters, and to refrain from rendering the slightest insult to Ottoman subjects in these same waters.

Then, at the end of February 1754, at two in the morning, Grimani wrote again:[29]

> I have just now received the news that the corsair ship has returned to the port of Chieri, followed by a tartan which should presumably be taken for his prize. I have no doubt that, without the slightest regard to his country's commitment or to the very important interests of the Serene Republic, he has again dared to cause molestation within Venetian waters and to insist on remaining in those parts. However, in order to ascertain ourselves of the true facts and of all the circumstances, you are kindly requested to proceed personally to the Riva di Chieri, to take accurate note of what type of boat (*legno*) is that which the corsair has

---

[27] Ibid., fols 8r–11v.

[28] Ibid., fol. 5r: Copia di lettera scritta da S. E. Francesco Maria Grimani, Provveditor del Zante all'Illustrissimo Signor Console di Malta Giovanni Ferendino li 23 Gennaio 1753 S[tile] V[eneto].

[29] Ibid., fols 5r–5v: Copia di lettera scritta da S. E. Francesco M. Grimani, fu Provveditor del Zante all'Illustrissimo Signor Console di Malta Giovanni Ferendino li 30 [*sic*] Febbraio 1753 S[tile] V[eneto] alle due ore della notte.

conducted into the harbour, and to which nationality it belongs, to be able to report back to me with precision every bit of information. You should then again proceed to order firmly the said corsair to distance himself from Venetian waters, adding all the other instructions which I had given you in my previous letters. I look forward to receiving your report on the outcome of your operations.

Had Ferrendino disobeyed any of these instructions, Grimani would have known instantly and taken the necessary measures. 'There was no need,' remarks Pinto, 'for the French consul to go out of his way to indicate this in his *querela* to the *Provveditore General da Mar* seven months later.'[30]

The second serious allegation concerned Ferrendino's purchase of the stolen silk. In the declaration made under oath in February 1754 at the *Magistrato della Sanità* in Zante, that is several months before Reynaud's *querela*, Marco di Gligori, the Greek merchant who had fallen victim to Marassi, reveals that the silk he had on board belonged to Greek merchants at Coron and not, as Reynaud claimed, to the French dragoman. This was confirmed by every witness under cross-examination. Indeed, they all claimed certain knowledge that the silk had been sold by the corsair for two Venetian *zecchini* the *ocha* to a dyer (*tintore*) from Zante, whose name they could not recall. At no stage of the transaction was the name of Ferrendino ever mentioned. Even for the sake of argument, Pinto remarks in one of his several observations on the case, had Ferrendino in fact bought the silk, this would in no way imply any modicum of guilt, even had the silk really belonged to the French dragoman. 'Whoever buys from corsairs,' he argues, 'does not seek to find out who originally owned the goods he is purchasing.'[31]

Pinto calls the *querela* 'full of deceitful charges', and its author 'an imposter', one whose ultimate objective was to defame and damage Ferrendino's reputation. The firm stance Pinto had adopted in defence of his consul was to be ultimately justified, as early indications appear to suggest. Some time between March and May 1754, a manuscript note, undated and unsigned, reports that on the basis of the findings of the *processo informativo*, the French *Homme du Roi* in Malta, M. de Boccage, had acquitted Ferrendino of Reynaud's charges.[32] Then, on 21 August 1754, at Zante, three indigenous merchants – Statti Lisgarà, Giorgio Flemotorno, and Giacomo Papadato – were found guilty *in absentia* of having secretly bought the silk from on board Marassi's privateer to have it eventually sold in the city, evading customs duty, and

---

[30] See ibid., fols 19r–21r, *passim*.

[31] APV, *Sezione* III, *Affari marittimi*, *busta* 42, fols 19r–21r.

[32] Ibid., fol. 20: 'Dopo il Ferandino ha fatto constare la sua innocenza mediante l'annesso giuridico Processo formato in Malta, il quale fu communicato al ministro della Corona di Francia, da cui fu assoluto per quello riguarda la querela contro Lui prodotta dal Console Francese.'

daringly defying all health regulations. They were condemned to fifteen years' exile from Venice's mainland and maritime domains.[33]

*   *   *

What impact did this gaudy episode of Venetian retaliation have on the historical development of Veneto-Hospitaller relations? The essence of Venetian strategy on this occasion appears to have been to win swiftly and with the minimum of damage to the republic's rapport with the Ottoman Porte. To achieve this objective its public representatives on Zante and Cephalonia disregarded all niceties of honour, at times even of decency. At the root of Ferrendino's case lay, in their view, the Order's recent crusading warfare in the Levant, for behind Marassi's defying venture there loomed large the pervasive protection which Hospitaller Malta had long been extending to its corsairing industry. This view of the situation emerges in a very explicit form from Grimani's already cited letters to Ferrendino. In one of them, he refers to the Grand Master as the 'Superior' ultimately responsible for the corsair's 'unfair and irregular behaviour'; in both, this behaviour is termed offensive to Venetian interests and to Marassi's own country's 'promises' or 'commitment'.[34] One clause of the 1747 settlement between the two states, it is well to recall, had guaranteed precisely the prevention of any further Hospitaller or Maltese privateering in Venetian waters.[35]

Was Venice's alacrity in dealing with Ferrendino, therefore, a bargaining ploy on the part of the republic? If so, what concessions did it gain, or hope to gain, from the Hospital on other issues in return for what eventually turned out to be an implicit admission of having acted too hastily? In 1752 Pinto's dismissal of his consul in Venice, Gio Batta Zocchi,[36] proved propitious to the republic in more than one sense. It immediately raised the question of the Order's consular representation on Venetian islands; prompted one other timely practical alternative to the traditional *sequestro* approach to its commitment to counter Hospitaller warfare, which she so rapidly endorsed; and, thirdly, exposed the republic's real need to regularize its position on the central Mediterranean island.

Venice moved quickly from the idea to its general practical significance. The image it had always entertained of Hospitaller Malta was that of a lair of

---

[33] Ibid., fol. 25: Copia tratta dalla Raspa delle Sentenze Criminali tenuta nell' Officio della cancelaria dell'illustrissimo et Eccellentissimo Signor Agostin Sagredo Provveditore General da Mar. G. Boerio defines *raspa* as 'quel libro su cui si registravano le sentenze criminali d'ogni sorta.' *Dizionario del Dialetto Veneziano* (Venice, 1856), *sub voce*.

[34] APV, *Sezione* III, *busta* 42, fol. 5.

[35] See Mallia-Milanes, *Venice and Hospitaller Malta*, p. 205.

[36] See the *Cinque Savii*'s report, 15 July 1752, in ASV, *Senato, Roma Ordinaria, Secreta, filza anno* 1752.

corsairs, where transgressors were permitted to escape punishment either through barefaced protection or through cunningly disguised statutory technicalities.[37] While the issue of Ferrendino was far from closed,[38] the republic was endeavouring to secure a strategic position on the island where it could witness infractions at first hand; indeed, intervene directly through its representatives in matters where the interests of Venetian merchants and sailors were of primary concern. In theory there should have been at least two possibilities open for the republic: the setting up of a Venetian consulate and the dispatch of a resident ministry. In reality there was a clear incompatibility between international norm and Hospitaller disposition. The situation on Hospitaller Malta, as on Hospitaller Rhodes, was totally different. To protect magistral prerogatives and safeguard the interests of the principality against any possible jurisdictional intrusion on the part of foreign states, traditional practice on either Hospitaller island consistently and indiscriminately required all foreign consuls be appointed, removed or assigned other duties by the Grand Master and be answerable to him alone.[39] To Venice the system appeared, as it would later appear to England, odd by international criteria, stale and unenviable. With the meagre services offered by the local consular agencies, the republic claimed to have suffered explicit disabilities.[40] But when the senate, on the advice of the *Cinque Savii alla Mercanzia* (the Venetian magistracy of trade), declared its intention to establish its own consulate on the island in June 1754,[41] its attempt to bypass these agencies was a quick failure, and the issue was not raised again.

There was, however, a second, indeed a more ingenious possibility, suggested the *Cinque Savii*, one capable of circumventing the Hospital's whole consular system. Several European states elected a Knight of St John, a native subject residing on Malta, and entrusted him with the protection of his co-nationals on the island. If this person was then assigned an annual stipend sufficiently decent to enable him to keep in his employ an official whom he could trust with minor duties (which could be of a consular nature), the proposal would have the advantage of blending the two characters harmoniously into one person, that of a resident minister and that of a consul. The senate's choice fell on the Paduan knight Hospitaller, Massimiliano Buzzaccarini

---

[37] See, for example, Giacomo Capello's dispatches from Malta to Venice and his later account on Malta in *Descrittione di Malta, Anno 1716: A Venetian Account*, ed. V. Mallia-Milanes (Malta, 1988). In 1716 Capello, the Venetian resident minister at Naples, was on an official visit to Malta.

[38] Notwithstanding the criminal proceedings against the three from Zante and their forced exile, Ferrendino was still writing to the Order's ambassador in Rome on 10 December 1754. He had not yet been reinstated in his consular office, nor had his confiscated property been restored. APV, *Sezione III, busta* 42, fol. 14, Copia di lettera dal Signore Gio. Ferrendino Console di Malta al Zante in data delli 10 Dicembre 1754 al Bali Solaro di Breglio.

[39] Mallia-Milanes, 'Malta and Venice', *passim*.

[40] For details, *idem, Venice and Hospitaller Malta*, pp. 211–14.

[41] ASV, CSM, *Diversorum, busta* 403, 25 July 1754.

Gonzaga, who was about to leave his native city to take up residence at the convent in Malta.[42] It was a very subtle proposal, shrewd and perspicacious, but it too would have almost certainly been rejected by the Grand Master had it not been for Fra Maurizio Solaro di Breglio. The Order's ambassador to the Holy See counselled reluctant Pinto that to deny Venice local facilities that had been for long accorded to so many other states, the principality of Monaco included, would be tantamount to sustaining her long-standing suspicion of Hospitaller duplicity.[43]

Buzzaccarini Gonzaga arrived in Malta in an official capacity as *Huomo della Repubblica* on 4 December 1754. Venice's resolve had been successfully translated into a rewarding capacity for direct intervention in what it had traditionally held as a major *radix malorum* in the Mediterranean. There is ample archival evidence that Buzzaccarini Gonzaga's presence at Valletta not only provided his accrediting republic with immediate understanding of the true nature of its subjects' grievances.[44] His access to the Grand Master's court and to those of other resident ministers also influenced central decisions in matters pertaining to privateering – and this no longer in a climate of deeply rooted sentiments of mutual animosity.[45]

---

[42] On Buzzaccarini Gonzaga, see Mallia-Milanes, *Venice and Hospitaller Malta, passim.*

[43] Malta, Cod. 1355, fols 149–150, 8 September 1754; also Mallia-Milanes, *Venice and Hospitaller Malta*, pp. 214–19.

[44] See *idem*, 'Poised between Hope and Infinite Despair'.

[45] For Veneto-Hospitaller relations in the second half of the eighteenth century, *idem*, *Venice and Hospitaller Malta*, ch. 8.

15

Literacy and Learning in the Military Orders during the Twelfth and Thirteenth Centuries

Alan Forey

Welfare and warfare: the main functions of military orders were of a practical nature, involving physical tasks, and rather different from the activities pursued in contemplative religious houses. Is it to be assumed, therefore, that military orders consisted predominantly of uneducated and unlearned brethren,[1] or did they include men of intellectual attainments, and did the implementation of their tasks in fact require some intellectual skills? Although it will not be possible to cover fully all the matters raised by these questions, and although there will have to be some generalization which will tend to underplay regional and chronological diversity, the present paper seeks to confront a number of the more important issues.

The first concerns literacy, which in the twelfth and thirteenth centuries commonly meant at least an ability to read and understand Latin. Chaplains were obviously assumed to possess this skill, but the majority of brethren were laymen. In the leading Orders these consisted of knights and sergeants, of whom the former in the thirteenth century were expected to be of knightly descent, while the latter rank excluded serfs; and certainly in the Temple and the Hospital sergeants considerably outnumbered knights. Discussion therefore mainly concerns laymen who were free but not noble, and is to be related to claims that from the twelfth century onwards considerable numbers of laymen did have some knowledge of Latin.[2]

---

[1] Discussion will be restricted to male members of military orders.

[2] M.B. Parkes, 'The Literacy of the Laity', in *Literature and Western Civilisation, 2: The Medieval World*, ed. D. Daiches and A. Thorlby (London, 1973), pp. 555–77; R.V. Turner, 'The *Miles Literatus* in Twelfth- and Thirteenth-Century England: How Rare a Phenomenon?', *American Historical Review*, 83 (1978), 928–45; M.T. Clanchy, *From Memory to Written Record: England, 1066–1307* (London, 1979), pp. 182–91.

Direct statements about the extent of literacy among lay brothers, in the sense of an ability to read Latin, are few and not altogether consistent. The most positive claim is found in the Teutonic Order's rule, the surviving version of which dates from the mid-thirteenth century. The eighth clause in the Latin text asserts that many, or even most, of the lay brothers understood Latin: '*plerique laycorum litterati sunt*'. But this text was apparently not written by a brother of the Order, and the vernacular versions are usually more guarded in their wording.[3] The most negative statements occur in the records of the trial of the Templars. In 1309 it was said of the Aragonese Templars besieged at Monzón – seventy-two brothers were reported to have been in the castle at one stage in the siege – that 'they are laymen and do not understand Latin' ('*son lecs et no entenen lo lati*').[4] The papal commissioners in Paris were similarly told by brethren that 'almost all are illiterate' ('*fere omnes sunt illiterati*')[5] – a claim that applied not only to the rank-and-file brethren. The Grand Master, James of Molay, described himself as 'an illiterate knight' ('*miles illiteratus*').[6] But Templars made these comments in Paris when they were attempting to avoid the burden and responsibility of conducting their own defence, and in this context the word '*litteratus*' may have been used – as it was on some other occasions – to signify a certain degree of learning rather than just an ability to read Latin, which seems to be the usage in the Teutonic Order's rule.[7]

In the testimonies of those who appeared before the papal commissioners, some lay brethren were in fact described as being '*litteratus*' or, more frequently, as understanding Latin. Twenty out of some 200 lay brothers were singled out in this way.[8] Of these, seventeen are known to have been sergeants and two were knights. But this does not mean that there were proportionately more literate sergeants, for sergeants comprised about 90 per cent of the lay brothers questioned. Only nine of the literate brothers were said to be preceptors, although it is possible that others had held office in the past,[9] and several had been in the Order for too short a time to have acquired a post. It is, of course,

---

[3] *SDO*, Regel 8, pp. 34–5; cf. ibid., pp. xlvii–xlviii; H. Grundmann, 'Deutsches Schrifttum im Deutschen Orden', in his *Ausgewählte Aufsätze*, 3 vols, Schriften der Monumenta Germaniae Historica, 25 (Stuttgart, 1976–8), 3, p. 118.

[4] H. Finke, *Papsttum und Untergang des Templerordens*, 2 vols (Münster, 1907), 2, doc. 100, p. 180; Barcelona, Archivo de la Corona de Aragón, Cancillería real, Cartas reales diplomáticas, Templarios, 546.

[5] *Procès*, 1, p. 101.

[6] Ibid., 1, p. 42; cf. ibid., 1, p. 88. The author of an Anglo-Norman version of the Hospitaller rule had earlier commented on the illiteracy of brethren in positions of authority: *The Hospitallers' Riwle*, ed. K.V. Sinclair, Anglo-Norman Text Society, 42 (London, 1984), p. 18, lines 601–4.

[7] They also employed the words '*laici*' and '*simplices*' in the same context: *Procès*, 1, pp. 28, 136, 144, 281–2.

[8] Ibid., 1, pp. 241, 254, 296, 379, 474, 538, 560, 606; 2, pp. 11, 107, 141, 143, 204, 209, 225, 227, 236, 256, 261, 267.

[9] They are not, however, among the preceptors listed in E.G. Léonard, *Introduction au cartulaire manuscrit du Marquis d'Albon* (Paris, 1930).

not known how systematically information about literacy was noted: the Templar treasurer in Paris, for example, was not among those described as literate.[10] The figures are minimum numbers, and lower than estimates of lay literacy derived from some late thirteenth- and fourteenth-century English sources;[11] but it is difficult to make valid comparisons and to be sure that like is being compared with like. In this context it may be noted that some of the statements contained in the Paris proceedings seem to have been based merely on a brother's own assertion, and could have implied varying degrees of competence: not all who claimed to know Latin were able to say whether Templar priests omitted the words of consecration in the Eucharist.[12]

Not surprisingly, only occasional comments are found in the records of the Templar trial about the literacy of chaplains, but clearly some had only a limited knowledge of Latin: of Aymeric of Bures the papal commissioners remarked that 'he did not understand Latin well' ('*nec intelligebat bene Latinum*'); and a group of twenty Templars, which included two chaplains, apologized for the mistakes ('*falsis Latinitatibus*') in a document which they had drawn up and which was certainly riddled with error.[13]

While direct statements about literacy are few, various sources imply a contemporary assumption that the bulk of lay brothers were unable to understand Latin. Regulations concerning the holding of services assume that these brethren would not usually be able to participate actively. Templar customs, for example, state that 'when ... matins are sung, all should remain silent and hear the service quietly and in peace' ('*quant ... les matines se chantent, chascun doit tenir silence et oyr le servise belement et en pais*'), and a thirteenth-century version of the rule of Santiago similarly decrees that 'they are to keep silent in church while divine service is being held' ('*silencio tengan en la ecclesia mientre que el servimiento de Dios se fiziere*').[14] Lay brethren were merely expected to say a certain number of paternosters for each office. The same practice was, of course, adopted for Cistercian *conversi* and the lay brothers and sisters of hospitals.[15] The Hospitaller *usances* admittedly instructed brethren to genuflect when they heard certain Latin words or phrases said during services, and

---

[10] *Procès*, 1, pp. 595–601.

[11] Clanchy, *Memory to Written Record*, pp. 175–6; R.W. Kaeuper, 'Two Early Lists of Literates in England: 1334, 1373', *English Historical Review*, 99 (1984), 363–9.

[12] For example, *Procès*, 1, p. 256. This was, in fact, a common admission by Templars questioned, and could be taken as a further implied statement of illiteracy.

[13] Ibid., 1, pp. 120–4, 320.

[14] *RT*, § 282 (p. 171); D.W. Lomax, *La orden de Santiago (1170–1275)* (Madrid, 1965), §§ 6,7 (pp. 222–3); cf. J. Leclercq, 'La vie et la prière des chevaliers de Santiago d'après leur règle primitive', *Liturgica*, 2 (1958), 353–4; *RSJ*, §§ 5, 6 (pp. 88–90); *CH*, 2, no. 2213, §§ 123–4 (pp. 536–61).

[15] J. Leclercq, 'Comment vivaient les frères convers', in *I laici nella 'Societas Christiana' dei secoli XI e XII* (Milan, 1968), p. 169; J. Dubois, 'L'institution des convers au XIIe siècle: Forme de vie monastique propre aux laics', in ibid., pp. 217, 239–42; N. Orme and M. Webster, *The English Hospital, 1070–1570* (New Haven, 1995), p. 52.

similar injunctions are found in the regulations of some other orders;[16] but this does not signify that lay brothers would always have understood the meaning of the words. In some instances priests also helped brethren by saying '*flectamus genua*' ('let us kneel') or '*levate*' ('arise') – phrases whose sense would quickly be learnt by those who had no general familiarity with Latin.[17] Yet regulations about the conduct of services also indicate that not all lay brothers were assumed to be illiterate. The eighth clause of the Teutonic Order's rule starts by stating that all brothers should attend services, with the clerics 'singing and reading' ('*cantantes et legentes*'), while the lay brethren were to say a number of paternosters, but adds that literate lay brethren could participate in the saying of offices – it is in this context that the statement about the numbers of literate lay brethren is made – and a similar ruling occurs in the regulations of the Order of the Blessed Virgin Mary, drawn up in 1261.[18] Literate lay brothers were in some cases thought to be sufficiently numerous to merit a mention in regulations.

Assumptions that most lay brothers were illiterate were apparently still being made in various parts of the West during the Templar trial. The noting in Paris of those who did understand Latin itself implies an assumption that literacy was considered unusual. Furthermore, when brothers appeared before their interrogators, it was common in many places for lists of accusations, records of testimonies and other documents drawn up in Latin to be expounded in the vernacular so that Templars could understand them. When this was done in the presence of a group of Templars it is not necessarily very significant: it could merely mean that those in charge of investigations assumed that there would be some who could not understand Latin. Yet it is clear that it was also a normal practice to translate from Latin when information was being conveyed to individual Templars. In the Papal State and the Abruzzi the articles of accusation were expounded in the vernacular to each of six lay Templars questioned – though not to the one chaplain – and their testimonies were later read back to them in the vernacular, even though they were recorded in Latin.[19] In Roussillon in 1310 the charges were expounded in the vernacular to each of the twenty-five Templars interrogated.[20] It was similarly reported

---

[16] *CH*, 2, no. 2213, § 124 (pp. 536–61); *RT*, §§ 295, 342, 344–5 (pp. 176, 196–8); Leclercq, 'Vie et prière', 353.

[17] *RT*, §§ 342, 345 (pp. 196–8). When Templar regulations allude to the hearing or saying of offices, the saying at least in some cases refers to the recital of paternosters: ibid., §§ 266, 300, 306 (pp. 163, 178, 180).

[18] D.M. Federici, *Istoria de' cavalieri gaudenti*, 2 vols (Vinegia, 1787), 2: *Codex diplomaticus*, p. 21.

[19] A. Gilmour-Bryson, *The Trial of the Templars in the Papal State and the Abruzzi* (Vatican City, 1982), pp. 131, 135, 146, 156, 172–86, 188–99, 201–12, 214–25, 250, 253–5, 257, 261; cf. K. Schottmüller, *Der Untergang des Templer-Ordens*, 2 vols (Berlin, 1887), 2, pp. 125, 132 for interrogations at Brindisi.

[20] *Procès*, 2, pp. 423–515.

that the Templars who were questioned before the pope at Poitiers in the summer of 1308 had their testimonies read back to them 'in the vernacular or mother tongue' (*'in vulgari seu in lingua materna'*) and 'in their Gallic mother tongue' (*'in lingua gallica et materna'*).[21] Individual Templars for whom documents were translated included the Grand Master himself, James of Molay.[22] Although in Paris literate brothers were listed and a literate Templar knight who was interrogated there examined the charge sheet himself,[23] the practice of translating elsewhere for each Templar appears to imply an assumption that the great majority of brethren did not have sufficient Latin to understand articles of accusation or testimonies which were not in the vernacular: inquisitors merely surmised ignorance without ascertaining whether it really existed. Had they inquired, the practice of translating would probably not have been so uniform.

The argument has admittedly been advanced that the translating of documents was sometimes occasioned by defiance on the part of Templars. This has been claimed with reference to the translating of articles of accusation for seventeen of the twenty-nine Templars denying the main charges at Clermont in 1309: it is pointed out that it was apparently not necessary to translate for any of the forty who did confess to more serious charges.[24] If this argument is accepted, then all those questioned at Clermont would have had a working knowledge of Latin. Perhaps a more plausible explanation is that the scribes recording the proceedings did not systematically note when charges were translated: this would certainly not be the only variation in the formulae used in the wording of these records. There was also an occasion in March 1310, however, when over 500 Templars assembled in Paris said that they were content with hearing a Latin version of the commission's instructions and the articles of accusation. Yet this was done not because they understood Latin but because 'they did not want such disgraceful matters – which they said were wholly false and not fit to be mentioned – to be expounded to them in the vernacular' (*'non curabant quod tante turpitudines quas asserebant omnino falsas et non nominandas vulgariter exponerentur eisdem'*).[25] The wording seems in fact to imply that most did not know Latin and did not want to hear charges in a language which they could understand.

Although assumptions about illiteracy were being made, the twelfth and thirteenth centuries were a period of increasing reliance on written records, and

---

[21] Schottmüller, 2, pp. 16–32, 55–6. This statement was not made of the group beginning on p. 34, but the explanation probably lies in scribal inconsistency. See also Finke, *Papsttum*, 2, no. 155 (p. 340).

[22] *Procès*, 1, pp. 33–4.

[23] Ibid., 1, p. 379; cf. ibid., 1, p. 421.

[24] *Le procès des Templiers d'Auvergne, 1309–1311*, ed. R. Sève and A.-M. Chagny-Sève, Mémoires et documents d'histoire médiévale et de philologie, 1 (Paris, 1986), p. 53.

[25] *Procès*, 1, p. 100.

the military orders were not immune to this trend. Acquisitions of rights and privileges were recorded in writing; and to ensure that such records were preserved cartularies were compiled, though not systematically, and archives established at various levels: in the later thirteenth century, for example, the Aragonese Templars had a provincial archive at the convent of Miravet, on the Ebro, although some charters and privileges were also kept more locally.[26] Estate management produced documentation which included inquests, surveys and rentals, the best-known example being the English Templar inquest of 1185.[27] When the Templar castle of Monzón fell to James II of Aragon in 1309, it was reported that twenty-five books and *cuadernos* detailing rents and dues were seized.[28] It was also normal practice to draw up inventories of goods in a brother's keeping: these would range from lists of the personal effects of an individual to records of all goods coming into an order's treasury. A Hospitaller statute of 1301 furthermore reminded the brother in charge of the store at the Order's headquarters that he should obtain a receipt for any item he assigned to brethren-at-office, although it is not known what form the receipt took.[29]

Officials were also expected to render accounts. In the Teutonic Order the treasurer and other central officials who distributed goods or disbursed money had to account before the Master at the end of each month, and a Hospitaller statute in 1283 similarly stated that the Master should audit the treasury accounts monthly, although the wording implies hearing rather than reading on the Master's part.[30] In these Orders the Master was, of course, the senior official, but in the Order of Calatrava the Master himself had to render account before the visitor, who was a Cistercian abbot.[31] Leading central officials and those in charge of provinces or of local houses had further to answer before the appropriate chapter. In the Hospitaller general chapter central officials had to present a roll detailing the state of their offices.[32] Officials in the Teutonic Order were to present written 'accounts of debts and rents and a statement about their houses' ('*computaciones debitorum, reddituum et statum domorum*') when

---

[26] A.J. Forey, 'Sources for the History of the Templars in Aragon, Catalonia and Valencia', *Archives*, 21 (1994), 16–17.

[27] B.A. Lees, *Records of the Templars in England in the Twelfth Century: The Inquest of 1185*, Records of the Social and Economic History of England and Wales, 9 (London, 1935).

[28] Archivo de la Corona de Aragón, Canc. real, registro 291, fol. 323v; cf. *CH*, 3, no. 3039, § 23 (pp. 43–54).

[29] *CH*, 4, no. 4549, § 1 (pp. 14–23). Other regulations on inventories include ibid., 1, no. 70, § 6 (pp. 62–8); 3, no. 3317, § 6 (pp. 186–8); 3, no. 4022, § 8 (pp. 525–9); 4, no. 4549, § 38 (pp. 14–23); *RT*, §§ 111, 491 (pp. 94–5, 260); *SDO*, Regel 5 (pp. 31–2); Ges. I(i) (p. 58); Gew. 17 (pp. 101–2); Madrid, Biblioteca Nacional, MS 8582, fol. 64.

[30] *SDO*, Gew. 31 (p. 107); *CH*, 3, no. 3844, § 2 (pp. 450–5); see also ibid., 4, no. 4549, §§ 1, 14, 15 (pp. 14–23).

[31] D.W. Lomax, 'Algunos estatutos primitivos de la orden de Calatrava', *Hispania*, 21 (1961), 493.

[32] *CH*, 2, no. 2213, § 109 (pp. 536–61).

resigning their posts at provincial chapters; in some Templar provinces, on the other hand, heads of convents merely brought to the provincial chapter a statement of what goods their houses contained.[33] Among other matters recorded in writing were announcements of appointments made by the central authorities of an order, and recalls and transfers of brethren.[34]

Documents were also to be drawn up with reference to some judicial matters arising within an order. The Hospitaller rule states that brothers who persistently offended were to be sent to the Master with a written report of their failings, and also that brothers were to inform the Master in writing of the faults of any colleague who refused to amend his conduct;[35] and the Templar customs required the almoner to record when a brother who had been deprived of his habit began his penance.[36] Correspondence was, of course, also received from, and sent to, outsiders, although there is no evidence by the end of the thirteenth century of any system of registration of letters issued in the names of officials of military orders. Nevertheless, for the administration of a military order and its possessions, recourse to writing was the norm and the need for this was increased by the international character of leading orders: information and instructions were being sent over long distances.

Nor was only a small proportion of an order's membership involved in administrative activities. Many houses of the leading Orders in Western countries, such as France and England, contained no more than a handful of brethren, at least several of whom would have administrative responsibilities. Some brethren were also employed in administrative capacities by popes and kings,[37] and some orders, especially the Temple, were engaged in banking and moneylending activities, which – like some aspects of estate administration – required both numeracy and literacy.[38]

The growing use of written records has, of course, been one reason for postulating an increase in literacy among laymen. Yet, before conclusions can

---

[33] *SDO*, Ges. II(b) (pp. 59–60); Gew. 7*, 18 (pp. 96–7, 102). Some Templar statements apparently presented to the Aragonese provincial chapter in 1289 have been published in J. Miret y Sans, 'Inventaris de les cases del Temple de la Corona d'Aragó en 1289', *Boletín de la Real Academia de Buenas Letras de Barcelona*, 6 (1911), 62–9; cf. J.F. O'Callaghan, 'The Earliest "Difiniciones" of the Order of Calatrava, 1304–1383', *Traditio*, 17 (1961), § 16 (265).

[34] *CH*, 3, no. 3670, § 1 (pp. 368–70); 3, no. 4022, § 22 (pp. 525–9); A.J. Forey, *The Templars in the Corona de Aragón* (London, 1973), no. 44 (pp. 414–15); H. Finke, 'Nachträge und Ergänzungen zu den Acta Aragonensia (I–III)', *Spanische Forschungen der Görresgesellschaft: Gesammelte Aufsätze zur Kulturgeschichte Spaniens*, 4 (1933), no. 14 (451–2).

[35] *CH*, 1, no. 70, §§ 12, 17 (pp. 62–8).

[36] *RT*, §§ 489, 654 (pp. 259, 335).

[37] On the Templars, see M.L. Bulst-Thiele, 'Templer in königlichen und päpstlichen Diensten', in *Festschrift Percy Ernst Schramm*, ed. P. Classen and P. Scheibert, 2 vols (Wiesbaden, 1964), 1, pp. 289–308; Forey, *Templars in Aragon*, pp. 344–5.

[38] L. Delisle, *Mémoire sur les opérations financières des Templiers* (Paris, 1889); J. Piquet, *Des banquiers au moyen âge: les Templiers* (Paris, 1939).

be drawn from the Orders' reliance on writing, it is necessary to consider the language in which documents were written, the degree of linguistic skill required, the frequency with which material had to be read, and also the assistance available to those who could not read.

The spread of the vernacular as a language of record was uneven. It was already being used in the twelfth century in some parts of southern France and in the thirteenth century in Castile, but in many areas Latin was still the norm in 1300. It is probably true that letters and communications transmitted within orders were written increasingly in the vernacular, even in districts where Latin was still the language of record, and regulations usually existed in vernacular versions;[39] but some internal correspondence was certainly still in Latin at the end of the thirteenth century.[40] Even if the use of the vernacular was spreading, it was sometimes necessary to refer back to earlier documents. In this context it may be noted that cartularies compiled for military orders before 1300 normally retained the language in which the documents had originally been written, although in the later thirteenth century the Aragonese Templars did have vernacular versions made of a general Latin cartulary.[41]

In 1300 a knowledge of Latin was still needed for reading administrative records, but not all documentation in Latin required a uniform level of linguistic skill. A rental could be understood with very little knowledge of Latin. The perusal of charters entailed a somewhat greater command of the language, but formulae were, of course, commonly employed. A much greater competence was needed for documents which did not in the main adhere to set phrases: failure to identify the mood or tense of a verb in a royal or papal letter might have awkward consequences. A command of Latin that would make such documents easily intelligible was not to be acquired through a little perfunctory instruction, as sometimes seems to be suggested.

Some documents would only rarely be read. Once charters had been compiled, they would normally be consulted only if disputes arose. Reference to rentals usually occurred only when payments or services were due. Letters of an administrative character would be read when they arrived but, although some royal chanceries were issuing innumerable documents of this kind, the numbers reaching many Western convents may not have been very large. Some who occupied minor administrative positions in the Orders were probably not constantly using documentation written in Latin. When lay officials did need to peruse documents, they usually had access to men who could read

---

[39] J. Delaville Le Roulx, 'Les statuts de l'ordre de l'Hôpital de Saint-Jean de Jérusalem', *Bibliothèque de l'Ecole des Chartes*, 48 (1887), 345, states that in the early thirteenth century the Hospitaller Master Alfonso of Portugal decreed that statutes and privileges should be translated into the vernacular; but he provides no reference.

[40] See, for example, H. Finke, *Acta aragonensia*, 3 vols (Berlin, 1908–22), 3, no. 18 (p. 31); Forey, *Templars in Aragon*, no. 46 (p. 419); Grundmann, pp. 100–1.

[41] Forey, 'Sources', 21.

Latin. Convents normally had chaplains, whether they were brethren or secular priests, and recourse could also be made to professional notaries, some of whom are found in the employment of Orders.[42] It is questionable, therefore, whether the existence of documentation in Latin necessitated a high degree of literacy on the part of large numbers of brothers involved in administrative tasks. No doubt there were some for whom an ability to read Latin was essential, but in an age when knowledge of foreign languages is not considered a prerequisite for international political discussion and the use of interpreters is an accepted practice, it should not occasion surprise that at an earlier time some sought assistance in coping with written material. Although there were some lay brethren who could read Latin to a greater or lesser extent, the surviving evidence cannot be taken to indicate that competence in the language was common; and there was a contemporary assumption that illiteracy was widespread.

Since the use of the vernacular was spreading, there is also the question of reading ability in languages other than Latin. On this point it may be noted that it was the custom for information to be conveyed orally even when it was contained in vernacular sources. It was not, for example, assumed that brethren would routinely refer to vernacular versions of rules and regulations. According to a thirteenth-century description of the Templar admission ceremony, the receiving brother was to tell a recruit about the penalties for various offences as well as other details of the daily routine and Templar life;[43] and that guidance was in fact given in this way is apparent from the testimonies of many Templars questioned in the early fourteenth century. As this form of instruction could not by itself be altogether adequate, Templars were further advised to seek guidance from senior brothers.[44] In all military orders additional instruction was also provided through periodic public readings of rules and regulations: at one time brethren of the Teutonic Order were to have their rule read to them at least six times a year.[45] Although the Teutonic Order sought to make this possible by decreeing that each house should have a copy of the rule,[46] it was not the practice to ensure that copies of regulations were available to most brothers. The Templar customs decree that 'no brother is to have a copy of the rule and statutes, unless he has it with the consent of the convent' ('*nul frere ne doit tenir retrais ne regle, se ne les tient par le congié dou couvent*'): only officials were normally allowed to have one. Similar restrictions were imposed by

---

[42] See below pp. 197–8 and notes 70–4.

[43] *RT*, §§ 678–86 (pp. 345–50).

[44] Ibid., §§ 679, 686 (pp. 346, 350); *Procès*, 1, pp. 360, 382, 539, 546; D. Wilkins, *Concilia magnae Britanniae et Hiberniae*, 4 vols (London, 1737), 2, p. 334.

[45] *SDO*, Ges. III(b) (p. 63); cf. ibid., Ges. 17, 27 (pp. 71, 74); *CH*, 3, no. 4234, § 7 (pp. 638–40); *RT*, § 532 (p. 279); Lomax, *Santiago*, § 50 (p. 227); *RSJ*, §§ 7, 45 (pp. 92, 122).

[46] Cf. C.R. Cheney, *Episcopal Visitation of Monasteries in the Thirteenth Century* (Manchester, 1983 edn), pp. 157, 168.

some other orders.[47] A literate Templar interrogated during the trial in fact said that copies had been taken away from brethren.[48] Although during their trial a few Templars claimed to have read their rule,[49] it is clear from the wording of testimonies that many brothers had not: they could only state what they had been told and had heard. There were, therefore, in military orders various practices which might be seen as characteristic of a mainly non-literate society. Such practices do not, of course, necessarily signify that the large majority of lay brothers could not read in the vernacular: they could merely represent the survival of antiquated customs. Proficiency in reading, however, depended not only on initial instruction but also on regular practice, and the lack of any need – or ability – to consult written regulations about conventual life would have served to discourage the maintenance of any skills which some brothers may once have possessed.

To assess how many brethren could in fact read in the vernacular is not easy. Scribes were little interested in reporting reading ability other than in Latin. It may be assumed that chaplains could do so, but it is difficult to estimate what proportion of lay brothers had this ability. The most worn part of a Catalan version of Templar regulations is that relating to the admission ceremony, which suggests that it was often used by officials, who would mainly have been lay brothers, when admitting recruits;[50] and several Templars reported that, when they were admitted, regulations had been *read* to them, though not necessarily by the receiving official.[51] It may also be noted that the records of the Templar trial refer to a few lay brothers who read out documents in the vernacular, written in some cases by themselves.[52] On the other hand, some Templar testimonies suggest that the brother admitting a recruit did not always provide instruction by reading out regulations. One knight said that the official merely mentioned some points which he could remember, although this particular comment may have had its origins in the wording of Templar regulations themselves.[53] It should, however, be remembered that copies of regulations were not always in the local vernacular: the three copies of Templar regulations seized in the Valencian convent of Peñíscola in 1307 were in

---

[47] *RT*, § 326 (p. 189); *CH*, 3, no. 3844, § 7 (pp. 450–5); Madrid, Bib. Nac., MS 8582, fol. 56.

[48] *Procès*, 1, pp. 388–9; cf. ibid., 1, p. 614; Finke, *Papsttum*, 2, no. 155 (p. 336).

[49] *Procès*, 1, pp. 387–8, 473, 569; 2, pp. 73, 111, 445.

[50] J. Delaville Le Roulx, 'Un nouveau manuscrit de la règle du Temple', *Annuaire-bulletin de la Société de l'Histoire de France*, 26 (1889), 186.

[51] *Procès*, 1, p. 243; Wilkins, 2, p. 334.

[52] *Procès*, 1, pp. 36, 37, 140, 169.

[53] Ibid., 1, p. 382; *RT*, § 678, p. 346. Hospitaller regulations for the holding of general chapters include the provision that senior brethren should recite customs they could remember: *CH*, 2, no. 2213, § 109 (pp. 536–61); but these were presumably observances which at the time had not been set down in writing.

French, as were most versions later in the hands of the Aragonese kings.[54] This situation is encountered not only with regard to regulations. A letter sent by the Templar commander of Alfambra to the Grand Master James of Molay was in Catalan, and conversely some letters dispatched from the Templar headquarters in the East to the Aragonese province were in French.[55] Some lay brothers may have been able to read, but not to understand the particular vernacular in which a document was written.

In studies of more modern periods, when literacy did not involve Latin, an ability to write one's name has often been used as a criterion, and it might be argued that for the Middle Ages it could indicate an acquaintance with writing, if not with Latin. Yet, whatever the validity of this criterion for other periods, it is of little use for the twelfth and thirteenth centuries, for it was not then the custom even for brothers who knew Latin to write their own names at the end of documents.[56]

A further approach to the problem of the extent of vernacular literacy – as well as literacy in Latin – is provided by examining the books possessed or read by lay brethren, although those who fell into the category of what has been termed 'cultivated readers' were presumably fewer than so-called 'pragmatic readers'. Much evidence is inevitably imprecise or anecdotal. The statutes issued by the Hospital in 1262 refer to brothers who read works in the vernacular while in the infirmary, and also to breviaries, psalters and other books belonging to deceased brethren; and, although later regulations of the Teutonic Order envisage that only chaplains would leave books, the Hospitaller *usances* assume that breviaries and psalters might be found among the possessions of dead bailiffs and brethren-at-arms.[57] A Templar knight told the papal commissioners that he used to have a copy of St Bernard's *De laude*, and Berenguer of Cardona, Templar provincial Master in Aragon at the end of the thirteenth century, possessed a version of Genesis.[58] Some lay brothers are known to have

[54] J. Rubió, R. d'Alós and F. Martorell, 'Inventaris inèdits de l'orde del Temple a Catalunya', *Anuari de l'Institut d'Estudis Catalans*, 1 (1907), no. 4 (393–6); F. Martorell y Trabal, 'Inventari dels bens de la cambra reyal en temps de Jaume II (1323)', ibid., 4 (1911–12), 553, 562–6; J.E. Martínez Ferrando, 'La Cámera real en el reinado de Jaime II (1291–1327). Relaciones de entradas y salidas de objetos artísticos', *Anales y Boletín de los Museos de Arte de Barcelona*, 11 (1953–4), no. 134 (193–8); J. Massó Torrents, 'Inventari dels bens mobles del rey Martí d'Aragó', *Revue hispanique*, 12 (1905), nos 6, 39, 53, 154, 285 (415, 420, 422, 435, 453).

[55] Finke, *Papsttum*, 2, no. 24 (p. 37); Forey, *Templars in Aragon*, no. 36 (pp. 405–6); Finke, 'Nachträge', no. 14 (451–2).

[56] There are a few apparent exceptions: see, for example, Archivo de la Corona de Aragón, Canc. real, pergaminos, Jaime I, 95, 96, 2234.

[57] *CH*, 2, no. 2213, §§ 113, 116 (pp. 536–61); 3, no. 3039, §§ 39, 42 (pp. 43–54); *SDO*, Capitelbeschlüsse II(1) (p. 135); H.-D. Kahl, 'Zur kulturellen Stellung der Deutschordensritter in Preussen', in *Die Rolle der Ritterorden in der mittelalterlichen Kultur*, ed. Z.H. Nowak (Toruń, 1985), pp. 45–6.

[58] *Procès*, 1, p. 389; Rubió, Alós and Martorell, no. 9 (p. 400).

commissioned translations, just as lay nobles were doing in the same period.[59] A French version of the Book of Judges was made in the twelfth century, apparently in England, for two Templars, and at Temple Bruer, in Lincolnshire, translations of several works were undertaken for another Templar, Henry Darcy.[60] About the year 1300 a translation of the psalter was dedicated to the Hospitaller Simon Rat, and his colleague William of Santo Stefano similarly commissioned translations of Cicero's *De Inventione* and of the *Rhetorica ad Herenium*. His writings also make reference to Gratian as well as early Christian writers, although it is difficult to judge the exact extent of his reading.[61] Several gifts of books are also recorded: in the later thirteenth century the Hospitaller Boniface of Calamandracen was given a translation of Albertus Magnus's *Libellus de Alchimia* by an Armenian king, and two books were assigned to an ex-Templar knight by James II of Aragon in 1316.[62] It has admittedly been suggested that illuminated religious manuscripts were regarded almost as relics,[63] but the commissioning of translations implies that these were meant to be used.

Nevertheless, such evidence relates to only a handful of lay brothers, and the inventories of Templar goods compiled after the arrest of brethren suggest that many convents possessed only liturgical books; and in some cases these books were explicitly stated to have been found in the conventual chapel.[64] There are, however, exceptions, which in some instances could imply regional differences. A Templar house at Arles, which possessed over forty volumes,

---

[59] Parkes, pp. 556–7.

[60] M. Melville, *La vie des Templiers* (Paris, 1951), pp. 80–3; J. Folda, *Crusader Manuscript Illumination at Saint-Jean d'Acre, 1275–1291* (Princeton, 1976), pp. 61–5; R.C.D. Perman, 'Henri d'Arci: the Shorter Works', in *Studies in Medieval French Presented to Alfred Ewert* (Oxford, 1961), p. 279; *Le Livre des Juges. Les cinq textes de la version française faite au XIIe siècle pour les chevaliers du Temple*, ed. Marquis d'Albon, Société des Bibliophiles Lyonnois (Lyon, 1913).

[61] *Histoire littéraire de la France*, 37 (Paris, 1936), 441–2; L. Delisle, 'Maître Jean d'Antioche, traducteur, et frère Guillaume de Saint-Etienne', ibid., 33 (Paris, 1906), 2, 32–5.

[62] A.T. Luttrell, 'The Hospitallers' Interventions in Cilician Armenia, 1291–1375', in *The Cilician Kingdom of Armenia*, ed. T.S.R. Boase (Edinburgh, 1978), p. 121; Martínez Ferrando, no. 82 (pp. 110–11).

[63] M.T. Clanchy, 'Looking Back from the Invention of Printing', in *Literacy in Historical Perspective*, ed. D.P. Resnick (Washington, 1983), p. 14.

[64] Published texts or summaries of individual inventories include *Le dossier de l'affaire des Templiers*, ed. G. Lizerand (Paris, 1964), pp. 46–55 (Baugy); A. Higounet-Nadal, 'L'inventaire des biens de la commanderie du Temple de Sainte-Eulalie du Larzac en 1308', *Annales du Midi*, 68 (1956), 258–60; W.H. Blaauw, 'Sadelescombe and Shipley, the Preceptories of the Knights Templars in Sussex', *Sussex Archaeological Collections*, 9 (1857) 240–1, 253–4; H.E. Chetwynd-Stapylton, 'The Templars at Templehurst', *Yorkshire Archaeological and Topographical Journal*, 10 (1889), 432–3; T.H. Fosbrooke, 'Rothley. The Preceptory', *Transactions of the Leicester Archaeological Society*, 12 (1921–2), 32–4; *Victoria County History: Cambridge and the Isle of Ely*, 2 (London, 1948), pp. 260, 262–3 (Denney, Duxford and Wilbraham); Rubió, Alós and Martorell, no. 4 (pp. 393–6); Martínez Ferrando, no. 32 (pp. 38–44) (Peñíscola). An analysis of French inventories is provided by A.-M. Legras and J.L. Lemaître, 'La pratique liturgique des Templiers et des Hospitaliers

had copies of the *Dialogues* of Gregory the Great and the *Historia Scholastica* of Peter Comestor.[65] These works, together with writings by St Ambrose and Hugh of St Victor, were also among the non-liturgical books seized when the Aragonese castle of Monzón fell to James II in 1309.[66] A further list of Templar books sent in 1308 to the Aragonese king, possibly from the convent of Tortosa, includes the *Codex* of Justinian, a copy of the *Chirurgia* of the Dominican Theoderic, and a version of John XXI's *Thesaurus pauperum*.[67] The books in this last list were in the vernacular, but those from Monzón were apparently in Latin. It is not known how the Templars obtained possession of such works, or to what extent they were read, particularly by lay brethren. Certainly they are rather different in kind from most of the known commissioned writings. The possession of books in the vernacular and the spread of vernacular languages in documentation suggest that, although reading was commonly taught through Latin works,[68] there were, by the later thirteenth century, some lay brethren who could cope better with the written vernacular than with Latin. Templar inventories suggest that such brothers – their numbers are unknown – used the skill mainly for administrative purposes, rather than for 'cultivated reading'; and the latter activity does not seem to have been very characteristic even of Templar chaplains.

An ability to read was not the only intellectual skill which might be required in military orders. Documents had to be written as well as read. Although some charters and letters were composed by chaplains – the use of ordained brothers as scribes may have been most widespread in some convents of clerics, such as Santiago's house of Vilar de Donas[69] – this task was most commonly undertaken by outsiders. Leading central officials normally had hired scribes in their entourage. Although the Hospitaller Grand Master in 1126 had a chancellor who was apparently a brother, it was not until the early fourteenth century that the post was formally established in the hands of a member of the

---

de Saint-Jean de Jérusalem', in *L'écrit dans la société médiévale: divers aspects de sa pratique du XIe au XVe siècle*, ed. C. Bourlet and A. Dufour (Paris, 1991), pp. 99–106, 121. On surviving liturgical books, see ibid., p. 78; C. Dondi, '"Missale Vetus ad usum Templariorum": l'ordine dei cavalieri templari in area modenense nei secoli XII–XIV', *Aevum*, 68 (1994), 339–42. On gifts of liturgical books to Templar houses, see E. Barthélemy, 'Obituaire de la commanderie du Temple de Reims', in *Mélanges historiques*, 5 vols, Collection de documents inédits sur l'histoire de France (Paris, 1873–86), 4, p. 328; V. Carrière, *Histoire et cartulaire des Templiers de Provins* (Paris, 1919), no. 86 (p. 106).

[65] Legras and Lemaître, pp. 121–2.

[66] Rubió, Alós and Martorell, no. 5 (pp. 396–7); Martínez Ferrando, no. 48 (pp. 70–1).

[67] J. Villanueva, *Viage literario a las iglesias de España*, 22 vols (Madrid, 1803–52), 5, pp. 200–2; see also Martorell y Trabal, pp. 562–7; Martínez Ferrando, no. 134 (pp. 193–8).

[68] On teaching methods, see D. Alexandre-Bidon, 'La lettre volée. Apprendre à lire à l'enfant au moyen âge', *Annales. Economies, Sociétés, Civilisations*, 44 (1989), 953–92.

[69] See the thirteenth-century documents published in J.L. Novo Cazón, *El priorato santiaguista de Vilar de Donas en la edad media (1194–1500)* (La Coruña, 1986).

Order, and even then it was not permanently maintained.[70] In regulations of
the later thirteenth and early fourteenth centuries the Hospitaller Grand
Master was in fact assigned two scribes.[71] In the West a list of secular scribes
of the Hospitaller prior of Navarre can be compiled, although the position was
briefly held by a brother in the mid-1240s,[72] and in the Aragonese province of
the Templars the Master in the later thirteenth century had his own public
notary.[73] A number of Aragonese Templar houses also had secular scribes
among their employees.[74]

Military orders required the composition of cartularies and surveys, as well
as charters and letters, and it is usually difficult to discover who produced such
volumes in the twelfth and thirteenth centuries; but the compilation of a
cartulary for the Templar house of Vaour was undertaken by the commander's
nephew, who was a canon of Saint-Antonin, and a large part of the Douzens
cartularies was written by William de Palatio, who was apparently not a
Templar.[75] It is also clear that some copies of rules and customs were made by
outsiders: a public notary who testified before the papal commissioners in
Paris during the Templar trial stated that he had made a copy of Templar
regulations.[76] Documents and books were in fact compiled by a wide variety
of scribes, but the Orders did not usually have *scriptoria* manned by brethren.
It is true that the Templar James of Garrigans, who knew how to 'write in an
elegant hand and to illuminate with gold' ('*escriure letra formada e illuminar ab
or*'), was commissioned by the Aragonese king James II to make a book of hours
while he was in custody during the Templar trial, but he was exceptional.[77]
There is no evidence to suggest that the illuminator who has been designated
'the Hospitaller master' was a brother of the Hospital;[78] and the binding of the
English Templar inquest of 1185 was apparently the work of a London binder.[79]

---

[70] A.T. Luttrell, 'Notes on the Chancery of the Hospitallers of Rhodes: 1314–1332', *Byzantion*, 40 (1970), 408–16; *CH*, 1, nos 77, 399 (pp. 72–3, 272–3).

[71] Ibid., 3, no. 3317, § 1 (pp. 186–8); 4, no. 4574, § 4 (pp. 36–41); cf. B. Casado Quintanilla, 'La cancillería y las escribanías de la orden de Calatrava', *Anuario de estudios medievales*, 14 (1984), 79–80.

[72] See the documents published in S.A. García Larragueta, *El gran priorado de Navarra de la orden de San Juan de Jerusalén*, 2 vols (Pamplona, 1957), 2 *passim* (nos 307, 309 [pp. 301, 303–4] for the brother scribe).

[73] Forey, *Templars in Aragon*, p. 315.

[74] Ibid., p. 288.

[75] *Cartulaire des Templiers de Vaour*, ed. C. Portal and E. Cabié (Albi, 1894), p. i, no. 115 (pp. 103–4) (the cartulary is in fact in more than one hand: ibid., pp. ii–iii); *Cartulaires des Templiers de Douzens*, ed. P. Gérard and E. Magnou, Collection de documents inédits sur l'histoire de France, 3 (Paris, 1965), pp. xii–xiv; cf. D. Le Blévec and A. Venturini, 'Cartulaires des ordres militaires, XIIe–XIIIe siècles (Provence occidentale, basse vallée du Rhône)', *Les cartulaires*, Mémoires et documents de l'Ecole des Chartes, 39 (Paris, 1993), pp. 453–4.

[76] *Procès*, 1, p. 643.

[77] Archivo de la Corona de Aragón, Canc. real, Cart. real. dipl., Templarios, 157.

[78] Folda, p. 52.

[79] Lees, p. xxiii; G.D. Hobson, *English Binding before 1500* (Cambridge, 1929), p. 4.

In protecting their rights, military orders were often involved in litigation, and it is known that in the twelfth and thirteenth centuries they did include a few brothers who were knowledgeable in law. In that period, however, the Orders appear to have relied mainly on professional lawyers, although the situation changed in the fourteenth century.[80] If Orders were not usually represented by brothers in litigation, they did engage in law-making and the codification of laws. The Hospital's rule was drawn up by Raymond du Puy, with the counsel of his chapter, and it is clear from internal evidence that sections of the Templar customs were compiled by a brother, while at the end of the thirteenth century William of Santo Stefano made a compilation of his Order's regulations.[81] It was usual for general chapters to issue statutes, and Orders also provided codes of customs for communities of vassals. But not all regulations were new enactments – St Thomas of Acre, for example, borrowed from the Teutonic Order – and several foundations, such as Calatrava, had some rulings imposed by outsiders.[82]

A number of orders also, of course, undertook the care of the sick; and all military orders had to contend with diseased and wounded brethren. Among Templar brothers in Aragon at the turn of the twelfth and thirteenth centuries there was an Arnaldus Medicus, and a Hospitaller – also named Arnold – was in the early fourteenth century described as *medicus* and *magister*, while two Templar books seized in Aragon were medical works.[83] But the significance of names is not always certain, and it is not known if the books were used. It is clear, however, that Orders normally relied on outsiders for medical skills. The physicians and surgeons mentioned in Hospitaller regulations in the twelfth and thirteenth centuries were always spoken of as outsiders; and the same is true of those referred to in the rules and customs of the Temple and the Teutonic Order.[84] No doubt there were brothers who acquired a certain amount of practical experience in medical matters: this would explain, for

---

[80] J.A. Brundage, 'The Lawyers of the Military Orders', in *MO*, 1, pp. 346–57; A.T. Luttrell, 'Fourteenth-Century Hospitaller Lawyers', *Traditio*, 21 (1965), 449–56; Forey, *Templars in Aragon*, pp. 320, 338 note 110. For further references to advocates employed in the thirteenth and the beginning of the fourteenth centuries by the Aragonese Templars, see Archivo de la Corona de Aragón, Canc. real, pergaminos, Jaime I, 1100, 1122, 1966, 2093, 2159; registros 142, fols 44v, 100v; 291, fols 191, 217v–218.

[81] *CH*, 1, no. 70 (p. 62); *RT*, §§ 233, 447, 459, 485, 521, 559 (pp. 155, 241, 246, 256, 275, 292) (in these the author writes of 'our' house and brothers, and gives his opinion as a brother); Delisle, 'Maître Jean', pp. 23–5.

[82] A.J. Forey, 'The Military Order of St Thomas of Acre', *English Historical Review*, 92 (1977), 487; J.F. O'Callaghan, 'The Affiliation of the Order of Calatrava with the Order of Cîteaux', *Analecta sacri ordinis Cisterciensis*, 15 (1959), 188–91; Lomax, 'Estatutos primitivos', 483–94.

[83] Forey, *Templars in Aragon*, pp. 423, 443; A.T. Luttrell, 'The Hospitallers' Medical Tradition: 1291–1530', *MO*, 1, p. 76. The medical works were the *Chirurgia* and the *Thesaurus pauperum*.

[84] *CH*, 1, nos 627, 690 (pp. 425–9, 468); 3, no. 3039, § 33 (pp. 43–54); no. 3317, § 1 (pp. 186–8); no. 4515, §§ 5, 18 (pp. 810–16); *RT*, § 197 (p. 141); *SDO*, Regel 6, 24 (pp. 32, 48); Ges. 11 (p. 69); cf. E. Wickersheimer, 'Organisation et législation sanitaires au royaume franc de Jérusalem

example, the statement in the rule of Santiago that commanders of infirmaries should accompany armies on campaign 'with the necessary equipment, so that they can minister, as is required, to brothers and others of the faithful in the army, if they happen to fall sick' ('*con aquel appareiamento con el qual a los freyres e a los otros fieles de la hueste, si ad algunos conteciere de enfermar, que ellos les puedan aministrar assi como conviene*').[85] Yet, like the regulations of many other hospitals,[86] the military orders' decrees concerning the care of the sick emphasize the provision of bedding and adequate food, and spiritual welfare,[87] rather than medical treatment by brethren.

In pursuing their function of warfare, rather than welfare, Orders based in the Holy Land had frequent diplomatic contacts with neighbouring Muslim powers, and occasional references occur to brethren who had a knowledge of Arabic, such as the Templar who negotiated the surrender of Safed in 1266.[88] But as most brothers in the East came from western Europe, such knowledge does not seem to have been widespread. The Orders usually employed interpreters, as in Joinville's account of discussions between the Grand Masters of the Temple and Hospital and an envoy of the Assassins during Louis IX's stay in the Holy Land, and they probably used the Saracen scribes listed in the households of some leading officials.[89]

Even if the Orders had to rely on outsiders for some skills required for the functioning of these institutions, there was a limited amount of other intellectual and literary activity among brethren, apart from the 'cultivated reading' which has already been mentioned. The Hospitaller William of Santo Stefano is well known for producing a discussion of the different kinds of law and of the application of legal principles, with particular reference to the Hospital.[90] More common, though still not numerous, are historical writings relating to the Orders, although of course some compositions of this kind have not survived. Lost accounts of some early developments relating to the Teutonic Order in the Baltic were written probably in the thirteenth century,

---

(1099–1291)', *Archives internationales d'histoire des sciences*, 4 (1951), 689–705; J. von Steynitz, *Mittelalterliche Hospitäler der Orden und Städte als Einrichtungen der sozialen Sicherung* (Berlin, 1970), p. 43; C. Probst, *Der Deutsche Orden und sein Medizinalwesen in Preussen* (Bad Godesberg, 1969), pp. 36, 160–1.

[85] Lomax, *Santiago*, § 39 (p. 226); *RSJ*, § 35 (p. 114).

[86] M. Carlin, 'Medieval English Hospitals', in *The Hospital in History*, ed. L. Granshaw and R. Porter (London, 1989), p. 31.

[87] See also L. Le Grand, 'La prière des malades dans les hôpitaux de l'ordre de Saint-Jean de Jérusalem', *Bibliothèque de l'Ecole des Chartes*, 57 (1896), 325–38; K.V. Sinclair, 'The French Prayer for the Sick in the Hospital of the Knights of Saint John of Jerusalem in Acre', *Medieval Studies*, 40 (1978), 484–8.

[88] *Gestes des Chiprois*, cap. 347 (p. 180).

[89] *La vie de Saint Louis*, ed. N.L. Corbett (Quebec, 1977), cap. 454 (p. 177); B. Altaner, 'Zur Kenntnis des Arabischen im 13. und 14. Jahrhundert', *Orientalia Christiana Periodica*, 2 (1935), 441; *RT*, §§ 77, 99, 110, 120, 125 (pp. 75, 86–7, 94, 100, 102); *SDO*, Gew. 11 (p. 98).

[90] Delisle, 'Maître Jean', pp. 27, 32–9.

and a reference by Matthew Paris to a *liber Templariorum* has led to the
suggestion that the Templars produced a work on the Fifth Crusade.[91] It has
further been argued that a life was written of Pelayo Pérez Correa, who was
Master of Santiago for over thirty years in the mid-thirteenth century.[92] The
sole surviving chronicle providing continuous coverage of a considerable
period is the *Livländische Reimchronik*, written in the last decade of the thirteenth
century.[93] A short set of annals compiled at Santiago's convent of Uclés was
written possibly before the end of the thirteenth century, but it contains few
entries about the Order itself.[94] There were other historical compilations,
however. Lists of leading officials were kept in the twelfth and thirteenth
centuries: William of Santo Stefano included one of Hospitaller Grand Masters
in his writings.[95] The most common form of historical composition, however,
seems to have been on the origins of Orders. The prologue of the rule of
Santiago recounts the foundation of that Order,[96] and differing accounts of the
origins of the Hospital have survived: legends grew up tracing the foundation
of the Order back before the time of Christ, who himself was said to have
frequented the hospital in Jerusalem; an early Anglo-Norman version of these
legends was composed in the later twelfth century.[97] These views were
rejected, however, by William of Santo Stefano, who provided a version similar
to that given earlier by William of Tyre.[98] An account of the origins of the

---

[91] Grundmann, pp. 108–9; K. Helm and W. Ziesemer, *Die Literatur des Deutschen Ritterordens*
(Giessen, 1951), pp. 145–6; G. Eis, 'Die Literatur im Deutschen Ritterorden und in seinen Ein-
flussgebieten', *Ostdeutsche Wissenschaft*, 9 (1962), 80–1; Matthew Paris, *Historia Anglorum*, ed. F.
Madden, 3 vols, RS, 44 (London, 1866–9), 2, p. 232; M.L. Bulst-Thiele, *Sacrae domus militiae Templi
Hierosolymitani magistri: Untersuchungen zur Geschichte des Templerordens, 1118/9–1314* (Göttingen,
1974), p. 168.

[92] D.W. Lomax, 'A Lost Medieval Biography: the Corónica del Maestre Pelayo Pérez', *Bulletin
of Hispanic Studies*, 38 (1961), 153–4; J.B. Avalle-Arce, 'Sobre una Crónica medieval perdida', *Boletín
de la Real Academia Española*, 42 (1962), 255–97.

[93] Ed. L. Meyer (Paderborn, 1876).

[94] D.W. Lomax, 'The Medieval Predecessors of Rades y Andrada', *Iberoromania*, 23 (1986), 82,
89–90.

[95] Delisle, 'Maître Jean', p. 26; cf. *The Cartulary of the Knights of St John of Jerusalem in England,
secunda camera, Essex*, ed. M. Gervers (Oxford, 1982), pp. 568–9.

[96] Leclercq, 'Vie et prière', 351–3; *RSJ*, pp. 76–82.

[97] *Hospitallers' Riwle*; on the date, see pp. xlv–xlviii. For other versions of the legends, see ibid.,
pp. xix–xxii; *RHC Occid*, 5, pp. cxii–cxx, 405–21; K. Borchardt, 'Two Forged Thirteenth-Century
Alms-Raising Letters Used by the Hospitallers in Franconia', in *MO*, 1, pp. 52–6. On claims that
the Order of Santiago was founded earlier than 1170, see J.L. Martín, *Orígenes de la orden militar
de Santiago (1170–1195)* (Barcelona, 1974), pp. 11–15. On the document entitled *Haec est institutio
militiae Pererii*, which provides an account of the alleged origins of Alcántara, and which was first
published by A. Manrique, *Annales Cistercienses*, 4 vols (Lyons, 1642–59), 2, p. 280, see J.F.
O'Callaghan, 'The Foundation of the Order of Alcántara, 1176–1218', *Catholic Historical Review*,
47 (1962), 471–7; R.P. de Azevedo, 'A ordem militar de S. Julião do Pereiro depois chamada de
Alcântara', *Anuario de estudios medievales*, 11 (1981), 715–24.

[98] *RHC Occid*, 5, pp. 422–7; WT, XVIII.4, 5 (pp. 814–17).

Teutonic Order is provided both in some versions of the prologue to the rule and in *De primordiis ordinis Theutonici narracio*, which was composed shortly after 1244.[99] Such writings were not, of course, entirely without a practical purpose. This was sometimes to enhance the reputation of an order and to attract support, either by providing an idealized account of what had actually happened or by seeking to assign a spurious antiquity to an order; and the composition of the *Narracio* has been linked with the dispute about the Hospital's claim to authority over the German Order.[100]

Although the authorship of William of Santo Stefano's writings is established, in most cases the writers of these historical works cannot be definitely identified. Assumptions have to be made on the internal evidence of texts. Thus the Anglo-Norman version of Hospitaller legends has been attributed to a Hospitaller chaplain, possibly resident at Clerkenwell, and the *Livländische Reimchronik* to a knight of the Teutonic Order;[101] but much remains uncertain and it cannot always be assumed that authors were actually brethren.

Besides the information set down in these works, a certain amount of comment about the past was made in other writings, such as obituary lists,[102] charters and the records of disputes: in 1198 Innocent III received two conflicting versions of the recent history of Mountjoy from rival factions of brethren.[103] Information is also found in inscriptions, such as that recording the death of the Hospitaller Grand Master, Peter of Vieillebride, discovered in 1962.[104]

Such comments usually related to recent events, and historical writings were the work of a few. The question therefore arises of the extent of knowledge about the more remote history of their Orders among brethren in general. The *Livländische Reimchronik* was intended to be read aloud[105] and such readings would have served to inform members of the Teutonic Order about its history; conversely, historical writings were to some extent based on information which had been transmitted orally.[106] Some historical knowledge

---

[99] *SDO*, pp. 22–3, 159–60; U. Arnold, 'De primordiis ordinis Theutonici narratio', *Preussenland*, 4 (1966), 17–30.

[100] Ibid., p. 25; H. Boockmann, 'Die Geschichtsschreibung des Deutschen Ordens: Gattungsfragen und "Gebrauchssituationen"', in *Geschichtsschreibung und Geschichtsbewusstsein im späten Mittelalter*, ed. H. Patze, Vorträge und Forschungen, 31 (Sigmaringen, 1987), p. 450. For a later parallel in the Order of Santiago, see D.W. Lomax, 'The Order of Santiago and the Kings of Leon', *Hispania*, 18 (1958), 3–10.

[101] *Hospitallers' Riwle*, pp. xl–xlv; L. Mackensen, *Zur deutschen Literatur Altlivlands*, Ostdeutsche Beiträge aus dem Göttinger Arbeitskreis, 18 (Würzburg, 1961), p. 53.

[102] Barthélemy, p. 318.

[103] A.J. Forey, 'The Order of Mountjoy', *Speculum*, 46 (1971), 259–60.

[104] J. Prawer, 'Military Orders and Crusader Politics in the Second Half of the XIIIth Century', in *Die geistlichen Ritterorden Europas*, ed. J. Fleckenstein and M. Hellmann, Vorträge und Forschungen, 26 (Sigmaringen, 1980), p. 223.

[105] Mackensen, p. 30.

[106] Ibid., p. 44; Boockmann, p. 449.

was clearly circulating within Orders, although not all of it was accurate. The situation is illustrated by the testimony of a public notary who appeared before the papal commissioners in Paris during the Templar trial.[107] He reported that when he had been in Templar service in the East he had often ('*pluries*') heard from brothers that the Order had been founded by two Burgundian nobles and that its first task was to defend a pass later known as Château Pèlerin, where pilgrims were being robbed and killed. This work was continued for nine years, during which time only nine brothers were received. The Templars then gained papal confirmation. For a long time only those of noble and knightly descent were admitted to the Order: sergeants were paid employees. Lack of funds had led, however, to the admission of sergeants as brothers. Some of these comments are familiar, but not all are accurate. Although in the Temple's early years there was only one rank of lay brethren, the distinction between knight and sergeant brothers was being made before 1140. The testimony of the Templars themselves during the trial also occasionally throws light on their historical knowledge. Some spoke of St Bernard as the founder of the Order, and author of some regulations; and Hugh of Payns was mentioned as the first Grand Master.[108] Some knew that the Order did not at first have brother chaplains and that there had at one time been a probationary period, although there were others who were of the opinion that a novitiate had never existed.[109] In their trial Templars tended, of course, to mention only points which arose in connection with the accusations, but it is clear that some historical knowledge was not unusual.[110]

Some historical writings, such as the Livonian chronicle, were written in verse, but before 1300 there was also poetry associated with military orders on other topics. Problems, however, commonly exist about precise dating and authorship, and it is often difficult to state whether a writer was in fact a brother. Yet the Orders certainly produced poets: Hugo of Langenstein, who wrote a long work on St Martina at the end of the thirteenth century, was a priest in the Teutonic Order, while Templar poets in the thirteenth century included Olivier and Bonomel.[111] These two were commenting on

---

[107] *Procès*, 1, p. 643.

[108] Ibid., 1, pp. 121, 122, 145, 603, 613, 616; 2, pp. 223, 228, 231, 232; Finke, *Papsttum*, 2, no. 155 (pp. 333, 335); Schottmüller, 2, p. 67.

[109] *Procès*, 1, pp. 141, 237, 387–8, 424; 2, pp. 215, 437, 481.

[110] The development of oral traditions can also be traced in other Orders: see, for example, Forey, 'St Thomas of Acre', 482.

[111] For poetry linked with the Teutonic Order, see Helm and Ziesemer; Eis; M.E. Goenner, *Mary-Verse of the Teutonic Knights* (Washington, 1943). On the Templars, see P. Meyer, 'Les derniers troubadours de la Provence', *Bibliothèque de l'Ecole des Chartes*, 31 (1870), 436; M. Milá y Fontanals, *De los trovadores en España* (Barcelona, 1966 edn), p. 335; A. de Bastard, 'La colère et la douleur d'un templier en Terre Sainte: "Ir'e dolors d'es dins mon cor asseza"', *Revue des langues romanes*, 81 (1974), 333–73.

contemporary events, particularly crusading, whereas the poetry linked with the Teutonic Order usually had a religious theme.

Although there were some brothers with intellectual and literary interests,[112] as institutions the Orders appear to have done only a little to educate brethren. It has been suggested that bestiaries were utilized in monasteries for the instruction of lay brothers, partly through the use of pictures, and it is possible that the bestiary mentioned in the inventory of the English Templar house of Shipley served this purpose.[113] More generally, recruits were expected to familiarize themselves with their Order's regulations and, if necessary, to learn the paternoster, Ave Maria and creed; brothers in the Teutonic Order were given six months for the latter task, while a Templar ruling allowed learning in the vernacular.[114] An increased understanding of the faith was provided by readings at mealtimes and by sermons, which were sometimes delivered by outsiders, such as friars.[115] James of Vitry, when arguing that lay brothers in military orders should not usurp the functions of priests, advocated further education of some brethren: he wanted literate brothers to be sent to schools of theology, so that the Orders would have 'literate priors and priests, adequately instructed in God's ordinance' (*'priores et sacerdotes litteratos, et in lege Dei sufficienter instructos'*).[116] Yet, although the Temple and Hospital may in the mid-thirteenth century have rented houses in Paris to students,[117] there is no evidence of their sending their own brethren to universities. The Orders apparently did not avail themselves of the medical training available in the thirteenth century; and the Templars described as 'skilled in law' (*'jurisperiti'*) in the records of their trial had gained their knowledge and skill before entering the Order: Hugh of Marchant had joined the Temple when he was aged about forty after 'he had studied law for a long time' (*'studuerat longo tempore in legibus'*), and John of Folhayo, named as a doctor in civil law, had become a Templar only two years before the arrests.[118]

---

[112] J. Ferreiro Alemparte, 'Hermann el alemán, traductor del siglo XIII en Toledo', *Hispania sacra*, 35 (1983), 35, 47–50, suggests that this translator was a member of the Teutonic Order; but convincing evidence is lacking. I am grateful to Manuel Rodríguez de la Peña for drawing my attention to this.

[113] W.B. Clark, 'The Illustrated Medieval Aviary and the Lay Brotherhood', *Gesta*, 21 (1982), 70–1.

[114] *SDO*, Ges. II(e) (p. 61); A. Knöpfler, 'Die Ordensregel der Tempelherren', *Historisches Jahrbuch*, 8 (1887), 692.

[115] *RT*, §§ 24, 187, 288 (pp. 34, 136–7, 173–4); *SDO*, Regel 13 (p. 41); Lomax, *Santiago*, § 32 (p. 225); *RSJ*, § 28 (p. 110); *Procès*, 1, pp. 141, 181.

[116] J.B. Pitra, *Analecta novissima. Spicilegii Solesmensis altera continuatio*, 2 vols (Paris, 1885–8), 2, p. 412; cf. A. Stroick, 'Collectio de scandalis ecclesie', *Archivum Franciscanum Historicum*, 24 (1931), 57.

[117] *Chartularium Universitatis Parisiensis*, ed. H. Denifle and E. Chatelain, 4 vols (Paris, 1889–97), 1, nos 138, 203 (pp. 179, 232–3).

[118] *Procès*, 1, pp. 183, 379, 422, 598; 2, p. 277; Finke, *Papsttum*, 2, no. 155 (p. 341).

There is little evidence of academic instruction of outsiders within the Orders' convents. The Hospitallers were admittedly under an obligation to admit abandoned children,[119] and it was not uncommon for children to be placed in convents of military orders by their parents. But such arrangements were often made in wills, and the purpose appears to have been primarily to provide for the guardianship and support of children.[120] There also seems to have been a practice of having sons of nobles reared in the house of an Order instead of in a noble household or other religious house. Yet, whereas in noble households and monasteries boys might be taught to read,[121] there is no evidence to indicate that sons of nobles normally received any instruction in letters in convents of military orders: when the Templar commander of Peñíscola was instructed by the Aragonese provincial Master to receive the son of a certain knight, he was merely told to rear him 'in good customs' ('*en bons costums*'), which seems to refer to conduct rather than instruction in reading.[122] It is, of course, possible that teaching of the latter kind was sometimes provided by chaplains, but the only formal requirement for the academic instruction of children comes from the Order of Santiago. Its primitive rule states that sons born of serving brothers were to be nurtured in the Order's houses and instructed in letters, and later versions of the rule also refer to the instruction of daughters.[123]

Nor is there evidence of active participation in schooling outside convents. Although it has been suggested that the Hospitallers had 'a kind of school' annexed to their convent of Bargota in Navarre, the wording of the source in question is not sufficiently precise to substantiate this claim.[124] It is clear, on the other hand, that the Teutonic Order was given responsibility for a school at Altenburg in 1272, but both then and later the schoolmaster was not a brother.[125]

There are, in fact, signs of a reluctance to encourage learning within military orders. The reading of vernacular works in the infirmary was in the Hospital put on a par with eating prohibited food. In the Teutonic Order illiterate brothers were forbidden to learn to read without permission, although those who could read were allowed to use their skill; and priests were not to attend a *Hochschule* (university) without the Master's permission.[126] Such rulings

---

[119] *CH*, 1, no. 627 (pp. 425–9).

[120] Forey, *Templars in Aragon*, no. 13 (pp. 379–80); García Larragueta, 2, nos 95, 382 (pp. 97, 388–90).

[121] N. Orme, *From Childhood to Chivalry: The Education of the English Kings and Aristocracy, 1066–1530* (London, 1984), cap. 2.

[122] Archivo de la Corona de Aragón, Cart. real. dipl., Templarios, 458.

[123] Leclercq, 'Vie et prière', 354; Lomax, *Santiago*, § 19 (p. 224); *RSJ*, §§ 15, 40 (pp. 102, 118).

[124] García Larragueta, 1, p. 248; 2, no. 369 (pp. 374–5).

[125] *Altenburger Urkundenbuch (976–1350)*, ed. H. Patze (Jena, 1955), nos 227, 420, 529 (pp. 172–3, 339, 421–2).

[126] *CH*, 3, no. 3039, § 39 (pp. 43–54); *SDO*, Ges. 1 (p. 64); Capitelbeschlüsse I(3) (p. 134); cf. Dubois, p. 217.

could be seen mainly as attempts to discourage what were viewed as distractions from the proper functions of brethren of a military order, rather than as a sign of outright hostility to learning. The wording of the Teutonic Order's regulation does not imply that permission would always be withheld, but a literate Templar knight appearing before the papal commissioners in 1311 did impute hostility by commenting that 'there was a widely held view in the Order, among the older brethren, that because there had been literate brothers among them the Order had not progressed as it should have done' ('*erat vox communis in ordine, inter antiquos ordinis, quod ex quo litterati fuerant inter eos, ordo non fecerat profectum suum*').[127] There may have been personal reasons for this comment, but a disdain for learning was still being expressed, at least in some quarters, in the thirteenth century outside military orders,[128] and it is possible that such notions were held by some brethren who felt that the practical tasks to which they devoted themselves, especially warfare, were superior to book-learning.

---

[127] *Procès*, 1, p. 389.
[128] Clanchy, *Memory to Written Record*, p. 23.

16

A New Edition of the Latin and French Rule of the Temple[*]

Simonetta Cerrini

The Rule of the Temple is the text through which the Templars expressed their ideal way of life. This was a religious ideal hitherto unknown to Christianity, a new development which Peter of Cluny, among others, saw as flashing '*velut rutilum novi syderis*',[1] as brilliantly as a new star.

Yet, if we wish to read the Rule, we are currently forced to resort to the 1886 edition of Henri de Curzon, who published the French text of the Rule and the *retrais* as given by three manuscripts,[2] and to the 1908 edition of Gustav Schnürer, who published the Latin text as preserved in two manuscripts.[3] Hitherto, these have been the only critical editions worthy of the title.[4]

However, during this century research has evolved a long way, and we now find ourselves in possession of six Latin and four French manuscripts which supply us with the text of the Rule.[5] Meanwhile the corpus of the *retrais*, that

---

[*] This article is a product of my work to establish a new critical edition of the Rule of the Temple in Latin and Old French which forms part of a doctoral thesis at the University of Paris IV–Sorbonne under the supervision of Mme Geneviève Hasenohr.

[1] Petrus Venerabilis, *The Letters of Peter the Venerable*, ed. G. Constable (Cambridge, Mass., 1967), 1, no. 172 (p. 407).

[2] *La règle du Temple*, ed. H. de Curzon, Société de l'Histoire de France (Paris, 1886).

[3] *Die ursprüngliche Templerregel, kritisch untersucht und herausgegeben*, ed. G. Schnürer (Freiburg i. B., 1903).

[4] This is not the case for the editions produced by L. Dailliez, such as *La Règle des Templiers* (Nice, no date: 1977), as I have already noted. S. Cerrini, 'Nuovi percorsi templari tra i manoscritti latini e francesi della Regola', in *Atti del convegno I Templari in Piemonte, dalla storia al mito. Torino 20 ottobre 1994*, ed. R. Bordone (Turin, no date: 1995), pp. 36–7, 51–2 note 14.

[5] For the Rule and the *retrais* see Cerrini, 'Nuovi percorsi templari', 35–56 ; the same subject, with supplementary details, was developed in S. Cerrini, 'La tradition manuscrite de la Règle du Temple. Etudes pour une nouvelle édition des versions latine et française', in *Autour de la première Croisade. Actes du Colloque de la Society for the Study of the Crusades and the Latin East (Clermont-Ferrand 21-25 juin 1995)*, ed. M. Balard (Paris, 1996), pp. 203–19.

is to say the individual statutes which applied to the officials of the Order and the Order's other legal material, has come down to us in five French manuscripts while three Latin manuscripts preserve only brief fragments of the *retrais* and the list of feast days and fasts which were to be observed.[6] However, here we shall be concerned with the original Rule only.

For this reason a new edition is essential: an edition which, for the first time, compares the two versions and clarifies various points. In this article I shall briefly confront the questions: what is the manuscript tradition of the Rule of the Temple? and why is the order of chapters in the Latin and French texts of the Rule so different?

WHAT IS THE MANUSCRIPT TRADITION OF THE RULE OF THE TEMPLE?

Tables 16.1 and 16.2 show the complete contents of the manuscripts which contain the text of the Rule. At first sight, the divergence between the Latin tradition and the French tradition is striking. The Latin version is placed alongside very different works, although their authors are often contemporaries of the Rule and derive from a monastic milieu, particularly Cistercian; the context is always literary. On the other hand, the French Rule is always followed by a list of feasts and fasts, the *retrais* and the Templars' legal corpus; no space is given to other important texts. We may deduce from this that the Latin text circulated within a predominantly monastic or canonical network of intellectuals, and it was the French text that the Templars used for their everyday observance.

Nevertheless, a more extensive analysis forces us to moderate this first impression. The text of the Rule fills, on average, around fifteen folios, that is to say around thirty pages: yet such a document could only with great difficulty be handled as a separate unit without being lost or damaged. Moreover, as far as we know, the bulk of the Order's legal material, which could amount to around a hundred folios, was composed directly in French and during the thirteenth century.

How can we account for the presence of the Latin text of the Rule in these composite manuscripts, whose compiler and date of compilation is unknown? Of six Latin manuscripts written in the course of the twelfth century, we have two which have only the text of the Rule and a third which adds fragments of the Order's legal texts in Latin before and after the Rule. The three remaining manuscripts, those of Brugges, Nîmes and Paris, are characterized by the presence of the *Littera de laude novae militiae* which St Bernard wrote at the request of Hugh of Payns, the founder of the Order. Yet, neither of these could have been created for the Templars. The Paris manuscript contains

---

[6] For the list of feast days and fasts see also: S. Cerrini, 'Festività templari', in *Templari a Piacenza. Le tracce di un mito* (Piacenza, 1995), pp. 80–3.

Table 16.1 Contents of the Latin manuscripts of the Rule of the Temple

Manuscript							
Brugge, Stedelijke Openbare Bibliotheek, MS.131	REGULA	Bernard o.Cist. (†1153) *De laude*	Bernard o.Cist., *Liber apologeticus*	William of St.-Thierry o.Cist. (†1149) *Epistola aurea*	Gerhoch can. reg. (†1169) *De simonia*	*Epist. Ad Raynardum abbatem Morimundi*	Peter of Cluny, o. Clun (†1156), *Ep. 28 ad Bernardum*
London, British Library, Cotton, Cleopatra B III. 3	Ailred of Rievaulx o.Cist. (†1167) *Genealogia regum Anglorum*	Ralph of Diss (†1199/1200) *Abbreviationes chronicarum*	*De concurrentis De epactis*, Tables	Calendar	REGULA	*Statutes of the Golden Fleece (1431)*	Nigel of Long-champs (†1200) *Contra curiales et clericos; Versus ad Guilelmum Eliensem*
München, Bayerische Staats-bibliothek, Clm 2649	*Retrais* in Latin (ed. Curzon 224–232; texte ajouté au XIIIe siècle)	REGULA	*Retrais* in Latin *Acta capituli Mausonii*	Feasts and fasts in Latin (ed. Curzon 74–76)	*Ars dictandi*	*Varia theologica*	
Nîmes, Bibliothèque Municipale, MS 37	Augustine, *Sententiae*	REGULA	Hugo of Payns, *Christi militibus*	Bernard o.Cist. (†1153) *De laude*	*De consan-guinetatibus*		
Paris, Bibliothèque nationale de France, lat. 15045	REGULA	Bernard o.Cist. (†1153) *De laude*	Prayers	Anselm of Canterbury (†1109) *Orationes et meditationes*	*Psalmi* and hymns	Anselm of Canterbury (†1109) *Orationes et meditation*	Godfrey of Saint-Victor (†1196) *Sequentia de sancto Victore*
Praha, Národní knihovna, XXIII G 66	REGULA						

annotations and the text of a *Sequentia Sancti Victoris* in the hand of Godfrey of St Victor, a restless Victorine intellectual who had been driven from his abbey but returned at the end of the twelfth century.[7] The Nîmes manuscript, which opens with Saint Augustine's difficult *Quaestiones LXXXIII*, also leads us to the Victorines because it contains a letter addressed to the knights of Christ in the Temple at Jerusalem (that is, the Templars) which, according to the rubric, should be attributed to Hugh of St Victor; but this attribution has been keenly contested, and I am now convinced that it should be attributed to Hugh of Payns.[8] In any case, we are faced with three manuscripts of the Rule which probably have a canonical origin, or monastic, and that reveal to us the interest which the intellectual religious of the era took in the Templars.

Table 16.2 Contents of the Romance Manuscripts of the Rule and the Retrais

BALTIMORE, Walters Art Gallery, W. 132	RULE	Feasts and fasts in French (ed. Curzon 74–76)	*Retrais* (ed. Curzon 77–635)	Ballad *Si je ne chant si souvent*
(DIJON) Archives de la Côte-d'Or, MS. H111) ms stolen	RULE	Feasts and fasts in French (ed. Curzon 74–76)	*Retrais* (ed. Curzon 77–223)	
PARIS, Bibliothèque nationale de France, fr. 1977	RULE	Feasts and fasts in French (ed. Curzon 74–76)	*Retrais* (ed. Curzon 77–686)	
ROMA, Accademia dei Lincei, 44. A. 14	RULE	Feasts and fasts in French (ed. Curzon 74–76)	*Retrais* (ed. Curzon 77–686)	
BARCELONA Arxiu corona Aragó Codices Varia IX		Retrais 224–686 in the *langue d'oïl* with many characteristics of the *langue d'oc* and catalan script		

In fact it is plausible that the Bruges manuscript was compiled very early on by the Cistercians of the abbey of Dunes. The Munich manuscript, which must

---

[7] Gilbert Ouy established that the *Sequentia* were written by Godfrey himself: F. Gasparri, 'Textes autographes d'auteurs victorins du XIIe siècle', *Scriptorium*, 35.2 (1981), 277–84; G. Ouy, 'Manuscrits entièrement ou partiellement autographes de Godefroid de Saint-Victor', *Scriptorium*, 36.1 (1982), 29–42. On the other hand, Mme Françoise Gasparri, whom I requested to examine the manuscript, informed me that Godfrey also wrote out a transliteration of a curious holy Tetragrammton into the Latin alphabet: Cerrini, 'Nuovi percorsi templari', pp. 42, 56 notes 40–3.

[8] I have set out the evidence in my PhD thesis, and I concur with the opinion of Dominic Selwood, set out in '*Quidam antem dubitaverunt*: the Saint, the Sinner, the Temple and a Possible

have originated in a Templar house, came later – as a present or by request, for instance – to the Cistercian abbey of Aldersbach in Baveria.

Here again the indication is that the other contemporary religious orders felt a sense of attraction towards the new Order. It remains to say that, among the three Latin manuscripts which contain only the Rule – or, rather, fragments of legal texts, as is the case with the Munich manuscript – some material must have derived from the Temple. There was thus a 'Templar' distribution network for the Latin text of the Rule; evidently this was particularly the case outside France. Yet, in the thirteenth century, the presence of the *retrais*, which were mostly composed in French, probably induced the Templars, even those who were not French, to abandon progressively the Latin text of the Rule and to adopt a Romance version, particularly one in French.

This said, it is necessary to recognize that to all appearances the surviving French manuscripts did not have a 'literary' diffusion, but were composed for the Templars. Among these, the Rome manuscript must have left the *scriptorium* of Acre before 1291, when the Templars established themselves on Cyprus after the fall of the city.[9] It is also possible that the manuscripts of Baltimore and Paris originated in the East. Evidence of the use of the Romance Rule by others than the Templars themselves comes only after the trial; among the few books of Pope Clement V which were found in his room when he died in 1314 appeared '*duo libelli de regula Templi*' ('two little books of the Rule of the Temple'),[10] which were described as follows: '*Item duo parvi libri in romancio, cooperti corio tannato cum sera ferrea, eiusdem tenoris, continentes regulam Templariorum*' ('Item, two small books in the "romance" language, covered with tanned leather with an iron lock, with the same contents,

---

Chronology', in *Autour de la première croisade*, pp. 221–30. There is a wealth of scholarship on this problem: J. Leclercq, 'Un document sur les débuts des Templiers', *Revue d'histoire ecclésiastique*, 52 (1957), 81–91 (reprinted in his *Recueil d'études sur Saint Bernard et ses écrits*, 2, Storia e letteratura. Raccolta di Studi e Testi, 104 [Rome, 1966], pp. 87–99), attributed the letter to Hugh of Payns. Ch. Sclafert is for Hugh of St Victor: 'Lettre inédite de Hugues de Saint-Victor aux Chevaliers du Temple', *Revue d'ascétique et de mystique*, 34 (1958), 275–99. R. Baron is for Hugh of Payns: 'Hugues de Saint-Victor. Contribution à un nouvel examen de son oeuvre', *Traditio*, 15 (1959), 296–7. Some other historians have not taken sides in the debate: R. Goy, *Die Überlieferung der Werke Hugos von St. Viktor. Ein Beitrag zur Kommunikationsgeschichte des Mittelalters*, Monographien zur Geschichte des Mittelalters, 14 (Stuttgart, 1976), p. 483; J. Châtillon, '*La transmission de l'oeuvre de Hugues de S. Victor*. A propos d'un livre récent de Rudolf Goy', *Mittelateinischen Jahrbuch*, 15 (1980), 57–62, 59; J. Fleckenstein, 'Die Rechtfertigung der geistlichen Ritterorden nach der Schrift "De laude novae militiae" Bernards von Clairvaux', in *Die geistichen Ritterorden Europas*, ed. J. Fleckenstein and M. Hellmann, Vorträge und Forschungen, 26 (Sigmaringen, 1980), pp. 9–22, 10 and note 9.

[9] Its Acre provenance was established by Dr Peter Edbury, to whom I showed reproductions of the manuscript (letter of 9 September 1996).

[10] F. Ehrle, *Historia bibliothecae romanorum pontificum tum Bonifatianae tum Avenionensis*, 1 (Rome, 1890), no. 3 (pp. 260–1).

containing the Rule of the Templars').[11] Thus, by the time that the Order of the Temple disappeared, it was no longer the Latin text of the Rule which was regarded as the official version.

WHY IS THE ORDER OF THE CHAPTERS IN THE LATIN TEXT AND FRENCH TEXT OF THE RULE SO DIFFERENT?

We have said that we have two versions of the Rule of the Temple at our disposal, one in Latin and the other in French. It has already been established that the Rule was first composed in Latin and was subsequently translated into French. This is confirmed by the dating of the manuscripts: those in Latin are all from the twelfth century, or at the very latest the beginning of the thirteenth, whereas those in French are datable to the thirteenth century, including the Dijon manuscript which could belong to the second half of the thirteenth; although, as it was stolen in 1985, we are now unable to verify this. From the point of view of content, the French text is a true French translation of a Latin text and, despite or thanks to its faults, it assists us in establishing the original by indirect tradition.

But now let us consider Table 16.3. The first column shows us that Henri de Curzon's division of the manuscript does not always respect the manuscript tradition, adding chapter divisions where the manuscripts had none. But what is most striking here is that the order of chapters in the Latin text is completely different from that of the French text, although the content is almost the same, with the exception of two Latin chapters which are omitted.

The Prologue gives us a possible explanation for this, for here we find, at line 9, the following words: '*et modum et observantiam equestris ordinis* per singula capitula *ex ore ipsius predicti magistri Hugonis audire meruimus*' ('and we have been able to hear the customs and observances of the knightly order *chapter by chapter* from the mouth of the aforesaid Master Hugh himself'). So the founder of the Order, Hugh of Payns, set out orally before the Council of Troyes a Rule which was already organized into chapters.

Thus, our hypothesis is that the chapter order presented to us in the French version may correspond to the draft followed by Hugh of Payns, whereas the order followed by the Latin version is that laid down by the '*scriba*', the official redactor of the Rule, that is to say 'Johannes Michaelensis', following the decisions of St Bernard and the council. The draft which the Master used would have remained in the Templars' possession, and when they decided to translate the Rule into French the translator chose to make use of this document which was guaranteed to have the required authenticity.

---

[11] They are included in the catalogue of the papal library established at Avignon in 1369 by Pope Urban V, and were located in St Michael's chapel: Ehrle, no. 1174 (p. 375) and note 375.

Table 16.3 Concordance of the French edition of Henri de Curzon (C) with the new French edition, and of the new French edition with the new Latin edition

Edition of Henri de Curzon	The New French edition	The New French edition	The New Latin edition
1	Pr. 1–3	Pr. 1–22	Pr. 1–22
2	Pr. 4–7		
3	Pr. 8–10		
4	Pr. 11–13a		
5	Pr. 13b		
6	Pr. 14–18		
7	Pr. 19–20		
8	Pr. 21–22		
9	1 (9C + 10C)	1	1
10	1 (9C + 10C)		
11	2	2	55.1–3
12	3 (12C + 13C)	3.1	61.4
13	3 (12C + 13C)	3.2	61.6
		3.3	61.5
		3.4–6	61.7–9
		3.7–8	54
14	4	4.1–4	59
		4.5	55.4
15	5 (15C + 16C)	5.1–2	6.1–2
16	5 (15C + 16C)	5.3	57
		5.4–6	6.3–5
17	6 (17C + 18C + 19C)	6.1–2	19.1–2
18	6 (17C + 18C + 19C)	6.3	21
19	6 (17C + 18C + 19C)	6.4–9	19.3–8
		6.10	22
		6.11–12	19.9–10
		6.13	26
		6.14	19.11
		6.15	24
		6.16	19.12
20	7	7	66.1
21	8	8.1–6	67
		87–10	27
22	9	9.1–2	28.1b–2a
		9.3	28.1a
		9.4	28.2b
		9.5	28.3
		9.6	28.4
23	10	10	7

Table 16.3   Continued

Edition of Henri de Curzon	The New French edition	The New French edition	The New Latin edition
24	11	11	8
25	12	12	10
26	13	13	9
27	14	14	11
28	15	15	12
29a	16	16	13
29b	[17]	[17]	14
30	18	18	15
31	19 (31C + 32C)	19.1 + 19.3	16.1
32	19 (31C + 32C)	19.2	16.2
		19.4–9	16.3–8
33	20	20.1–3	17
		20.4	om.
34	21	21	18
35	22	22	36
36	23	23	56
37	24	24	61.1–3
38	25	25	51
39	26 (39C + 40C + 41C)	26.1	32.1
40	26 (39C + 40C + 41C)	26.2	om.
41	26 (39C + 40C + 41C)	26.3–10	32.2–9
42	27	27	38
43	28	28.1	40.2
		28.2	40.1
		28.3	40.3
		28.4–5	41
44	29	29.1–2	39.1–2
		29.3	41.3
		29.4	39.3 + 41.4
45	30	30.1	64.1
		30.2	64.3
46	31 (46C + 47C)	31	65
47	31 (46C + 47C)		
48	32	32	68
49	33	33	42
50	34	34	33
51	35	35.1–2	29
		35.3–4	30
52	36	36.1	34.1
		36.2	om.
		36.3–4	34.2–3

Table 16.3   Concluded

Edition of Henri de Curzon	The New French edition	The New French edition	The New Latin edition
53	37	37	35
54	38	38	37
55	39	39.1–3	43
		39.4–7	44
56	40	40.1	45.1
		40.2	om.
		40.3–4	45.2–3
57	41	41	48
58	42	42	63
59	43	43.1–2	46.1–2
		43.3	47
60	44	44.1	60.1
		44.2	60.3
		44.3	60.2
61	45	45.1–3	49
		45.4	50.1
		45.5	50.2a
		45.6	50.3
		45.7	50.2b
62	46 (62C + 63C)	46.1–5	2
63	46 (62C + 63C)	46.6–10	5.2–6
64	47	47	3
65	48	48	4
66	49	49	31
67	50	50	58
68	51	51	20
69	52	52	52
70	53	53	53
71	54	54	69
72	55	55	[70]
73	56	56	[71.1]

Key: The chapter numbers in the first column refer to Henri de Curzon's edition, while the other columns use the numeration employed in the new editions, which appear in my doctoral thesis. Pr. = Prologue; 1C = chapter 1 of Curzon's edition; 1.1–2 = the two first clauses of chapter 1 (the subdivision of the rule into clauses was an editorial decision, which has no basis in the manuscript tradition).

In conclusion: study of the manuscript tradition of the Rule of the Temple, with systematic research into its sources, can throw new light on its text and development. Thus a close reading of the Prologue, for example, gives an insight into how the Rule was formed and the role played in its creation by the persons therein named.

17

Wind Beneath the Wings: Subordinate Headquarters Officials in the Hospital and the Temple from the Twelfth to the Early Fourteenth Centuries[*]

Jochen Burgtorf

One day during Peter of Montaigu's mastership (1219-32), the commander of the vault, an official in the Templars' headquarters in Acre, ordered a shipload of grain that he had just bought to be stored in the grain store. The brother of the grain store objected, arguing that the grain, still damp from shipment overseas, should be spread out on the terrace to dry, otherwise it would certainly rot, and then he would not assume any responsibility. However, the commander insisted; it was put in the grain store, and when he had second thoughts and had it spread out on the terrace, a considerable portion was indeed rotten. In chapter, he pleaded for mercy, but lost his habit since he had caused damage knowingly.[1] This incident presents an amazing variety of aspects concerning the Order's headquarters: supplies, buildings, offices, titles, hierarchy, obedience, stewardship and the penal system.

In the course of the twelfth and thirteenth centuries, the headquarters of the Temple and the Hospital became complex institutions. Their internal structures, shaped during the Jerusalem period, had to be adapted when the kingdom's capital and the Orders' headquarters moved to Acre in 1191, and again when relocation to Cyprus in 1291, intended to be merely a temporary

[*] I should like to thank Professor R. Hiestand for the opportunity to use his collation of edited Hospitaller charters with the Malta originals, and his transcription of the 'Inventaire de Manosque a. 1531', Marseille, Archives départementales (Bouches-du-Rhône), 56 H 68. I am indebted to him, Dr M. Riethmüller and Mr R. Klug for their helpful comments on earlier versions of this paper.
[1] *RT,* § 609; cf. § 260; J. Delaville Le Roulx, 'Un nouveau manuscrit de la Règle du Temple', *Annuaire-Bulletin de la Société de l'Histoire de France*, 26 (1889), 185–214 (at p. 192). Cf. M.L. Bulst-Thiele, *Sacrae domus militiae Templi Hierosolymitani magistri (Untersuchungen zur Geschichte des Templerordens 1118/19–1314)* (Göttingen, 1974), pp. 170–88 (at p. 184).

solution, dictated further modifications.[2] Leadership in these headquarters came, above all, from the Master and a group of high dignitaries: grand commander (or seneschal), marshal, drapier, treasurer and – in the Order of the Hospital – conventual prior and hospitaller.[3] This paper is not devoted to these well-known 'providers of leadership', rather to their subordinate officials, that is, those responsible for the daily routine, and to the headquarters' internal structures. On the basis of the Orders' rules, statutes and charters, three aspects will be addressed: (1) the interpretation of early headquarters structures; (2) strategies for adapting to new challenges; and (3) regulations concerning interaction and internal control mechanisms.

*   *   *

As a consequence of the First Crusade, the number of pilgrims to the Holy Land rose tremendously, and those institutions in Jerusalem occupied with the pilgrims' well-being had to adjust somehow – among them, the Hospital of St John whose basic internal structures may have dated from before 1099,[4] and the new Order of the Temple founded to escort and protect the pilgrims. As these two institutions grew by attracting manpower which the kingdom of Jerusalem was so notoriously lacking, their influence increased and their Masters' social status changed: by the time of the Second Crusade, these Masters found themselves at the royal court as the king's valued advisers.[5] What happened in the Orders' headquarters during these times? Whenever an institution assumes more responsibility it has to fine-tune its administration, and as regards the Order of the Hospital it has been said that it first 'experimented' with various officials, that 'none of these survived' and that eventually the group of high dignitaries mentioned earlier emerged.[6] This view may have to be modified.

During the Hospital's early history, everything revolved around the Master, and it is thus in his immediate vicinity that the first officials should be expected. Indeed, a chancellor and a constable appear as early as 1126;[7] however, in order to get straight to the point they shall be ignored here. In 1141,

---

[2] For the Orders' headquarters, see J. Riley-Smith, *The Knights of St John in Jerusalem and Cyprus (c. 1050–1310)* (London, 1967), pp. 34–5, 198, 248–9; M. Barber, *The New Knighthood (A History of the Order of the Temple)* (Cambridge, 1994), pp. 6–7, 241–3, 312.

[3] A. Forey, *The Military Orders from the Twelfth to the Early Fourteenth Centuries* (London, 1992), p. 156.

[4] The Hospital's rule mentions no officials except for the Master and priests, cf. *CH*, 1, no. 70 (1125–53).

[5] R.C. Smail, *Crusading Warfare, 1097–1193*, 2nd edn (Cambridge, 1995), pp. 95–6.

[6] Riley-Smith, pp. 279–80.

[7] *CH*, 1, no. 77.

we encounter a seneschal[8] and in 1150, we find the first preceptor,[9] that is, the prototype of the grand commander. It is important to note here that the office of seneschal did not disappear. He only moved into the Master's personal entourage, as we can see from charters of 1199 and 1201, the statutes of Margat (1204/6) and those of 1302.[10] The list of the Master's entourage contained in the statutes of 1302 is particularly interesting, for it features, next to the seneschal, several other 'experiments', officials that had allegedly disappeared long ago: the Master's cupbearer, chamberlain and chaplain. Together with the seneschal they form a group that strikingly resembles the group of officials found at royal courts since at least early medieval times. A direct line may now be drawn from 1302 back to 1141. In three charters of 1141, issued by Patriarch William I of Jerusalem, we find among the witnesses a group of Hospitallers with rather revealing cognomina: Raymond of the Palace (*de Palacio*), Stephen of the Chapel (*de Capella*), Peter the treasurer (*thesaurarius*) and Gerard the cupbearer (*pincerna*); one of these charters also mentions Robert the seneschal, and two of them list a second treasurer (also named Raymond).[11] Raymond of the Palace and Stephen of the Chapel continue to appear in the charters of the following years, and in 1147 they witness a charter of King Baldwin III, again together with Peter the treasurer and Gerard the cupbearer.[12] It seems reasonable to assume that cognomina such as '*de Palacio*' and '*de Capella*' are, just like '*thesaurarius*' and '*pincerna*', not family names, but titles of headquarters officials (whose responsibility has yet to be examined).

In a recent study, W. Rösener has convincingly shown that during the twelfth century German dukes, counts, bishops and abbots began to surround themselves with groups of court officials – an indication of *imitatio regis*.[13] We may have an interesting parallel here: all the charters cited earlier involve the Hospital's Master, the famous Raymond du Puy, during whose mastership many interesting developments occurred, and three of them also involve the king. The position that the Masters of the Hospital and the Temple held at the court of Jerusalem by the middle of the twelfth century may be compared

---

[8] *CH*, 1, no. 138.

[9] *CH*, 1, no. 192.

[10] *CH*, 1, nos 1085, 1096; 2, nos 1145–6, 1193; 4, no. 4574.

[11] *CH*, 1, nos 138 (with Robert the seneschal and Raymond the treasurer), 139; *Le Cartulaire du Chapitre du Saint-Sépulcre de Jérusalem*, ed. G. Bresc-Bautier (Paris, 1984), no. 107 (with Raymond the treasurer).

[12] *CH*, 1, no. 173. *RRH*, no. 244 omits the title 'cupbearer' because J. Delaville Le Roulx was unable to make out the word following Gerard's name in the text; the word in question is '*pincerna*' (R. Hiestand's collation with the Malta original). Cf. *CH*, 1, no. 150; *Cartulaire du Saint-Sépulcre*, no. 38 (Stephen of the Chapel).

[13] W. Rösener, 'Hofämter an mittelalterlichen Fürstenhöfen', *Deutsches Archiv für Erforschung des Mittelalters*, 45 (1989), pp. 485–550.

to that of powerful barons, and they had to represent their Orders appropriately. The cupbearer and the chamberlain may have become subordinate headquarters officials eventually, but their importance for the Masters' social status should not be underestimated. Rösener's type of *imitatio regis* may have been an 'international' phenomenon in the twelfth century, encompassing the Latin East. By 1302, when the personal entourage of the Hospital's Master numbered about forty, the Order's grand commander and marshal had their own cupbearer and chamberlain. That is not surprising: as these high dignitaries became representatives of the Order's tongues, they surrounded the Master as barons surrounded a king.[14] Unfortunately, we do not have the sources to prove a parallel development for the Order of the Temple – which did have a seneschal as early as 1130[15] – but the description of the Master's entourage in that Order's *retrais* suggests that it was probably similar.[16]

*   *   *

In the second half of the twelfth century, the German pilgrim John of Würzburg went to Jerusalem and admired the Hospital's many charitable works, but assumed that even the officials of the house would be unable to keep an account of these activities: '*quod certe summa sumptuum nequaquam potest deprehendi, etiam ab eius domus procuratoribus*' ('In no way can a reliable total of the expenses be obtained, even from the managers of the house').[17] As we have seen, the growing institution generated more elaborate forms of representation, but it also demanded adequate adjustments on the part of the administration. Sooner or later even new offices proved to be too much work for those appointed to them, and other strategies had to be tested: one could invent more new offices, subordinate assistants to offices already existing,[18] appoint two brethren for any job that had proven too much work for one alone (and thereby institute mutual control),[19] hire non-members for special tasks (doctors and scribes)[20] and, last but not least, employ new brethren in the trade they had learned before entering the Orders. The last was in fact a basic policy in the Order of the Hospital.[21] Candidates asking for reception into the Order of the Temple were told that they would very likely be asked to do

---

[14] Cf. *CH*, 4, no. 4574, §§ 4–6.

[15] *Chartes de Terre-Sainte provenant de l'abbaye de N.-D. de Josaphat*, ed. H.-F. Delaborde (Paris, 1880), no. 17.

[16] Cf. *RT*, §§ 77–9.

[17] *Peregrinationes tres: Saewulf, John of Würzburg, Theodericus*, ed. R.B.C. Huygens, Corpus Christianorum, Continuatio Mediaevalis, 139 (Turnhout, 1994), pp. 131–2.

[18] Cf. *CH*, 1, no. 372; 4, p. 248 (*subthesaurarius*). Similarly, ibid., no. 508 (*custos helemosine* and *helemosinarius*).

[19] *CH*, 1, no. 138; *Cartulaire du Saint-Sépulcre*, no. 107.

[20] *CH*, 1, no. 627; 3, nos 3317, § 1 and 4515, § 5; cf. Riley-Smith, p. 240. *RT*, §§ 77, 197.

[21] *CH*, 2, no. 1193. One possible example for this policy: *CH*, 1, nos 754, 941 (Peter *de Coquina*).

things they would not want to do;[22] however, this should be interpreted as a means to test the applicants' sincerity, for it is hardly conceivable that the Templars would have wasted the expertise of a skilled brother.

As the headquarters' internal structures changed, so did the responsibility and the titles of the officials working there. The Hospital's Latin statutes of 1182 call the brother charged with the repair of old shoes simply *frater expertus*, while the French translation written later already gives him the title of *frere corvoisier*.[23] The Templars' Latin rule calls the brother charged with the brethren's clothing *'procurator hujus ministerii'*, *'frater cujus est ministerium'* or *'procurator [id] e[s]t dator pannorum'*, while the French translation written later calls him *'celui qui tient cel office'* or *'le drapier'*.[24] The drapier's department would later be called *'parmentarie'*, and in the Templars' *retrais* we encounter the subordinate officials working there, the *parmentiers*, that is, the tailor brethren.[25] By the first half of the thirteenth century, one of the Hospital's *parmentiers* had been promoted to the status of an intermediate headquarters official, who – together with the infirmarian and the master esquire – was responsible for the belongings of the headquarters' deceased brethren.[26]

The Orders' headquarters were complex institutions, and there seem to be headquarters officials that have escaped notice so far. The Hospital and the Temple possessed considerable real estate, first in Jerusalem and then later in Acre. For the Templars, this real estate was administered by the treasurer;[27] it was probably the same in the Hospital, as that Order's treasurer appears in several twelfth-century charters concerning real estate in and around Jerusalem.[28] When Acre became the capital, its real estate became the focus of attention. In the Hospital's charters issued between 1219 and 1260, we encounter three brethren with the cognomen 'of the houses' (*de Domibus*), and it is quite revealing that the charters in question deal with revenues from houses in Acre, the exchange of houses in Acre, a land donation in the plains of Acre and the donation of a house in Acre.[29] Considering the extent of real estate acquired by the Hospital in Acre over the years, the institution of a brother 'of the houses' charged with the administration of this real estate in and around the capital makes perfect sense. In the Order's hierarchy one would expect this

---

[22] *RT*, § 661; cf. § 662. However, see also *RT*, § 647 (work during penance).

[23] *CH*, 1, no. 627.

[24] *Die ursprüngliche Templerregel, Kritisch untersucht und herausgegeben*, ed. G. Schnürer (Freiburg i. B., 1903), §§ 18, 25; BN, nouvelles acquisitions latines 66, fol. 35 (Marquis d'Albon's transcription of the Nîmes manuscript); *RT*, §§ 18–19.

[25] *RT*, § 130.

[26] *CH*, 2, no. 2213, § 110.

[27] *RT*, § 118.

[28] *CH*, 1, nos 115, 249, 312, 375, 603, 663.

[29] *Guillelmus de Domibus* (1219), *Renaldus de Domibus* (1235) and *Girardus de Domibus* (1255–60): *CH*, 2, nos 1656, 2126, 2714, 2949.

official as a subordinate of the grand commander and/or the treasurer. Perhaps he was the colleague or forerunner of the Hospital's *casalarius* who, in 1273 and 1275, also concerned himself with houses in Acre (and should not be confused with the Order's *casalarii* who were in charge of local villages).[30]

* * *

One of the three vows in the military orders was that of obedience. Commands had to be obeyed, but not blindly: there were regulations and other internal control mechanisms concerning the interaction between commanders and subordinates. Brethren of the Temple could ask to be released from executing 'unreasonable' orders[31] and, as we have seen, if a commander ignored their objections he had to assume full responsibility for the consequences. According to the Hospital's thirteenth-century customs, brethren had to demand *esgart*, that is, the ruling of the brethren, when they found a command to be contrary to the good usages and customs of the house.[32]

Forcing brethren from different departments to work together was an excellent control mechanism.[33] The Templars' commander of the house, a subordinate of the seneschal, and their infirmarian had to work together; however, there was – understandably enough – a loophole. The commander of the house was in charge of all meal preparations, with the exception of the infirmary table,[34] and several sub-departments were under his command – the wine store, the great kitchen, the oven, the pigsty, the henhouse and the garden – but it was left to his discretion whether or not he would allow the infirmarian access to these sub-departments; alternatively, he could give him money.[35] Maybe this was simply a mechanism to prevent chaos. One can easily imagine various sergeant brethren, including some from the infirmary, arriving at the great kitchen and demanding food at the same time. Situations like this obviously occurred, as we can see from stipulations in the rule of the Templars prohibiting self-service in sub-departments and workshops, and regulating how provisions, goods and materials should be demanded and distributed properly.[36]

---

[30] *Reginaldus, casalarius Hospitalis* (1273) and *Bernardus casalarius domuum Hospitalis* (1275): *CH*, 3, nos 3514, 3557; Marseille, Archives départementales (Bouches-du-Rhône), 56 H 68, 'Inventaire de Manosque a. 1531', 33 L fol. 331' (R. Hiestand's transcription).

[31] *RT*, § 313.

[32] *CH*, 2, no. 2213, § 88.

[33] For example, joint administering of the belongings of deceased brethren: *CH*, 2, no. 2213, § 110. Similarly, the *arbalesterium*: *CH*, 3, no. 3317, § 1; 4, nos 4549, § 36, 4613, 4617; for officials working there, cf. *CH*, 1, nos 317, 754.

[34] *RT*, § 184.

[35] Ibid., § 196.

[36] Cf. ibid., §§ 321, 591; BN, nouvelles acquisitions latines 68, fol. 136 (Marquis d'Albon's transcription of the Barcelona manuscript).

Another control mechanism was the rendering of accounts.[37] We have already been introduced to the 'vault'. The vault was a structure existing in both Orders in Jerusalem, Acre and Cyprus.[38] In the Hospital, the vault served as a storage place for food, but it also contained workshop and other non-food supplies. The brethren-at-office were supposed to pick up supplies there after presenting a written and sealed receipt. The brother of the vault, a subordinate of the vault's commander, had to collect these receipts and submit them at the treasury's monthly audit.[39] The Hospital's statute of 1301 instituting this audit is interesting for another reason. While the Templars' statutes often start with a rather self-incriminating 'it happened that', the Hospitallers' statutes usually begin with the much more neutral 'if it happens'. However, the paragraph instituting this monthly audit reveals that the Hospitallers merely covered up their background stories in a more subtle way, for it closes by saying: '*Encore quant le frere de la vote donra char salée ou fromage à la cusine, que le frere de la cusine soit en pre[se]nse*', ('Again, when the brother of the vault gives salted meat or cheese to the kitchen, the brother of the kitchen should be present').[40] One may reconstruct the background story from there. Had someone come to the vault and demanded food for the kitchen which had then never, or only in part, reached the kitchen? Had the brother of the kitchen forgotten or refused to present a receipt, thereby causing confusion at the monthly audit about salted meat and cheese not accounted for? Maybe a close reading of the Hospital's statutes would reveal yet more background stories, and thus show how that Order's internal control mechanisms developed.

*   *   *

A few observations may serve as a conclusion. The military orders' early headquarters structures, namely the first group of officials surrounding the Master of the Hospital, can be interpreted as a response to the demand for more administration, but also as a response to the need for appropriate representation, probably even as *imitatio regis*. For the study of the Orders' internal structures, it may be useful to look for parallels not just in other religious institutions, but also in the households of kings and nobles. Moreover, even early structures survived; they merely moved into the background making space

---

[37] For the Hospital, cf. *CH*, 2, no. 2213, § 109.

[38] For the Hospital's vault in Jerusalem, cf. *CH*, 1, no. 249; for the Hospital's commander of the vault in Acre, Thomas Mausus (1264), cf. *CH*, 3, no. 3105. For the Templars' commander of the vault in Cyprus (1292), cf. A. Forey, *The Templars in the Corona de Aragón* (London, 1973), pp. 405–6.

[39] *CH*, 4, no. 4549, § 1. See earlier (1300): *CH*, 3, no. 4515, § 15. For the annual written report that the Hospital's infirmarian had to present, see *CH*, 4, no. 4672, § 11.

[40] *CH*, 4, no. 4549, § 1.

for the emerging group of high dignitaries whose functions would soon go far beyond those of court officials.

Concerning the Orders' developing of new structures and offices, it seems that their charters' witness lists have yet more to tell. It seems reasonable to assume that headquarters officials are hidden behind such cognomina as *de Palacio, de Capella, de Camera, de Fabrica* and, as argued above, *de Domibus*.[41] An in-depth study of these cognomina might help other levels of headquarters structures to be revealed.

In the courtyard of Jerusalem's Rockefeller Museum stands the thirteenth-century tombstone of a Templar mason showing the tools of his profession: hammer and angle-iron. An inscription featuring the utensils of a cook, presumably a Templar, was found close to the Templars' headquarters at Jerusalem's Haram al-Sharif.[42] Not too much source evidence remains to tell us the story of the Templars' and Hospitallers' subordinate headquarters officials. However, it was they who kept the Orders' headquarters running, thereby enabling the governing of two complex international organizations. Even back in the twelfth and thirteenth centuries, the work of these officials may have been largely invisible to people outside the Orders – invisible, but nevertheless indispensable, like 'wind beneath the wings'.

---

[41] For *de Camera*, cf. *CH*, 1, nos 192, 202; for *de Fabrica*, cf. *CH*, 2, no. 1656.

[42] *A Display of Crusader Sculpture in the Archaeological Museum (Rockefeller) on the Occasion of the Second SSCLE Conference (Jerusalem and Haifa, July 2–6, 1987)* (Jerusalem, 1987), p. 23; S. de Sandoli, *Corpus Inscriptionum Crucesignatorum Terrae Sanctae (1099–1291)*. Studium Biblicum Franciscanum, 21 (Jerusalem, 1974), pp. 120–1.

18

The *Sergents* of the Military Order of Santiago

Carlos de Ayala Martínez

BACKGROUND

Few institutions can reflect the sociological reality of the Middle Ages better than the military orders. They are, so to speak, a scale model of its structure, reflecting its most significant nuances. This is especially true in relation to that paradigmatic medieval institution that was the cavalry. It has been said that medieval society was organized by and for war,[1] and it is clear that 'the only warrior worthy of the name was, in the eyes of his contemporaries, the one who fought on horseback'.[2] This fact, although it helps us to explain the knight's pre-eminent role in medieval society, can also mislead us; for not all the warriors who fought on horseback were, from a social point of view, knights.

We do not intend to enter the worn-out historiographical debate over the evolution of the term *miles* (knight) to its unequivocally aristocratic meaning. We will limit ourselves to identifying the different kinds of soldiers who could be found fighting on horseback in the society of the Christian West during the central Middle Ages. Philippe Contamine has categorized them into four fundamental groups.[3] In the first place, the proper knights, those who were confirmed as sharing in the social and economic hegemony of knighthood through having been admitted into the restricted and, to a certain degree, consecrated circle of the military aristocracy through the ceremonial ritual of the *cingulum militiae*. Not all the components of this first and most character-istic social sector of the cavalry possessed the same status. It is clear that from the beginning of the thirteenth century a knightly elite of *adalides* – the

---

[1] J.F. Powers, *A Society Organized for War. The Iberian Municipal Militias in the Central Middle Ages, 1000–1284* (University of California, 1988).

[2] G. Duby, 'Les origines de la chevalerie', in *Hommes et Structures du Moyen Age* (Paris, 1973), p. 331; tr. C. Postan as 'The Origins of Knighthood', in *The Chivalrous Society* (London, 1977), p. 163.

[3] P. Contamine, *La guerre au Moyen Age* (Paris, 1980), pp. 161–6.

From *The Military Orders. Volume 2. Welfare and Warfare*. ed. Helen Nicholson. Copyright © 1998 by Helen Nicholson. Published by Ashgate Publishing Ltd, Gower House, Croft Road, Aldershot, Hampshire, GU11 3HR, Great Britain.

Castilian *ricahombría* – were of higher social standing than the ranks of gentlemen *bacheliers* – the Castilian *infanzones* – who were financially more modest.

There was also a second rank of cavalry composed of freeholders whose position in the social hierarchy varied. They were vassals who were free from servile burdens but whose land holdings were insufficient for them to enter the select group of the knightly class. In fact, sometimes they themselves did not wish to commit themselves to fulfilling the sacred and unavoidable mesh of obligations this involved, irrespective of the privileges they would receive in exchange. Also forming part of this group were people who had risen from the ranks of the commoners, sheltered by lordly protection and promoted, thanks to this protection, to positions of personal dependence very close to noble circles. The heterogeneous composition of this numerous group of soldiers fighting on horseback is reflected by the assortment of terms used to describe them, for example: *satellites equestres, clientes, servientes* or *sergents*.

These two groups are those most customarily identified with the soldiers who fought on horseback. They were distinguished by the different mounts and variety of equipment available to them and by their different appearance under arms, which varied according to individual rank, but not by their military tactics nor by the manner in which they faced the enemy in the battlefield. Their conception of warfare was similar, but their ideals of action and lifestyle were separated by a social abyss.

The two other groups of soldiers fighting on horseback – consisting of light cavalry and mounted archers respectively – had very little to do with the previously mentioned groups. The fact that they were invariably of common extraction, when not servile, meant that their loyalties were far removed from the vassalic spirit, depending on the mercenary sale of their services. These two groups used similar weapons and combat strategies which were completely alien to the conventional practices of the traditional cavalry, thus placing them outside the normal social structure. However, the military importance of these groups rose to increasingly higher levels in time, as circumstances changed.

As we have said, all the military orders had these different groups of cavalry in their own forces or incorporated into them through feudal connections and mercenary dependencies. On the following pages we will concentrate on the second of the groups described, the *sirvientes* or *sergents*. They were documented under this name in the 'international' military orders – the Temple, Hospital and Teutonic Order[4] – and also formally defined in this way in the most important Spanish Order, that of Santiago. We have devoted this short study

---

[4] A. Forey, *The Military Orders. From the Twelfth to the Early Fourteenth Centuries* (London, 1992), pp. 54–5.

to outlining the social and functional contours of the *sergents* of Santiago, and describing their evolution.

DATA

In fact there is very little evidence in the records of the Order of Santiago which alludes unequivocally to the *sergents*. We can find some allusions in the rule, some statutory prescriptions in the *establecimientos* of the chapter, and isolated documental references. Consequently, there has been hardly any specialized historical study on this issue, except for a few lines written on the subject by Professor Lomax.[5] The profile remains obscured of an institution that was certainly more important than the poor documental trail allows us to trace.

Possibly the only way to define the ultimate profile of the *sergents* is by an in-depth examination of the meagre testimonies about them that have come to our attention. First, we know that they did not exist at the Order's beginnings, since we find no reference to them in the most ancient texts of the rule (those of the end of the twelfth century).[6] We must wait for the vast draft of the first half of the thirteenth century to find an unequivocal allusion to them, which appears in one of the rule's numerous penitential prescriptions: a *freire* who beat or injured his *sergent* would incur a half-year's penance, though, in the case of a knight, would not be deprived of his military equipment.

We can make two basic observations on this text. From a strictly termino-logical point of view, the word *sergent*, which is present only in the thirteenth-century version of the rule translated into Spanish (*Regla romanceada*), corresponds to the word *serviens*, which possessed the double meaning of servant and squire.[7] Both meanings are obviously related, but here *serviens* understood as *armiger* (squire) appears more socially relevant than *serviens* as the equivalent of the simple *famulus* (servant). It is evident that the *sergents* of the military orders were *armigeri*, and appear clearly identified as such in the Latin version of the rule of Santiago (*'frater qui armigerum vel servientem suum ...'*). In the later translated version of the fifteenth-century rule this expression was translated as the meaningful term *page de lança* (*'el freyle que a su siruiente o page de lança ...'*). Nevertheless, the ambiguity of the Latin word from which the word *sergent* originated means that in the same text of the rule we find the expression *serviens* or its translation, *servant*, designating the lowest social category of those who were entrusted with the lowliest occupations: the *freires* punished with a year's penance were obliged to share the food and work of the *servants*.

---

[5] D.W. Lomax, *La Orden de Santiago (1170–1275)* (Madrid, 1965), p. 89.

[6] On the rule, see Lomax, pp. 51–3; E. Benito Ruano, 'Establecimientos de la Orden de Santiago en el siglo XIII', in his *Estudios Santiaguistas* (León, 1978), pp. 175–8; and E. Sastre Santos, *La Orden de Santiago y su Regla* (Universidad Complutense of Madrid, 1982).

[7] Du Cange, *Glossarium: serviens*.

Of course, the diffuse definition of the *sergents* is not a consequence of chance, but, in a contradictory way, underlines their social origin; an origin that, however, their own rule did not acknowledge. For instance, there was no effective difference between the penitential treatment of the *freires* involved in an assault against another *freire* (presupposed to be of aristocratic origin) and the punishment laid down for an assault on a simple *sergent*.[8] The servant–squire condition peculiar to the *sergents* is underlined by the little documentation we do possess from the Order on this subject, thanks to which we infer that they entered the Order formally, though without any religious connotations that implied the taking of vows. An interesting primitive text originating from the *Tumbo Menor de León*, published by Lomax, indicates what must have been customary practice: in 1202 Juan de la Pellecería was admitted in the Order as *freire* without dispensing with 'his man' ('*su hombre*', whose name, significantly, is ignored), who was also admitted by the Master into the institution as a *sergent, secundum Deum et secundum ordinem*.[9]

This probably does not mean that the *sergents* remained linked in a systematic and definite way to the noblemen with whom they entered the Order. It is very probable that, once within the Order, they would be distributed according to the service or assignment criteria that the Master and chapter determined. Otherwise, it would not be easy to explain why the first *establecimientos* promulgated by Master Pelayo Pérez Correa, probably in 1251, envisaged the systematic assignment of squires to commanders, bailiffs and conventual brothers. Squires and pages, who are undoubtedly identifiable with *sergents*, are clearly differentiated from the *rapazes* and *criados* that also appear in the text.[10]

However, we should not think that the *sergents* were always of servile origin or linked to the personal service of noblemen who were entering in the Order as *freires*. This would lead us to deduce that the *sergents* were socially immobile and that it was impossible for them to rise, sooner or later, to the condition of *freire*. Let us start by considering that probably not all the *sergents* were of servile

---

[8] '*Frater qui frater suum percusserit et non cum armis vel qui fratrem suum minatus fuerit cum armis, non tantum percusserit, poeniteat per suscriptam poenitentiam dimidii anni. Haec est penitentia dimiddi anni. In primis tollatur signum crucis fratri de veste, uerberetur regularibus disciplinis et si miles fuerit, auferatur ei equus et arma, et si miles aut non, in terra sine mantilibus de cibo seruientium comedat et eorum seruitia faciat...*': *RSJ*, p. 134.

[9] Lomax, pp. 239–40.

[10] '*... Stablesçemos que los comendadores de los Regnos que traigan dos **escuderos** e dos azemilas con sus ommes e sendos vasos de plata e dos taças, e por todo esto si menester fuere a los mayordomos destos comendadores sean dos **escuderos** con sendas bestias e ningund otro baylio nin otro freyle del convento que non traygan azemilas sin liçençia del maestre o del comendador. El freyre que la truxere sin liçençia pierda el azemila e tome por ella quinze viernes (...) Todos los baylos trayan sendos **escuderos** e dos **rapazes**, e los priores mantenganse commo los comendadores mayores, e estos stablesçimientos ansy los usen los clerigos commo los cavalleros (...) Stablesçido es que ningund comendador ni otro freyre ninguno non fagan pegujares a sus **criados** nin a sus ommes en la heredad de la Orden nin en otra heredad...*': Biblioteca Nacional de Madrid (hereafter BNM), MS 8.582, fols 57–59r.

origin. The 1259 *establecimientos* of Santiago determined that if any faithful *sergent* sought to enter the Order, he should not be admitted until he became a knight: '*si algun escudero fidalgo quisiere resçebir nuestra orden, que non gela den a menos que sea ante cavallero.*'[11] Does this mean that such noble pages and squires were directly rejected by the Order, or simply that it was not lawful for them to receive the sacred knightly status of the *militia*? Without any doubt this last is more likely, if we consider the subsequent *establecimientos*, promulgated in Mérida in 1274.[12] Here it is emphasized that the Order's habit could not be given to a nobleman who had not already received the order of knighthood, and adds: '*si lo dieren a otro, denlo como a sirviente.*' That is to say that entry into the Order was possible for noblemen who were not knights, but with the status of *sergent*, not of *freire*. Evidently, the *sergents* could be of noble birth and, as such, owners of possessions of certain importance that, as the *establecimientos* determine, automatically came under the Order's control at the moment of the new *sergent*'s entry. In this respect, the consequences of this vow were the same for *sergents* of noble origin – though theoretically they were not subject to the poverty vow – as for the *freires*, being deprived of their possessions upon entering the Order.

The heterogeneity of the *sergents*' social origin can be explained, to a certain extent, by the fact that their military functions were comparable to those of the *freires*. Thus, in the *establecimientos* of 1274 are mentioned ten '*freyres escuderos de cavallo*' that would have to accompany the Master. In spite of the anomalous, but very meaningful, *freires* designation that exceptionally appears here, we have no doubt that the *establecimientos* are speaking about *sergents*, as they are well differentiated from thirty *onbres de pie* who also constituted the Master's retinue. In fact, in this case these *sergents* fought on horseback in a quite similar way to the *freires* although they would not share the same military

---

[11] AHM OO.MM, *Uclés*, carp. 214, doc. 16; AHN, *Sellos*, carp. 63, doc. 5; BNM, MS 8.582, fols 64–65r.

[12] '*... Otrosi establesçemos que el maestre ni los comendadores non den el el* (sic) *habito de nuestra Orden sinon a omme fidalgo e que sea primeramente cavallero asi como desuso abemos stablesçido. E si lo dieren a otro, denlo como a sirviente dando de sus heredades a la Orden de que la Orden se aproveche. E otramiente mandamos en virtud de santa obediencia que tal omme non sea acogido, e si fuera acogido, si non commo dicho abemos, seale tirado el abito e sea echado de nuestra Orden (...) Otrosi que en tiempo que la Orden non oviere guerra con los moros nin el Rey llamare a su serviçio, el maestre traiga consigo diez freyres estuderos de cavallo e treynta onbres de pie e los ofiçiales que menester ovieren de poner de pie e de cavallo (...) Otrosi los priores traiga cada uno consigo tres freyres clerigos e tres escuderos de cavallo e dos ommes de pie, e de ofiçiales commo dicho es (...) Otrosi que los comendadores mayores cada uno traiga consigo un capellan e quatro freyres de convento e seys escuderos de cavallo e quinze ommes de pie, e de ofiçiales commo dicho es (...) Otrosi que todos los otros comendadores traygan consigo un freyle morador e dos ommes de cavallo e çinco ommes de pie porque en el tiempo de la guerra cada uno ha de yr lo mejor acompañado que pudiere (...) Otrosi que los freyres que tienen los castillos fronteros tengan ommes de pie e de cavallo los que menester ovieren e podieren mantener. Pero si algun comendador oviere mas menester de pie que de cavallo para el serviçio de su Orden, puedanlos traer todavia con liçençia del maestre...*': BNM, MS 8.582, fols 45v–47.

equipment nor, above all, the social status that conditioned their own attitude to the combat.

However, both *freires* and *sergents* bore the habit, and this general similarity of appearance not only allowed, as we have seen, the latter to be designated with the title of the former (though this is an exceptional case), but resulted in the *sergents* being considered as a special category, midway between the *freires* and the laity, being well differentiated from those of the latter who were linked to the Order or were serving it. Thus, in the Portuguese *establecimientos* of 1327, a clear distinction is made between *freires cavaleiros, freires clerigos, sergentos* and *outros hommes segraaes*.[13]

EVALUATION

But what was the real importance of the *sergents* in the evolution of the Order of Santiago? It is not easy to answer this question with the scarce information that we have. The few references on which we rely belong almost entirely to the area of disciplinary regulations and, even here, there is an obvious gap in the period between the *establecimientos 'postpelagianos'* (at the beginning of the fourteenth century) and the *ordenamiento* promulgated by Alonso de Cádernas in the Great Chapter of Uclés-Ocaña-Corral de Almaguer-Llerena that took place in 1480–1, the penultimate of those celebrated by the Order of Santiago as a independent institution. We will here consider the references in the aforementioned Great Chapter which relate to the *sergents*; but before doing so, we must emphasize the silence of the disciplinary sources on this subject, a century's silence (1327–1480) unbroken even by the most important *establecimientos* of Lorenzo Suárez de Figueroa (beginning of the fifteenth century).[14]

In fact, this silence is still more striking if we take into account that the documentation of the Order of Santiago preserved in the Archivo de Uclés and in the rest of the Order's archives almost completely ignores the figure of the *sergent*, and that not even the *Chronicle of Rades* includes the most minimal allusion to it. All the data – or rather, the obvious shortage of data – indicates the marginal position and the relative unimportance of the *sergents* in the Order's institutional, socio-economic and even military development.

However, the title of the twelfth *establecimiento* promulgated by Alonso de Cárdenas in 1480, the one referring to the *sergents*, reveals that they had a greater level of importance than has been indicated so far.[15] The disciplinary text, as

---

[13] Arquivo Nacional Torre do Tombo, Lisbon, *Ordem de Santiago*, Livro (das Tábuas Ferradas) 141, fols 2v–3r.

[14] Mérida, 1403: BNM, MS 8.582, fols 68–86r.

[15] '*Titulo XII. De los sergentes. Porque en nuestra Orden ay mucha confusion por los sergentes que son resçebidos a nuestro abito fuera de lo antiguamente stablesçido por la dicha nuestra Orden, de lo qual viene perjuizio a nos en lo forma* [sic] *de la dacion del habito que los priores lo dan sin nuestra liçençia e provision commo se requiere segund el dicho stablesçimiento antiguo, e a los pueblos viene asimismo daño e perjuizio por los pechos que suelen pagar de que se esentan los dichos sergentes e carga sobre los otros pecheros de los*

was customary, began by denouncing an abuse. It said that the habit of Santiago had been conceded to new *sergents* without observing the most minimal prescriptions of the ancient rule, and that this was prejudicial to the Master, the city councils (*concejos*), the commanders and the Order at large. To the Master, because the priors were admitting the new *sergents* without his licence, dishonouring his mandatory provision; to the *concejos*, because as long as the *sergents* were exempt from personal taxes (*pechos*), the collectors of city taxes were imposing greater pressure on the rest of the taxpayers; to the commanders, because after the *sergents'* admission they no longer received from them the tithes that the *sergents* had to pay before their admission; and, finally, to the Order at large, because the *sergents* failed to carry out the obligatory transfer of their goods that the ancient *establecimientos* had prescribed.

The accusation puts us on the track of some interesting problems, and confirms some data already known. To begin with, the increase in the number of *sergents* must have been sufficiently significant to necessitate giving attention to the problems their position caused. Furthermore, we know that the *sergents*, whose admission into the Order normally required provision from the Master, were enjoying a double fiscal exemption: at the *concejos* level they were considered not taxable, and at the ecclesiastical level, they remained, *de facto* though not *de iure*, exempt from paying tithe. Apart from this, there is confirmation of their formal use of the habit and the continuing observance, at least theoretically, of the *establecimientos* of Mérida (1274) that prescribed the automatic transfer of a new *sergent's* property to the Order.

The measures taken by the Master to deal with the problem of the *sergents* are no less illuminating of their condition and circumstances in the second half of the fifteenth century. Alonso de Cárdenas invoked previous *establecimientos* – promulgated by himself, it seems – and, supported by them, confirmed arrangements designed to correct abuses, also adding new measures. These measures can be summarized as follows:

---

lugares donde biven, e a nuestra Orden viene asimismo perjuizio que no le dan nin dexan sus bienes segund thenor del dicho stablesçimiento, e a los comendadores viene daño de los diezmos que se les pagan dixiendo ser esentos dellos.

Mandamos que de aqui adelante ningunas ni algunas personas non sean resçebidos por sergentes al abito de nuestra Orden sin nuestra liçençia espeçial e mandado siguiendo los stablesçimientos nuestros e dexando a la dicha nuestra Orden la quinta parte de los bienes commo en el dicho stablesçimiento se contiene, e que paguen los diezmos de sus labranças e crianças donde antes estavan en costunbre de las pagar, pero que en su vida pueda gozar del usofruto de sus bienes que asi diere e dexare a la dicha Orden, e si no toviere fijos que todos sus bienes queden a la dicha Orden, e teniendolos, que les quede el quinto segund dicho es.

E porque los tales sergentes sean conosçidos entre los cavalleros, mandamos que el abito que traxeren sean braços sin dedos.

Pero que los dichos priores puedan resçebir por sergentes sin liçençia nuestra los que fueren de fuera de nuestra Horden e bivieren en lo realengo o de otros señores.': BNM, MS 8.582, fols 244–278.

1. No subject of the Order could obtain the habit of *sergent* without the Master's express licence. Only an aspirant not subject to the Order could be admitted by the priors without the Master's licence.
2. The new *sergents* were obliged to deliver a fifth of all their goods to the Order, though this portion would be enjoyed by them in usufruct for life. The rest of their goods were left for their descendants. If they had no descendants, the whole of their possessions would pass to the Order.
3. The *sergents* were obliged to pay the mandatory tithes of their *labranças e crianças*, as they had done before entering the Order.
4. Finally, the *sergents* had to wear habits that allowed them to be distinguished from the knights.

These four measures are extraordinarily revealing. The first clarifies the problem that has been outlined above: it was necessary to restrict the number of *sergents* originating from the Order of Santiago's lordships because from the institution's point of view the fiscal advantages that they enjoyed were not compensated for by the mandatory – but theoretical – delivery of property that must accompany the taking of the habit. On the other hand, this explains why the Order did not place even the most minimal impediment on those from the royal demesne (*realengo*) or other lordships who wished to become *sergents* in the Order of Santiago.

The second measure indicates the change that had occurred in the disciplinary tradition concerning the *sergent*'s possession of property. The ancient *establecimientos* of 1274 were firm on this point: all the goods of those aspiring to become a *sergent* had to be delivered to the Order. The Order's slow but progressive 'privatization' of common property in the fourteenth century, which meant the relaxing of the poverty vow for the *freires*, gave the *sergents*, who were excluded from the poverty vow, the possibility of not resigning more than a fifth of their patrimony. It seems that some unknown *establecimientos* of the above-mentioned Alonso de Cárdenas, prior to those of 1480–1, must have allowed the *sergents* free disposal of their property, except for the fifth which must be delivered to the Order. This allows us to establish another important fact: the change in the social sector from which the majority of the *sergents* originated, from positions close to servitude towards the comfortable enjoyment of certain economic potential. That is the only way to explain the Order's preoccupation with this matter.

The third measure, the re-establishment of the tithes payment, was unavoidable. Successive *establecimientos* promulgated throughout the fifteenth century, including those of Cárdenas, insist on the fact that the *freires* were subject to a mandatory tithes payment. Obviously, when the *sergents* refused to pay tithes to their commanders they were committing a notorious abuse which damaged the whole of the community of Santiago. At any rate, and once again, the Order's preoccupation with not being deprived of this revenue indicates its high value, and, consequently, the clear socio-economic evolution of the people who were subjects of Santiago.

We must interpret the last of the agreed measures on the same lines: it was necessary for the *sergents'* habit clearly to differentiate their social position from that of the knights. The expression *'brazos sin dedos'* ('arms without fingers'), mentioned by *establecimientos* to designate the specific habit of the *sergents*, would put an end to the increasingly arrogant career of apparent social ascent that certain subjects of the Order would have begun as *sergents*. Wearing the Order's habit, in which all symbolic codes which revealed the social origins of the wearer had been erased, had allowed them to display their social ascent publicly.

19

Hospitaller and Templar Commanderies in Bohemia and Moravia: their Structure and Architectural Forms

Libor Jan and Vít Jesenský

This article deals with the economic basis of the Hospitaller and Templar commanderies in Bohemia and Moravia and principally with the architectural and structural forms of their houses in this area. For reasons of space we omit the third military order, the Teutonic Order, which in fact played an equally important role in the area under examination.

The Order of St John of Jerusalem was introduced into Prague in 1169 by the Czech king Vladislav II in conjunction with his closest counsellors. During the next thirty years the other Přemyslid princes endowed it with relatively extensive landholdings, largely in long-settled areas: in the vicinity of Prague, around Litoměřice and Plzeň.[1] The activity of some aristocratic families, the Markwartingers from northern Bohemia and the Bavors of Strakonice from southern Bohemia, further enlarged the landed possessions of the Order in the first half of the thirteenth century. In Moravia, even before the end of the twelfth century, the Order acquired Ivanovice na Hané and some time later Grobniki, which today is in Poland. The knights also gained a firm foothold in Kroměříž and Brno and in some smaller localities.[2]

From the beginning of the thirteenth century the Hospitallers converted the existing Slavic villages to the emphyteutic system; that is, they settled sparsely inhabited areas with predominantly German colonists. The only documents

---

[1] M. Skopal, 'Založení komendy johanitů na Malé Straně', *Pražský sborník historický*, 26 (1993), 7–36; L. Jan and V. Jesenský, 'K funkci a stavební podobě johanitských komend na Moravě', *Průzkumy památek*, 1 (1996), 75–86.

[2] L. Jan, 'Ivanovice na Hané, Orlovice a johanitský řád', *Časopis Matice moravské*, 111 (1992), 199–226; J. Šebánek, 'Z problémů slezského kodexu', *Slezský sborník*, 49 (1951), 1–16; J. Svátek, 'Johanité v Kroměříži', *Studie Muzea Kroměřížska* (1986), 25–40; J. Vodička, 'Počátky špitálu sv. Ducha na Starém Brně', *Sborník Matice moravské*, 78 (1959), 161–204; T. Edel, 'Blahoslavená Zdislava a řád sv. Jana Jeruzalémského', *Zprávy památkové péče*, 51 (1992), 28–30.

Figure 19.1   Hospitaller commanderies in Bohemia and Moravia

which give us a more precise idea of the economic power of particular
commanderies date from the second half of the fourteenth and the beginning
of the fifteenth centuries. According to the visitation of 1373, the most
important commanderies within the Prague archbishopric were in Prague,
Strakonice and Český Dub, while the commanderies in Manětín and
Ploskovice also deserve particular attention.[3] All of these were centres of real
lordship, while the other preceptories were more like large rectories. This was
also reflected in the terminology of the privilege granted by King Venceslas
IV in 1384, in which Prague, Strakonice and Český Dub are called *monasterium*
and *conventus*; Manětín, Ploskovice, Velky Tynec (Grosstinz in Silesia) and
Vratislav (Wrocław – Breslau, also in Silesia) are called simply *domus*; while the
third group consists of the parish churches (*ecclesias parochiales, domos parochiales*)
in Kadaň, Horažďovice, Pičín, Mladá Boleslav at the church of St Guy and St
John the Baptist, Zittau, Hirschfelde, Kladsko (Klódsk – Glatz), Dzierzoniów
(in Silesia) and Strzegom (again in Silesia).[4] The visitation of 1373 classified
the commanderies as *domos conventuales* (Prague, Strakonice, Manětín,
Ploskovice, Český Dub and Mladá Boleslav at St Guy) and *domos parochiales*
(Pičín, Kadaň, Mladá Boleslav at St John, Zittau, Kladsko and Hirschfelde).

   In 1373, the annual income of the Order's house in Prague, which held
diverse forms of property (tributary land, their own manors, town payments),

---

[3] 'Inquisitio domorum Hospitalis S. Johannis Hierosolimitani per Pragensem archidiocesim facta
anno 1373', ed. V. Novotný, *Historický archiv*, 19 (1901), 11, 23, 25, 27, 32–3, 38, 43–4.
   [4] Státní ústřední archiv Praha, Archiv Velkopřevorství maltézského, no. 995.

reached almost 900 threescores (*sexagenae*, or sixties) of Prague *grossi*.[5] The income in Strakonice, Český Dub and Manětín ranged between 200 and 300 threescores; the income of Ploskovice was a little over 100 threescores.[6] The other commanderies received only several tens of threescores. In 1418, the Knights of St John in Bohemia, where the king considered himself the legal successor of the founders and enjoyed the rights of a founding patron, paid 330 threescores of a special royal tax (*berna specialis*) per year.[7] For comparison, the Teutonic Order as a whole paid 200 threescores,[8] and the largest monasteries paid sums similar to the Hospitallers' payments (Chotěšov 330 threescores, Břevnov and Kladruby 300 threescores, Pomuk 270 threescores).[9] It can be judged from this that the property of the Hospitallers in the whole of Bohemia was comparable to that of two or three of the largest Premonstratensian or Benedictine monasteries.

The situation in Moravia is much less clear. The centre of real lordship was Ivanovice (or Orlovice), the annual income of which would be about the equivalent of around 150 or 200 threescore *grossi*. At the same time, the nearby lordship of the Teutonic Order in Slavkov (Austerlitz) with a similar area and structure, returned roughly 180 marks of rent from tributary fields and several tens of marks from manors per year[10] – a mark being theoretically equivalent to one threescore of *grossi*. The possessions of the commandery and the hospital in Staré Brno (Old Brno) were heterogeneous. It acquired, besides the Hospitallers' manors in the close vicinity of Brno, and town payments, revenue from two villages and pieces of land around Křižanov in the Bohemian–Moravian uplands, and from patronage of several local churches. The income of the preceptory can be estimated to have been between 50 and 100 marks.[11] The Order's houses in Horní Kounice and Přibice, which were founded in the villages originally donated to the Lower Austrian commandery in Mailberg, and the house in Mutěnice (*Crux, Kreuz*) received payments from serfs' farmsteads in these villages, which belonged in their entirety to the Order. The size of these payments could range in particular cases from twenty to fifty threescores per year. The commandery with a hospital in Kroměříž had two tributary villages. In contrast, the hypothetical preceptory in Brtnice was no more than a large rectory. The majority of the Hospitallers' preceptories

---

[5] The Prague *grossi* or groats were originally minted at sixty to the mark, and even when this was no longer so, they were still reckoned in sixties: see P. Spufford, W. Wilkinson and S. Tolley, *Handbook of Medieval Exchange* (London, 1986), p. xxiii.

[6] 'Inquisitio', pp. 70–1.

[7] K. Krofta, 'Začátky české berně', *Český časopis historicky*, 36 (1930), 464, 471–2.

[8] Ibid., p. 471; J. Hemmerle, *Die Deutschordens-Ballei Böhmen in ihren Rechnungsbüchern 1382–1411*, QuStDO, 22 (Bonn, 1967), p. 96.

[9] Krofta, 471–2.

[10] Hemmerle, p. 60.

[11] L. Jan, 'Účet starobrněnského špitálu z roku 1367', *Forum brunense* (1993), 9–20.

were destroyed during the Hussite wars in the 1420s; only Strakonice and Staré Brno survived.[12]

The Templars came to the Czech lands as late as the 1230s. In contrast with the Hospitallers and the Teutonic Order, which appeared in Prague and Opava at the turn of the thirteenth century, they came without the king's support, which resulted in their receiving a rather modest endowment of property. The Templars had their seats in two commanderies in Bohemia: in Prague at the church of St Lawrence and in the nearby village of Uhříněves; they also had two houses in Moravia, in Jamolice (and in the castle of Tempelštejn) and Čejkovice. At the turn of the fourteenth century, the dominant commandery was Čejkovice (for instance, the *commendator provincialis* for Bohemia, Moravia and Austria often had his seat there). Some small estates in Vienna and its surroundings were also controlled from there because the Templars had no houses in Austria. But even Čejkovice did not become the centre of a more extensive complex of Templar properties. The Order held only this large village and a small one not far from it. Between 1297 and 1308 the Templars began more intensive colonizing activity in the newly acquired area around the River Bečva and in the area surrounding Vsetín, but this activity was interrupted by the abolition of the Order.[13]

The Templars' commandery in Čejkovice, which was later rebuilt as a Renaissance and baroque castle, was placed in an elevated position protected on two sides by lakes. The precinct had a roughly oval shape, 60 m in circumference, and was enclosed by a defending wall.[14] Parts of this wall and the bulky tower are probably the only remains of the original commandery[15] from the 1240s and 1250s.[16] As the parish church is outside the commandery, we can assume that a chapel was situated within the complex. The form of this commandery allows us to describe it as almost a small castle rather than simply a stronghold. It may be an example of the military orders' custom to have the seat of the preceptor of that country or province in their castle nearest to the state capital.

The commandery of Jamolice was founded soon after the commandery in Čejkovice, but we do not know of any building remains, nor of the commandery's precise location. Remarkably, it was later removed to the

---

[12] Jan and Jesenský, 77–8.

[13] L. Jan, 'Pečeti rytířských duchovních řádů v Čechách a na Moravě 1189–1310' (s přihlédnutím k dalšímu vývoji), *Zprávy Krajského vlastivědného muzea v Olomouci*, 246 (1987), 1–27; J. Šebánek, 'Tři nejstarší doklady o Vsetíně', *Sborník prací filosofické fakulty brněnské university*, 8 (1961), 77–93; A. Mailly, *Der Tempelherrenorden in Niederösterreich in Geschichte und Sage* (Vienna, 1923), pp. 9–22.

[14] J. Tribula and J. Bednaříková, 'Archeologický výzkum gotické tvrze v Čejkovicích', *Vlastivědný věstník moravský*, 32 (1980), 202–7. *Idem*, 'Průzkum čejkovické tvrze', *Malovaný kraj*, 18 (1982), 5–6.

[15] M. Plaček, *Hrady a zámky na Moravě a ve Slezsku* (Prague, 1996), p. 126. B. Samek, *Umělecké památky Moravy a Slezska*, 1 (Prague, 1994), p. 346–7.

[16] J. Eliáš, 'Čejkovice, Stavebně historický průzkum, zámek (tvrz)', (Brno, 1993). Unpublished report held in the archives of the Office for Conservation in Southern Moravia in Brno.

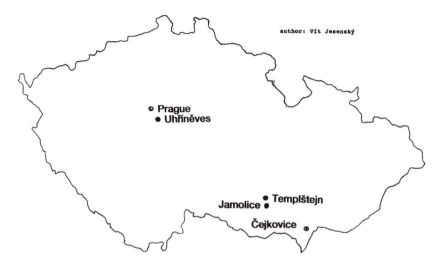

author: Vít Jesenský

Prague
Uhříněves

Jamolice • Templštejn

Čejkovice

Figure 19.2   Templar commanderies in Bohemia and Moravia

nearby castle of Templštejn, which was built by the Templars between 1281 and 1298. This castle, which survives as ruins, has become the subject of a debate over its typological classification;[17] but this does not alter the fact that it is, with the Hospitallers' Orlov, a rare unambiguous example of an isolated medieval castle built by a military order in Moravia. The location of another such castle, Freundsberk, which should have been founded within the Templars' estates around the town of Vsetín, can only be guessed at, and it was probably never finished. The Templars' colonization activities provide a general context for these building activities, but research is needed to clarify their purpose further.

The Prague commandery, the only Templar commandery within a town in Bohemia, was founded some time shortly after 1230. The Templars, undoubtedly after an invitation or donation from an unknown feudal baron, settled on the right bank of the River Vltava, close to Judit, later Charles, Bridge. They possessed the area around the rotunda, which perhaps originated in the first half of the twelfth century. Today, the site is occupied by a former Dominican nuns' convent dating from the fourteenth century.[18] Probably even before the second half of the thirteenth century the Templars extended the rotunda by building the nave with an apse. The other known remains of the commandery buildings are two cellars attached to the north side of the

---

[17] P. Bolina, 'Hrad Templštejn, k.ú. Jamolice, okr. Znojmo a jeho vztah k chronologii hradu s plášt'ovou zdí na Moravě', *Archaeologia Historica*, 5 (Brno, 1980), 267–74. Plaček, p. 341.

[18] V. Procházka, 'K dějinám stavebního vývoje kostela sv. Anny, sv. Vavřince a kláštera dominikánek na Starém Městě pražském', *Umění*, 3 (1954), 124.

Figure 19.3   The castle in Čejkovice, former Templar commandery

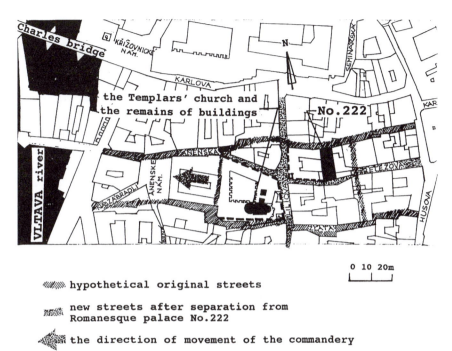

0 10 20m

/////// hypothetical original streets

*new streets after separation from
Romanesque palace No.222*

the direction of movement of the commandery

*Figure 19.4   The Templar commandery in Prague – location and hypothetical
development*

church.[19] A very small amount of the church's masonry has survived, and in
1954 it was excavated under the floor of the nuns' church[20] which had been
converted for storage after secularization.

Analysis of the broader urban relations of the known Romanesque structures
in the area under examination suggests a possible relationship between the
commandery and the nearby Romanesque palace No. 222.[21] Its owner is not
known but he must have been of a status corresponding to the high architectural quality of the building.[22] Perhaps he donated part of his town plot to the

---

[19] D. Líbal and M. Vilímková, 'Č.p.211–I, Anenský klášter. Stavebně historický průzkum'
(SÚRPMO, 1962). Typed report, held in the archives of SÚRPMO (Státní ústav pro rekonstrukce
památkových měst a objektů, the State Institute for the Reconstruction of Historical Towns and
Buildings) and in the Prague Office for Conservation.

[20] I. Borkovský, 'Objev templářského kostela v Praze', *Archeologické rozhledy*, 9 (1951), 500. *Idem*,
'Kostel řádu templářů na Starém Městě', *Kniha o Praze* (1959), 35.

[21] V. Jesenský, 'Stavební vývoj anenského kláštera a jeho okolí do začátku 14. stol.', unpublished
thesis (Faculty of Architecture, Prague Technical University, 1985), p. 40.

[22] V. Píša, 'Románský palác na Starém Městě pražském', *Kniha o Praze* (1958), 45. *Idem*,
'Kunštátský dvorec', *Ochrana památek* (1959), 47–74. Líbal and Vilímková, p. 66. D. Líbal, 'Stručný
přehled urbanistického i architektonického vývoje oblasti anenského kláštera' (SÚRPMO, 1962).
Typed report held in the archives of SÚRPMO and in the Prague Office for Conservation.

The Templars' church (the nave attached to the older Romanesque rotunda) excavated under the church of St. Anna and the remains of the attached hypothetical wing of the commandery

Drawn by Vít Jesenský following I. Borkovský and D. Líbal

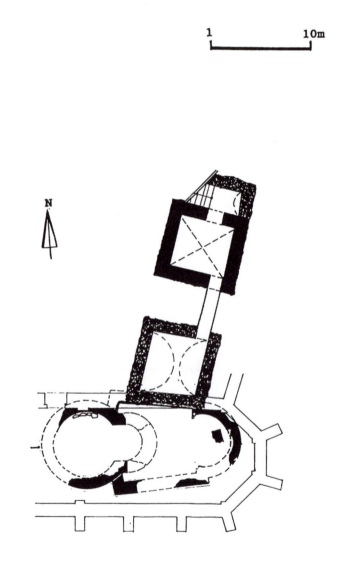

Figure 19.5   The Templar commandery in Prague – plan of the church and wing

Templars. This is also indicated by a hypothetical reconstruction of the Romanesque structures and streets, and the possibility that the commandery developed only on the western side of the remains discovered of a wing of the commandery which was attached to the church.[23] Nevertheless, the greatest architectural rarity seems to be the plan of the Templars' church: the longitudinal walls of its nave were intentionally convergent. The most probable explanation for this is that it was an adaptation of the rotunda of the Holy Sepulchre in Jerusalem[24] rather than an attempt to prolong the interior visually through the effect of perspective. One could speculate further about the meaning of the architectural form; but in any case this opens up the interesting problem of standard iconographical and architectural 'types' of military order church, in the form of a rectangular nave linked to a round chancel, or vice versa. The intentionally convergent walls of the nave form a significant architectural element which demands comparison.

The Prague Hospitaller commandery at the Church of Our Lady under the Chain became one of the most important centres of the Order in Europe, and its form and development reflected this. It is a very well known site, and therefore it is only necessary to remind readers that the original Romanesque basilica, standing on the site of the present courtyard in front of the Gothic presbytery, had on the southern side a contiguous regular building of typical monastic plan around a cloister. Another building, probably with a courtyard but with no clear function, adjoined the northern side of the church. Substantial discoveries have provided evidence for other agricultural, industrial and residential buildings within the enclosed precinct.[25]

The commandery in Strakonice in southern Bohemia is an example of a seat of the Order existing in symbiosis with a secular castle belonging to the donor, Bavor of Strakonice. It is a very familiar structure whose form is substantially preserved and supported by historical documents. Nevertheless, it is worth mentioning that in recent years previous theories that the castle was founded for both secular purposes and those of the Order simultaneously have been gradually corrected.[26] It is now considered possible that the castle was founded by the donor around 1220, and the commandery was built in the south-eastern part within the subsequent twenty years. The so-called chapter hall lay in the western part; the northern wing and the church with a gallery on the eastern

---

[23] Jesenský, *Stavební vývoj anenského kláštera*, p. 45.

[24] V. Denkstein, 'K archeologickému výzkumu kláštera sv. Anny na Starém Městě pražském', *Kniha o Praze* (1959), 47.

[25] V. Hlavsa and J. Vančura, *Malá Strana* (Prague, 1983), pp. 18, 19, 45, 106, 107, 244, 247. D. Líbal, 'Architektura', *Praha středověká* (1983), 100, 102, 281, 282. A. Merhautová, *Raně středověká architektura v Čechách* (Prague, 1971), pp. 245, 246. V. Richter, 'Maltézský kostel P. Marie na Malé Straně v Praze ve středověku', *Památky archeologické*, 38 (1932), 40. M. Vilímková, 'Urbanistický vývoj maltézské jurisdikce', *Pražský sborník historický* (1966), 72.

[26] J. Varhaník, 'Neznámý prostor strakonického hradu', *Průzkumy památek*, 2 (1995), 77–84.

side; and the cloister was built between them, probably being added in later. The origin of the Hospitallers' hospital, which is documented in 1318 as standing outside the castle at the town bridge, is unclear.

The third significant Hospitaller preceptory was founded in Český Dub in northern Bohemia shortly after 1237. Continuous archaeological excavations in recent years have gradually uncovered an extraordinarily interesting structure in the area. This is probably one of the most fruitful discoveries in Bohemia for evidence of the form of buildings and the functioning of Hospitaller commanderies.[27] The preceptory was established by the owner of the village of the time, Havel of Lemberg, at the little Romanesque church with a cemetery. This was probably the centre of the settlement, the structure of which was respected by the development of the new precinct.

In the first phase, a room vaulted by two cross vaults and probably even a late Romanesque chapel continuing towards the south were annexed to the original church. The chapel has a square nave and three-sided chancel. It was vaulted by a cross vault without ribs and had an upper floor. On the southern side a two-storey palace wing was possibly added, which on the ground floor comprised a hall with three cross vaults separated by pointed arches, while a similarly vaulted room was added at the northern end. The remains of the enclosure wall were found in front of the western front of the pre-Hospitaller church. Without a broader knowledge of the layout of the commandery, the existence of two little churches separated only by one room in the same wing is startling.

This situation probably lasted for almost all of the thirteenth century. The northern church was destroyed by fire before 1291 and the wing of the preceptory was extended on to this site. At the same time the parish church of the Holy Spirit, whose Romanesque tower is preserved today, was erected on the northern side between the precinct of the commandery and the market square. The ruins of a possible hospital dating from the end of the fourteenth century have been located adjoining the northern side of this church. It will undoubtedly be interesting to observe the excavations in the possible western part of the commandery area. The importance and position of the commandery in Český Dub could indicate a similar building layout as in Prague and Strakonice. In spite of this, we rather doubt the possibility of a plan with a regular cloister.

In Moravia the commandery at Ivanovice na Hané, which was founded before 1286, is among the most remarkable from the point of view of architecture and typology. Its remains became the core of a surviving Renaissance castle. It is a two-storey tower building with two barrel-vaulted rooms on the ground floor in the north-western corner of the castle. The area of the precinct, standing in the neighbourhood of a parish church, could have

---

[27] T. Edel, *Příběh ztraceného kláštera Blahoslavené Zdislavy* (Prague, 1993).

been roughly identical to that of a square, fortified, late Gothic stronghold which was built in the area of the commandery without the Hospitallers' participation, probably at the end of the fifteenth century. Before 1328 the Order built a medieval castle above the nearby village of Orlovice. This castle unfortunately survives only as ruins, from which it is apparent that part of the structure, mainly the cylindrical tower, was built of brick. The castle was the seat of the preceptor; nevertheless, after 1328, on some occasions the Hospitallers also used the more spacious and comfortable stronghold in Ivanovice.[28]

A detailed, historical structural analysis of the site of the commandery in Horní Kounice, which is mentioned for the first time in 1248, has produced valuable information about the form of this site.[29] It was a fairly regular oblong manor house enclosed by a wall and doubtless by a moat, probably together with the church opposite. At least one stone building stood within the precinct, which can be considered a two-storey hall typical of the commanderies of the military orders with a residential, meeting and warehousing function. It is preserved in the walls of a baroque granary, including the pointed sandstone portal of an entrance and a pointed double window. The gateway out of the village was protected by a gatehouse. Other agricultural and residential buildings were certainly located within the manor; it may be theorized that the stone-vaulted cellar in the north-western corner represents their remains. Further evidence for the development of the area is the fact that the church nave has been significantly extended. In the analysis of the site, this extension was attributed to the Hospitallers, in connection with the village's change of status to a town in 1318.

Despite a wide variety of buildings and the limited preservation of Hospitaller commanderies in Moravia, we have suggested that they may be categorized into two groups.[30] The first group is defined as commanderies with 'spitals' (hospitals) in the towns, and is represented by Staré Brno and Kroměříž. The physical layout and form of these ensembles were dependent on the geography of the site, previous building, the economic prosperity of the commandery, the time of foundation, location inside or outside the town walls, and so on. The second group is represented by the commanderies in Horní Kounice, Přibice, Ivanovice, Mutěnice and Brtnice. They are a type of village commandery which fulfilled economic and administrative duties as centres of the Order's estates. These preceptories took the form of an enclosed manor house and precincts standing in close proximity to parish churches, in which the Hospitallers met the spiritual needs of the settlers. The churches

---

[28] Plaček, pp. 177, 268. Jan and Jesenský, 75–86.

[29] V. Jesenský, 'The Commanderies of the Order of the Knights of St John in Moravia – an Investigation into their Building Form', unpublished final thesis from the Department of Advanced Studies in Art and Architecture of the Central European University (Prague, 1995), 20–31; Jan and Jesenský, 81–3.

[30] Ibid., 84.

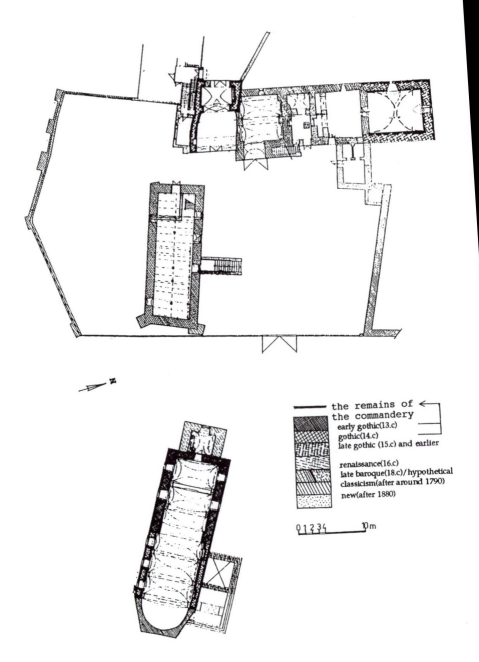

the remains of
the commandery
early gothic(13.c)
gothic(14.c)
late gothic (15.c) and earlier

renaissance(16.c)
late baroque(18.c)/ hypothetical
classicism(after around 1790)
new(after 1880)

0 1 2 3 4   10 m

Figure 19.6   Horní Kounice – plan of the ground floor

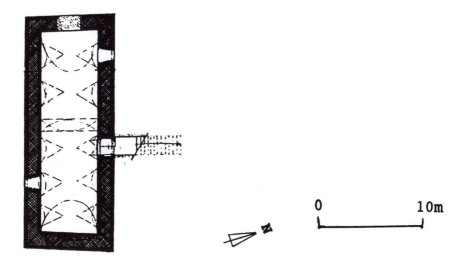

0   10m

Figure 19.7   Horní Kounice – plan of the granary basement

were either included in the walled enclosure of the commandery or walled separately and linked with it. There is no evidence in Moravia of the existence of special chapels such as are known from similar research in other countries.[31]

The differences between these two groups of manor houses were not reflected in variations in their physical size but rather in the number and quality of the buildings. From an architectural point of view, the Orders' building production in Moravia does not present any specific and characteristic features of construction, typology, iconography or art. On the contrary, it was adapted relatively flexibly to regional influences, both in details and construction techniques. It is not certain that the commanderies had a predominantly protective role; the form of walls and other defensive elements depended on the importance of the seat. The architecture was not found to reflect any strategic or purely military function. The Orlovice commandery represents a specific type, namely a castle or significantly fortified stronghold, for which deeper analysis and clarification of role and function are still required. Nevertheless, it is apparent that it was influenced by the design of the Orders' castles in Palestine.

We can deduce a number of methodological conclusions from our work. The history of the military orders in Bohemia and Moravia is reflected in the extensive destruction of the remains of their commandery buildings. Investigation of the forms and function of these buildings can only be productive if a multi-disciplinary approach is adopted, which requires the cooperation of

---

[31] R. Gilchrist, *Contemplation and Action. The Other Monasticism* (London, 1995), pp. 62–105.

Horní Kounice - the Hospitallers' commandery

1 the portal to the basement of the granary
2 the gothic window walled up in the facade of the granary
3 the manor from the East

2

1

3

Figure 19.8   Horní Kounice – three photographs

20

Christ, Santiago and Avis: an Approach to the Rules of the Portuguese Military Orders in the Late Middle Ages

Paula Pinto Costa and António Pestana de Vasconcelos

This article will focus on the study of three Portuguese documents, written in 1503,[1] 1509[2] and 1516,[3] containing regulations relating to the Orders of Christ, Santiago and Avis respectively. These texts in effect represent the first time that the Orders of Santiago and Avis in Portugal acted on their own, independently from the main convents in Castile. The Order of Christ, on the other hand, had not originally been dependent on a Castilian order, although it had later become affiliated to the Order of Calatrava. Its foundation was the consequence of a political decision taken by the Portuguese monarchy after the extinction of the Templars, whereby the Order of Christ inherited all the possessions belonging to the Templars in Portugal.[4]

By the early fifteenth century, the Portuguese military orders felt the need to reorganize and to readapt themselves to their fundamental goal: the fight against the infidel. Throughout western Christendom in general there was an urgent desire for religious reform, due to the fact that from 1378 to 1415 the Catholic Church was divided between two obediences: Rome and Avignon. The resulting instability was responsible for a certain disorganization in everyday life. To this instability was added the fact that, as far as Portugal was concerned, the Reconquest had reached its end in 1249.

---

[1] Arquivo Nacional/Torre do Tombo (hereafter AN/TT), Série Preta, no. 1393.

[2] Ibid., no. 872.

[3] Biblioteca Nacional de Lisboa (herafter BNL), Res. 3008 V.

[4] Other works on the military orders in Portugal include: I.M.G.F.C. Lago Barbosa, 'A Ordem de Santiago em Portugal na Baixa Idade Media', unpublished MA thesis (University of Oporto, 1989); M. da Silva Castelo Branco, 'As Ordens Militares na Expansão Portuguesa: Vice-Reis e Governadores da Índia que, no século XVI, tiveram os hábitos de Avis, Cristo e Santiago', in *As Ordens Militares em Portugal, Actas do 1o Encontro sobre Ordens Militares*, ed. P. Pacheco and L. Pequito Antunes (Palmela, 1991), pp. 57–66; M. Cocheril, 'Calatrava y las Ordenes Militares Portuguesas',

The establishment of the Order of Christ in Portugal in 1319 later made possible a new approach in the field of overseas conquests, moving from a war against an enemy within the peninsula to a war against an enemy overseas. This new approach developed further following the accession in 1420 of Prince Henry, whose reform of the Order was intended to prepare it for its participation in maritime expansion.[5] In 1434 this same objective prompted Pope Eugenius IV to put the bishop of Lamego in charge of revising and reorganizing the Order,[6] although his reorganization took place only in 1449, due to the opposition of the Master of Calatrava and of the abbot of Alcobaça, the latter being the perpetual visitor and corrector of the Order.[7] Their attitude is understandable when we consider that one of the results of this reform would be to break the links with Calatrava once and for all. After the beginning of the sixteenth century the link of Avis and Christ to Calatrava and that of Santiago to Uclés were no longer meaningful.

Cistercium, year 10, no. 59 (Sept.–Dec. 1958), 331–9; M. Cocheril, 'Les Ordres Militaires Cisterciens au Portugal', *Bulletin des Etudes Portugaises*, new ser. 28–29 (1967–68), 11–72; A.L. Conde, 'Tipologia de la vida religiosa en las Ordenes Militares', in *Actas del Congreso Internacional Hispano-Portugues (1971)*, *Las Ordenes Militares en la Peninsula durante la Edad Media* (Madrid and Barcelona, 1981), pp. 33–58; P.M.C. Pinto Costa, 'A Ordem Militar do Hospital em Portugal (Sécs. XII–XIV)', unpublished MA thesis (University of Oporto, 1993); M.C. Almeida e Cunha, 'A Ordem Militar de Avis (das Origens a 1329)', unpublished MA thesis (University of Oporto, 1989); M.R. de Sousa Cunha 'A Ordem Militar de Santiago (das origens a 1327)', unpublished MA thesis (University of Oporto, 1991); C.M. De Witte, 'Les Bulles Pontificales et l'Expansion Portugaise au XVe Siècle', *Revue d'Histoire Ecclésiastique*, 48 (1953), 683–718; 49 (1954), 438–61; 51 (1956), 413–53, 809–36; 53 (1958), 5–46; 54 (1959), 443–71; J. Leclerq, 'La vie et la prière des chevaliers de Santiago d'après leur règle primitive', *Liturgica*, 2 (1958), 347–57; *Nova História de Portugal. Portugal na Crise dos Séculos XIV e XV*, ed. J.S. Marques and A.H. de Oliveira Marques, 4 (Lisbon, 1987); J.F. O'Callaghan, *The Spanish Military Order of Calatrava and its Affiliates* (London, 1975); M.C.G. Pimenta, 'A Ordem Militar de Avis, durante o mestrado de D. Fernão Rodrigues Sequeira', unpublished MA thesis (University of Oporto, 1989); M.C.G. Pimenta and I.L. Morgado Sousa e Silva, 'Castro Marim: uma comenda da Ordem de Cristo', *Cadernos Históricos*, 3 (1992), 62–93; M. Rivera Garretas, 'Los Ritos de Iniciacion en la Ordene Militare de Santiago', *Anuario Estudios Medievales*, 12 (1982), 279–301; E. Sastre Santos, *La Orden de Santiago y su Regla* (Madrid, 1982); I.L. Morgado Sousa e Silva 'A Ordem de Cristo durante o mestrado de D. Lopo Dias de Sousa (1373?–1420)', unpublished MA thesis (University of Oporto, 1989).

[5] J.P. Oliveira Martins, *Os filhos de D. João I*, 7th edn (Lisbon, 1947); J. Bensaúde, *A Cruzada do Infante D. Henrique* (Lisbon, 1943).

[6] *Monumenta Henricina*, ed. Comissão Executiva das Comemorações do V Centenário da Morte do Infante D. Henrique, 15 vols (Coimbra, 1960), 5, no. 49 (pp. 113–15).

[7] Ibid., 10, no. 84 (pp. 125–37); A.M.F. Pestana de Vasconcelos, 'A Ordem Militar de Cristo na Baixa Idade Média. Espiritualidade, Normativa e Prática', unpublished MA thesis (University of Oporto, 1995); E.J.N. Alves Jana, 'Considerandos sobre a presença da Ordem de Cristo no Ultramar Português', in *Actas do Congresso Internacional de História da Missionação Portuguesa e Encontro de Culturas*, Universidade Católica Portuguesa e Comissão Nacional para as Comemorações dos Descobrimentos Portugueses, Fundação Evangelização e Culturas, 3 (Braga, 1993), p. 436.

The three texts studied here, which date from the early sixteenth century, are the best examples of the attitude towards autonomy assumed by the military orders in Portugal.

We have divided the various regulations into three main groups:

1. internal way of life;
2. religion and spirituality;
3. patrimony and administration.

INTERNAL WAY OF LIFE

The fundamental concerns here were admission to the Order, how and in what circumstances the habit should be used, the distribution of duties among various dignities and positions, and when and how the Order's leadership should function, as well as behaviour within the house.

The conditions for recruitment of new members were important, as it was necessary to set out the requirements which were to be observed by all the candidates. They all had to go through a year of probation, so that they could be integrated into the Order's customs and practices. Finally, the ceremony of profession would take place.[8]

Likewise, the procedures for professing the faith and receiving the habit were laid down. The habit was of particular importance as it was the unifying and representative symbol of the group in contrast to the external world. This is demonstrated through the various specific clauses which oblige the Order's members to wear it on certain occasions, such as the main religious festivals, in the general chapter, and during funerals of brethren; although it should not be forgotten that the daily use of the Order's habit was compulsory. Apart from these details, consideration was given to the colour, material, size, dimensions and the places where this habit was worn.[9]

These regulations also applied to specific offices, such as the responsibilities of the *comendador-mor* (principal commander), prior and *claveiro* (key-keeper), among others. In the Orders of Christ,[10] Santiago[11] and Avis[12] it was obligatory to have a master of grammar in the house, whereas only the Order of Christ seems to have had a musician.[13] Again, only the rule of the Order of Christ laid down that a physician must also be present in the house.[14]

---

[8] AN/TT, Série Preta, no. 1393, fols 20–20v.

[9] Ibid., no. 872, fols 36–36v, 91; BNL, Res. 3008 V, fols 7–10; AN/TT, Série Preta, no. 1393, fols 5v–6, 22–23, 24–24v, 34; ibid., no. 872, fols 9v; 75v–78, 89–89v; BNL, Res. 3008 V, fols 11; 18v, 50–50v.

[10] AN/TT, Série Preta, no. 1393, fols 25–25v.

[11] Ibid., no. 872, fol. 101v.

[12] BNL, Res. 3008 V, fol. 51.

[13] AN/TT, Série Preta, no. 1393, fol. 28v.

[14] Ibid., fols 28v–29; no. 872, fols 10, 98.

Nevertheless, one of the obligations of the brethren of the Order of Santiago was to care for the old brethren and the wounded, as well as giving hospitality to the poor or guests; this is not surprising if we consider that in the Order of the Hospital of St John, another military order, this preoccupation with welfare towards pilgrims and the sick and wounded was the original reason for its existence. The fact that the rule of the Order of Santiago did not insist that a physician must be present in the house may indicate that the infirmaries of the Order, like most hospitals in western Europe in the Middle Ages, were, rather, nursing homes, in which case the presence of a physician would not be necessary.

To fulfil the vow of obedience, the knights of the Order of Christ who had been given castles to look after had to pay homage to the Master[15] and they were not allowed to leave the kingdom without his permission.[16] In the same way, the brethren could not leave the house enclosure without previous authorization from the prior.[17] The same applied to the *comendadores* (commanders), who were required to reside within their own *comendas* or benefices.[18] The knights, especially those who received an income, were compelled to serve the Master during war, and in his absence they were supposed to be faithful to the Order's banner.[19]

There is also a set of directions relating to the organization of the Order, which defines the brethren's conduct although some of these directions related to the Order's patrimony. The most significant cases are the procedures to follow when Masters were elected,[20] the conditions required for brethren to be accepted on the *treze*, or council,[21] as well as their behaviour in the general chapter.[22] If brethren disobeyed the rules for behaviour within the community, they were subject to punishment. In 1509, the Order of Santiago stressed this aspect by listing twenty-four instances where there should be a close correspondence between the crime and the punishment to be inflicted.[23]

RELIGION AND SPIRITUALITY

Each military order admitted new members by means of a religious ceremony; nevertheless, there was a clear distinction according to whether the candidate was a knight or a cleric. If a brother desired to abandon the Order after profession, he was compelled to enter another order with a similar lifestyle.

---

[15] Ibid., no. 1393, fol. 32.

[16] Ibid., fol. 38.

[17] Ibid., fols 25v–26.

[18] Ibid., fols 35v–36.

[19] Ibid., fols 6v–7v; no. 872, fols 92, 103; BNL, Res. 3008 V, fols 52–52v.

[20] AN/TT, Série Preta, no. 1393, fols 8, 29–32; no. 872, fol. 12.

[21] Ibid., no. 1393, fol. 8; no. 872, fols 12, 94.

[22] Ibid., no. 1393, fol. 33v; no. 872, fols 5, 12, 39, 40–45; BNL, Res. 3008 V, fols 26v–29v.

[23] AN/TT, Série Preta, no. 872, fols 14–18v.

Only the clerical brethren of the military orders were under an obligation to pray, but there were other obligations imposed on both knights and chaplains, notably to fulfil the three basic vows,[24] to say the hours,[25] to hear mass,[26] to attend the main religious festivals in the convent,[27] as well as to confess and to receive communion.[28] In relation to confession, the Orders of Santiago and Avis stress its importance by listing each and every step a brother should follow to redeem all his sins – the 'Confessional of the Order'.[29] All the brethren were obliged to attend mass on the day devoted to each patron saint.[30]

In the Order of Christ the priests who were not hebdomadaries were expected to say mass once a week, while the others had to receive communion six times a year. In this Order, all the prior's liturgical responsibilities were set out, as he was the leading religious dignitary of the Order. The regulations of the Orders of Santiago and Avis do not give such details about chaplains. As for the knights, who were not obliged to take part in liturgical ceremonies, they were expected to recite the same daily prayers as the clerical brethren. However, owing to the fact that they were knights and had made a vow to fight in defence of the faith of Christ, if the Master agreed, they could be exempted from this recitation in times of war.[31] War was itself a kind of prayer in the service of God.

Besides all this, the brethren were also required to fast. This had to take place on specific days of the week, namely on Mondays, Wednesdays and Fridays in the Order of Christ. However, by papal dispensation this obligation was reduced to once a week (Fridays), apart from the days appointed by the liturgical calendar.[32]

In the Order of Avis, the brethren who did not fast were obliged to feed a poor man or, otherwise, give a poor person ten meals. Related to the practice of fasting was the prohibition on eating meat.[33]

PATRIMONY AND ADMINISTRATION

The bodies charged with the administration of the whole Order were the Master, the chapters, and the council or *treze*, constituted of thirteen of the oldest brethren.

---

[24] Ibid, fol. 9; BNL, Res. 3008 V, fols 10–11, 37–38.
[25] AN/TT, Série Preta, no. 1393, fols 14–14v; no. 872, fols 4, 5; BNL, Res. 3008 V, fols 11v, 16–17v.
[26] AN/TT, Série Preta, no. 1393, fols 14, 15, 24; no. 872, fols 5, 10.
[27] Ibid., no. 1393, fols 38–38v.
[28] Ibid., fols 7, 17v–18, 38–38v; no. 872, fols 88v–89; BNL, Res. 3008 V, fols 12, 44–48.
[29] AN/TT, Série Preta, no. 872, fols 9–9v, 68–74, 88–88v; BNL, Res. 3008 V, fols 44–48.
[30] Ibid., fol. 50v.
[31] *Monumenta Henricina*, 10, no. 84 (pp. 125–37).
[32] AN/TT, Série Preta, no. 1393, fol. 7v; no. 872, fols 5, 7, 75v–77v; BNL, Res. 3008 V, fols 11–12.
[33] Ibid., fol. 55v.

The Master, as the head of the Order and as responsible for the administration of all its possessions, created the *priorados* and benefices and looked after
all the needs of the brethren who did not receive their own income. He also
had to intervene in disputes between the Order and any other religious entity
and judge quarrels among the brethren.[34] However, his freedom of action was
limited in certain ways by the general chapter, notably in the concession of
benefices. His main role was in wartime, when his intervention was particularly
important in carrying out certain aspects of the rule, such as praying, fasting
and dress. The Master was allowed to decide how often, how and when these
obligations should be carried out.[35]

The general chapter was the most important administrative organ. The
elections of the *treze*, the Master and the visitor took place during these
sessions. Its tasks also included other more delicate decisions concerning
possible amendments to the rule and the nomination of brethren to certain
positions.[36] The Order of Christ was an exception to the other military orders
because of its national character and participation in the expansionist project,
and it had the particular privilege of assigning overseas benefices as well as
being responsible for spiritual jurisdiction overseas.[37]

As already mentioned, the visitors were elected in the general chapter.
The many regulations referring to visitation of all the possessions of these three
Orders demonstrates the Orders' concern for the preservation of their entire
patrimony.[38] This preoccupation is also noteworthy in the regulations for
keeping records, according to which all the possessions and rights belonging
to a certain area had to be registered. Clearly, their patrimony was very
important to these institutions, both to maintain the community and in allowing
them to exert power, accumulate rights and broaden their jurisdiction.[39]

Lastly, another administrative function was to agree to whom the benefices
of the deceased brethren would belong,[40] as well as the payments received by
each brother according to his position.[41]

To sum up, we might perhaps say that at the beginning of the sixteenth
century the regulations of each of the Portuguese military orders demonstrated
a very similar internal organization independently of their basic spiritual roots,
though there are some differences between the Orders when minor details are

---

[34] AN/TT, Série Preta, no. 872, fol. 103; BNL, Res. 3008 V, fol. 61v.

[35] AN/TT, Série Preta, no. 872, fols 92, 103v–104; BNL, Res. 3008 V, fol. 11v.

[36] AN/TT, Série Preta, no. 1393, fols 8, 29–32, 33v–34v; no. 872, fols 5, 12, 39, 40–49v, 78–80;
BNL, Res. 3008 V, fols 26v–31v.

[37] AN/TT, Série Preta, no. 1393, fols 48–48v.

[38] Ibid., fols 34v–35v; no. 872, fols 52–67; BNL, Res. 3008 V, fols 30v–44.

[39] AN/TT, Série Preta, no. 1393, fols 37v–39v; no. 872, fols 105–108; BNL, Res. 3008 V, fols
56–58.

[40] AN/TT, Série Preta, no. 1393, fols 9v–10; no. 872, fols 99–100; BNL, Res. 3008 V, fols 54v–55.

[41] AN/TT, Série Preta, no. 1393, fols 43–45v; no. 872, fols 104–105; BNL, Res. 3008 V, fols
42v–43v.

analysed. The greatest differences were in the rules concerning marriage and welfare. For instance, from the time of the foundation of the Order of Santiago the brethren had been allowed to marry, as opposed to the practice in the other Orders, in which this permission was not given by papal disposition only until in the fifteenth century.[42]

In the case of warfare, the main objective for both the Orders of Christ and Avis, although this was less stressed in the latter, was the fight against the infidel. The Order of Christ, as the king's right hand in the development of his expansionist policies, had received on 8 January 1455 the bull *Romanus Pontifex* of Nicholas V, which granted it power, dominion and spiritual jurisdiction over all overseas lands from Cape Bojador, all through Guinea and the southern coast of Africa to the Indies.[43] On the other hand, the Order of Santiago, besides its involvement against the infidel (not forgetting its role in the conquest of the Algarve)[44] also paid great attention to the welfare of the sick and poor.

In terms of religion and spirituality, at the beginning of the sixteenth century there was a concern to regulate and define various forms of prayer as well as fundamental religious practice. If, on the one hand, this leads us to suspect that previously this aspect was sometimes neglected, on the other, one of the objectives was to adapt the brethren of the different Orders to activities more suited to the functions they were supposed to fulfil, bearing in mind that they were members of a religious institution as well as a military one and viewed this latter role as more and more difficult to achieve.

The administration of the patrimony continued to be an important part of the regulations because, as the owners of extensive wealth and property, the military orders had to adopt procedures similar to all other landlords. All three Orders recognized this need by adopting the same means of control: Master, chapter, the *treze*, and visitors.

At the end of the Middle Ages in Portugal, the military orders were part of a political project led by the monarchy. The princes, and later the king himself, became the most important figures in the hierarchy of these institutions. In 1551 the military orders were annexed to the Crown.[45]

---

[42] On 20 February 1440 Pope Eugenius IV gave permission for the brethren of the Order of Calatrava to marry (*Monumenta Henricina*, 7, no. 43 [pp. 58–60]), and on 20 June 1496 Pope Alexander VI gave the same right to the brethren of Avis and Christ, in accordance with the request of the king D. Manuel: AN/TT, Ordem de Cristo, Codex 234, part 1, fols 60–60v, and Gaveta VII, *maço* (bundle) 3, no. 32, and *maço* 7, no. 11; published by A.C. de Sousa, ed. M. Lopes de Almeida and C. Pagado, 6 vols, in *Provas de História Genealógica da casa real portuguesa* (Coimbra, 1946–1954), 2.1, pp. 326–8, with an incorrect date: 20 June 1492.

[43] AN/TT, Bulas, *maço* 7, no. 29 (the original version).

[44] J. Marques, *Os Castelos Algarvios da Ordem de Santiago no reinado de D. Afonso III* (Braga, 1986).

[45] AN/TT, Gaveta IV, *maço* 1, no. 18. Published in *As Gavetas da Torre do Tombo*, ed. Arquivo Nacional, Lisbon (Lisbon, 1960–), 2, pp. 60–8.

21

Fifteenth-Century Hospitaller Architecture on Rhodes: Patrons and Master Masons

Fotini Karassava-Tsilingiri

The question of whether the builders of Rhodes were native Rhodians or invited from abroad has long been debated. From the mid-nineteenth century to the present day there have been various approaches to the subject.[1] Most of them, however, have been based on the traditional attribution to Italian military engineers of the sixteenth-century updating of the fortifications. Italians did work on Rhodes in the sixteenth century, if to a lesser degree than initially believed,[2] but if we look for a Rhodian Hospitaller architecture we must keep in mind that the foundations for its creation were laid in the fifteenth century,[3] and we must look for its creators among the Rhodian builders active in that period, as well as among their patrons.

In the *capitula* issued for the construction of the new hospital on 20 March 1441[4] it was ordered that ten *magistri muratores* were to be retained at the building works of the hospital. These *magistri* were to be free from military service, and the same exemption applied to the three brethren assigned to the same work. The team would be provided with sufficient grain from the Order's granary, and the builders were allowed to quarry stone for the works from a

---

[1] See mainly A. Gabriel, *La cité de Rhodes*, 1 (Paris, 1921), p. 113–17; G. Gerola, 'Il Contributo dell' Italia alle Opere d' Arte Militare Rodiesi', *Atti dell Reale Istituto Veneto di Scienze, Lettere ed Arti*, 89 (1930), 1015–27. A thorough account of the evolution of the question up to 1930 is given in R. Santoro, 'Giuseppe Gerola e Albert Gabriel sui Bastioni di Rodi', *Atti dell' Istituto Veneto di Scienze, Lettere ed Arti*, 147 (1988–9), 31–4, 41–7. Santoro's own views on the subject in ibid., 47–51. E. Kollias, *The City of Rhodes and the Palace of the Grand Master*, 2nd edn (in Greek) (Athens, 1994), pp. 83–4, discusses the question. Z. Tsirpanlis, *Unpublished documents concerning Rhodes and the Southern Sporades from the Archives of the Knights of St John*, 1 (1421–1453) (in Greek) (Rhodes, 1995), pp. 77–9, is based on primary sources and focuses on defining the meaning of *protomastoras*.

[2] Gabriel, 1, pp. 115–16.

[3] F. Karassava-Tsilingiri, 'The Architecture of the Fifteenth-Century Hospital of Rhodes: A Historical Approach', PhD thesis (University of London, 1994) pp. 202–30, 249–54.

[4] Text in Tsirpanlis, *Documents*, pp. 403–4.

From *The Military Orders. Volume 2. Welfare and Warfare*. ed. Helen Nicholson. Copyright © 1998 by Helen Nicholson. Published by Ashgate Publishing Ltd, Gower House, Croft Road, Aldershot, Hampshire, GU11 3HR, Great Britain.

specific site in the city of Rhodes. The whole team was under the control of
the prior of the Church, Jean Morelli. The composition of the team is rather
unusual by Western standards.[5] The ten *magistri* seem to have been employed
in all kinds of building tasks, for example in quarrying stone or fetching
timber, without any hierarchical discrimination or specific job description.
There is no team leader among them, and apart from their supply of grain no
other payment is mentioned.[6] The role of the three brethren assigned to the
building works is not clear in the text.

Sixteen years after the appearance of the *capitula*, in 1457, a commemora-
tive inscription was mounted on the fortification wall of the city.[7] This
inscription, we are informed from its text, was mounted by permission of the
then Master, Fr. Jacques de Milly; it is bilingual in Italian and Greek, and it
records the work of the master builder Manolis Kountis. In the Italian text
Kountis is recorded as '*muradur*' and '*protomagistro de tutta la muralia nova de
Rodo*', while in the Greek text he writes in the first person, saying that 'the
present wall of Rhodes was built and I was the master builder'. In the Italian
text the fact is recorded that the inscription was mounted by licence of the
Master, while the Greek text omits this.

While Manolis Kountis was the only master builder to have received such
an honour in recognition for his work, his is not the only name of a master
builder that we know. Other names, like those of Georgios Singan, alias
Turco, who was active in the first decades of the fifteenth century in building
the castle of Bodrum;[8] Michalis Tangris, mentioned in 1452 as *magister serviens
castri nostri Lyndi* and entrusted with financing and carrying out the repairs and
extension to the church of Hagios Nicolaos in Psartos;[9] Antonio tu Papa who
was active in Rhodes and other places in the Hospitaller domain towards the
end of the century;[10] and Theodoro Stradioti[11] are recorded in the sources, not

---

[5] D. Knoop and G. Jones, *The Medieval Mason* (Manchester, 1933), pp. 15–43, 73–108, 151–84;
J. Harvey, *Medieval Craftsmen* (London, 1975), pp. 123–34, 147–58.

[6] Payrolls have not been discovered, but see Gabriel, 1, p. 114 for methods of financing works;
here, too, reference is made to block pricing without allusion to payment of builders.

[7] Text and reproduction of the inscription in Gabriel, 1, p. 98; see also ibid., p. 113 and pl. XIX.
A slightly different, and more convincing, transcription in P. Egidi, 'Di un' Inscrizione Medioevale
Italo-Greca sulle Mura di Rodi', *Atti della Reale Academia delle Scienze di Torino*, 63 (1928), 61–9.

[8] A. Luttrell, *The Later History of the Maussolleion and its Utilization in the Hospitaller Castle at
Bodrum*, 2.ii of *The Maussolleion at Halikarnassos: Reports of the Danish Archaeological Expedition to
Bodrum* (Aarhus, 1986), p. 161 note 84.

[9] Text in Z. Tsirpanlis: *Rhodes and the Southern Sporades at the Time of the Knights of St John*, (in
Greek) (Rhodes, 1991), p. 279.

[10] Much of the controversy on the nationality of the builders has been based on misreading this
master mason's name as Antonio lu Papa: Gerola, 1022; Gabriel, 1, p. 148; Santoro, 46, goes as far
as suggesting that it is a common southern Italian name. In most documents, though, it appears
as Antonio or Antoni tu Papa, a common form of surname in Rhodes meaning 'son of the priest'.
See Kollias, p. 83 and note 93, for discussion.

[11] Text in Tsirpanlis, *Documents*, pp. 490–1.

always in connection with building works, but with their profession usually mentioned. Special treatment was often reserved for them in reward for their services to the Order: Manolis Kountis rented in 1437 saltworks at lower than the market price.[12] In 1448 a magistral bull emphasized that Theodoros Stradioti and his family would belong to the class of *marinarii* and not to the lower class of the *parichi*, as a reward for Theodoros's good services to the Order.[13]

Although there is no definite proof for it, there must have been some sort of hierarchical distinction between the *magister muradur* and the *protomagistro*. The *magistri muratores* were probably experienced in building stone, but not every one of them was distinguished. As the document of 1441 testifies, in the case of the hospital they were organized in a team, but no leader is mentioned. On the other hand, the wording in the Greek text of the 1457 inscription designates Kountis as the leader of a team,[14] while in some other cases builders are referred to as *protomagistores*. However, and contrary to western tradition, we have no notion of hierarchical grades among the *magistri muratores*. From the names that have come down to us the majority of master builders seem to have been Greeks, although it is probable that there were builders from other parts of the multinational Rhodian society: Georgios Singan, alias Turco, whose main surname may mean gypsy, may have been a converted Muslim. It is probable that around the middle of the fifteenth century there was at least one woman among the master builders: in 1452, Anna Maistrissa, widow of Petros Mulas, was allowed to spend the rest of her life in the monastery of St John Agallianos in the city of Rhodes, repairing and restoring its church and cells and looking after the buildings.[15] It has been suggested that her surname may mean that she was a schoolteacher,[16] but the phrasing of the document shows her to have had the same responsibilities as Michalis Tangris. Female builders were not unknown in the medieval West, particularly wives or daughters of master builders.[17]

Magistri muratores often worked side by side with *magistri marangones* or carpenters. In a miniature of 1483 a team of carpenters is depicted kneeling before the Master, Pierre d'Aubusson, who receives them in front of the city wall under construction.[18] *Pelecanos* probably were those who chiselled quarried stone, as the term is still in use in this sense in Greek.[19] We can only speculate

---

[12] Text in ibid., pp. 282–3.

[13] Text in ibid., pp. 490–1.

[14] Discussion in Tsirpanlis, *Documents*, p. 79.

[15] Text in Tsirpanlis, *Rhodes*, p. 280.

[16] Ibid., p. 262.

[17] C. Opitz, 'Life in the Late Middle Ages', in *A History of Women in the West*, 2, ed. C. Klapisch-Zuber (Cambridge, Mass., 1992), p. 301.

[18] BN, Cod. Lat., 6069, fol. 9v.

[19] Tsirpanlis, *Documents*, p. 77, believes they were carpenters.

as to the probable role of the *architectus* who is mentioned once in the texts[20] in connection with the construction of the cloistered walk of St John's lodge. In this text Morelli is allowed to order from this architect all the 'ornament' he might need for building a residence for the prior of the Church. The term appears rarely in medieval texts[21] and then with various meanings, often different from the modern one; in the later Middle Ages, its most frequent use is as a synonym to *cementarius*, or mason.[22] Morelli's architect, who had been in charge of the cloisters and the library, seems also to have had a good knowledge of the standard ornament used by the Order.[23]

Although the Byzantine tradition of being organized and employed in teams may have been maintained in the Hospitaller period,[24] the building methods and wall techniques as seen in constructions built by the Order, particularly those dated after 1440, were not by any means Byzantine. Structures firmly dated in the fourteenth century or in the first few decades of the fifteenth are few and far between, their stones irregularly cut and with brick and pot shards in the joints.[25] Those dated between 1428 and 1445, dates provided by the arms of the Catalan Grand Master Fr. Antoni Fluviá and those of his successor, Fr. Jean de Lastic, show signs of belonging to a transitional period. The stones are regularized, although with less care than in later constructions, but the joints are still filled with ceramics. Sculpted architectural ornament of set patterns appears for the first time on the up-to-the-minute austere façades. Although dating Rhodian Hospitaller structures has never been a simple affair, we can certainly assume that at some point in Rhodian building history, probably in the period between 1428 and 1445, builders were trained in employing new forms and building techniques. At the moment it is not possible to tell by whom, but perhaps the *architectus* who provided Morelli with the sculpted ornament for the priors' residence had a part in this.

Master builders often had some sort of supervision by specially assigned brethren.[26] We have evidence that this happened in constructions financed by

---

[20] Text in ibid., p. 295.

[21] Knoll and Jones, p. 108; N. Pevsner, 'The Term "Architect" in the Middle Ages', *Speculum*, 17 (1942), 554.

[22] Pevsner, 555–7.

[23] Malta Cod. 352, fols 145–6: '*(duximus annuendum) tenore presentium vobis venerabili priori ad tam comunem ornamentum parato, antedictum locum siue tectum lobij ab architectu supra versus celum et similiter supra librariam.*' Tsirpanlis, *Documents*, p. 295, gives a slightly different reading.

[24] Gabriel, 1, p. 113 note 5, also compares Rhodian with Byzantine teams; on the survival of Byzantine teams of stone masons, N. Moutsopoulos, 'Koudaraioi Makedones kai Ipirotes Mastores' in *Protoi Ellines Technikoi Epistimones* (Athens, 1976), p. 358; D. Phillipidis, *Neoelliniki Architektoniki* (Athens, 1984), pp. 61–2. The situation in fifteenth-century Crete is briefly outlined in C. Maltezou, 'Métiers et Salaires en Crete Venitienne', *Byzantinische Forschungen*, 12 (1987), 321–7.

[25] On Rhodian Byzantine and fourteenth-century building techniques, see M. Acheimastou, 'I Panagia tou Kastrou Rhodou', *Archeologikon Deltion*, A, 23 (1969), 221–83.

[26] Gabriel, 1, p. 114, believes that every new structure needed approval by the Council, but this seems to have been a rule mainly for public works.

the Order such as the new hospital, parts of the fortification wall[27] and the wall at Bodrum,[28] to name but a few. The supervision must have concerned finances, the provision of materials, seeing to the needs of the building teams, and usually there was a brother in the committee for taking over finished structures, along with the *protomastores* commissioned. When the tower of Italy was being built in 1445, two Italian brethren were empowered to contract the master masons necessary to carry out the works.[29] The *scriba* of such works was usually a brother, and in one case Fr. P. Clouet, who was the *scriba* of the fortification works in 1474, acted as building contractor for the Order in several other works, such as finishing the new hospital and later its garden,[30] and renovating the *Auberge* of France. Clouet, who seems to have been entrusted with such matters by the Master, Pierre d'Aubusson, was also responsible for keeping the financial records for building works between 1483 and 1489.[31]

In many cases, as in the new hospital, the building works were directed by a specially assigned dignitary of the Order. We have already seen that Morelli, who was prior of the Church around the middle of the fifteenth century, was put in charge of the construction of the new hospital. This was not the first construction Morelli had undertaken. As we have seen, in 1437 the then Master, Antoni Fluviá, had given him permission to build the residence of the prior of the Church near the conventual church, the library and the *Auberge* of Provence, following his supervision of the construction of the library a few years earlier.[32] Morelli also participated in teams supervising building works in Rhodes and other islands.[33] In November 1436 Fr. Angelino Muscetula undertook the repairs of all the churches and houses of the Order in the preceptory of Cyprus, of which he was then in charge.[34] Even Clouet, who is first mentioned in 1475 merely as the *scriba* of the repair works on the fortifications,[35] held higher office during much of his career as Aubusson's building contractor; he became infirmarian in the years after 1482 and by 1489 he was preceptor of Villedieu.[36] The brethren in charge of major works were in all

---

[27] Gabriel, 1, pp. 114–15.

[28] Luttrell, *Later History*, p. 161.

[29] The text is published in S. Fionini and A. Luttrell, 'The Italian Hospitallers at Rhodes: 1437–1462', *Revue Mabillon*, 68 (1996), 209–33 (at 229–30).

[30] Malta Cod. 380, fols 205–205v.

[31] Malta Cod. 390, fols 162–163.

[32] The building mentioned in document no. 56 in Tsirpanlis, *Documents*, p. 295, lines 20–2, is in my opinion the library and not, as Tsirpanlis suggests (ibid., p. 298 note 1), the *canonica*, whose existence separate from the priors' residence cannot be proven. See also A. Gabriel, 2 (1923), p. 86 note 5.

[33] Tsirpanlis, *Documents*, no. 187 (pp. 499–500).

[34] Malta Cod. 351, fol. 153. It appears that the works were still in progress in June 1437: Malta Cod. 352, fols 191–192v.

[35] Malta Cod. 383, fol. 216.

[36] Malta Cod. 380, fols 205–205v.

probability responsible for financing and final accounts, but it is also probable that they enforced certain building rules. Such rules concerned, perhaps, the amount and form of architectural ornament, the layout of buildings in cases where there was a rough layout to which builders should remain faithful (the hospital was probably one such case), and perhaps a certain number of planning rules. Brethren do not seem to have interfered with the internal organization and function of the teams of builders. Although the evidence is inadequate, one may assume that these teams continued to work as they were accustomed to do so, in a way comparable to teams on the Greek mainland, but under close supervision by authorized members of the Order and following their instructions to some extent.

The status of the master builders was further enhanced by their taking part in committees which inspected castles, churches and other buildings both in Rhodes and in other parts of the Hospitaller domain.[37] For example, a committee of three brethren was sent in 1440 to inspect the state of the buildings on the islands of Kos, Nisyros and Leros which Fr. Fantino Quirini had just left, and these brethren were to be helped in completing their task by builders and carpenters.[38] It is interesting that the head of the committee was the Latin archbishop of Rhodes, a position held by Morelli at the time. But *protomastores* such as Antonio tu Papa were themselves sometimes members of such committees, holding the same rank as the assigned brethren,[39] or they acted as technical advisers in their own right.[40] On the other hand it seems that lay people, subjects of the Order in Rhodes or the other islands, were not free to employ builders directly, at least in the case of public works such as castles or churches. Thus, in 1453, the inhabitants of Nisyros had to ask the Master in writing for a *protomastoras* as well as for a 'master of the pit' to slake lime for their castle which was in need of repair.[41] It is noteworthy that while the thickness of the wall and the provenance of the materials were settled by a committee of brethren, it was up to the Master to appoint the *protomastoras*.

To recapitulate, fifteenth-century building in and around Rhodes was carried out by professional master builders, working in teams. It is probable that these teams were organized in a manner similar to that which survived on the Greek mainland for several centuries, and which may have existed in pre-Hospitaller Rhodes. Although the Order exerted its control by employing brethren, often experienced in supervising building works, the builders had

---

[37] See Luttrell, *Later History*, p. 161 and note 84 for cases of *protomagistri* and teams of builders at work outside Rhodes.

[38] See note 33 above.

[39] Gabriel, 1, p. 148.

[40] Gabriel, 1, p. 145.

[41] The text, which is in Greek, was first published by F. Miklosich and J. Muller: *Acta et Diplomata Graeca Medii Aevi*, 3 (Vienna 1865), pp. 288–90; more recently in Tsirpanlis, *Rhodes*, pp. 197–200.

22

'The Rights of the Treasury': the Financial Administration of the Hospitallers on Fifteenth-Century Rhodes, 1421–1522

Jürgen Sarnowsky

During the second century of the Hospitallers' domination of Rhodes and its neighbouring islands, from the death of Master Fr. Philibert de Naillac in 1421 to the final Ottoman siege in 1522, the Order and its territories in the East faced increasing danger from Muslim attacks.[1] The precondition for an effective defence was the continuous supply of men and money from the West. This required a financial administration which was able to control the periodical payments imposed on the houses in the West. As one document of 1501 put it, the defence of Rhodes and the territories of the Order in the East was impossible 'without the imposition and payment of the rights of the treasury upon all and single priories, the castellany of Amposta, the bailiwicks, preceptories and benefices of this Order'.[2] Keeping the deficiencies of a

---

[1] For a survey of this period see E. Rossi, 'The Hospitallers at Rhodes, 1421–1523', *Crusades*, 3, pp. 314–39; H.J.A. Sire, *The Knights of Malta* (New Haven and London, 1994), pp. 37–9, 51–8. The most complete account is still I. Bosio, *Dell'istoria della sacra religione et illustrissima militia di S Giovanni Gierosolimitano*, 2, 2nd edn (Rome, 1629). For the second half of this period see also N. Vatin, *L'Ordre de Saint-Jean-de-Jérusalem, l'Empire ottoman et la Méditerranée orientale entre les deux sièges de Rhodes 1480–1522*, Collection Turcica, 7 (Paris, 1994). A general outline of the problems is given in A. Luttrell, 'The Hospitallers of Rhodes: Prospectives, Problems, Possibilities', in *Die geistlichen Ritterorden Europas*, ed. J. Fleckenstein and M. Hellmann. Vorträge und Forschungen, 26 (Sigmaringen, 1980), pp. 243–66, repr. in *idem, Latin, Greece, the Hospitallers and the Crusades, 1291–1440* (London, 1982), 1. The research for this article has been made possible by a Heisenberg scholarship of the Deutsche Forschungsgemeinschaft. I also wish to thank Dr Jens Röhrkasten, Birmingham, and Matthew Caldwell, Hamburg, who read and corrected the first English version of this paper, and Dr Anthony Luttrell, Bath, for his helpful suggestions. The faults that remain are mine. The following abbreviation is used: ASVat, Archivio Secreto Vaticano.

[2] '*Gravissimum pondus ipsius ordinis nostri consistit in manutencione et defensione fidei catholice contra inimicos et conservacione Rhodie urbis, castellorum, oppidorum, insularum, locorum et populorum chris-ticolarum in Oriente dicioni dicti reverendissimi domini et ordinis subditorum, quorum impensis gravioribus*

modern public financial administration in mind, it is easy to imagine that late-medieval institutions were even less perfect. Thus the difficulties encountered time and again by the Hospitallers come as no surprise. Since they also experienced grave problems of morale concerning the regular payments from the houses in the West, they incurred heavy debts; in fact there was an endless process of raising and repaying loans. In this short paper I intend to show how the Order managed to survive some of its financial crises. Some general remarks on the Order's financial administration will be followed by a summary of developments from 1421 to 1522, especially of the measures taken to secure the Order's solvency.

When the Order's statutes were revised in 1489, under the direction of its vice-chancellor, Guillaume Caoursin, one entire section was devoted to regulations concerning the treasury.[3] It began with a passage that referred to ancient custom but which also described the practice of the fifteenth century. Since, according to the statute, all property of the Order went back to pious donations, it had to be administered in a way which met the donors' intentions and which permitted the spiritual, charitable and military tasks undertaken by the Order to be fulfilled. From this followed the need to establish a financial administration which also had to retain a portion of the Order's incomes in order to have reserves in cases of emergency. Thus, in times of peace, a fifth or a quarter of all the revenues had to be paid into the treasury; in times of danger and need, even a half or three-quarters could be required – though it is not clear how these incomes were determined. The rates of the 'responsions', as these financial obligations on the priories and commanderies of the Order were called, and the methods of payment were fixed by the chapters general which assembled about every five years during the fifteenth century.[4] The decisions made by the chapters were written down and transmitted to the priories and the castellany of Amposta (which in fact was the priory of Aragon). There the chapters' directions had to be carried out and transgressors punished.[5] Though this outline of the Order's financial administration is basically correct, there

---

in dies emengentibus suppleri nullo modo potest) absque imposicione et solucione iurium communis thesauri super universis et singulis prioratibus, castellania Emposte, baiuliatibus, preceptoriis [sic] *et beneficiis eiusdem religionis* ...', Malta, Cod. 284, fol. 17v, letter of Master Fr. Pierre d'Aubusson of 26 August 1501 concerning the decisions of the chapter general.

[3] Here Guillaume Caoursin's version of the statutes is used in the good and early manuscript in NLM, Libr. 244; the section on the treasury covers fols 47v–57r.

[4] For the chapters general see J. Sarnowsky, 'The Oligarchy at Work. The Chapters General of the Hospitallers in the XVth Century (1421–1522)', in *Autour de la première Croisade*, ed. M. Balard (Paris, 1996), pp. 267–76; B.Waldstein-Wartenberg, *Rechtsgeschichte des Malteserordens* (Vienna and Munich, 1969), pp. 110–11. For two of the chapters general, see C. Tipton, 'The 1330 Chapter General of the Knights Hospitallers at Montpellier', *Traditio*, 24 (1968), 293–308; and R. Valentini, 'Un capitulo generale degli Ospitalieri di S Giovanni tenuto in Vaticano nel 1446', *Archivio Storico di Malta*, 7 (1936), 133–68.

[5] NLM, Libr. 244, fols 47v–48r.

were other 'rights of the treasury' (a term frequently employed), such as rights
to the property of deceased brethren, to incomes from vacancies, and other
fixed payments. The Order and its Masters (who had their own financial
administration) also had incomes from the sale of sugar, from local taxes,
customs and so on.

All the revenues from the houses in the West and from the Order's
possessions in the East had to be paid into the treasury at Rhodes. Until the
first half of the fourteenth century, the head of the treasury was the treasurer
of the Order, at that time one of the conventual bailiffs, that is, one of the main
officials in the convent. Some time between 1330 and 1344, the treasurer lost
his prominent position and was subordinated to the grand preceptor, another
conventual bailiff.[6] In the fifteenth century the treasurer still participated in
settling the accounts, but his main task then was to keep the iron seal of the
convent.[7] The treasury was at that time headed by the grand preceptor, who
was assisted by several other officials. First there were two proctors of the
treasury: two experienced brethren, carefully chosen by the Master and council
for a one-year term only. Each of the proctors and the grand preceptor held
one of the three keys of the treasury; they were responsible for the regular
book-keeping of two other officials – the conservator general and the scribe
of the treasury. Any money coming in or going out had to be registered. If
financial transactions had been ordered by the Master and convent and made
known to the grand preceptor, the money was taken in or paid out by the
conservator general. Quarrels between the *langues* or tongues, that is the
groupings of brethren from the same area of Europe living in the convent, at
the chapter general in Rome in 1446 led to reforms concerning financial
administration.[8] As a consequence, the conservators general had to be elected
by chapters general, and from different tongues. Also at that time, a group of
brethren made up of one brother from each of the *langues* became the auditors
of the accounts, whose duty was to control the books of the treasury once
weekly.[9] Thus the grand preceptor was aided (and partly controlled) by the
proctors, the conservator general, the auditors of the accounts and by the
scribe of the treasury.

---

[6] See A. Luttrell, 'Papauté et Hôpital: l'Enquête de 1373', *L'Enquête Pontificale de 1373 sur l'Ordre
des Hospitaliers de Saint-Jean de Jérusalem*, ed. J. Glénisson, 1: *L'Enquête dans le Prieuré de France*,
ed. A.-M. Legras (Paris, 1987), pp. 3–42 (at p. 3 note 2); Valentini, 135–6. For the treasurer
during the twelfth and thirteenth centuries see J. Riley-Smith, *The Knights of St John in Jerusalem
and Cyprus, c. 1050–1310* (London, 1967), pp. 310–12.

[7] See NLM, Libr. 244, fol. 78r, a statute from the time of Master Fr. Jean de Lastic (1449);
according to this statute, the treasurer was a capitular bailiff to be elected from the French *langue*.
For the role of the treasurer see Waldstein-Wartenberg, p. 117.

[8] See Valentini, 142–4.

[9] For the proctors of the treasury, the conservator general and the auditors of the accounts see
NLM, Libr. 244, fols 51r–52v; for statutes from the time of Master Fr. Jean de Lastic, see also
Waldstein-Wartenberg, p. 116.

These officials were all based in the convent on Rhodes; therefore others were needed to secure the collection and transfer of the monies from the West. After the chapter general in Rhodes under Fr. Roger des Pins in 1358, there were receivers in every priory and the castellany of Amposta, who were also chosen by the Master and convent.[10] They collected the responsions and other payments, and sent them to Rhodes. They also had to render an account at the provincial chapter of each priory in which they could demand the payment of debts, yet they were obliged to settle their own accounts only with Master and convent. The most important official in the West was the receiver general in Avignon who organized the transfer of money to the East and paid out larger sums to merchants, creditors of the Order and others.[11] Thus the receiver general functioned as a kind of 'long arm' of the treasury.

The administration of the treasury by the grand preceptor, the proctors, the conservator general and their staff was designed for times of peace and stability. However, during the fifteenth century, the Order's situation became more and more unstable and even precarious. Difficulties began with the Mamluk attacks on Cyprus in 1424–6, and continued with the growing threat to Rhodes and its neighbouring islands from 1440 onwards, posed first by the Mamluks and then by the Ottomans.[12] It is likely the first problems arose in 1427/28 when the Order contributed 15,000 florins for the ransoming of King Janus of Cyprus who had been captured by the Mamluks.[13] By that time, the Order had borrowed from Rhodian, merchants in England, and probably in other places as well, to the extent of pawning plate and jewels.[14] Because of the Anglo-French and other wars in Europe responsions were coming in slowly, with the result that the chapter general in May 1428 decided to sell life annuities in the French priory for up to 10,000 écus.[15] The Master, Fr. Antoni Fluviá, promised an additional 12,000 florins from his own incomes, and in turn took over the administration of the preceptory of Kos.[16] It seems that these measures were not very successful, because some months later the Order turned to a form of administration of the treasury which was soon to become common in times of

---

[10] NLM, Libr. 244, fol. 49v(–50r); the original (more extensive) statute, for example, in NLM, Libr. 501, fol. 134v (a fifteenth-century Italian version of the statutes).

[11] For the receivers general of the fourteenth century see, for example, J.E. Nisbet, 'Treasury Records of the Knights of St John in Rhodes', *Melita Historica*, 2 (1957), 95–104 (at pp. 95–6), and the account book of Fr. Pierre de Provins in Malta, Cod. 48. On the election of the receivers general there is a statute of 1493 in NLM, Libr. 244, fol. 125r.

[12] As note 1. For the Mamluk attacks on Cyprus 1424–6 see also N. Housley, *The Later Crusades. From Lyons to Alcazar, 1274–1580* (Oxford, 1992), p. 196; J. Riley-Smith, *The Crusades. A Short History* (London, 1987), pp. 218–19.

[13] For this see Rossi, p. 318; Bosio, 2, p. 200.

[14] Malta, Cod. 347, fol. 162 (new foliation: 174)r–v; 348, fol. 162bis (165)v (a list of Rhodian creditors from 1428, still smaller sums). For a loan of 1,000 English marks see Malta, Cod. 347, fol. 172(184)v.

[15] Malta, Cod. 348, fols 203(197)r–204(198)v; see also Bosio, 2, p. 201.

[16] Malta, Cod. 348, fol. 201(195)v, dated 28 May 1428.

crisis: the Master himself undertook 'the rule, government, burden and load of the common treasury' for three years starting in June 1429 – though it is not clear under what conditions this took place.[17]

When the administration of the treasury by Fr. Antoni Fluviá expired in June 1432, financial problems remained. In December 1433, Pope Eugenius IV made an appeal to Emperor Sigismund to induce the Order's officials in the Empire to pay their responsions and other monies due to the treasury.[18] It appears that at that time the other priories were also well behind with their payments. This situation was worsened by the Mamluk attacks on Rhodes and the other territories of the Order in the East after 1440. Therefore the chapter general at Rhodes in November 1440 decreed additional payments of one-fifth from all the incomes of the brethren who stayed in the West, and one-tenth from the incomes of those who were to come to Rhodes. This was to last for five years.[19] These decisions were enforced by Pope Eugenius who ordered that the clergy, bishops and archbishops should help the receivers and the deputies of the Master and convent in estimating the real value (*verus valor*) of the incomes of the Order's officials and in securing the transfer of the money to the treasury.[20] Similar measures were taken by the chapters general in 1445, 1446 and 1449.[21] In September 1449, because of the Muslim threat and because of the interest due to be paid on the debts incurred meanwhile, the chapter general ordered the payment of two responsions for one year to be paid in June 1450, that is, half of all the incomes of the Order which were estimated at 200,000 florins.[22] This led to quarrels about the distribution of the sums to be sent to the treasury and, in consequence, in 1450 the Master and convent authorized brethren to carry out visitations in some priories.[23] By that

---

[17] '*Cuius communi thesauri regimen, gubernacionem, sarcinam et onus habebamus ...*', Malta, Cod. 349, fol. 12v. Since the registers for the years 1429 to 1432 are lost, there are only accidental hints on the administration of the treasury by Fr. Antoni Fluviá; see also ibid., fols 34r and 54v.

[18] ASVat, Reg.Vat. 372, fols 242v–243v.

[19] The imposition of higher responsions was also common in the fourteenth century, see, for example, J. Sarnowsky, 'Die Johanniter und Smyrna (1344–1402)', *Römische Quartalsschrift für christliche Altertumskunde und Kirchengeschichte*, 86 (1991), 215–251 (at 246–7), and 87 (1992), 47–98 (at 72–3, 81–2, 84–5 [nos 48, 66, 70–71]).

[20] ASVat, Reg.Vat. 375, fols 204v–205v, dated 14 March 1441.

[21] For the Roman chapter of 1446 see Valentini; J. Sarnowsky, 'Der Konvent auf Rhodos und die Zungen (*lingue*) im Johanniterorden (1421–1476)', *Ritterorden und Region – Politische und soziale Verbindungen im Mittelalter*, ed. Z.H. Nowak, Ordines militares, 8 (Torun, 1995), pp. 43–65 (at pp. 54–5).

[22] Malta, Cod. 361, fols 16r–17r, letter of the chapter general to the prior of *Francia*, Fr. Nicole de Giresme, dated 21 September 1449; the regular responsions (a quarter) were estimated at 50,000 florins. See also ASVat, Reg.Vat. 393, fols 99v–100v, papal confirmation of the decisions of the chapter, from 6 November 1450.

[23] See, for example, Malta, Cod. 362, fols 131(132)v–132(133)r, 140(141)v–142(143)v and 143(144)r–145(146)v, the last one giving a list of all the payments due from the West: old responsions, fifth and tenth (of the 1440 chapter general), one year's income (*annata*) (of 1446), *arreragia* from these, simple and double responsions (of 1449), monies from the property of deceased brethren and from vacancies.

time the debts had once more increased. When the castellan of Amposta and the prior of Catalonia received orders to pay back 20,000 florins which had been lent by a merchant of Barcelona, they first had to serve the life annuities which the Order meanwhile had sold in Barcelona.[24] From March to November 1450 more money was borrowed and the Order engaged itself in somewhat mysterious transactions. On the one hand, the Order purchased large quantities of pepper at a high price but promised to pay for it only after a given period of time (normally within six to twelve months). On the other hand, contracts were made concerning the Order's sale of large quantities of pepper at a low price which the merchants immediately paid into the treasury, though they were to receive the pepper only after a fixed period of time (again within about six to twelve months).[25] The sense of these commercial arrangements is not quite clear. Perhaps the Order had hoped for gains from piracy (where else would the pepper have come from which it had sold to the merchants?), but in the end these operations probably led to increasing debts and thus to another crisis.

In this situation, the Master, by then Fr. Jean de Lastic, again took over the administration of the convent and treasury for three years, starting in June 1451, under conditions which were fixed in a special agreement between his lieutenant and the brethren in the convent.[26] The convent's maintenance costs were estimated at 54,000 florins a year: 20,000 florins were to be paid by the houses in the West; 18,000 florins and additional sums by the officials in the East. While the Master himself promised to contribute 12,000 florins from his own incomes, the remaining responsions from the West were obviously designated to satisfy the Order's creditors. Since the Master now had responsibility for the finances of the convent and for the treasury, he was allowed to appoint the officials on Rhodes and at St Peter's castle at Bodrum. For extraordinary expenses such as the hiring of mercenaries the Master would receive another 1,700 florins.

When Lastic died, the new Master, Fr. Jacques de Milly, followed in his footsteps and was confirmed as administrator of the convent and treasury by the chapter general in 1454.[27] This time, only 50,000 florins were reserved for the maintenance of the convent, plus 1,000 florins for the conventual church.

---

[24] Ibid., fol. 62(63)r, dated 16 April 1450.

[25] See ibid., 362, fols 149(150)r–160(161)v. The pepper was bought at 80–100 ducats per quintal (100 pounds); it was sold at 50 ducats per quintal, and if the Order was not able to deliver the pepper within the given time it had to pay back 56 or 62 ducats.

[26] Ibid., 363, fols 226v–228r, dated 6 June 1451. For some financial details of this agreement see Bosio 2, p. 239; Z. Tsirpanlis, *Anekdota eggrapha gia te Rodo kai te Noties Sporades apo to archeio ton Ioanniton Ippoton* (Unpublished Documents concerning Rhodes and the South-East Aegean Islands from the Archives of the Order of St John), 1: *1421–1453* (Rhodes, 1995), p. 163; A. Luttrell, 'La funzione di un ordine militare: Gli ospitalieri a Rodi, 1306–1421', (forthcoming), note 8.

[27] See Malta, Cod. 282, fols 19r–20v, 17 November 1454, especially fol. 19v: '*Quod ... magister capiat conventum et comunem tesaurum* [sic] *ad manus suas*'.

Additional sums were assigned for extraordinary expenses. After that, a similar contract was made between the conventual bailiffs and the brethren in the convent during the chapter general of 1459. Then, in 1462, administration of the convent and treasury reverted to the grand preceptor, the proctors, and the conservator general, with detailed regulations concerning the payment of the Order's debts.[28] But in February 1467, during the long Roman chapter general, Fr. Pere Ramon Zacosta, who was Master at the time, again took over responsibility for the Order's finances. Meanwhile the Order's debts had reached the sum of about 250,000 écus plus about 40,000 écus for life annuities in Catalonia.[29] In order to pay back the loans and to secure the maintenance of the convent it was ordered that the Western priories should again give half of their incomes for five or, if necessary, six years. Again, the maintenance costs of the convent were estimated at 27,000 écus or 54,000 florins of which 36,000 should come from the West, mainly from France and Italy, and 18,000 from the East. The incomes from Spain, England and other priories were to be used to redeem the debts. The pope, Paul II, decreed a moratorium on the interests due from the Order, at first for six years, then, in January 1471, for an additional two years.[30] This was confirmed by the new pope, Sixtus IV, in 1472, and the respite became effective for another three years. During that time, an equal part of the debts was to be discharged each year.[31]

Zacosta died shortly after the Roman chapter but his successor, Fr. Giovanbattista Orsini, also undertook the administration of the convent and treasury, with slight changes concerning the endowment of the convent.[32] This arrangement expired with the general chapter in November 1471, when about 130,000 écus of the debts of 1467 had been repaid. Control over the treasury reverted to the grand preceptor and the other officials in the convent, but the state of emergency persisted. Since the number of brethren living in the East had been increased to 450, 32,000 écus a year were reserved for the convent. For another four years, the houses in the West had to give half of their incomes to the treasury.[33] Similar measures were taken at the chapters general of 1475

---

[28] Ibid., fols 83–86r, 27 October 1459; fols 117r–119v, 6 November 1462, also during a chapter general.

[29] See the papal confirmations of the decisions of the chapter general in Malta, Cod. 283, fols 29v–32v (= ASVat, Reg.Vat. 527, fols 30r–311r) and 33r–36r, dated 12 February 1467. For the 'budget' of 1467 see Luttrell, 'La funzione', note 8; for the chapter general of 1466/7 see Bosio, 2, pp. 299–310; G. Bottarelli, *Storia politica e militare del sovrano ordine di S.Giovanni di Gerusalemme detto di Malta*, 1: *Dalle origine alla caduta di Rodi* (Milan, 1940), pp. 223–6.

[30] ASVat, Reg.Vat. 537, fols 137v–141v.

[31] Ibid., 554, fols 123r–126v; the idea was to pay back a fifth of the remaining debts in each of five years.

[32] See the papal confirmations of two (inserted) magisterial bulls dated 19 August 1468 in ASVat, Reg.Vat. 537, fols 120v–122r and 141v–143r (from 20 January 1471).

[33] See Malta, Cod. 283, fols 81v–87r (= ASVat, Reg.Vat. 554, fols 49r–57v) and 87v–91r, papal confirmations dated 25 June 1472.

and 1478, but in 1478 it was again the Master, this time Fr. Pierre d'Aubusson, who himself took over the administration of the convent and treasury. Since 1471 at least, Aubusson had been one of the brethren working together with the grand preceptor and the other officials governing the treasury: therefore he had long experience of the problems involved.[34] Though he repeatedly complained of his duties, he was always persuaded by the participants of several successive chapters general to continue as administrator, and served until his death in 1503.[35] By that time, it had almost become custom for the Master to be also head of the treasury, and therefore Aubusson's successors, Fr. Émery d'Amboise and Fr. Fabrizio del Carretto, followed in his footsteps.[36] The earlier contracts between the Masters and the convent formed a pattern which could easily be adapted to face new difficulties. Thus at the chapter general in 1514, during the mastership of Carretto, about 40,000 écus were assigned to the maintenance of the convent, where at that time about 550 brethren would have been in residence. Since the debts had been reduced, the Western priories had to send to Rhodes only one-third of their incomes. As before, additional monies from the East were reserved for extraordinary expenses such as the 'great ship' of the Order, artillery, embassies to the West, and the defence of Rhodes. And, as had become customary since the time of Lastic, the Master was entitled to appoint the Order's officials on Rhodes, Kos and Cyprus.

Faced with increasing outside pressure and with growing debts between 1428 and 1451, the Order had resorted to higher impositions on the Order's incomes and to more intensive central control. From at least 1454 onwards, a series of chapters general commissioned the Masters to deal with the Order's finances and to guard 'the rights of the treasury'. After 1478, the Masters continuously functioned as administrators. What began as an emergency measure during times of crisis had developed into a regular form of financial administration.

---

[34] Aubusson is mentioned as one of the administrators in 1471, see Malta, Cod. 283, fol. 90r; the document of 1478, ibid., fols 184v–186v, mentions that Aubusson '... *tam in minoribus constitutis quam post suam promocionem ad magistratum functus est*' the administration of convent and treasury (fol. 184v). A 'budget' from about 1478 which probably belongs to Aubusson's takeover of the treasury has been analysed by A. Luttrell, 'La funzione', text to note 8.

[35] The last contract between Aubusson and one chapter general dates from 26 August 1501, see Malta, Cod. 284, fols 22r–25r.

[36] See, for example, Malta, Cod. 284, fols 57r–66r, 17 December 1504, and 285, 8 February 1514 (also for the following).

23

Hospitaller Record Keeping
and Archival Practices

Theresa M. Vann

Readers may speak metaphorically of heavy scholarship and dense prose. But students of the crusades, especially of the Order of the Hospital, may speak literally of weighty tomes. One of the major collections of diplomas for the crusader states is Delaville le Roulx's four-volume *Cartulaire général de l'ordre des Hospitaliers de S. Jean de Jérusalem (1100–1310)*, which weighs an estimated sixty-five pounds.[1] I am not mocking the *Cartulaire*, for Delaville le Roulx monumentally contributed to scholarship by collecting and publishing Hospitaller charters from European archives. His *Cartulaire* has become the primary resource for the diplomatic history of the Order of St John of Jerusalem, supplanting earlier collections.[2] But the physical appearance of the *Cartulaire* has indirectly influenced the modern conceptualization of crusader sources. The *Cartulaire* appears substantial and complete, but the user must realize that Delaville le Roulx compiled a modern cartulary that recreates the contents of a central depository that never existed in this form. The organization of the *Cartulaire* does not duplicate the Order's main archives on the island of Malta, which Delaville le Roulx described in detail in a previous work.[3] In the *Cartulaire*, Delaville le Roulx published transcriptions of the charters, but he lacked the capacity to analyse every charter. This is a fine distinction, but one that is essential for interpreting the diplomatic and legal development of the crusader kingdoms. In order to advance Hospitaller studies to a new level,

---

[1] The shipping scale of St John's University Alcuin Library provided the approximate weight.

[2] S. Pauli, *Codice diplomatico del sacro militare ordine Gerosolimitano oggi de Malta*, 2 vols (Lucca 1733–7), published only the charters available to him in the archives of the National Library, Valletta, Malta.

[3] J. Delaville le Roulx, *Les archives, la bibliothèque et le trésor de l'Ordre de Saint-Jean de Jérusalem à Malte* (Paris, 1883).

From *The Military Orders. Volume 2. Welfare and Warfare*. ed. Helen Nicholson. Copyright © 1998 by Helen Nicholson. Published by Ashgate Publishing Ltd, Gower House, Croft Road, Aldershot, Hampshire, GU11 3HR, Great Britain.

researchers must consider the appearance of charters and their method of transmission to answer questions of Hospitaller record keeping and notarial forms.

The Hill Monastic Manuscript Library (Collegeville, Minnesota) preserves medieval manuscript libraries on microfilm and provides open access to these materials. The Library has filmed the Archives of the Order of St John from the National Library in Valletta, Malta, which are available through its Malta Study Center (see Table 23.1). The Archives are organized into seventeen sections, covering the period between 1100 and 1798. Section I contains original medieval parchments, registers of *responsions*, letters, and bulls from Syria, Rhodes and Malta. Scholars are familiar with a portion of this material through the *Cartulaire*, which contains the charters and other materials dating from between 1100 and 1310; but the scope of the materials in Section I extends well beyond Delaville le Roulx's cut-off date of 1310, and their format consists of original diplomas, copies in codices, or single registers from incomplete series. In addition to the registers in Section I, three series of registers date from the Order's tenure of the island of Rhodes: Section II, the register of the deliberations of the council of the Order (1459); Section IV, the registers of the acts of the chapter general (1330); and Section V, the registers of the Grand Masters' bulls (1346). Three more sections contain medieval texts in later registers or transcriptions: Section VII (papal bulls) and Section XIII (the Church) preserve the text of twelfth-century papal bulls in a series of registers compiled in the sixteenth, seventeenth and eighteenth centuries; Section X (law) contains seventeenth- and eighteenth-century printed works and transcriptions of some of the original parchments found in Section I. These extensive resources do not comprise all the surviving medieval Hospitaller material in Europe, which is not duplicated in Malta.[4]

After a preliminary inventory, the Library has begun cataloguing the contents of Section I using the microfilms in the Malta Study Center with the intention of electronic publication. The catalogue of Section I produced by the National Library of Malta is helpful, but it does not provide the details that modern researchers require.[5] The first fourteen containers (each called an 'Archive') of Section I consist of folders containing parchment charters. The cataloguers, Antony Zammit Gabarretta and Joseph Mizzi, refer to these folders as volumes, implying that they are bound and printed. The cataloguers registered only the date and grantor of individual charters, based on the handwritten list pasted inside each folder. Some of these identifications are inaccurate, but fortunately Zammit Gabarretta and Mizzi cite the published

---

[4] See *CH*, 1, pp. xxvii–ccxxx, and *PUTJ*, 1, pp. 47–170, 2, pp. 19–64, for a survey of the Order's holdings in European archives.

[5] A. Zammit Gabarretta and J. Mizzi, *Catalogue of the Records of the Order of St John of Jerusalem in the Royal Malta Library*, 1 (Malta, 1964).

edition of each charter. Still, this is not the best method for handling archival material, which should at least be sorted by date and indexed for the convenience of researchers. Finally, the catalogue does not address questions of diplomatic practices, notarial development, and record keeping in the Order of the Hospital or the crusader states.[6]

Cataloguing microfilms is not the same as working with the original materials. All descriptive comments are based upon the filmed image, which limits discussion of size, coloration or surface irregularities, although the initial observations have been verified by subsequent examination of the originals. It is possible to tell if a charter was sealed, but surviving seals may not have photographed well. The microfilm shows that many of the charters appear to have sustained substantial damage and undergone major repairs that have obliterated portions of the text. However, the physical appearance of the artifacts in the Hospitaller archives can tell the researcher as much about the uncertainties of Latin settlement in the crusader states and the development of Hospitaller estates as the published transcriptions.

Delaville le Roulx did not always indicate the extent of the damage to the charters, although when the charter is badly rubbed or the text obscured in other ways he published only an abstract. For example, he cited an original bull of Odo des Pins dated 31 March 1295, but did not publish the text. Delaville le Roulx described it as 'orig. bullé, mauv. état' and cited Sebastiano Pauli, *Codice Diplomatico del Sacro Militare Ordine*, 2, p. 1, no. I, for the published text. This citation, however, points to a papal bull of Nicholas IV dated 1292 (*Dura nimis*); Pauli does not appear to have published the bull of Odo des Pins. The bull itself is damaged and stained, but most of the text is readable.[7]

It is amazing that any material survives from the crusader states, since the Hospitallers had more than one opportunity to lose all their archives during their long history. The fall of Jerusalem in 1187, the fall of Acre in 1291[8] and the loss of Rhodes to the Ottomans in 1522 were probably also marked by the destruction of Hospitaller records. The sixteenth-century historian Giacomo Bosio, who wrote the first history of the Order based on archival sources, did not have the Order's surviving Syrian charters for his first volume, and claimed in 1594 that there was little material for the period before 1350 except for chronicles.[9] Some of the Hospitaller charters predating 1300 may have been shipped to Provence, because in 1742 Grand Master Pinto ordered that the

---

[6] See H. Mayer, *Die Kanzlei der lateinischen Könige von Jerusalem*, 2 vols, in Monumenta Germaniae Historica, Schriften, 40 (Hanover, 1996), for the latest research into the chanceries of the crusader states.

[7] For example, *CH*, 3, no. 4276, p. 662, cited Malta, Cod. 16, no. 8.

[8] A. Luttrell, 'The Hospitallers' Historical Activities: 1291–1400', in his *The Hospitallers in Cyprus, Rhodes, Greece and the West, 1291–1440* (London, 1978), p. 2.

[9] *Idem*, 'The Hospitallers' Historical Activities: 1530–1630', in his *Latin Greece, the Hospitallers and the Crusades* (London, 1982), p. 63.

Syrian charters in the archives of the priory of St Gilles be returned to the main archives in Malta.[10]

The Hospitallers began preserving their manuscripts before the evacuation of Acre in 1291. By 1303 William of Santo Stefano, the preceptor of Cyprus, had made two compilations of the Order's rules, statutes, *esgards* and customs covering the period from 1125 to 1304, although the bulk of the material is contemporary to his era.[11] These compilations are not cartularies in the monastic sense, since William omitted charters that established rights to Hospitaller properties in the former crusader states. Exceptions to this are the text of a magisterial bull of Grand Master Jobert dated 1176 concerning the production of white bread for the hospital in Jerusalem, and the text of a donation of doubtful authenticity attributed to Godfrey of Bouillon.[12] William included Godfrey's supposed gift of European property in the *Exordium hospitaliorum* as proof of the early origins of the hospital in Jerusalem. The donation is, however, too early for Hospitaller acquisition of property outside the crusader states, nor is it supported by any subsequent confirmations. In 1110 Baldwin I confirmed a grant of an estate and properties in Jerusalem and Galilee that Godfrey had made to the hospital of Jerusalem.[13] This brief description in an original charter bearing Baldwin's signature is far more credible than the full, laudatory text copied out by William of Santo Stefano.[14]

The Hospitallers' long tenure on Malta ensured the continuity of its later records, but even after the Order established itself on the island its remaining archives suffered additional dispersals. Delaville le Roulx reiterated that the Knights of Malta preserved their archives through all their moves, yet he found that after 1798 Napoleon Bonaparte took sections of the Order's Maltese archives to the National Archives in France, and he speculated that the Order's materials for the period 1798–1810 remained in St Petersburg after Grand Master Ferdinand von Hompesch's brief stay at the tsar's court.[15] There were

---

[10] J. Delaville le Roulx, 'Inventaire de Pièces de Terre Sainte de l'Ordre de l'Hospital', *ROL*, 3, pp. 36–43; *PUTJ*, 1, pp. 51–67.

[11] Rome, Vatican, MS 4852 and BN, French MS 6049; J. Delaville le Roulx, 'Les statuts de l'Ordre de l'Hospital', *Bibliothèque de l'Ecole des Chartes*, 48 (1887), 347–8; Luttrell, 'Hospitallers 1291–1400', p. 3; J. Riley-Smith, *The Knights of St John in Jerusalem and Cyprus, 1050–1310* (London, 1967), pp. 272–3, 299.

[12] BN, French MS 6049, published in *CH*, 1, pp. 339–40; *RHC Occid*, 5, pp. 425–7.

[13] *CH*, 1, no. 20 (pp. 21–2); Malta, Valletta, Section I, Archive 1, nos 3, 5, 6.

[14] The charters in William of Santo Stefano can still confuse the unwary. For example, see T. Pichel, *History of the Sovereign Order of Saint John of Jerusalem Knights of Malta* (Shickshinny, PA, 1970), p. 95, who accepts the authenticity of William's text of the charter and prints an English translation.

[15] *CH*, 1, pp. xiv, lxiv; Delaville le Roulx, *Archives*, p. 8, for Russian archival material; see also A. Tardieu, 'Archives de l'ordre de Malte', *L'intermédiaire des chercheurs et curieux*, 38 (1902), 908, for Bonaparte's transportation of the archives. If there is Hospitaller archival material in Russia it would appear to have been generated on the spot, and not transplanted from the main archives.

also two folders, formerly Archives 5 and 7, which disappeared from Section I after Pauli included them in the *Codice diplomatico*. These were missing by the time Delaville le Roulx began his work.[16] By then the archival numbers had been reassigned, so that the modern Archive 5 was originally Archive 6.[17] Pauli is the only available source for the previous archival designations. The archives now designated 6 and 7 were compiled at some date after Pauli completed his *Codice*, but their origins are not precisely known. In his *Codice*, Pauli drew the texts of the bulls now in Archive 7 from a volume in the *Liber consilium* and from original bulls in the Malta archive, identifying the latter by the same charter number that they bear today. Therefore, the current Archive 7 probably formed part of the original papal bulls in Section I. The modern Archive 6 contains five papal bulls issued by three different popes. Pauli published one of these, which he identified as number 4 rather than by its current number, 1.[18] The modern Archive 6, therefore, may have been created from stray bulls culled from elsewhere in the collection.

The current organization of the Hospitaller archives demonstrates the Order's administrative priorities on Malta. Unlike monastic or cathedral archives, which organized records to establish a legal claim to rights or property, the archives of the Order reflect the priorities of a sovereign international religious corporation. The registers provide quick access to the seventeenth- and eighteenth-century records of the councils of the Order on Malta, yet the organization of the medieval material does not facilitate rapid retrieval of specific materials for modern scholars. The royal diplomas in Section I are bundled together based upon their approximate date of issue. The papal bulls are filed by the name of the pope, so all bulls issued by popes named Urban, Alexander and Clement are grouped together regardless of their period.

At some point the Hospitallers systematically classified their charters. Aside from the two lost folders, Pauli's published edition shows that the current numbering system of the charters in Section I has not changed much since the eighteenth century, and that the charters had been systematically classified prior to his work. The modern archival classification number is usually written in ink on the top front of each charter. The charters are also labelled on the reverse. The earliest dorsal label was a one-word identification of the property mentioned in the charter written in a thirteenth- or fourteenth-century hand. The second classification was a longer abstract of the charter, written in a later hand. Some charters also bear markings on their back that may correspond to another, unidentified, filing system.

---

[16] Delaville le Roulx, *Archives*, pp. 23–7, contains a discussion and reconstruction of the missing Archive 5 based on Pauli; he does not discuss the missing Archive 7, although he notes it as lost in his citations to the appropriate charters in *CH*.

[17] Zammit Gabarretta and Mizzi, pp. 2–3; see p. 219 for a reconstruction of the two lost containers.

[18] Pauli, 1, doc. 2 (p. 269) (Calixtus II, *Ad hoc nos*, 19 June 1119).

There is no evidence of a Hospitaller cartulary predating 1300 that established claims to lands in the crusader states. However, the Malta archives of the Order contain copies of charters from the Latin rulers in the East that established legal claims to properties lost after the fall of Jerusalem in 1187. Many of the texts of the early crusader charters survive only in later thirteenth-century copies. This pattern of survival raises serious questions of interpretation. The charters may tell us more about the thirteenth-century Hospitallers than about the settlement patterns of the twelfth-century kingdom.

The Hospitallers in the thirteenth-century crusader states used the vidimus, a French diplomatic instrument common in the thirteenth century, to produce notarized copies of their Syrian charters.[19] The vidimus is a confirmation of an earlier charter that attests to the appearance, validity, and the text of the original. The *inspeximus* was a similar form of confirmation used in the English chancery, which did not contain any affirmations aside from the reproduction of the text.[20] The French royal chancery, the papal chancery, and the English chancery used these instruments to validate and confirm earlier royal and papal charters. The act of confirming charters not only validated their authenticity (which can be real or imagined) but also assured institutional continuity. The monarch confirmed the acts of his dead predecessors to guard the rights of that undying institution, the Crown. In the crusader states the vidimus served a different purpose: it became a useful instrument that could regularize any gaps in the institutional continuity brought about by Saladin's conquests of 1187. The prelates of the crusader states, not the rulers, issued the vidimus for the royal and papal charters that survive in the Hospitaller archives. Considering the circumstances, this was probably the best solution to the record-keeping difficulties peculiar to the Latin states in the East. The diocesan clergy apparently were working on behalf of the Order, which may have been part of the Order's overall strategy of consulting outside legal experts.[21] But the vidimus could also legitimize charters of dubious provenance to establish firm territorial claims via the papal and ecclesiastical courts.

The mixture of the genuine and the spurious characterizes at least one *inspeximus* dated *c.* 1250.[22] The parchment contains two texts: Hans Mayer has established that the top text, labelled 'b', dated May 1122, is almost certainly a forgery.[23] The bottom text, labelled 'a', is a copy of a genuine charter dated 29 April 1166.[24] The genuine charter had been issued by Baldwin of Ibelin and

---

[19] A. Giry, *Manuel de diplomatique* (Paris, 1925), p. 20; *Vocabulaire international de la diplomatique,* ed. M. Cárcel Ortí (Valencia, 1994), nos 67, 68, pp. 34–5.

[20] H. Hall, *Studies in English Official Historical Documents* (New York, 1969 [1st edn 1908]), p. 242.

[21] J. Brundage, 'The Lawyers of the Military Orders', in *MO*, 1, pp. 349–50.

[22] NLM, Section I, Archive 2, nos 41a, 41b; *CH*, 1, nos 59, 354 (pp. 49, 245).

[23] H. Mayer, 'Carving Up Crusaders: The Early Ibelins and Ramlas', in *Outremer: Studies in the history of the Crusading Kingdom of Jerusalem,* ed. B.Z. Kedar, H.E. Mayer and R.C. Smail (Jerusalem, 1982), pp. 101–18; Pauli, 1, no. 191 (p. 236); *CH*, 1, no. 59 (p. 49).

[24] NLM, Section I, Archive 2, no. 40; *CH*, 1, no. 354 (p. 245).

confirmed earlier gifts of properties and incomes that the Ibelins had given to the Order. Mayer established the forgery from textual evidence concerning the genealogy of the Ibelin family. He suggested that the forged portion was created when the charter was drawn up in Acre around 1250 to establish that the Order's claim to the tithes of Mirabel predated 1166. But the appearance of the charter is also highly irregular. The *inspeximus* consists of the texts of the authentic and the forged charters, with a row of circles marking the end of each one. There is one text block of confirmation for both charters. One of the confirmers, Adam, the archdeacon of Tyre, was active in the 1250s, but the identification of the other confirmer as *J. abbas sancti Sepulchri* is unique to this charter, and the date is not correctly recorded.[25]

This individual instrument served its purpose and cemented the Order's shaky claims to a specific property, but it probably would not have stood in the papal court. When the Order had to defend its controversial acquisition of the monastery of Mount Tabor from Pope Alexander IV in 1255, it or its advisors created a file of vidimus seeking confirmation of every charter that defined Mount Tabor's properties and incomes.[26] For example, Baldwin I's original donation to the monastery of Mount Tabor (1107) is the oldest surviving royal diploma in the Hospitaller archives. Its appearance is unprepossessing. Although it had been pierced for a seal (now missing), it lacks other accoutrements such as a notarial mark, witnesses or any other guarantor of authenticity. In comparison, the vidimus of Baldwin's donation is an elegant instrument that is more impressive in appearance than the original.[27] The first part of its four-part structure consists of the affirmation of Giles, archbishop of Tyre, and Joscelin, archbishop of Caesarea, that they had examined Baldwin's original bull at the request of the Master and brothers of the Hospital of St John in Jerusalem. It describes Baldwin's seal that was then attached. The second part is a transcription of the text of the earlier charter. The third part contains the attestation of the two prelates that the original charter had not been cancelled in any way, as well as their order that Aliottus, the public notary, transcribe the original charter.[28] The final section identifies Aliottus as the scribe of the vidimus, contains his notarial mark (a stylized fleur-de-lys) and his affirmation that he transcribed the original exactly, according to the commands of Giles and Joscelin, with the date and place (23 July 1255, Acre). Aliottus did not produce an exact transcription in the modern sense of the term, since his instrument contains some variations in punctuation and spelling that do not, however, alter the meaning of the text.

---

[25] Mayer, 'Carving Up Crusaders', pp. 110, 112.

[26] Riley-Smith, pp. 413–17.

[27] NLM, Section I, Archive 1, nos 1, 2; Pauli, 1, no. 1, p. 1. The charter was not included in *CH*.

[28] Mayer, *Die Kanzlei*, 1, p. 336 and note 12, identifies him as Aliotto Uguccio, a scribe of the *Cour des Bourgeois* in Acre. As at 24 August 1244 Aliottus was the imperial notary: see NLM, Section I, Archive 5, no. 25; *CH*, 2, no. 2330 (p. 619).

Table 23.1   Archives of the Knights of Malta, in Valleta, Malta, Biblioteca Nacional

Section	Name	# of Mss Documents	Date of Documents	Registration Date	Contents	Publications and Catalogues
I	Original documents	1,500	1100s–1798	1107–1798	Charters letters and bulls	Catalogue: *Catalogue of the Order of St John of Jerusalem in the Royal Malta Library*, vol. I (Malta, 1964). Published: S. Pauli, *Codice Diplomatico del Sacro Militare Ordine Gerosolimitano oggi di Malta*, 2 vols (Lucca, 1733–1737) J. Delaville Le Roulx, *Cartulaire General de l'Ordre des Hospitalliers de S. Jean de Jerusalem* (1100–1310) 4 vols (Paris, 1894–1906)
II	*Liber conciliorum*	186	1459–1797	15th–18th c.	Deliberations of the Council of the Order	Catalogue: *Catalogue of the Order of St John of Jerusalem in the Royal Malta Library*, vol. 2 (Malta, 1970)
III	*Liber Conciliorum Status*	26	1623–1798	17th–18th c.	External affairs and matters of state handled by the Council	Catalogue: *Catalogue of the Order of St John of Jerusalem in the Royal Malta Library*, vol. 3 (Malta, 1965–1966)
IV	*Chapter General*	37	1330–1776	14th–18th c.	Thirty-six Chapters General of the Order, their proceedings and enactments	Catalogue: *Catalogue of the Order of St John of Jerusalem in the Royal Malta Library*, vol. 4 (Malta, 1964)
V	*Libri bullarum*	320	1346–1798	14th–18th c.	Magisterial bulls	Uncatalogued
VI	The Treasury	606	1604–1798	17th–18th c.	Financial and administrative documents from Malta and from the Langues	Uncatalogued
VII	Papal Bulls	58	1100s–1797 1503–1798	16th–18th c.	Papal bulls issued to the Order, the Grand Masters, and individual knights	Catalogue: *Catalogue of the Records of the Order of St John of Jerusalem in the Royal Malta Library*, vol. 7 (Malta, 1964)
VIII	Petitions	18	1603–1798	17th–18th c (Italian)	Petitions to the Grand Master (in *John of Jerusalem*, vol. 8 (Malta, 1967).	Catalogue: *Catalogue of the Records of the Order of St*

Table 23.1 Concluded

Section	Name	# of Mss Documents	Date of Documents	Registration Date	Contents	Publications and Catalogues
IX	Correspondance	464	1530–1798	16th–18th c.	Foreign correspondence and ambassadorial reports	Uncatalogued
X	Constitutions	77	1100s–1798	17th–18th c.	Manuscripts, printed books and pamphlets on the Rule, Statutes, and Privileges of the Order	Catalogue: *Catalogue of the Records of the Order of St John of Jerusalem in the Royal Malta Library*, vol. 10 (Malta, 1969)
XI	The Hospital	46	1730–1798 1503–1798	16th–18th c.	The Hospital's administrative documents and wills	Catalogue: *Catalogue of the Records of the Order of St John of Jerusalem in the Royal Malta Library*, vol. 2 (Malta, 1969)
XII	The Navy	181	1600–1798	17th–18th c.	The Navy's administrative documents, log books, reports, shipyard records and other material	Catalogue: *Catalogue of the Records of the Order of St John of Jerusalem*, vol. 12 (Malta, 1968)
XIII	The Church	194	1156–1798	16th–18th c.	The records of the Conventual Church in Malta, and the administration of the Order's churches and monasteries throughout Europe	Catalogue: *Catalogue of the Records of the Order of St John of Jerusalem in the Royal Malta Library*, vol. 13 (Malta, 1967); Ibid., *Archives 2038–2071* (Malta, 1990)
XIV	Deliberations of the Langues	157	pre 1530–1798	14th–18th c.	Deliberations of the Langues of the Order; the responsions of the Langues	Uncatalogued
XV	Proofs of Nobility	3349	1100s–1798	17th–18th c.	Genealogical records showing the noble status of individual knights	Uncatalogued
XVI	Cabrei (Visitations)		1530–1798	16th–18th c.	Descriptions of visitations to lands belonging to the Order	Uncatalogued
XVII	*Miscellanea Generale*		1530–1804	16th–19th c.	Miscellaneous documents, some records of post-1798 French Administration	Uncatalogued

In the month of July 1255 this Acre team produced three other vidimus that are almost identical in form to this one. They confirmed a papal bull of Paschal II originally dated 1103, a charter issued by Gibelin of Sabran, papal legate, in 1112 and a papal bull of Eugenius III issued in 1146.[29] The original bulls of Paschal II and Gibelin of Sabran do not survive, while Eugenius III's bull survives in a copy in Marseilles.[30] These bulls formed part of the Order's case before Alexander IV, who confirmed them in October 1256.[31]

The vidimus underwent a period of development before it reached the standards of Aliottus' elegant instruments, as demonstrated by a suit between the Order of the Hospital and the county of Tripoli over the castle of Maraclea that reached the papal court in the 1230s. Bohemond of Tripoli granted the castle of Maraclea to the Order in 1199 after he became prince of Antioch. He then revoked the donation on the understanding that it would revert to the Order upon his death.[32] The succession to Antioch was contested and Bohemond's successors did not honour the agreement. The case took the long route of most medieval litigation and eventually wound up before the pope. The Order presented various examples of vidimus as part of their case. The most irregular charters in appearance are the two earliest vidimus, dated *c.* 1215–20, affirmed by Eustorgius of Montaigu, archbishop of Nicosia, and Peter, archbishop of Caesarea. Unlike later vidimus, these two charters merely transcribed the text of the original and affirmed that neither added nor subtracted from the text. Peter, archbishop of Caesarea, either confirmed the vidimus at a later date or signed the parchment himself instead of creating new documents.[33] The formula indicates that the Order of the Hospital requested the production of the vidimus. One charter still bears a damaged Hospitaller seal that depicts on one side a kneeling figure before a cross, while the other side shows a reclining figure under a dome with the legend '*iherusalem hospitalis*'.[34]

In conclusion, a systematic examination of original charters is rewarding, even when the texts have been published. The appearance and organization of material can and does influence historical interpretation. The researcher must be aware of forgeries and recreation. Many of the records of these now-defunct states have been lost, and no medieval chancery had a stake in policing forgeries. What survives may tell us more about the hopes and desires of the

---

[29] NLM, Section I, Archive 6, no. 2 (29 July 1103, vidimus 23 July 1255); Archive 1, no. 7 (1112, vidimus 6 July 1255); and Archive 8 no. 3 (4 May 1146, vidimus 23 July 1255); in *CH*, 2, nos 2832, 2829 (pp. 826–28, 899 iv).

[30] *CH*, 2, no. 2829 (pp. 823–4).

[31] Ibid., nos 2829, 2832 (pp. 823–8).

[32] Riley-Smith, pp. 152–62, 452; NLM, Section I, Archive 1, nos 20, 21; in *CH*, 1, nos 1085, 1096 (pp. 674–5, 682–3).

[33] NLM, Section I, Archive 1, nos 20, 21.

[34] Ibid., no. 20.

thirteenth-century crusading effort than about earlier settlements. Therefore, a clear understanding of the process of document survival is vital in order to avoid tainted interpretations. But, due in part to these circumstances, the entire archives of the Order remain a rich, under-utilized source of information on the Hospitallers and the crusading movement. These court cases are just two examples taken from the archives that demonstrate how the Order of the Hospital consciously manipulated its written records to secure rights to property and income. A thorough case study provides us with a better idea of the legal processes in the crusader states. Much more analysis of crusader charters remains to be done to find additional evidence for social, economic, legal and notarial developments in the Latin East.

24

Exemption in the Temple, the Hospital and the Teutonic Order: Shortcomings of the Institutional Approach

Luis García-Guijarro Ramos

Research on the military orders is generally built on what is thought to be firm ground. Historians take it for granted that the inner meaning of the topic they are dealing with is obvious, and they regard their contributions as new storeys added to a solid edifice. This present-day confidence relies on substantial foundation work carried out in the past, mainly by German or French scholars who, in accordance with positivist aspirations of making history 'scientific', followed institutional approaches based on exhaustive and careful treatment of the written sources, the exact wording of which was considered the bedrock of historical explanation. The most influential works were not only those specifically devoted to the military orders – books and articles by H. Prutz and J. Delaville le Roulx among others – but also those general or particular analyses of other monastic institutions which could be easily applied to the new *militiae*.

The uncritical acceptance of the institutionalist view has detached specialized studies from necessary reconsiderations of positivist theories in this field. This tendency has resulted in the coexistence of traditional ideas about the military orders alongside valuable research that has unearthed unknown aspects of their history; yet questions about the global significance of these institutions in Latin Christendom have been lacking in the proliferation of fragmented studies. Knowledge about the Orders has without doubt greatly increased in the last decades; it is time to start thinking in wider terms, to suggest elements of a more comprehensive history of the military orders in the Middle Ages that might break the intellectual limits of the formalist view.

When asked for a short description of these institutions, many historians fall back on a well-known label: 'warrior monks'. This poor definition makes clear the relevance of one part of the compound name: 'monks'. The peculiarity of

From *The Military Orders. Volume 2. Welfare and Warfare*. ed. Helen Nicholson. Copyright © 1998 by Helen Nicholson. Published by Ashgate Publishing Ltd, Gower House, Croft Road, Aldershot, Hampshire, GU11 3HR, Great Britain.

religious men fighting has traditionally been considered the distinctive character of the military orders; at the same time, this feature has puzzled a good number of scholars who link monasticism with contemplation or, at the most, with peaceful activities. A redefinition of these *militiae* must bring into consideration their central, not peripheral or exotic, position in the Latin Church; their emergence is only understandable within the context of ecclesiastical reform, which developed an active and positive acceptance of a certain kind of war. The encouragement of practices hitherto regarded as being contrary to the religious profession fitted in with the reformist wish to widen the roads to spiritual perfection, which until then had been limited to contemplation in its diverse forms. Charitable activities, redemption of captives and 'proper' fighting were set on an equal footing with traditional monastic life. The unified diversity of the new Orders helps us to understand the deep affinity between Cistercians and Templars, monks with apparently different, almost opposite vocations.

The unifying factor behind such different kinds of spiritual pursuits lay in the type of monasticism promoted by ecclesiastical reform. The military orders should be seen as part of a wide spectrum of monastic foundations; their common features show the depth of character of the *militiae*, which were significant not merely for their engagement in war, but mainly for their place in the structure of the Latin Church. Twelfth-century monasticism differed from the old Benedictine form in two basic aspects. The new monastic foundations were spread all across the Christian world in a network very different from the highly autonomous diffusion of individual pre-reformist coenobitic houses. This network had an apex: Rome. Direct dependence on the papacy was the element that connected the network of institutions which emerged all over Latin Christendom to the Church as a whole. This privileged bond with the Apostolic See showed the pope's desire for control over an expanding Church as well as his greater strength, and was far distant from the nominal links sought by some monasteries in pre-Gregorian times.

The basic trait of the military orders was thus a submission to Rome that meant freedom from any other ecclesiastical power and consequently suppression of any secular or diocesan intervention. This *maior libertas* has traditionally been called 'exemption'; the way this tie has been understood and defined by modern historiography has conditioned the very concept scholars have of these Orders. The institutionalist approach developed for reformist monasticism by G. Schreiber and J.B. Mahn was and still is extended to the military–religious foundations.[1] This view is based mainly on four assumptions.

---

[1] G. Schreiber, *Kurie und Kloster im XII Jahrhundert. Studien zum Privilegierung, Verfassung und besonders zum Eigenkirchenwesen der vorfranziskanischen Orden, vornehmlich auf der Grund der Papsturkunden von Paschalis II bis auf Lucius II (1099–1181)* (Stuttgart, 1910). J.B. Mahn, *L'Ordre Cistercien et son gouvernement des origines au milieu du XIIIe siècle (1098–1265)*, 2nd edn (Paris, 1982).

First, exemption has basically been regarded as freedom from the punitive powers of the bishop, that is to say from episcopal interdict and excommunication. Secondly, historians developed the idea that this central liberty was given in a specific document. Thirdly, this assumption fixed a clear distinction between papal protection and exemption; both were considered essentially different privileges which were granted at separate times with no necessary union between them; the Roman *tutela* did not always lead to formal liberation from diocesan jurisdiction. Finally, when exemption was awarded, it has been supposed that it became expressed in subsequent documents by certain sets of *formulae*, which have helped past and present scholars to establish whether a certain order did enjoy the *maior libertas* or not.

All these assumptions can be submitted to criticism. The relevance of the *formulae* is less conclusive in signalling exemption than historians have thought. They are, in fact, no real test for proving the existence of this supreme liberty, because there are actually many instances in the new Orders of explicit freedom from excommunication alongside a wording that denotes just the opposite, if the rules pre-established by historians are followed. Outside the boundaries of the military institutions, the Orders of Camaldoli and of Vallombrosa are good examples of this lack of concordance between evidence and the institutional theory.[2]

The whole formalist argument relies on the specific document that grants *maior libertas* to each order. There is no instance among the various *militiae* and other institutions, such as the Cistercians, of such types of privilege. The absence of central documentation for the Temple, whose Outremer archives disappeared during the Turkish invasion of Cyprus – as R. Hiestand has consistently proved[3] – gives no satisfactory explanation, because, had it ever existed, this most important papal grant would have been copied many times in the West. The idea that the text was written during the long pontificate of Alexander III has been sustained by A.J. Forey, but there is no clear documentary evidence to support it;[4] a thirteenth-century bull, Honorius III's *Ex autentico* from 4 December 1219, confirms exemption to the Order and vaguely refers the liberty back to the times of Alexander III, but this obscure reference does not permit us to think in terms of a specific document issued by that pope or by some other predecessor.[5]

Delaville le Roulx's *Cartulaire* offers no clue to this question in the Order of the Hospital. No satisfactory answer is found in the bull that the French

---

[2] L. García-Guijarro, *Papado, Cruzadas y Órdenes Militares, siglos XI–XIII* (Madrid, 1995), pp. 90–1.

[3] R. Hiestand, 'Zum Problem des Templerzentralarchive', *Archivalische Zeitschrift*, 76 (1980), 17–37.

[4] A.J. Forey, *The Templars in the Corona de Aragón*, London, 1973, p. 167.

[5] Archivo de la Corona de Aragón, Cancillería Real, Pergaminos, Legajo IV, no. 7 (copy of 8 January 1274). Hiestand publishes a somewhat earlier version, of 13 November 1219: *PUTJ*, 1, no. 238 (pp. 413–14).

historian assigned to Clement V with the date 17 April 1309; regardless of
modern assumptions of a much later promulgation by Clement VI, this papal
document seems to be just a ratification, in no way the establishment of
exemption.[6] The documentary sources of the Teutonic Order point in the same
direction. E. Strehlke's compilation contains a bull of 15 December 1220, traditionally considered as the grant of exemption.[7] As shown in other cases, it
was just a confirmation of the Order's direct link with the papacy which freed
it from diocesan dependence; a previous bull of 1 October 1218 makes this
meaning clear when it states that the Teutonic brethren had no bishop other
than the pope.[8]

Historians have devoted much effort to identifying the exemption grant for
a particular privilege, and to getting nearer to it by reading too much into other
extant documents. This road has borne little fruit and takes no account of the
basic fact that the much searched-for bull has not been discovered because it
was probably not granted. There was no need for it, as dependence on Rome,
established through papal protection, meant an overall submission to the
pope that implicitly included *libertates* from punitive action by diocesans;
these and other liberties existed from the time when these institutions became
firmly linked to the Holy See, regardless of whether the military orders were
or were not strong enough to put them into practice. So there was no real
distinction between protection, that is supreme dependence to the pope, and
exemption. When this concept is looked at from this particular angle, the
restrictive idea of freedom from excommunication gives way to a wider notion
of global liberty implicit in the protection of the highest authority of the
Latin Church.

Thus, following ecclesiastical reform, the *tutela apostolica* became the
dividing line between *maior libertas* and other fragmented and less embracing
privileges enjoyed previously by these institutions or in general by other
monastic orders not linked to Rome. The text that granted protection could
be laconic or could describe in detail the liberties that a certain *militia* had
received. The difference was quite irrelevant. The key aspect was admission
into the circle of papal protégés; this was the source of any kind of privilege
that, in consequence, did not need to be precisely specified in order to exist.
On many occasions, the present-day preconception which assumes that rights
must have a specific legal expression to be of any significance has been
projected into the medieval world; yet, at that time, it was dependence alone
which modelled liberties – liberties that emerged from the link that

---

[6] *CH*, 4, no. 4858 (pp. 210–12).

[7] *Tabulae ordinis Theutonici ex tabularii regii Berolinensis codice potissimum*, ed. E. Strehlke (Berlin,
1869, repr. Toronto and Jerusalem, 1975), no. 306 (pp. 275–9). The bull was reissued on 28 July
1227 (Strehlke, no. 424 [pp. 343–4]).

[8] Strehlke, no. 305 (p. 275). This bull was reissued on 16 January 1221 and on 27 June 1226
(Strehlke, nos 313 [p. 284], and no. 397 [p. 331]).

dependence established. The everyday existence of these liberties was related to the power that those who benefited from these privileges had to impose them, and not so much to their being clearly specified in a grant.

Exemption was thus the greatest liberty accorded to the highest connection any human could achieve: papal protection. It could be presented with considerable detail, as in the bull *Omne datum optimum*, granted by Innocent II to the Templars in 1139.[9] The prolific description of the Order's rights in this bull meant considerable weakening of diocesan jurisdiction over the Temple. This apostolic privilege dealt a blow to the control the patriarch of Jerusalem had had over this institution, whose original obedience to the most important Church authority in Outremer had been reaffirmed years before at the Council of Troyes, where the patriarch was given permission to alter the rule.[10] The firm bond with Rome shaped in 1139 prevented such future metropolitan interventions; *Omne datum optimum* established that statutes could be altered only by the Master with the consent of the general chapter.[11]

On the other hand, the Order of the Hospital had received in 1113 a short privilege, *Pie postulatio voluntatis*, important because it established the *tutela apostolica*, the basis of all liberties subsequently specified up to 1154, when the Order was allowed to have its own clergy in the bull *Christiane fidei religio*.[12] The four fundamental papal texts that registered specific liberties in the first half of the twelfth century always referred back to apostolic protection. When the bull *Quam amabilis Deo* urged diocesans to procure lay alms for the Hospital, the Roman link became the decisive argument in favour of this request.[13] In the same way, the Teutonic Knights were granted a brief protection privilege by Clement III in 1191;[14] its extremely concise form cannot conceal the ultimate fact of apostolic dependence, which contrasted with the subjection of the pre-1187 German hospital at Jerusalem to the Hospital.[15]

The texts granted by the Roman *Curia* in 1113, 1139 and 1191 were the starting point of the *maior libertas* the three Orders enjoyed, and they are the basic documents which allow us to understand the real meaning of these *militiae* in the twelfth and thirteenth centuries. No wonder that we find many copies of them in the cartularies and other documentary sources, while precise exemption grants are lacking.

---

[9] *CT*, bullaire, V, pp. 375–9. *PUTJ*, 1, no. 3 (pp. 204–10); a textual study of this privilege is in *PUTJ*, 2, pp. 67–103.

[10] *RT*, § 4, p. 15.

[11] *CT*, p. 376; *PUTJ*, 1, pp. 206–7.

[12] *Pie postulatio voluntatis*: *CH*, 1, no. 30 (pp. 29–30); *PUTJ*, 2, no. 1 (pp. 194–8). *Christiane fidei religio*: *CH*, 1, no. 226 (pp. 173–5); a textual study of this bull is in *PUTJ*, 2, pp. 104–35.

[13] *CH*, 1, no. 130 (pp. 107–8). A textual study of this privilege is in *PUTJ*, 2, pp. 136–62.

[14] Strehlke, no. 295 (pp. 263–4).

[15] *CH*, 1, no. 154, pp. 123–4.

25

The Hospitallers in Pomerania: Between the Priories of Bohemia and *Alamania*

Karl Borchardt

Centralized religious orders – Cistercians, Hospitallers, Templars, Dominicans, Franciscans – offer an opportunity to study central and local government in medieval times. The appointment of officers, the payment of money and the circumscription of provinces within these orders can be compared with general ecclesiastical or secular administration. Regional divisions of these orders were determined not only by ecclesiastical, but also by political, economic and cultural factors. Changes of such divisions were sometimes due to political pressure by local rulers, sometimes to more subtle, but equally powerful, social or national forces. From the 1180s the Hospitallers in central Europe had two priories, a western one called *Alamania* for Germany and an eastern one, mainly for Slav countries, usually called Bohemia, sometimes Moravia and sometimes *Polonia*.[1] In 1238 the three Hospitaller centres in Pomerania – at Stargard on the River Ihna, at Schlawe and at Stargard on the River Ferse – together with the house at Posen in Poland belonged to the eastern priory, as

---

[1] The titles vary: in 1205 the chief official was entitled prior for Bohemia and Moravia, and separately Master for Silesia: *CH*, 2, nos 1224 ff., in 1230 Master for Boemia, Moravia, Polonia and Pomerania: *CH*, 2, no. 1961, *Pommersches Urkundenbuch* (hereafter *Pomm. UB*), 7 vols, 2nd edn (Cologne and Graz, 1970 [1st edn 1877]), 1: 786–1253, no. 267; in 1238 prior for Moravia: *CH*, 2, nos 2191–2194; in 1246 prior for Poland: *CH*, 2, no. 2426. Finally, the eastern priory was divided into four subregions, Bohemia, Moravia, Austria and Poland (Silesia). For general reference see W.G. Rödel, *Das Großpriorat Deutschland des Johanniter-Ordens im Übergang vom Mittelalter zur Reformation anhand der Generalvisitationsberichte von 1494/95 und 1540/41*, 2nd edn (Cologne, 1972); E. Opgenoorth, *Die Ballei Brandenburg des Johanniterordens im Zeitalter der Reformation und Gegenreformation*, Beihefte zum Jahrbuch der Albertus-Universität Königsberg, 24 (Würzburg, 1963); B.B. Szczesniak, *The Knights Hospitallers in Poland and Lithuania* (The Hague and Paris, 1969), pp. 14–40, 45 ff. (not always reliable); B. Waldstein-Wartenberg, 'Die Kommenden des Großpriorats Böhmen', in *Der Johanniterorden/der Malteserorden: Der ritterliche Orden des hl. Johannes vom Spital zu Jerusalem. Seine Geschichte, seine Aufgaben*, ed. A. Wienand, 3rd edn (Cologne, 1988), pp. 383–408.

From *The Military Orders. Volume 2. Welfare and Warfare*. ed. Helen Nicholson. Copyright © 1998 by Helen Nicholson. Published by Ashgate Publishing Ltd, Gower House, Croft Road, Aldershot, Hampshire, GU11 3HR, Great Britain.

four letters of Gregory IX demonstrate.[2] By 1269, however, it was the prior of *Alamania* who sought papal protection for Stargard on the Ihna.[3] After 1278, Fr. John of Rochow, a nobleman from Brandenburg in Germany, became commander of the Hospitaller possessions in Eastern Pomerania.[4] Again, in the fourteenth century the preceptor of Saxony, who was subject to the prior of *Alamania*, was responsible for Pomerania. His title read '*preceptor generalis per Saxoniam, Marchiam, Slaviam et Pomeraniam*' (in German '*Gebietiger von Sachsen, der Mark, Wendland und Pommern*').[5] This paper discusses why and how the Hospitallers in Pomerania were transferred from the eastern to the western priory.

Pomerania was not converted to Christianity before the 1130s, but as early as 1182 the pope was writing to the Hospitaller preceptor *in Boemia, Polonia et Pomerania*.[6] Foundation charters are not extant for the three Pomeranian centres of the Order, but the founders were commemorated by the Hospitallers and mentioned by Gregory IX in his four letters of 1238. By 1182 there were at least two Hospitaller foundations in Pomerania, which were probably Stargard on the Ferse in the east and Stargard on the Ihna in the

---

[2] See below, notes 8–11. Hospitallers in Pomerania: H. Hoogeweg, *Die Stifter und Klöster der Provinz Pommern*, 2 (Stettin, 1925), pp. 869–904; W. Hubatsch, 'Der Johanniterorden in Ost- und Westpreußen', *Zeitschrift für Ostforschung*, 21 (1972), 1–19; *Handbuch der historischen Stätten Deutschlands*, 12: Mecklenburg, Pommern, ed. R. Schmidt (Stuttgart, 1996), pp. 270 ff. (Schlawe), 276–9 (Stargard), 324 ff. (Zachan); ibid., 13: Ost- und Westpreußen, ed. E. Weise (Stuttgart, 1966), pp. 122 (Liebschau), 181 (Preußisch Stargard), 207 (Schöneck). The Church in Pomerania: J. Petersohn, *Der südliche Ostseeraum im kirchlich-politischen Kräftespiel des Reichs, Polens und Dänemarks vom 10. bis 13. Jahrhundert*, Ostmitteleuropa in Vergangenheit und Gegenwart, 17 (Cologne and Vienna, 1979).

[3] Straßburg, 12 August 1269: *CH*, 3, no. 3365; *Pomm. UB*, 2: 1254–1286 (Stettin, 1881/85, repr. Aalen, 1970), no. 891.

[4] Fr. John of Rochow 1291, 1312 and 1313: *Pommerellisches Urkundenbuch*, ed. M. Perlbach (Danzig, 1881/1916, repr. Aalen, 1969) (hereafter *Pommerell. UB*), no. 476; *Pomm. UB*, 5: 1311–1320 (Stettin, 1905, repr. Aalen 1970), no. 2704, *Preußisches Urkundenbuch* (hereafter *Preuß. UB*), 2: 1309–1335, ed. M. Hein and E. Maschke (Königsberg, 1932/39, repr. Aalen, 1962), no. 97; without surname, 1289 to 1305: *Pommerell. UB*, nos 456, 467, 470, 471, 631. For donations in 1278 and 1287: *Pommerell. UB*, nos 300, 425.

[5] J. v. Pflugk-Harttung, *Die Anfänge des Johanniterordens in Deutschland, besonders in der Mark Brandnburg und in Mecklenburg* (Berlin, 1899); idem, 'Die Anfänge des Johanniter-Herrenmeistertums', *Historische Vierteljahresschrift*, new ser., 2 (1899), 189–210; Opgenoorth, *Ballei Brandenburg*, pp. 29–47; idem, 'Die Kommenden der Ballei Brandenburg', in Wienand, pp. 372–82.

[6] Velletri, 23 October 1182: *CH*, 1, no. 643. For the history of Pomerania: M. Wehrmann, *Geschichte von Pommern*, 2 vols (1919/21, repr. 1982); K. Slaski and B. Zientara, *Historia Pomorza*, 1 (to 1466), 2nd edn (Poznan, 1972); J. Spors, *Dzieje polityczne ziem sławieńskiej, słupskiej i białogardzkiej XII–XIV w.* (Poznan, 1973); idem, *Podziały administracyjne Pomorza Gdańskiego i Sławieńsko-Słupskiego od XII do początku XIV wieku* (Słupsk, 1983); B. Śliwiński, *Urzędnicy Pomorza Wschodniego do 1309 roku Spisy* (Wrocław, 1989).

west, both in old places (Stargard means 'old town') and both on roads from Poland to the shores of the Baltic.[7]

At Stargard on the Ferse the *princeps Pomeranie* Grimislaw was commemorated as founder. He was said to have donated the castle which protected the important road from Danzig to the south when it crossed the Ferse. This road was still called *via Grimislai* in the fourteenth century. In 1198 the same Grimislaw granted to the Hospital the church of Holy Trinity at Liebschau. Recently the hypothesis was advanced that Grimislaw could have been a Polish noble sent to Pomerania by the Piasts as a check on the native princes. This hypothesis can be supported by the history of the Hospitaller possessions, because in 1317 the commander of Liebschau and Schöneck was still responsible for estates not only in Cujavia (Nemoiov and Scheblenz) but also in Little Poland (Zagost). Zagost had been given to the Hospitallers in the 1150s and was confirmed in 1172. The Hospitallers who received the Eastern Pomeranian properties which Grimislaw donated may have come from Zagost.[8]

Stargard on the Ihna is said to have been founded by Duke Bogislaw I (d. 1187) and his son Bogislaw II (d. 1220). The Hospitallers held the parish church at Stargard, whose patron saint was St John the Baptist, probably because the Hospitallers had founded the church. Bogislaw I may have summoned them from Posen when he visited that place and married the daughter of the Polish duke Mieszko;[9] Mieszko (d. 1202) and his son Władysław (d. 1231) were commemorated as founders of the Hospitaller house in Posen.[10]

The third of the Hospitallers' centres in Pomerania, Schlawe, was said to have been founded by the *princeps Pomeranie* Ratibor and his son Boleslaw. There were, however, two rulers named Ratibor at Schlawe; the first died in 1156 and had a son Boleslaw, the second died in 1228 without a male heir. But the patron saint of the Hospitaller parish church at Schlawe was not St John the Baptist:

---

[7] Schlawe, the third Hospitaller centre, was on major north–south routes (predominant in the twelfth century) as well as west–east routes (predominant in the thirteenth century): K. Slaski, 'Die Landhandelsstraßen Pommerns und Pommerellens vom 11. bis zum 13. Jahrhundert', *Beiträge zur Geschichte Pommerns und Pommerellens*, with preface by K. Zernack, ed. H.G. Kirchhoff (Dortmund, 1987), pp. 74–93 with map.

[8] '*a clare memorie Grimislao, principe Pomeranie*' Lateran, 12 March 1238, extant as vidimus from 1269: *CH*, 2, no. 2193; *Pommerell. UB*, nos 64, 241; *Preuß. UB*, 1/2 no. 290. 1198 alleged original *CH*, 1, no. 1043; *Pommerell. UB*, no. 10; *Pomm. UB*, 1, no. 133; vidimus 1262 with different text *CH*, 1, no. 1042; *Pommerell. UB*, no. 9; *Pomm. UB*, 1, no. 134, 2, no. 723; on these forgeries J. v. Pflugk-Harttung, 'Unechte Urkunden des Johanniter-Ordens aus dem 12. und 13. Jahrhunderte', *Forschungen zur brandenburgischen und preußischen Geschichte*, 11 (1898), 301–9. 1317: *Codex Diplomaticus Maioris Poloniae* (hereafter *CD Mai. Polon.*), 5 vols, (Poznan, 1877–1908), 2, no. 567. Szczesniak, pp. 23 ff., there is a photograph of the 1172 charter for Zagost following p. 16; Rödel, p. 432.

[9] '*[a] clare memorie B., duce Cassubie, ac B. filio eius necnon successoribus*', Lateran, 19 March 1238: *CH*, 2, no. 2192; *Pomm. UB*, 1, no. 355. In 1229 Duke Barnim I confirmed donations to Stargard by his father Bogislaw II and grandfather Bogislaw I, extant as vidimus from 1262: *CH*, 2, no. 1936; *Pommerell. UB*, no. 42; *Pomm. UB*, 1, no. 257, 2, no. 724. Hoogeweg, pp. 870–2.

[10] '*clare memorie M. ac V., filius eius, duces Polonie*', Lateran, 23 March 1238: *CH*, 2, no. 2194. Szczesniak, pp. 26 ff.

it was first St Adalbert and then St James. So Schlawe was probably not given to the Hospitallers by the elder, but by the younger Ratibor when the church already existed, and the Hospitallers took over its patron saint. This must have occurred in the 1220s at the latest. In 1223 a princess of Schlawe was married to Count Henry of Schwerin who founded the Hospitaller house at Kraak. Perhaps the Hospitallers came to Schlawe from Saxony (Werben, Kraak) or Denmark (Andvorskov).[11] Schlawe is therefore probably the youngest of the three Hospitaller foundations in Pomerania.

Among the Pomeranian princes, the Griffins in the west maintained some independence from Poland in the twelfth century by paying homage to Henry the Lion of Saxony, to Frederick Barbarossa and then to the kings of Denmark, Canute VI and Waldemar II. This independence was reflected by ecclesiastical divisions. The Griffin bishopric, which was first established in 1140 at Wollin, then moved to the Premonstratensian convent of Grobe on Usedom and finally in 1175/6 to Kammin, was exempt from both Gnesen in Poland and Magdeburg in Germany, and subject only to the Holy See.[12] The Premonstratensians in the Griffin territory had an independent *circaria Slavia*, which bordered on the *circaria Polonia* to the south and *circaria Saxonia* to the west. Cistercians and Premonstratensians were called in not only from Germany or Poland, but also from Denmark.[13] In Central and Eastern Pomerania, Polish influence remained stronger during the twelfth century. Ecclesiastically, these regions belonged to the Polish bishopric of Leslau, and politically the Piast seniors were for a time able to prevent the native princes, the Samborids, from forming a hereditary duchy by relying on nobles like Grimislaw.

In the early thirteenth century the political situation as well as the social and ethnic structure of the Pomeranian regions changed. The Danish hegemony over the Baltic countries broke down following the battle of Bornhöved in 1227. Polish power broke down, too, when in 1227 the Piast senior, Leszek the White, was assassinated by the Samborid Swantopluk. In general, the Germans gained predominance over the Baltic countries, Lübeck with the *Hanse*, the Teutonic Knights in Prussia and the Swordbrothers in Livonia. The Ascanian margraves of Brandenburg[14] expanded towards the Baltic shores and towards the east,

---

[11] '*clare memorie Rateborius, princeps Pomeranie, ac Boleslaus filius eius*', Lateran, 16 March 1238: *CH*, 2, no. 2191; *Pomm. UB*, 1, no. 354.

[12] Petersohn, pp. 262–315; R. Benl, 'Gründung, Vorgeschichte und Frühzeit des pommerschen Bistums', *Baltische Studien*, new ser., 78 (1992), 7–16.

[13] N. Backmund, *Monasticon Praemonstratense, id est historia Circariarum atque Canoniarum candidi et canonici ordinis Praemonstratensis*, 1, 2nd edn (Straubing, 1983 [1st edn 1949]), pp. 323–31; B. Krings, 'Das Ordensrecht der Prämonstratenser vom späten 12. Jahrhundert bis zum Jahr 1227', *Analecta Praemonstratensia*, 69 (1993), 107–242.

[14] Especially John I (1220–66) and his brother Otto III (1220–67): J. Schultze, *Die Mark Brandenburg*, 1 (Berlin, 1961, repr. 1989), pp. 113–57; E. Schmidt, *Die Mark Brandenburg unter den Askaniern 1134–1320*, Mitteldeutsche Forschungen, 71 (Cologne and Vienna, 1973); recently H. Assing, 'Die Landesherrschaft der Askanier, Wittelsbacher und Luxemburger (Mitte des 12. bis Anfang des 15. Jahrhunderts)', in *Brandenburgische Geschichte*, ed. I. Materna and W. Ribbe (Berlin, 1995), pp. 85–168 (at pp. 94–8).

trying to subjugate the counts of Schwerin, the lords of Mecklenburg and the Pomeranian princes, the Griffins in the west and the Samborids in the east. All local rulers, whether of German or Slav origin, called on German nobles and peasants to found new villages, and German merchants and craftsmen to found new towns.[15]

The Hospitallers of Saxony readily adapted to this new situation. Their principal establishment at Werben now received estates in Slav lands – among them Kraak – to be colonized. The count of Schwerin donated the church at Eichsen and some villages around Sülstorf in the 1220s, later administered by a commander at Kraak. The *dominus Slavorum* Henry Borwin, the native prince of Mecklenburg, donated Mirow in the 1220s, soon itself the seat of a commander. At Kraak and Mirow noble brethren from Saxony and the mark of Brandenburg began to colonize the countryside in the same way as lay nobles colonized estates donated by local rulers.[16] Under the hegemony of the Danish king, *rex Danorum et Slavorum*, the region between the Elbe and the Oder had been called *Slavia* (*Wendland* in German); their towns formed the *Wendisches Quartier* of the *Hanse*. The term *Slavia* included the Griffin territory of Western Pomerania, since the Griffins were Danish vassals. As Danish hegemony broke down, they began to call themselves *dux Slavorum*, while the title *dux Pomeranorum* was reserved for the Samborids. The Hospitallers may have had the impression that Stargard on the Ihna was not actually in Pomerania at all but in *Slavia*, and this may have eased the transfer of their Western Pomeranian possessions from the eastern to the western priory.[17]

Another factor that may have eased this transfer was the administration of the two priories by one and the same person. This began with Fr. Clement in 1249. As *magnus preceptor* or Master for *Alamania*, Bohemia, Moravia and Poland, Fr. Clement and his successor Fr. Henry of Fürstenberg installed separate priors for Poland (Fr. Geldolf, from Lower Germany, mentioned 1251 and 1255) and for Bohemia (Fr. *Johannes*). But for the next seventy years the two priories of *Alamania* and Bohemia frequently, though not always, had the same brother as grand preceptor or as prior, while Poland sometimes had a different prior. Under Fr. Geldolf the Hospitallers in Stargard on the Ihna – properly part of the Eastern priory – may have begun to regard themselves as part of the western priory.[18]

---

[15] C. Higounet, *Die deutsche Ostsiedlung im Mittelalter*, tr. from French by M. Vasold (Berlin, 1986) with excellent bibliography.

[16] G.C.F. Lisch, 'Zur Geschichte der Johanniter-Ordens-Comthurei Mirow', *Jahrbücher des Vereins für Mecklenburgische Geschichte und Altertumskunde*, 2 (1837), 53 ff.

[17] G. Renn, *Die Bedeutung des Namens 'Pommern' und die Bezeichnungen für das heutige Pommern in der Geschichte*, Greifswalder Abhandlungen zur Geschichte des Mittelalters, 8 (Greifswald, 1937); R. Benl, 'Slawische Stammesnamen in pommerschen Urkunden und die Frage der pommerschen Reichszugehörigkeit', *Baltische Studien*, new ser., 72 (1986), 7–23. As early as 1238 Gregory IX called the Griffin prince *dux Cassubie* and reserved the term *Pomerania* for the eastern part of the country (see notes 8–9 above).

It was probably while Fr. Geldolf was prior of Poland that the *dux Slavorum*, the Griffin Barnim I (1220–78), founded a German town at Stargard on the Ihna. Later, this duke, his nobles and the abbot of Kolbaz occupied several Hospitaller possessions: the town of Stargard, the castle of Reetz and six villages. The Master of *Alamania* and his brethren complained to Clement IV. On the pope's command in 1269 Albert the Great, the famous Dominican scholar, who was frequently employed as papal judge delegate, excommuni- cated the duke, the abbot and thirty named nobles. When the duke imprisoned two Hospitallers, the priest Fr. *Petrus* and the deacon Fr. *Ludovicus*, both from Mirow, Albert put him and his supporters under interdict in 1271. The reasons for the conflict are hard to discern.[19] Barnim had quarrelled with the Ascanian margraves of Brandenburg; he had to pay heavy indemnities to them and to give fiefs to their vassals. He may have confiscated Hospitaller property to compensate himself for his losses; he could do so because the Hospitallers were not protected by the Ascanians. No Ascanian founded a Hospitaller house between 1160 (Werben) and 1298 (Nemerow); instead, the Ascanians promoted the Cistercians and Templars. In general their distant relations with the Ascanians may have made the Hospitallers more acceptable to the counts of Schwerin, the lords of Mecklenburg, the Griffins and the Samborids, who were habitual opponents of the margraves. In this particular case, however, Albert the Great could not give much help to the Hospitallers because the Ascanians did not support the Order.[20] The Hospitallers lost the castle of Reetz and most of the villages and kept only the parish at Stargard. As a consequence they moved the seat of the commandery to the countryside, to Copan and later to Zachan.[21]

In Eastern Pomerania the Samborid Swantopluk (d. 1266) and his son Mestwin II (d. 1294) were supported by the Hospitallers during family quarrels and duly rewarded them with landed estates for colonization. The Hospitallers already held the church at Liebschau when Mestwin II granted that village to the Hospital at Stargard on the Ferse in 1278. In 1288 the duke added the licence to hold a market. Since Mestwin II also ruled Schlawe, the Hospitaller

---

[18] Lists of priors: Wienand, pp. 652–5; Fr. Clement and Fr. Henry of Fürstenberg: *CH*, 2, nos 2493, 2505, 2547, 2568, 2611, 2713; their lieutenants Fr. Geldolf and Fr. Johannes: *CH*, 2, nos 2547, 2611, 2713. *The Times Atlas of the Crusades*, ed. J. Riley-Smith (London, 1991), p. 91 depicts the ephemeral priory of Poland.

[19] 1269: above, note 3; Cologne, 9 April 1271: *CH*, 3, no. 3420; *Pomm. UB*, 2, no. 914 (erroneously 16 April 1270); H. Frederichs, 'Herzog Barnim I. im Streit mit dem Johanniterorden', *Baltische Studien*, new ser., 36 (1934), 256–67. For the foundation of the town of Stargard see *Pomm. UB*, 1, no. 572 (date 1243, but certainly after 1248, perhaps 1253).

[20] D. Lucht, 'Die Außenpolitik Herzog Barnims I. von Pommern 1220–78', *Baltische Studien*, new ser., 51 (1965), 15–32.

[21] Hoogeweg, pp. 874 ff.; Copan from 1284, Zachan from 1295. Copan probably lay near Stargard and Zachan but the exact site is not known.

parish priest there was made subordinate to the noble commander of Stargard on the Ferse. In 1291 one Fr. John of Rochow (in the Mark of Brandenburg) was living at Liebschau; by 1312 he was commander of the Hospitaller possessions in Eastern Pomerania. In 1324 his successor as commander in Eastern Pomerania was Fr. Conrad of Dorstadt (in Saxony), who was commander at Schöneck. This was a town founded around 1320 by the Hospitallers on their estates.[22]

By the 1260s, then, the Hospitallers from Saxony and the Mark had taken over western Stargard (on the Ilna) and, by about 1290, eastern Stargard (on the Ferse) with Schlawe. Some thirty Hospitallers are mentioned in Pomerania from 1250 to 1340, but it is not always possible to decide whether they were Slav or German: a *frater Johannes* might be of any origin. Most priests may still have been Slavs. The leading persons, commanders such as Fr. John of Rochow, Fr. Conrad of Dorstadt, Fr. John of Bortfeld, were nobles from the Mark, Thuringia or Saxony.[23] In the long run, the Hospitallers had to reach arrangements with Brandenburg as the main regional power. In 1298 Fr. Ulrich Schwabe, commander of Brunswick and Gardow, founded the commandery of Nemerow in the Mark.[24] After 1312, when Clement V suppressed the Templars, six Templar commanderies – Tempelhof, Lietzen, Rörchen, Quartschen, Zielenzig and Tempelburg – were a welcome addition, although the Hospitallers struggled until the 1340s to secure them. From then onwards their preceptor general in Saxony, the Mark, *Slavia* and Pomerania controlled houses from the Weser to the Vistula.

The change in the regional divisions of the Hospitallers had no parallels with the Teutonic Knights, the Templars, the Hermits of St Augustine, the Carmelites or the Dominicans; the only similarity was with the Franciscans. The Teutonic Knights had no establishments at all in Pomerania, Poland, Silesia, Meißen or Brandenburg, while the Templars did not have as many commanderies as the Hospitallers and could administer them through one master for all central Europe.[25] The four provinces of the Dominicans, *Teutonia*, *Saxonia*, Bohemia, and *Polonia*, differed from the Hospitallers in the south, since Bohemia and *Polonia* were separate and since Austria belonged to *Teutonia*

---

[22] E. Waschinski, *Geschichte der Johanniterkomturei und Stadt Schöneck in Westpreußen* (Danzig, 1904), pp. 8–14.

[23] John of Rochow 1291 to 1313: above, note 4; Conrad of Dorstadt 1321 to 1334: *Pomm. UB*, 6: 1321–5 (Stettin, 1907, ND Aalen 1970), no. 3761, 7: 1326–30 (Stettin 1934/40, repr. Aalen 1958), nos 4156–59, *Preuß. UB*, 2, nos 330, 402, 820s; John of Bortfeld 1334 to 1335: *Preuß. UB*, 2, nos 818–21, 843, 870.

[24] Since Ulrich used his private money to buy the village, he was allowed to hold the new commandery for life: *CH*, 3, no. 4417. Pflugk-Harttung, *Anfänge*, pp. 78 ff.; G.C.F. Lisch, 'Geschichte der Johanniter-Comthureyen Nemerow und Gardow', *Jahrbücher des Vereins für Mecklenburgische Geschichte und Altertumskunde*, 9 (1844), 32 ff.

[25] For the Templars in Germany see M. Schüpferling, *Der Tempelherrnorden in Deutschland*, phil. diss. Fribourg (Bamberg, 1915); M.–L. Bulst-Thiele, *Sacrae Domus Militiae Templi Hierosolimitani*

(Upper Germany), although in the north their boundaries were similar, since all convents in Prussia and Eastern and Western Pomerania belonged to *Polonia*.[26]

The Franciscans allotted their houses in central Europe in 1230 to a south-western province along the Rhine and to a north-eastern province. Ten years later the huge north-eastern province was subdivided into three separate provinces, *Saxonia, Dacia* (Scandinavia) and Bohemia. In 1240 Bohemia with Austria, Moravia, Silesia, Poland, Eastern Pomerania and Prussia corresponded exactly to the Hospitaller priory of Bohemia with one exception: Stettin and its subordinate convents were considered as part of *Slavia* and belonged to *Saxonia*. After a first attempt in 1263, in 1272 the Franciscans transferred convents in Prussia (Thorn, Kulm), in Silesia (Breslau, Goldberg) and in Lusatia (Bautzen) from Bohemia to *Saxonia*; for, as they were settling in pre-dominantly German towns, the Franciscans had to consider the language of the people to whom they preached. In Upper Silesia the convents stayed with Bohemia, because there the towns were not exclusively German. But the changes had a political background, too. They affected the territories of the Teutonic Order, of the dukes of Lower Silesia except Glogau (which had its own duke and stayed with Bohemia) and of the margraves of Brandenburg (in Lusatia). At the same time and for merely political reasons the Franciscans temporarily allotted Cracow to Hungary and Moravia to Austria.[27] Obviously, the Franciscans and the Hospitallers acted in similar or parallel ways and the changes were determined by both the ethnic change through colonization and the political situation.

Political quarrels continued to affect the Hospitallers in Pomerania. When Mestwin II died in 1294, his inheritance was disputed between the margraves of Brandenburg and the dukes of Poland. Finally, in 1308–9, the Teutonic

---

Magistri: Untersuchungen zur Geschichte des Templerordens 1118/19–1314 (Göttingen, 1974), pp. 372–9; M. Starnawska, 'Notizie sulla composizione e sulla struttura dell'Ordine del Tempio in Polonia', in *I Templari: Mito e storia*, ed. G. Minnucci and F. Sardi (Sinalunga and Siena, 1989), pp. 143–51.

[26] P. v. Loë, *Statistisches über die Ordensprovinz Saxonia*, Quellen und Forschungen zur Geschichte des Dominikanerordens in Deutschland, 4 (Leipzig, 1910); J. Kłoczowski, *Dominikanie polscy na Śląsku w XIII–XIV wieku* (Lublin, 1956).

[27] C.C. Baran, *Sprawy narodowościowe u franciszkanów śląskich w XIII wieku*, Studia historico eccle-siastica, 9 (Warszawa, 1954); J.B. Freed, 'The Friars and the Delineation of State Boundaries in the Thirteenth Century', *Order and Innovation in the Middle Ages: Essays in Honor of Joseph A. Strayer*, ed. W.C. Jordan, B. McNab and T.F. Ruiz (Princeton, 1976), pp. 31–40, 425–8; J. Kłoczowski, 'Die Minderbrüder im Polen des Mittelalters', in *800 Jahre Franz von Assisi*, Katalog des Niederöster-reichischen Landesmuseums, new ser., 122 (1982), pp. 318–31, especially 322–4, emphasizes the factors other than the national quarrels. For a debate, see L. Teichmann, 'Die "polnische" Franziskanerprovinz in Schlesien im 13. Jahrhundert', *Archiv für schlesische Kirchengeschichte*, 42 (1984), 145–58; W. Irgang, 'Zur Frage der polnischen Franziskanerprovinz im 13. Jahrhundert', ibid., 43 (1985), 251–61; and L. Teichmann, 'Eine polnische Franziskanerprovinz in Schlesien im 13. Jahrhundert?', ibid., 45 (1987), 251–6.

Knights from Prussia occupied Danzig and the eastern parts of Mestwin's lands with Stargard on the Ferse, Liebschau and Schöneck, but left the western parts with Schlawe to a Brandenburg vassal. Brandenburg sold its rights in Schlawe to the Griffins who reassumed the title *dux Pomeranorum*. For the Hospitallers this meant that Schlawe was separated from Schöneck; as a consequence, the parish priest at Schlawe became a deputy of the commander at Zachan.[28]

The Hospitaller possessions on the Ferse remained in territory controlled by the Teutonic Order. The Hospitallers supported the Teutonic Order and the Bohemian king John of Luxembourg (1310–46) who claimed the throne of Poland. The Polish opposition rallied around the Piast Władysław Łokietek, who was crowned king of Poland at Cracow in 1320, while the Silesian and Mazovian princes became vassals of the Bohemian king. Władysław tried to secure the inheritance of Mestwin II against the Teutonic Order both by waging war and by appealing to the papal *Curia*. In this context Władysław and his supporter, the bishop of Leslau, confiscated the Hospitaller estates of Nemoiov, Scheblenz and Zagost. The Hospitallers retaliated by occupying property belonging to the bishop of Leslau in Eastern Pomerania; they also appealed to the pope. Hearings began in 1319, and in 1330 the parties agreed not to claim back the property confiscated or occupied.[29]

In general the transfer of the Pomeranian Hospitallers from one priory to another cannot be explained as merely the natural result of German colonization. That process affected all regions east of the Elbe and the Saale, yet only in Pomerania did it bring about a change of boundaries; it did not do so, for instance, in Silesia where the Hospitallers also colonized villages and administered parishes in German towns.[30] While the Franciscans changed their provincial boundaries in Silesia as well as in Pomerania, the Hospitallers did not do so, perhaps because the Bohemian prior controlled Silesia more closely than remote Pomerania. So far, no other instances are known of the Hospitallers changing the boundaries of their priories. Such attempts may have been made after the Sicilian Vespers, when the priory of Messina had difficulties in controlling mainland Calabria; or when the Aragonese conquered Sardinia in the fourteenth century.[31] For Pomerania, no ratification of the transfer from Bohemia to *Alamania* by senior officials of the Order is known, either in the

[28] Hoogeweg, pp. 869 ff., 881–4.

[29] Sources: *CD Mai. Polon.*, 2, no. 567; *Preuß. UB*, 2, nos 229, 287, 327, 346, 473; *Preuß. UB*, 3, 3 parts: 1335–41, ed. M. Hein (Königsberg, 1944 and Marburg, 1958/61, repr. Marburg, 1975), part 1, no. 138. I. Ziekursch, *Der Prozeß zwischen König Kasimir von Polen und dem Deutschen Orden im Jahre 1339* (Berlin, 1934); H. Chłopocka, *Procesy Polski z Zakonem Krzyżackim w XIV wieku* (Poznan, 1967); *idem*, 'Die Zeugenaussagen in den Prozessen Polens gegen den Deutschen Orden im 14. Jahrhundert', in *Der Deutschordensstaat Preußen in der polnischen Geschichtsschreibung der Gegenwart*, ed. U. Arnold and M. Biskup (Marburg, 1982), pp. 165–88; H. Boockmann, *Ostpreußen und Westpreußen*, Deutsche Geschichte im Osten Europas (Berlin, 1992), pp. 155–70.

[30] Szczesniak, pp. 16–20; Waldstein-Wartenberg, pp. 383–408.

thirteenth century or later. Nor did the senior officials of the Order protest against Władysław's confiscations in Poland at the Council of Constance – where the records of the quarrel between the Teutonic Knights and Poland were produced and the status of the Hospitaller commandery at Posen was discussed.[32] Pomerania was so remote from both the Bohemian priory and the Order's headquarters that local forces decided for themselves and managed to secure unobserved the transfer to the priory of *Alamania*. In a strict sense, the Hospitallers in Pomerania were not transferred, but transferred themselves from the eastern to the western priory. The central government failed to react against Władysław Łokietek, but it was precisely this lack of effective control that allowed the Hospitallers to adapt to and profit from the political, social, national and cultural changes in thirteenth-century Pomerania.

THE MAP

The map which follows (Figure 25.1) depicts houses, parishes and stations of the Hospitallers and the Templars that existed about 1300–20. Possessions that had been lost by that time or that had been moved to other places are shown as hollow symbols. Outside Pomerania the map is incomplete, since detailed studies would be necessary to differentiate between commanderies and other possessions. The names are usually given in English or German; Polish (P) or Czech (Cz) equivalents are: Bahn (P) Banie; Böhmisch Aicha (Cz) Český Dub; Breslau (P) Wrocław, (Cz) Vratislav; Brieg (P) Brzeg; Brünn (Cz) Brno; Czeikowitz (Cz) Čejkovice; Eger (Cz) Ohře; Eiwanowitz (Cz) Ivanovice; Elbe (Cz) Labe; Ferse (P) Wierzyca; Glatz (P) Kłodzko, (Cz) Kladsko; Glogau (P) Głogów; Gnesen (P) Gniezno; Goldberg (P) Złotoryja; Gröbnig (P) Grobniki; Groß-Tinz (P) Wielki Tyniec; Ihna (P) Ina; Jung-Bunzlau (Cz) Mladá Boleslav (two commanderies); Kaaden (Cz) Kadaň; Kammin (P) Kamień [Pomorski]; Klein Oels (P) Mała Oleśnica; Kolbatz (P) Kołbacz; Krakau (P) Kraków; Kremsier (Cz) Kroměříž; Lebus (P) Lubusz; Leobschütz (P) Głubczyce; Leslau (P) Włoclawek; Liebschau (P) Lubiszewo; Lietzen (P) Lesnica; Löwenberg (P) Lwówek; Lossen (P) Łosiów; Lukow (P) Łuków; Manetin (Cz) Manětín; March (Cz) Morava; Moldau (Cz) Vltava; (P) Nemoiov Schönwiese; Netze (P) Noteć; Oberkaunitz (Cz) Horní Kounice; Oder (P) and (Cz) Odra; Peilau (P) Piława; Posen (P) Poznań; Ploskowitz (Cz) Ploskovice; Prag (Cz) Praha; Quartschen (P) Chwarszczany; Reetz (P) Recz; Rörchen (P) Rurka;

---

[31] A. Luttrell, 'Gli ospedalieri e un progetto per la Sardegna 1370–1374', in *Società, istituzioni, spiritualità: Studi in onore di Cinzio Violante* (Spoleto, 1994), pp. 503–8. I am extremely grateful to Dr Luttrell for his comments on possible parallels.

[32] Confirmation of Posen by Master Fr. Philibert de Naillac, Constance, 3 September 1417: Malta, Cod. 340, fols 131v–134r (edition prepared by E. Schöffler and K. Borchardt in collaboration with A. Luttrell). For negotiations between the Teutonic Order and Poland–Lithuania at Constance see H. Boockmann, *Johannes Falkenberg, der Deutsche Orden und die polnische Politik* (Göttingen, 1975); *idem, Ostpreußen und Westpreußen*, pp. 170–200.

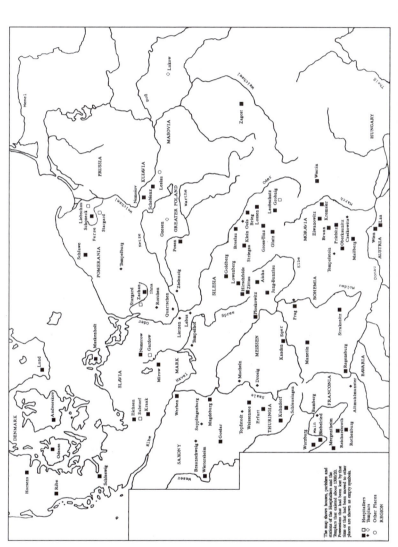

Figure 25.1   Houses, parishes and stations of the Hospitallers and Templars in Pomerania, Poland, Bohemia and northern Germany, c. 1300–20

Scheblenz (P) Zbląg; Schlawe (P) Sławno; Alt Schlawe (P) Sławsko; Schöneck (P) Skarszewy; Stargard (P) Stargard [Szczeciński]; [Preußisch] Stargard (P) Starogard; Strakonitz (Cz) Strakonice; Striegau (P) Strzegom; Tempelburg (P) Czaplinek; Tempelstein (Cz) Tempelštejn; Warthe (P) Warta; Weichsel (P) Wisła; Wien (Cz) Vídeň; Wollin (P) Wolin; Wsetin (Cz) Vsetín; Zachan (P) Suchań; Zagost (P) Zagość; Zielenzig (P) Sulęcin; Zittau (Cz) Žitava.

26

The Beginnings of the Military Orders in Frisia

Johannes A. Mol

The settlement and expansion of the military orders in Frisia are remarkable in at least three ways. In the first place the number of houses they came to possess in this region is striking. Of the eighty religious houses that were founded before 1350 in the Frisian territories along the Dutch and German North Sea coast no less than eighteen, nearly one in four, belonged either to the Order of St John or to the Teutonic Order.[1] That is quite a lot if one bears in mind that in the middle of the fourteenth century both Orders together possessed no more than twenty-five commanderies in the whole of the Netherlands. However, it has to be observed that not all these Frisian foundations of the military orders were rich and populous; most of them in fact were very modest or even poor.

Another particular aspect of these Frisian Hospitaller and Teutonic Orders' settlements is that they lacked the military element.[2] None of them housed any knight brethren. They were populated by small religious communities of priests or nuns, under the direction of a priest commander, mostly with a group of lay brothers attached to them for housekeeping and farm management. Their main task was to sing divine office and pray for the well-being of their benefactors. Some of the Frisian priest brethren were also active as parish ministers. If not for the cross on their habits, they were hardly distinguishable from Benedictines, Augustinian canons or Premonstratensians.

Related to their monastic character was the relative autonomy of these houses *vis-à-vis* the provincial superiors and central authorities of their

---

[1] See the surveys in J.A. Mol, *De Friese huizen van de Duitse Orde. Nes Steenkerk en Schoten en hun plaats in het middeleeuwse kloosterlandschap* (Leeuwarden, 1991), pp. 31–4; *Groninger kloosters*, ed. C. Tromp (Assen and Maastricht, 1989); and M. Smid, *Ostfriesische Kirchengeschichte* (Pewsum, 1974), pp. 87–114.

[2] Mol, *Friese huizen*, pp. 64–91.

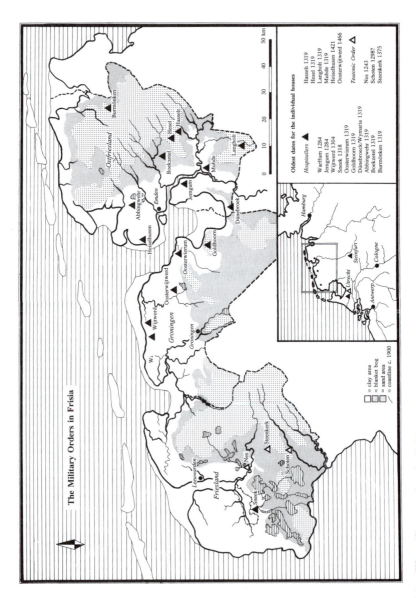

The Military Orders in Frisia

Oldest dates for the individual houses

Hospitallers	▲	Hasselt 1319
		Hesel 1319
Warffum 1284		Langholt 1319
Jemgum 1284		Muhde 1319
Wijtwerd 1304		Heiselhusen 1421
Sneek 1318		Oosterwijtwerd 1466
Oosterwierum 1319		
Goldhoorn 1319		*Teutonic Order* ◣
Dünebroeck/Wymaria 1319		
Abbingwehr 1319		Nes 1243
Boekzetel 1319		Schoten 1298?
Burmönken 1319		Steenkerk 1375

Figure 26.1   The military orders in Frisia

respective Orders. Wherever there was a real community, the male members
– including in some commanderies the *conversi* or lay brothers, which seem to
have had the status of sergeant brothers – elected their own commanders in
the fourteenth and fifteenth centuries. There is also evidence that they
themselves made decisions on the entry of new brothers and sisters. This was
the case for both the three houses of the Teutonic Order, which were under
the bailiwick of Utrecht, and the fifteen Hospitaller settlements. The latter did
not constitute a provincial circle on their own – as, for example, the Frisian Premonstratensian monasteries did – but were brought into two different districts
under the authority of provincial commanders outside Frisia: one of them, the
Hospital on the Mount of St John (*in Monte sancti Johannis*) in Sneek, in the
present-day Dutch province of Friesland, belonged to the circle of St
Katherine's convent in Utrecht; the other fourteen, situated in both the Dutch
province of Groningen and the German *Landschaft Ostfriesland*, were under the
commandery of Steinfurt near Münster, which was the central house in the later
bailiwick of Westphalia.

How can we explain the large number of these houses, their monastic
outlook and their autonomy, if not independence? Although we are hampered
by the scarcity of sources, it seems possible to come close to the answer by
taking a fresh look at the earliest data on the origins of the individual houses.
But first the region that is the focus of this paper should be sketched in a
few words.

Frisia in the high and late Middle Ages is best described as a sociocultural
entity, in the sense that people here had their own laws and language.[3] In the
political respect fragmentation is the key word, mainly because of the specific
geophysical structure of the Frisian lands. Settlement was originally limited to
the very long but narrow strip of fertile clay soils along the North Sea, which
ran from the northern part of Holland as far as the Danish border, intersected
by many tidal streams, river outlets and small estuaries. Since Roman times or
even before, people here had protected themselves against floods and storm
surges by artificially raising the height of their places of residence on so-called
terpen (mounds). There never developed a real centre of power that covered
the separate subregions. The Frankish conquest, which was realized in phases,
had the long-term effect of bringing the whole area into the hands of different
lords outside Frisia. This situation is reflected in the division of the various
Frisian lands over four dioceses: Utrecht, Osnabrück, Münster and Bremen.

In the twelfth and thirteenth centuries the possessors of comital rights,
among others the count of Holland and the bishops of Utrecht and Münster,
were impeded from extending and developing their jurisdictions into real
territorial dominions by the long distances involved. In consequence, no feu-

---

[3] B.H. Slicher van Bath, 'The economic and social conditions in the Frisian district from 900
to 1500', *A.A.G. Bijdragen*, 13 (1965), 97–133.

dalization took place, which in turn opened up the way for the small allodial nobility to organize a kind of semi-communal government in each region. The result was the development of a series of miniature republics, called *terrae* or 'lands', which were not subject to an overlord, except in theory to the German emperor. This situation was only altered in the course of the fifteenth century when the *terrae* came to be absorbed by the neighbouring territorial states.

We may now ask at what time the Hospitallers and Teutonic brethren made their first appearance into Frisia, and how we should envisage the coming into existence of their houses. A serious problem in doing so is that little has been preserved of their archives. For the Hospitaller houses nearly all thirteenth-century documents are missing. For the Teutonic Order the situation is less problematic, thanks to the preservation of some early charters from the commandery of Nes in the archives of the still-existent bailiwick of Utrecht.

These charters show us that the house of Nes already existed in 1243. In that year the brethren were given by the bishop of Utrecht the very important *ecclesia matrix* of Oldeboorn on the River Boorne.[4] The year 1243 is also the earliest *datum ante quem* for the foundation of any Frisian house of the military orders. The earliest reliable date for the existence of Frisian Hospitaller houses is 1284, the year in which the bishop of Münster sold some Frisian property he had bought from the Benedictine abbey of Werden to the commander of Steinfurt, for the benefit of his houses in Warffum and Jemgum.[5] This fact demonstrates that these two commanderies originally depended on the house of Steinfurt near Münster in Westphalia.

Schöningh, the first historian to study the settlements of the Hospitallers in *Ostfriesland*, concluded that the brethren of St John had by then already resided in the region for at least a decade.[6] He found an indication for this in a charter from 1276, issued to end a quarrel between the bishop of Münster and four united Frisian *terrae*, in which the commander of Steinfurt acted as an arbitrator, along with some Cistercian and Premonstratensian abbots.[7] The Steinfurt commander would never have been asked by one of the parties to mediate if he had not had some possessions in the regions concerned. Schöningh did not dare to date this involvement much earlier than about 1270. He related the appearance of the Hospitallers to the crusade of St Louis, in which many Frisians from the Groningen region and *Ostfriesland* participated, as we know from the chronicle of the Premonstratensian abbey of Wittewierum.[8]

---

[4] *Archieven der Ridderlijke Duitsche Orde, balie van Utrecht*, 2 vols, ed. J.J. de Geer tot Oudegein (Utrecht, 1871), no. 522.

[5] *Oorkondenboek van Groningen en Drenthe*, 2 vols, ed. P.J. Blok *et al.* (1896–9), no. 164.

[6] E. Schöningh, *Der Johannieterorden in Ostfriesland* (Aurich, 1973), pp. 10–12.

[7] *Oorkondenboek Groningen en Drenthe*, nos 147, 150, 151.

[8] *Kroniek van het klooster Bloemhof te Wittewierum*, ed. H.P.H. Jansen and A. Janse (Hilversum, 1991), pp. 422–40.

1270, however, remains a relatively late date: late when we realize that the property of the richest and oldest Hospitaller houses in Groningen and *Ostfriesland* – Warffum, Wijtwerd and Jemgum – nearly came to equal that of the youngest Benedictine, Cistercian and Premonstratensian houses which had been founded in the first decades of the thirteenth century.[9] 1270 is a late date, too, when we consider that the Teutonic Order, which in the end was not as successful in expanding as the Order of St John, had already founded a house in West Friesland before 1243.

The development of the Hospitaller house of Sneek, near the Teutonic house of Nes, gives us another reason to assume a much earlier arrival of the brethren of St John in the Frisian lands. The Hospital of Sneek is mentioned for the first time in a charter as late as 1318, but it must have existed for quite a few decades by then.[10] Retrospective research into the extent and location of its landed property shows that the core complex consisted of the glebe of the tenth-century St Martin's church of Sneek, which was originally an *Eigenkirche* (proprietary church) of the bishop of Utrecht. That makes us strongly inclined to think that the bishop was involved in the early patronage, if not in the foundation, of the house, in the same way as he was with Nes in 1243. He alone could have made possible the incorporation of the parish church into the house of the Hospitallers. Because the church of Sneek was older, richer and more important than the Oldeboorn church, we may even assume that its donation was made at an earlier stage than the gift of the latter to Nes. In the end the Hospital house of Sneek certainly owned more property than Nes, accounted for more brethren and had more parishes to care for, which all in all does presuppose an earlier start.

Against this background it seems worthwhile to take a fresh look at the available Hospitaller sources, in search of evidence of earlier relations between Steinfurt and the Frisian part of the Münster diocese. Luckily, I recently found such an indication on the seal of a certain Brother Henry of Steinfurt. This seal is attached to a charter from 1240, issued for the benefit of the commandery of St John in Arnhem.[11] In the text Henry is called 'prior of the Hospital of St John in the diocese of Utrecht' (*'prior hospitalis beati Iohannis per dyocesam Traiectinam'*). The title and office are unknown to us but they were obviously only created for the occasion, because the seal gives a different title. It is the 'SIGILLVM of H [for Henricus] PRIORIS STEVERDIE ET [and there is apparently a letter missing] RISIE.' So Steinfurt is not to be taken as the place of Brother Henry's origin but as the name of the house he governed

[9] J.A. Mol, 'Aduard 1192–1594', in *Geschiedenis van Aduard, Den Ham en Den Horn*, ed. J. Arkema *et al.* (Bedum, 1992), pp. 19–36 (at p. 19).

[10] J.A. Mol, 'De Johanniters fan Snits: nammen, komôf en karrières', *Fryske Nammen*, 10 (1996), 117–54.

[11] *Corpus sigillorum Neerlandicorum*, 2 vols, ed. H. Brugmans and K. Heeringa (The Hague, 1937–40), no. 375.

as a prior. But what is more important, the uncomplete name 'RISIE' can only be 'FRISIE', with an 'F' for the missing character. In other words, in 1240 Steinfurt already had so much property in the Frisian part of the Münster diocese that it was necessary to have it named separately when defining the office of its prior.

This also brings the *datum ante quem* for the arrival of the Hospitallers in the Groningen and *Ostfriesland* areas of medieval Frisia back to the beginning of the 1240s. Combine this with the data already given for Nes and Sneek and the conclusion is that in the decade(s) before 1240 benefactors in at least two separate Frisian regions sought contact independently of each other with three different provincial centres of the military orders outside Frisia. This in turn leads to the presumption that these people must have become simultaneously acquainted with the work of these Orders. One does not need a lot of imagination to assume that this happened during a crusade.

But which crusade? Frisians have been reported as participating in nearly all the crusades, from the first to the last.[12] They fought as *milites Christi* in the Holy Land, near Lisbon, in Lithuania and even in their own backyard against the so-called heretic Stedingers and Drents rebels. However, it is not necessary to ponder for long over the crusade in question here. The first crusade in which Frisians from the whole coastal area took part *en masse*, sailing towards the East in more than 200 ships, was the fifth, which brought the Christian fighters to Damietta in the years 1217–21.[13] The Frisian contribution is recorded in many contemporaneous chronicles and has left an indelible impression in later Frisian historiography. The Fifth Crusade was also the only one in which the Teutonic Order, along with the Order of St John, played a major role in organization and actual warfare. The massive Frisian interest was to a great extent the work of the papal envoy Oliver of Cologne who, in the years 1214–15, preached the Cross all over Frisia, supported by the abbots of all newly founded monasteries.[14]

It can safely be assumed that a number of Frisian crusaders made a donation to the above-mentioned military orders during or shortly after the campaign; donations which some time before 1240 resulted in the foundation of separate houses. The earliest of these houses were founded in the prosperous and long-occupied clay regions. Along with the already named houses of Nes and Sneek in West Friesland, we count among them the commanderies of Warffum, Wijtwerd and Oosterwierum in Groningen, and of Jemgum in *Ostfriesland*.

After the crusade in Egypt, in 1224, Oliver of Cologne appeared once more in Frisia to rouse enthusiasm for the next crusade, with as much success as

---

[12] H. Brassat, *Die Teilnahme der Friesen an den Kreuzzügen ultra mare* (Berlin, 1970).

[13] J.M. Powell, *Anatomy of a Crusade, 1213–1221* (Philadelphia, 1986), pp. 61, 75, 109; *Kroniek Wittewierum*, pp. 58–82.

[14] J.M. van Moolenbroek, 'Signs in the Heavens in Groningen and Friesland in 1214: Oliver of Cologne and Crusading Propaganda', *Journal of Medieval History*, 13 (1987), 251–72.

before. It seems, however, that in the end the Frisian fleet did not depart, as no mention is made of further Frisian participation in the crusade of Frederick II. It is not impossible that the military orders in the region profited from the untimely end of the Frisian expedition by taking in donations for the redeeming of crusading vows.

There is an indication in that direction, albeit rather vague. The reliable chronicle of Wittewierum informs us of the violent death of the nobleman Eltetus of Middelstum, who had taken the Cross at that time and was accompanying Master Oliver on his tour through the Groningen area.[15] This Eltetus is honoured by the Ewsum family of Middelstum as their progenitor. Strikingly, the Ewsum family in the fifteenth century not only claimed to have founded the Hospitaller house of Wijtwerd – which claim was supported by a forged charter – but it actually controlled the election and appointment of the *commendator in loco*.[16] Possibly this patronage was the result of an exaggerated reminiscence of the crusade donations of their ancestor, the *miles Christianus* Eltetus.

In the case of the Hospitallers, foundation in the third or fourth decade of the thirteenth century meant that the patrons or benefactors had to seek a connection with existing houses in their dioceses. The brethren of St John already had a foothold in both the Utrecht and Münster dioceses at that time. The commandery of Steinfurt, dedicated to St George, was founded around 1190.[17] The foundation date of the Utrecht convent of St Katherine is not known exactly, but there is every reason to believe that it was already in existence before the end of the twelfth century.[18] That was not the case with the later centre of the bailiwick of the Teutonic Order of Utrecht, the commandery of St Mary in the city of Utrecht. This house came into being as late as 1231. If its later Frisian daughter house of Nes was founded earlier – which is not impossible – then it must have had an early connection with the mother house of the Utrecht convent, Aldenbiesen in Belgium, between Hasselt and Maastricht.

In all three cases a relationship of dependency was created, which in the course of time did not appear to be a very close one. From the few fourteenth-century documents on the Frisian houses of the military orders, we know that they all, independently of one another, came to enjoy the same, relatively free form of autonomy. This autonomy was not automatically granted. It had to be

---

[15] *Kroniek Wittewierum*, pp. 164–8.

[16] G.F. Noordhuis, *De Johannieters in Stad en Lande. Geschiedenis van de Johannieters in de provincie Groningen (13de–17de eeuw)* (Warffum, 1990), pp. 35–41; M. Hartgerink-Koomans, *Het geslacht Ewsum* (Groningen and Batavia, 1938) pp. 38–40.

[17] B. Regelmeier, *Die Johanniterkommende zu Steinfurt* (Münster, 1912), p. 310.

[18] J.M. van Winter, 'De heren van Sint-Catharijne te Utrecht', in *Bewogen en bewegen*, ed. W. Frijhoff and M. Hienstra (Tilburg, 1986), pp. 349–64; Mol, 'Johanniters Snits', 127.

won by the Frisian brethren from their superiors in hard bargains; which is why these documents were produced and preserved.

To get an idea of the way in which this extraordinary development could take place it seems useful to take a close look at one of these charters. The one that is chosen here is a charter of compromise of 8 September 1319 by which the quarrels over their reciprocal rights and duties between the *commendator* of Steinfurt and the commanders and convents of twenty Hospitaller houses in Groningen and *Ostfriesland*, cited by name, were ended[19] The case can also easily be illustrated by some articles of similar documents for Sneek/Utrecht and Nes/Utrecht from 1320 and 1350,[20] but the Steinfurt charter of compromise is older and gives more details. The charter contains a judgment pronounced by three ecclesiastical and two lay authorities. Their first five clauses are formulated as follows:

(1) Primo, quod quilibet commendatorum domorum et conventuum predictorum renun-ciaverunt omnibus actionibus, literis papalibus et instrumentis aliis obtentis, quibus utrobique, quilibet per se vel coniunctim, causam suam possent aliquo modo promovere et defendere contra alium, vel alios, hinc et inde.

(2) Deinde commendatores Frisie domorum sancti Johannis predicti, cessantibus aliquomodis exactionibus personarum, de novo ab eisdem recipiendarum, et equorum decedentium commendatorum domorum sancti Johannis ibidem, quadraginta quattuor marcas sterlingorum [...] dabunt in subsidium in elemosinam Terre Sancte, annis singulis, magistro seu commendatori Stenfordie seu conventui ibidem [...]

(3) Item magister sive commendator domus Stenfordie relinquet electionem novi com-mendatoris fratribus domorum sancti Iohannis per Frisiam, de maiore parte fratrum canonice faciendam, et per ipsum magistrum Stenfordie postmodum confirmandam.

(4) Item si super electione commendatoris nequiverint concordare, magister Stenfordie, cum maiori et saniori parte fratrum, electionem celebret, prout ipsis et conventui videbitur salubrius expedire.

(5) Item si quis commendatorum domorum Frisie predictarum inutilis fuerit, conventu conquerente, probata eius negligentia, de consilio magistri Stenfordie [...] et voluntate sanioris partis conventus, commendator alius assumetur.

([1] First, that each of the commanders of the aforesaid houses and convents renounced all actions, papal letters and other legal instruments which they have obtained, by which they each could, singly or together, prosecute or defend their case against another or others on either side.

[2] Next, all exactions from persons newly admitted by the commanders of the houses of St John aforesaid in Frisia and from the horses of the departing commanders of the houses of St John there will cease ... and the commanders of the houses of St John in Frisia will give each year to the master or commander of Steinfurt or the convent there forty-four marks sterling in support of alms for the Holy Land. ...

---

[19] *Oorkondenboek Groningen en Drenthe*, no. 264.

[20] Mol, *Friese huizen*, pp. 97–8, 105–6.

[3] Again, the master or commander of the house of Steinfurt will surrender to the brothers of the houses of St John throughout Frisia the [right to control the] election of the new commander. The election should be carried out canonically by the greater part of the brothers, and afterwards confirmed by the master of Steinfurt himself.

[4] Again, if they cannot agree over the election of the commander, the master of Steinfurt, with the greater and more sensible part of the brothers, will make the election as seems most suitable and expedient for them and the convent.

[5] Again, if any of the commanders of the aforesaid houses of Frisia should prove to be useless, on the complaint of the convent, if his negligence is proven, another commander will be appointed with the advice of the most sensible part of the convent.)

The first two articles show clearly that the Steinfurt commander had until then claimed and collected the entrance fees of all new members of the Order in Frisia, entirely against the wishes of his subordinate commanders and brethren there. Furthermore it can be deduced that he also had reserved for himself the appointment of Frisian commanders. This may not surprise students of Hospitaller statutes, which allow the Master and his delegates all rights to appoint whomever they want, without giving brethren at the lowest level a say in these matters. But obviously in Frisia there was a gap between theory and practice. As seen from the first clause, the Frisian brethren had appealed to lay courts in their own region, to the bishop and to the pope, and in the end apparently had the Steinfurt commander exactly where they wanted him. Provided the Frisians paid him forty marks yearly as their *responsio*, he promised not to collect any more entrance fees. In my opinion, this does not mean that new members of the Order did not have to pay such fees. It was now up to the Frisian brethren to collect them, and thus to determine who was to be admitted to their houses and Order.

Very important also is the third clause, in which the Steinfurt commander is judged to leave the right to elect new commanders in Frisia to the Frisian brethren, that is to the *maior pars* or the elder and most experienced among them. The text may lead some readers here to the conclusion that because of the use of the singular form *commendator*, the election in question concerns just one person for all houses.[21] In that case the commander would have been a sort of regional officer to overlook and represent all Frisian houses. This is very unlikely, however. In the first place it is hard to imagine how such an election could have been organized practically, because it required the involvement of the brethren from twenty different remote houses and granges. In the second place – and this is more convincing – it is stated in the following clause that if any of the Frisian commanders proves to be ineffective in his management,

---

[21] A. Luttrell, 'The Hospitaller Province of Alamania to 1428', in *Ritterorden und Region – politische, soziale und wirtschaftliche Verbindungen im Mittelalter*, ed. Z.H. Nowak, Ordines militares, Colloquia Torunensia Historica, 8 (Torun, 1995), pp. 21–42 (at pp. 32–3).

the commander of Steinfurt has the right to intervene in the appointment of a new one. Here the plural *commendatores* is used. As this clause complements the foregoing, we cannot but conclude that the use of the singular in the latter relates to the election of the commander in each individual house in Frisia. And, last but not least, there are striking parallels for the Hospitallers of Sneek *vis-à-vis* their superior in Utrecht, and for the Teutonic brethren of Nes *vis-à-vis* their provincial commander, also in Utrecht. They too succeeded in obtaining the right to elect their own commander and decide on the admission of new brothers and sisters to their houses.

The cession of these rights opened the way for a unique form of autonomy – unique, at least for the military orders – which, given that the oldest houses were not founded before the third and fourth decades of the thirteenth century, does not appear to have had its origin in privileges of an earlier date.[22] We must seek another explanation. In doing so, it must be stressed that what all Frisian commanderies had in common, along with being populated by Frisians of course, was that they did not have knight brethren as members of their communities. I have simply never encountered a Frisian knight brother in the documents. Most of these commanderies housed small communities of chaplains and lay brothers. Some of them were nunneries. The available documents reveal that most of them started as double convents or at least as houses with a mixed population, which differed hardly at all from the religious houses of the Benedictines, the Augustine canons, the Premonstratensians and even the Cistercians. Like these, the rich ones developed either into real nunneries or convents of sisters with a small staff of priests and lay brothers, or into monasteries with a male population in which most brethren were active as pastors in incorporated parishes. The poor Hospitaller houses in the East Frisian heath and moor areas lost their communities in the course of time and ended up as granges with only one or two brethren as administrators.

It is striking that the West Frisian houses of both Orders lost their female populations, while nearly all large Groningen and East Frisian commanderies developed into nunneries. The cause has to be sought in the different ways in which the bishops of Utrecht and Münster patronized their Frisian religious houses in general. The bishop of Utrecht gave them churches, while his colleague in Münster limited his benefactions to the donation of land. In consequence, the West Frisian commanderies had to specialize in pastoral work, the East Frisian in singing divine office. In both cases we are looking at monastic or canonical settlements, rather than centres for recruitment and collecting money for the Holy Land. Monastic communities always tend to stress their autonomy, not least because they have to keep to the *stabilitas loci*. It is therefore very possible that the efforts of the Frisian Hospitallers and Teutonic brethren to reach a sort of self-government were strongly encouraged

---

[22] Mol, *Friese huizen*, pp. 91, 107–8.

by the example of the neighbouring monasteries and convents, which were nearly identical in function and outlook. With this conclusion, the problem shifts to the question of why the Frisians did not have or did not want to have knight brethren in their houses. The answer must be sought in the peculiar political structures that developed in the thirteenth century in this region.[23] As this is a theme in itself, this development can only be described here briefly. The thirteenth-century chronicles lead to no other conclusion than that there was by that time an allodial, self-styled noble elite in Frisia, from which knight brethren could have been recruited. The example of the aforementioned *miles Christianus* Eltetus makes it clear that people recognized and appreciated the idea of secular knighthood in service of the Church. Knighthood in the service of a lord, the worldly counterpart, however, was an unknown phenomenon. It probably could have been developed if some count had succeeded in establishing a territorial government. The count of Holland, for example, twice had the chance of reaching that distance but he lost both his battles against the united Frisians, who did not want to meet his conditions. In consequence, no feudalization took place, with the result that the Frisian elite had little understanding of the knightly ideal of serving a lord. Knighthood and territorial lordship were closely connected with each other. As most of them did not want the latter, the Frisian noblemen were not enthusiastic towards the knighthood of the military orders. They preferred to see them as monastic or hospital orders whose houses they could easily control at home.

---

[23] On this theme, see O. Vries, *Het Heilige Roomse Rijk en de Friese vrijheid* (Leeuwarden, 1986), pp. 14–31.

27

Alfonso X and the Teutonic Order: an Example of the Role of the International Military Orders in Mid Thirteenth-Century Castile

José Manuel Rodríguez García

Among the Salazar collection of papers in the Biblioteca de la Real Academia de la Historia, Madrid, is a letter from the Teutonic Order addressed to King Alfonso X of Castile.[1] It is a plea for assistance which describes Louis IX's first crusade to the Levant (1248–54) and the pitiful situation of the forces that remained in the East after his departure, with particular reference to the disastrous condition of the German Order. According to Salazar, the document is a fifteenth-century copy of a thirteenth-century original. Quite apart from its interest for the study of Louis's crusade, the letter is most useful for broadening our understanding of the relationship between the Castilian king and the Teutonic Order. I will take this relationship as a starting point for comparing the roles of the international military orders in mid thirteenth-century Castile.

Although the letter is undated, I have argued in a previous study that it was written by *frater Petrus*, the marshal of the Order in the Holy Land, before the end of May 1254, soon after Louis IX left the Holy Land (24 April).[2]

ALFONSO X AND THE TEUTONIC ORDER: ALFONSO AS GERMAN PRINCE

The letter contains three references to Alfonso X as a German prince. First, it speaks of the German origin of the Order and identifies Alfonso with the

---

[1] Madrid, Biblioteca de la Real Academia de la Historia: Colección Salazar, G 49, fol. 453, Sig. 9/946. Index number 33005: 'Carta de la Orden Teutónica a Alfonso X. (no place, no date)'.

[2] Lines 50–1. J.M. Rodríguez García and A. Echevarría Arsuaga, 'Alfonso X, la Orden Teutónica y Tierra Santa. Una nueva fuente para su estudio', in *Las Ordenes Militares en la Península Ibérica*, ed. R. Izquierdo Benito (Ciudad Real, 6–9 May 1996, forthcoming). This study contains a transcription of the full text of the letter, to which all the line numbers refer.

German nation (lines 3–4). Secondly, at lines 39–43, we have another appeal to a natural link to the Castilian king's ancestors as founders of the Order. The third reference, which again points out the important role of Alfonso's forefathers as protectors of the Order, appears in lines 46–8. So, we can see that Alfonso is repeatedly mentioned as a descendant of those German princes who helped to establish and protect the Order. It should be remembered that he was the son of Beatrice of Swabia, a daughter of Duke Philip of Swabia.[3] This acknowledgement of the Castilian king as a German prince, which can only be explained through his claim to the title of duke of Swabia, anticipates by almost a year Pope Alexander IV's support for Alfonso's claims to the duchy.[4] While it is true that, within the framework of the struggle against the German emperor, Frederick II, the papacy had already given its backing to the Castilian claims by 1246,[5] it is also true that this apparent endorsement lapsed after the emperor's death. It would seem, therefore, that the Teutonic Order's support for Alfonso preceded and was more long-lasting than papal support.

The first and main possession of the Order in Castile was the commandery of Sta María de los Caballeros, or de la Mota de Toro, given by the new queen, Lady Beatrice, in 1222.[6] Later, in 1231, Fernando III gave the lordship of Higares to the Teutonic Order.[7] From these bases the Teutonic Knights participated actively in Fernando III's campaigns in Andalucía, where they were granted properties and privileges in Córdoba, Jaén, Carmona and Seville in return for their services.[8] Nothing else is known about the presence of the Order in the thirteenth century except the fact that for a long time the commanders of the Order in Spain were Germans (in 1255 we find a *commendatori domus Theutonicorum in Hispania*, Eberhard of Morsberg, and from 1270 to 1288 Volmar of Bernhausen was *Provinciale Hispaniae*). Alemparte could add only one point relating to Alfonso X's reign: in 1258 he confirmed the original donation of the commandery of Sta María de los Caballeros to the Teutonic Order.[9] Is this confirmation connected with the 1254 plea for aid?

---

[3] A. Ballesteros-Beretta, *Alfonso X, el Sabio* (Barcelona, 1966); K. Forstreuter, *Der Deutsche Orden am Mittelmeer*, QuStDO, 2 (Bonn, 1967); U. Arnold, 'Eight Hundred Years of the Teutonic Order' in *MO*, 1, pp. 236–44.

[4] *La Documentación Pontificia de Alejandro IV, 1254–1256*, ed. I. Rodríguez de Lama (Rome, 1976), no. 23 (Lyons, 4 February 1255).

[5] M. Burriel, *Memorias para la vida del santo rey Don Fernando III* (Madrid, 1800), p. 488 (Innocent IV: Lyons, 3 May 1246).

[6] J. Ferreiro Alemparte, 'Asentamiento y extinción de la Orden Teutónica en España', *Boletín de la Real Academia de la Historia*, 168 (1971), 227–74.

[7] Sto Domingo de Silos, 20 September 1231: Duque de Alba, 'Documentos sobre propiedades de la Orden de los Caballeros Teutones en España', *Boletín de la Real Academia de la Historia*, 122 (1948), 17–21; Burriel, p. 393.

[8] M. Nieto Cumplido, *Corpus Medievale Cordubense*, 1 (Córdoba, 1980), pp. 8–32; J. González, *Libro del Repartimiento de Sevilla* (Seville, 1954); A. Sancho and F. Collantes, *Colección diplomática de Carmona* (Seville, 1966); Ferreiro Alemparte, p. 254.

[9] Ferreiro Alemparte, p. 248.

It is my belief that the confirmation must be linked to events after the spring of 1256, and not to the 1254 letter. Once the Pisans had offered Alfonso the imperial throne in April 1256, he pursued a clear European policy designed to achieve that aim. It was then logical for Alfonso to try to win as many German allies as possible to strengthen his candidature. Christiansen goes beyond the historical evidence when he connects the introduction of the Order into the Tajo area (1231) and Andalucía (1248) to Alfonso's imperial claims, which only dated from 1256.[10] Alfonso seems to have obtained the Order's support for his imperial claim, and even at the imperial election of 1273 the Teutonic Master or one of his commanders seems to have been present, although it is not clear whom he supported on that occasion.[11] It is also possible to go further and establish some kind of relationship between the creation of the Castilian military order of Sta María and the Teutonic Order, as the pope seemed to do in 1272.[12]

IMAGE AND CRITICISM OF THE MILITARY ORDERS

It seems clear from the letter that the Teutonic Order was well aware of its role and image as defender of the Holy Land and Christendom, as well as of its charitable role, especially in relation to the Germans: '... our Order, as light and mirror to the Christians, has been existing in the Kingdom of Jerusalem until the present ...' (lines 31–3); and near the end of the document: '... because we have suffered so much for the defence of the Christian faith and the extermination of the pagans, our Order, which exists in the Holy Land for the special care of the poor and as the Teutons' only home, is now under destruction ...' (lines 42–4). Nevertheless, the Order was also aware of the increasing criticism against the military orders in general,[13] including criticism of their wealth and its misuse. Other criticisms were directed specifically against the Teutonic Order, in particular at its excessive interest in the Germans and at its role as an instrument of imperial policy. Accordingly it was in the Order's interest to stress that: '... we spent much in obedience to him [Louis IX], so much so that our expenses exceeded our resources. We did this that we might serve him, and God, with the greatest dignity, in order that no one could blame us falsely, saying that we would have served him better if he had been of our tongue or if we had had possessions and convents within his dominion' (lines 7–10).

---

[10] E. Christiansen, *The Northern Crusades* (London, 1980), p. 76.

[11] Ballesteros-Beretta, p. 703.

[12] *Les Registres de Grégoire X (1272–76)*, ed. J. Guiraud and L. Cadier (Paris, 1898), no. 200 (Orvieto, 23 October 1272); Rodríguez García and Echevarría Arsuaga, in Izquierdo Benito; A. Rodríguez de la Peña, 'Las Ordenes Militares como instrumento de la corona. Una panorámica europea, s. XIII', in Izquierdo Benito.

[13] A. Forey, *The Military Orders from the Twelfth to the Early Fourteenth Centuries* (London, 1992), pp. 204–20; H. Nicholson, *Templars, Hospitallers and Teutonic knights: Images of the Military Orders, 1128–1291* (Leicester, 1993).

Nevertheless, it is possible to see throughout the text an element of resentment against Louis IX, both for not having fulfilled his promised rewards in the crusade (lines 6–7, 12–13, 23–4) and for leaving the Order in such a pitiful situation without enough resources – both material and human – to defend themselves and the Holy Land (lines 50–1). In facing the economic strains, the Order could point to the enormous expenses which it had borne in fulfilling its mission: '... in his business [Louis IX's crusade] we spent more than we had, for the honour of our Order, so that it should not appear that we gave up our dignity ...' (lines 26–9).

We cannot find any serious reason for criticism of the international military orders in Castile in the mid-thirteenth century. There were the inevitable tensions which arose from problems with the Church, with the nobles and even with the other Orders over territorial jurisdiction and rights which resulted in papal letters protecting the Orders' properties and members. The military orders – and their members – were, however, highly appreciated. Two examples of this can be seen in Alfonso's *Cantigas* and in the crusade song *Ay, Jerusalem!*: the former spoke of being a member of a military order as the highest post which a cleric could achieve;[14] the latter praised the work of the military orders as defenders of the Holy Land, while asking for help against the Moors.[15] Appreciation of the international military orders can also be seen in the wills of some noblemen who gave weapons and horses to the Hospital or the Temple, normally intended for use in the Holy Land.[16] Despite his poor relationship with the Hospitallers in Castile after 1278, Alfonso X bequeathed his bed, bedding and robes together with 1,000 silver marks to the 'poor of the Hospital of St John in Acre' in his will.[17] Of course, such things did not entail royal submission to the international military orders and their work in the Levant, as none of the Castilian kings would allow their resources to be diverted from the Reconquest; nor would they renounce their policy of putting the Orders under royal control – and Alfonso was no exception.

Alfonso, following Fernando III's practice, had the Masters of the military orders, both national and international, among the members of his privy council. We can find these men attending all the royal assemblies that took place in Castile at the time. They also frequently appeared confirming royal letters and privileges, but more often it was the Masters of the Spanish Orders rather than the international ones who did so. Members of the Orders were also sent on various embassies.[18] We must also take into account that the reign of

---

[14] *Cantigas profanas*, ed. J. Paredes Nuñez (Granada, 1988).

[15] Between 1254 and 1274. *Poesía Española*, 1: *Edad Media: Juglaría, Clerecía y Romancero*, ed. F. Gómez Redondo (Barcelona, 1996).

[16] C. Barquero Goñi, 'Los Hospitalarios en Castilla y León (Siglos XII y XIII). Señoríos de la Orden de San Juan', PhD thesis (Univ. Autónoma de Madrid, 1995), pp. 876–90.

[17] M. González Jiménez, *Diplomatario Andaluz de Alfonso X el Sabio* (Seville, 1991), no. 521 (1283).

[18] *Crónica de Alfonso X*, ed. C. Rosell, Biblioteca de Autores Españoles, 66 (Madrid, 1953 repr.), X–XVI (pp. 8–13); *Memorial Histórico Español*, 1 (Madrid, 1898), p. 231.

Alfonso X coincides with a period (the 1260s and 1270s) when the Masters of the various Orders were distancing themselves from the other brothers of their Orders and becoming very important landlords in their own right. In all the Orders the position of Master was becoming the object of ambition for the highest Castilian nobility and even the royal family – something which made it more in the king's interests to maintain his control over all these people.[19]

THE ROLE OF THE INTERNATIONAL MILITARY ORDERS

The letter under consideration offers us clear examples of the roles of the Orders both in the Levant and in the West. There is no need to stress the fundamental martial and charitable role that the international military orders played in the Holy Land, but these two roles were also transferred to two European fronts: the Baltic area and the Iberian Peninsula. We know that all the Spanish military orders, as well as the Orders of St John and St Lazarus, had hospitals in the Iberian Peninsula which were used for two purposes: the care of the poor and wounded, and redemption of Christian prisoners in Muslim hands.[20] Even the Templars, with their commanderies along the road to Santiago, seem to have played some kind of charitable role.[21] It is difficult to establish whether the Teutonic Order had a proper hospital or not. Its commandery in Castile, Sta María de los Caballeros, had a great house and a convent with a church. Its position, very close to the road to Santiago, and the fact that the grant of the commandery was made by Beatrice of Swabia, who was familiar with the practices of the Order, lead us to believe that they did develop a charitable role in the area.[22]

The martial role of the international military orders in the Peninsula is still under discussion. Latest research stresses the idea of their active participation in the Reconquest.[23] There is no general study for Castile, and we do not have any discussion of quantitative matters such as the exact numbers of knights

[19] C. de Ayala Martínez, 'Maestre y Maestrazgos en la Corona de Castilla, s. XII–XV', in Izquierdo Benito.

[20] J.W. Brodman, *L'Orde de la Mercé* (Barcelona, 1990); A. Forey, 'The Military Orders and the Ransoming of Captives from Islam', *Studia Monastica*, 33 (1992), 259–79; C. de Ayala Martínez, 'Ordenes Militares Hispánicas: reglas y expansión geográfica' (forthcoming).

[21] J.V. Matellanes Merchán and E. Rodríguez-Picavea Matilla, 'Las Ordenes Militares en las etapas castellanas del camino de Santiago' in *El Camino de Santiago, la hospitalidad monástica y las peregrinaciones*, ed. H. Santiago-Otero (Salamanca, 1992), pp. 346–63.

[22] Tomás López, 'Atlas Geográfico de los reinos de España', Biblioteca Nacional de Madrid, MS 7310, caja 11, pp. 145–50.

[23] For: M. Ledesma Rubio, *Templarios y Hospitalarios en el Reino de Aragón* (Zaragoza, 1982); M. Bonet Donato, *La Orden del Hospital en la Corona de Aragón. La castellanía de Amposta* (Madrid, 1994); and Barquero Goñi, pp. 879–88. Against: S. García Larragueta, *El gran priorado de Navarra de la Orden de San Juan de Jerusalén (S. XII–XIII)* (Pamplona, 1957); J. González, *El reino de Castilla en la época de Alfonso VIII* (Madrid, 1960); R. Serra Ruiz, 'La Orden de San Juan de Jerusalén en el reino de Murcia (S. XIII)', *Anuario de Historia del derecho español*, 38 (1968), 563.

or troops that an Order could raise. From a general point of view the military importance of the Orders in the Peninsula was much less than in the Baltic or the Levant, where they bore the main burden of defence and were more independent from royal power. The Castilian kings' own resources, together with those of their towns and nobles, provided enough for a successful war against the Moors. But we cannot underestimate the role of the Orders. They were a permanent and trained force ready to fight at any moment. We can see their Masters at the councils called by the king before any campaign, and we can see them riding with the king in the main belligerent actions of the mid-thirteenth century: Seville (1248), Niebla (1262) and the Mudejar revolt (1264).[24] The Spanish military orders were entrusted with the defence of most parts of the Andalusian frontier, something which was stressed after the Mudejar revolt of 1264, while the international Orders were kept as the rearguard.[25] In any case, the importance of the international military orders in the defence of the kingdom was less than the national ones.

Apart from their martial and charitable functions, the international Orders had two other important roles. One of them – and the letter is best proof of it – was their function in providing fast messenger services between the crusader states and Europe. This activity flowed from the Orders' own initiative or from the pope's command. He used the members of the Orders as examples of crusading and as witnesses to the events in the Holy Land in order to inform and encourage Western rulers to participate in crusading and papal enterprises. We have instances of members of the Orders as papal envoys to all the European courts:[26] for example, an earlier letter mentioned in our text (lines 18–19, 48–9), which we do not have but which must have existed, as did the Hospital's letter to the king of Navarre from around 1246,[27] and the Templar embassy sent to Alfonso by the pope in order to mediate in the struggle between France and Castile in 1280.[28]

The other role, or rather, *use* of the military orders – especially of the international ones – was as 'defenders' of neutral zones between the Christian kingdoms. This can be seen in the area of 'El infantazgo' (Castronuño) on the Castilian–Leonese frontier where the Orders of Santiago and the Hospital were each granted five castles to create that neutral zone in 1181–3. In the case of

---

[24] Ballesteros-Beretta, pp. 260, 360.

[25] Forey, *The Military Orders*, pp. 89–91; C. de Ayala Martínez, 'La monarquía y las Ordenes Militares durante el reinado de Alfonso X', *Hispania*, 51 (1991), 409–65; M. González Jiménez, 'Relaciones de las Ordenes Militares Castellanas con la Corona (1152–1284)', *Historia, Instituciones y documentos*, 18 (1991), 209–22.

[26] W.C. Jordan, *Louis IX and the Challenge of the Crusade: a Study in Rulership* (Princeton, 1979); C. Tyerman, *England and the Crusades, 1095–1588* (Chicago and London, 1988).

[27] E. Asensio, 'Ay, Jerusalén! Planto narrativo del S. XIII', *Nueva revista de Filología Hispánica*, 14 (1960), no. 13 (pp. 247–70).

[28] *Registres de Nicolas III (1277–1280)*, ed. J. Gay (Paris, 1898), nos 676 (20 February 1280), 680 (31 March 1280).

the double donation of Albufera to the military order of Avis by both Alfonso III of Portugal (1256) and Alfonso X (1257), we see the struggle for the sovereignty of that area; it was given to an Order as a first solution.[29] Even the Teutonic commandery of Sta María was located on the frontier between Castile and Leon at the time of its donation by the Lady Beatrice.[30] However, all these examples did not mean that such 'neutral areas' were going to be neutral for ever. Over a period of ten years, in the 1270s, Alfonso X managed to obtain some castles in strategic areas in the Algarve (Mouroa and Xerpa on the Portuguese frontier) from the Hospitallers in exchange for certain properties in Castile. In this case Alfonso broke down the 'neutral area', which he himself had created in 1259, for his own benefit.[31]

Theoretically the main role of the international military orders in Europe was to obtain sufficient resources to maintain their forces in the Levant. The struggle for resources was a permanent cause of tension between the Castilian monarchy and these Orders. As is well known, the Castilian kings had little inclination to divert resources from their kingdom to any business outside their territory,[32] and this policy clashed drastically with what was commonly regarded as the principal role of these Orders outside the Holy Land. We know that the Hospitallers, and probably the Templars and Teutonic Order as well, had to collect one-third of the annual rents in each of their European commanderies – the so-called '*responsion*' – to send to the Holy Land.[33] The *responsion* was usually paid in cash, although they also sent horses, weapons and armour, grain and textiles.[34] Presumably the Orders raised other kinds of taxes which were also sent to the Levant including, perhaps, an annual collection of alms for the Holy Land. In 1265 Alfonso allowed the Hospitallers to collect alms for the Holy Land, and so lifted the prohibition on raising money not destined for the crusade in Castile.[35] However, they always had to face royal opposition in one way or another. For example, in 1278 the pope, at the petition of St John and St James, had to remind Alfonso X that all the military orders were exempt from paying the crusade tithe because of their work against the infidel.[36] We do not

[29] M. Cunha and M.C. Pimenta, 'Algunas consideraçaos sobre as relaçaos entre os monarcas castelanos e a orden de Avis no século XIII', *Boletín do Arquivo Distrital do Porto*, 2 (1985), 47–55.

[30] E. Fernández Prieto, 'Una encomienda de la Orden de los caballeros teutónicos en el territorio Castellano-Leonés', *Hidalguía*, 136 (1976), 379–83.

[31] C. de Ayala Martínez, 'Alfonso X y la Orden de San Juan de Jerusalén' in *Estudios de Historia Medieval en homenaje a Luis Suárez Fernández*, ed. V.A. Alvarez Palenzuela (Valladolid, 1991) pp. 35–40.

[32] Ballesteros-Beretta, p. 400.

[33] Rule of 1182: E. King, *The Rule, Statutes and Customs of the Hospitallers, 1099–1310* (London, 1934).

[34] Barquero Goñi, pp. 876–9.

[35] 28 July 1265: *Libro de los Privilegios de la Orden de San Juan de Jerusalén en Castilla y León, S. XI–XV*, ed. C. de Ayala Martínez, C. Barquero Goñi, *et al.* (Madrid, 1995), no. 342. Sancho IV reissued it in 1285.

[36] *CH*, 3, no. 3677 (p. 373).

know exactly which routes the Castilian resources took on their journey to the Holy Land or indeed to the Baltic region. It seems that initially the international Orders sent their resources via the ports of southern France,[37] but in 1271 Alfonso established Cartagena and Alicante as the ports from where all merchandise had to be sent to the Levant.[38] On the other hand, it seems that Alfonso X was never in debt to the international military orders, nor did these Orders ever act as treasurers to Fernando III or Alfonso.

THE ECONOMIC SITUATION OF THE MILITARY ORDERS

Forey has already pointed out that the financial health of the military orders at the beginning, and especially by the middle, of the thirteenth century was far from satisfactory.[39] It is our opinion that this document confirms that view. On the one hand we are reminded of the heavy expenses that the Orders were facing as the almost sole defenders of the Levantine kingdom's main strongholds. On the other, the defeat in Egypt and its heavy losses in both men and materials were also stressed. The outcome of all this was the pitiful situation of the Orders generally (lines 33–6) and of the Teutonic Order in particular. It was claimed that the commanderies in Livonia and Prussia could hardly sustain themselves, and that the struggle between the Empire and Rome obstructed any European project to aid the Levant (lines 35–48).[40] The author of the letter might be exaggerating – after all, his intention was to petition Alfonso for economic assistance – but the general context seems to be undeniable.

What was the economic situation of the international military orders in Castile at this time? It is almost impossible to answer this question at present. While studies on the Spanish military orders in Castile are diverse and increasing, we cannot say the same for the other Orders.[41] There are some basic problems, such as the loss of most of the Templars' documents in the kingdom of Leon and Castile; perhaps we just have to search more carefully and in different places. Although regional studies of the various commanderies and lordships are increasing, there is no general, comprehensive research into the subject.

We must remember that at least from 1230 the military orders, in common with the rest of Spanish society, had been involved in a permanent offensive

---

[37] S. García Larragueta, 'Relaciones comerciales entre Aragón y el Hospital de Acre', *VII Congreso de Historia de la Corona de Aragón* (Madrid, 1994), 42–3.

[38] J. Torres Fontes, 'La Orden de Santa María de España', *Miscelánea Medieval Murciana*, 3 (1977), 73–118.

[39] Forey, *The Military Orders*, pp. 91–131.

[40] Christiansen, pp. 89–152. *The Atlas of the Crusades*, ed. J. Riley-Smith (London, 1991), p. 74.

[41] D.W. Lomax, *Las Ordenes Militares en la Península durante la Edad Media* (Salamanca, 1976); C. de Ayala Martínez, C. Barquero Goñi, *et al.*, 'Las Ordenes Militares en la Edad Media peninsular', *Medievalismo*, 2, (1992), 119–69; 3 (1993), 87–144.

against the Moors, with its toll in terms of men and materials. If it is true that this expansion also involved an increase in the Orders' patrimony, it is also true that the profits were not so high as one might have expected. The Castilian Church also suffered in this respect.[42] Although we can see that the military orders had reached the height of their expansion by the 1270s, their territorial gains did not reflect a healthy economic situation.[43] We have to take into account the policy of Alfonso X, who drastically reduced the number of new concessions to the military orders while at the same time maintaining royal prerogatives. All this was part of his wider scheme of increasing and centralizing royal power at the expense of the lordships.[44]

Central to the question of the wealth of the international Orders is the use to which it was put. One-third of all the income of each commandery was destined for the Levant. From the remaining two-thirds the commandery had to sustain itself and fulfil its everyday duties, as well as maintain its hospitable and military activities, all of which were quite expensive in the Castilian Reconquest. Furthermore, we must add that a certain proportion of the income, resources or properties was likely to be lost to other social agents such as the monarchy, towns or higher nobility. It is difficult to avoid the suspicion that certain of the Orders' properties were alienated at the Masters' or the commanders' own hands.

---

[42] P. Linehan, *The Spanish Church and the Papacy in the 13th Century* (Cambridge, 1971).

[43] Of the international military orders that received lands after the fall of Seville, only the Hospitallers seem to have obtained really profitable estates in the rich lowland area of Seville. But even they came a poor fourth after the Spanish military orders in terms of the value of the concessions they obtained: C. Segura Graiño and A. Torreblanca, 'Alfonso X y las Ordenes Militares: Andalucía', *Alfonso X: vida, obra y época*, 1 (Madrid, 1989), pp. 123–34; C. de Ayala Martínez, 'Alfonso X y la Orden de San Juan', pp. 29–50; M. González Jiménez, 'Las Ordenes Militares en Andalucía: De la expansión a la crisis (1225–1350)', in Izquierdo Benito.

[44] J.M. Rodríguez García, 'Idea y Realidad de Cruzada en tiempos de Alfonso X el Sabio, 1252–1284', MA diss. (Univ. Salamanca, 1997).

28

The Trial of the Templars Revisited

Malcolm Barber

Thus disappeared, virtually without a struggle, an organisation which was regarded as one of the proudest, wealthiest, and most formidable in Europe. It is not too much to say that the very idea of its destruction could not have suggested itself, but for the facilities which the inquisitorial process placed in able and unscrupulous hands to accomplish any purpose of violence under the form of the law. If I have dwelt on the tragedy at a length that may seem disproportionate, my apology is that it affords so perfect an illustration of the helplessness of the victim, no matter how highly-placed, when once the fatal charge of heresy was pressed against him, and was pressed through the agency of the Inquisition.[1]

In this way, Henry Charles Lea, the great American historian of the Inquisition, concluded his account of the Templars' trial in volume three of his *History* published in 1889. According to Norman Cantor, 'no book written about the European Middle Ages before 1895 or so is still worth reading'.[2] Lea's arguments in favour of the Templars' innocence, however, still retain their force: that no single Templar was prepared to die for the beliefs which the French government alleged permeated the Order from top to bottom, that no verifiable concrete evidence in the form of idols was ever found (nor has been since), that there was no external evidence against the Order, leaving only confessions extorted by torture as the basis for the belief in guilt. Thus, as Lea says, 'If we accept the evidence against the Templars we cannot reject it in the case of the witch'.[3] Lea believed his formidable German contemporary, Hans Prutz, had wasted his time in making a minute study of the Templar depositions. Prutz had concluded that the Order had indeed rotted from

---

[1] H.C. Lea, *A History of the Inquisition in the Middle Ages*, 3 (New York, 1889), p. 334.

[2] N.F. Cantor, *Inventing the Middle Ages. The Lives, Works, and Ideas of the Great Medievalists of the Twentieth Century* (New York, 1991), p. 44.

[3] Lea, p. 267.

From *The Military Orders. Volume 2. Welfare and Warfare.* ed. Helen Nicholson. Copyright © 1998 by Helen Nicholson. Published by Ashgate Publishing Ltd, Gower House, Croft Road, Aldershot, Hampshire, GU11 3HR, Great Britain.

within as a result of its members' addiction to a combination of devil-worship and Catharism.[4]

Although a much larger edifice was constructed during the course of the trial – which lasted for five years from 1307 to 1312 – the essence of the accusations about which Lea and Prutz so profoundly disagreed is contained in the French chancellery's order for the arrests issued on 14 September 1307. On entry, novitiates were obliged to deny Christ three times, then, naked, they were kissed by the receptor on the base of the spine, the navel and the mouth, and finally, they took an oath to submit to what is described as 'the horrible and detestable vice of *concubitus*'. Once in the Order, the new recruit found it was 'dedicated to the cult of idols'.[5] Late twentieth-century historians have, almost without exception, been prepared to accept Lea's verdict about these charges, although some have apparently done so with reluctance, despite having what Cantor sees as the inestimable advantage of not being Victorians. Jean Favier, for instance, in his study *Philippe le Bel* (published in 1978) believes that the Order as an institution could not have been corrupt and that its faults were those of lax, weak, ignorant or even forgetful individuals. Pursuing his rather dubious distinction between the Order and the individuals within it (a distinction he has in fact borrowed from the trial proceedings), he says that the Templars were 'rough men, living in the East too near to other civilisations not to be contaminated by osmosis which often drew in the worst before the best, insufficiently instructed to be able to see the difference between true and false, the inoffensive and the criminal'. As a consequence, what he describes as their 'initiation rites' (a loaded term for what was in fact a reception ceremony) were full of religious profanity and '*bizuthage*'. 'Absence of women, the influence of the East,' he continues, 'all contributed to the *fact* [my italics] that sodomy had entered deeply into the customs of the Temple. The enemy of the Temple was not Sodomy [capital 'S'], it was the closed house.'[6]

Two years later the American historian, Joseph Strayer, published *The Reign of Philip the Fair*, which was the fruit of a long lifetime's study of the monarch and his activities. He, like me, must have wasted some of his time reading Henry Charles Lea, since his conclusion that the charges were baseless derives in part from his observation that 'those Templars who were burned at the stake were executed because they had repudiated their confession, not because they wanted to defend their beliefs'. He contrasts this with the attitude of the thirteenth-century Cathars, willing to prove their devotion in the fires of the crusaders. Like Favier, though, his verdict is in essence grudging, and indeed, essentially the same. Homosexuality, he thinks, was inevitable in such an all-

---

[4] H. Prutz, *Geheimlehre und Geheimstatuten des Templerherren-Ordens* (Berlin, 1879), pp. 62, 86, 100.

[5] *Le Dossier de l'Affaire des Templiers*, ed. and tr. G. Lizerand (Paris, 1923), pp. 18–21. '*Concubitus*' is given as 'copulation' by Lewis and Short.

[6] J. Favier, *Philippe le Bel* (Paris, 1978), pp. 473, 444, 447. '*Bizuthage*' is given as 'ragging' in standard French dictionaries.

male institution. He goes on, 'That there were barrack-room obscenities and blasphemies in the houses of the Templars is again what might be expected of such a group, especially when new members were being initiated.' Unlike Favier, he does concede that they might have been 'intelligent enough' to create a coherent set of heretical doctrines, but cannot see any reason why they should have tried to do so.[7] The struggle in Strayer's mind between historical analysis and personal prejudice is all too evident here. He may, too, have found it difficult to shake off the influence of his friend, Robert Fawtier, who believed that there was no point in agonizing over the issue, when the simplest explanation – that the Templars were condemned because they were believed to be guilty – was the most likely.[8] In a footnote, Strayer says that Fawtier once told him in conversation that the Templars were 'dirty men'. In fact, it is a historian of an earlier generation, Guillaume Mollat, who is most unequivocal in his views. 'The absence of material proof, the improbability of the charges, the contradictory nature of the statements, the brutal methods used at the enquiry, the number of recantations, the courage of those who defended the order – all go to prove the Templars' innocence. Their trial was a trumped-up affair and bears the unmistakable mark of Guillaume de Nogaret.'[9]

Apart from an occasional bout of homophobia, therefore, there seems to be a fairly general consensus among modern historians that the Templars were not guilty as charged. There is much less agreement on the questions implicit in all the above views. If the Templars were not blasphemers, idolaters and sodomites, why were they arrested and tried in the first place and, indeed, how was it possible to bring down a privileged order of the Church which, for nearly two centuries, had formed the core of the Christian armies in the crusader states?

It is clear that historians like Favier and Strayer, while refusing to accept the panoply of charges brought by the French government, do not think that all was well within the Order, although neither considers why this particular generation of Templars should have been more prone either to 'Eastern influence' in the form of non-Christian ideas or to homosexuality and horseplay, than the Templars of any other period. If they mean, on the other hand, that such beliefs and practices were endemic, they make no attempt to explain why it took nearly two centuries for the authorities to take action. It is in fact very difficult to find much evidence of internal 'decadence' at or before the time of the trial. Historians are fond of claiming that the military orders showed little sense of the need for the frequent internal reform which, they allege – and in this they are in harmony with both Thatcherites and Maoists – is necessary for

---

[7] J.R. Strayer, *The Reign of Philip the Fair* (Princeton, 1980), pp. 291–2.

[8] R. Fawtier, *L'Europe Occidentale de 1270 à 1380*, Histoire du Moyen Age, 6 (Paris, 1940), pp. 416, 423–4.

[9] G. Mollat, *The Popes at Avignon*, tr. J. Love (London, 1963, tr. from 9th French edn, 1949), p. 245.

the continuing health of any long-standing institution. It is true that the Templars in the thirteenth century did not produce a Stephen of Lexington, a man acutely aware of the failings of his own Cistercian order and equally willing to do something about it. It is also true that in 1307 the leadership of the Order was elderly: James of Molay, the Grand Master, had served forty-two years, Hugh of Pairaud, the visitor, forty years, and Geoffrey of Charney, preceptor of Normandy, thirty-seven or thirty-eight years.[10] Arguably, this can produce a conservative ethos, especially when the majority of the membership in France was middle-aged, as can be seen from the trial depositions. Molay's remark that 'never or rarely is there innovation without the risk of great dangers' perhaps serves to confirm this.[11]

Nevertheless, the rule of the Temple was not a static entity unresponsive to changing needs: extensive additions in French were made between 1165 and 1187 and again between 1257 and 1267. These clauses describe an elaborate system of penances, carefully graded in seriousness, and, under the mastership of Thomas Bérard between 1256 and 1273, they incorporated detailed case histories to aid the interpretation of the Templar authorities when imposing punishments. These covered simony, internal security, homicide, theft, conspiracy, desertion to the Saracens, lack of Christian belief, homosexuality, flight from the battlefield and ordination without permission,[12] as well as many lesser offences, amounting to 112 clauses in total. This preoccupation with systematic legislative action on penances was fully in keeping with contemporary practices within the Church as a whole in the development of both canon law and the construction of detailed penitentials. It seems that both the Hospitallers under Hugh Revel (1258–77) and the Templars under Thomas Bérard were undertaking internal reviews of their Orders at about the same time, possibly in response to their perception of the dangers inherent in rivalry between the two (they had taken opposite sides in the civil war of 'St Sabas' between 1256 and 1258) at a time when the threat from both Mongols and Mamluks was becoming acute.[13]

The recognition of the need to monitor and correct internal failings was matched by continuing attention to their functions as protectors of pilgrims and defenders of the Holy Land. According to the anonymous account of the rebuilding of the castle of Safed in Galilee by the Templars (written some time

---

[10] *Le Dossier*, pp. 34–5, 38–9, 30–1.

[11] Ibid., pp. 4–5.

[12] *RT*, §§ 544–86 (pp. 285–305).

[13] On Hugh Revel's reputation as a reformer, see J. Riley-Smith, *The Knights of St John in Jerusalem and Cyprus c. 1050–1310* (London, 1967), p. 187. Latin text of Hugh Revel's statutes in *CH*, 3, nos 3075 (pp. 75–7), 3104 (p. 91), 3180 (pp. 118–21), 3317 (pp. 186–8), 3396 (pp. 225–9); English translation, E.J. King, *The Rule, Statutes, and Customs of the Hospitallers, 1099–1310* (London, 1934), pp. 53–78. Hugh Revel's statutes were followed by a further series of reforms by his five successors.

between 1261 and 1266), one of the many advantages of its completion was that 'now the famous places which are in the district of the castle of Safed can be visited',[14] thus regaining access to the Galilean sites for pilgrims. The disasters of 1291 did nothing to change the Order's basic aims. James of Molay pursued an active crusading programme from the beginning of his mastership in *c.* 1293. There is, for example, a clear realization that, at least for the immediate future, the war in the eastern Mediterranean would be primarily at sea. Among the Templar efforts were the fitting out for Cypriot waters of six galleys in Venice in 1293; a combined naval attack on the Egyptian and Palestinian coasts in 1300; and the well-known attempt to establish a garrison on the island of Ruad, off Tortosa, between 1300 and 1302, which was presumably intended as a preliminary to the recovery of the Templar base in the city itself. At the same time, supplies of money and materials, and fresh manpower, were being shipped from France, England and Sicily. Molay himself visited Pope Boniface VIII at Christmas 1294, and during the following year undertook an extensive tour of France and England, where he held important chapter meetings of the Order. Contact was maintained throughout with Charles II of Naples and James II of Aragon.[15] This task was not easy, for all four monarchs were deeply concerned about their relations with each other, despite their professions of support for the crusade. Nevertheless, it was only possible to arrest the Templar leaders in Paris because they were in France in 1307 to discuss future crusading plans with Pope Clement V.

This very positive approach could not have been pursued without the requisite manpower. Recent research into the age structure of the Templars in the late thirteenth and early fourteenth centuries, based upon the trial depositions, shows that the Order continued to send younger men overseas to fight, while the preceptories in the West were served by the older Templars. Anne Gilmour-Bryson has shown that knights were generally younger when they joined than either serving brothers or priests, a pattern which seems to reflect the perceived difference in functions. Nearly 65 per cent of the knights were under twenty-one at the time of admission. In Cyprus, which was the Order's front line after 1291, her estimates of the age of thirty-seven knights (the highest possible number given the data available) show only one to have been over fifty (he was perhaps fifty-two), while among those present in Cyprus in 1310, only two had joined before the fall of Acre. If knights and sergeants are taken together, under 7 per cent of the Templars in Cyprus were fifty or over, in contrast to the figure for the Parisian hearings, which is 40 per cent.[16] This difference is confirmed by Alan Forey. Among those interrogated

---

[14] 'De constructione castri Saphet', ed. R.B.C. Huygens, *Studi Medievali*, ser. 3, 6 (1965), 386.

[15] See M. Barber, 'James of Molay, the Last Grand Master of the Temple', *Studia Monastica*, 14 (1972), 94–100.

[16] A. Gilmour-Bryson, 'Age-Related Data from the Templar Trials', in *Aging and the Aged in Medieval Europe*, ed. M.M. Sheehan (Toronto, 1990), pp. 130–42.

in the West between 1309 and 1311, the highest percentage with less than ten years' service was found in the British Isles, with 36 per cent. Yet in Cyprus, the figure is 64 per cent: here forty-six of the seventy-two Templars questioned in 1310 had joined the Order since 1300.[17] In the light of these figures and the work of Elizabeth Siberry, Norman Housley and Sylvia Schein, which has stressed the wider crusading continuities of the late thirteenth and early fourteenth centuries,[18] I would now be more cautious than I was twenty years ago about presenting the Order of the Temple as rising and falling in relation to a crusading movement which supposedly peaked in the twelfth and early thirteenth centuries.[19] The evidence, then, does not suggest that Philip the Fair attacked an apathetic, decadent or redundant Order in 1307 and it seems doubtful that any historian would have suggested this, had the trial not brought the Order to such a dramatic end.

If it is difficult to find reasons for the trial which are intrinsic to the Order, it might be more fruitful to examine the role and motivation of its accusers. Here, the desire to lay hands on the wealth of the Order seemed as obvious to me as it did to H.C. Lea. 'For an explanation of Philippe's action, however, we need hardly look further than to financial considerations,' he said.[20] Far from seeing Philip IV as a 'great king', as Fawtier did,[21] it seemed to me that he presided over a series of never-ending crises, lurching from one to another with little idea of how to resolve them. The reign started badly, burdened with debts from his father's disastrous Aragonese crusade, which had cost at least 1.22 million *livres tournois* (a useful measure of comparison is St Louis's lavish expedition between 1248 and 1254 which cost 1.5 million *livres tournois*).[22] Yet, from 1294, the king embroiled the country in a new series of conflicts with Edward I. Malcolm Vale suggests that Philip had felt a degree of humiliation when Edward I, 'technically a vassal of the French crown', had presided over the end of the Aragonese–French conflict in 1287–8. Certainly, Edward I clearly did not see himself in any way inferior in status to the house of Capet.[23] If this is true, Philip was prepared to spend heavily to restore Capetian pride: the minimum cost of the war with England between 1294 and 1299 was 1.73

---

[17] A.J. Forey, 'Towards a Profile of the Templars in the Early Fourteenth Century', in *MO*, 1, pp. 196–204.

[18] See E. Siberry, *Criticism of Crusading 1095–1274* (Oxford, 1985); S. Schein, *Fideles Crucis. The Papacy, the West, and the Recovery of the Holy Land 1274–1314* (Oxford, 1991); N. Housley, *The Later Crusades. From Lyons to Alcazar 1274–1580* (Oxford, 1992).

[19] See M. Barber, *The Trial of the Templars* (Cambridge, 1978), p. 5.

[20] Lea, 3, p. 254.

[21] R. Fawtier, *The Capetian Kings of France*, tr. L. Butler and R.J. Adam (London, 1965, originally 1941), p. 35.

[22] J.R. Strayer, 'The Crusade against Aragon', *Speculum 28* (1953) 102–13; W.C. Jordan, *Louis IX and the Challenge of the Crusade* (Princeton, 1979), pp. 78–9.

[23] M.Vale, *The Angevin Legacy and the Hundred Years War 1250–1340* (Oxford, 1990), pp. 177–8.

million *livres tournois*, leaving the Crown with 'enormous debts'.[24] The graph of Capetian financial profligacy therefore continued on its upward course, reinforced by the Crown's inability to achieve decisive victory, either in this war or in the conflict with Flanders which included the new shame of defeat at Courtrai in 1302. Strayer's detailed analysis of the government's finances, published as long ago as 1939, shows the often frantic search for new sources of income coupled with the failure to establish an adequate and regular system of taxation.[25] The confrontation with Boniface VIII over clerical taxation (1296–7), the debasement of the coinage between 1294 and 1306, and the seizures of the property of the Lombards and the Jews in 1291 and 1306 respectively, surely offer convincing evidence of what today we would call the chronic 'short-termism' of government policy. In Vale's words, 'The conduct of successful war, as the French learned in Aragon and Flanders, the English in Scotland, and both discovered in Aquitaine, demanded resources in money, manpower and supplies which ultimately lay beyond their available means.'[26] Not surprisingly, as Sophia Menache has shown, many contemporaries and later medieval observers outside France, especially among the nobles and prelates, were unconvinced by the government's claim that it had been forced to act because of the dangers arising from a heretical conspiracy uncovered within the Order.[27]

This is worth bearing in mind since, unlike Lea, recent historians *have* thought it necessary to look beyond financial considerations, focusing their attention particularly upon the personality of Philip the Fair and upon his relationship with his prominent counsellors. Fawtier's view, indeed, is diametrically opposed to that of Lea: 'The slowness with which the affair was undertaken, the king's scant resistance on the question of the goods of the Temple, the fact that he could obtain from the Temple the money which he needed, permit [us] to set aside the motive of cupidity.' Fear of the Temple he finds equally unconvincing, given the relative ease with which the arrests were made. The answer, he feels, is to be found in a combination of circumstances arising from Philip's piety. The king – 'ardently desiring a crusade', which he believed a union of the military orders would facilitate – found

---

[24] J.R. Strayer, 'The Costs and Profits of War: The Anglo-French Conflict of 1294–1303', in *The Medieval City*, ed. H.A. Miskimin, D. Herlihy and A.L. Udovitch (New Haven and London, 1977), pp. 272–3; Vale, pp. 207–8, 225–6.

[25] J.R. Strayer and C.H. Taylor, *Studies in Early French Taxation*, Harvard Historical Monographs, 12 (Cambridge, Mass., 1939), pp. 3–105.

[26] Vale, p. 176.

[27] S. Menache, 'Contemporary Attitudes Concerning the Templars' Affair: Propaganda's Fiasco?' *The Journal of Medieval History*, 8 (1982), 135–47, and *idem*, 'The Templar Order: a Failed Ideal?' *The Catholic Historical Review*, 79 (1993), 1–21, where she argues that the attack on the Templars was part of a wider policy aimed at removing 'outsiders' (including the Lombards and the Jews) from their important roles in governmental financial administration, thus opening the way for indigenous bourgeoisie.

James of Molay equally strongly opposed to the idea just at the time that accusations were being made against the Order. Philip accepted these as true, an opinion strengthened by the first confessions. The confessions, Fawtier says, were 'probably *accompanied* [my italics] by torture ... This could, in our eyes, diminish the value of the depositions obtained in this way. But for the people of the beginning of the fourteenth century, this was normal procedure, used in all criminal trials.' Philip had been revolted by what he had learned, and feared that the Church would be too indulgent to its own, so he pursued the Templars with Christian fervour. The affair of the Templars was 'an act of faith' for the king.[28]

Fawtier's view was admittedly only a small part of a general textbook on the period between 1270 and 1328. More detailed analysis has been offered in a long and brilliant article by Elizabeth Brown; she argues that, despite the problems of the evidence, it is possible to reconstruct the main character traits of the king and to show their relationship to the many 'dramatic and important events' of the reign.[29] As she sees him, the key lies in his moralistic and censorious nature, largely moulded by a childhood during which he was reminded constantly of the saintly qualities of his grandfather, whose reputation grew as that of his own father's sank. At the same time he lived in a world of unexplained deaths, sinister rumours and potential threats to his own safety. Following the early deaths of his mother and two of his brothers, his stepmother, Marie of Brabant, was accused of poisoning the brothers (one of whom had been the heir to the throne). Gossip had it that she planned to gain the throne for her own son, Louis of Evreux who, arguably, had a better claim in that he had a more direct descent from Charlemagne. Philip grew into an adult well known for his personal piety, expressed through penances and abstinences, even to the wearing of a hair shirt. In view of his childhood experiences, the degree of paronoia which he seems to have exhibited is not perhaps too surprising. For Brown, then, the evidence reveals him as 'a captious, sternly moralistic, literalistically scrupulous, humorless, stubborn, aggressive, and vindictive individual, who feared the eternal consequences of his temporal deeds'.[30] His policies reflected this personality and, as such, show a fundamental consistency. They were marked by 'the unprecedented insistence on the connection between the king's causes and those of God and

---

[28] Fawtier, *L'Europe Occidentale*, pp. 423–4. Fulk of Villaret, the Master of the Hospital, had also been asked for his opinion, but his report has not survived. Schein, p. 197, thinks that other sources indicate he might have been more favourable to the idea of union. Strayer, however, believed that Philip lost interest in crusading as a consequence of the Aragonese disaster, and that this memory moulded his attitude towards the papacy and its policies thereafter; 'Crusade against Aragon', 102, 113.

[29] E.A.R. Brown, 'The Prince is Father of the King: the Character and Childhood of Philip the Fair of France', *Medieval Studies*, 49 (1987), 282–334.

[30] Brown, 315.

Jesus Christ'. Specifically, she says: 'Many of the acts of Philip's reign – the campaigns against Boniface VIII and the Templars, the efforts to humiliate the Flemings, the prosecution of the lovers of the king's daughters-in-law – suggest that the person responsible for these acts identified himself with higher powers and was determinedly censorious in exposing and seeking temporal retribution for what he perceived as moral lapses.'[31]

The contemporary climate should not be ignored here since the trial of the Templars was not an isolated event. Apart from the other proceedings in France itself, there are signs of an increasing sense of Christian exclusivity manifested in the hardening of attitudes towards religious minorities across Europe, ranging from the expulsion of the Jews of England in 1290, to the deportation of the Muslims of Lucera in 1300, as well as the identification of lepers, homosexuals and witches as antisocial forces ready to undermine the cohesion of the Christian community. The sudden destruction of the Muslim Luceran community is instructive in this context, since it has provoked the same kind of debate about Charles II's motives as we have seen in the case of Philip the Fair and the Templars. At this time Charles was spending massive sums in a huge effort to regain the island of Sicily from Frederick of Aragon. As in France, warfare provoked financial crisis. However, David Abulafia has looked for an explanation which is not so 'crudely materialistic', and suggests that Charles – the nephew of Louis IX – might well have believed that it was his duty to clean up what he described as the pollution of the land, where Saracens did 'detestable and horrible things inimical to the Christian name'. For Abulafia, though, the material and the religious are not necessarily mutually exclusive. 'To insist on the importance of religious motives is not to deny that Charles was enthused by the prospect of making short-term profits from the sale of the inhabitants, their livestock and their crops, to help pay his war costs.'[32]

It can hardly be a coincidence that the accusation of institutionalized homosexuality was made overtly against the Templars, while that of witchcraft was at the very least implicit in the allegations. Homosexuality is a subject given much attention by historians recently. Although they differ in emphasis, there is in fact a broad consensus between Michael Goodich, John Boswell and James Brundage, who have all published on this theme since the late 1970s, which is that there was a growth in hostility towards homosexuals from at least the mid-thirteenth century, that this was reflected in harsh laws concerning what was described as a 'crime against nature', and finally that it was

---

[31] Ibid., 288–9.

[32] D. Abulafia, 'Monarchs and Minorities in the Christian Western Mediterranean around 1300: Lucera and its Analogues', in *Christendom and its Discontents. Exclusion, Persecution and Rebellion, 1000–1500*, ed. S.L. Waugh and P.D. Diehl (Cambridge, 1996), pp. 234–63.

increasingly associated with heresy.[33] Pauline and Augustinian condemnation had been translated into law by Justinian, whose constitutions of 538/9 and 559, significantly, in view of the accusations against the Templars, claimed that homosexuality was diabolical in origin. Toleration could only bring disaster upon the land. By the late twelfth century, canonists had taken this up so completely that even incest between mother and son was considered a less serious offence. Not surprisingly, contemporary writers alleged that both internal and external enemies – that is, the Cathars and the Muslims – were particularly prone to homosexual behaviour, while, as Robert Lerner has shown, the link between heresy and fornication established itself as a topos of the thirteenth century.[34] The French government used this not only against the Templars, but against Boniface VIII and Guichard of Troyes as well. There is perhaps some irony in the fact that the Templars themselves seem to have been equally affected by these attitudes, for they were more reluctant to confess to sodomy than to any other accusation, including the denial of Christ.[35] As described by Brown, Philip the Fair would appear to have been particularly susceptible to this climate of opinion. His outrage in the case of the lovers of his daughters-in-law in 1314 is testimony to 'his sensitivity to charges of sexual morality'. More specifically, in 1276 his own father, Philip III, had been accused of 'sinning against nature', an accusation accompanied by the dire warning that, if he did not reform, one of his sons would die within six months. The death of Louis, heir to the throne, did indeed occur within the same year.[36] To Philip the Fair, the story of the destruction of Sodom and the lessons to be drawn from it was much more than the tired old cliché of second-rate chroniclers that it appears to us today.

By the early fourteenth century the stereotype of the sodomist as an antisocial force, often linked to heresy or even Islam, was well established. Witchcraft was less clearly delineated, but nevertheless was evidently thought

---

[33] M. Goodich, *The Unmentionable Vice: Homosexuality in the Later Medieval Period* (Santa Barbara and Oxford, 1979), pp. xv, 51–88; J. Boswell, *Christianity, Social Tolerance and Homosexuality. Gay People in Western Europe from the Beginning of the Christian Era to the Fourteenth Century* (Chicago and London, 1980), pp. 37–8, 269–91; J. Brundage, *Law, Sex, and Christian Society in Medieval Europe* (Chicago and London, 1987), pp. 313, 398–9, 472–3. An index of the way the climate of opinion has changed on this subject can be seen by the fact that, when I first looked at this subject in the early 1970s, the staff of the British Museum apparently believed that a scholarly treatment such as D. Sherwin-Bailey's *Homosexuality and the Western Christian Tradition* (London, 1955) could only be read in a special seat in the North Library directly in front of the superintendent. Such attitudes go a long way to explain the views of Strayer and Fawtier on this subject.

[34] Brundage, pp. 121–2, 399; R.E. Lerner, *The Heresy of the Free Spirit in the Later Middle Ages* (Berkeley and London, 1972), pp. 20–5.

[35] The depositions made in Paris in October and November 1307 show three Templars admitting to homosexual acts out of a total of 138, *Procès*, pp. 290, 294.

[36] Brown, 326, 332. For a recent survey which puts this subject in its wider historiographical context, as well as examining the validity of Templar 'confessions' in detail, see A. Gilmour-Bryson, 'Sodomy and the Knights Templar', *Journal of the History of Sexuality*, 7 (1996), 151–83.

to exist. While the accusation against the Templars is not as explicit as that of homosexuality, the allegations do centre upon secret ceremonies central to which is the denial of Christ and the adoration of an idol, apparently representing demonic forces whose existence in large numbers was accepted by thirteenth-century writers. In *Europe's Inner Demons* published in 1975, Norman Cohn devotes a chapter to 'the crushing of the Knights Templars', which he sees as an important stage in the development of the medieval concept of witches, largely because the renunciation of Christ was, for the first time, at the core of the alleged depravity.[37] Richard Kieckhefer, whose *European Witch Trials* (covering the period between 1300 and 1500) was published almost simultaneously in 1976, equally places the period of the trial as one of growing belief in witchcraft or at least in its efficacy as an accusation against those identified as enemies. He found little material which predates 1300, but discerned a burst of activity between 1300 and 1330, when in Europe as a whole there was, on average, one witch trial per annum, just over half of which took place in France. These included the famous cases of Boniface, the Templars and Guichard of Troyes under Philip IV, that of the former chamberlain, Enguerran of Marigny under Louis X, and a further seven cases between 1316 and 1331, which Kiechkhefer associates with the anxieties of a dynasty facing possible extinction despite having held power since the tenth century.[38] He does not mention the panic caused by the alleged 'plot' by the lepers, the Jews, and rulers of Granada to take over Christendom, which temporarily rocked the government of Philip V in 1321 but which, it seems to me, certainly falls within his definition of witchcraft and exhibits similarly feverish paranoia.[39] At the same time, the French pope, Jacques Duèze, who became John XXII in 1316, was equally obsessed, making the atmosphere at the papal court little different from that of the last Capetians. Jacques Duèze was very familiar with the trial of the Templars as he had been one of the prelates who had prepared a report on the proceedings for Clement V at the Council of Vienne in 1311. He had recommended the suppression of the Order on the grounds of apostasy, so he apparently believed that the Order had been penetrated by anti-Christian doctrines.[40] Kieckhefer notes that the trials most frequently involved high-profile groups or individuals, either as victims or perpetrators, and that they all had a highly political character.[41]

---

[37] N. Cohn, *Europe's Inner Demons* (London, 1975), pp. 75–98, esp. p. 98.

[38] R. Kieckhefer, *European Witch Trials. Their Foundations in Learned and Popular Culture, 1300–1500* (London, 1976), pp. 10–14 (especially the graph on p. 11), 108–12.

[39] M. Barber, 'Lepers, Jews and Moslems: the Plot to Overthrow Christendom in 1321', *History*, 66 (1981), 1–17; F. Beriac, 'La persécution des lépreux dans la France méridionale en 1321', *Le Moyen Age*, 93 (1989), 203–21.

[40] See V. Verlaque, *Jean XXII, sa vie et ses oeuvres* (Paris, 1883), pp. 52–3.

[41] Kieckhefer, p. 10.

Kieckhefer's survey produces a conclusion which is very pertinent to our subject. Basing his argument on evidence drawn from thirty-five trials in the fourteenth and fifteenth centuries, he maintains that, while most people believed in sorcery (that is, positive acts of harm through disfiguring images or concocting poisons), the idea of diabolism (that is, the worship of the devil or demons in some form of assembly) was 'the product of speculation by theologians and jurists'[42] who imposed their views and extracted confessions appertaining to these views through inquisitorial procedures. Since the educated could not conceive of sorcery in a vacuum, they necessarily sought a controlling force in the form of the devil or demons. The concept of the corrupt Templar reception ceremony is therefore much more likely to be the product of Philip IV's jurists than that of the Templars themselves who, whatever their talents, cannot be seen as representatives of what Kieckhefer calls 'the learned tradition'.

R.I. Moore has taken this further, arguing that by the late twelfth and early thirteenth centuries it is possible to discern the foundation of what he calls 'a persecuting society', driven not by popular prejudice or mob violence, but by the rise of the *literati*, intent on consolidating their new power derived from service to the king and willing both to create and to persecute defined groups in order to maintain their superiority. In Moore's thesis, these people were determined to put down competition in the form of Lombards and Jews, while at the same time holding in contempt those they saw as their inferiors, not equipped with literary and administrative skills, whom they presented as 'rustics' and 'idiots'. To achieve their aims they exaggerated the importance and coherence of Catharism and used the accusation of 'unnatural vice' against political opponents. For Moore, persecution is inseparable from their rise to power.[43] Moore's book does not run beyond *c.* 1250, but presumably he would see the following period as a time when these trends were accentuated. The accusers of the Temple were, after all, in a position to manipulate clerical beliefs about the enemies of Christianity. As early in the crusade era as 1108, when the Franks were besieging Sidon, the German chronicler of the First Crusade and its aftermath, Albert of Aachen, associated mockery of the Cross, in particular spitting and urinating upon it, as characteristic of apostates and Saracens, actions which were quite specifically alleged against the Templars.[44] Do Philip the Fair's lawyers – particularly Nogaret and Plaisians – exhibit the characteristics of the *literati*, using accusations of conspiracy to strengthen their position, knowing that the king was only too willing to see the world in this way? King James II of Aragon apparently thought so. In December 1307

---

[42] Ibid., p. 36.

[43] R.I. Moore, *The Formation of a Persecuting Society. Power and Deviance in Western Europe 950–1250* (Oxford, 1987), especially pp. 124–53.

[44] Albert of Aachen, 'Historia Hierosolymitana', in *RHC Occid*, 4 (Paris, 1879), X.48 (pp. 653–4).

he told Clement V that 'we suspect that the pious credulity of this king could be deceived by the persuasion of others'.[45] Robert-Henri Bautier, in contrast to most other historians, agrees with this view. He sees the king as largely in the hands of these ministers, especially after the death of his wife, Jeanne of Navarre, in 1305. Bautier argues that the itineraries and diplomata of the king show him to be increasingly preoccupied with visiting monasteries, going on pilgrimage and making grants to religious institutions. When William of Nogaret became keeper of the seals on 22 September 1307, he exploited this state, so that it was not difficult to convince the king that certain actions had to be taken to protect the faith and the realm. Bautier quotes the note made by the chancellery scribe that day: 'The seal was surrendered to the Lord William of Nogaret, knight, where there was discussion concerning the arrest of the Templars.'[46] Brown believes that Philip remained in much firmer control of affairs than Bautier would admit, but even she concedes that 'these men influenced the king; they spoke for him, they interposed themselves between him and his subjects; they sometimes flaunted their authority'.[47]

Moore's thesis can be challenged on a number of counts, not the least of which is the usual point that the evidence we have comes from a literary elite who were not interested in the thoughts of the mass of the people, or perhaps did not even believe they had any. Bernard Hamilton has, moreover, argued that, for instance, legislation against lepers seems to have arisen largely from fear of contagion, while the crusades, rather than the jealousy of the *literati*, provided the context for popular attacks upon the Jews.[48] Indeed, to be consistent with Moore's thesis we should equally expect to see that the pope and his entourage were convinced of the Templars' guilt. Their conduct throughout the trial shows quite clearly that they were not: Clement V, for instance, is reported by the St Albans chronicler, William Rishanger, as saying that the Templars were of good repute, which was why they had been enriched and privileged by the Church, and why he had found the allegations against them astonishing.[49]

However, the evidence that we have about the Templars' own post-1291 efforts and about public attitudes towards them during this period has perhaps

---

[45] H. Prutz, *Entwicklung und Untergang des Templeherrenordens* (Berlin, 1888), p. 348.

[46] R.-H. Bautier, 'Diplomatique et histoire politique: ce que la critique diplomatique nous apprend sur la personnalité de Philippe le Bel', *Revue Historique*, 259 (1987), 3–27.

[47] Brown, 288.

[48] B. Hamilton, review in *The Heythrop Journal*, 31 (1990), 337–9. It seems most likely that sometimes the impetus for persecution came from above, sometimes from below, and sometimes from a combination of the two. Moore's view seems too schematic to fit all cases during these centuries. See, too, the criticisms of R. Chazan, 'The Deteriorating Image of the Jews – Twelfth and Thirteenth Centuries', in *Christendom and its Discontents*, pp. 220–33.

[49] William Rishanger, *Chronica et Annales*, ed. H.T. Riley, RS, 28, pp. 496–7. Cf. the report of the Aragonese ambassador, Jean Bourgogne, on the papal speech at Poitiers in June 1308, H. Finke, *Papsttum und Untergang des Templeordens*, 2 (Münster, 1907), pp. 148–50.

made this debate less relevant to the trial than it might have been. It now
appears obvious that there was no widespread public belief in Templar
'heretical depravity', nor indeed in the actual concept of diabolism until it was
announced to the world by Philip the Fair's lawyers. Thus the claim of William
of Plaisians that 'it was through their fault [*defectum*] that it is said the Holy Land
was lost and it is said that they often made secret pacts with the Sultan'[50] – apart
from misleading a whole generation of crusade historians – is in fact irrelevant,
since the issues at stake were more concerned with French domestic politics
than with the Templar contribution to the crusade effort. The final satisfaction
for Philip's lawyers can be found in the humbling of the once proud Templars.
At one point in the trial James of Molay abjectly describes himself just as they
would have wished when he says that he is *miles illitteratus et pauper*, thus
inviting (and receiving) the patronization of William of Plaisians.[51]

Therefore, reading books written before 1895 is not perhaps so futile after
all. Have Lea's 'able and unscrupulous hands' transformed themselves by 1941
into Fawtier's royal servants who 'had become more royalist than the king',[52]
only for us to find that by 1987 they reappear as Moore's rising *literati*? Perhaps,
as he would certainly have liked, we can leave the last word with William of
Plaisians: 'God,' he said, 'has chosen such ministers for this victory who do not
seek in these matters anything for themselves, but that which is Christ's,
setting aside from themselves all cupidity and vainglory.'[53]

---

[50] *Le Dossier*, pp. 122–3.
[51] Ibid., pp. 164–5.
[52] Fawtier, *Capetian Kings*, p. 182.
[53] *Le Dossier*, pp. 114–15.

29

'An Island Called Rhodes' and the 'Way' to Jerusalem: Change and Continuity in Hospitaller *Exordia* in the Later Middle Ages

Mark Dupuy

By most accounts, the body of John the Baptist was put to rest in Samaria. According to at least one medieval tradition, however, his head began its own circuitous journey to Constantinople after translations to both Alexandria and 'an island called Rhodes'.[1] In the fourteenth century the Hospitallers, whose traditions usually honoured John as 'certainly the patron of our house',[2] likewise landed upon the shores of Rhodes, and the island became crucial to the survival of the Order over the course of the next two centuries. In various forms, Hospitaller propaganda proved flexible enough to incorporate the new conquest into their foundation myths, while retaining a conservative element – glimpsed in at least one pilgrim's guide appended to the Hospitallers' rule – which embraced an historic ideal of the Order, namely, the care and control of pilgrim routes to the Holy Land. Rhodes offered the Order those benefits it needed, and as such, the 'way' back to Jerusalem lay through 'an island called Rhodes'. It served as an operations base for future efforts to regain a foothold in the Holy Land and justified the Order's existence at a time when its usefulness was coming under increasing scrutiny, from both opponents and proponents of the idea of crusade. For various reasons, however, the Hospitallers' operations from Rhodes resembled rearguard actions more than earnest attempts to recover the Holy Land.

---

[1] Theodoricus, in *Peregrinationes tres: Saewulf, John of Würzburg, Theodoricus*, ed. R.B.C. Huygens, with a study of the voyage of Saewulf by J.H. Pryor, Corpus Christianorum, Continuatio Mediaevalis, 139 (Turnhout, 1994), p. 188, lines 1389–92.

[2] '*Ce est le privilegi que le duc godefroy de buillon fist alhospital en jerus por le quel sont tesmoynes molt debiens spirituales estre fays nostre maysson en jerus e par lequel est tesmonignt que le patron denostre maysson est Saint johan babtist certainement ...*' Biblioteca Vaticana, Vatican, MS Vaticana Latina (hereafter Vat. Lat.) 3136, fol. 20.

From *The Military Orders. Volume 2. Welfare and Warfare*. ed. Helen Nicholson. Copyright © 1998 by Helen Nicholson. Published by Ashgate Publishing Ltd, Gower House, Croft Road, Aldershot, Hampshire, GU11 3HR, Great Britain.

After the capable if corrupt magistracy of Fulk of Villaret, the Order suffered from a general lack of leadership, both from within the Order and from its theoretical head, the papacy.[3] The Hospitallers were led further and further away from Jerusalem, from their early plans to strike at the Mamluk forces in Cairo,[4] to their participation in the capture of and increasing responsibility for the port-city of Smyrna, and culminating in their involvement in the disaster at Nicopolis in 1396. As the Order struggled with various Islamic powers over the course of the fifteenth century, it tenaciously defended the bulwark at Rhodes, losing the island only at the beginning of 1523. Yet in the transitional years, after the suppression of the Templars and the initial campaigns against Rhodes, the Hospitallers had to assimilate the island by the pen as well as by the sword. Similarly, the Order had to reconcile itself with its expulsion from Palestine. An examination of the Order's *Miracula* and a pilgrims' guide appended to the Vaticana Latina 3136 version of the rule offers us one glimpse of the Hospitallers' efforts to adjust to their new circumstances.

The *Miracula* are the Hospitallers' foundation myths, tales about the supposed origins of the Hospital and its history in the Holy Land. They constitute, in the words of one historian, 'an attempt to give the foundation of the Hospital a venerable antiquity'.[5] The *Miracula* trace a series of gifts, donations and miracles involving the Hospital from the time of Judas Maccabaeus to the time of Godfrey of Bouillon who, some Hospitaller traditions claimed, granted special privileges to the Order, privileges confirmed by Pope Eugenius III. In the years between Judas and Godfrey, the myths claimed that governance of the early hospital in Jerusalem passed from Zechariah, father of John the Baptist, to a mythical figure named Julian the Roman, during whose incumbency Christ himself was supposed to have frequented the hospital.

The central elements of Julian's story are usually these: that he and other 'good men' were travelling east to gather the tribute of the Jews, and that somewhere in the sea of Crete their boat foundered upon an island, killing all save Julian, who then spoke with the Lord and continued on to Jerusalem, where he played out his role in the Hospital's traditions. Most extant versions of the *Miracula*, however, differ in their identification of the island upon which Julian landed.

The Anglo-Norman verse version of the *Riwle* and *Miracula*, datable to the reign of King Henry II of England, states merely that 'God appeared to Julian ... and bore him safely to land.'[6] By the thirteenth and fourteenth centuries,

---

[3] A. Luttrell, 'Hospitallers at Rhodes, 1309–1421', in *Crusades*, 3, p. 289.

[4] R. Irwin, 'How Many Miles to Babylon?: The *Devise des Chemins de Babilione* Redated', in *MO*, 1, pp. 57–63.

[5] J. Riley-Smith, *The Knights of St John of Jerusalem and Cyprus, c. 1050–1310* (London, 1967), pp. 32–4.

[6] The Hospitallers' *Riwle*, ed. K.V. Sinclair, Anglo-Norman Text Society, 42 (London, 1984), p. 7: '*Mes le fis Dieu li apparut/Qui a ses meinz sus le saka/E sein a tere enporta ...*'

many manuscripts had become more specific in their descriptions of Julian's disaster. Various thirteenth- and fourteenth-century versions of the *Miracula* state that Julian's boat was in the sea of Crete when it was broken up near an island called varyingly 'Joa' or 'Joha'.[7] Other versions – including Vatican Latina 3136, which originated at Rhodes – note that the boat ran aground near or on an island known varyingly as 'Elos', 'Roas', 'Rody', or 'Rodes'.[8] Judging from the extant versions, by the fourteenth century Rhodes had been worked into Julian's tale as a popular variant; by the fifteenth century, the 'Joa' version no longer appears in the manuscripts, which employ either Rhodes or a form of Telos as Julian's 'port of call'.

Several Latin and French versions of the *Miracula* have been transcribed and edited in the *Recueil des Historiens des Croisades: Historiens occidentaux*. The origins of the tales are obscure, and the relationship between most of the extant manuscripts is still unclear. Sections of Riant's editions of the *Miracula* in the *Recueil* relied quite heavily upon Delaville Le Roulx's *De Prima Origine hospitalariorum Hierosolymitanorum*, and in addition Charles Kohler admitted that a more rigorous classification of the manuscripts, such as some sort of stemma, should replace his own grouping of the manuscripts into three rather general redactions. Further investigation into the provenance and relationship of the extant versions of the *Miracula* might shed light on the manner by which Rhodes was grafted into many versions of the foundation myths. Perhaps Antoine Calvet's forthcoming study of the *Miracula*[9] will reveal the relationships of the manuscripts to each other. In any case it is clear that during the fourteenth century, in some versions of the *Miracula*, Rhodes began to replace Joa, described by Kohler as 'an unknown place ... [which] we have sought in vain on the journey to Jerusalem ...'[10] Elos, the most popular variant in extant fifteenth-century documents, is probably a form of Telos, a small island north-west of Rhodes and within its sphere of influence.[11]

---

[7] The manuscripts referring to 'Joa' are Munich, Bibliotheque Royale, lat. 4620 (thirteenth-fourteenth century); BN, MSS latine 5515 (fourteenth century); and 14693 (fourteenth century). The reference to 'Joha' is in BN, MS français 6049 (fourteenth century). All citations from these manuscripts in this article are taken from *RHC Occid*, 5. BN, MS français 6049 has been dated to 1302: J. Delaville Le Roulx, *De Prima Origine Hospitalariorium Hierosolymitanorum* (Paris, 1885), p. 57.

[8] BN, MS latine 1080 (fifteenth century) also uses 'Rodes'. For 'Roas', see BN, MS français 1978 (fourteenth century) and Montpellier, fac. de médecine, 372 (fourteenth century); for 'Rody', see Toulouse, Archives Départementales, St Jean, 1 (fifteenth century); for 'Elos' see BN, MS français 13531, (fourteenth century), BN, MS français 1079 (fifteenth century), and BN, MS français 17255 (fifteenth century) – printed in *RHC Occid*, 5. BN, MS français 1978 has been dated to 1315: Delaville Le Roulx, pp. 56–7.

[9] See A. Luttrell, 'The Hospitallers' Medical Tradition, 1291–1530', in *MO*, 1, p. 66 note 11.

[10] '*Locus incertus, forte Ionicum littus. In itineribus Hierosolymitanis haec frustra quaesivimus ...*', *RHC Occid*, 5, p. 407 note a.

[11] E. Rossi, 'The Hospitallers at Rhodes, 1421–1523', in *Crusades*, 3, p. 324. See also S. Pauli, *Codice Diplomatico del sacro ordine militare ordine Gerosolimitano* (Lucca, 1733–7), 2, pp. 502–3.

For the Hospitallers of the fourteenth and fifteenth centuries, Rhodes was both literally and metaphorically the 'way' to Jerusalem, for documents appended to their rule indicate that a return to the Holy Land continued to be their primary goal. The existence of a pilgrims' guide at the end of one fourteenth-century compendium of the rule, statutes, usages and customs of the Order is evidence of this lofty ideal. Vaticana Latina 3136 contains a French version of the rule and associated documents, as well as copies of both the *Miracula* and the *Chronicles of the Deceased Masters*. Its Latin *explicit* informs us that it was copied at Rhodes in 1342.[12] Near the end of the codex – after the *explicit*, but before a final section which refers back to the *usages* – is a pilgrims' itinerary which begins, 'These are the roads on which one can rightly go from the city of Acre to Jerusalem and the pilgrimages to the Holy Places which are part of a just life ...'[13] This guide is known to modern scholars as the *Chemins et pelerinaiges de la terre sainte*.[14] While the codex as a whole has not escaped historical inquiry, the *Chemins* has attracted little attention.

'First one goes from Acre to Haifa', suggests the guide.[15] The trip continues to Caesarea and then down the coastal road towards Arsūf and Jaffa. After pointing out how far Ascalon is from Jaffa – but never going there – the itinerary turns inland past Blanchegarde and Bayt Nūbā to the zenith of any pilgrimage, Jerusalem.

Once there, the guide describes the different gates, or *intrees*, to the city and the various holy places one must see and at which one must worship.[16] After an erratic tour of the Holy City, the guide then leaves Jerusalem and describes the road to Quarantene. The next path goes south again, this time to Bethlehem, and then north to Nāblus, Samaria and Mount Tabor. Having travelled thus far north, the description stops, begins anew at Acre, and follows the road from Acre to Nazareth. The guide ends with a comment on the purpose of pilgrimage, which is made because such an effort 'might be to the profit of our bodies and to the exaltation of our souls'.[17]

---

[12] '*Expliciunt statuta et usatica bona n non regula sancte domus hospitalis sancti john jeros que hodie fratres dictae domus tenent facta fine pia te laudo virgo maria yic liber scriptus est ad honorem [[ ]] de sancto [[ ]] per manum [[ ]] de Ro des [[ ]]is anno domini m ccc quadregesimo y et [[ ]] menssis November apud civitatem colocenssem in loquo vocato lo co lac in capite in ssule Rodi. amen. qui scripssit scribat ssemper cum domino vivat ...*', Vat. Lat. 3136, fol. 129v.

[13] '*Ces sont les chamins que droytament vuet aler dela cite dacre en jerus eles pelerintages de los sains eles luoqs que sont en la droyte vie ...*', ibid., fol. 130.

[14] See *Itinéraires à Jerusalem et descriptions de la Terre Sainte, rédigés en français aux xie, xiie & xiiie siècles*, ed. H. Michelant and G. Raynaud (Geneva, 1882).

[15] '*Primerament l'on vait d acre a caiphas*'; '*hont habitans les ermitans latins que len apele fratres dou carme ...*', Vat. Lat. 3136, fol. 130.

[16] '*Ces sont les intrees dela sainte cite de jerusalem eles luoqs sains quelon doit faire et adhorer ...*', ibid., fol. 131v.

[17] '*Ce est le chamin dacre a nasaret ... ssains pelerinatges ... illi ssoit au proffit de nos cors et ad exaltation de nos armes*', ibid., fols 134v–135v.

The composition of the *Chemins* has been dated to between 1265 and 1290, and it is apparently extant in only two versions. Its nineteenth-century editor, Gaston Raynaud, reached no conclusion on its authorship, remarking only that the Vatican version originated in the fourteenth century and was copied by a Provençal scribe. Neither he nor Delaville le Roulx, who mentioned the Vatican codex in a variety of works,[18] made any attempt to address the question of how or why such an account came to be included within a compendium of Hospitaller documents.

Unlike the *Devise de Chemins de Babilione*, this itinerary had no military use; but it can perhaps tell us something about Hospitaller ideology and the state of devotional piety within Christendom in the fourteenth century. The Hospitaller version was copied into this particular manuscript in the 1340s, a period which Jean Richard claims saw a sudden rise in the number of European pilgrimage accounts.[19] Henry Savage has likewise shown that the popularity of Christian pilgrimage to the Holy Land remained consistently high even after the fall of Acre.[20] The inclusion of this itinerary in a Hospitaller codex corroborates the assessments of Savage and Richard.

More specifically and more recently, Anthony Luttrell has argued that in the latter half of the fourteenth century the Hospitallers began to take an active interest in pilgrim traffic to Jerusalem, although even in the final quarter of the century they lacked adequate resources to attract to Rhodes western pilgrims *en route* for Jerusalem.[21] Nevertheless, a good number of travellers visited the island,[22] and Luttrell's assertion that Rhodes was the centre of a 'spiritual and physical axis' between Tuscany and Jerusalem may perhaps be extended to Western Christendom as a whole.[23] The guide in Vaticana Latina 3136 may be an early manifestation of Hospitaller interest in regaining a share of the pilgrim trade. The alms-raising function of the *Miracula* has recently been attested,[24] and it is possible that the itinerary served a similar purpose, calling the faithful to take up the pilgrim's staff and to book their passage for Palestine, a passage which, had the Hospitallers' wishes materialized more fully, would probably have carried them through Rhodes at one point or another.

---

[18] For instance, Delaville le Roulx, *De Prima Origine*, and 'Les Statuts de l'Ordre de Saint-Jean de Jérusalem', *Bibliothèque de l'École des Chartes*, 48 (1887), 341–56.

[19] J. Richard, *Les Récits de Voyages et de Pèlerinages* (Bruges, 1981), pp. 22–3.

[20] H. Savage, 'Pilgrimages and Pilgrim Shrines in Palestine and Syria after 1095', in *Crusades*, 4, p. 66.

[21] A. Luttrell, 'Rhodes and Jerusalem: 1291–1411', in his *The Hospitallers of Rhodes and Their Mediterranean World* (Aldershot, 1992), X, p. 192.

[22] *Idem*, 'The Hospitallers Between Tuscany and Jerusalem', *Revue Mabillon*, 64, new ser. 3 (1992), 129.

[23] Ibid., 118.

[24] K. Borchardt, 'Two Forged Thirteenth Century Alms-Raising Letters used by the Hospitallers in Franconia', in *MO*, 1, pp. 52–6.

The audience for such a guide could hardly have been the brethren themselves, as canon law forbade them from going on crusade, and their own rule denied them the privilege of leaving the cloister to go on pilgrimage, for which magisterial licence was required.[25] Perhaps they saw Rhodes acting for their own Order as Marienburg would for the Teutonic Knights, as a lightning rod for both Western chivalric and devotional sentiment. The *Chemins* may have been an early attempt at sustaining western interest in pilgrimage to the Holy Land. By placing their island at the centre of the 'axis' between Jerusalem and the West, the Hospitallers could put themselves in a position to strengthen ties between themselves and noble pilgrims overseas. The *Chemins*, like the *Miracula*, harks back to a time when the routes to all the holy places were easily accessible by any earnest pilgrim. The *chemins* of the guide were the roads of the twelfth and thirteenth centuries, roads which the Hospital guarded precisely so that pilgrims could visit the holy sites in Jerusalem and its countryside.

With hindsight, it is clear that by the fourteenth century those were the paths of a bygone era. Yet the situation was not necessarily so clear at the time, and many recent crusade historians, most notably Norman Housley and Sylvia Schein, agree that a return to the Holy Land was still a legitimate goal in the minds of crusade proponents.[26] Until such time as a return to the Holy Land could be achieved, however, the Hospital had to content itself with solidifying its position at Rhodes. Its presence there presented both a challenge and an opportunity for the Order, the challenge of assimilating the island into its 'history', and the opportunity to use its location to the Order's advantage. Documents appended to various copies of the Hospitaller rule show that the Order attempted both to meet that challenge and to make the most of that opportunity. The island had a place in its tradition, or so it could claim, and by holding on to it the Hospitallers might one day return to Jerusalem. Maintaining their position at Rhodes would require external support, the likes of which the Hospitallers might have marshalled by assuming a greater role in the increasingly lucrative fourteenth-century pilgrim trade. Ultimately, however, their designs to do so were aborted. Like their mythical ancestor, Julian the Roman, the Hospitallers found safe haven at Rhodes in a time of dire need; unlike Julian, however, they would not continue on to the Holy Land.

---

[25] The privileges granted to the Master – 'and no other' – in the *usances* include the right to undertake a pilgrimage. See E.J. King, *The Rule, Statutes and Customs of the Knights of St John* (London, 1933), p. 175. For the granting of licences, see Luttrell, 'Rhodes and Jerusalem', pp. 191–2, and 'Hospitallers Between Tuscany and Jerusalem', 132.

[26] N. Housley, *The Later Crusades* (Oxford, 1992), and S. Schein, *Fideles Crucis* (Oxford, 1991) agree on the vitality of the idea of crusade in the later Middle Ages.

30

The Hospitallers and the Kings of Navarre in the Fourteenth and Fifteenth Centuries[*]

Carlos Barquero Goñi

The relationship between the Hospital of St John and the kings of Aragon during the last two centuries of the Middle Ages has been the subject of in-depth analysis by Anthony Luttrell and María Bonet.[1] However, no such detailed studies have been carried out for the rest of the Spanish monarchies, and in the case of Navarre, only a single study has appeared, on the fourteenth century.[2] In this paper I shall attempt to broaden our knowledge of how relations between the Hospitallers and the Spanish kings evolved in the later Middle Ages by an examination of the ties between the Hospitallers and the kings of Navarre in the fourteenth and fifteenth centuries based on documents from the archives of the Hospitaller priory preserved in the Archivo Histórico Nacional.[3]

The first royal donations to the Hospital in Navarre date from the time of Alfonso I, king of Navarre and Aragon, who also bequeathed one-third of his kingdom to the Hospitallers in his will of 1131.[4] Alfonso I's will was never

---

[*] This paper was prepared with the aid of a postdoctoral grant from the 'Caja de Madrid' Foundation.

[1] A. Luttrell, 'The Aragonese Crown and the Knights Hospitallers of Rhodes, 1291–1350', and 'La Corona de Aragón y las Ordenes Militares durante el siglo XIV', in his *The Hospitallers in Cyprus, Rhodes, Greece and the West. 1291–1440* (London, 1978), nos XI–XII; *idem*, 'Hospitaller Life in Aragon, 1319–1370', and 'Las Ordenes Militares en la Sociedad Hispánica. Los Hospitalarios aragoneses, 1340–1360', in his *The Hospitallers of Rhodes and their Mediterranean World* (Aldershot, 1992), nos XV–XVI; M. Bonet Donato, *La Orden del Hospital en la Corona de Aragón. Poder y gobierno en la Castellanía de Amposta (ss. XII–XV)* (Madrid, 1994), pp. 59–80.

[2] S. García Larragueta, 'La Orden de San Juan de Jerusalén en Navarra. Siglo XIV,' in *Las Ordenes Militares en el Mediterráneo Occidental. Siglos XIII–XVIII*, no editor (Madrid, 1989), pp. 103–38.

[3] C. Gutiérrez del Arroyo, *Catálogo de la documentación navarra de la Orden de San Juan de Jerusalén en el Archivo Histórico Nacional. Siglos XII–XIX*, 2 vols (Pamplona, 1992).

[4] S. García Larragueta, *El gran priorado de Navarra de la Orden de San Juan de Jerusalén (siglos XII–XIII)* (Pamplona, 1957), 2, pp. 12, 14–21.

From *The Military Orders. Volume 2. Welfare and Warfare*. ed. Helen Nicholson. Copyright © 1998 by Helen Nicholson. Published by Ashgate Publishing Ltd, Gower House, Croft Road, Aldershot, Hampshire, GU11 3HR, Great Britain.

carried out, but his successors on the throne of Navarre, García Ramírez and Sancho VI, granted several privileges and donations to the Hospital, perhaps in an attempt to compensate for this loss.[5] Although these donations were significant, they were neither numerous nor lavish.[6] During the reign of Sancho VII and of the kings of the Champagne dynasty some donations and at least one exchange were granted by the monarchs to the Hospital of St John.[7] In return, the high officials of the Hospital rendered services to Sancho VII, Theobald I and Henry I.[8] Even the Master of the Order himself maintained correspondence with the kings of Navarre, keeping them apprised of news in the East and requesting their assistance.[9] Nevertheless, monarchs sometimes acted against the interests of the Hospitallers,[10] and the prior of St John was among those present at an assembly of 1298 during which a number of demands were made of the monarchs of France and Navarre, Philip IV and his wife Jeanne I.[11] In short, it appears that although the Navarrese Hospitallers enjoyed royal support during the twelfth and thirteenth centuries, this support was neither intense nor lacking in crises.

The majority of the kings of Navarre during the fourteenth century expressly safeguarded the rights of the Hospital. Yet, although Sancho VI had already forbidden attacks on the Order's members and holdings back in 1173,[12] this was the only grant of formal protection until the fourteenth century,[13] and no further examples of similar grants of protection are known for the fifteenth century. It is usually stated in such documents that they were issued at the request of the priors of the Hospital of St John, which leads us to question how far the monarchs were in favour of such grants and whether they were effective. In this case, we should perhaps question whether the Order really did enjoy special royal protection in Navarre during the fourteenth century, especially under the Evreux dynasty. However another possible indication of special royal backing is the fact that in the fourteenth century the monarch awarded some tax concessions that would have benefitted the Hospitallers.[14]

In the twelfth and thirteenth centuries the kings of Navarre made a few donations of royal property to the Hospital, but none at all in the fourteenth and fifteenth centuries. However, the kings did contribute to the expansion

---

[5] A.J. Martín Duque, 'La restauración de la monarquía navarra y las órdenes militares (1134–1194)', *Anuario de Estudios Medievales*, 11 (1981), 65–71.

[6] García Larragueta, *El gran priorado*, 2, pp. 22–3, 25–6, 35, 44, 49, 65.

[7] Ibid., pp. 79–80, 93–4, 101–2, 263–4, 335–6.

[8] Ibid., pp. 183–4, 249–50, 252, 439–41.

[9] Ibid., pp. 85–90, 297–8.

[10] Ibid., pp. 352–4, 430–1.

[11] J. Salcedo Izu, 'Las Cortes de Navarra en la Edad Media', in *Las Cortes de Castilla y León en la Edad Media*, no editor, 2 vols (Valladolid, 1988), 2, pp. 588–9.

[12] García Larragueta, *El gran priorado*, 2, p. 44.

[13] *CH*, 4, no. 4764 (p. 154). AHN OO.MM, carpeta 849, nos 14, 15. ibid., legajo 8569, no. 39.

[14] Ibid., carpeta 849, nos 16, 20; carpeta 905, nos 7–8.

of the Navarrese priory with property from other sources.[15] It should be emphasized that the monarchy raised no objection to the incorporation of the Templars' Navarrese holdings into the Hospital at the beginning of the fourteenth century.[16] This was property which, while not particularly significant, was nonetheless worth acquiring.[17]

In general, some monarchs pursued a policy of protection and defence of the property of the Hospital of St John.[18] Examples of this policy in practice include, for instance, the kings' repeated orders to officials to confiscate the property of those who did not pay rent to the Order. This suggests that one of the Order's main problems was that those who cultivated its lands frequently neglected to pay rent, and that the only option open to the Order was to appeal for royal assistance.[19] Again, on one occasion the Navarrese king assisted in returning to the priory several commanderies that had been illegally occupied.[20] Only once did a king take some property from the Order, for which the Order was duly compensated.[21] The Crown also guaranteed the transportation and trade of all Hospitaller products throughout the kingdom.[22]

Yet the monarchy's policy of protecting the Hospitallers was limited: the kings fiercely reserved the exercise of final jurisdiction within the Order's dominions for themselves.[23] This situation continued at least until the end of the fifteenth century when the kings acted to preserve the remaining rights of the Order.[24] Among those monarchical actions with the greatest repercussions on the Hospitallers were the decisions given in legal disputes affecting the Order. We have therefore attempted to piece together royal policy in this area, although our sources on this subject are limited because – with only two exceptions we have found[25] – the Order generally only preserved records of cases which were decided in its favour.

The majority of the judicial decisions that we have discovered date from the second half of the fourteenth century. Most of the cases were between the Hospital of St John and its tenants, and the monarch systematically gave sentence in favour of the Order.[26] Nevertheless there was one case which was

[15] Ibid., carpeta 849, no. 19.

[16] J. Delaville le Roulx, *Les Hospitaliers à Rhodes jusqu'à la mort de Philibert de Naillac (1310–1421)* (Paris, 1913), p. 45. García Larragueta, 'La Orden', 109–10.

[17] S. García Larragueta, 'El Temple en Navarra', *Anuario de Estudios Medievales*, 11 (1981), 635–61.

[18] AHN OO.MM, carpeta 887, nos 265, 281; carpeta 850, no. 26.

[19] Ibid., carpeta 921, no. 67; carpeta 898, no. 22; carpeta 925, nos 37–38; carpeta 850, nos 22, 31.

[20] Ibid., legajo 8533, no. 33.

[21] Ibid., carpeta 936, no. 26; carpeta 888, no. 287.

[22] *CH*, 4, no. 4774 (p. 159). J. Zunzunegui, *El reino de Navarra y su obispado de Pamplona durante la primera época del Cisma de Occidente. Pontificado de Clemente VIII de Avignon (1378–1394)* (San Sebastián, 1942), pp. 331–3.

[23] AHN OO.MM, legajo 8510, no. 11; carpeta 897, no. 19.

[24] Ibid., legajo 8516, no. 18.

[25] Ibid., carpeta 897, no. 19; legajo 8542, no. 37.

[26] Ibid., carpeta 849, no. 18.; carpeta 910, no. 27; carpeta 921, nos 67, 68, 78.

ultimately lost by the Order, perhaps because the opposing party, the council of Tudela, enjoyed equal power and influence over the monarch.[27] It appears that the monarch's decisions were in favour of the Hospitallers where the opposing party was inferior in rank, and particularly if it consisted of persons dependent upon the Order, but not when the interests of the monarch or another important power were at stake.

During the fourteenth and fifteenth centuries, the priors of the Hospital maintained close ties with the monarchy. The prior of the Hospital was very prominent at the Navarrese court throughout the reigns of Charles II and Charles III,[28] and was a member of the royal council.[29] During both Kings' reigns, the prior took part in several important acts and performed important duties.[30] In addition, the Hospital of St John provided Charles II with troops for his wars.[31] During the reign of King John II and his wife, Queen Blanca, the prior of the Hospital, John of Beaumont, was the guardian of Charles, prince of Viana, and chancellor of the kingdom.[32] He was a member of the prince's household, enjoying certain privileges in consequence.[33] The prior also attended parliamentary sessions;[34] at the end of the fifteenth century, the monarch had to resolve a peculiar dispute between the prior of the Hospital and the prior of Roncesvalles over seat preference in the Navarrese parliament.[35] In the last years of the fifteenth century the prior of the Hospital enjoyed a close relationship with the king and queen of Navarre. Some interesting correspondence survives in which Queen Catherine of Foix addresses him on very friendly terms.[36]

Even though relations between the priors of the Hospital of St John and the Navarrese monarchy were, for the most part, favourable throughout the later Middle Ages, the archives provide evidence of three crises. The first of these occurred in the middle of the fourteenth century, and appears to have been the result of a jurisdictional conflict. The governor's lieutenant at the time, Gil García Dianiz, at the request of the king's procurator, confiscated all of the

---

[27] Ibid., legajo 8542, no. 37.

[28] García Larragueta, 'La Orden,' 123, 127–8, 132–3. J. Zabalo Zabalegui, *La administración del reino de Navarra en el siglo XIV* (Pamplona, 1973), p. 60.

[29] Ibid., p. 93.

[30] *Crónica de Garci López de Roncesvalles. Estudio y edición crítica*, ed. C. Orcastegui Gros (Pamplona, 1977), p. 108. Zunzunegui, pp. 96, 143. J.R. Castro, *Carlos III el Noble, rey de Navarra* (Pamplona, 1967), pp. 169, 176, 179, 180, 255, 305, 598.

[31] Zabalo Zabalegui, p. 325. Zunzunegui, p. 81.

[32] J.M. Lacarra, *Historia política del reino de Navarra desde sus orígenes hasta su incorporación a Castilla* (Pamplona, 1972–1973), 3, p. 245. E. Ramírez Vaquero, *Solidaridades nobiliarias y conflictos políticos en Navarra, 1387–1464* (Pamplona, 1990), pp. 132–3.

[33] AHN OO.MM, carpeta 847, no. 3.

[34] Zabalo Zabalegui, p. 345. Zunzunegui, pp. 216, 252, 282. Salcedo Izu, 592–3. AHN OO.MM, legajo 8496, no. 1.

[35] Ibid., carpeta 850, nos 32, 33; legajo 8496, no. 1.

[36] Ibid., carpeta 847, nos 8, 43, 44.

Order's assets, properties and income in the name of the king. Nevertheless in 1355 Charles II, at the petition of the prior and all the brethren, decided to grant them a pardon and return all the Hospital's assets to them, on condition that they would repair and duly maintain all their palaces, houses and estates.[37]

The second conflict between the prior of the Hospital of St John and the monarchy occurred in the fifteenth century and was far more serious and lasting. We are referring to the participation of Prior John of Beaumont in the revolt of the prince of Viana against King John II, beginning in 1451. His support for the party opposing the monarch was due to his kinship with a powerful noble family, the Beaumonts. Eventually he even became one of the leaders of the revolt.[38] The reaction of John II was to confiscate not only the prior's own properties, but also everything he managed in the name of the Order.[39] The revolt ended provisionally in January of 1460 with the Concord of Barcelona,[40] one of whose articles stipulated that their properties and ecclesiastical revenues be returned to the prince's followers. Accordingly, John of Beaumont asked the king to return everything that had been confiscated from him, which included the priory of St John with all its possessions, as well as the commanderies of Melgar and Cogullo, Iracheta, Ribaforada, Fustiñana and Cabanillas. On 26 April 1460, John II ordered the Princess Leonor, his lieutenant-general in Navarre, and all his officials in the kingdom to return all the property that had belonged to both John of Beaumont and the Order prior to the 1451 revolt.[41]

This situation did not last long. Following the arrest of the prince of Viana by his father in December 1460, the Beaumont family resumed the struggle.[42] As the Navarrese prior of St John fought in favour of King Henry IV of Castile and against John II in Catalonia, all the fortresses and properties which he had owned in Navarre, together with their corresponding revenues, were confiscated. In August 1464 he aligned himself with King John II and once again these possessions were returned to him.[43]

A new Beaumont revolt began in 1471,[44] and once again the Hospitaller prior, John of Beaumont, was involved. He was declared a traitor and once again was forced to endure the confiscation of all his properties and revenues, including the revenues of four commanderies: Cabanillas, Fustiñana, Buñuel and Ribaforada. But it appears that the monarch's confiscation of the priory's

---

[37] Ibid., carpeta 849, no. 17.

[38] Ramírez Vaquero, pp. 67, 132–3, 215, 216, 220, 221, 228, 241–2, 254, 263, 264, 270, 273, 274, 279, 282–3.

[39] M.P. Huici Goñi, *La Cámara de Comptos de Navarra entre 1328–1512 con precedentes desde 1258* (Pamplona, 1988), p. 154.

[40] Lacarra, 3, pp. 288–91. Ramírez Vaquero, pp. 285–7.

[41] AHN OO.MM, legajo 8510, no. 20.

[42] Ramírez Vaquero, pp. 294–7.

[43] Lacarra, 3, pp. 313–15.

[44] Ibid., pp. 328–30.

revenue during this revolt did not include the suspension of the taxes payable to the Order's central convent in Rhodes. The king therefore made a distinction between the prior and the Hospital's highest authorities.[45]

The last conflict between the rulers of Navarre and the Hospital of St John during this period occurred in 1491. Apparently the monarchs, John of Albret and Catherine of Foix, sequestered the Hospitaller priory of Navarre in order to prevent an outsider from taking possession. However, they were satisfied when Commander Berenguer of Berrozpe showed them a papal bull from Pope Innocent VIII by which the said priory was reserved for Berenguer himself with the approval of the Master and the entire convent of Rhodes. As Berenguer of Berrozpe was their subject and faithful servant, King John and Queen Catherine lifted the seizure from the priory and ordered their officials to allow Berenguer of Berrozpe to take possession of it.[46]

The price paid by the Navarrese Hospitallers for their proximity to royal power was increasing intervention by the Crown in the priory's internal affairs throughout the fifteenth century. It appears that the kings of Navarre believed they had the right to use the Order's holdings for their own purposes. At first this was done cautiously.[47] Then, under John II, the Crown blatantly utilized Hospitaller holdings to support its men.[48] A further step was taken at the end of the fifteenth century, when the kings of Navarre began to propose candidates for the Order's vacant posts within the kingdom.[49]

In short, it seems that the Hospital, the only military order with a significant presence in the kingdom, enjoyed the continuous support of the Navarrese monarchy during the later Middle Ages. Analysis of the relations between military orders and the Spanish kings in the fourteenth and fifteenth centuries indicates that, in general, the Navarrese model follows the Aragonese model of close collaboration and ties as opposed to the Castilian model, which was one of frequent conflicts.[50] There was only one period, in the middle of the fifteenth century and during the era of Prior John of Beaumont, in which there was a deviation towards the Castilian model, although this was not consolidated. In any event the final result, the Crown's increasing interventionism, was common to all.

---

[45] AHN OO.MM, legajo 8510, no. 24.

[46] Ibid., carpeta 850, no. 29.

[47] Ibid., carpeta 907, no. 6.

[48] Ibid., carpeta 847, nos 4, 5.

[49] Gutiérrez del Arroyo, 1, p. 24. AHN OO.MM, carpeta 847, nos 7, 9.

[50] Luttrell, 'The Aragonese Crown', pp. 18–19; idem, 'La Corona de Aragón', pp. 76–7.

31

Strategies of Survival: the Military Orders and the Reformation in Switzerland[1]

Christoph T. Maier

In memoriam Hans R. Guggisberg (1930–1996)

During the Reformation the military orders of the Knights of St John and of the Teutonic Knights lost a number of their houses in the Protestant cantons of the Swiss confederation. This in itself is not surprising since elsewhere, too, the Orders were forced to surrender their properties in areas which turned away from Catholicism. It is more remarkable that the Orders managed to hold on to some of their houses in the newly reformed cantons of Switzerland. In all three main centres of the Reformation in Switzerland, the cantons of Basel, Bern and Zürich, the Order of St John and the Teutonic Knights managed to continue or, after a short interruption, resume their presence as the only Catholic institutions throughout the sixteenth century and beyond. There was no breakaway movement forming a Protestant branch within the Orders as elsewhere in the German-speaking areas.[2]

The Reformation in Switzerland happened within a relatively short period of time. The canton of Zürich formally rejected Catholicism in 1525/6, Bern

---

[1] For clarity's sake I use the following, sometimes anachronistic, English translations for the contemporary German terms: 'Switzerland' and 'Swiss confederation' for '*Eidgenossenschaft*'; 'canton' for '*Ort*' or '*Stand*'; 'commandery' and 'commander' for '*Komturei*' or '*Kommende*' and '*Komtur*'.

[2] For previous studies of this topic see W.G. Rödel, 'Die Johanniter in der Schweiz und die Reformation', *Basler Zeitschrift für Geschichte und Altertumskunde*, 79 (1979), 13–35 and *idem*, *Das Grosspriorat Deutschland des Johanniter-Ordens im Übergang vom Mittelalter zur Reformation anhand der Generalvisitationsberichte von 1494/95 und 1540/41*, 2nd edn (Cologne, 1973), pp. 57–113. For studies on the military orders in Switzerland in general see C. Maier, 'Forschungsbericht zur Geschichte der geistlichen Ritterorden in der Schweiz (12.–19. Jahrhundert)', *Schweizerische Zeitschrift für Geschichte*, 43 (1993), 419–28.

followed in 1528, Basel a year later in 1529. After a short military conflict between the Catholic and the Protestant cantons, an agreement – the so-called *Kappeler Landfrieden* – was struck in 1532. At a very early stage compared to the rest of Europe, this led to peace between the confessions and established a *modus vivendi* which allowed the confederation to survive and function as a multiconfessional entity. In essence the agreement was that the confessional *status quo* of 1532 was to be preserved and respected by all cantons.[3]

In the sixteenth century Switzerland was still a confederation of largely autonomous cantons with their own governments. The cantons had a common foreign and defence policy, however, and they jointly governed the *Gemeine Herrschaften*, territories which were administered by two or more cantons jointly in the name of the confederation. For this purpose meetings of the representatives of the cantons took place frequently at irregular intervals, often several times a year. These so-called *Tagsatzungen* were opportunities to settle conflicts and affirm good relations within the confederation. They also served to mediate conflicts between individual cantons and with outside powers and institutions. By the sixteenth century the confederation had established a fairly sophisticated culture of political power-broking and conflict management at these *Tagsatzungen*. The military orders profited hugely from these mechanisms when putting forward claims, with the support of the Catholic cantons, to keep their properties in the Protestant territories.

The Reformation was, however, not the only threat to the military orders in Switzerland in the early sixteenth century. The Orders also came under increasing pressure from the cantonal governments, both Catholic and Protestant. The cantons tried to get a better grip on their own territories by asserting widespread fiscal and jurisdictional authority. This affected ecclesiastical institutions such as the military orders, even though they tried to escape formal control by the cantons by calling on their many privileges and exemptions. One way of trying to break up the Orders' autonomy was to accuse them of mismanagement of their estates and of improper use of their funds.[4] When, for example, the news of the fall of Rhodes reached Switzerland, accusations were bandied around that the disaster could have been avoided if the houses of the Order of St John had been run properly and all the proceeds used in the fight against the Turks.[5] The canton of Lucerne even went as far

---

[3] For the most recent survey of the Reformation in Switzerland see the chapters by H. Berner, U. Gäbler and H.R. Guggisberg in *Die Territorien des Reichs im Zeitalter der Reformation und Konfessionalisierung, 5: Der Südwesten*, ed. A. Schindling and W. Ziegler (Münster, 1993), pp. 278–323.

[4] See for example H. Bühler, 'Geschichte der Johanniterkomturei Tobel', *Thurgauische Beiträge zur Vaterländischen Geschichte*, 122 (1985), 5–312 (at 22–33).

[5] *Amtliche Sammlung der älteren Eidgenössischen Abschiede*, 8 vols, ed. J. K. Krütti *et al.* (Berne *et al.*, 1839–1890), 4.1a, pp. 363–4. See also H. Lehmann, 'Das Johanniterhaus in Bubikon. Geschichte, Baugeschichte und Kustdenkmäler', *Mitteilungen der Antiquarischen Gesellschaft in Zürich*, 35, nos 1–3 (1945–7), 1–219 (at 160–2).

as sequestrating the commandery of Hohenrain and temporarily putting it under cantonal control.[6]

Another blow to the Orders was the Peasants' War of 1524/5 which hit some of the commanderies very hard when the peasantry defied their authority and plundered their properties.[7] This contributed to the general impression that the Orders were not administering their estates well. Some houses belonging to the two Orders such as Hitzkirch, Hohenrain, Tobel and Bubikon had substantial holdings which were of great economic and fiscal interest to the cantons.[8] It was generally believed that some degree of governmental control over the Orders' houses would enhance the prosperity of the cantons and their subjects. .

In addition, some of the commanderies, such as Leuggern, Wädenswil and Biberstein, were of military importance because of their fortifications and their defensive locations on the edge of the Swiss confederation or on the borders between cantons.[9] During the *Schwabenkrieg* of 1499, for example, the troops of the confederation occupied the commandery of Leuggern as one of their stationary defensive positions on the Rhine.[10] The military potential of these commanderies was also a reason for some cantons to impose increasing control over the Orders. In 1524, for example, the confederation demanded successfully that the commander of Leuggern spend most of his income of the following years on restoring the commandery's fortifications.[11]

At the time of the Reformation the military orders were thus already in a defensive position. When their houses in the Protestant cantons were threatened with dissolution alongside all other Catholic institutions, their situation looked very bleak indeed. And yet, they managed to survive.

Generally speaking, the military orders retained their houses in the Protestant cantons only if they put up a fight. Their easiest case was probably Basel, where the Reformation was formally introduced in April 1529.[12] Almost immediately the Catholic Orders and the clergy were called upon to swear allegiance to the government and their properties were sequestrated. The commanders of the houses of the Order of St John and the Teutonic Knights, however, refused to swear the oath, asking for time to consult their superiors.[13] The commander of the Hospitallers, Peter of Englisberg, who lived in Bern, refused to

---

[6] Rödel, *Das Grosspriorat Deutschland*, pp. 95–6.

[7] See for example Bühler, pp. 22–4; R. Fröhlich, *Die Eigenleute des Johanniterhauses Bubikon. Eigenschaft und Leibeigenschaft im Herrschaftsbereich der Johanniterkomturei Bubikon 1192–1789*, Zürcher Studien zur Rechtsgeschichte, 25 (Zurich, 1993), pp. 292–8.

[8] See the entries for the individual houses in Maier, 422–7.

[9] Ibid.

[10] *Amtliche Sammlung der älteren Eidgenössischen Abschiede*, 4.1d, p. 354.

[11] Ibid., 4.1a, p. 506; 4.1d, p. 354.

[12] *Die Territorien des Reichs im Zeitalter der Reformation*, pp. 290–4.

[13] *Aktensammlung zur Geschichte der Basler Reformation in den Jahren 1519 bis Anfang 1534*, 3, ed. P. Roth (Basel, 1937), pp. 437–40.

collaborate with the government in Basel, and his administrator for the house at Basel left the town taking the administrative records with him.[14] This was to prove a crucial move for, although the cantonal authorities did sequestrate the house and establish their own administrator, it was of little use to them. Without the administrative records, the town encountered problems in levying tithes and other income, especially from the numerous properties of the Order to the north of Basel which lay outside the sphere of influence of the canton and the confederation.[15] If Basel wanted to administer the commandery properly and obtain all its income, it needed the collaboration of the Order. This put the Hospitallers in a strong bargaining position.

Between February and June 1530 the grand prior of Germany, John of Hattstatt, who was resident at Heitersheim in Alsace, negotiated an agreement with the government of Basel whereby the Hospitallers were allowed to keep their commandery with all its rights and possessions but had to pay an annual rent of 12 guilders and a contribution towards feeding the poor.[16] This agreement served both sides well: the Order kept its property and the canton of Basel secured some income from the Order without antagonizing it. The fact that there was still a Catholic order inside the Protestant town, where Catholic mass was celebrated for the members of the Order, does not seem to have bothered the cantonal government greatly. For its part, the Order did not mind having to pay for the upkeep of its former chaplain who had converted to Protestantism.[17] The main objective for both sides seems to have been the preservation of the commandery as an economic unit from which a financial profit could be gained.

The Teutonic Order made a very similar arrangement for its commandery in Basel seven years later. There is not as much information about how this came to be, but it seems clear that the arrangement was modelled on the earlier one with the Hospitallers, since both contain almost exactly the same points.[18] It was only logical that the government of Basel treated the two military orders alike, even though the house of the Teutonic Knights seems to have been much less prosperous than that of the Hospitallers.

The two houses of the military orders in Protestant Basel were preserved mainly because of the initiative taken by the grand prior of the Hospitaller province of Germany. John of Hattstatt was a man of some stature and authority. When he began negotiating the fate of the priory in Basel in 1530 he had only just come back from the siege of Vienna where he had fought

[14] G. Wyss, 'Das Basler Ritter-Ordenshaus St Johann und die Stadt Basel', *Basler Zeitschrift für Geschichte und Altertumskunde*, 37 (1938), 167–93 (at 172–4).

[15] Ibid., 174–9; *Amtliche Sammlung der älteren Eidgenössischen Abschiede*, 6.1b, p. 400.

[16] MS Basel, Staatsarchiv, Johanniterorden, Pergamenturkunde 9. See also Wyss, 181–8.

[17] J. Hennig, 'Zur Stellung Basels in den Urkunden des Johanniterordens der Royal Malta Library', *Basler Zeitschrift für Geschichte und Altertumskunde*, 70 (1970), 131–44 (at 139).

[18] MS Basel, Staatsarchiv, Deutscher Orden, Pergamenturkunde 5/6.

against the Turks.[19] He was therefore in a good position to argue to the Basel government that his Order was not like the other orders of the Church and therefore should be treated differently. He stressed the fact that his Order was rooted as much in a tradition of chivalrous nobility as in an ecclesiastical tradition. He also pointed out that it fulfilled a valuable task in the defence of Christendom as a whole.[20] From a man like Hattstatt these were strong arguments. Still, it is unlikely that Hattstatt's negotiations would have been successful without the material advantages which the Protestant government of Basel drew from the agreement with the Order.

The relatively easy and peaceful settlement in Basel set a precedent for the way in which the question of the houses of the military orders was solved in other Protestant territories. After his success in Basel John of Hattstatt went on to negotiate with the newly reformed cantons of Zürich and Bern. With the support of the Catholic cantons, he also intervened against the confiscation of the Order's properties at the federal *Tagsatzungen*.[21]

The situation in Zürich was difficult. Both the Commander of Küsnacht, Conrad Schmid, and the chaplain and administrator of Bubikon, Johannes Stumpf, became ardent supporters of the Reformation in the 1520s.[22] The Commandery of Küsnacht was run by clerical brothers of the Order, who were in charge of their own parish church and hospital, but no large estate. These were not favourable conditions for survival in a Protestant territory. When the newly converted Commander of Küsnacht died in 1531, the canton of Zürich simply took over both parish and estate;[23] the Order seems to have accepted this without resistance. A similar process occurred in the other priestly commandery of the Order in Switzerland at Biel, which was dissolved alongside all other monasteries when the Reformation was introduced in the town in 1529.[24] It seems that the hierarchy of the Order was realistic enough to realize that it could not keep these priestly commanderies. Catholic parishes and public mass were unthinkable for the authorities in the Protestant territories. Küsnacht and Biel, which also had very small estates, were the only Hospitaller commanderies that the Order never tried to regain.

The Hospitaller commandery of Bubikon was of particular importance to the Order since it was a *camera prioralis* of the grand prior of Germany. This meant that John of Hattstatt himself actually served as its commander during

---

[19] Wyss, 181–2.

[20] MS Basel, Staatsarchiv, Johanniterorden, F 1. See also Wyss, 182.

[21] See *Amtliche Sammlung der älteren Eidgenössischen Abschiede*, 4.1c, p. 128.

[22] A. Egli, 'Komtur Konrad Schmid, ein Weggenosse Ulrich Zwinglis', *Jahrhefte der Ritterhaus-gesellschaft Bubikon*, 54 (1990), 11–23; F. Blanke, 'Johannes Stumpf in Bubikon', *Jahrhefte der Ritterhausgesellschaft Bubikon*, 12 (1948), 19–26; Rödel, *Das Grosspriorat Deutschland*, pp. 58, 92; Lehmann, pp. 159–60.

[23] Rödel, *Das Grosspriorat Deutschland*, pp. 92–3.

[24] Ibid., p. 107.

the negotiations with Zürich.[25] After 1528 the government of Zürich tried to enforce sequestration. However, it was only in 1532 that proper negotiations took place, when Zürich came under increasing pressure from the Catholic cantons after losing the battle of Kappel. Zürich finally had to allow the Order to keep its commandery and estates on the condition that they were administered by a Protestant citizen of Zürich on behalf of the Order. In addition, the Order had to continue financing the parishes within their estates which were now run by Protestant clerics.[26]

The Hospitaller house at Wädenswil, a *membrum* of Bubikon, seems to have encountered serious economic and administrative problems at the beginning of the sixteenth century. Even before the Reformation there were complaints from the government of Zürich about its administration and difficulties with the peasants in the countryside. As early as 1524 the Order tried to sell the house to the canton of Zürich.[27] In 1536, after the Reformation in Zürich, this was discussed again, but the canton was cautious about buying. The house at Wädenswil was heavily fortified and lay near the border with the Catholic cantons of Zug and Schwyz. Zürich's acquisition of Wädenswil would have been considered by its Catholic neighbours to be an offensive act. This led to the paradoxical situation of the Hospitallers keeping Wädenswil although the Order was happy to sell and Zürich in favour of buying.[28] It was only in 1550, after long negotiations between the Catholic cantons and Zürich, that the Order was able to sell the house on the condition that its fortifications be demolished.[29]

Developments in the third Protestant canton, Bern, also proved not to be straightforward. Here there were three Hospitaller houses: two commanderies at Thunstetten and Münchenbuchsee and a fortified house at Biberstein, which was a *membrum* of the commandery of Leuggern. The Teutonic Knights had two houses at Sumiswald and Köniz.[30] All of these were sequestrated by the government of Bern in 1528/9. The only negotiations that took place concerned the Hospitaller commanderies of Münchenbuchsee and Thunstetten, which their commander, Peter of Englisberg, sold to the Bernese government under uncertain circumstances, without the approval of the Order's hierarchy.[31]

---

[25] Lehmann, pp. 164–5; Rödel, *Das Grosspriorat Deutschland*, pp. 57–8.

[26] Lehmann, pp. 167–9; Rödel, *Das Grosspriorat Deutschland*, p. 59.

[27] P. Ziegler, *Die Johanniterkomturei Wädenswil, 1287 bis 1550* (Wädenswil, 1987), pp. 83–5, 93; Rödel, *Das Grosspriorat Deutschland*, pp. 64–5.

[28] Rödel, *Das Grosspriorat Deutschland*, p. 65.

[29] Ziegler, pp. 93–8.

[30] See the entries for the individual houses in Maier, 422–7.

[31] E.-F. von Mülinen, 'Der Johanniter- oder Malteserorden, seine Verfassungsgeschichte und seine Niederlassungen in der Schweiz, speziell das Johanniterhaus Buchsee (Münchenbuch-see)', *Archiv des Historischen Vereins des Kantons Bern*, 7 (1868), 33–62 (at 57–9); R. Petitmermet, 'Münchenbuchsee, die letzten Jahre und die Reformation', *Jahrhefte der Ritterhausgesellschaft*

It seems that Bern later came under increasing pressure from the Catholic cantons to enter into formal negotiations with the military orders after the example of Basel and Zürich. An easy solution was found for the fortified Hospitaller house at Biberstein. As early as 1535 John of Hattstatt, the grand prior of Germany, formally sold it to the canton of Bern.[32] He knew that Bern would not give it up because of its strategic military importance near the borders of the Catholic cantons of Solothurn and Lucerne. John of Hattstatt was also realistic enough to realize that he could do nothing about the two commanderies of Münchenbuchsee and Thunstetten after the deal which Peter of Englisberg had struck. This turned out to be a fair judgement. Even though the sale of 1529 had not been approved by the hierarchy of the Order, it constituted some kind of formal agreement. When the Order tried to regain Münchenbuchsee in the 1540s and 1550s this proved to be in vain. The government of Bern chose a legalistic line of argument, pointing out that the matter had long been settled with Peter of Englisberg.[33]

The lack of a formal agreement following the sequestration of the Teutonic Order's houses at Köniz and Sumiswald did, however, pose a problem for the Bernese government. In 1550 Sigmund of Hornstein, the commander of the bailiwick of Alsace–Burgundy, with the assistance of the Catholic cantons, demanded the return of the two houses. Since Bern was not able to document the legality of its possession of the two houses, it was in a weak bargaining position. When the government of Basel offered to mediate, the Bernese finally agreed to negotiate. Basel had after all struck a viable agreement with the Teutonic Order back in the 1530s. The result was a very similar arrangement to the one in Basel. The Order regained its possessions, but had to give assurances that the houses would be run properly and without harm to the Protestant religion. As elsewhere, the Order also had to finance the Protestant parishes within its estates.[34] In this way the canton of Bern avoided a quarrel with the Catholic cantons as well as long-drawn-out litigations.

Thus during the Reformation the Order of St John lost four commanderies in the newly reformed territories of Switzerland, but it managed to hold on to two of the most prosperous ones: Basel and Bubikon. The Teutonic Order even

Bubikon, 30 (1966), 11–29 (at 18–23); M. Jufer, 'Die Johanniterkommende Thunstetten', *Jahrhefte der Ritterhausgesellschaft Bubikon*, 37 (1973), 14–28 (at 25–6); Rödel, *Das Grosspriorat Deutschland*, p. 102.

[32] A. Lüthi, 'Biberstein – eine kleine Johanniterkommende im unteren Aareraum', *Jahrhefte der Ritterhausgesellschaft Bubikon*, 38 (1974), 15–33 (at 28–30; *Amtliche Sammlung der älteren Eidgenössischen Abschiede*, 6.1a, p. 1343; 4.1b, pp. 1401–3, 1424; 4.1c, pp. 514, 912, 948.

[33] Ibid., 6.1e, pp. 934, 1059–60, 1125–6, 1150–1, 1163, 1241, 1252–3. See also Rödel, *Das Grosspriorat Deutschland*, pp. 103–4.

[34] *Amtliche Sammlung der älteren Eidgenössischen Abschiede*, 6.1e, pp. 451–2, 467, 590–1, 602–4. See also F. Stettler, *Versuch der Geschichte des deutschen Ritterordens im Kanton Bern. Ein Beitrag zur Geschichte der Stadt und des Kantons Bern* (Bern, 1842), pp. 76–8; H.C. Zeininger de Borja, 'L'Ordre Teutonique en Suisse', *Schweizerische Zeitschrift für Geschichte*, 7 (1957), 487–97 (at 494–6).

managed to keep or regain all three houses at Basel, Köniz and Sumiswald. The two Orders certainly profited from the rivalry between the Catholic and Protestant cantons. Because the presence of Catholic military orders in Protestant areas was of symbolic importance, the Protestant cantons wanted to eliminate them while the Catholic cantons tried to protect them. The balance of power within the confederation and the rules established to deal with confessional issues were, however, favourable to the military orders. With the help of the Catholic cantons the Orders managed in most cases to exploit the culture of conflict management and the legalistic approach to solving confessional issues which had been adopted by the Swiss confederation in 1532.

Nevertheless the question of religion was not the prime issue. As both sides pointed out, the military orders were considered orders of worldly chivalry as much as religious orders of the Church. In addition, they fought for the defence not just of the Catholic Church but for the whole of Christian Europe.[35] This presumably was the rationale which allowed the Protestant cantons to justify the existence of the military orders as the only Catholic institutions in Protestant Switzerland. It also allowed the military orders to enter into negotiations with the Protestant cantons and to strike deals that in some aspects, such as the funding of Protestant parishes within the Orders' estates, compromised their commitment to the Catholic cause.

The question of the survival of the military orders in the Protestant cantons was ultimately a matter of economics and of political control. The forces which advocated good government, efficient administration and the maximization of income were paramount on both sides of the confessional divide. In fact, most of the houses of the military orders in Protestant territories stopped functioning as religious houses, and few of them were ever inhabited permanently by members of the Orders. The Hospitallers and the Teutonic Knights nevertheless managed to continue to draw an income from their estates because they agreed to pay taxes and abstained from interfering in political and religious matters. The mutual goodwill and the amicable *modus vivendi* which the Orders eventually established with the Protestant authorities was thus primarily based on an economic partnership.[*]

---

[35] See also Rödel, *Das Grosspriorat Deutschland*, pp. 103–4.

[*] I should like to thank Cathy Aitken for her help and advice in preparing this paper.

32

The Order of St John as a
'School for Ambassadors' in
Counter-Reformation Europe

David F. Allen

This paper draws attention to one of the Order of St John's characteristic activities even more neglected by the historians of Counter-Reformation Europe than its military or hospitaller functions. Diplomacy was the Order's forte both for preserving its own privileges and for interacting with the respective foreign policies of its principal protectors, namely the papacy, and the Spanish and French monarchies. The former was the Order's supreme protector and the latter were the natural sovereigns of so many Knights of St John. In 1655, Cardinal Mazarin put into the mouth of his master, the young Louis XIV, this definition of the Order of St John: it was an army whose function was to fight the enemies of Christendom, 'and to work for the unification of Christian princes'.[1] So lofty an expectation chimed in with the Order's political thought, still centred on that notion of a supranational Christian republic which had antedated the building and consolidation of nation states in Renaissance and Counter-Reformation Europe. At the same time, Knights of St John also served their own monarch or prince, sometimes as naval or military officers, sometimes as colonial governors and often as ambassadors. The tensions resulting from serving simultaneously up to three masters, namely the reigning pontiff, Grand Master and monarch, were familiar to any Knight of St John who was able and ambitious enough to focus his career during middle age at one of the courts of Catholic Europe rather than remaining content to reside at his commandery or in the convent at Malta.

So much of the Order of St John's history remains wrapped up in its diplomacy. What follows are some reflections from the period on the ideal of 'the perfect ambassador' and the readiness of several popes, Grand Masters and

---

[1] Malta Cod. 1200, fols 449–50; 1776, fols 309–11.

From *The Military Orders. Volume 2. Welfare and Warfare.* ed. Helen Nicholson. Copyright © 1998 by Helen Nicholson. Published by Ashgate Publishing Ltd, Gower House, Croft Road, Aldershot, Hampshire, GU11 3HR, Great Britain.

princes to seek its embodiment in particular Knights of St John. The Order of St John's embassies to the courts of Rome, Madrid and Paris will be highlighted. The strain imposed upon the Order of St John's ideal of neutrality in disputes between Christian princes will be examined by reference to one of the numerous Franco-Spanish conflicts of the period which had its expression in the revolt of Naples in 1647. How this uprising against the Spanish monarchy affected the ambassadorial career of the French Knight of St John, the *bailli* de Valençay, and increased his hatred for his Spanish rival, Prior Redin, will form the tail end of my paper.

In his evergreen study of Renaissance diplomacy, Garret Mattingley has analysed those manuals which had appeared between 1540 and 1620 with the purpose of describing the ideal ambassador. To be impervious to fear, to be handsome, of noble blood and rich enough to keep up the proper state of an embassy were four commonplace requirements for would-be ambassadors in the respective treatises of Dolet, Braun, Maggi, Le Vayer, Gentili, Pasquale and De Vera.[2] Since Knights of St John were also expected to be valiant, of commanding presence (if not handsome), to be of noble birth and rich enough to maintain the honour both of their own house and of their Order, overlapping manifestations of aristocratic behaviour become discernible between Mattingley's canon of books describing the perfect ambassador and those treatises written between the sixteenth and eighteenth centuries which addressed themselves to the awesome duties of a Knight of St John. During the Knights' early years at Malta, the Italian style of diplomacy had already taken root in the greater courts of Europe, and diplomatic service had become a recognized stepping stone in the courtier's career. Similarly Knights of St John, once they had served their *carovane* from Malta and once they had acquired their commandery in continental Europe, might have found themselves elected by their Grand Master and council as their Order's own ambassador, or they might have been sent as ambassador by their natural sovereign to represent him at one of the courts of Catholic Europe.

In either case, such knightly ambassadors assumed the shape not of angels (the supposed predecessors of all ambassadors) but rather of what we might call a halfway figure between the churchmen who had dominated medieval diplomacy and the secular gentlemen of early-modern diplomacy.[3] The sacred character of the ideal ambassador had been well expressed in the fifteenth century by Ermolao Barbaro. His Venetian ambassador was required to possess 'hands and eyes as pure as those of the priest officiating at the altar. Let him remember that he can do nothing more meritorious for the Republic than to lead an innocent and holy life.' Later Thomas More's Utopians selected their

---

[2] G. Mattingley, *Renaissance Diplomacy* (London, 1955), pp. 211–22. Cf. J.J. Jusserand, *The School for Ambassadors and Other Essays* (London, 1929), p. 29.

[3] For the supposedly angelic origins of ambassadors, see the material cited by Jusserand, p. 14.

ambassadors, like their priests, from their Order of the Learned. Much later Louis XIV employed spies to tell him whether his ambassadors heard Mass every day. The ideal ambassador's espousal of Christian morals, coupled with scriptural knowledge, perfected his grounding in the secular arts or sciences such as oratory, history, literature, the fine arts, music, mathematics, navigation and warfare. At bottom this paragon was, in the words of Jusserand, 'a kind of lay priest, with a sacred task and moral duties to fulfil, of interest to the whole of mankind.'[4]

These indirect references both to God and to a Christian republic which had antedated that *ragione di stato* so beloved of early-modern political theory provide a backdrop against which the diplomatic employments of Knights of St John in Renaissance and Counter-Reformation Europe might be highlighted. Of course the Order of St John found it easier to describe its own *raison d'être* by reference to this Christian republic, a figment which was still to be invoked in the Treaties of Westphalia in 1648 and of Utrecht in 1713, and which Louis XIV had sometimes invoked to further French interests.[5] Just as this notional Christian republic was being challenged by the *realpolitik* of individual rulers and states, so too this ideal ambassador of the manual writers was daily challenged by moral contingencies which he confronted with the beauty of his character as often as with the advice of his confessor. Lying abroad in the service of one's country, or dissimulation at least, was every ambassador's lot, and one for which the manual writers refined their advice about 'an honourable mode of deception'.[6]

Familiarity with this tension between the utilitarian and the good provided the daily experience of Knights of St John. 'I am a person of faith and integrity and know several languages and am a seaman' was how the Order's former ambassador to the Holy See requested Cardinal Barberini in 1639 for a new position in Urban VIII's service.[7] Some sixty years earlier, the Order of St John's prior of Capua had been sufficiently literate, when serving as the Grand Duke of Tuscany's ambassador at the Sublime Porte, to publish an account of Constantinople and the customs of that court.[8] Because of their noble birth, education at Jesuit schools and experience of baroque courts, Knights of St John

---

[4] Ibid., pp. 20, 24, 26–7.

[5] C.R. Steen, 'Christendom as a Representation of Belief in European Unity at the time of Louis XIV', *Proceedings of the Western Society for the Study of French History*, 2 (1975), 48–58; *idem*, 'The Fate of the Concept of Christendom in the Policy of Louis XIV', *European Studies Review*, 3 (1973), 283–9.

[6] '*Embajada Española*. An Anonymous Contemporary Spanish Guide To Diplomatic Procedure in the Last Quarter of the Seventeenth Century', ed. H.J. Chaytor *Camden Miscellany XIV* (London, 1926), p. 31.

[7] Biblioteca Apostolica Vaticana (hereafter BAV), MSS Barberini Lat (hereafter Barb. Lat.), 6697, fol. 45.

[8] B. Gianfigliazzi, *La relazione della città di Constantinople e de' costumi di quella corte*, cited by Marchese Villarosa, *Notizie di alcuni cavalieri del Sacro Ordine Gerosolomitano illustri per lettere e per belle arti* (Naples, 1841), p. 161.

were influenced as much by the political thought of the Counter-Reformation as by its spirituality. This political thought had an anti-Machiavellian bias, as Professor Bireley has demonstrated.[9] Against Machiavelli's assertion that the sincere Christian could never succeed in politics, Catholic writers familiar with the statecraft of baroque courts argued that there need not be such a polarity between Christianity and politics. Writers such as Botero, Lipsius, Ribadeneira, Contzen, Scribani or Saavedra raised pragmatic questions of government, diplomacy and warfare which were entirely familiar to Knights of St John who represented their Order or their prince at the courts of Catholic Europe. What was a just war? Was it a noble's destiny to discover himself through fighting? Was he permitted to duel in defence of his honour?

The anxiety of the Order of St John's ambassador to the Holy See about papal appropriation of the Order's Italian priories related precisely to an anti-Machiavellian treatise published at Venice in 1589 by the former Jesuit, Giovanni Botero, who had also tutored Prince Filiberto of Savoy who became a senior Knight of St John. In his *Della ragion di stato*, Botero asserted that soldiers should be properly rewarded, and mentioning them in the history books was necessary to preserve their memory and honour. Also Botero provided the Order of St John with a Counter-Reformation updating of traditional writing about the waging of holy war. Botero focused on Machiavelli's assertion that foreign wars were useful to a prince who wished to keep peace in his own state. Botero advised his own Christian prince that the Turks were always there to be attacked by the prince's own restive population. Botero's last chapter called for a concerted Christian campaign against the Turks, in passionate language which recalled the final chapter of Machiavelli's *Prince* and its plea to drive the barbarians from Italy. Once Botero had updated the notion of holy war, it contributed to the language of diplomacy at baroque courts and so reinforced the rightful presence there of the Order of St John's ambassadors, even if no actual crusade was ever inaugurated.[10]

The reality of divine providence in history was a belief which underlay the Order of St John's diplomacy – a belief which was also being reformulated against Machiavelli's denial by many of the Counter-Reformation theorists in Professor Bireley's canon. Whenever the Order's Grand Masters explained their defeats, they did so by reference to the timeless teaching of Scripture that defeat was God's punishment for sin into which the good might have fallen temporarily. Once Lipsius's theory of the rise and fall of kingdoms had been linked with Christian providence and once the Spanish diplomat Saavedra had explained 'the decline of Spain' in 1643, the Order of St John had access to a rich imagery or vocabulary with which to comfort itself, whenever during its

---

[9] R. Bireley, SJ, *The Counter Reformation Prince. Anti-Machiavellism or Catholic Statecraft in Early-Modern Europe* (Chapell Hill, 1991).

[10] Ibid., pp. 68, 71.

survival into modernity it might have felt unwanted or overlooked by the greater powers of Europe.[11]

The Order of St John's singular survival into the world of early-modern nation states is a further reminder alongside the Papal State, the republic of Venice and the composite state of Piedmont-Savoy, how that world remained incorrigibly plural despite the outpouring of contemporary literature in praise of the centralizing state. These examples are not drawn at random. The diplomatic processes which assisted the Order of St John's survival, and at which it excelled, had been created largely by the Holy See and Venice, appealing likewise to successive rulers of Turin, as these played off one greater power against another. The papacy was the Order of St John's 'supreme protector', although this fact alone never guaranteed smooth relations between Rome and Valletta. As for Venice, just as that republic's diplomacy often masked its declining power, so too the Order of St John's diplomacy remained out of proportion to the Order's actual size or power. The Order could never make policy independently of the powers who protected it. The Order often ended by confusing policy with the rituals of diplomacy, of which its ambassadors were past masters. The relations between Venice and Malta have been treated thoroughly by Professor Victor Mallia-Milanes, and we would add only this gloss by Grand Master Lascaris in 1644, since his comment revealed a distinctive diplomatic attitude towards his contemporary world of territorial nation states. Thanking France's ambassador at Venice for his recent mediation in the Order's long-standing disputes with the republic, Grand Master Lascaris complained how Venice had 'acted towards us not as religious but almost as enemies. A military order should not be treated in this way but it holds back from expressing its rightful resentment because it is religious.'[12]

Outside the Order of St John, its diplomatic sensitivity as a multilingual and supranational religious corporation which exercised sovereignty within no clearly marked territorial borders was best understood by Rome and Turin. Since all the Order's roads led to Rome, let us first mention Turin, if only because the Order expected diplomatic precedence equal to Savoy's at the courts of Rome and France. Close links existed between the duchy of Savoy and the Order of St John, perhaps because neither could be pigeon-holed neatly in the geography or history of Europe. There were shared memories of the crusader kingdom of Cyprus, to which the dukes of Savoy had acquired legal title, although that island had actually fallen to the Ottomans in 1571. Another link had been forged in 1527, when Charles III of Savoy had made Knights of St John welcome at Nizza and Villafranca.

---

[11] T.G. Corbett, 'The Cult of Lipsius: A Leading Source of Early–Modern Spanish Statecraft', *Journal of the History of Ideas*, 36 (1975), 139–52; G.A. Davies, 'The Influence of Justus Lipsius on Juan de Vera y Figueroa's *Embaxador* (1620)', *Bulletin of Hispanic Studies*, 42 (1965), 160–73.

[12] Malta Cod. 1552, despatch of 21 December 1644; V. Mallia-Milanes, *Venice and Hospitaller Malta, 1530–1798* (Malta, 1992).

Returning now to Rome, Grand Master Pinto in 1763 described his Order of St John as 'an open door, whose keys are always in the hands of His Holiness.'[13] Whether the pontiff of the moment used his keys to lock the Order of St John into a particular project or pattern of behaviour depended on the interplay at Rome between the Order's representatives and various officials of the papal court. Besides the Order's ordinary ambassador to the Holy See, an extraordinary ambassador was sometimes sent from Malta to expedite delicate negotiations. These senior Knights of St John were conscious that the Holy See was already well informed about Malta from a source they often regarded as hostile to their interests, namely, the apostolic delegate and inquisitor of Malta, a prelate sent from the Holy See who corresponded regularly with the cardinal secretary of state. The pontiff and his court recognized the Order of St John's ambassador as a public minister who enjoyed comparable status to the ambassadors from Savoy and Tuscany.

Finding the appropriate Knight of St John to represent their Order at Rome was always a headache for Grand Masters and their councils since, as one Knight of St John expressed it in 1739, such a position of trust could be handed only to the wisest and most experienced brethren.[14] Should an ambassador ignore his instructions or pursue his own agenda at the court of Rome, his Grand Master became compromised. By December 1628, for example, the French Grand Master de Paule had had enough of the *commandeur* de Saint-Léger, their Order's ambassador in Rome, and wrote to Cardinal Richelieu in Paris, requesting the latter's assistance in recalling this Knight of St John to France in the king's name, since this ambassador had already refused his Grand Master's order to return to Malta from Rome.[15] France's ambassador to the Holy See was expected to help the Order of St John in any difficulties it might encounter there, when so requested by the French monarch, because the French Knights of St John were serving their sovereign on land and sea.[16] Grand Master Wignacourt, for example, petitioned the French ambassador in Rome to ask Clement VIII to permit the convening of his Order's chapter general in 1603, since the Grand Master did not wish to proceed without papal approval.[17]

Ambassador Knights of St John were expected to liaise in Rome with their Order's prior of Rome as well as with their Order's cardinal protector, the cardinal nephew of the reigning pontiff. During 1639–40, Urban VIII's cardinal nephew, Francesco Barberini, was put on the spot by a blazing row between Grand Master Lascaris and the latter's chosen ambassador to the Holy See, the *bailli* Henri d'Estampes de Valençay. At first the Grand Master had been

---

[13] NLM, Libr. MS 421, fol. 13.

[14] Luc de Boyer d'Argens, *Réflexions politiques sur l'état et les devoirs des chevaliers de Malthe* (La Haye, 1739), p. 98.

[15] *Papiers d'état de Richelieu*, ed. P. Grillon, 3 (Paris, 1979), pp. 586–7.

[16] BAV, Barb. Lat., 5036, fol. 11.

[17] BN, Fonds français, 3491, fol. 81.

attracted by the younger knight's mental agility and social finesse, as well as by his reputation for piety and prudence, since he had avoided horseplay and duelling as a novice Knight of St John.[18] Valençay's competence and energy were engaged by his Grand Master in plans to reform the administration of their embassy in Rome.[19]

Trouble appeared in the garrulous form of Valençay's uncle, himself a senior Knight of St John resident at Rome, perpetually intriguing for promotion within his Order or for honours elsewhere, any of which Grand Master Lascaris as well as Louis XIII and Cardinal Richelieu were determined to block because of the contempt in which they all held his character. Achille d'Estampes de Valençay had always been an ambiguous role model for his nephew Henri, exemplifying the military rather than the hospitaller character of their Order of St John. This uncle had won renown as a soldier and as a duellist. The elder Valençay was a *creatura* of the Barberini, who recruited his nephew as their *creatura* at the time of his appointment to Rome as his Order's resident ambassador. Because of this Barberini patronage, both uncle and nephew considered themselves independent agents in Rome, unruffled by their Grand Master's dissatisfaction with his ambassador to the Holy See.

By April 1640, Grand Master Lascaris was complaining to Cardinal Francesco Barberini that he could no longer trust his own ambassador Valençay and would therefore communicate to him only the public business of their Order, retaining truly private matters for communication via the agent, Fr. Rosa, whom the Grand Master trusted *because he was a priest*![20] Valençay had upset and angered his Grand Master by allegedly appointing a secretary at the embassy whom Lascaris considered to be his 'personal enemy'. Further allegations followed. Valençay had tampered with the Grand Master's seals and had tried to poison Cardinal Barberini's mind against Lascaris. Above all, Valençay had fallen under the thumb of his uncle, who had misled Urban VIII and the Barberini into supporting his unsuitable promotion as marshal of their Order of St John, when the Grand Master and the French court had already decided on a worthier candidate for this illustrious office. Fortunately God had seen through such machinations and the Holy Spirit had guided His Holiness to cancel the brief which had given such offence at Paris as well as Valletta.[21]

Trusting his Barberini patrons to calm down his Grand Master, and confident in their need of his uncle's military skills in the Papal State, the younger

---

[18] As is clear from a notice in F. Cagliola, *Disavventure marinaresche* (Malta, 1929).

[19] The plans amounted to saying that there was no need to maintain both an ambassador and an agent at the Holy See. Fr. Rosa, who had performed well as agent, was to be recalled and one of the Order's conventual chaplains was to be appointed for three years as the new ambassador's secretary, with the task of making an inventory of all the embassy's registers, books and papers. See BAV, Barb.Lat., 6690, fol. 189; ibid., 6700, memorial 75.

[20] My italics.

[21] BAV, Barb. Lat., 6690, fols 244–5, 249.

Valençay brushed aside Lascaris's allegations. Valençay told Cardinal Barberini that Lascaris's dislike of his uncle had rubbed off on to himself, and more than once he had requested to be relieved of his embassy in Rome. It had even been alleged that Valençay had invited the Turks once more to besiege Malta, in order to secure his uncle's promotion as marshal of their Order. The younger Valençay reminded Barberini of his twenty or so years of service to the Order of St John.[22] He was addressing the converted. In 1643 his uncle Valençay was to be created a cardinal by Urban VIII, as reward for his command of papal troops against the duke of Parma in the War of Castro. The elder Valençay's elevation displeased not only the queen regent of France and her minister Cardinal Mazarin but also Grand Master Lascaris. Benefiting from his uncle's disturbing adornment of the Sacred College, the younger Valençay became one of Mazarin's *créatures* and an important agent in the cardinal minister's Neapolitan policy during 1647, as we shall see below. At the same time, the younger Valençay remained a *creatura* of the Barberini, who had been, of course, the young Mazarin's patrons in Rome before his ministry in France.

Besides the Order of St John's representation at the Roman court of its supreme protector, the Order's resident ambassadors at the courts of Spain and France sought to maintain their Order's protection by these respective monarchs who were the natural sovereigns of so many brethren. The Order's embassy to Madrid was important not only because the Spanish monarch was *Signor diretto di Malta* in consequence of Charles V's donation of 1530 but especially because the Order's fortress in the central Mediterranean depended upon regular provisioning from Sicily, another of the Catholic monarchy's kingdoms beyond the Iberian peninsula.[23] Whenever a new viceroy of Sicily had been appointed from Madrid, the Order of St John sent its extraordinary ambassador to Palermo with the *benvenuta* and also to seek confirmation of the Order's concession of buying grain for Malta at favourable prices. However, these negotiations were often difficult, with the result that the Order's resident ambassador at the court of Madrid was obliged to remind ministers that his Order was paying for Sicily's grain from the income it had received from its estates in Castile and Portugal. In other words, the Order was helping to distribute wealth between the disparate kingdoms of the Spanish monarchy, a point noticed by French ministers such as Richelieu, Mazarin and especially Colbert, who was to drop heavy hints that the Order of St John's revenues from its estates within France should also be spent within that kingdom.[24]

Besides watching the limiting consequences of this dependence on Sicily, the Order of St John's resident ambassador in Madrid had to defend his Order's rule against charges by Maltese subjects that it was oppressive. Once,

---

[22] BAV, Barb. Lat., 6693, fols 60–2.
[23] BAV, Barb. Lat., 5036, fol. 11; Malta Cod. 1766, fol. 145.
[24] Malta Cod. 1767, fols 12, 14.

during the early seventeenth century, the Order's ambassador was paid 100 ducats by Spanish ministers towards his expenses incurred while travelling from Malta to Madrid, in order to refute a 'popular memorial' that the Maltese people should be entitled every three years to elect their own ambassador to Madrid as a counterweight to the Order's ambassador to the Spanish court. Although the Order saw off this challenge, the Spanish ministers advised the viceroy of Sicily to appoint an intelligent priest from among the regulars in Malta to inform him secretly about Maltese public opinion, so that neither Palermo nor Madrid would remain so dependent upon the Order's ambassador for information about Malta.[25]

Like the envoys representing greater powers, the Order of St John's ambassadors were preoccupied with diplomatic precedence and ceremonial at the courts where they were accredited. Indeed, too hasty a reading of the archival evidence might lead the historian to think that such a preoccupation left the Knights of St John with no time to fight the Turks or to heal the sick. Because this religious, military order was protected by the Holy See, it remained sensitive to how pontiffs such as Julius II and later Urban VIII ranked the various rulers or states of early-modern Europe.[26] The monarchs of Spain and France, who disputed their respective rankings beneath the Holy Roman Emperor, remained the Order of St John's secular protectors because so many Spanish, Portuguese, Neapolitan, Sicilian, Lombard or French Knights of St John were serving their respective natural sovereign. Although they were brethren of a supranational military order which harked back to a Christian republic, Knights of St John contributed to the military and bureaucratic processes of state building and consolidation in early-modern Europe. For this reason, their visible profile at the court of Madrid was matched by a similar presence at the court of France.

There were many reasons why the Order of St John needed to send its ambassador to France, 'to negotiate such business as we normally have at the court', as Grand Master de Valette wrote to the French monarch just one year after the Ottomans' siege of Malta in 1565.[27] So long as St Louis continued to inspire Valois and Bourbon alike, the Order of St John's ambassador at the French court remained a visible prompter of the monarchy's crusading traditions.[28] There still lingered the notion that this 'eldest son of the Church' might lead a crusade against the Ottomans after having pacified Europe, even though the Wars of Religion and later the Franco-Spanish war during the ministries of Richelieu and Mazarin provided obstacles to such a crusade. As late as 1663, when Louis XIV became embroiled in a dispute with Alexander

---

[25] BAV, Barb. Lat., 6700, memorial 20 (undated).

[26] Cf. W. Roosen, 'Early Modern Diplomatic Ceremonial: A Systems Approach', *Journal of Modern History*, 52 (1980), 452, 460–1.

[27] BN, Nouvelles acquisitions françaises, 2160, fols 73–7.

[28] Cf. C. Beaune, *The Birth of an Ideology* (Berkeley, 1991), pp. 93, 103–17.

VII, the Cardinal Knight of St John Antonio Barberini wrote to the superior general of the Jesuits: 'I can only renew my prayers to God that He might permit His Holiness to win back this eldest son of the Church, so that the king [viz. Louis XIV] might then use his armies in the zealous defence of Christendom.'[29] Always more real than this phantom of the crusade were the Order of St John's priories and commanderies within France, as well as the preponderance of French brethren, many of whom were serving their natural sovereign in France's armies or navies or in colonial enterprises. For all these reasons, the king of France had more interests at stake in the Order of St John than any other temporal monarch in Christendom.[30]

At the court of France, the Order of St John's ordinary and extraordinary ambassadors supplemented a network of intelligence gatherers in the persons of their brethren priors, commanders, receivers and agents. Consequently their Order's Grand Master was better informed about France than was His Holiness in Rome, frozen out by Gallic sensibilities. This contrast was made by Richelieu's uncle, Frère Amador de la Porte, a senior Knight of St John and his Order's sometime ambassador to the French court.[31] At the court of Henry IV, the Order of St John's ambassador was the *commandeur* de Sillery, whose diplomatic skills were then recruited for the French embassy to the Holy See. First as his Order's ambassador to the French court, Sillery had chalked up certain successes. He had ensured that, when his Order sent an extraordinary ambassador to commiserate with the royal widow after Henry IV's assassination in 1610, this embassy had been received with similar pomp as marked the reception at the French court of the ambassadors of crowned heads.[32] The practice of sending a French Knight of St John to represent France at the Holy See was exemplified in the reigns of Henry IV and Louis XIV by the *commandeurs* de Sillery and de Valençay, respectively. In between Richelieu had thought of sending his uncle, the *commandeur* de la Porte, to represent Louis XIII at Rome but decided to keep this Knight of St John as governor of Angers.[33]

The quintessential character of the Order of St John's representation at the French court was well expressed in 1638–9 by the *bailli* de Forbin's extraordinary embassy to Louis XIII and Queen Anne of Austria, in order to convey his Grand Master's congratulations for the unexpected birth of the dauphin, the future Louis XIV, on 5 September 1638. At Malta a *Te Deum* was sung in St John's and the French Grand Master Lascaris compared his own joy to Simeon's, when the infant Jesus had been presented in the Temple.[34] To mark

---

[29] Quoted by P. Pecchiai, *I Barberini* (Rome, 1959), p. 248.

[30] Cf. BAV, Barb. Lat., 5036, fol. 11.

[31] Malta Cod. 1969, fol. 40.

[32] Ibid., 6428, fols 230–3.

[33] *Papiers d'état de Richelieu*, 1 (Paris, 1975), p. 574.

[34] Malta Cod. 58, fol. 56.

so important an event, the Grand Master and his council wanted to send a gift even choicer than the Maltese falcons or Maltese oranges which they were in the habit of despatching to the French court.[35] With Urban VIII's approval, the Grand Master sent their secular protector one of his Order's oldest treasures, dating from the Knights' presence in the holy city of Jerusalem. This was no parchment, yet it combined the Order's history, political thought and spirituality. It linked the Order of St John's past in Jerusalem, Cyprus and Rhodes with its presence in Malta.

This relic of a finger of St Anne, the mother of the Virgin Mary, was to have an extraordinary effect on its recipient Queen Anne, not only because St Anne was her patron but also because Queen Anne had been intending to found a new convent of the Order's *dames hospitalières* at Paris. Far from remaining an exalted object of passive veneration, this relic of St Anne had a dynamic presence in Queen Anne's household. The queen ordered the relic to be carried to the dauphin's wet-nurse, a woman called Pierette, whose breasts had dried up in consequence of her suffering a fever. Once the relic had touched her breasts directly, this royal wet-nurse recovered her health and her milk flowed for the dauphin. Queen Anne spoke of this as a miracle. A year later, when the queen was in labour with her second son, Anne attributed his speedy delivery to the effect of St Anne's relic.[36]

Their precious relic's association with pain and humiliation had been appreciated by the Order of St John before it was presented to Queen Anne. When the Order's ambassador explained to the French court what his brethren were parting with, he emphasized two characteristics of his Order. Despite Erasmus and Calvin, the first was the Order of St John's continuing devotion to the saints and veneration of relics associated with men and women proven to have led a holy life. Despite Machiavelli, the second and related characteristic was the Order of St John's continuing belief in the workings of divine providence in history. 'This Order', declared ambassador Forbin, 'has always held God and His saints in the highest esteem. Throughout its defeats, its sieges, its retreats and losses, it has always venerated relics with the profoundest respect.' In the history of France, continued Forbin, it was divine providence which had converted Clovis, struck, like St Paul before him, by a divine light. As Clovis's successor, Louis XIII was God's lieutenant to carry forward unwittingly the divine plan for mankind. The Order of St John rested its hopes on the dauphin, willing him to mature and impose his universal peace throughout Christian Europe, prior to his leading a crusade against the Ottomans and liberating the Holy Places from their tyranny. Since Malta itself was blessed with two secure harbours, it would be the ideal point of departure for such a crusade.

---

[35] Such gifts were expressive of that contemporary *mentalité* analysed so imaginatively by S. Kettering, 'Gift-Giving and Patronage in Early Modern France', *French History* 2 (1988), 131–51.

[36] NLM, Libr. MS 258, fols 24, 95–6, 125; Malta Cod. 1213, fol. 185; ibid., 58, fol. 76.

Overshadowing Forbin's embassy of 1638–9 was the Franco-Spanish war. During this conflict, as in previous ones, the Order of St John's official neutrality in disputes between Christian princes was suspect at the French court, despite protestations from the Grand Master at Malta, in a Spanish zone of influence. French dismay had greeted Charles V's donation of 1530, whereby he had locked the Order of St John at Tripoli, Malta and Gozo into his own strategic defence of the Iberian and Italian coasts against Ottoman or Barbary raids. A further complication for the Order of St John's diplomacy in this period had been the Franco-Ottoman accord. In 1558 the sultan had requested the French monarch to recall from Malta all the French Knights of St John, in consequence of the recent capture of an Ottoman galley off Rhodes, in which only French Knights of St John had been the aggressors. To Ottoman protests the cardinal of Lorraine replied that this skirmish just proved that the only effective Knights of St John were the French brethren – 'for the knights are the warders of King Philip [viz. Philip II of Spain], placed and kept by him in that site for his individual service, rather than neutral men.'[37]

Given this Valois characterization of the Order of St John, it was not surprising that later both Richelieu and Mazarin continued to be suspicious of the Order's neutrality during the Franco-Spanish war of their own times. The Grand Master might well insist on that fine distinction between his Order's neutrality and the predetermined duty of Spanish and French brethren to serve their respective natural sovereign. But to the ears of secular ministers at both courts, such a distinction was almost fine enough to amount to casuistry. In 1638, when the viceroy of Sicily successfully demanded the Order's galleys for the defence of Spain's coasts from French aggression, the Order's ambassador at the French court faced Richelieu's anger, by referring to an excess of zeal among his Spanish brethren at Malta. But the ambassador was rattled, writing to his Grand Master: 'Let me say how dangerous it is, in these present times, to mix up the Order's galleys with those of kings ... the kings will never be offended when we stay within the bounds of our establishment.' Despite the ambassador's assurances to Richelieu about his Order's neutrality, two years later the cardinal minister issued his terrible threat to withdraw all French Knights of St John from Malta to *les îles d'Hyères*, off the coast of Provence, unless the Order would observe a strict neutrality between France and Spain. Soothing words from his uncle, now Grand Prior de la Porte, prevented Richelieu from carrying out this threat. The Order's ambassador wrote from Paris to warn his Grand Master that their Order's galleys should serve nobody but themselves and certainly not the king of Spain.[38]

The near-impossibility of the Order of St John's neutrality in disputes between the two Crowns of Spain and France was starkly revealed in 1647–8

---

[37] *Calendar of State Papers Venetian, 1557–1558*, ed. R. Brown (London, 1884) no. 1172 (pp. 1454–5).

[38] Malta Cod. 1213, fols 106, 145–6, 178.

by the revolt in Naples, a constituent kingdom of the Spanish monarchy. Louis XIV's and Mazarin's dependence on French Knights of St John to lead France's naval intervention in the Two Sicilies augured turbulent diplomacy for the Order of St John. Mazarin's hesitation has been emphasized by historians benefiting from hindsight. But there had been nothing enigmatic about the command of French ships and galleys in the Bay of Naples by senior French Knights of St John, including Philippe des Gouttes, formerly his Order's marshal, and the *bailli* Henri d'Estampes de Valençay, whom we have already encountered as his Grand Master's distrusted ambassador at the Holy See. Spanish Knights of St John in the Two Sicilies such as Gregorio Carafa and Martin de Redin, prior of Navarre, both of whom were later to become Grand Masters, were then defending not only Spain's interests in the Italian peninsula and in Catalonia but also the retention of their convent at Malta within the Spanish zone of influence. Where the rivalry between Redin and Valençay was intense, their octogenarian Grand Master Lascaris tried to maintain his Order's ideal of neutrality between Spain and France.

The sudden explosion of the Neapolitan Revolt in July 1647 took by surprise not only Grand Master Lascaris but most other European ministers and diplomats, whose attention was then concentrated at Münster on trying to make a general peace after nearly thirty years of war. Although the Order of St John could not be comprehended within the contemporary model of the early-modern state because it lacked national frontiers, standing armies or bureaucratic structures to underpin an absolute monarch or prince, its apparent singularity was not so visible in the kingdom of Naples. Here fifteen thousand or so barons and other nobles comprised less than one per cent of the population but expected the Spanish viceroy's principle of government to be 'according to (noble) blood'. These aristocratic expectations had never been challenged effectively, either in Neapolitan culture or in the outlook of Spanish viceroys, by any theory of centralism and royal absolutism.[39] Complacently for decades, while straddling its frontier between Europe and Africa, the 'aristocratic republic' of knights at Malta had heard comforting echoes of its own values and prejudices from its nearest Christian neighbour of the Two Sicilies.

French perceptions that Spanish resistance during this last phase of the Thirty Years' War depended almost entirely on Neapolitan war aid to Madrid explain the despatch of a French fleet to Naples before, during and after the actual revolution of 1647–8. The prominence of French Knights of St John in these naval manoeuvres was the result of Richelieu's creation of a French galley fleet with the advice and assistance of French Knights of St John. Richelieu's had been the opposite policy from that followed by his Spanish rival, the Count-Duke Olivares, who had neglected the galleys of Spain in the western

---

[39] R. Villari, *The Revolt of Naples* (Cambridge, 1993), p. 21.

Mediterranean.[40] Inheriting Richelieu's Italian policy, Cardinal Mazarin made exceptional efforts to drive the Spaniards from the peninsula before the Fronde imperilled the continuation of his ministry within France.[41]

Mazarin also inherited some of Richelieu's clients within the Order of St John, attracting some new ones to his service and for despatch to Naples. However brave he might be, or however experienced in naval warfare, no French Knight of St John in this period could rely solely on his native talents, which had to be developed, or were to be constrained, by networks of patrons and clients which had existed from before his own birth and profession within his Order of St John. That reality of elites within French society, as described by Professor Mousnier and Professor Kettering, comprehended also the French Knights of St John. So Grand Prior des Gouttes, *bailli* Jacques de Souvré and *bailli* de Forbin became Mazarin's clients, alongside newly recruited clients such as the *chevalier* Paul and the *bailli* Henri d'Estampes de Valençay.[42] Valençay merits attention because his actions and letters reveal him to have been Mazarin's man first and a Knight of St John second. His Grand Master Lascaris had judged him correctly during the days of his Roman embassy.

Writing in November 1647, awaiting a favourable wind to carry his squadron to Naples, Valençay declared, 'besides my disposition to serve His Eminence, I can think only of ending my days with my breviary and of following the path which a religious like me should follow.' Valençay's correspondent was not His Eminence, Grand Master Lascaris but rather the French secretary of state for foreign affairs, the count of Brienne, and the eminence referred to was, of course, Mazarin. Much later Valençay was to write of Mazarin: 'The world already knows that Mazarin is the miracle of our times, the hero of this age, the glory of Italy and the reputation of France – he does not need *my* praises.'[43] Loathing the 'intrigues' of his Spanish brethren in the Order of St John, Valençay's whole life was devoted to plotting the predominance of France. At bottom he was a religious man. When French ambassador at the Holy See between 1649 and 1653, Valençay was to secure from Innocent X certain privileges for Vincent de Paul's *Congrégation de la Mission*.[44] This subtle soldier and diplomat knew enough of his Order of St John's history from the Middle

---

[40] Ibid., p. 24; I.A.A. Thompson, 'Aspects of Spanish Military and Naval Organisation during the Ministry of Olivares' in his *War and Society in Habsburg Spain* (Aldershot, 1992), IV (p. 4).

[41] G. Dethan, 'La politique italienne de Mazarin' in *La France et l'Italie au temps de Mazarin*, ed. J. Serroy (Grenoble, 1986), pp. 27–31.

[42] Cf. S. Kettering, *Patrons, Brokers and Clients in Seventeenth-Century France* (Oxford, 1986). One Knight of St John prominent in the French fleet who was not Mazarin's client but rather the client of Mazarin's enemy, the count d'Alais, governor of Provence, was the *chevalier* Philandre de Vincheguerre.

[43] *L'Expédition du duc de Guise à Naples. Lettres et instructions diplomatiques de la cour de France*, ed. J. Loiseleur and G. Baguenault de Puchesse (Paris, 1875), pp. 183–4; Biblioteca Angelica, Rome, MS 1654, fol. 262.

[44] Vincent de Paul, *Correspondance*, ed. P. Coste, 13 vols (Paris, 1920–24), 5, p. 134.

Ages to appreciate that it had been hospitaller before it was ever militarized. During Valençay's service to Mazarin both at Naples and later in Rome, this hospitaller vocation remained for him 'the chief foundation of our religion'.[45] Echoing Machiavelli, Valençay advised Mazarin that the bravery of the lion had to be joined with the cunning of the fox, if France were to benefit from the dissension at Naples.[46]

In return Mazarin expected a great deal from Valençay. This experienced Knight of St John was to advise the French fleet's eighteen-year-old commander-in-chief, the duc de Richelieu, who happened to be the client of Mazarin's enemy, the count d'Alais. Valençay's second task – bearing in mind the declaration of a republic at Naples in October 1647 – was to ascertain whether the people of Naples would permit themselves to be ruled by Louis XIV or by another francophile prince nominated by Mazarin, possibly Prince Thomas of Savoy. Valençay's third task at Naples was to buy for Mazarin's personal collection fine furniture and tapestries as well as horses, using as money for this purpose whatever he happened to have in hand.[47]

The details of how French policy failed to prevent the viceroy's reassertion of Spanish rule at Naples need not concern us here. Rather let us complete this paper by referring to Valençay as French ambassador to the Holy See between 1649 and 1653 and his eventual failure as Mazarin's candidate for the magistracy of his Order of St John. Soon after Valençay's posting as French ambassador to the Holy See, his Grand Master Lascaris complained to the French secretary of state for foreign affairs, Brienne, that Valençay was not behaving as a dutiful religious should, since Valençay had neglected to write any letter from Rome to his Grand Master in Malta. When Brienne passed on the Grand Master's complaint to Valençay, the latter replied that the Grand Master should have written to him first! Valençay reminded Brienne that he was now the ambassador of a crowned head and no longer the ambassador merely of the Order of St John. Valençay assured Brienne that he understood this protocol better than the elderly Grand Master. With a reference to his own reading of Rabelais, Valençay highlighted for Brienne the Grand Master's 'monkish peevishness' in Lascaris's apprehension as to whether Valençay would cede him precedence on his forthcoming visit to Rome from Malta. So long as he continued to serve the king of France at the Holy See, declared Valençay, he would remain indifferent to His Eminence of Malta! And if Lascaris was Grand Master, let nobody forget that Valençay was a Grand Cross! Valençay assured Brienne that all this bad blood between himself and his Grand Master

[45] BN, Nouvelles acquisitions françaises, 3101, fol. 189.

[46] C. de la Roncière, *Histoire de la marine française*, 6 vols (Paris, 1909–32), 5, p. 134.

[47] Kettering, *Patrons*, pp. 161–2; La Roncière, 5, pp. 132–3; *L'Expédition du duc de Guise*, p. 167; *Lettres du Cardinal Mazarin*, ed. M.A. Chéruel and G. d'Avenel, 9 vols (Paris, 1872–1906), 2, pp. 546–7.

had been caused by the mischief of the Spanish knights at Malta, especially by the prior of Navarre, Martin de Redin.[48]

Anti-Spanish, pro-Neapolitan prejudices continued to animate Valençay during his embassy in Rome. The court of Rome, like his Order of St John, presented itself to Valençay's mind as being divided between 'them' and 'us' – 'them' being the Spaniards and their sympathizers, including Innocent X himself, many cardinals and most of the Italian princes. How fortunate it was for France that the Barberini cardinals were still on her side and, of course, that Valençay himself was there as French ambassador! His *palazzo* was feeding daily one hundred or so refugees from Naples. Unknown to Grand Master Lascaris, Valençay continued to send French agents at Elba such information as came his way about Spanish troop movements in the peninsula.[49]

Although the years of Valençay's embassy coincided with that epic struggle for Crete between Ottoman besiegers and a fragile alliance of defenders which included the Knights of St John, Valençay behaved in Rome not as a Knight of St John but as the ambassador of a Catholic country which notoriously had its own understanding with the Sublime Porte. When this Franco-Ottoman accord was criticized by the Venetian ambassador in Rome, Valençay rebuked him. And when news reached Rome of some Venetian success at Crete, Valençay refused to light fireworks outside the French embassy in imitation of other Christian ambassadors who had illuminated the Roman night. Valençay explained to the Venetian ambassador that he meant no disrespect to his republic but he had too much respect for the delicate position of the French ambassador at the Sublime Porte.[50]

This wily streak in Valençay was detected by Cardinal de Retz, who recorded how Innocent X became terrified by his audiences with the French ambassador and tried to avoid them. Retz was convinced that Valençay was seeking a cardinal's hat for himself.[51] Probably this was true. After representing the French monarchy at the Holy See, Valençay hoped to be rewarded by being nominated France's candidate in the next creation of cardinals. As a cardinal Knight of St John, Valençay might have ended his dual career as a religious and as a *politique* with some resolution of integrity. But Mazarin kept Valençay dangling throughout the 1650s between the claims of his own French service and the prospect of promotion within the Order of St John. Mazarin was promising that Valençay would be France's candidate, not for the college of cardinals, but for the Grand Mastership, once the ailing Lascaris had died. Valençay's bugbear was Redin. But Redin was elected Grand Master to

[48] BN, Fonds français, 18028, fols 45, 128, 260–4.
[49] Ibid., 18025, fol. 2; 18028, fols 90, 31, 33; 18027, fol. 54.
[50] Ibid., 18028, fol. 1134; 18027, fol. 51.
[51] Cardinal de Retz, *Mémoires*, ed. S. Bertière (Paris, 1987), 2, 158, 304, 495.

succeed Lascaris in August 1657. Mazarin, Valençay and the Order of St John's ambassador at Paris, Souvré, had all failed to stop the prior of Navarre.

Let me conclude with this final thought about the value of studying the Order of St John as 'a school for ambassadors' in early-modern Europe. Unlike the Order's military history which remains visible in the fortifications of Malta, and unlike the Order's spiritual history which remains an atmospheric presence in Our Lady's sanctuary at Zabbar in Malta,[52] the Order's political history remains invisible in diplomatic archives beyond Malta and throughout Europe. If the resources of an international team of historians could be directed to such archives, emerging information would interest not only the Order of St John's historians but also those historians of early-modern Europe who study courts and the attendant predicaments of noble lifestyles. My own instinct is that, however valuable the Order of St John's military and spiritual character might have been in early-modern Europe, its greater value to contemporary popes, cardinals, monarchs and princes was as a quarry of patronage, guarded by Grand Masters too weak to prevent its excavation. Further study of diplomatic archives in Catholic Europe will reveal, I suspect, what I have only hinted at in this paper: namely, that the Order of St John was as much 'a school for ambassadors' as it was ever 'a school for soldiers' because it needed to defend its offices, estates and possessions from the predatory interest of its self-styled protectors, especially at the courts of Rome, Madrid and Paris.

---

[52] D. Allen, '"A Parish at Sea": Spiritual Concerns aboard the Order of St John's Galleys in the Seventeenth and Eighteenth Centuries', in *MO*, 1, p. 113; J. Zarb, *Zabbar Sanctuary and the Knights of St John* (Malta, 1969).

33

The Bailiwick of Brandenburg and the Prussian Monarchy 1701–1810

Johannes Schellakowsky

This paper sets out to examine the relationship between the bailiwick of Brandenburg and the Prussian monarchy in the eighteenth century with regard to the changing relations between monarchy and aristocracy and between the governmental administration and the estates. Based on prosopographical and statistical data it focuses on two coalescing lines of development; its purpose is to piece together the complex process of political centralization, bureaucratic administration or, generally speaking, modernization in Brandenburg-Prussia on the one hand, and, on the other, the development of the bailiwick of Brandenburg, the Lutheran branch of the Catholic Order of St John during the last hundred years of its existence. Following a brief sketch of the historical background and the geographical distribution of the commanderies during the seventeenth century, the receptions of knights and the commanders' biographies will be analysed. Finally, the history of the bailiwick of Brandenburg in the eighteenth century will end with a survey of its situation in Prussia under the *ancien régime*.[1]

During the turbulent first half of the seventeenth century the small electorate of Brandenburg greatly enlarged its territory and rose to be one of the leading

---

[1] For a brief summary of the bailiwick of Brandenburg, see W. Hubatsch, 'Die Geschichte der Ballei Brandenburg bis zur Säkularisation', in *Der Johanniterorden, der Malteserorden*, ed. A. Wienand, 3rd edn (Cologne, 1988), pp. 303–11. For the history of the bailiwick of Brandenburg, see also E.L. Wedekind, *Geschichte des Ritterlichen St Johanniter-Ordens, besonders dessen Herrenmeisterthums Sonnenburg oder der Ballei Brandenburg* (Berlin, 1853); C. Herrlich, *Die Balley Brandenburg des Johanniter-Ordens von ihrem Entstehen bis zur Gegenwart und ihren jetzigen Einrichtungen* (Berlin, 1886); R.K. Freiherr von Finck, *Übersicht über die Geschichte des souveränen ritterlichen Ordens St Johannis vom Spital zu Jerusalem und der Balley Brandenburg* (Leipzig, 1890); E. Opgenoorth, *Die Ballei Brandenburg des Johanniterordens im Zeitalter der Reformation und Gegenreformation*, Beihefte zum Jahrbuch der Albertus-Universität Königsberg, 24 (Würzburg, 1963); B. Waldstein-Wartenberg, *Rechtsgeschichte des Malteserordens* (Vienna and Munich, 1969), pp. 190–3.

---

powers in the Holy Roman Empire. The Hohenzollern dynasty ruled a string of heterogeneous principalities scattered across the northern parts of Germany from Poland to the Netherlands. The elector of Brandenburg had acquired these principalities almost without military effort and mainly in consequence of dynastic family agreements.[2] The emergence of dynastic absolutism profoundly modified the traditional political order and the social system throughout early-modern Europe. The destruction of territorial autonomy, the political enervation of the estates, the centralization of financial and military administration, foreign policy exercised without consent, the introduction of permanent taxation and the maintenance of a standing army meant the end of the so-called '*Ständestaat*'.[3] In all these areas the elector established dynastic monopolies which may be interpreted as a revolutionary break with the old forms and concepts of government. The landed nobility, on the other hand, was able to consolidate the institution of *Gutsherrschaft* (manorial estate) in East Elbia. Through an increasing control of the agrarian economy, as well as of the provincial administration, the nobility and the estates maintained a strong position.[4]

The changing political, economic and social situation and the impact of the Thirty Years' War profoundly affected the bailiwick of Brandenburg in the first half of the seventeenth century. Since most of the commanderies and properties had been devastated or occupied by foreign troops the bailiwick was reduced to the verge of ruin.[5]

---

[2] Cf. H. Rosenberg, *Bureaucracy, Aristocracy and Autocracy. The Prussian Experience 1660–1815*, Harvard Historical Monographs, 34, (Cambridge, Mass., 1966, 1st edn 1958), pp. 27–45. For the seventeenth century in general see, for example, F.L. Carsten, *The Origins of Prussia* (Oxford, 1954), pp. 162–277. For the biography of the great elector cf. *idem* 'The Great Elector and the Foundation of the Hohenzollern-Despotism', *English Historical Review*, 65 (1950), 175–202; E. Opgenoorth, *Friedrich Wilhelm, der Große Kurfürst*, 2 vols (Göttingen, 1971/1978); G. Oestreich, *Friedrich Wilhelm. Der Große Kurfürst* (Göttingen, 1971); L. Hüttl, *Der Große Kurfürst. Friedrich Wilhelm von Brandenburg* (Munich, 1981), and, most recently, *Ein sonderbares Licht in Teutschland. Beiträge zur Geschichte des Großen Kurfürsten von Brandenburg (1640–1688)*, ed. G. Heinrich, Zeitschrift für Historische Forschung, Beiheft 8 (Berlin, 1990).

[3] See O. Hintze, *Die Hohenzollern und ihr Werk* (Berlin, 1915), pp. 202–21. Cf. also *Ständetum und Staatsbildung in Brandenburg-Preußen*, ed. P. Baumgart (Berlin and New York, 1983); C. Fürbringer, *Necessitas und Libertas. Staatsbildung und Landstände im 17. Jahrhundert in Brandenburg* (Frankfurt and Bern, 1985). For the fundamental studies of Otto Hintze cf. G. Oestreich, 'Ständestaat und Ständewesen im Werk Otto Hintzes', in *Strukturprobleme der frühen Neuzeit. Ausgewählte Aufsätze*, ed. B. Oestreich (Berlin, 1980), pp. 145–60; *Otto Hintze und die moderne Geschichtswissenschaft*, ed. O. Büsch and M. Erbe, Einzelveröffentlichungen der Historischen Kommission zu Berlin, 38 (Berlin, 1983).

[4] Rosenberg, pp. 42–5; cf. also P. Baumgart, 'Zur Geschichte der kurmärkischen Stände im 17. und 18. Jahrhundert', in *Ständische Vertretungen in Europa im 17. und 18. Jahrhundert*, ed. D. Gerhard, 2nd edn (Göttingen, 1974), pp. 131–61. See also W. Neugebauer, 'Brandenburg im absolutistischen Staat. Das 17. und 18. Jahrhundert', in *Brandenburgische Geschichte*, ed. I. Materna and W. Ribbe (Berlin, 1995), pp. 291–394.

[5] Hubatsch, p. 310. For the situation after 1648 cf. also J.G. Dienemann, *Nachrichten vom Johanniterorden, insbesondere von dessen Herrenmeisterthum in der Mark, Sachsen, Pommern und Wendland (...)*, ed. J.E. Hasse (Berlin, 1767), pp. 89–93.

As a result of the Peace Treaty of Westphalia the commanderies of Mirow and Nemerow were secularized. According to the stipulations of article 12, §3, Mirow was given to the duchy of Mecklenburg-Schwerin, whereas Nemerow was to belong to the duchy of Mecklenburg-Güstrow. The two commanderies were to continue to pay their *responsiones* to the Order and the electorate of Brandenburg. Moreover, the privilege of patronage over the Hospitallers was granted officially to the elector.[6] Although the Hohenzollern dynasty had converted to Calvinism in 1613, it did not try to impose Calvinism on the bailiwick of Brandenburg. But the influence of the ruler and the dynasty on the Order was growing. It was only a small group of nobles who identified themselves with the absolutist state. Because of their Calvinist confession they had been excluded from office in the *Ständestaat* government by the parochially minded Lutheran majority among the officials, but they were welcomed and richly rewarded by the ruler.[7] With the increasing influence of absolutist government the Hospitallers of Brandenburg lost their traditional identity as a member of the universal Order of St John.

After 1648 the bailiwick of Brandenburg[8] included the following eight commanderies:

Wietersheim (about 1322–1799/1811), located in the former principality of Minden, which had been secularized in 1648 and had been given to Brandenburg-Prussia.

Süpplingenburg (1357–1811), located in the duchy of Braunschweig-Lüneburg

Werben (1160–1811), mark of Brandenburg (Altmark)

Lietzen (1318–1811), mark of Brandenburg (Mittelmark).

Gorgast (1768–1811), separated from Lietzen in 1768.

Lagow (about 1350–1811), mark of Brandenburg (Neumark).

Burschen (1768–1811), separated from Lagow in 1768.

Schivelbein (1540–1811), located in Pomerania.

Except for the commandery of Süpplingenburg, which was located in the duchy of Braunschweig-Lüneburg, all the Hospitallers' commanderies were

---

[6] Hubatsch, p. 310. For the Peace Treaty of Westphalia cf. *Instrumenta Pacis Westphalicae. Die Westfälischen Friedensverträge 1648*, ed. K. Müller, Quellen zur Neueren Geschichte, 12/13, 2nd edn (Bern, 1966), p. 60.

[7] O. Hintze, 'Kalvinismus und Staatsräson in Brandenburg-Preußen zu Beginn des 17. Jahrhunderts', in *Regierung und Verwaltung. Gesammelte Abhandlungen zur Staats-, Rechts- und Sozialgeschichte Preußens*, ed. G. Oestreich, 2nd edn (Göttingen, 1967), pp. 255–312; G. Oestreich, 'Calvinismus, Neostoizismus und Preußentum', *Jahrbuch für die Geschichte Mittel- und Ostdeuschlands*, 5 (1956), 157–81; idem, 'Fundamente preußischer Geistesgeschichte. Religion und Weltanschauung in Brandenburg im 17. Jahrhundert', in Oestreich, *Strukturprobleme*, pp. 275–97; B. Nischan, 'Kontinuität und Wandel im Zeitalter des Konfessionalismus. Die Zweite Reformation in Brandenburg', *Jahrbuch für Berlin-Brandenburgische Kirchengeschichte* 58 (1991), 87–133.

[8] For a survey cf. Hubatsch, and E. Opgenoorth, 'Die Kommenden der Ballei Brandenburg', in Wienand, pp. 372–7. A map is given in Wienand.

situated in the territory of Brandenburg-Prussia. And except for the commanderies of Wietersheim and Schivelbein, they were situated in the central region, the Mark, the historical nucleus of Brandenburg-Prussia. The bailiff, or *Herrenmeister*, had his residence at Sonnenburg, which was administered by him directly without a commander.[9] The castle of Sonnenburg had been rebuilt after the Thirty' Years War under Johann Moritz von Nassau-Siegen, the *Herrenmeister* from 1661 to 1667. In 1792 the administrative district of Sonnenburg included ten villages, thirty-seven newly founded settlements (*Colonien und Etablissements*), six farmsteads, six watermills and two windmills. It could be seen as a big *Gutsherrschaft*.[10]

From 1693 to 1811 the *Herrenmeister* was always a member of the house of Hohenzollern; the first two *Herrenmeisters* came from the collateral line of Brandenburg-Schwedt.[11] Their office was used as a way of supplying members of that line with an adequately high-ranking post. This line had its origin in the great elector's second marriage with Dorothea of Holstein-Sonderburg-Glücksburg.[12] From 1693 to 1695 the third son of the marriage, Carl Philip, margrave of Brandenburg-Schwedt (1673–95), was *Herrenmeister* at Sonnenburg.[13] His elder brother, Margrave Albert Frederick (1672–1731), succeeded him and ruled at Sonnenburg for more than thirty years.[14] Although King Frederick William I viewed the independent policy and the status of that collateral line with distrust and suspicion, and although he left their members in no doubt about his legitimate and exclusive demand for sovereignty in Brandenburg-Prussia, as he put it in his political testament of 1723, the connection between the Order and the Prussian monarchy became very close during those years. After Margrave Albert Frederick, his son Frederick Carl Albert (1705–62)[15] became *Herrenmeister* at Sonnenburg; his successor in 1763 was a son of King Frederick William I, August Ferdinand, prince of Prussia (1730–1813).[16] The connection with the house of Hohenzollern, which so far has not been studied thoroughly, existed throughout the eighteenth century

---

[9] Hubatsch, 307. See also Waldstein-Wartenberg, pp. 190–3.

[10] *Berlin und Brandenburg*, ed. G. Heinrich, Handbuch der Historischen Stätten Deutschlands, 10, 2nd edn (Stuttgart, 1985), p. 464. Cf. also B. Schulze, *Besitz- und siedlungsgeschichtliche Statistik der brandenburgischen Ämter und Städte 1540–1800* (Berlin, 1935), pp. 110–15, which gives a list of the Hospitallers' properties in the mark of Brandenburg.

[11] Cf. Hintze, *Hohenzollern*, pp. 256–7. For a detailed history of the collateral line of Brandenburg-Schwedt, see L. Böer, *Das ehemalige Schloß zu Schwedt/Oder und seine Umgebung* (Augsburg, 1979).

[12] Cf., for example, Hüttl, pp. 524–31.

[13] Hubatsch, pp. 310–11; see also J.C. Dithmar, *Genealogisch-Historische Nachricht von denen Hochwürdigsten und Durchlauchtigsten Herren-Meistern des Ritterlichen Johanniter-Ordens (...)* (Frankfurt an der Oder, 1737), p. 112.

[14] Ibid., p. 113.

[15] For a short biography see Dithmar, p. 114–28; K. von Priesdorff, *Soldatisches Führertum*, 1 (Hamburg, 1937), pp. 205–6.

[16] Ibid., pp. 405–7.

and is of fundamental importance to the Order. This can be demonstrated through two examples: (1) the reception of knights and (2) the appointment of commanders during the eighteenth century.

RECEPTION OF KNIGHTS (*RITTERSCHLÄGE*)

According to the printed sources available, the total number of knights' receptions between 1550 and 1764 was 521.[17] During the period from 1550 to 1697 there were 199 receptions; between 1704 and 1764 there were 322. This means that the number of receptions almost quadrupled during the eighteenth century. These figures, which could be expanded from unprinted sources, correspond to the increasing number of noble creations in Brandenburg-Prussia during that period.[18] As far as the chronological distribution is concerned, the number of receptions increased greatly during and after the Seven Years' War (1756–63), in which many Hospitallers lost their lives as officers in the Prussian army.[19]

An important factor during the eighteenth century was the ranking of expectancies for the commanderies. By this ranking the possibility of rivalry and conflict among the knights was reduced, because each knight could calculate exactly when he would receive a commandery. Some particular persons admitted to the Order, such as members of ruling houses, even received two or three expectancies.[20]

Another question to analyse is the distribution of knights according to the different aristocratic classes or ranks: members of ruling houses, counts, counts of the Empire (*Reichsgrafen*), barons, barons of the Empire (*Reichsfreiherrn*) and simple noblemen. During the eighteenth century the percentage of Hospitaller commanders who belonged to ruling houses decreased from about 7 per cent in 1731 to about 4 per cent in 1764.[21] This may be interpreted as a

---

[17] The following analysis is based on the printed lists of knightings given by Dithmar and Dienemann: for the knightings of 1731 and 1735, see Dithmar, pp. 3–13 (8 August 1731), 53 (20 September 1731), 57–63 (26 October 1735); for those between 1736 and 1764, see Dienemann, pp. 166–8 (17 August 1736), 183–8 (26 February 1737), 244–59 (14 September 1762), 332–49 (1 October 1764).

[18] For a survey of knightings, see Dienemann, pp. 125–6; cf. also Waldstein-Wartenberg, pp. 191–2. For the noble creations in Brandenburg-Prussia cf. A.M.F. Gritzner, *Chronologische Matrikel der Brandenburg-Preußischen Standeserhebungen und Gnadenakte (...)* (Berlin, 1874), pp. 16–23; F. Martiny, *Die Adelsfrage in Preußen vor 1806 als politisches und soziales Problem. Erläutert am Beispiel des kurmärkischen Adels*, Beiheft 35 zur *Vierteljahrsschrift für Sozial- und Wirtschaftgeschichte* (Stuttgart and Berlin, 1938), pp. 72–80.

[19] Dienemann, p. 126.

[20] According to Waldstein-Wartenberg, p. 191, from the seventeenth century onwards in some cases more than one expectancy was conferred on a knight.

[21] For the different classes of nobility in the Empire cf. J.G. Gagliardo, *Reich und Nation. The Holy Roman Empire as Idea and Reality, 1763–1806* (Bloomington and London, 1980), pp. 12–15, and the recent study of J. Dewald, *European Nobility, 1400–1800*, New Approaches to European History (Cambridge, 1996), pp. 15–59.

result of the decreasing influence of foreign dynasties on the Order. On the other hand, the proportion of simple noblemen was constant in that period at about 60 per cent, whereas the number of counts and barons increased slowly.[22]

As far as their profession was concerned, the great majority of Hospitallers were officers. In the eighteenth century this percentage was between 55 per cent and 65 per cent, whereas the proportion of officials was 15 per cent and that of courtiers 10 per cent. The majority of their members being officers, the Hospitallers were still a military order. The close connection to the state of Brandenburg-Prussia was also emphasized by the fact that nearly 75 per cent of all new members served in Prussia.[23] Aristocrats serving in the Empire, for other territories or even for foreign powers were a small minority. The predominance of officers is made more apparent by the list given below.[24] Among those who were in Prussian service at the reception of knights between 1735 and 1764, there were:

	1735	1736	1737	1762	1764
Officers	81%	77%	81%	45%	76%
Courtiers	–	8%	5%	29%	12%
Officials	13%	15%	14%	23%	10%

COMMANDERS (*KOMTURE*)

According to the manuscript personnel lists kept in the Geheimes Staatsarchiv Preußischer Kulturbesitz (Berlin),[25] the commanderies of the bailiwick of Brandenburg had sixty-five commanders during the eighteenth century. The distribution of different aristocratic classes was as follows:

Members of ruling houses/princes	11%
Counts of the Empire	15%
Barons of the Empire	3%
Counts	12%
Barons	9%
Simple noblemen	50%

The predominance of simple noblemen probably arose from the fear that high-ranking nobles might bring in foreign influence and problems of interference.

---

[22] Cf. also Dienemann, pp. 106–26.

[23] For the policy of the Prussian kings towards their nobility cf. E. Schwenke, *Friedrich der Große und der Adel* (Berlin, 1911); F.L. Carsten, *Geschichte der preußischen Junker* (Frankfurt am Main, 1988), pp. 40–54. (Published in English as *A History of the Prussian Junkers* (Aldershot, 1989); here at pp. 33–48.)

[24] Dieneman, pp. 332–49.

[25] Geheimes Staatsarchiv Preußischer Kulturbesitz, Berlin-Dahlem, B 9.

An analysis of the commanders' professions again shows the predominance of officers in the Order with about 45 per cent, whereas the proportion of courtiers was 11 per cent and that of officials 12 per cent. For about 32 per cent there is no further information; probably most of those commanders had been land owners (*Gutsherren*). Nearly 60 per cent of all commanders in the eighteenth century were in Prussian service.[26]

The statistical data given here should be supplemented with some more or less ceremonial aspects and symbols which illustrate the growing connection between the Prussian monarchy and the Order of St John. During the reign of the Elector Frederick III, who represented the peak of baroque absolutism[27] in Brandenburg-Prussia, a new and much more splendid ceremony for the *Herrenmeister*'s investiture was introduced.[28] Furthermore, several military units of the Prussian army began to use the Hospitallers' cross on their flags.[29] At the Hospitallers' request Frederick the Great issued an order in 1745 which allowed the commanders and all members 'for the glory of the Order' to wear the royal crown above the Hospitallers' cross.[30] It may also be interpreted as a sign of honour for the Hospitallers that the *Herrenmeister* of Brandenburg, Albert Frederick, prince of Prussia, was the third person to be given the Order of the Black Eagle when it was founded in 1701 at the coronation of Königsberg.[31] By bringing together both Orders, the traditional religious one and the newly founded royal one, the Prussian king made it clear to everybody that the two Orders were of more or less equal ranking.

The increasing presence of the Order in the royal capital of Berlin was made apparent by the acquisition of an urban palace built in an area that was an extension of the Friedrichstraße district. Since the first owner of that palace, the Prussian general Carl Ludwig Truchseß, count of Waldburg, died in 1737, King Frederick William I had to find another financially strong investor. As protector of the Order the king offered the palace to his relative, the *Herrenmeister* Margrave Frederick Carl Albert.[32] The negotiations between the heirs of Waldburg and the Hospitallers were at first unsuccessful, because the Hospitallers refused to finance such an expensive building. This caused the king's indignation and he forced the Hospitallers to accept the high costs

---

[26] Cf. Dienemann, pp. 327–31.

[27] Cf. P. Baumgart, 'Epochen der preußischen Monarchie im 18. Jahrhundert', *Zeitschrift für Historische Forschung* 6 (1979), 287–316; L. and M. Frey, *Friedrich I. Preußens erster König* (Graz, Vienna and Cologne, 1984).

[28] Cf. Hubatsch, p. 310.

[29] Cf. ibid., p. 310–11.

[30] Order from 23 February 1745; cf. Dienemann, p. 219.

[31] See L. Schneider, *Das Buch vom Schwarzen Adler-Orden* (Berlin, 1870). For the members of the Order of the Black Eagle, see *Die Ritter des Königlich Preußischen Hohen Ordens vom Schwarzen Adler und ihre Wappen* (Berlin, 1881).

[32] For a detailed analysis, see the recent study of L. Demps, *Berlin-Wilhelmstraße. Eine Topographie preußisch-deutscher Macht* (Berlin, 1994), pp. 48–50.

for that project in 1738.[33] This case raised sharply the problem of royal influence on the Order, whose social and charitable intentions were strongly affected by that expensive project. The palace served as the *Herrenmeister*'s residence in the capital until 1919.[34]

In general it can be said that after 1648 there was a period of consolidation and continuity during which the Order was prospering and was honoured by the Hohenzollern rulers. During the reign of Frederick William I, between 1713 and 1740, there was an increasing integration of the Hospitallers into the state, although the king was always distrustful of the aristocracy and the Order's activities.[35] The Order's contributions made during the reign of Frederick the Great to the Silesian wars, and also to the colonization of the Warthebruch in 1772, should be mentioned.[36]

The history of the Hospitallers in Brandenburg-Prussia shows the development from a traditional religious military order to a royal order, which was closely connected with the ruling dynasty. It should be noted, however, that the Brandenburg Hospitallers never disclaimed their connections with the Catholic Order in Malta. They regularly paid their *responsiones* throughout the eighteenth century.[37] In the eighteenth century the idea of secularization and the general discussion about the status of religious powers in the Holy Roman Empire also influenced the Order. Not only authors who wrote on public law in Germany, but also Johann Gottfried Dienemann, a deacon at the Hospitallers' church of Sonnenburg, took part in this discussion.[38] In his successful book *Principia Juris publici Imperii Romano-Germanici*, Johann Jakob Mascov (1689–1761)[39] described the historical development and the status of both the Teutonic Order and the Hospitallers. This detailed inquiry, which was first published in 1729 and reprinted several times, reflected the discussion on religious principalities in the Empire and in Europe. In the political thinking and enlightened absolutism of Frederick the Great, the Teutonic Order and the Hospitallers were mere historical phenomena; he considered them as outdated.[40] With this view the end of the bailiwick of Brandenburg in 1811 becomes much more understandable. In this sense, for eighteenth-

---

[33] Ibid., pp. 50–3, 61–3.

[34] Cf. ibid., p. 311.

[35] Cf., for example, Rosenberg, pp. 57–74; Carsten, *Geschichte*, pp. 40–54.

[36] Hubatsch, p. 311.

[37] Malta Cod. 893 (payment of *responsiones* 1761–77), 894 (1777–97).

[38] See, among others, K.O. Freiherr von Aretin, *Heiliges Römisches Reich 1776–1806*, 2 vols (Wiesbaden, 1967); Gagliardo, pp. 206–21. For the contemporary discussion, see also Dienemann, pp. 127–62.

[39] J.J. Mascov, *Principia Juris publici imperii Romano-Germanici, ex ipsis legibus, actisque publicis eruta et ad usum rerum accomodata* (Leipzig, 1729), libr. VI. Cf. also M. Stolleis, *Geschichte des öffentlichen Rechts in Deutschland*, 1, *1600–1800* (Munich, 1988), pp. 298–309.

[40] Cf. G. Heinrich, *Geschichte Preußens. Staat und Dynastie* (Frankfurt am Main, Berlin and Vienna, 1984, 1st edn 1981), p. 74. For the political and religious situation in the age of enlightened

century Prussia the famous quotation of Frederick William I concerning his aristocracy could also be applied to the Hospitallers, 'to acknowledge no master but God and the King in Prussia'.[41]

---

absolutism in Prussia, see G. Birtsch, 'The Christian as Subject. The Worldly Mind of Prussian Protestant Theologians in the Late Enlightenment Period', in *The Transformation of Political Culture. England and Germany in the Late Eighteenth Century*, ed. E. Hellmuth, Studies of the German Historical Institute London (Oxford, 1990), pp. 309–26.

[41] Cf. Rosenberg, p. 45. The famous quotation of Frederick William I is from the king's instruction to his successor (1722), see *Acta Borussica. Denkmäler der Preußischen Staatsverwaltung im 18. Jahrhundert, Behördenorganisation*, 3, ed. G. Schmoller, O. Krauske and V. Loewe (Berlin, 1901), p. 451, and *Die politischen Testamente der Hohenzollern*, ed. R. Dietrich, Veröffentlichungen aus den Archiven Preußischer Kulturbesitz, 20 (Cologne and Vienna, 1986), p. 229: 'Keinen herren Kennen als Gott und den Köhnig in Preussen'.

Select Bibliography

U. Arnold, ed., *Von Akkon bis Wien. Studien zur Deutschordensgeschichte vom 13. bis zum 20. Jahrhundert. Festschrift zum 90. Geburtstag von Althochmeister P. Dr. Marian Tumler O.T.* (Marburg, 1978).

U. Arnold, ed., *Zur Wirtschaftsentwicklung des Deutschen Ordens im Mittelalter* (Marburg, 1989).

U. Arnold and M. Tumler, *Der Deutsche Orden. Von seinem Ursprung bis zur Gegenwart*, 5th edn (Bad Münstereifel, 1992).

M. Barber, *The Trial of the Templars* (Cambridge, 1978).

M. Barber, *The New Knighthood. A History of the Order of the Temple* (Cambridge, 1994).

M. Barber, ed., *The Military Orders. Fighting for the Faith and Caring for the Sick* (Aldershot, 1994).

M. Barber, *Crusaders and Heretics, Twelfth to Fourteenth Centuries* (Aldershot, 1995).

F. Benninghoven, *Der Orden der Schwertbrüder* (Cologne, 1965).

M. Bonet Donato, *La orden del Hospital en la Corona de Aragón. Poder y gobierno en la Castellanía de Amposta (ss XII–XV)* (Madrid, 1994).

R. Bordone, ed., *Atti del convegno I Templari in Piemonte, dalla storia al mito. Torino 20 October 1994* (Turin, 1995).

F. Bramato, *Storia dell'ordine dei Templari in Italia* (Rome, 1991).

M.L. Bulst-Thiele, *Sacrae Domus Militiae Templi Hierosolymitani Magistri: Untersuchungen zur Geschichte des Templerordens 1118/9–1314* (Göttingen, 1974).

M. Burleigh, *Prussian Society and the German Order. An Aristocratic Corporation in Crisis c. 1410–1466* (Cambridge, 1984).

A. Demurger, *Vie et mort de l'ordre du Temple*, 3rd edn (Paris, 1993).

K. van Eickels, *Die Deutschordensballei Koblenz und ihre wirtschaftliche Entwicklung im Spätmittelalter* (Marburg, 1995).

S. Ekdahl, *Die Schlacht bei Tannenberg 1410. Quellenkritische Untersuchungen*, 1: *Einführung und Quellenlage* (Berlin, 1982).

M.-L. Favreau, *Studien zur Frühgeschichte des Deutschen Ordens* (Stuttgart, 1974).

L. Fenske and K. Militzer, *Ritterbrüder im livländischen Zweig des Deutschen Ordens* (Cologne, Weimar and Vienna, 1993).

J. Fleckenstein and M. Hellmann, eds, *Die geistlichen Ritterorden Europas* (Sigmaringen, 1980).

A.J. Forey, *The Templars in the Corona de Aragón* (London, 1973).

A.J. Forey, *The Military Orders. From the Twelfth to the Early Fourteenth Centuries* (London, 1992).

A.J. Forey, *Military Orders and Crusades* (London, 1994).

K. Forstreuter, *Der Deutsche Orden am Mittelmeer* (Bonn, 1967).

L. García-Guijarro Ramos, *Papado, cruzadas y órdenes militares, siglos XI–XIII* (Madrid, 1995).

S. García Larragueta, *El gran priorado de Navarra de la Orden de San Juan de Jerusalén (siglos XII–XIII)*, 2 vols (Pamplona, 1957).

M. Gervers, ed., *The Cartulary of the Knights of St John of Jerusalem in England*, Part 2: *Prima Camera, Essex* (Oxford, 1996).

J. Hemmerle, *Die Deutschordens-Ballei Böhmen in ihren Rechnungsbüchern, 1382–1411*, (Bonn, 1967).

E. Hume, *Medical Work of the Knights Hospitallers of St John in Jerusalem* (Baltimore, 1940).

H. Kluger, *Hochmeister Hermann von Salza und Kaiser Friedrich II* (Marburg, 1987).

D.W. Lomax, *La orden de Santiago, 1170–1275* (Madrid, 1965).

D.W. Lomax, *Las Ordens Militares en la Península durante la Edad Media* (Salamanca, 1976).

A. Luttrell, *The Hospitallers in Cyprus, Rhodes, Greece and the West: 1291–1440* (London, 1978).

A. Luttrell, *Latin Greece, the Hospitallers and the Crusade: 1291–1400* (London, 1982).

A. Luttrell, *The Hospitallers of Rhodes and their Mediterranean World* (Aldershot, 1992).

V. Mallia-Milanes, *Venice and Hospitaller Malta, 1530–1798: Aspects of a Relationship* (Malta, 1992).

V. Mallia-Milanes, ed., *Hospitaller Malta 1530–1798: Studies on Early Modern Malta and the Order of St John of Jerusalem* (Malta, 1993).

K. Militzer, *Die Entstehung der Deutschordensballeien im Deutschen Reich* (Marburg, 1981).

G. Minnucci and F. Sardi, eds, *I Templari: Mito e Storia. Atti del Convegno Internazionale di Studi alla Magione Templare di Poggibonsi-Siena, 29–31 Maggio 1987* (Siena, 1989).

J.H. Mol, *Die Friese huizen van de Duitse Orde. Nes Steenkerk en Schoten en hun plaats in het middeleeuwse kloosterlandschap* (Leeuwarden, 1991).

H. Nicholson, *Templars, Hospitallers and Teutonic Knights: Images of the Military Orders, 1128–1291* (London, 1993).

G.F. Noordhuis, *De Johannieters in Stad en Lande. Geschiedenis van de Johannieters in de provincie Groningen (13de–17de eeuw)* (Warffum, 1990).

Z.H. Nowak, ed., *Ritterorden und Region – politische, soziale und wirtschaftliche Verbindungen im Mittelalter*, (Toruń, 1995).

Z.H. Nowak, ed., *Ritterorden und Kirche im Mittelalter* (Toruń, 1997).

A. Nowakowski, *Arms and Armour in the Medieval Teutonic Order's State in Prussia*, (Łódź, 1994).

J.F. O'Callaghan, *The Spanish Military Order of Calatrava and its Affiliates* (London, 1975).

Las Ordenes Militares en el Mediterráneo Occidental. Siglos XIII–XVIII (Madrid, 1989).

P. Pacheco and L. Pequito Antunes, eds, *As Ordens Militares em Portugal: Actas do 1o Encontro sobre Ordens Militares* (Palmela, 1991).

J.P. Phillips, *Defenders of the Holy Land. Relations between the Latin East and the West, 1119–87* (Oxford, 1996).

D. Pringle, *The Churches of the Crusader Kingdom of Jerusalem: A Corpus*, 3 vols [in progress] (Cambridge, 1993–).

D. Pringle, *Secular Buildings in the Crusader Kingdom of Jerusalem: An Archaeological Gazetteer* (Cambridge, 1997).

J. Riley-Smith, *The Knights of St John in Jerusalem and Cyprus, c. 1050–1310* (London, 1967).

W.G. Rödel, *Das Grosspriorat Deutschland des Johanniter-Ordens im Übergang vom Mittelalter zur Reformation anhand der Generalvisitationsberichte von 1494/95 und 1540/41*, 2nd edn (Cologne, 1972).

J. Sarnowsky, *Die Wirtshaftsführung des Deutschen Ordens in Preussen (1382–1454)* (Cologne, 1993).

E. Sastre Santos, *La Orden de Santiago y su Regla* (Madrid, 1982).

H.J.A. Sire, *The Knights of Malta* (New Haven and London, 1994).

B.B. Szczesniak, *The Knights Hospitallers in Poland and Lithuania* (The Hague and Paris, 1969).

F. Täubl, *Der Deutsche Orden im Zeitalter Napoleons* (Bonn, 1966).

F. Tommasi, ed., *Acri 1291. La fine della presenza degli ordini militari in Terra Sancta e i nuovi orientamenti nel XIV secolo* (Perugia, 1996).

N. Vatin, *L'Ordre de Saint-Jean-de-Jérusalem, l'Empire ottoman et la Méditerranée orientale entre les deux sièges de Rhodes, 1480–1522* (Paris, 1994).

A. Wienand, ed., *Der Johanniterorden/Der Malteserorden: Der ritterliche Orden des hl. Johannes vom Spital zu Jerusalem. Seine Geschichte, seine Aufgaben*, 3rd edn (Cologne, 1988).

Index

C Order of Calatrava   H Order of St John   S Order of Santiago   T Order of the Temple
TK Teutonic Order

INDEX OF PERSONS

Note: names have been listed in the form
which is given in the text, which is normally
the form best known to English-speaking
readers.

Abulafia, David, historian, 337
Adam, archdeacon of Tyre, 281
al-'Ādil (al-Malik al-'Ādil Saif al-Dīn Abū
    Bakr Aḥmad ibn Ayyūb), 92, 95, 107
Agnes Goby, 167
Ahmad ibn Tulun, 11
Albert of Aachen, German chronicler, 103,
    340
Albert of Brandenburg-Ansbach, grand
    master of the TK, 70
Albert of Milan, papal chaplain, 154
Albert the Great (Albertus Magnus), 196,
    300
Alberti family of Florence, 166
Albert Frederick, margrave of
    Brandenburg-Schwedt and Herren-
    meister of the H, 384, 387
Alcobaça, abbot of, visitor of Order of
    Calatrava, 252
Alexander III, pope, 84–8, 291
Alexander IV, pope, 281, 284, 320
Alexander V, pope, 165–7
Alexander VI, pope, 257 n. 42
Alexander VII, pope, 371–2
Alfonso I, king of Aragon and Navarre,
    349
Alfonso III, king of Portugal, 325
Alfonso VII, king of Castile and León, 94
Alfonso X, king of Castile and León,
    319–27

Alfonso of Portugal, grand master of the
    H, 192 n. 39
'Alī ibn al-'Abbās al-Majūsī, 12, 30–1, 38
Aliottus, public notary, 281, 284
Alonso de Cádernas, master of S, 230–3
Amalric (Amaury), king of Jerusalem, 84,
    86, 116–17
Amanieu, archbishop of Auch, 161
Amaury of Lusignan, lord of Tyre, 158
Ambroise, Anglo-Norman trouvère, 92
Andronicus II, Byzantine emperor, 156
Angelino Muscetula, H, 168, 172, 263
Anna Maistrissa, 261
Anne of Austria, queen of France, 370,
    372–3
Anton Victor, grand master of the TK, 72
Antoni Fluviá, grand master of the H,
    169, 262–3, 270–1
Antonio tu Papa, 260, 264
(Pseudo) Apuleius, 29
Aristotle, 29
Armand of Périgord, grand master of the
    T, 96
Arnaldus *Medicus*, T, 199
Arnold *Medicus*, H, 199
Arnold of Oudenaarde, 76 n. 7
Ascanian family of Brandenburg, 298, 300
August Ferdinand, prince of Prussia, Her-
    renmeister of the H, 384
Avicenna, 31
Aymeric of Bures, T, 187
'Aziz al-Dīn, 7
Azo, chaplain of Yāzūr, 92

Baldwin I, king of Jerusalem, 103, 278,
    281

INDEX OF PLACES

INDEX OF SUBJECTS

Σίμωνας